Hobby
GUNSMITHING

By Ralph T. Walker

Edited by Jack Lewis

DIGEST BOOKS, INC., NORTHFIELD, ILLINOIS

DEAN A. GRENNELL
Technical Editor

TOBY BRIDGES
Research Editor

RAYMOND H. BISHOP
Art Director

JUDY K. RADER
Production Director

THE COVER:

Custom rifle at left was built by E. W. Patrick of Phoenix, Arizona. It's chambered for the .17 Javelina cartridge on an L-46 Sako action. The stock is of birdseye maple, consuming some 220 man-hours. Inlaid acorn and oak leaves, plus the fish scale checkering were executed with chisels made by Patrick for project. Scalloped area around the trigger guard is inlaid with ironwood; guard is of brass stock and gold-plated, as are Redfield mounts holding Leupold variable scope. Richly decorated handguns show possibilities for the talented do-it-yourselfer, while photo at lower right is of completed custom rifle and stock of another that still is in process of being checkered.

Produced by
Charger Productions

ISBN 0-695-80361-1

Library of Congress Catalog Card Number 72-86644

TABLE OF CONTENTS

DEDICATION

Franklin Riley Walker, my grandfather and one of the oldtime gunsmiths that I, as a boy, watched for hour after fascinating hour as his slow and careful strokes with a file, fashioned a precision gun part out of what but a short while before had been a scrap piece of metal. He planted the seed that grew into a love of guns and things mechanical. To him, this book is respectfully dedicated.

INTRODUCTION

My favorite uncle served for many years as captain of a fire department in one of the major cities of the South. After a disastrous chemical fire his health deteriorated to the point of mandatory medical retirement. He had been a man full of energy, always on the go — hunting, fishing or engaged in other physical activity. But his health now prevented any such outings and time hung heavy on his hands.

Always interested in guns and hunting, he was fascinated by my work as a gunsmith. I spent a few hours teaching him how to refinish the stock of one of his guns. All of his old energy seemed to come back and the light danced in his eyes as he worked, carefully refinishing that one old gunstock.

He bought a few simple tools, commandeered one of my aunt's kitchen tables and set up a small workshop in one of their spare rooms. The sandpaper shavings and dust were an inch deep on the floor as he refinished one after another of the stocks of his personal guns. Finishing these, he started in on his son-in-law's guns. Soon, any gun within a six block area was in dire danger of coming under his hand.

In the few years since he began his career as a hobby gunsmith, he has developed into a first class stock refinisher, doing work equal to that of a professional. And those many hours that would have been empty otherwise have been filled in the pursuit of a useful hobby. I might get some argument from his doctors that this hobby has helped him health-wise, but there can be no question that it has given him a lot of happiness and pride in doing useful work.

A businessman in a neighboring town is a combination gun buff and gun collector. Like most of us, his financial obligation to his family limited his collection, leaving large gaps that could be filled only by the expensive and hard-to-find models. Several of the gaps had been filled by buying damaged guns and having a professional gunsmith rebuild them, but even this was limited due to the expense. He began tinkering on the kitchen table, doing part of the work himself and haunting the gun shop to watch the professional finish the gun.

His kitchen table and tool box work began to grow to the point that he was forced to build a small shop in his backyard. He filled it with used machine tools and a lot of homemade equipment with plenty of storage space for parts. His original plan was to use it to restore guns for his collection and as a tool room for household needs.

Friends began dropping guns by for repair, and he soon was spending all of his spare time on general repair and none on his own collection. Finally, he hit on the idea of working only on restoring antiques with the accompanying large amount of handmade parts. All general gunsmithing was forwarded to a fulltime shop in his town. Since that time he has become something of an artist in restoration. The income from this work has been poured into his collection, which has grown into one of the best in the country. Many pieces are the result of several reworked specimens being traded for one needed rare model. His shop is self-supporting and no funds are taken from his regular work for his hobby. The shop is what a lot of gun buffs dream of, filled with good tools and equipment.

Hardly a week goes by that a customer doesn't ask me for advice on some gun project he has going. They are farmers, doctors, lawyers, pilots, policemen and general working types ranging in ages from 15 to 70. They all have one thing in common: a fascinating hobby that has doubled their enjoyment of firearms. In this day of mass production, nearly everyone yearns to create things with his own hands. When you succumb to that yearning and see things improved or made completely with your own hands, it instills something that might be called inner peace. The tensions and worry of everyday modern life seem to melt away.

No tranquilizing pill has ever been made that is its equal for helping you face the daily grind.

The Author

Ralph Thomas Walker was born at Selma, Alabama, in 1931. The Walker family had settled in Selma in 1821 and a great-great grandfather of Ralph's served as a sniper with the Confederate Army in the War Between the States. His grandfather, Franklin R. Walker, was a well-known local gunsmith who taught the present author skills and secrets of the trade while the latter still was in knee britches.

Walker attended Trinidad State Junior College, graduating with an AA degree in Gunsmithing. P.O. Ackley was chief instructor and Walker worked part-time in the Ackley shop before enlisting in the army in July, 1951.

He took basic training and attended NCO school at Fort Jackson, South Carolina, going on to graduate from OCS at Aberdeen Proving Grounds, Maryland. Further specialist schools from which he graduated included Small Arms Maintenance, Enemy Arms and Material, Explosive Ordnance Demolition and Military Attache. Ordered to Formosa, Walker served as senior small-arms advisor to the Nationalist Chinese Ordnance Corps, setting up their smallarms rebuilding facilities and assisting in the design and production of two Chinese smallarms: the sub-machine-gun and sniper rifle. He saw combat on Taichen and Quemoy while serving as smallarms advisor to irregular guerrilla troops and received a commendation from Nationalist China. Returning to the USA, he served as commanding officer of the 95th Ordnance Company at Camp Stewart, Georgia, until leaving the service in 1955.

In civilian life, Walker started a small backyard gunsmithing operation, but quickly outgrew its facilities. He moved to the location of his present shop in Selma. He incorporated his activities in 1971, serving as president and presently has three shops: the original one in Selma, others in Griffin, Georgia, and Joplin, Missouri, with a fourth scheduled for Chicago.

Walker commenced writing for the firearms press some years ago and has been writing for GUN WORLD Magazine since 1970.

GETTING STARTED

Gunsmithing Is A Term Full Of Mystery —
Even Fear Of The Unknown —
But It Doesn't Have To Be That Way!

MOST SPORTSMEN AND gun buffs, at one time or another, think about doing a little gunsmithing themselves. It may be the result of a professional gunsmith's estimate of repair on a favorite gun with the estimate more than the market value of the gun. Sometimes it is a desire to own a custom-made gun with a pocket-book falling a mite short of the required funds. Still other times it is just a desire to tinker with a gun in an attempt to make it function better. Whatever the reason, often it is the beginning of a lifetime of hobby gunsmithing.

Unfortunately, most of the time the reverse is true and the desire falls by the wayside. The biggest single reason that most fail to follow their desire is just plain lack of confidence. They take a look at the internal components of a gun or perhaps glance through a book on gunsmithing and their immediate reaction is that they never could do work like this. It just looks too complicated and they mentally compare gunsmithing to working on a fine watch or taking up brain surgery as a pastime.

Virtually any man who has sense enough to tie his shoes can do some form of gunsmithing! I do not mean that you just yank a fellow off the street, lock him in a well equipped gun shop and expect him to exit a couple of days later with a premium grade rifle he has built. A large portion of gunsmithing does require a good bit of technical knowledge with the accompanying skill, and most major mechanical repairs and alterations should be left to the professionals. On the other hand, quite a bit of gunsmithing

Chapter 1

Watching a professional gunsmith as he goes through his routine daily work is perhaps the best way to learn his tricks of the trade.

Tools and other equipment, such as a good strong vise, are important to gunsmithing, observant beginner should take notice.

There is a right way and a wrong way to do nearly everything. A just starting gunsmith should perfect the first, avoid the latter.

is not complicated and is well within the capability of anyone willing to devote a little time to learning a few simple skills. Gunsmithing is like many other skills in that it requires patience, practice, concentration and, most of all, a willingness to learn. From here on, it is just a matter of applying yourself and taking one step at a time. How far you advance into the more technical aspects of gunsmithing is strictly up to you. Some hobby gunsmiths limit their work to minor adjusting of guns and possibly refinishing stocks with a cigar box full of tools and the kitchen table as their workbench. Others find a place for a small workshop, add a few power tools and go in for the more advanced forms of gunsmithing including the building of custom guns. In the majority of cases, it is a matter of increasing need for more work area and tools as knowledge and skills increase.

The next obvious question involves acquiring the necessary knowledge and skills. On-the-job training in a professional gun shop is by far the best way, but the hobbyist's financial obligations and regular occupation usually prevents it or the professional gunsmith simply does not have the time to train him. In just about every case, the knowledge is obtained by reading books such as this one and steadily progressing by reading other books and magazine articles about gunsmithing. Knowledge is a matter of building, for you build on what you already know with each tiny new scrap of information a building block. The skill is acquired slowly by repeatedly putting the knowledge into practical application; each time you perform a certain task you will do it a little bit better. No artist or craftsman ever has done his best work on the first try.

Constructive criticism of your work by a professional gunsmith can be a tremendous help to you, for he will notice and point out small mistakes that otherwise would go unnoticed. If this help is not available, you will have to be your own critic. Compare your work with a similar job done by a professional gunsmith or even a photograph of similar work and note every difference. Inspect your finished product carefully and try to find everything you can that is wrong with it, then make mental notes to correct this on your next attempt.

Usually you will find the mistakes occur when you hurry or reach a point where you are not sure of yourself. Take your time, work slowly and perform every tiny part of the task to the best of your ability. This attention to the tiny details is the mark of a craftsman and will affect the quality of the entire job. If you are not sure of a certain point, seek the help of someone more advanced in gunsmithing than yourself. If this help is not available, research the subject to clarify it in your own mind. Most of all, do not become discouraged in this self-criticism, for no true craftsman is ever completely satisfied with his work.

As your skill and knowledge increases, you will find hobby gunsmithing pays off in many ways. If you count it money-wise, you probably could earn more by digging ditches in your spare time. In this day of mass machine production, nearly everyone yearns to create something with his own hands. When you succumb to that yearning and see things improved or made completely with your own hands, it instills pride and something that might be called inner peace.

One of the biggest faults we all have is putting off the things we really want to do with the excuse that we are too busy. One of the best pieces of advice I ever received came from an old gentleman who could not even write his name. He said, "My friend, life is a short road at best and instead of running down it at full speed, you had better slow down to a walk and look around, for you will pass this way only once."

If you have ever thought about doing gunsmithing as a hobby, there will never be a better time to get started than now. You have today; tomorrow is but a promise.....

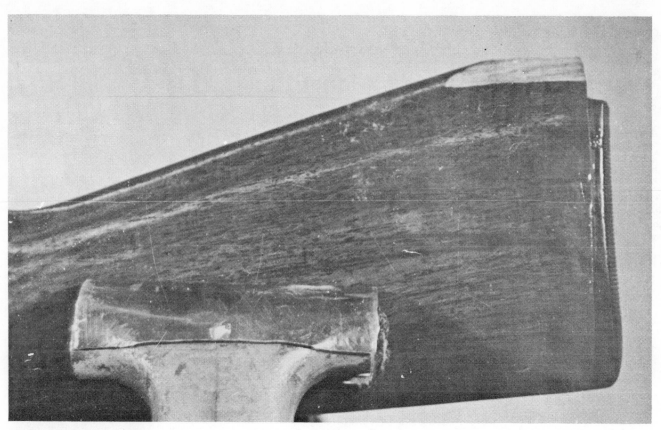

Chapter 2

THAT FIRST PROJECT

Here Is A Beginning To Determine Whether Gunsmithing Is Really Your Bag!!

THE TWO MOST COMMON mistakes beginners make in gunsmithing are first, tackling too big a job and, second, getting tool happy. This can be compared to turning a student driver loose in the 6 p.m. getting-home traffic in a five thousand dollar automobile. Nine times out of ten, disaster is in the making and the beginner loses confidence both in himself and in the entire idea. This does not mean that the first gunsmithing project has to be dull and of no practical use. It just means it should not be something like attempting to refinish your Browning over-and-under shotgun. Instead, hedge your bet and spend your learning period on a less expensive gun. The time will come eventually when you can refinish that Browning and do a beauti-

ful job of it, experience is gained through a series of simple projects.

A hobbyist with tools galore at his disposal usually ends up without the skill to use any of them properly, while one starting with a few hand tools will learn to use each of them well. Simply buy tools when you no longer can work efficiently without them. The need will present itself soon enough and you will know exactly what you want as well as what you need. Too often the beginner is presented with a couple of pages listing a bunch of tools and equipment that would ruin a thousand dollar bill. One glance at such a list will cool the ardor and ambition of a hobby gunsmith quicker than anything I know.

Most beginning hobbyists probably will have a few hand tools that are used for the hundred and one things that have to be repaired around a home. Many of these tools have no use in gunsmithing and occasionally you will have to purchase one or two new ones at the beginning of a project. Others can serve as the beginning of your gunsmithing tools. You also will find that many of the tools needed in gunsmithing simply are not available on the market and will have to be fabricated by hand. Most full-time professional gunsmiths spend part of each week either making a tool, modifying a tool or putting together a jig for a specific job.

Toolmaking can be a rewarding part of gunsmithing and I always have felt sorry for the fellows who buy all of their tools. In my apprentice days, special gunsmithing tools were few and we spent a good bit of our time making our own. If you use good materials, these homemade tools will last for years. I have some in daily use that I made well over twenty years ago.

Basically, guns are made from two things: steel and wood, if you don't count the present day aluminum, pot metal, and bent beer cans from which some of the guns are made.

The hobbyist will find that wood should be his first interest for several reasons. First, the cost of tooling for wood work will be minor in comparison to the tooling for metal. It is easier to learn to work with wood than with metal and it requires less working area. Metal work uses some of the basic talents that are learned in woodworking and the transition will be much easier for the hobbyist who has mastered woodworking first.

There are dozens of possible projects we could use for our first job, but let's choose one that is simple and inexpensive. Nearly every sportsman has an old single-barrel shotgun around the house. If not, now is a good time to buy one, not only for your first project but as a loaning gun to save scratches and nicks from being put into one of your good guns. Telling Cousin Mortimer that this is the only extra gun you have is acceptable and will not be held against you, when you explain at the pearly gates about the time Mortimer used one of your good guns to club a half dead rabbit then remarked, when the stock shattered, that "they sure don't make guns like they used to!"

If you have to buy your first project, try to pick one of the more common currently manufactured models instead of one of the old odd-brand guns. Parts for the old guns are almost non-existent, since the wide variety of odd-brand names for old single barrel shotguns is exceeded in number only by the unkept promises of politicians. Any oldtime hardware store that would give a small gun manufacturer an order for a few hundred guns could have his or any name under the sun stamped on the receiver. This accounts for the terrific number of names encountered, often with the guns otherwise identical. These brand names are an interesting side issue as some were really awe inspiring with examples such as "Invincible," "Long Range Wonder" and I even ran across one with the confidence building name of "Top of the Tree." For the most part, selection of one of these for your project will end up in disaster, if a part proves defective and cannot be replaced. Spend a little extra for a modern gun.

Your first check should be the same one that is given to any gun you undertake to repair or refinish. All of the care and time in the world spent refinishing a gun is lost unless the gun is safe to use – antiques excepted.

With your single barrel, the most important feature to check is the fit of the barrel to the receiver. Hold your shotgun up against a strong light and look carefully at the juncture of the barrel to the receiver. If you can see light

between the barrel end and the receiver, there is a good chance that the gun has excess headspace and could be dangerous to fire. In such cases, seek the recommendations of a professional gunsmith before you go another step further.

The second basic safety check is the bore of the gun which should be as bright and shiny as possible. Quite often with used guns, this is not the case. A mild pitting of the bore will not overly affect the pattern of the gun and often these can be eliminated with a little careful lapping of the bore. The one to watch out for is the bore with holes impossible to remove and, in really severe cases, the deep pit can be a point where the barrel could burst.

To cover all of the necessary repairs, modifications, et al., involved in stock refinishing, it is necessary to invent a hypothetical single barrel shotgun to use as an example. So, we will describe the repair and refinishing of a stock that is about a half step from the junk pile. Most of the stocks that you will be working on will not be in this bad shape, but will be suffering one or more of the defects in our example.

Once a few basic fundamentals are understood and you have mastered them, the procedure will be about the same with any stock, whether it is a cheap single barrel shotgun or a fine, high quality custom rifle. As you refinish more stocks, you will pick up a lot of tricks and short cuts, but watch professional gunsmiths refinish stocks and read everything about stocks and stock refinishing that you can lay your hands on. Each gunsmith will use a slightly different process or method. Never hesitate to change your own procedure if his proves to be superior.

In a close look at our shotgun, the first thing we notice is that about one inch of the bottom part of the butt stock is broken off and will need a new piece of wood spliced on. This section of the stock carries the technical name of "toe" and the top rear part of the butt stock at the rear is called the "heel." The toe of the butt stock receives a lot of abuse and broken parts are common. People seem to take special pains to drop the gun on the toe, use it to pound rattlesnake heads or for similar sporting events.

As is usual on a stock such as this the butt plate is broken and will need to be replaced. Our example has its full share of dents distributed up and down the sides of the stock with practically none of the original finish remaining.

There is a small crack in the front of the stock where it joins the rear of the receiver. This front section of our stock is dark in color, indicating the usual soaking of the wood with oil that has drained back down the stock from the receiver and internal moving parts. The forearm has a couple of healthy dents and the screws that attach the wood to the forearm iron assembly are loose where they have chewed out the wood and someone has attempted to tighten it by jamming in pieces of paper.

Before we can start sanding or refinishing the stock we will first have to remove any lingering trace of the old finish, plus the accumulated grease, grime, dirt and what not, ground into the wood over the years. One can do a fair job of cleaning with plain soap and water, but you cannot remove the old finish this way. Commercial paint stripper will do the work much better and faster with a lot less elbow grease.

I have tried dozens of different brands of paint stripper and they all seem to do a fair job on stocks but some work better. The cheap ones all have one thing in common; you must wash the stock with soap and water after application. No matter how much you wash and scrub the stock, you never can seem to remove completely all the stripper remaining on the stock and these small traces will affect the finish when it is applied to the stock. The best types con-

INSTRUCTIONS FOR PROPER CUTTING OF STOCK FOR RECOIL PAD INSTALLATION

Illustrated in Fig. 1 below are the average shotgun dimensions for proper trigger pull length and drop at comb and heel as well as dimensions from trigger to heel and toe.

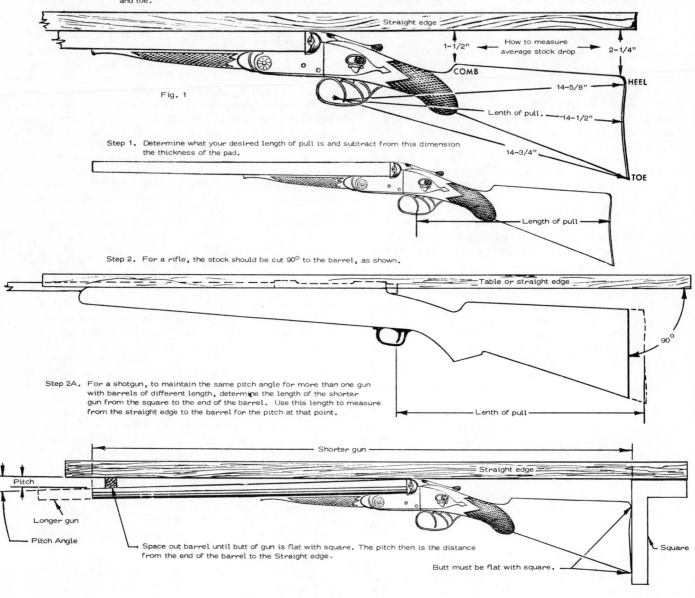

Straight edge

1-1/2"   How to measure average stock drop   2-1/4"

COMB

HEEL

14-5/8"

Fig. 1

Lenth of pull.   14-1/2"

14-3/4"

TOE

Step 1. Determine what your desired length of pull is and subtract from this dimension the thickness of the pad.

Length of pull

Step 2. For a rifle, the stock should be cut 90° to the barrel, as shown.

Table or straight edge

90°

Step 2A. For a shotgun, to maintain the same pitch angle for more than one gun with barrels of different length, determine the length of the shorter gun from the square to the end of the barrel. Use this length to measure from the straight edge to the barrel for the pitch at that point.

Lenth of pull

Shorter gun

Straight edge

Pitch

Longer gun

Pitch Angle

Space out barrel until butt of gun is flat with square. The pitch then is the distance from the end of the barrel to the Straight edge.

Square

Butt must be flat with square.

Step 3 Slide the square along the table to the length of pull, less the pad dimensions and mark or scribe the stock. Recheck before cutting.

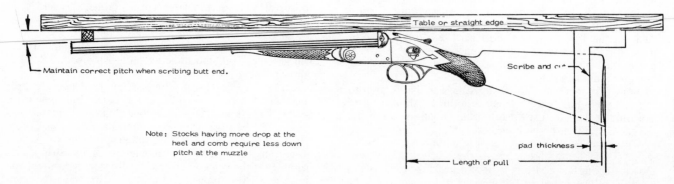

Table or straight edge

Maintain correct pitch when scribing butt end.

Scribe and cut

Note: Stocks having more drop at the heel and comb require less down pitch at the muzzle

pad thickness

Length of pull

12

tain a chemical that eliminates the need for washing or rinsing the stock after the stripper has done its job. All of the paint strippers that contain this chemical will have a sentence on the can reading "does not require washing or rinsing after application." Look for this instead of a certain brand name. A pint of stripper will be more than enough for several stocks.

When buying the paint stripper, pick up a cheap two-inch paint brush, a pack of double ought (00) steel wool, and a pack of triple ought (000) steel wool. The more oughts (0) in the designation, the finer the steel wool and the finer the cut it will make. After the ought designations you move up through the coarser grades of steel wool designated as 1, 2, 3 and so on. Grades coarser than No. 2 are of little practical use around a gun shop and are used, I suspect, mainly to clean the hides of elephants. Four ought (0000) steel wool is seldom used on stock work but is good to have around the shop to remove rust. In a tight spot, you can use it for stock work and eliminate the triple ought (000).

Paint stripper is safe to handle and use as long as you do not try to make a cocktail out of the stuff and provided you follow the manufacturer's directions. It is best to use it outdoors, for any spatter will do an excellent job of removing the finish from your furniture. This is sure to bring some smart remark from your wife.

It is a good idea to pour a small amount into a dish and place some old newspaper under the dish to soak up the overflow. The actual application of the stripper to the stock is better done with the cheap paint brush than any attempt to dip the stock.

Paint stripper will cause some people to break out in a small rash where it touches their skin, and will crack the skin of others as it removes all of the oil from the surface. If you have extra-tender skin, wear rubber gloves when working with the stripper. If your skin just cracks, this can be corrected with a good hand lotion containing lanolin, but regardless of whether you wear gloves, be sure to wash your hands thoroughly. Your eyes always should be protected with some type of safety glasses or goggles, since a

speck of stripper in your eye can cause some extra fancy foot work and cussing, even if no permanent damage is done. There is no need to fear paint stripper, but treat it with respect.

With the stock removed from the metal receiver and its butt standing flat on a piece of newspaper, hold the stock with one hand and pick up the paint brush with the other. Dip the brush in the dish containing the paint stripper and, with long unbroken strokes, start painting the stock with the stripper. This is not the place to be stingy, so get it on the stock good and heavy, being sure to cover every part of the outside of the stock. Once you have the stock completely covered, stand it up against something and allow the stripper to do its work. Usually about fifteen minutes will be sufficient, but check the directions on the can and follow the manufacturer's directions if more time is recommended. Do not rub the stock while the stripper is working.

After the correct amount of time has elapsed, you will see that the old finish has puckered up somewhat like a prune, and the dirt and grime in the stock will have been brought to the surface and appear as loose mud. When it has reached this stage and the old finish and grime are loose, it can be wiped from the stock. Rags can be used for this, but a piece of double ought steel wool about the size of an orange will do a much better job. Make your stroke in one direction only and do not break the stroke. Do not make a back stroke, for to do so will just wipe the muck back on the stock and press it down into the grain of the wood compounding the problem of getting it off. The pad of steel wool will clog up, so rotate it in your hand and always present a clean section for each wipe. The steel wool can be washed clean of the residue and used over and over.

Go over the stock thoroughly until all of the muck has been removed, then take a piece of old bath towel and rub the stock in a one way continuous stroke. Keep repeating this with a clean piece of cloth until there is no lingering trace of the old muck and grime. Finish up by giving the stock a thorough and hard rubbing with a clean piece of towel, this time, in all directions. Your stock now should be clean as a hound's tooth.

Left: Drawing is courtesy of Pachmayr Gun Works. (Below) Using clean steel wool, wipe old finish off with one clean stroke. Do not make a backstroke, as this will simply wipe old finish back onto the stock, into pores.

Stock dents are raised by using moist blotter or a gun patch, hot metal rod pressed against it. The water turns to steam, which raises the compressed wood fibers in the dent. Rod shown is quarter-inch copper with dowel handle.

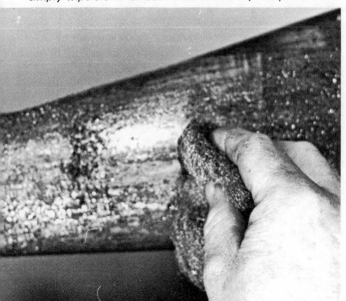

Stand the stock up, preferably in the sunshine, and allow it to dry by itself without applying any heat, such as a torch. This will give you time to repeat the same procedure on the forearm. After the stock is dry, you will notice that it not only is clean but somewhat faded in color. The sanding will go past this fading and expose the regular wood color underneath. If you are refinishing a good sound stock that will not require repairs, quite often you can give the stock a mild sanding or hard scrubbing with the double ought steel wool and go right into the refinishing process.

Many old stocks have the front section soaked in oil which must be removed as the stock finish will not stick to such a surface. There are dozens of ways to go about removing this oil with perhaps the simplest being, just hold the wood near a heat source and wipe away the oil as it thins and comes up. The only thing wrong with this method is that it is as slow as a tax refund and does not completely remove all of the oil. The best method that I have found so far is to use household bleach which is applied in full strength to the stock with a paint brush, similar to the method used with the paint stripper. The stock then is hung in the sunshine and allowed to dry.

The wood will turn white on the surface but this is easily cut down to the normal colored wood underneath with a little sanding. The oil in the stock brought to the surface is virtually dissolved. If you have a heavily oil-soaked stock, try the heat method first, then follow up with the household bleach. These two combined usually get the job done completely. Occasionally you will find a real stubborn stock and will have to make two applications of the bleach. In the event two applications fail, forget it and live with the oil; continued bleaching will require quite a bit of sanding and lose the lines of the stock.

With the old finish and the oil removed, our next problem is the dents in the stock and forearm. Sanding down past these dents will require the removal of too much wood, so we will raise the dents back level with the surface of the stock! This has its limitations, however, as you cannot raise a dent, if the fibers of the wood down in the dent have been broken. Dents such as these can be helped by the process but they will not be removed completely. Those dents where the wood has not been broken can be removed, usually without a trace remaining.

To raise the dent we will need two pieces of simple equipment, both of which are probably already available in your home. The first is some form of heated metal such as an electric soldering iron, but even this is not an absolute necessity as almost any kind of metal can be used. Even one of your wife's old tablespoons will work. If you use a spoon, grind the handle down to a point and drive on a piece of wood as a handle to protect your paws when the metal is hot. Another similar tool can be made by driving a piece of copper tubing up into a common file handle, give it a slight bend and hammering the exposed end flat. The second piece of equipment is a piece of common ink blotter or you can substitute a gun patch or similar cloth.

To remove the dent, heat your piece of metal over the kitchen stove, if you are not using an electric soldering iron. The metal should be only slightly hot, about like your wife's clothes iron; excessive heat will only burn the wood. Next, wet the blotter or gun patch with clean water and lay it directly over the dent. Apply the heated metal to the wet blotter or patch. The water will be condensed quickly into steam which will, in turn, flow into the bent fibers of wood and swell them.

The wood fibers in the dent then take the path of least resistance and return to their original shape and your dent is gone. One application usually is sufficient, but some stubborn dents will take two or even more applications before they are level with the rest of the surface of the stock. Be sure to use a new piece of wet blotter or wet patch with each steaming.

If the wood fibers have been broken and the dent is small, it probably will be best to try to sand the stock down enough to eliminate it this way. Should the dent be too deep or perhaps a piece of wood is gouged out, it will have to be filled or patched. Patching the stock should be a last resort, as it is difficult to match perfectly the grain and color of two pieces of wood. Rather than try to hide the defect by blending in a similarly colored piece of wood, some gunsmiths prefer to patch it with a piece of contrasting wood. Either way, cut the gouge out to the shape of a diamond about one-eighth inch deep. Now, make a patch to match the diamond and glue it into the recess leaving a little sticking up over the surface of the stock. After drying, the patch-diamond is sanded even with the surface of the stock.

Some find it easier to make the diamond replacement first, then cut the gouged stock out to match the pre-cut diamond patch. If you wish, there is a wide variety of manufactured plastic and pre-cut wood diamonds that you can purchase from gunsmith supply houses. Any contrasting color always should be located in a position on the stock that will add to the appearance rather than just be placed in some odd section of the stock. Personally, I have never taken a liking to the Buck Rogers inspired multicolored plastic inserts. In my opinion, they cheapen a stock.

If you have trouble with inletted patches, there is another simple and easy way to get rid of the gouges. This is accomplished first by cleaning out the gouge, removing all loose fibers as well as any lingering dirt and grease. The next step is to mix up a batch of good glue such as epoxy and dump in a spoonful of sawdust from the stock you are working on. This is stirred until the sawdust mixes completely with the glue taking on the appearance of putty. The material then is pressed down into the recess until the gouge is filled and slightly overflowing. With a flat piece of metal such as a common dinner knife, press hard on the mixture working it in firmly and expelling any trapped air.

When sanding the stock, always sand with the wood grain and never across it. Sanding block shown is inexpensive commercial model. It is available at hardware stores.

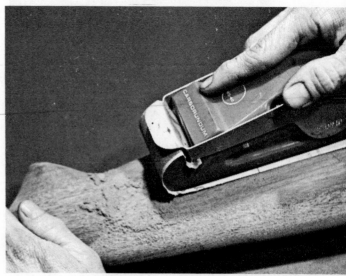

Add more mixture as needed and pile on a little afterwards over the filled gouge to allow for shrinkage.

Set the stock aside and allow the mixture to dry thoroughly. The final step is to sand the mound down even with the surrounding stock surface and your gouge will be as invisible as it is possible to obtain. If you are using glass bedding material, this can be substituted for the mixture of glue and sawdust, but most gouges filled with glass will be slightly darker in color than one using the glue and sawdust.

We now have our stock stripped of the old finish, grease and dirt, the dents have been duly raised and the gouges filled or hidden. We now are ready to tackle the major repair of the stock, which as you will remember, is a section of the toe of the stock broken off and a broken butt plate. We also have a large crack in the stock up at the front where it joins the receiver. Normally you would make both of these repairs at the same time, but for clarity, we will treat each as a separate repair. Let's tackle the crack first, then come back to the broken toe.

There must be a thousand or more different types of glue that can be used to repair gunstocks and the majority of them will do a good job. Many oldtime gunsmiths swear by such ill-smelling home concoctions as hide glue, all of which are mixed with glee at midnight over a smoking pot. This is a double-barrel mixture that will glue things together and open up the clogged sinus of a dead man. My nasal passages need no clearing and all I want is a glue that is easy to mix and that will bond things together with as little fragrance as possible. I feel that all glues for gun stocks became obsolete with the invention of epoxy.

Epoxy comes in two separate tubes, one the resin and the other the hardner. When the two are mixed and applied correctly to a stock, the resulting bond is much stronger than the wood surrounding it! An added advantage is that the glue does not depend on outside heat for hardening, it makes its own heat by chemical action. This may not seem much of an advantage, until you have worked with it during extreme temperature conditions and still get a terrific bond where other glues would fail.

About the only mistake you can make with epoxy is not mixing it in equal parts or not stirring the two parts until they turn to a cream color. It is best to mix the glue on a

In selecting a piece of wood for replacing the broken toe of a stock, try to match the color and grain, as here.

piece of paper or aluminum foil that can be discarded when you are finished, for it is next to impossible to remove any left-over epoxy from a container.

Our cracked stock is prepared first by flushing the crack with a few drops of lighter fluid or alcohol. Care should be taken when using such fluids, as both are highly flammable and you can end up with a mighty charred stock or gunsmith. It's about like the old joke that ducks have flat feet from stamping out flaming forest fires and elephants have flat feet from stamping out flaming ducks. Such fluids can prove quite useful around a gunshop but must be treated with the necessary respect and caution.

Allow the fluid to evaporate completely and repeat this a couple of times to be sure you have flushed away any oil in the crack, as oil is the enemy of epoxy. If any oil is present on the surface of the wood, the epoxy will not stick to the wood no matter how much or how carefully you apply the glue.

Mix up a batch of epoxy and fill the crack until it is overflowing. Then light a large kitchen match and hold it for a moment or two about an inch above the glue. This warming of the glue does not effect its hardening or binding, but it does thin the glue and allows it to flow down deep into the crack covering the exposed wood completely. If the crack soaks up all of the glue, repeat the whole process including the match trick; keep repeating it until the crack has absorbed all of the glue it can. If possible, squeeze the crack together, with a C-clamp or a large rubber band for a good tight joint. The glue will dry completely in a few hours and the excess can be sanded away leaving an almost invisible joint.

To repair the split toe of the stock we will first have to prepare it to receive a new piece of wood by cutting the ragged break smooth and even. A plane works best for this, but it can be done with a wood rasp or even a pocket knife. Of course, since I use planes, which are a necessity in stockmaking and stock repairing, I guess this is as good a place as any to stop and discuss the different types of planes available, their uses and also make a few recommendations as to choice.

There are five basic types of planes, the largest being the fore plane which is about eighteen inches long and is used mainly by carpenters and cabinet makers to plane long straight surfaces, making it about useless in stock work. Next in length is the jack plane, about a foot long and the basic plane of all carpenters. Again, due to its length, little practical use will be found for it in stock work. The third type looks like a bob-tailed jack plane. About eight or nine inches long, it is known as the bench plane or smooth plane. This is the one for the stockmaker to choose for the heavy stock work. It is short enough to get into close places that the fore or jack plane cannot reach, yet it is long enough to keep the surfaces of the stock smooth and is rugged enough to remove a mountain of wood in a hurry. Next in length is the block plane which, unlike the other planes, is designed to be held with one hand. Its best use is in the finish work on a stock, but if finances dictate, it can be substituted for the bench plane and will accomplish the same work in a longer span of time.

The smallest of the five is the model makers plane which is about three inches long, usually costing only a couple of dollars. It is worth ten times this amount to the gunsmith as it will get down into the tiny spaces that the other planes will not reach and can be used to take that final hair-thin cut from the stock.

Getting back to the split-off toe of our stock; we first remove the broken butt plate and closely examine the remaining wood of the stock as well as the roughness of the break. Most split-off stock toes are rough and ragged which eliminates any chance of trying to match pieces of wood to this surface.

With the stock held firmly in a vise, we begin to carefully plane the rough surfaces away and remove a chunk of the entire toe of the stock. Go slowly, removing only a little wood at a time and continue until the rough surface has been eliminated and the surface of the cut is absolutely smooth and level. To check the accuracy of your cut, lay a flat-edged ruler or piece of metal on the planed surface and hold it up to eye level against a strong light. Any dips or waves in your work will be detected instantly. Additional strokes of the plane will get the surface smooth and level as needed. Once this is accomplished, lay the stock aside, being careful not to get the newly prepared surface contaminated with grease and dirt.

The stock surface prepared, we can begin our patch to take the place of the section of the stock we removed, as well as the part that was broken off. First, however, we must look closely at the lines of a good stock of similar design, preferably with the stock in our hands, but a photo is better than nothing. Notice that the line of the bottom of the stock is straight from the pistol grip right down to the toe of the butt plate. Our job will be to make our patch blend with the same bottom line of our stock. With what the finished stock should look like firmly in our mind, we select a piece of wood that matches the color and grain as closely as possible.

If you intend to work on many stocks in the future, now is the time to start saving every piece of walnut, maple and similar stock wood that you can lay your hands on. Old broken stocks usually have plenty of good solid wood left on them for repairing other stocks and the age of the old stock will match more closely a used stock being repaired than new wood. In addition, many broken stocks have beautiful sections of wood in them that can be made into pistol grips, shotgun and rifle grip caps, forend tips and

even butt plates.

With a handsaw, cut off a big chunk of wood and with your plane make a piece about the same basic size as the missing toe section of our stock. The surface of the replacement piece that will match the prepared surface of our stock must be as flat and level as our stock. It is a good idea to leave the replacement piece about an eighth or even a quarter of an inch larger on all sides to allow for final shaping. Any excess can be rasped or planed off until the patch blends into the lines of the stock. If you make the mistake of cutting the replacement too small to begin with, then you are up the proverbial creek. With the replacement shaped and ready, mix up a batch of epoxy glue and, using a small piece of clean wood as an applicator, smear the glue on the prepared surface of the replacement wood that will be joined to the stock. These two joining surfaces must be covered completely with glue. To assure this coverage, press the two glue-covered surfaces firmly together and slide them back and forth to be sure both surfaces are covered completely. Align the replacement piece with the stock correctly and press the two together firmly and wipe away any excess glue that is squeezed from the joint.

Clamps can be used to hold the two pieces together while the glue is drying, but due to the angle of the stock and the patch, this is usually not a simple job. A much easier method is to use two large rubber bands which are rolled together, then stretched over the stock and the patch. If the patch joint is a long one, use two or three sets of the rubber bands to exert pressure equally. If the patch has a tendency to slip while the rubber bands are in place, it can be secured with several strips of tape which can be almost any kind that is available, including plain masking tape.

When applying the tape, start halfway on one of the sides of the stock, cross over the patch and prevent any movement. A couple of such layers of tape, one at each end, may be necessary for long patches. Make a final check

Section of wood matching grain of stock as closely as possible is glued to stock after surfaces have been planed to match. Epoxy is used, with rubber bands to hold the two sections together; tape prevents slipping.

and carefully lay the stock where it will not be bumped and allow the glue to dry overnight.

The next day the tape and rubber bands are removed and the patch checked to be sure that it still is in the correct position. It is a good idea to look at the lines of a similar stock again and compare it to your patched stock. Thus you determine how much of the wood must be removed from the patch and where it must come off to get the stock lines correct. The spliced-on piece of wood can be shaped fully with the plane and sandpaper, but a wood rasp will prove invaluable and eliminate a lot of sanding.

Rasps come in a wide variety of cuts, shapes and lengths, all of which can be used on gun stocks at one time or another. However, the beginner can buy one special rasp and do about seventy-five percent of the rasping required on gun stocks. There are two names for this special rasp, four-in-hand and shoe rasp. Regardless of which name you prefer, the rasp usually can be purchased at any hardware store for approximately two dollars in the eight-inch size.

It is, as the name implies, actually four different rasps in one. One side is flat and the other side is slightly rounded. The flat side is divided in half with one half being rough cut and the other half a smooth cut. The rounded side is made exactly the same with half of it a rough cut and the other a smooth cut. In use, the rasp is extremely fast, as it can be changed from rough to fine cut, either flat or round side with just a quick twist of the wrist. As there is no handle on the rasp, those with tender hands will find a light leather glove useful, until their hands toughen up a bit.

With your rasp and plane, slowly and carefully shape the spliced-on piece of wood until it is almost flush with the original lines of the stock and also, the surface of the stock. From there it is best to attack the remaining surplus wood with varying grades of sandpaper, finishing up with an extra fine grit. If you do your work well, the spliced-on wood will match perfectly with the old stock and only a hair line will be visible at the joint. If the shade of the new piece of wood is different from that of the stock, this can be corrected by applications of wood stain and bleach in varying degrees until the two pieces match closely.

Speaking of rasps, you will need to add a few as each new need presents itself. Always buy the best grade of rasp that your pocketbook will allow, for you will find that in rasps, quality usually goes hand-in-hand with price. One rasp often overlooked by the beginner is actually not a rasp at all, but a large metal file which allows you to work the surface of the stock down almost to the finish line, instead of doing it with sandpaper. Most machine shops throw away large metal files when they become dull for metal work and usually they are yours for the asking. Soak these in mineral spirits for a day and clean them thoroughly with a file card or steel wool to remove any lingering rust and packed-in grease.

Wood hand-scrapers also will prove invaluable in stock work and can be either purchased or made from any good piece of flat steel not over a quarter of an inch thick. File the edge of your homemade scraper exactly level and square the sides, for the edge is what does the cutting. To use, the scraper is cocked at a slight angle and pulled toward you, allowing the sharp edge to cut a thin curl of wood. Some beginners use a piece of broken glass as a substitute, but this is not a good idea as broken glass can quickly slice your finger to the bone.

Sandpaper, another necessary tool in stock work, is nothing but fine particles of selected stone or artificial cutting compounds glued to stiff pieces of paper or cloth. There are three basic types of sandpaper used in stock work, any of which can be used for the entire job or you

Glue dried, rubber bands and tape are removed. Section is shaped with rasp to blend with shape of the original. Finish is with sandpaper decreasing in grit size until only the faint line of joining is evidence of the repair.

can use a combination, if you prefer. The least expensive is garnet paper but the most practical use for this paper is in the rough cuts, for it tends to clog quite easily in the finer grits. The second type, and a bit more expensive, is silicon carbide which will last much longer than garnet paper and does not clog as quickly. The third type and the best of them all is aluminum oxide which will last much longer than the other two, as well as resist clogging.

All three types usually are sold in hardware stores in coarse, fine and extra fine grades. This simplified system of grading the grit is fine for the average citizen who wants to sand the back door or the dog house, but too often each manufacturer decides what is coarse and what is fine with little or no comparison in grit to another manufacturer's products. Sometimes they will designate it as 3/0, 8/0 etc., which can be equally as confusing. The best method of identification is to buy the grit expressed in units of 10, which will generally be printed on the back of the sandpaper, in addition to the other designations. The only thing to remember is that, as the number becomes larger, the size of the grains of grit will decrease in size and will give you a finer cut when the sandpaper is used. The sizes most used in stock work will be numbers starting with 120 as the most coarse, followed by 220, 280, with 320 about the finest grit necessary. Grit size 400 will be needed occasionally when you are working with an especially dense piece of wood.

If there is a glass cutting business located in your town, ask them for some of their discarded sanding and cutting belts. These are usually about four inches wide with a stiff cloth backing and use aluminum oxide as a cutting agent. These belts are almost indestructible and you can sand with a piece of it hour after hour without ever getting it clogged.

If it does clog for some reason, a few quick swipes across the grit with a piece of steel wool and it is ready to go again, cutting like it was new. This stuff has to be extra tough to cut and smooth the edge of glass! When it gets too worn for the glass cutter, it is just right for the woodworker. I have used it for many years and never actually have worn out a piece of it on wood. I have even used it for rough cutting steel with cutting oil and power feed and even then, the stuff lasted for a long time.

An electric hand sander is fast but is not an absolute necessity. Also, it requires a good bit of experience to use correctly on gun stocks. If you decide to buy one, check to see that it vibrates straight back and forth. The more common orbital sander will cut across the grain as well as with the grain when used and the cross-grain cuts will produce scratches that are difficult to remove. Oddly enough, the straight back and forth type is usually the cheaper of the two types. Hand-held belt sanders are available, but for the most part, they are heavy and difficult to use on stocks, being limited to the wide straight sections of the stock. Most hardware stores sell a small hand sanding block for around a dollar with clamps at each end to hold the sandpaper in place as it is used.

If you wish, you can make these quite easily, for all you really need is a piece of wood with a small piece of cloth behind the sandpaper, and instead of the metal clamps to hold the sandpaper in place, you just hold it with your fingers as you sand. The good part about these homemade sanding blocks, besides saving money, is that you can make them in all sizes and shapes to reach those close sections of the stock with all of those odd curves and edges. Even your old finger itself can be used as a sanding block by simply wrapping a piece of sandpaper around it.

Before we start our sanding, the decision has to be made as to whether the gun will be reblued. If the gun is to be reblued, the butt stock can be left attached to the receiver during the sanding operation and make the entire job of sanding a lot easier. Any run-over from the sandpaper will cause scratches on the metal, but if the gun is to be reblued, these scratches will be removed during the polishing operation prior to rebluing. However, if the metal is not to be reblued, such scratches will stand out like a sore thumb. Protect the metal by covering it with plastic electrician's tape and be extra careful not to hit the metal with the sandpaper. You can still do a good job and not touch metal so long as you do not go sanding away like a mad man. The butt stock can be removed from the action for the sanding operation, if desired, but I do not recommend this, as it takes a lot of practice to keep from rounding the edges of the stock where it joins the metal and being sure not to sand the wood down below the level of the metal where they join.

There is one cardinal rule that must never be violated in sanding a stock: Always sand with the grain of the wood and never across it. Sanding with the grain will produce an

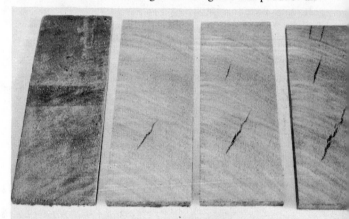

Hasty, forced curing of a walnut stock blank can be the cause of problems such as this. Section at left was sawed from end of blank, did not show any sign that the blank was ruined by cracks and checked areas.

Here are six typical tools used in fitting and bedding barrels and actions to stocks. From left: two gouges, a circular scraper and three rasps differing in size.

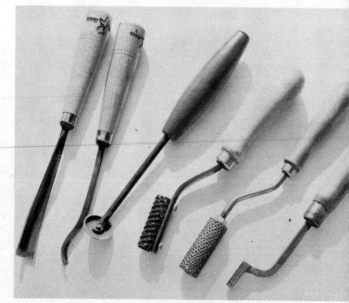

even appearance and any scratches put into the wood will be hidden and blended with the grain in the wood. Sanding across the grain, even with the finest of grits, will produce scratches that stand out like a Republican at a Democratic fund-raising dinner. Such scratches are difficult to remove and require extensive elbow grease and sweat that could be put to better use sanding the stock in the correct manner. Many beginners go at the job of sanding as if they were erasing their mother-in-law, when smooth and even strokes with a steady pressure will remove more wood. In the long run, both you and the sandpaper will last longer.

After you have taken the wood down as far as possible with the plane, rasp and scraper, begin sanding your stock with the number 120 grit to remove the roughness and blend any parts such as the spliced-on section in with the lines and level of the rest of the stock.

Go over the entire stock with this grit, then wipe the stock to remove the dust from the sanding. An old T-shirt or bath cloth will do an excellent job of removing the dust. If you are lucky enough to have compressed air, a quick short blast of the air will clear the dust better than any cloth.

When you have finished with the 120 grit, drop down to the next finest grit that you have and go over the stock for a second time, sanding with this grit just as you did with the 120. Again wipe or blow the dust away and have a go at the stock with the next finest grit that you have available. Keep repeating this, dropping to a finer grit each time, until you have the stock completely sanded smooth with all dips, waves and roughness eliminated.

Keep the lines of the stock straight and refer to your example of a similar stock if there are any questions in your mind. The correctness and throughness of your sanding will contribute fully seventy-five percent to the appearance of your finished stock. If you have been careless or too hurried in your sanding, this will be quite evident when the finish is applied; the best finishing material and method cannot hide a poorly sanded stock. Take your time and do it right.

When you have sanded the stock as slick as a greased eel, it still is hiding a feature that will ruin your sanding efforts, as well as the best of any finish that is applied. The problem is that, while sanding, you are cutting the fibers of the

Stock layout templates of sheet plastic are handy if you plan to produce many stocks. Transparent material permits you to pick out choicest grain. These two are for shotgun stocks; line on lower is for Win. Model 12.

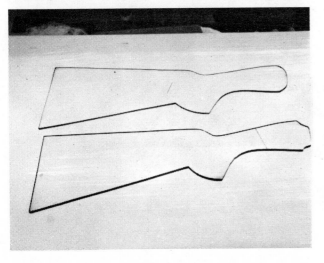

wood and many of the ends of the fibers break loose from the body of the wood and look like the end of a rope unraveling. If left alone, these loose fiber ends will stick straight up when the finish is applied and the entire surface of the stock will feel much like a day's growth of beard. Because of this similarity they are called "whiskers," and the process of removing them from the stock is known as "whiskering the stock."

Sometimes the wood is hard enough that this process is not needed to any great extent, while other woods that are on the soft side will look like a shaggy dog. Regardless of how hard the stock appears, it is a good idea to go through the process once to make absolutely sure no whiskers remain when you begin applying the finish.

To whisker the stock, thoroughly wet a section of bath cloth or a piece of sponge, then wring it out until it is just damp. Now, wipe one side of the stock with the moist cloth or sponge, covering all areas of this side. You are not trying to give the stock its Saturday night bath, so just dampen it. When you have the side completely covered, hold this damp section about six inches over the stove burner with the flame set on low, if you are using a gas stove.

Be careful not to burn the wood, hold it only close enough and long enough for the heat to evaporate the moisture you have put in the stock with the damp cloth or sponge. Keep moving the stock across the heat source until all parts of the stock are again dry, then closely look at the surface of the stock. You will see those loose fiber whiskers standing tall! As the water evaporates, the resulting steam produced in the wood raises the splintered fiber ends above the surface of the stock where you can get at them. Repeat the whiskering of the stock until you have every inch raised before you start removing the whiskers.

There are two basic ways to remove the whiskers with some gunsmiths swearing by one, others standing pat for the second method. One method uses a piece of worn sandpaper or a new section of grit size 320 or 400, with all strokes made against the grain to cut the whiskers from the wood. This will do an excellent job and is recommended when you are working with a particularly open grain stock with many tough whiskers to remove.

The second method uses a wad of double ought steel wool instead of the sandpaper, and again, with the strokes against the grain of the wood to cut the whiskers from the stock. Regardless of your choice of method, under no circumstances make a back stroke, for if you do you will just press the whiskers back down into the grain of the wood and will have to repeat the entire process to correct the back stroke.

Make your strokes from the small section of the stock toward the thicker and higher sections and you will be right ninety-nine percent of the time in not cutting against the grain. If the section of the stock is level, move your finger lightly first one way, then the other against the stock and you can determine instantly which way to make your cutting stroke. Of the two methods, I prefer steel wool, as it removes the whiskers more quickly, but you must examine the wood closely afterwards to be sure no tiny fibers of steel wool remain imbedded in the surface of the stock.

When you have finished removing the whiskers, wet the stock again and repeat the same procedure. Only when your wetting efforts produce no whiskers can you consider the job finished. It is a good idea to allow the stock to stand in a warm, dry part of the shop overnight to remove any lingering traces of moisture in the wood before you begin applying the finish.

I cannot overstress the importance not only of correct sanding but complete sanding as well. Too often I have seen a beginner tire of the work and stop short of the finish line. The resulting stock is a sorry sight to behold, with rough sections standing out like a sore thumb on what otherwise would have been a beautiful stock. The quitter would have been far better off to have hired a professional to do the work or to have forgotten the whole idea. The amount of sanding will depend on many things, including the condition of the stock before the sanding even begins. If the stock is old, oil-soaked and rough, you probably will have to start with the coarsest grit available and work slowly up to the finish grit, step by step.

On the other hand, if you are refinishing the stock of a relatively new gun, the coarse grit will not be needed and you usually can start with a medium grit. I have seen stocks that required only light sanding with the finest grit. About the best rule to follow is to use the finest grit that you can get away with and still have the stock surface in correct condition to receive the finish. If the stock is clean with no dents, gouges or scratches after stripping, skip the heavy grit. In a few rare cases, even whiskering is not necessary.

With the butt stock of our shotgun now repaired, sanded and whiskered, we can turn our attention to the forearm. We have stripped the forearm of all remaining finish and removed the oil that was soaked into it. We raise the dents and make any necessary filling operations if gouges are present just as we did on the butt stock.

Before we start the sanding and whiskering operation on the forearm we will have to make a few repairs to put the forearm in order. The metal forearm assembly must be held tightly to the wood and ours falls short, as the screw holes are worn and wallowed out. Our first step is to remove any slivers of loose wood in the forearm screw holes and get the holes clean of any oil and grime. Rotten and damaged wood must be cut away with a knife until we are down to good solid wood, but no attempt is made to get the holes nice and round. Flush the holes with lighter fluid and we are ready to make our repair.

As stated, epoxy glue will not stick to any oily surface, but otherwise will bond just about anything together including wood to steel. We will fill those ragged screw holes with a batch of epoxy, reassemble the metal to the forearm wood and insert the screws down into the epoxy-filled holes. When the epoxy has hardened, it not only will have filled the holes completely, but with the screws in position, we will have a sort of hard epoxy "nut" surrounding the screws and holding them secure.

However, if we do this without first taking one preventative step, the epoxy will bond to the screws permanently and prevent any further removal of the screws. So lets put that to work for us in a positive way. We will coat the screws with an oily substance before we insert them down into the epoxy filled holes and thereby prevent the bonding

Here's an assortment of coarse and fine wood rasps in several basic shapes, all handy for working on stocks.

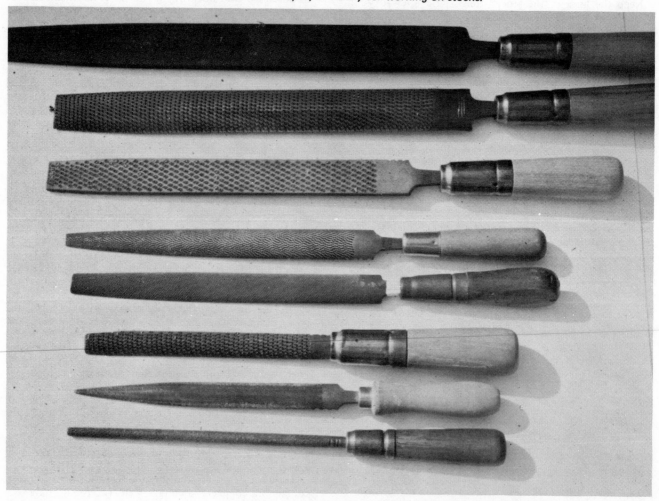

of the epoxy to the screws, but not the epoxy to the wood. There are many substances that can be used as a release agent for the screws such as heavy grease but any oil or grease has a tendency to soak into the wood and prevent the epoxy from bonding to the wood.

I prefer to use regular floor paste wax as a release agent. Besides, it has many other uses around a gun shop in addition to this duty. A regular can will last indefinitely. You can apply the wax to the metal cold, but this carries with it the possibility that some small surface will not be covered and the epoxy will bond to it.

The best way to assure that all surfaces are covered with the wax is to dump a couple of spoonfuls of wax into a tin can and hold it near a heat source until it melts. (Remember that some waxes are flammable, so keep the heat far enough away to just melt the wax and not burn it.)

When the wax is melted, dunk the screws into it, being sure that they are submerged completely. The bottom of the forearm metal components also must be covered with wax as they will come in contact with the epoxy and possibly bond to it. This is done best with a small brush dipped into the molten wax and painted on the metal surfaces thoroughly, taking care that all exposed surfaces are covered. Don't get careless with the application of the wax; if you do a halfway job and leave some surface uncoated, you are in for quite an interesting time getting the epoxy-bonded wood and metal apart. Cover every surface and take a second look just for good luck.

When all metal parts have been wax coated, fill the screw holes in the wood forearm with epoxy and set the forearm metal assembly into position. Next, seat the screws through the metal assembly, pressing them down firmly and finish with a couple of twists of each screw to seat them solidly in the epoxy and force out any trapped air. Should the epoxy flow back up through the screw holes in the forearm metal assembly, remove the screws and wipe away the excess glue

before reseating the screws. The screws must be wiped clean, for if the screw holes in the forearm metal assembly are countersunk, the epoxy would harden into these recesses and prevent removal of the assembly.

To hold the forearm metal assembly firmly to the wood while the epoxy is hardening, use a couple of C-clamps. You will need C-clamps continuously in gun work, so now is a good time to purchase a couple in the three-inch size. The size of all C-clamps is designated by the maximum opening of the clamp. Place the two clamps on the forearm directly over the screws, pressing them down into place and then set the forearm aside to allow the glue to harden overnight.

The next day, remove the C-clamps and the screws. The screws may resist removal and require considerable pressure of the screwdriver to free them from the skin-tight fit of the hardened epoxy.

With the screws removed, tap the forearm metal assembly lightly and rock it back and forth until it is free. You will notice that the epoxy has filled the old ragged holes completely and we now have a perfect and permanent epoxy nut seat for the screws. In this example we have used epoxy, but if you are using glass bedding material on the stock, it can be used for this same purpose in exactly the same way, including the use of the wax as a release agent.

With our stock and forearm repaired, the dents raised, the gouges filled, the oil removed and the stock thoroughly sanded plus whiskering, we are ready to apply the finish. Before we undertake this final phase of our stock refinishing, stop and remember for a moment the processes and methods we have used up to this point. These will serve you many times in the future in your newly found hobby. There is no magic in it, no secret, dark formula that would prevent any average person from refinishing gun stocks.

The only things actually used besides the material are a little knowledge, a little sweat and a lot of gol-danged determination.

Useful for roughing out large amounts of excess wood, this open-cut rasp is inexpensive, found in many shops.

Tools such as these are handy for removing small, precise amounts of wood in fitting stocks to the action. In center is a curved, fine-cut wood rasp for flat work.

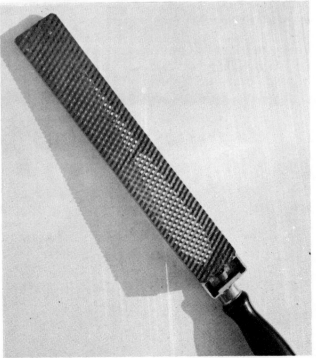

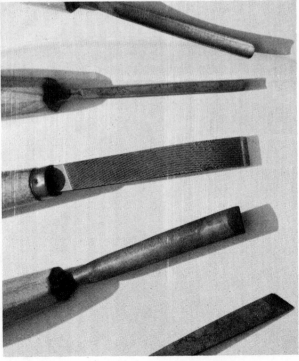

Chapter 3

STOCK FINISHING

The Basics Of This Art Should Be Among The First Perfected In Learning The Gunsmithing Crafts!

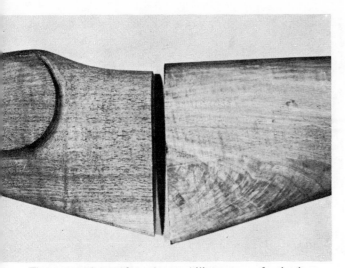

These two pieces of stock wood illustrate perfectly the differences between dense and porous woods. The stock at the left with the check piece is much more porous.

THERE ARE THREE separate phases to finishing any stock, regardless of whether it is a new stock or an old stock being refinished. Each of these steps provide a definite and useful service and all should be included in every finishing job.

The first step is sealing the surface of the wood against moisture, grease and dirt. Preventing these and other out-side elements from entering the fibers of the wood will increase the useful life of the stock indefinitely. If these elements are allowed to enter the fibers of the wood, they will slowly break down the fibers or change their structural shape and warp the stock.

The second step — filling — eliminates the pockmarked surface of the wood caused by the pores of the wood. Filling these pores until level with the surrounding surface of the stock will improve the appearance of the stock after the finish has been applied.

The final step is the finish itself. This is the main defense the stock has against all of the ills that befall a gun stock. Depending on the process being used, these three steps can be accomplished with three different materials or, in some cases two materials, while still other processes will use one material for all three steps. Yet, in every case, there are always three steps: seal, fill and finish.

The old classic finish is supposed to be linseed oil that has been kettle-boiled slowly, then lovingly rubbed into the wood with tender care, month after month, until a deep and wonderful finish is obtained.

When I was a youngster I read with awe the starry-eyed spiels by some of the oldtime writers about this classic finish. Deciding to refinish a favorite rifle this way, I made a trip into town and bought a half-gallon of the best linseed oil I could find. I figured that, like water, some it was going to boil away and I wanted to be sure I would have enough to carry me through those months of rubbing. I asked every paint dealer I could find just how to go about kettle boiling it and received some mighty strange and puzzled looks. I then searched through all of the glowing articles for this all-important detail. While the adjectives were many, the details on boiling were conspicuously lacking. I plunged ahead to find the answer for myself.

A good look at the mess in one of her best boilers on her stove and Mom gave explicit instructions and directions to the back yard. Deprived of my heat source and container, I then built a roaring fire with some hardwood. When this was reduced to glowing redhot coals, I suspended the lin-seed oil over them in an old iron pot. Stirring the smoking oil with a spoon in one hand, fanning the coals with the other, presented a sight not soon forgotten. I ended up with the gosh-awfullest gooey mess you ever saw. The contents of the kettle didn't appear to be the best thing for a gun stock, but mixed with a bag of down, it would have served a good duty in a tar and feather outing.

It was years before I learned that so-called kettle-boiled linseed oil was actually raw linseed oil cleaned of impurities with acid, with a special ingredient added to it to speed up the drying. Just as the oldtimers wrote, you can finish a stock with good commercial boiled linseed oil if you have the time and patience. If you enjoy doing things the hard way, like brushing your teeth while standing in a hammock, then this is just the finish for you.

Raw linseed oil on a gun stock is slightly better than burned motor oil. You can rub a stock with raw linseed oil until you reduce it to the size of a toothpick and never get a decent finish. As for drying, there is no drying! You can settle this question in your mind once and for all with a simple little experiment. Hold any oil finished military stock next to a heat source and watch the oil ooze out of the stock. Remember that these stocks were submerged in boiling linseed oil hot enough to blister a brick and still, the oil is not dry.

Many of our present firearms writers, while guarding against cheapening guns through modern mass production, tend to develop a hide about six inches thick that nothing can penetrate. Mention a new modern stock finish to one of them and he draws up on his pedestal, head held high, his gray locks blowing in the breeze, and starts quoting from the opened pages of a book he wrote in the 1920s about how nothing compares with the "London Hand Rubbed Oil Finish." This is like saying that grandma has a better remedy for pneumonia with her blackstrap molasses and sulphur than any newfangled thing like penicillin.

If you want a good rubbed oil finish, all you have to do is buy a bottle of one of the new stock finishes designed specifically for this purpose. These products beat the old home-brewed finishes without even getting a light sweat. However, they must be applied slowly and with care follow-ing the manufacturer's directions to the letter, instead of following the advice of an armchair gunsmith.

The finished stock will be one of which you can be proud and the method of application is simplicity in itself. Just rub the thin finish in well, and let it dry thoroughly before applying the next coat. Time, patience and correct application are the keys to any good stock finish. There are no dark and mysterious secret methods known only to a select gray-headed few.

Another of the old, often touted finishes is known as "French polish," which at one time was used widely on fine furniture, then adapted to gun stocks. Shellac, a waterproof material, was used as the basic material in French polish. As shellac has a tendency to shrink and crack, boiled linseed oil was added to the shellac to prevent this and the serve as a lubricant when applying it to the stock. A French polish-finished stock is nice in appearance but lacking in wearability and it will water spot.

If you want to try a French polish finish on one of your stocks, first buy a can of orange shellac (its natural color) and a small can of commercial boiled linseed oil.

The applicator is made by placing a thumbnail size wad of cotton inside of a piece of discarded women's nylon hose. Twist the hose around the cotton wad and make a working pad about the size of a marble. Dip the pad lightly in the shellac and let the cotton absorb only a couple of drops. The pad now is dipped ever so lightly in the linseed oil. Only one drop of linseed oil is needed and, if you wish, it can be applied to the cotton pad with a medicine dropper.

Apply the soaked pad to the stock surface and work one spot at a time in a hard circular rubbing motion. The area covered should be about the size of a silver dollar; about 1½ inches in diameter. Your pad will soon stop dragging and start to slide easily over the area as the shellac dries under the constant circular rubbing. As soon as this happens, stop and prepare another pad as you did the first time, but in another section of the hose and with another wad of cotton. The second working circle should just touch and blend into the first complete circle on the stock. Keep repeating this procedure and interlocking the circles until the entire stock has been covered. Look at the finished surface closely in bright sunlight. If, while making the circles, you have caused some ridges to be formed, they can be eliminated and the surface smoothed by soaking a pad in alcohol and wiping the surface of the stock lightly. You may have to make two trips over the stock to get a high finish, but one trip usually is sufficient.

Another popular stock finish is lacquer. Many of the inexpensive modern guns have their stocks finished with this. When used with a spray gun it will cover a stock fast and, as it is fast drying, any missed sections can be covered quickly without runs. The speed of its drying time is the main factor that endears it to manufacturers. Although the finish is not as good as most gun buffs like, it is a service-able finish that resists the elements quite well. There is a wide variety of lacquer types, most of which can be used on gun stocks.

I have experimented with automotive lacquer and it will do an acceptable job when used in a spray gun, but for those interested in a lacquer finish, I would recommend one of those available from the gunsmith supply houses that are designed especially for gun stocks. These are applied with a common paint brush and will give a nice finish to the stock. When shellac is thinned, it will go on evenly and, if cut extra thin, will serve as a good stock sealer. As a filler, it leaves a lot to be desired, as cutting off the excess with steel wool is a hard job.

Varnish is another widely used stock finishing material with the best of the bunch being spar varnish, specifically the type used for marine purposes. It is tough stuff and will resist scratches far better than regular furniture varnish.

While varnish can be applied directly to the stock with a brush, the results will be lacking in appearance. A much better way is to substitute varnish for shellac in the French polish method. If you want a faster finish, mix two parts varnish to one part of boiled linseed oil, add a bit of thinner and rub it into the stock in clean, even and long strokes. Spar varnish is one of the old favorite sealers and is still a good choice if it is cut thin with turpentine and brushed thoroughly into the wood.

The newest type of varnish is not a varnish but a plastic, and the name is retained only to avoid confused customers and make it sell faster. It is known by a variety of trade names but all are some form of polyurethane plastic. It is even tougher than spar varnish! Most major paint companies offer it in both a high gloss finish and a soft or satin finish. Its finest use on stocks is as a sealer and filler which requires that it be thinned with naphtha and brushed into the wood. When the stock has been covered, wait about fifteen minutes, then with a rag soaked in thinner, rub the stock cross-grain. This will remove the surface coat,

Stock hanging bracket is made from electrical conduit and affords a good handle for holding the stock, while the finish is being applied. Angle brackets hold up end.

but not harm the polyurethane that has soaked down into the wood. Follow this with a good overall rub down of the stock with a dry cloth and allow the sealer to dry for twenty-four hours before working on the stock again.

The Casey Chemical Company manufactures what I consider one of the best and most easily applied of all oil finishes, under the brand name of Tru-Oil. It is versatile and will forgive a multitude of errors and still produce a good finish. In fact, the stock can be sealed, filled and finished with Tru-Oil alone or the material can be used in con-junction with another type sealer and finisher. Several other companies manufacture a similar oil finish and, having tried some of them, I can find no fault. If you care to substitute one of these, the process will be about the same.

Wood has pores that are actually tiny holes in the wood similar to the pores of your skin. The number of pores and their size will depend on the closeness of the grain of the wood. In turn, the closeness of the grain is determined by the location of where the wood grew as a tree. If the tree grew high on a hill or in soil with a low water content, the growth rings of the tree will be close and tight. This results in close grain and few pores. If, however, the tree grew in a swamp, the growth rate was fast with big, fat growth rings and pores large enough for an ant to crawl in and out of. If the finish is applied without these pores being filled, the stock will look as though it has just recovered from a bad case of chicken pox.

Filler, as the name implies, is designed to fill these pores and in doing so, make the wood surface smooth and un-broken. Most fillers are composites of some holding agent and use fuller's earth as the actual filling substance. If you use one of these be sure it is designed for stock work and not general cabinet work. The latter often uses grains that are too large and some use other substitutes for fuller's earth. The wrong type can give the stock a rough finish and wreck a checkering tool in short order.

Your first reaction when opening a can of the average stock filler is to decide that some joker has sent you a can of mud. Reach in to the can, pull out about a tablespoon-full of the stuff and slap it on the stock. Rub it in, both with and across the grain, until the stock looks like some-thing pulled out of the swamp.

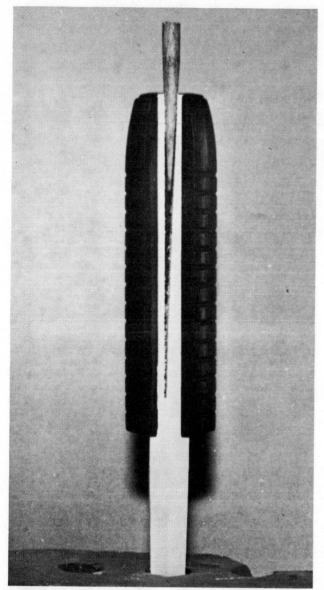

This forend holder is fashioned from 1X1 wood. It has been rounded at the top, saw cut with wedge to secure the holder to the forend. It can be set in a brick to hold it upright out of dirt or it can be hung from top.

Wait about five minutes and, with a piece of old towel, wipe across the grain to remove the excess. Continue wiping hard until the stock takes on a light sheen. Check closely to determine whether the pores have been filled or will need another coat or two. When you are satisfied that the filler has done its job, set the stock aside and allow the filler to dry thoroughly before you start applying the regular finish. The main thing to remember, when using a filler that has fuller's earth or similar material in it, is that you apply it both across the grain and with the grain, but you only remove it by wiping cross grain. If you wipe with the grain you will remove the filler.

Polyurethane, in addition to serving as a sealer, is a good filler and can be applied in two different ways. The whole secret in using this stuff as a filler is not to allow it to dry completely, which it will do in about twenty-four hours.

When it is dry, it is so hard and slick that even other coats of polyurethane will not stick to it. If you use a thinned coat of polyurethane as a sealer, follow this in about four hours with a good thick coat for the polyurethane as a filler. Do not allow the thin sealer coat to dry.

Brush your thick filler coat straight out of the can and get it on solid, both cross grain and with the grain. Don't be stingy when you are using it for a filler, as all pores must be filled completely.

This coat is allowed to dry for the full twenty-four hours, then cut back down with steel wool to the bare wood surface. Every pore will be filled completely and you can follow up with your regular finish. The only trouble with this system is that getting that thick coat off is a tough job and calls for a lot of sweat and elbow grease.

The second method is identical in that a thick coat is applied over the thinner coat before the thinner coat dries, only this time don't wait for the thick to dry. Instead, wait only about ten minutes, then wipe the filler coat of polyurethane off cross-grain with an old bath towel. Note that I specify cross grain and not with the grain. If the pores have not been filled with this filler coat, apply a second coat and, after ten minutes, again wipe it cross-grain. This is a bit on the messy side as the polyurethane feels like thick syrup under the towel and you will have to apply a considerable amount of pressure. It does, however, cut the work time and is the easier of the two methods to use. You then will have to wait the full twenty-four hours for the filler coat to dry and you probably will have a small amount of polyurethane remaining on the wood that must be cut off with steel wool as in the first method. The only difference between the two methods is that the second method leaves a lot less excess polyurethane to be cut off after it is dry. Either way, polyurethane will fill the pores completely and provide a smooth foundation for the finish.

Polyurethane also can be used for the final finish. In fact, some manufacturers offer it in spray cans for this purpose. The spray cans are a bit expensive, but for a one-stock job, they are to be recommended. They give you more control than a paint brush and there is no excess material left over to dry out. The material also can be applied with a good camel hair brush if it is thinned about fifty-fifty. Apply the material in long even strokes distributing the material equally over the stock and avoiding buildups that will cause runs. One good thing about polyurethane is that, if you apply it even halfway correctly it will flow together and erase any brush marks.

If you use it as the final finish, be sure to wait no more than twelve hours between coats so that the second and following coats will stick to the coats already applied. If a satin finish is desired it is best to select a polyurethane that specifies a satin or soft finish on the can However, if you have only the gloss type on hand, this can be rubbed down with a good stock rubbing compound after it is dry, to produce a soft velvet finish, but it requires a lot of rubbing. I have used polyurethane on quite a few stocks and I think it makes a good finish. My only objection is that it is too hard to control and there are easier ways!

The foregoing methods have been outlined to give a working knowledge of stock finishing by various methods. All of these and several others not mentioned will deliver good results provided you take your time and follow the manufacturer's recommendations. However, this book is for the hobbyist and not the professional, so we are interested in the simplest and easiest method that will produce good results.

Starting with a naked stock devoid of any sealing or filling, pour some Tru-Oil into the cap of a plastic pill bottle. Immediately put the cap back on the bottle of Tru-Oil, tighten it good and stand it upside down. The reason for this is that air will dry Tru-Oil rapidly and cause a film to cover the surface. Even if the bottle is sealed and stored upright, the small amount of air in the bottle will cause this film to appear.

If the bottle is stored upside down, this film will still appear, but when you turn the bottle right side up, the film will be on the bottom and only clear Tru-Oil will flow out of the bottle.

Always work with a small amount of Tru-Oil poured out in something like that pill bottle top instead of straight out of the bottle and not only will cut your material loss, but will avoid the film getting on the stock and spoiling the job.

Slop the first coat on cross-grain, with the grain, down the grain and any other way that you can get it on thickly and completely. This is no place to be stingy, for you are both sealing and filling with this coat. When the stock has been filled and will absorb no more oil, hang it outdoors and allow it to dry completely. The sunshine and the wind will dry the stock in short order. Take the stock back indoors and slop on a second coat as thick as the first one and again hang it out in the wind and sun to dry. Follow this with a third coat, with the wind-sunshine treatment. This time, allow the stock to dry for a full twelve hours. These three coats have sealed the stock and also filled the pores of the wood, but the finish leaves a lot to be desired in appearance.

With a handful of medium-cut steel wool, scrub the stock until all of the Tru-Oil is removed and you are back down to the bare wood. All of the pores should be filled and the surface of the stock is smooth and unbroken by dimples. If any dimples remain, repeat one or two more sloppy coats, allow it to dry and again cut the finish back to the wood with steel wool. Even the most porous woods should be filling by now. Never start the final finishing coats until all the pores of the wood are filled, for if any remain, you will never arrive at a smooth finish. When the stock is filled, wipe the stock thoroughly with a dry towel to be sure no tiny bits of steel wool are sticking to the wood.

The secret of a good Tru-Oil finish is not in the thickness of the final coats but the reverse. The thinner you can apply the coats, the better the finish! You will need to be a miser with the Tru-Oil from now on. Start by touching your finger tips in the oil and carrying only a drop or two to the stock. Some people prefer to smooth the oil on the stock with their finger tips and this works fine. I use the heel of my hand to spread it, as I can get it to flow and blend better this way. Stretch these drops to the absolute maximum and continue rubbing them in until the finish starts to "pull." At this point, dip back into the container for a couple of drops more and blend these in with the section you have just finished. Keep repeating this, going over the entire stock, but do not go back over the section you already have covered. If you do, the oil will start to streak and splotch. All of these strokes, made with the grain, should be as even and as long as possible to avoid lap marks. When you have finished with the first complete coat, check the stock to see if you have missed any spots.

If you are finishing a stock with the metal attached, pull the oil right up to the metal and over it. Oil that dries on the metal can be removed when you are through and, if you stop right at the metal, the oil will puddle and build up into a ridge.

Your hands will be sticky with the finish, but it can be removed by rinsing them in mineral spirits and finishing with soap and water. Mineral spirits will dry the oil nature

This drying room is 36 inches wide, 48 deep and six feet high, with plywood door. Hanging rod is from conduit; straightened wire clothes hangers are used for hanging; hot plate on floor with fan, aids drying.

provided in your skin and repeated use may cause your hands to crack. This can be avoided by applying hand lotion after washing.

With the first coat on the stock, hang it in the wind and sunshine to dry. Drying time will depend upon the temperature and the humidity.

You can make a good hanging rig for butt stocks with a small four-inch angle bracket from the hardware store. This should have holes in both ends, one to receive the butt stock screw attaching it to the stock, the other hole to accept a wire to support the bracket and the stock from an overhead bar or nail.

An even better hanging rig can be made from scrap

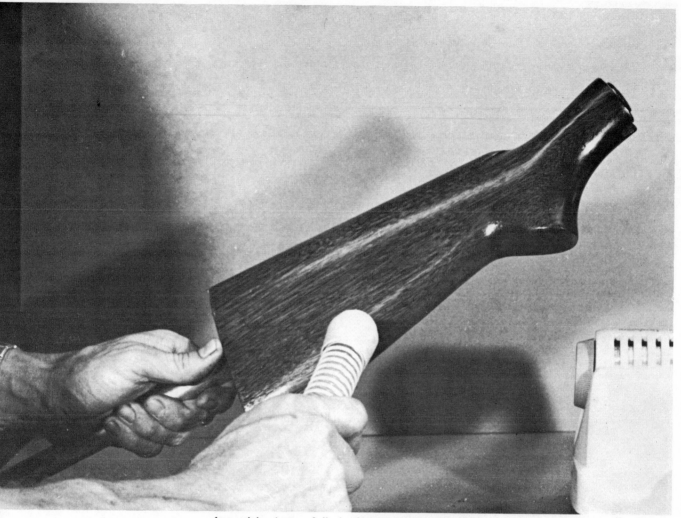

As explained more fully in the text, a hair dryer or even a vacuum cleaner can be used to speed drying of finish. With latter, be sure to empty vacuum bag first.

electrical conduit. Flatten one end of the conduit for about two inches and drill a hole in the flattened end. Now bend the flattened section at a ninety-degree angle. This section will attach to the butt stock. The other end is flattened and a hole drilled to accept the hanging wire.

A good hanging wire can be made from a clothes hanger that has been straightened and an open loop bent into each end. One loop goes through the stock hanging jig and the other goes over any convenient overhead rod or nail. These conduit stock holding jigs also provide a good handle for the stock while you are applying the finish.

Separate holding jigs for the forearms such as those found on pump and automatic shotguns can be made from one-inch wooden dowels with a cross nail through the dowel about a foot from the end. The dowel slips through the forearm hole from the outside and the cross nail limits its passage to provide a convenient handle and holding jig. If no dowel is available, you can use square wood stock with the edges rounded slightly for the same purpose.

If you want to hang them overhead, all that is needed is a hole through the upper end to receive the hanging wire. Another good way to hold the forend out of the dirt is to pick up a common brick, the type with holes through the center. The bottom end of the dowel or square holding jig

is inserted into one of the holes in the brick with the forend stopped by the cross nail. These simple jigs require only a couple of minutes to make, but save untold work if a stock slips and falls into the dirt and you have to do the entire job over again.

As any commercial shop has to turn out finished stocks regardless of the weather, we use a simple drying cabinet. This is nothing but an eight-foot high wooden box four feet square with a door and hanging racks inside. The racks are sections of electrical conduit inserted into blocks of two-by-four which are, in turn, nailed to the sides of the box. Down on the floor is a single unit electrical hot plate with a small portable electric fan blowing across it.

When the door is closed, the air inside is heated and circulated over the hanging stocks. Drying time is cut down about one-third over a similar stock out in the wind and sunshine. By keeping the drying cabinet clean, the finish does not pick up the dust particles it would if hanging in the open air.

The average hobbyist may not need such a large drying cabinet, but he can speed up stock drying with his wife's portable hair dryer. The machine set on high, the flexible hose is played up and down the stock, keeping the hose nozzle moving at all times. This heat and air will cut the

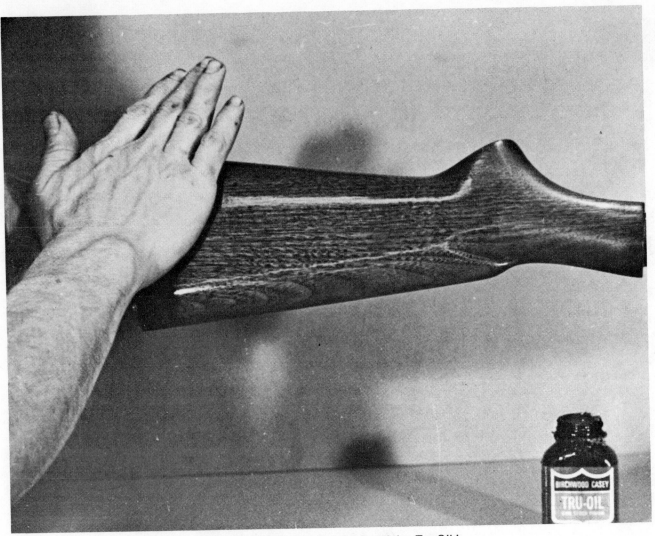

Walker feels that the best way of applying Tru-Oil is to work it in with the heel of the hand, making the oil stretch. Note first coat on pistol grip already is dry.

drying time of the finish considerably, yet cause the oil to penetrate more deeply into the stock during the first three filling coats.

The hair dryer can be utilized better by constructing a simple, inexpensive drying cabinet. Most furniture and appliance stores receive their wares in large heavy cardboard boxes which are usually available for the asking. Select one long enough to hold your stock when it is in the vertical position, allowing about six inches of clearance on both ends of the stock.

The first step is to cut a small door in one side of the box leaving the door attached on one side. To keep the door closed, you will need several strips of common masking tape or similar. A short rod, conduit or discarded broom handle is run through two sides of the box at the very top to provide a support rod from which to hang the stocks.

Next, cut a small circular hole about two inches in diameter on one side of the box down about six inches from the floor to serve as the entrance hole for the hair dryer hose. The top of the box should have an air exit hole of approximately the same diameter, although the size is not critical.

With your stock hanging inside and the door secure, insert the dryer hose through the bottom entrance hole and set the machine on medium warmth. Allow it to run for about an hour, then shut it off and, at the same time, plug the top air exit hole. The warm air will remain in the box for a considerable length of time.

If you do not have a hair dryer, you can make a similar arrangement by cleaning the bag of the vacuum cleaner, then inserting the hose in the exit or blower hole. This will provide the circulating air which will not dry the stock quite as rapidly as warm air, but still will speed drying time. If you do not clean the vacuum cleaner bag before doing this, you will blow all of the junk and dust in the bag into your drying cabinet and over the stock! An abandoned refrigerator stripped of its cooling mechanism will serve as a good drying cabinet and is more dust free than the cardboard box. You can use a hair dryer for the forced warm air or a hot plate and small portable fan arrangement. If no hot plate is available, you can rig up a heating coil stretched over an insulated frame in front of the fan and, in a pinch, even a common heat lamp can be employed with a fan. Be sure to remove the regular catch and substitute a common screen door hook to secure the door from the outside. This will prevent the door from locking from the inside.

Even a common vinyl garment bag like your wife uses to store off-season clothing can also be used for a dust-free drying cabinet. Select one that will provide ample clearance on the sides as well as the top and bottom. Vinyl will not stand much heat, but you can use the hair dryer without harm to the bag. If your working area is confined to your house, the bag will serve also as a storage place to keep the kids' fingers off the stock, while you are sanding it and applying the finish.

When your stock is dry from the first coat, remove it from the cabinet and examine it closely. The first coat probably will have soaked completely into the wood. Apply another coat of finish as you did the first coat and put the stock back into the drying cabinet. Don't forget to stretch that Tru-Oil out as far as possible to assure a thin, even coat over the entire surface. When the finish is dry, remove the stock from the cabinet and apply a third thin coat of finish. This apply and dry procedure is repeated until your stock starts to take on a light sheen. Usually about five coats will be necessary to obtain a good finish. Some woods will require more and still others, particularly those with the close grain, will take a good finish with as few as two coats.

You can stop right here and have a good serviceable finish, but a bit more work will turn a good finish into a professional job. To do this you will need to use a special stock rubbing compound. At one time or another, I have used a dozen or so different types, usually with good results. I argue with no man that his favorite brand will not do a good job.

One of the oldest stock compounds is rotten stone and, in the hands of a skilled craftsman with patience, it is hard to beat. For the beginner, it is best left alone until he gains more experience. Automotive body compound in extra-fine grit also can be used, but even the extra fine grit size is a little on the coarse side for most stock work. Use it only when nothing else is available and go easy on the application.

Most of the companies that manufacture semi-inletted stocks, as well as all of the gunsmith supply houses, offer stock rubbing compound of one brand or another. Just follow their instructions and you should have little trouble. With all brands, a small amount is spread thinly over a piece of good clean cloth, like an old T-shirt. This then is rubbed lightly, and I do mean lightly, over the entire stock surface. The idea is to cut the finish down to the point that all irregularities are smoothed out until the surface is even and unbroken. If you rub one spot too hard or too long, the rubbing compound will cut completely through the finish and down to the bare stock underneath. However, if you do it right, the finish will just lose some of its gloss as the irregularities are evened out the stock will take on a soft, warm glow. The finish can be left alone at this point and you will have something on the order of the classic London Hand-Rubbed Oil Finish only it is about ten dozen times more efficient in protecting the wood.

If you prefer a high gloss, just wipe the stock clean of any rubbing compound and apply one last and final coat of Tru-Oil, stretching it to the utmost and taking great care to get it on evenly. When this coat is dry, rub the finish briskly with a good, clean bath towel and you have the high gloss finish that is so popular with many hobbyists.

In either case, the final step is to wax the new finish job thoroughly and completely. Any good household paste wax will highlight the finish, adding even more protection. Many good commercial stock waxes are available and you seldom will go wrong, regardless of the particular brand. The final touch is to rapidly buff the stock from one end to the other with a piece of soft flannel.

I have left explaining bleaching and staining a stock to a specific shade until the end. This is a detailed and involved subject that could cover an entire chapter by itself. Staining has a multitude of uses. You will remember that we used a new piece of wood to repair the split off toe of the stock. Seldom will such a patch be the same color and shade as the original wood and, if left alone, the patch will be quite obvious. With correct bleaching and staining, the two woods can be blended to an almost perfect match in color and shade. New plain figured stocks usually can be improved with a little careful staining to bring out the grain structure and beauty of the wood. Many of the new semi-inletted stocks of economy grade have light streaks or some sap wood in one section that color up nicely with careful staining.

Matching two different pieces of wood is accomplished by first bleaching the more colorful piece of wood, usually the patch, until the color is more that of the less colorful piece. Commercial wood bleaches are available from stockmakers, gunsmith supply houses and most cabinet supply shops. Most brands will turn out an acceptable job.

I prefer to use a good household bleach, as the strength can be regulated with water, while most of the commercial bleaches require a special thinner. With the strength of a household bleach cut down about one-third with water, apply the solution with a regular paint brush to the surface of the more colorful piece of wood. The bleach can be accelerated by exposing the wood to sunshine, but this is not a necessity.

When the wood is dry, the bleach will have turned the surface of the wood almost white and you will need to cut the surface down lightly with sandpaper to expose the clear wood underneath. Compare the two pieces of wood and decide whether a second application will be necessary. If the two colors are reasonably close, stop with one application. Seldom will more than one application be needed.

As the strength of household bleaches varies with the manufacturer, make a trial application to a similar colored piece of scrap wood. Cut the bleach concentration and make more than one application rather than apply a concentrated solution and bleach the wood more than necessary.

The color match can be made even closer by applying a stock stain to the two individual pieces and varying the strength of the solution used on the two pieces. As the actual strength and number of applications will vary with each piece of wood as well as with the brand of stain, it is a wise hobbyist who experiments on scrap wood first! Most gunsmith supply houses offer commercial wood stains in orange, brown, black, scarlet and yellow. Each can be diluted or mixed with others to form just about any color combination required. A few companies offer stains specifically designed for gun stocks and are usually available in walnut, cherry, mahogany and brown mahogany. These usually are diluted with water to obtain a shade, but you can mix several for a specific need. I have found that stains will work better if you double the amount of dilution specified by the manufacturer and make several, rather than one, application. This gives far better shade control. Again, use scrap wood for experimenting with shades before applying it to your stock.

One of the favorite oldtime stains is potassium permanganate, a common antiseptic available at most drug stores. When in solution it is a deep purple color, which remains when the stain first is applied to the stock. Your first reaction is one of horror and you say nasty things about the fellow who recommended its use.

The average hobby gunsmith will be eager to get into this type of work, but a firm training program in the basics is something of a requirement before advancing.

The color is in the solution and not in the wood. When the solution is wiped off, the purple color goes with it and the wood underneath will appear to have aged with a deep shade of walnut color. With just a small amount of sanding to remove the surface of the wood, the figure of the wood will be brought out in sharp detail. The amount of stain, or rather the degree of darkening, is controlled first by the strength of the solution and second by the length of time the stain remains on the wood. There is little that can be given in the way of instructions, as the orignial color of the wood, its texture and age all contribute to the final color.

The best advice is to have your druggist make up a concentrated solution for you and try this on a piece of scrap wood for just a few seconds. Quickly wipe the stain away and note the shade. Next time, allow the solution to remain for a longer period before wiping it away. Finally, try diluting the solution to different strengths and varying the length of time. With a little experimentation you will become quite proficient with this stain and I believe it will become a favorite of yours, also.

After a little practice with bleach and stains you will be able to match woods closely and the results will be hard to detect. Another stain is nitric acid which will give colors in the yellow range up to a deep brown, if a ten percent solution is used. This is a good solution for new stocks, but is most useful in bringing life back to badly aged stocks. Quite often, a plain stock can be brought into beautiful and colorful array with careful application of different types of stain.

The old gunsmiths of the percussion and flintlock era often used a hot flame played with the grain to bring out grain structure that otherwise would not be visible. If the wood did not have any grain structure, they made cross or herringbone patterns in the wood by playing the flame back and forth across the stock.

For example, maple has little or no figure in most grades and the careful application of a flame can be used to greatly accentuate the wood structure, turning a plain stock into a thing of beauty.

The best tool for this is a common propane torch with the flame turned to the lowest position. Use a piece of scrap wood for your lessons and apply the torch to a stock only when you have acquired the knack. Usually you will need to sand the stock lightly after the flame to remove any scorched sections of wood. A good beginning lesson is to use the torch on a common piece of plywood, moving the torch over the visible grain structure and following its turns.

Just as the recent years have given us finishes superior to those available in the 1920s and 1930s, the future will give us even better finishes than we have today. As new products come on the market, regardless of the intended use, try them on old scrap stocks or pieces of wood. Quite often, you will find a solution or product that can be used in a way that the manufacturer never dreamed of when he offered it on the market. Many products used in furniture manufacture can be utilized in gun stock work. I believe the future will provide stock finishes far superior to the best we have today and my guess would be that they will be one of the new plastics. The new finish will be the answer to our wish for a soft and attractive finish that is impervious to rot, water and the hundred and one other troubles that befall the handles of our favorite smokepoles.

A RECOIL PAD CAN be a graceful addition to a stock or it can stand out like a bluetick hound at a French poodle family reunion. If the right type is chosen and fitted correctly, the pad will perform its primary purpose of softening the recoil, as well as adding to the overall appearance of the stock.

The first type pad to eliminate is the slipover pad. These come in a wide variety of models with various methods of attachment. Some are laced on the stock and some are variations of a rubber boot. Mount a gun to your shoulder equipped with one of these, and it feels about as correct as wearing your left shoe on your right foot! As for appearance, they ruin the lines of the stock, among other things. If left on a stock for any length of time, a slipover pad will destroy the stock finish under it. Their only use should be as a temporary stock adjustment.

The second type pad to eliminate is the cheap model that usually sells for about a dollar. These are made of a combination material with ground-up recap tires and tennis shoes as the main ingredients. They do a poor job of absorbing recoil. Some are about as soft as a rock and others spongy like foam rubber. When grinding one down, the material rolls off like sand and a smooth finish is impossible. It's money ahead, plus the saving of a lot of work, to buy a good pad to start with rather than pinching pennies for a pad that will have to be replaced after about a year's hard use.

Pads usually are designated as rifle or shotgun. I always have felt that three, rather than two, classifications are necessary. We will use three classifications.

The primary purpose of a rifle pad is not to absorb recoil, but to provide a non-slip surface against the

PADS, PLATES, SWIVELS AND WHAT TO DO ABOUT THEM

In Even The Most Simple Gunsmithing Chores, There Are Rights And Wrongs. Here's The Difference!

Chapter 4

shoulder. It is a shame that it's not used more often in place of the common plastic or similar material butt plate. A rifle so equipped will mount to the shoulder and stay there, shot after shot.

The second category is the special purpose pads. The trap pad is curved inward toward the middle of the pad similar to a half circle. This inward curve is useful on the trap range, as it aids in correctly positioning the pad on the shoulder. It is designed to provide maximum recoil reduction. The skeet pad is just the opposite in that it is the same thickness from top to toe. If ribs are used on the outside surface of the skeet pad, they are vertical to prevent catching on the clothes when the gun is mounted to the shoulder. This is a fine choice for the bird hunter who must mount his gun for a rapid snap shot. There also is a recoil pad that can be adjusted to vary the amount of drop in the stock.

The final and most common category is the field shotgun pad. These are a cross between the two extremes presented by the trap and skeet pads. There is a slight dip in the middle of the pad but not as pronounced as the trap model. A wide selection of field pads is available to meet any demand. Usually they are completely smooth on the outside or with lines running across the pad to prevent slipping. One version has a smooth center and scalloped edges, so it's all a matter of personal choice.

For the average shotgun hunter, the field pad will prove the best choice. They are available in different sizes, but I have always preferred the largest size field pad as it will fit just about ninety percent of all stocks when ground down to size. It is also a good choice for installing on a rifle where the recoil is heavy.

It is next to impossible to buy a pad that will just screw on the stock and fit correctly. Even the newly manufactured guns that come with a factory pad will give trouble if a replacement pad of the same make is installed. All of the edges will not line up right with the sides of the stock. For a correct fit, the pad will have to be bought oversize and be ground down to fit.

But, before we start putting the pad on the stock, we must arrive at the correct length of the stock. This measurement determined, the stock will be cut the right amount to allow for the thickness of the pad. The gun companies say they build the stock to fit the average man. This is fine as far as it goes, but is about like selling everybody a pair of size eight shoes. The short fat fellows and the beanpoles have to adjust their carcasses to fit the stock. If they become good shots with the gun, it is due to their adaptability rather than correct stock fit.

Normally a stock that is too short will kick like a ticklish mule in shoo-fly season. The stock that is too long will force the butt of the stock out on the muscles of the arm and turn the arm black and blue after a few shots. Either of these two situations will cause flinching and hits will become few and far between.

To make the stock fit the man instead of the man fit the stock is the answer to good accuracy and comfortable shooting. The biggest factor is the length of pull. This is the technical name for the distance from the middle of the trigger to the edge of the middle of the butt plate. The average length of pull as compared to a person's height will be as follows:

5 feet to 5 feet six inches	13½ inches
5 feet 7 inches to 6 feet	14 inches
6 feet 1 inch to 6 feet 6 inches	14½ inches

This will vary around a quarter of an inch, depending

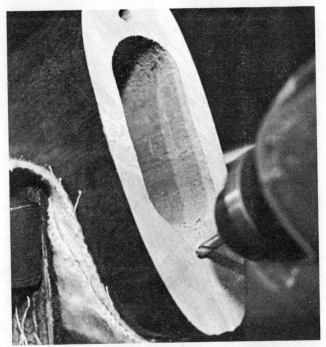

After marking through recoil pad with short nails, drill is used for hole in butt stock. Holes must be 90 degrees to back of butt stock. If this is not done, the pad will be buckled by the screws as they are pulled down tight.

Using two screwdrivers to pull the pad down evenly, make two or three turns with one, leaving it in place, then switch to other screwdriver for an equal number of turns.

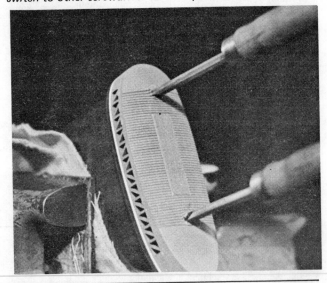

upon whether you are skinny or can't stay out of the cookie jar. A long or short neck also will vary the dimension slightly, as will the position of the cheek on the gun stock. I have often seen two men of almost identical build require as much as a half inch difference in stock length due to the way they position the stock.

A quick check of stock length is to bend your right elbow, place the butt of the gun inside the elbow and try to reach the trigger with your forefinger. If you are one of those left-fisted folks, reverse the arm used! If the finger

Grinding down the pad on a disk sander, the edge of the sander is kept on the pad's edge. Apply only light pressure in order to prevent uneven cutting of recoil pad.

The recoil pad also can be ground down with a rubber disk in a hand drill that is held firmly in padded vise.

must be stretched to fit the trigger naturally, the stock is too long. If the finger goes past the trigger almost to the third joint of the finger, the stock is too short. A correct fit is for the stock to fit naturally without stretching or bending the arm and the trigger rests halfway to the first joint of the trigger finger.

The above system is a quick check only and not to be relied on for a full and proper fit of the stock. Our British cousins use a "try gun." This is a special-built gun that can be adjusted in or out, up or down, until the right combin-

ation is determined. Measurements then are taken and the customer's gun altered to the dimensions indicated.

This is fine for the British, who use the double barrel shotgun almost exclusively, as one try gun will serve for several makes and models of guns. But, in America, our tastes in shotguns alone run to six different types. On top of this, the variations between a Remington M-1100 and a Browning five-shot automatic, would require two different try guns, not to mention all the other models.

There is a simpler way to find the correct length of pull and cost is almost zero. If the stock is too long, try removing the butt plate. Most butt plates are about a quarter-inch thick. It is surprising how many stocks can be correctly fitted with this small alteration. Try a few shots, mounting the gun rapidly. If this feels better but is still too long, cut a quarter inch off the stock for a total of one-half inch alteration from the original length. Again try a few shots. This should be enough alteration, but if not, you can cut another quarter inch off and try again. Don't worry about getting the stock too short, as the average thickness of a field recoil pad is one inch and the stock will be cut this additional amount to compensate for the pad thickness. You can cut up to three quarters of an inch and still bring the stock back to its original length. Just be careful not to split the wood when making the cuts.

If you have the length right, the gun should mount to your shoulder smoothly without catching on the clothes. The butt of the stock should fit into a sort of pocket that is formed about two inches in from the shoulder joint when the elbow of that arm is raised up level with the shoulder. Each time the gun is mounted, it should drop into this pocket smoothly. The secret of eliminating black and blue shoulders and arm muscles, is to fit the butt of the gun in this pocket. The chest muscles are thick here and will absorb a tremendous amount of pounding from a heavy recoiling gun without pain. The muscle of your arm out past the shoulder joint will start to turn blue on about the third or fourth shot.

About one out of every four stock fitting jobs will be with the stock too short to begin with. To make a temporary adjustment jig, cut out a piece of one-quarter-inch plywood in the shape of the butt plate. Drill the screw holes in this and slot the holes lengthwise for adjustment. The plywood jig is inserted between the stock and the butt plate and the screws reinstalled. By doing this, you will have lengthened the pull one-fourth inch. Try mounting the gun to your shoulder and firing a few shots. If it is still too short, remove the plywood jig and reinstall the butt plate. Now, slip one of the rubber pullover recoil pads on the stock. These pads are about one-half inch thick. Try a few shots.

Obviously if more length is needed, you can combine the plywood jig and the rubber pullover pad for a total gain in stock length of three-fourths of an inch. You can go to a full inch gain by cutting a second plywood jig and placing this between the regular butt plate and the recoil pad. I keep one of these pullover pads with the sides cut back for easy installing. It has helped find the right length of pull on a lot of stocks.

Any target shooter will tell you that he does his best shooting when the muscles of his body are relaxed, not strained. We fit gunstocks with this in mind.

First, stand at attention as you did in your army days, heels together, back straight and your shotgun or rifle at port arms. Reverse all of this if you are left-handed. Now face a wall and pick out a mark at eye level. If doing this by yourself, look in a mirror at eye level. Check to be sure the gun is empty.

You should be facing the wall. If a line were drawn from

one shoulder to the other, it would be exactly parallel with the wall. Now, take one normal step forward with your left foot, toe pointed at the target. Keep the heel of your right foot down in place, but rotate the toe out at a forty-five-degree angle to your right. Now shift your weight to your left leg and bend your left knee slightly. The right leg is kept straight. Keep your body straight, don't stoop down.

Now push the gun out away from you as far as you can, left hand on the forend and right hand in position on the grip. Bring it slowly back to your shoulder. As you do so, raise your right elbow level with your shoulder. The butt is placed in the pocket that is formed about two inches in from the shoulder joint.

Keep your head up straight. Do not bend the neck to place the face on the stock. If the stock is fitting you correctly, you should be looking at the front sight and the sight should be directly on the target. If by chance you have a long neck, a slight "nod" to the target should bring the face and shooting eye in position.

I try to fit the stock so this nod is not necessary. On a shotgun, your shooting eye is the back sight. Accurate shotgun shooting requires that the gun be mounted in the same way each time to bring the "back sight" into the same alignment with the barrel. Any shifting of face or position on the shoulder will make this alignment harder. If you can shoot with your head up straight or with the tiniest of nods, you are a mile ahead.

After the sights are aligned, step back to the attention mark and do the whole thing over again in slow motion. Repeat this several times without taking your eye off the target. Slowly speed up the mounting of the gun and the step forward. If you can mount the gun and have the stock settle in the same position on your shoulder each time with the sights lined up, you have a stock that fits you like a glove.

If the stock is too long, you will have a tendency to be off target slightly to the left each time. If it is too short, you will point more to the right. The closer you are to the target, the more pronounced this is. For the left-hand shooter, the stock that is too long will point to the right and the stock that is too short will point to the left.

I said in the beginning you should be relaxed, yet we have set up a strained position; this is just to get everything lined up. After you have the general idea, relax a bit but keep the left foot forward and the weight on the left foot. If your knee is bent and your weight forward, you have a built-in recoil mechanism, as the gun has to push you back up straight against your body weight. Using the weight of the body to absorb the recoil is the same principle a prize fighter uses, when he throws a punch with his body shifted forward to put his weight behind the punch.

Rifle stock fitting can be done the same way. If a scope sight is used, the scope may have to be shifted forward or backward somewhat to focus correctly. The more you can do to a stock to make it fit normally and feel comfortable without the body, arms or head going through various contortions, the more accurately you can shoot.

Several other stock alterations, such as changing the drop at the heel of the stock or the drop at the comb of the stock, may be necessary to arrive at this perfect fit. But this will be discussed later. Right now, the step forward position can be used in determining the correct length of pull.

When correct temporary length of pull has been found, you can proceed with cutting off the stock and fitting the pad to make the length permanent.

We must mark the stock at a point that, when it is cut, the overall length of the stock with the pad attached, will be equal to the temporary length of pull. A pair of dividers will be needed, but a common dime store compass can be substituted. Set the dividers at 15/16-inch to allow for the saw cut and sanding. Leave all temporary fittings on the stock and stand it on a table with the muzzle pointed to the ceiling. The butt must be flat against the table.

Set one end of the dividers on the table and rest the other end against the stock. Carefully slide dividers around the stock, keeping one end on the table and marking the stock with the other end as you go. The two arms of the divider must be kept vertical, for to slant one end forward or backward will result in shortening the distance between the table and the marked line on the stock. Go all the way around the stock, marking the line. If you have done it right, the two ends of the mark should join exactly when you complete the trip around the stock.

This end view of the recoil pad shows the four basic flat cuts required to align the pad with the lines of stock.

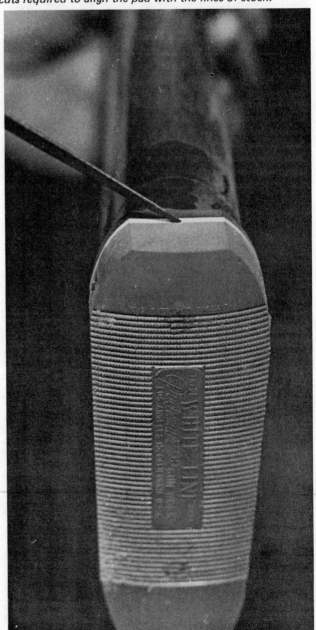

With the line established, remove any temporary jigs as well as the butt plate screws. The stock now is held firmly for sawing. There are a dozen different ways to cut the stock, but one of the simplest and best methods is the use of an eighteen-tooth hacksaw blade, good and tight in the hacksaw frame. This makes a good, smooth cut with little or no splintering of the wood. The cut must be made from top to bottom or vice versa. Never make the cut from one flat side to the other. When you start the cut, it must be continued through the stock. If you cut from the other end, the two cuts will not meet exactly and a step will be formed at the termination of the two cuts. As you cut, make even strokes and check to see that the saw is following the lines on both sides of the stock. Slow, steady strokes will get the job done better and faster than if you

Pad after flat cuts have been blended, rounded to match lines of stock. This can be done on disk sander. Clogged holes in pad are filled with dust from ground-off rubber.

Pad is finished up, using a vibrator sander. Note that this type of sander runs up to tape, not harming stock.

try to imitate a buzz saw.

With the cut finished, we need to straighten out any waves in the cut and even up the sides of the stock. To do this, we thumbtack a sheet of No. 150 grit sandpaper to a flat board with the grit side up. Place the butt against the sandpaper with the muzzle pointed at the ceiling. With the butt resting against the sandpaper, grasp the stock with one hand just under the pistol grip, with the other hand about three inches up from the bottom, on the top of the stock. Now, slowly push the stock away from you, sliding it across the paper. Be sure to keep it level and straight without rocking. Do not try to slide the stock back to you or it will chatter.

Pick the stock up, reposition it at the starting point, and again, slide it across the paper away from you. A half dozen strokes should have it good and smooth with all waves and nicks removed. The blade thickness making the cut, plus this sanding, will remove the remaining 1/16-inch of the stock. Combined with the 15/16 we cut off this will equal the one-inch thickness of the recoil pad. When the pad is fitted, the overall length will equal the length we determined with the jigs.

Pick up the recoil pad, look at the bottom and you will see two holes that do not go completely through the pad. We must get these holes all the way through, and there are several ways to do this. The screws can be reversed and pushed through or the pad can be slit with a knife. A simple way is to sharpen the points of two ten-penny nails, insert these in the two holes and push through the soft part of the pad. When the nails are removed, they will leave two small marks on the outside of the pad. Place the nails on the marks and push them through until the ends protrude about 3/8 of an inch. You can use these two points to see if the old screw holes in the stock will line up with the holes in the pad.

The bottom of the stock runs in a straight line from the pistol grip back to the toe of the stock. When the recoil pad is installed and cut down, this line must be continued, not bobbed off. Allow plenty of pad to protrude for the cutting line. A bobbed-off recoil pad toe makes the whole thing look like something added to the stock as an afterthought rather than blending with and becoming a part of the stock. The top of the stock is also straight and the pad must extend past the top line to allow for continuation of this line of the stock.

Looking down from the top of the stock, you will see that the sides of the stock get larger as you near the butt plate. This rate of size increase is constant and also presents a straight line on both sides for which allowance must be made. It is easy to see why a jumbo size pad usually works out as the best choice.

Hold the pad in the correct position against the butt and allow for the clearance of the top and bottom lines as well as the side lines. Now tap each of the marking nails with a hammer. When you remove the pad, you will see two small indentations in the stock made by the nails. Chances are high that the two marks will completely clear the two original holes. If one is close, try repositioning the pad slightly with one of the marking nails in the hole. If the stock lines can be held without being bobbed off, tap the other nail to mark its new position. Mark the old nail positions with an X as voided.

If the pad cannot be repositioned without being bobbed off, the old hole will have to be filled. If you try to drill the new hole close to the old one, the drill will slide into the old hole every time. Shape a plug of walnut, fill the hole with epoxy and drive the plug in tight. When dry, the excess is cut off and the end sanded flush with the stock. If

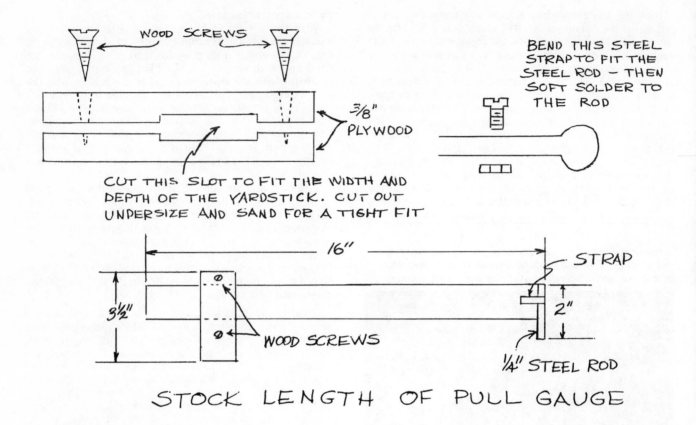

WOOD SCREWS

BEND THIS STEEL STRAP TO FIT THE STEEL ROD — THEN SOFT SOLDER TO THE ROD

3/8" PLYWOOD

CUT THIS SLOT TO FIT THE WIDTH AND DEPTH OF THE YARDSTICK. CUT OUT UNDERSIZE AND SAND FOR A TIGHT FIT

16"

STRAP

3½"

2"

WOOD SCREWS

¼" STEEL ROD

STOCK LENGTH OF PULL GAUGE

The pad installation has been completed. Note that all lines of stock are continued onto pad for neat appearance.

this is done correctly, you can drill into the side of the plug and still get the screw to pull up tight without the plug pulling out.

While the plug is drying is a good time to discuss another basic tool that you will need next, namely some form of drill. This can be the regular eggbeater hand drill purchased for approximately five dollars. If you buy this type, get the biggest one you can find. However, the hand drill has been put on the shelf by the electric drill except for one or two minor needs where absolute minimum slow speeds are needed. The lightest of the electric drills can be purchased for around ten dollars and, if used only for light work, will give a lot of service. It is always best, regardless of the type of tool, to buy the heavy duty size and the electric drill is no exception.

A 1/4-inch drill will do a lot of things besides drill holes. With attachments, it is one of the most versatile tools you can own. But what the quarter-inch-drill will do, the 3/8-inch size will do even better. The main difference between the two, besides the 1/8-inch capacity of the chuck, is the rpm (revolutions per minute) the drill turns at. The larger size version is available in several rpm ratings which, as a rule, are slower than the 1/4-inch size. The lower rpm allow you to do heavier work without burning up the drill. One of the more recent additions to the electric drill user is the variable speed version. The rpm are controlled by the amount of pressure that is applied to the trigger. Any speed from zero up to around 1200 rpm is available. Finally,

This view of the end of the stock length tool shows the method which has been used for attaching rod to the end.

Sliding block on the stock length tool is crude, effective.

Ground-down dowel is used to plug an existing screw hole that is in wrong place for a new butt plate, recoil pad.

some models come with an instant reverse feature that can get you out of a tight spot in a hurry. The king of them all is the 3/8-inch size with both the variable speed and instant reverse.

The number of available accessories would fill a book. The main accessory, of course, is a set of drills. A set running from 1/16 up to 3/8-inch in units of 1/16-inch will fill most stock requirements. You can buy drills larger than your chuck capacity, but they are seldom needed. The next most useful drills for the tool is a set of wood bits. These almost eliminate the need for a brace and bit. When buying these, always select the solid head type and never the replaceable head type. Get an extension for these for deepening stock bolt holes.

With the drill business settled and our plug dry and cut off, we are ready to drill the holes for the recoil pad screws. Screw dimensions always are given as minor and major diameter. The major diameter is the size of a hole that the threads will just clear with a tight fit. This is also given sometimes as "clearance size." While the major diameter is the outside size of the threads, the minor diameter is the size of the screw down at the bottom of the "V" of the thread. When boring a hole, be it wood or steel, the hole must be drilled at the size of the minor diameter of the screw. This allows for threads to be cut in the hole to accept and hold the screws.

With the wood screws, it is best to drill first with a drill that is the size of the minor diameter about one-fourth of

the way up the threads from the tip of the screw drilling the hole the length of the screw. Then use a second drill for the minor diameter of the wood screw about half way up from the tip of the screw and drill down about one-half the depth of the hole.

This takes a little more time but will provide a good bite for the screw without danger of splitting the wood. You can determine these drill selections by holding the two up to the light with the screw closer to your eye than the drill. The size is seen easily and the correct drill quickly selected.

If you plan to install several recoil pads, you can save time by purchasing a set of special two diameter wood screw drills. These should be the solid type with a depth stop. While all this might appear a waste of time, think about a stock splitting after you have worked for days because you chose the wrong drill size!

With both holes drilled for the recoil pad, rub a little wax or soap on the screws. This makes them go in more easily. Oil never should be used, as it will swell the wood and make removal of the screws difficult. With a screwdriver to match the screw slot, turn the first screw in for a couple of turns and stop. Switch to the other screw and take a few turns. Keep repeating the switching from screw to screw and take the pad down evenly. I like to use two screwdrivers for this, leaving one screwdriver sticking in the pad, while I turn the other one. Taking the screwdriver in and out chews up the hole through the pad. If two screwdrivers are used, this chewing will be prevented and will

The stud for this quick detachable sling swivel has been recessed correctly into the stock of this big bore rifle.

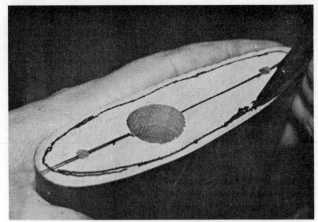

A rough line, approximately a quarter-inch from the edges, is drawn around the end surface of butt stock.

To install a curved butt plate, a template first is cut from a piece of stiff cardboard, then is held against the stock for rough outline's transfer to actual wood.

save a lot of time poking around trying to get the screwdriver bit back in the screw slot.

Some pads come with Phillips screw heads which are best, as the screwdrivers used are round and pad damage is almost nil. Why all pad manufacturers do not use Phillips head screws is beyond me, not only for the reason mentioned, but also for the ease in getting the screwdriver in the slot with this type screw. If you are stuck with the regular slot screw, you can cut down pad damage by rounding the edges of the screwdrivers on the sides of the blade.

Glue never should be used to attach a recoil pad to a stock. Epoxy will hold it firm and as well as screws, but if the day rolls around that the pad has to be removed for replacement or other reasons, get out a sharp knife and the cussin' dictionary, for you will need both of them. If screws are put in correctly, no glue is necessary for a hair line fit.

If you are refinishing a stock or putting the finish on a new stock, then the recoil pad should be installed before the sanding begins. The pad can be cut down and sanded with the stock for a perfect joint. If the stock is finished, it must be masked with tape to prevent the finish from being ruined. Any type of tape will protect the finish from the sandpaper, but I personally prefer one-inch electrical tape.

With the pad screwed down, and assuming we have a

stock with the finish already on it, start the tape on one of the sides with the edge of the tape just touching the recoil pad. Slowly lay the tape down on the stock, keeping the edge of the tape against the pad. Go all the way around the stock, keeping the edge of the tape against the pad. Go all the way around the stock and cut the tape in such a way that the two ends will just touch without a gap or lap over. Move over and start a second strip of tape with its edge just touching the edge of the first tape. Keeping the two edges touching, continue around the stock, ending as before. You will now have a two-inch wide band of tape around the stock. A final layer of tape is placed over the first one next to the stock. This strip should be started on the opposite side of the stock so the two joints will not be at the same place.

If only hand tools are available, start with the hacksaw with the blade turned sideways. Remembering the basic lines we set up, cut off the excess sections of the pad. Don't try to make this in one big whack but rather in small nibbling bites. With a little care and patience, the excess can be reduced close to the finish line.

Next, switch to the hand rasp. Carefully rasp the sides of the pad down, taking care not to hit the stock. The final shaping should be with old metal files, smoothing the rasp marks out. Finish up with a piece of sandpaper wrapped around the file. When the sandpaper is starting to cut the top layer of tape, remove it and switch to the finest cut file you have. Carefully filing, take the pad down until you are touching the bottom layer of the tape with the file and stop. You can go no further. Remove the tape. A small edge will remain on the side of the pad, the thickness of the tape, but it will be invisible, except on close inspection.

In place of the hacksaw and rasps, you can use a sanding disk chucked in your electric drill. This is a flexible round piece of rubber about six inches in diameter with a screw recessed in the center. Sandpaper disks are placed on the rubber and the screw, with a washer behind it, tightened into place to hold the sandpaper against the rubber. In use, the drill is secured to the table in a holder or placed in a vise. The rubber recoil pad then is pressed against the rotating disk to remove the excess. If hard pressure is used, the rotating disk will cut the soft part of the pad faster than the hard backing. The result will be a pad with the sides tapering to the back rather than continuing the straight lines of the stock. Light pressure will cut both at the same rate. Hold the stock firmly and let the outer edge of the

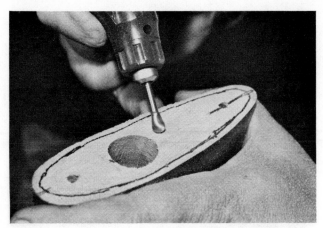

Wood inside the line is removed below the surface with a Dremel tool and router. When this is finished only the edge of the stock will need precision fit to butt plate.

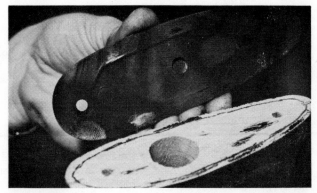

Butt plate is smoked with smudge pot, positioned on the stock, tapped. High spots on stock will be marked by the carbon from smoke; these are cut away carefully.

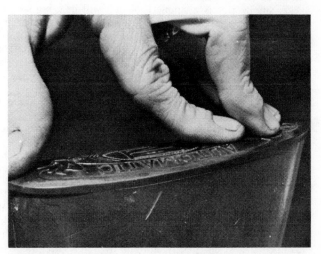

The curved butt plate, now matching the curve of the butt stock, is ready for screws to be installed and for trimming to match the overall lines of the stock.

disk do the cutting.

When you grind a pad down with a sanding disk, be prepared to be covered from head to toe with rubber dust. By all means, wear some sort of mask over your nose. If a regular respirator is not available, a damp handerchief a la bandit will do almost as well. As with any kind of grinding, protect your eyes with safety glasses or plastic goggles.

To hold the all important four lines, lay them out first before you start shaping the pad. Starting with the underside, press the pad against the revolving disk and, with a flat cut, remove the excess rubber down to within 1/16-inch of the tape. Repeat the same flat cut on the top and side line. I cannot overemphasize the necessity of making these four cuts, as shaping the pad is extremely difficult without them.

With the four lines established, begin removing the other excess with flat cuts. By making flat cuts to remove the excess rather than rounding cuts, we take the pad down evenly, holding all the lines of the stock straight. When all of the excess pad possible to remove with the flat cuts is finished, start rounding and blending the flat cuts together. The stock is rolled in the hand to make the blending cuts. You will find the flat cuts disappearing and the pad becoming a continuation of lines of the stock.

With the lines blended, you probably will start to touch the first layer of the tape with the disk. After you have had a little practice, you can remove the first layer of the tape and take the excess down still farther with the disc. But the beginner should lay the disc aside at this point and, with files and sandpaper, take the pad down the rest of the way via the hacksaw and rasp method.

By now, the holes in the side of the pad will be clogged with rubber dust. This can be removed by tapping on the pad with a hammer. If you have compressed air available, this can be used to remove the dust from the pad — and from yourself. If you want, you can take the recoil pad down a little closer after the plastic tape is removed by putting down a single layer of scotch tape and filing the side of the pad carefully.

Finish up the job by using a file to break the sharp edge on the back of the pad. This should be done lightly with a rounding stroke of the file. Any lingering glue on the stock from the tape can be removed by wiping with a cloth dampened in wood alcohol or lighter fluid. A little talcum powder rubbed into the sides of the pad will eliminate the newly cut appearance. If you have installed the pad before the stock is refinished, the pad should be masked with tape to prevent the stock finish from soaking into the pad.

If a standard butt plate is to be installed, the procedure is about the same as that for a recoil pad. Always try to get a replacement butt plate from the manufacturer of the gun as nothing looks tackier than, for example, a Winchester butt plate on a Remington model. If no butt plate is available, there are several models and styles available from the gunsmith supply houses. A Stevens M-311 butt plate can be used as a substitute, since it is fairly large and does not have any trade mark on it. Plastic butt plates will start to melt if any heat is generated by the sanding disk, so make the cuts light or use a file to shape the butt plate.

Horn butt plates always have been a favorite and will give a classic look to any stock. These are available in a wide assortment of sizes and styles. These should be cut down with file and sandpaper. If a sanding disk is used, the stink from the burning horn will gag a maggot!

Steel butt plates are attractive and practically indestructible. Properly fitted, they add quality to any stock. Since the amount they can be cut down is limited, it is best to fit them to only a new stock. The edges are blended in with the stock by filing with the plate being reblued after fitting. If you have the plate reblued, ask the gunsmith to strip the blue from the butt plate rather than polish it off. Polishing

39

will flatten the diamonds in the design.

Any time you have the choice, select a flat butt plate as these are a cinch to install as compared to a curved one. Cutting the curve just right to accept the plate can be frustrating. About the best way to start it is to make a cardboard template of the curve; hold this against the side of the stock and mark the outline of the curve. Cut the curve as closely as you can and finish up with a rasp and sandpaper wrapped around a dowel.

Some curved butt plates have a small ridge running around the bottom that will aid in getting a close fit, as the middle part is recessed and only the edge has to be fitted. If the plate you are using does not have this ridge, you can accomplish the same thing by cutting away some of the wood in the stock. To do this, set your dividers at 1/4-inch, place one leg on the edge of the stock and scribe a line all the way around the butt of the stock with the other leg. With a router or chisel, remove all the wood inside the circle down to a depth of about 1/32-inch to 1/16-inch.

A smoke pot is a simple tool that will be a big help in fitting any part to wood. Any old lamp, lantern, or even a candle may be used. If you use a lantern or similar pot, fill it with mineral spirits rather than kerosene, as mineral spirits will produce more smoke. The smoke will not stick to an oil surface, so clean the part well before smoking it. Hold the butt plate about two inches above the tip of the flame, move it around and check to see that all surfaces are covered.

When the butt plate is smoked well on the bottom, place it in position on the stock and tap with a hammer or piece of wood. Remove the butt plate and look at the wood. The high spots will be darkened by contact with the smoked surface, while the low spots will not be smoked as they did not touch the butt plate. Cut the high spots down, resmoke the part and try again. When the wood is in full contact, all parts of the wood bearing surface will show the smoke mark. Another trick in fitting a steel butt plate is to dampen the wood slightly and pull the screws up hard. The moisture softens the wood and allows it to be molded to the steel part. When the wood dries, the mold will hold and you have a perfect fit. Use this with caution, as excess moisture should be avoided.

Pistol grip caps are fitted the same way as a recoil pad or butt plate. They are available in plastic, horn and steel at a reasonable price. If you like things fancy, nickel, silver and even gold grip caps are available, plain or engraved. Most are attached with a single screw through the middle, while others are glued on. The main thing to remember is to get the surface of the wood exactly flat. The smoke pot comes in handy for this.

Old horn butt plates are a good source of material for grip caps. These can be cut and shaped with files. Small German silver shields, diamonds, et al., are inexpensive and, when fitted over the grip cap, will hide the screw and offer a place for the owner's initials to be engraved.

Some gun owners like a white spacer between the butt plate and the stock or under the grip cap. Sheets of suitable plastic can be purchased, but there is a cheaper source of supply. Your wife's discarded detergent bottles and bleach jugs offer a wide selection of colors. Cut the tops and bottoms off and slit one side. The plastic can now be laid out and pressed down to form a good usable sheet of plastic. The spacers can be cut in any design or shape from the plastic with a sharp knife point. Lay the spacer out to where the long part runs around the bottle rather than up and down, because the bottles usually are tapered with the thick part of the plastic on the bottom.

Sling swivels are fairly easy to install, especially with a little preparation. However, they can also split a stock or

A white plastic detergent bottle with top and bottom cut off can be utilized as material for a white line spacer.

The white plastic from the detergent bottle is marked with outline of the butt plate. In cutting, cut to the outside of the felt pen mark, then it is trimmed to fit.

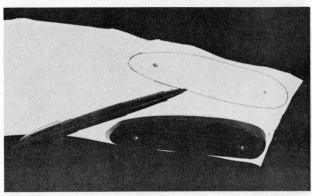

cheapen the appearance of the gun if carelessly installed. The most common type is the permanent swivel of either 7/8, 1, or 1¼ inches with the 1-inch the type most used on sporting slings. Quick detachable swivels, as the name implies, can be detached from the swivel stud and the sling and swivel bows removed as a unit and may be reinstalled in seconds. The Q-D style costs, on the average, a couple of dollars more than the permanent type. They are worth several times that amount, and if you use the permanent style, it will not take long for you to regret the choice.

Williams Gun Sight Company makes a little reamer that fits on a drill and greatly simplifies sling stud hole drilling for installing their swivels. But you can get the job done with a plain drill. Starting with the rear swivel which uses a wood screw, match up the minor diameter of the screw with a drill. Locate the position of the hole to be drilled at least two inches from the butt plate. Lock the stock in a vise, belly up, and with the bottom line of the stock on a horizontal level. Use a center punch to locate the hole. This must be exactly in the middle of the stock and not to one side. This is done best by positioning the punch and then sighting at eye level the length of the stock. You can easily tell if the punch is not centered. When lined up, tap the punch with a hammer to mark the stock.

If you are using a variable speed drill, your task will be simple as you need only touch the trigger lightly and let the

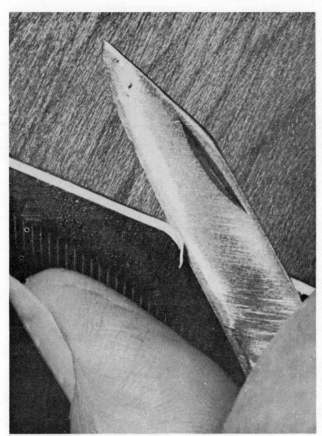

The spacer cut out and installed on the stock, trimming the excess plastic is done with a sharp knife. All of the cuts should be away from the stock to avoid scars.

There is any number of types of grip caps that can be used, including engraved metal, plastic, horn and rubber.

drill start at a very low speed. If you are using a drill without this feature, lightly tap the trigger button, let the drill rotate a couple of times and stop. Keep doing this until the drill has cut down a quarter-inch deep. The rest of the hole should be drilled as slowly as possible by touching and releasing the drill's trigger button. If you try to start the hole with the drill at full speed the drill will walk out of the punch mark and scar the stock.

You will notice that the swivel stud is round just above the screw. If installed in the hole we just drilled, the sides of the larger round section will hang over the sides of the stock. To make a neat job, the round section must be slightly recessed down into the stock. This is where the Williams jig comes in handy, as it cuts this recess, but a drill of the same size as the round section can be used to cut the recess. This time, get the drill going full blast and bring it down into the hole lightly. As soon as the drill cuts its full diameter, stop. If you try to use the drill at slow speed, the bit will splinter the wood around the hole. The hole you have drilled should be just deep enough to lightly recess the round section of the stud.

If you are using quick detachable swivels, remove the bow, insert a punch in the hole and use this to screw the stud into the wood. A little wax or soap on the threads will make the screw go in easier. Go slow and end up with the stud hole crossways of the stock to accept the swivel bow.

The forward swivel has a machine screw and nut instead of a wood screw. If a wood screw is used, it will protrude into the barrel channel as the stock is thin at this point. If made shorter, the screw would not be long enough to hold the swivel securely.

To install, determine the swivel's position by putting your gun to your shoulder and noting how far up on the forend you place your hand. A position about three inches back from the forend tip usually is about right. Again, place the center punch in the center of the forearm and tap it to make a mark. Select a drill that is the same size of the major diameter of the screw and drill through the forearm. Place the screw in the hole and see if it is going to protrude up into the barrel channel. If so, it must be shortened. Select another drill that is just a hair smaller than the nut and drill in the barrel channel deep enough to countersink the nut. Take care to drill only deep enough that the nut, when installed, will be below the barrel channel. Press the nut part of the way into the recess, install the screw from the other side and draw the nut down into the recess by turning the screw. Check again to be sure the nut and the screw will be below the barrel channel level.

Any accessory that you install or add to a stock must compliment the lines of the stock. A little planning, careful preparation, and correct installation all will play a part in determining whether the accessory will reflect the work of a craftsman or a jack leg.

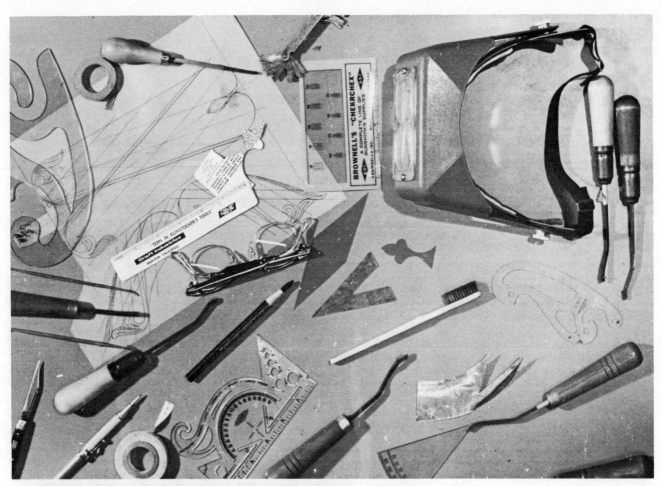

CHECKERING & CARVING

Chapter 5

These Arts Should Be Approached With Patience And A Willingness To Learn From Mistakes!

IN NO OTHER PHASE of gunsmithing does one have the opportunity to improve the appearance of a gun and express his artistic ability with a minimum tool requirement as in checkering. Every tool needed can be housed in a common cigar box except for the checkering cradle, which can be tucked away in a corner of a closet. Some stock scratchers manage to do beautiful checkering without a cradle, holding their work with one hand, pushing the tool with the other. But, if you are not an octopus or lack a grip like a vise, use a cradle. As for cost, a good set of checkering tools can be purchased for less than fifteen dollars. You can even make your own tools out of less than two dollar's worth of drill rod.

The fundamentals of checkering are relatively simple. The tools are inexpensive and easily stored. Even poor eye-

sight is not too great a drawback with a magnifying glass and short work periods. But checkering is slow, painstaking work and one who is short on the patience probably will be ahead to let someone else do his checkering. But if you take it easy and don't try to get the whole thing done between dinner and desert, you have the main problem licked. It is a matter of patience, criticizing your own work, practice, trying to do better on the next pattern — and more practice.

The first need in checkering probably will occur when one starts to refinish the stock on his favorite rabbit perforator. The stock will have a checkering pattern, or the remains of one, and the hobbyist is faced with three possible choices. He can sand the whole mess off and forget about it. You see a lot of stocks with the razor thin grip and

Nils Hutgren, a key man in the development of the early Winslow rifles line, is a member of a passing breed; a master, his stock carving is considered outstanding.

Stan de Treville No. 12 pattern is on Herter's cherry stock. Work takes time, but is classic to enthusiasts.

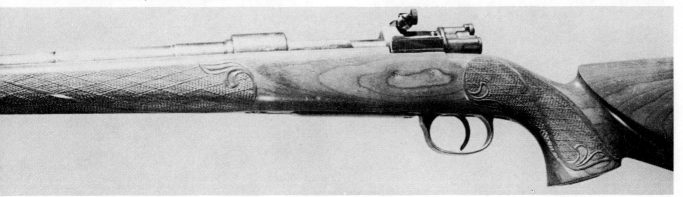

the dished-out section up on the forearm. He can ignore it and put finish right over the top of it. The final and best choice is to recut or trace the pattern. This process goes under a half dozen or so aliases such as recutting, retracing, pointing up, but the most commonly used phrase is "tracing." Not only will tracing the pattern improve and renew the general appearance of the stock, but will give the hobbyist an excellent opportunity to get the feel of checkering tools and learn the basic fundamentals. To get started in checkering, first recut a few patterns on old stocks.

Checkering is no more than a series of parallel V grooves cut to a depth of about 1/16-inch into a stock and crossed at a sharp angle by another similar series of parallel grooves of the same depth. The space between these two series or grooves are formed into hundreds of tiny pointed diamonds. The tools used to cut the grooves are very tiny saws with their cutting edge shaped in the form of a "V". While its primary purpose is to provide a better grip on the stock, checkering can be done in a way that will compliment and accentuate the lines of the stock. A properly chosen and executed checkering pattern can turn a plain piece of wood into a thing of beauty. At the same time, an elaborate, wild and glaring pattern can ruin the appearance of a fine piece of figured wood.

The basic tools used are the layout cutter (usually called the spacer) and the single cutter. The single cutter is shaped in the form of a V with the cutting edge on the sides of the V. When pushed across a piece of wood, these teeth cut into the wood and leave behind a groove, also in the shape of a V. The spacer cutter has two rows of teeth or two V's and, when viewed from the front, appear similar to the capital letter W.

The longest journey starts with the first step and that first step is to cut one straight V groove with the single cutter to full depth. To form the series of parallel grooves, you lay aside the single cutter and switch to the spacer cutter. Place one leg of the W cutter into the groove you have just cut and push the spacer cutter forward and away from you. The leg that is riding in the first groove will guide the tool while the other leg is cutting the second groove parallel to the first groove. When this new groove is cut to full length, the tool is lifted and the guide leg is placed into the second groove and the process repeated the same as before, to cut the third parallel groove and so on, until the whole series is completed.

The first groove that is cut is called either the guide line or base line and is cut to full depth. The other base line that will cross this line at an angle is also cut to full depth at the same time. These two lines are cut first before any others for all the additional lines will be based on these two. The angle at which they cross each other will determine the shape of the diamonds. This angle varies with the personal taste of the person doing the checkering, but a diamond that is 3½ times as long as it is wide is the accepted standard. If the diamond angle is much sharper, they have a tendency to break off, as their base will be too narrow to support them. At the same time, diamonds thicker than this will have a square, box-like appearance. A somewhat square form of checkering known as English flat checkering, is used seldom.

After the lines have been laid out straight and true, the diamonds in good proportions, the grooves must be cut to a depth that will bring the diamond to a point. The average beginner saws back and forth with the spacer tool in an attempt to cut the lines to this depth. The tool is a spacer and, as this name implies, it is used to lay out and space the lines only. When its work is finished it is put aside and the single cutter is used to bring each line to full depth. But even this must be done in at least two passes over the lines; sometimes three or more passes will be needed.

If the beginner thinks he can take a short cut and make one pass do it all, he will sail along fine in the first series of parallel grooves and probably compliment himself mentally upon how smart he is. But when he starts to cut the second series, the truth will hit him. The tool jams and digs in when it tries to cut across the full depth of the grooves in the first series. It is like trying to drive a car across a plowed field at a fifteen-degree angle to the furrows. The rows keep trying to turn your front wheels and make you follow their path. If one makes his first deepening pass to half depth or less, the second series will present little problem. As the next passes are made, the grooves will be deeper and provide a better guide, yet the lines they are crossing will be at equal depth.

When all lines have been brought to full depth, the diamonds should be pointed. A few usually are not, and the checkerer must make a pass or two with the single cutter to bring them to a point. All grooves and diamonds are combined into a group and called a pattern.

This is a simplified explanation of the mechanics of the checkering process that will give you some idea of how it is done and what is required in the way of patience.

Before you start refinishing your stock, take a close look at the checkering. If the lines are sharp, go ahead with the refinishing and forget about the pattern until the stock is finished. That of course, is assuming that you keep the sandpaper off the pattern. If the lines are shallow or parts of the pattern worn, you will have to deepen the lines before you start the refinishing. If you fail to do this at this time, the sanding process may remove what is left of the lines and retracing will be difficult, if not impossible.

Tracing before refinishing does not have to be to full depth. In fact, it would be a waste of time as the pattern will have to be gone over after the refinishing to remove any finish that has gotten into the grooves. Trying to mask the checkering with tape never seems to work to one hundred percent satisfaction and should be done only when the original checkering is of a quality that should not be traced. Masking must be done carefully with the tape right on the outside groove or border line and this takes time. It is a lot simpler to finish the stock as though the checkering were not there and clean the grooves out after the last coat has dried.

The best tool to trace the lines in the pattern is the regular checkering single cutter with the finishing touches being done with the commercial checkering file. If you have only one stock to do or would rather give checkering a whirl at the lowest possible cost then you can make a simple tool to do the job. I used one of these tools for quite a while, back in my early kitchen table gunsmithing days. It's simple, but I know one professional who still uses one for retracing, rather than a single cutter and he has a boxful of those.

To make the tool, you need a small triangular metal file, the smaller the better. A four-inch size with as little taper as possible is ideal. Hold the tang with a pair of pliers and heat the forward two inches of the file to a dull red. This can be done over the kitchen gas stove.

With a second pair of pliers, grasp the forward one inch of the file and bend it up in a slight gradual curve like that of a common kitchen fork. The outside of the curve must be directly on the edge of one of the points of the triangle, while the inside of the curve will be on the flat side opposite this point. If you do not have a second pair of pliers, catch the tip in a crack or other similar opening that

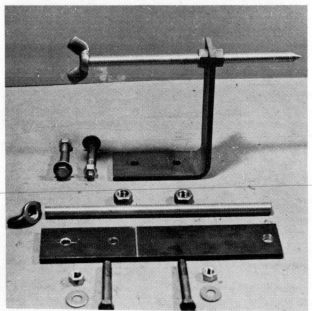

This is all of the metal necessary to build checkering cradle. In background is the unit after it is assembled.

New forearm is in checkering cradle, ready to receive the pattern. Holder is two-diameter wood dowel through the forearm, supported at each end by the cradle's uprights.

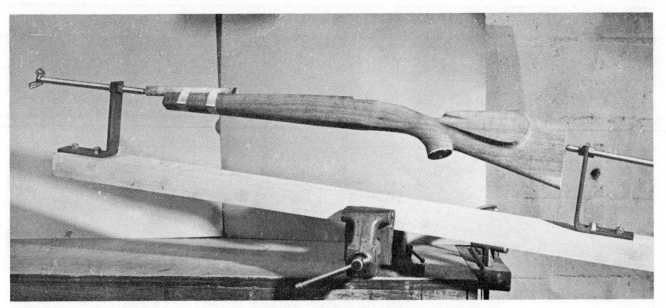

This simple checkering cradle, mounted on a 2X2 and held in a vise, has a stock in place, ready for work to begin.

will hold the tip, while you bend it. When you have finished bending the curve, the file will have cooled and be somewhat softer than originally but still hard enough to do the job in wood.

If you want it hard, all you have to do is heat it back to a dull red and quickly plunge it into a container of water. The colder the water, the harder the file will be. With the curve permanent, the next step is to break off the smooth tip that does not have any teeth on it. This can be done with the pliers or by catching the tip in a crack or laying it across a board and tapping it with a hammer. If you have a grinder handy, square up the break. You can remove the file teeth back of the bend if you wish, but this is not necessary.

In the checkering cradle described, the rear of the stock is supported by nothing more than point of threaded rod.

Finally, put some kind of handle on the file. Using a file without a handle, one slip and the tang can drive itself through your hand like an ice pick. Not only will this be painful but permanent damage can be done to the muscles and nerves of the hand.

File handles are inexpensive and available at just about any hardware store or you can make one out of a piece of old broom handle. Drill a small hole in one end to accept the tang or the hole can be burned into the handle with a nail heated red hot.

All else failing, you can fall back on the farmer's file handle — the corn cob. The old red corn cob finds itself being used for a lot of varied purposes around a farm.

The stock should be carried through the stripping stage before any checkering or tracing. This is to remove the dirt and grime that has worked its way down into the grooves along with the old finish. This dirt and grime will make short work of the file's sharpness and dull a checkering cutter. Allow the stock to dry fully and double check by holding it near a heat source. Trying to cut the grooves in a damp stock usually results in some of the diamonds being torn off.

In use, the homemade bent file is placed in one of the grooves of the checkering pattern with the tip slightly up and the bottom of the bend resting in the groove. The forefinger is rested on top of the file, pointing toward its tip. Most men find this the best way to hold any checkering tool, since it places the hand in a comfortable position with the forefinger acting as a pointer along the line.

With a smooth, steady stroke, push the file forward along the groove. Don't try to guide or aim the file, for to do so will cause the file to ride out of the groove. No one can guide a cutter and make a long cut without zigzagging or washing out the line. Instead, let the length of the file that is riding in the groove do the guiding. Remember, the file does the guiding, not you.

Don't try to cut the line to full depth, just deepen the line slightly. Repeat this half depth cut in all of the grooves in one series. If you are tracing a worn pattern, you can stop right here and finish up with a half depth cut in any border lines. The stock now can be whiskered and re-

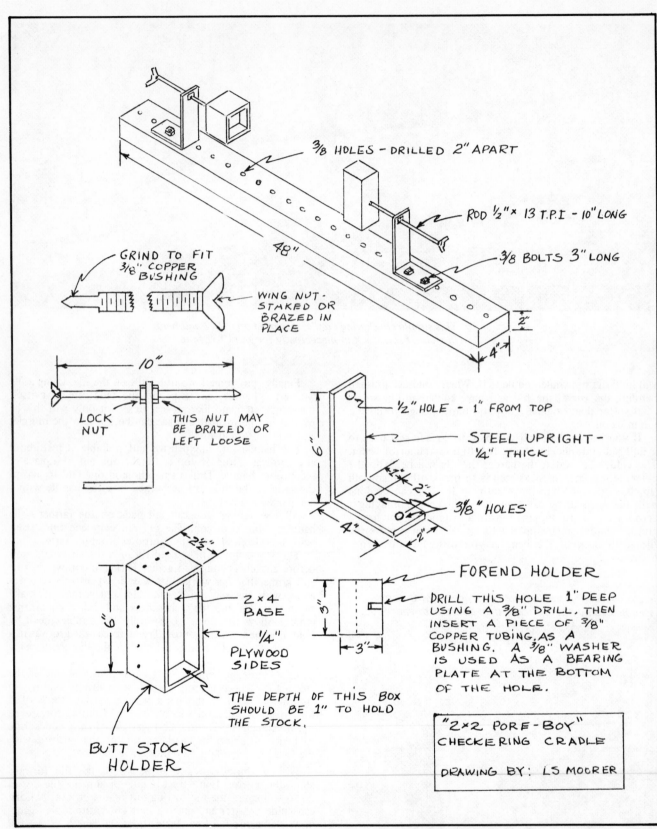

3/8 HOLES - DRILLED 2" APART

ROD 1/2" x 13 T.P.I - 10" LONG

3/8 BOLTS 3" LONG

48"

2"

4"

GRIND TO FIT 3/8" COPPER BUSHING

WING NUT - STAKED OR BRAZED IN PLACE

10"

LOCK NUT

THIS NUT MAY BE BRAZED OR LEFT LOOSE

1/2" HOLE - 1" FROM TOP

STEEL UPRIGHT - 1/4" THICK

6"

4"

2"

2"

3/8" HOLES

FOREND HOLDER

DRILL THIS HOLE 1" DEEP USING A 3/8" DRILL, THEN INSERT A PIECE OF 3/8" COPPER TUBING, AS A BUSHING. A 3/8" WASHER IS USED AS A BEARING PLATE AT THE BOTTOM OF THE HOLE.

2 1/2"

6"

2 x 4 BASE

1/4" PLYWOOD SIDES

THE DEPTH OF THIS BOX SHOULD BE 1" TO HOLD THE STOCK.

3"

3"

BUTT STOCK HOLDER

"2 x 2 PORE-BOY" CHECKERING CRADLE

DRAWING BY: LS MOORER

finished.

After the stock is refinished, the grooves are carried to full depth with a second or third pass over the lines. This is done as outlined, except the lines are carried right up to and joined to the border line. As you near the end of each line, rock the tool forward on its tip and cut the last quarter of an inch with the tip, stopping dead on the border line. This is the only time the tip is used in cutting the lines, all other cutting is done with the file right at the bend. You can make the strokes back and forth in a sawing motion, but go slow on the back stroke with less pressure on the tool. Let the tool do the guiding.

As you use the tool, you will find your speed picking up slowly until the stroke is quite rapid. In a short time you

To support rear of finished stocks, prevent scratching, this holder is built. It is block of wood with quarter-inch plywood to form sides.

The wooden boxes in which stock are held also contain foam rubber to act as added padding against scratching.

will have a feel of the tool and can make a smooth stroke. Tip the file forward for the last part of the line and stop it dead on a cat's whisker. You have to practice this stopping the lines at the border, for runovers are the signature of the careless worker.

When you have both series of lines at full depth and each line stopping right on the border line, check the points of the diamonds. If one is still flat, go back with the tool and point it up. This should be done starting about one inch before the offending diamond. Pass it and continue for another inch to blend the line. Start the cut shallow, deepen it as you come to the diamond and ease back out to a shallow cut. If you try to saw back and forth right at the diamond, you will dig a well. In all of the cuts, try to keep each of the lines to a depth the same as all other lines. One deep line will stand out sharply and destroy the quality of your work.

After all lines are cut, the diamonds pointed and the pattern even, switch your attention to the border line surrounding the pattern. This should be done with care, as the border line separates the pattern from the rest of the stock. If done carelessly, the whole process will have been in vain. The border lines usually catch the eye faster than

the pattern itself, so bear this in mind while making the border cuts. After you practice on the parallel lines and forming the diamonds, you should have little trouble cutting the border lines. It will help on the short curves of the border, if you again tip the file forward lightly and let the tip do the cutting. Be careful not to let the tool dig in and get away from you. If, while cutting one of the lines, you sneezed or kicked at the cat and ran over the border, you sometimes can fudge a bit on the border line cutting and hide your goof-up from the eyes of the critical world. When you come to the run over, lay the tool on its side slightly and file away the offending run over. This must be done gradually by starting the lay over before you get to the spot and carrying the lay over past the spot for an equal blending cut.

As you have been cutting all these lines, you probably noticed that they filled with wood dust and obscured the line. Use a dry tooth brush to remove the dust, but buy a new one as the frayed ends of a used brush will not reach into the grooves.

Another good checkering brush is the type ladies use to scrub their fingernails. Instead of a handle, it has two short stubs that curve over the back of the brush. In use, it is worn over the back of the fingers similar to brass knuckles. It is handy for a quick cleaning swipe at the checkering, yet is out of the way, allowing the hand to be used for other things until needed.

After tracing the pattern, cutting all the border lines and pointing the diamonds, the cleaned-out checkering will stand out white against the finished stock. To darken the lines to a color that will match that of the stock, use boiled linseed oil. Dip a second tooth brush into the oil and scrub it down into the grooves of one of the parallel series. Get it in with firm pressure, but don't try to drown the checkering with oil or it will build up in the grooves and ruin all of your work. Scrub it in, then repeat the scrubbing with the second series of parallel lines. After the oil has soaked into the lines, you can put a second coat of oil on the pattern and follow with a third, if necessary. Work to get the color of the checkering to match the color of the stock. In a pinch, you can use Tru-Oil, but it dries rapidly so use it sparingly, work with speed and stretch it to the utmost.

We have used a homemade tool to trace the checkering, but a regular single line cutter will get the job done more rapidly and easily. It is shorter in its cutting length and will make the short lines up in the corner of the pattern a lot easier to do. If by now you enjoy scratching lines on a stock, buy a regular single cutter for the next job, as well as a good checkering file. This is a small bent needle file similar to our homemade tool, but with the cuts on the file going right up to its fine tip. They come in size No. 0 for reworking old checkering and No. 2 for general diamond pointing, with the No. 4 for extra fine cuts. This file is rocked to one side to cut the wood and point the diamonds on one side of the line.

If you want one that does not have to be rocked, buy the ninety-degree checkering file. It is identical in appearance to the other type but will cut both sides of the line equally at the same time without rocking. It is available generally in No. 1 for coarse work and No. 3 for fine cutting.

Another checkering file variation is the riffler. This is a tool with a short bent file on each end and is used best to get into the corners of checkering where the regular single cutter or checkering file will not reach. It is especially useful in cleaning up checkering where some carving blends in with the pattern. This type is a bit more expensive than the regular checkering files and can be omitted from your tool kit, until you get into checkering new patterns. You will see checkering being referred to as 20 lpi, 18 lpi, and so on. This simply means that in this particular pattern there will be 20 parallel lines within a one-inch space. All of the lines in the pattern, both on the butt stock and on the forearm, should be the same number of lines per inch.

Regular checkering will run from 16 lines per inch as the coarsest, to 32 lines per inch as the finest. The 16 lines per inch size normally is found only on pistol grips or on a stock that requires a firm grip for some reason. The 18, 20 and 22 lines per inch sizes will be found on about seventy-five percent of the stocks you see, with the 22 lines per inch the accepted standard. The 24, 28 and 32 lines per inch are found on guns where appearance, rather than function, is primary. These last three sizes can be used only on close-grained wood. As the grain becomes more open, the more coarse the checkering size must be; to use a fine, close cutter on coarse, open-grained wood, would result in the diamonds shearing off. The number of lines per inch is determined by the spacer cutter.

The layout cutter — or spacer, if you prefer — usually is found with teeth cut on both legs of the W, but there is a cutter made with one of the legs free of teeth, the leg

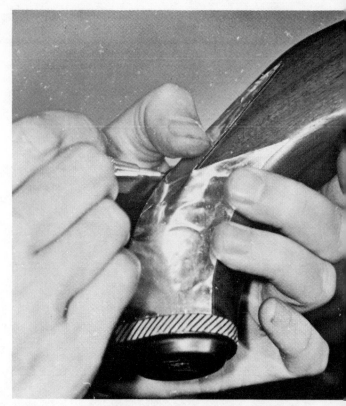

In transferring the foil pattern described in text to the pistol grip, the tooling foil is wrapped around the stock. This technique allows a close transfer of lines.

Second series of lines is being laid out to cross the first series. At this point, lines are mere scratches and are not cut to full depth on instrument's first pass.

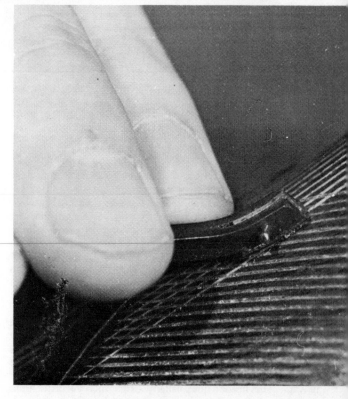

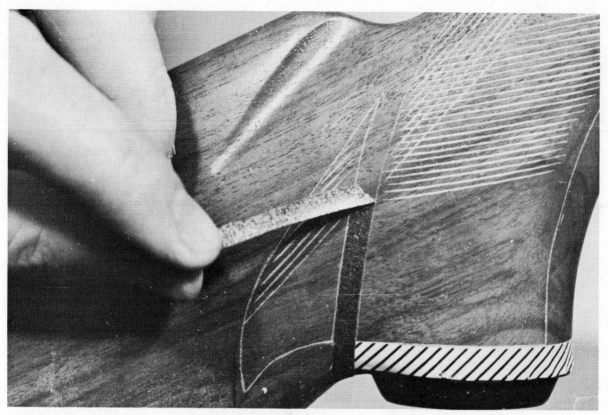

Strip of plastic tape is removed. It has been used to separate two sections of a pattern. Note plastic tape at bottom of pistol grip forms the bottom line of pattern.

perfectly smooth; the other leg has teeth cut in it as usual. In use, the smooth leg is placed in the groove to do the guiding while the leg with teeth does the cutting of the parallel line in the normal way. This absence of teeth on the leg makes it easier to keep it in the groove, as it has less tendency to ride out of the groove or dig in. It also allows the tool chauffeur to make his lines more equal as the guide leg is not cutting the guide line any deeper, and it is easier to maintain constant pressure with only one leg cutting. The only problem is that the two instruments are needed, one with the cutter on the left leg and the other with cutter on the right leg.

Spacer cutters with more than two rows of legs are also available. The most commonly used multi-leg cutter is the three-row version, but one with four legs also is available. The four-leg cut-an-acre-at-a-time model is best left alone until you have mastered the regular two-leg layout tool. But, when that time comes and you have a big space to cover, the multi-leg layout tool will prove a welcome addition to your tool kit.

The final variation in spacer cutters is the skip-line cutter. This usually is found as a regular four-leg cutter with one of the inside legs amputated. The missing leg produces a "skipped line" as the tool is pushed across the wood. This is worked into an effective, eye-catching skip-line checkering pattern that also is known as French checkering. Just like everything else, there are variations in this such as "skip-2-line" and "skip-3-line" cutters, but this gets a bit wild. Personally, I do not like two and three skip-line checkering, as I feel it begins to make the stock compliment the pattern rather than the other way around.

You can take a piece of drill rod, a few special files, a stone or two and, with some heat, build your own checkering tools. Quite a few of the top professionals make their own tools but I suspect this a holdover from the old days when no commercial tools were available, or when they wanted a special cutter that was not made commercially. I recommend that the hobbyist forget checkering tool manufacturing. I made a set once — and that was enough for me. Cutting all those little teeth was just a little easier than giving a rattlesnake a manicure. After cutting one pattern with the set, I gave them to a cousin. I never did like him anyway!

Your best bet is to buy a good set of tools. The price is reasonable and any brand that you buy will be superior to ninety percent of those you can make. The three most familiar brands are Dem-Bart, Full View and Gunline. You will not go wrong with any of these brands. Their main selling point is that all three use a replaceable cutter that fits in the forward end of the tool. These are held in place with a small cross pin. When the cutter becomes dull, out with the old one and in with the new cutter in just a few seconds.

As all of the replacement cutters are machine made, there will be no variation in the line spacing, which cannot be said for most of the homemade tools. Full View and the Gunline cutters can be sharpened with a stone to some degree, as their teeth are cut into the metal. The Dem-Bart cutting edge is sort of "teeth bent out of the metal," but the Dem-Bart cutters are the least expensive. All will do excellent work, so it's just a matter of personal preference.

The cutter is the least expensive part of the tool and, if you have enough time and are financially conservative, you can get away with one handle for the whole set. This gets old real soon, however, and you will end up buying more handles. You can economize by buying one handle for all of the spacer cutters as you will be needing only one size of these at a time on any given pattern.

The single cutter comes in three basic variations. The first is the coarse cutter generally used for deepening the lines; the second is the fine cutter which is used for pointing up the diamonds or cutting on close-grain wood. The third type is the short cutter about half the length of the other two and used to get up in the real close parts of the pattern.

A final word of advice is to write the size of the cutter and type on the handle with ink. A good place is on the belly of the handle, up near the front, as your finger normally does not come in contact with this part of the handle. When you need another cutter and look up from the pattern with your eyes crossed from following the lines, it sure is a lot easier to look for this easy-to-read number than trying to focus on the ant track-size number printed on the cutter. All the tools should be stored in a good box and not left where your wife can use them to scrape burned egg out of a frying pan.

Back in my army days, I served as a smallarms advisor to the Nationalist Chinese Ordnance Service. One of my assignments was to speed up rebuilding of rifles at their 44th Arsenal. One day, while I was doing a time and motion study of an assembly line, a Chinese translator made an observation that has stuck in my mind. A certain job required two Chinese to work two hours to complete. He observed if the same job were given to an English team, a German team and an American team, the following would result: the Englishmen would ask for two hours and fifteen minutes to include a tea break, the Germans would demand a complete set of blueprints and the Americans would spend an hour trying to figure out how to do the whole thing in ten minutes with power equipment!

It was only a matter of time for someone to devise power checkering equipment. There are two of these fine tools on the market to my knowledge. One is made by Dem-Bart and the other by MMC. The cutter is a small circular V-edge saw that is rotated by a flexible shaft hooked to a special electrical motor. Spacing is done by an adjustable shoe that rides in the guide groove while the little buzz saw cuts the next parallel groove. The shoe, by being adjusted toward or away from the rotating saw, allows a multitude of line spacing choices. These are precision instruments and the price is far from cheap. However, if a lot of checkering is to be done, it will soon pay for itself as it will get a pattern done quickly in the hands of a skilled user.

With the exception of a few specialized patterns, the skilled checkerer does not need a border tool. His checkering skids to a gnat's hair halt at the stop point and no further. If one of your fellow hobby checkerers gets to bragging about his checkering, ask to see some samples of his work. If the lines are straight with all diamonds pointed, by all means compliment him. Now look at the point where the lines stop. If there is no border and the whole pattern just seems to blend in together and come to a stop, tip your hat, and bow real low, for brother, you have met a real craftsman!

Most people are just not that good. Try as they may, the tool seems to sneak over the line and nick the other side. Some delightful soul, realizing the shortcoming of mortal man or to cover up his own mess, designed the border tool. This is shaped in the form of a letter U, except upside down. The space between is rounded for a purpose. In use, the border tool cuts a double line with the space between rounded to remove and eliminate the run over nicks in the wood. Border tools usually come in either wide or narrow spacing for different types of patterns.

Many of the stocks you refinish will have part of the checkering pattern worn off so much that the lines will not be visible or will be so faint that freshing them out will be

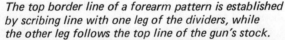

The top border line of a forearm pattern is established by scribing line with one leg of the dividers, while the other leg follows the top line of the gun's stock.

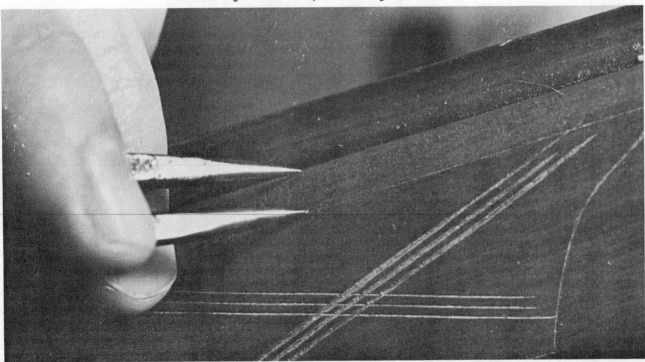

French curve, plastic tape and grease pencil are used to
lay out free-hand pattern. Grease pencil allows changes
before pattern is cut. Author says this system is useful
for one-of-a-kind pattern on stocks of irregular size.

impossible with the single cutter. Obviously the lines have
to be respaced with the spacer tool. But how many lines per
inch are there in the pattern? You can try several of the
cutters in the checkering lines to see if you can match them
up, but this system leaves a lot to be desired. The old way
was to use a screw thread gauge. This gauge consists of a
series of numbered blades with V teeth cut in them. In use,
the different blades are tried on the thread of a screw, and
when one series of Vs on a blade matches the threads on
the screw, the number of threads per inch is read off the
blade. While designed for threads on a screw, it can be used
to determine the number of lines per inch in a checkering
pattern by trying the blades against the lines until a match
is found.

A greatly simplified gauge is the Chekerchex, available
from Brownell's for less than a buck. This is a piece of
transparent plastic, with a series of parallel lines in groups
printed on the plastic. These series of parallel lines are of
different lines per inch spacing. The gauge is simply held
against the checkering pattern, moved about until one of
the series on the plastic matches the series of the checkering, and the lines per inch read from the Chekerchex.
The lpi size of each series is printed directly above the lines
on the gauge.

The number of lines per inch determined, the correct
spacing cutter is selected and two good sound lines in the
remaining part of the pattern picked out to become the
base lines. With the spacer cutter, go over the pattern,
laying in the missing lines and bringing the pattern back to
its original shape. The lines then are cut to half depth with
the single cutter and the refinishing of the stock done
before the final cut to full depth. This method of recutting

the lines can be done only if the general outline of the
original pattern is still visible and if two border lines can be
traced. Sometimes the general outline of the pattern is not
visible and it is impossible to determine the border lines of
the pattern, due to heavy wear or heavy-handed individual
sanding of the checkering pattern. When this happens, a
new approach has to be used.

Most patterns, such as that found on the pistol grip of a
stock, consist of two sections — one on each side of the
piece. These are normally mirror images of each other. If
one is still around, the worn pattern problem can be solved
with a transfer. This is done by placing a piece of typewriter paper against the side of the stock with the good
pattern and rubbing the side of a No. 2 pencil against the
paper. The side, and not the point of the pencil, must be
used. The whole area will be darkened, but the lines of the
pattern are below the surface and will not support the
pressure from the pencil. The paper bends down into the
groove and that part of the paper remains white, while the
surface surrounding the groove is darkened.

The rubbed tracing itself is hard to use, so we will make
a carbon copy of it. Place the rubbed tracing on top, then a
piece of carbon paper and a piece of typewriter paper on
the bottom. A couple of pieces of tape on the paper will
hold everything in place. Trace the border lines, keeping
them straight. We need two of the lines in the pattern for our
base lines, so pick out two that run through the middle of
the pattern. Don't try to trace these free-hand. Instead use
a ruler to keep the lines straight. When finished, remove the
rubbed tracing and the carbon; the pattern outline with the
two base lines will be on the paper underneath.

With a pair of scissors, cut the outside border line all the way around to get rid of the excess. Finally, hold the cut-out pattern against a window pane and draw the base lines on the other side of the paper pattern again, using the ruler to keep the lines straight. This paper pattern can be used on either side of the stock. On standard guns, the patterns are pretty constant, so this tracing can be used over and over. If you want to make it more permanent, make the transfer copy on thin plastic. The base lines can be scratched lightly on the plastic. Always write the make and model of the gun on the tracing to identify it.

One of the oldtime tricks with these cut-out patterns is to make them on thin sheet lead. The thin lead was bent easily to fit the contour of the stock perfectly and allowed close alignment with the old pattern. Unfortunately, sheet lead is about as plentiful now as hen's teeth. The trick has become a thing of the past.

One of my customers is a college professor who does checkering as a hobby. I consider it the equal to any done professionally, and some of his work is illustrated in this chapter. Professor Jack Ashworth stumbled across a cheap substitute for the hard-to-find thin lead that does an even better job. The material is tooling foil. This is the thin, flexible metal that is used in handcraft work to make the tooled-in-metal figures that most of you have seen. It is soft and, when any tool is pressed against it, the metal retains the impression. You should find it listed in the catalog of any company that sells handcraft materials.

To use tooling foil, the rubbed tracing is placed directly over the foil and a blunt end scribe used to mark the outline of the border. A sharp scribe then is used to place a few marks up and down the two base lines. When finished, cut the foil pattern out with a pair of scissors. Hold it against the sides of the stock and, with your hand, press it hard to shape and form the thin metal to the contours of the stock. The outline of the pattern can now be traced on the stock with a grease pencil or scribe. Where the two guide lines cross, press the sharp scribe through the metal into the wood. Make an identical mark where each of the guide lines joins the border line. Remove the metal pattern and it can be straightened by placing it between the pages of a thick book. It's a good idea to write on the pattern with the scribe the make, model and caliber or gauge of the gun from which it was taken.

If you are using a paper pattern cut-out, the process of transfer is about the same, except a few pieces of tape are used to hold the pattern against the stock. The paper pattern must be used carefully and held close to the stock as you make the tracing around the edge. Mark the guide lines the same way as with the tooling foil, by punching a hole through at the intersection of the lines and at their points. If you use plastic, the process is the same.

Whatever you use, keep the pattern and slowly build a catalog of them. Guns that come across your bench with a good pattern can be added to your collection of traced patterns with no ill effects to the stock. Some people are blessed with artistic ability and can sit down, design and draw a pattern from scratch. Most people are not this gifted and borrowed patterns are the answer to building a good catalog of patterns. Most can be used on more than one special make or model and the border lines can be adjusted to make it even more versatile.

Quite a few of the old classic stocks, such as those on an L.C. Smith or Parker shotgun, could come your way for retracing of the checkering. Some will require a completely new stock and your checkering pattern catalog will prove invaluable, as it is better to duplicate the original pattern than to come up with some wild child.

Connecting the base line points you pressed into the stock can be done in several ways. Perhaps the most

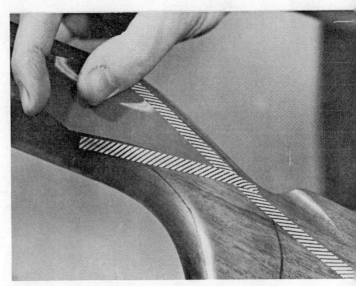

The plastic tape is used to lay out the two base lines with the aid of a large plastic diamond that's precut.

common is simply to connect them with a flexible plastic ruler and draw the lines with a scribe. A better way is to use quarter-inch plastic tape available at most stationery stores. Start a piece at one of the end points, bring it through the intersection mark and finish at the mark on the opposite end. The second line is laid out the same way. You can even use this tape to put in the border line. You can run the single cutter right up the side of the tape and keep the line straight as the tape will guide the cutter, or you can draw the line with the scribe and cut it after the tape is removed. A small V veining tool can be used to cut the base lines also.

If you are not interested in duplicating the original pattern, the best step with new patterns for the beginner is to use a decal checkering pattern. It is stripped free from its backing paper and pressed onto the stock in the desired position. Everything you will need, such as base lines, border lines, et al., are in the decal along with a few helpful hints. You simply cut the base line marked on the decal going through the decal and into the wood. The parallel lines then are laid out and the decal is cut away as you cut the pattern. The simplicity of this system, as well as the quality of the decal, can make the beginner look like a professional as long as he keeps his lines straight. Patterns are available in a wide selection with or without border carving; basket carving instead of checkering; pointed patterns; and so on. Most decals are the top designs of the best men in the checkering profession. I recommend that every beginner use at least one of the decal patterns, especially on that extra-special job. I believe you will find they are a big help.

The average gun owner looks at a checkering pattern with a ribbon running through it or the pattern broken up into a series of diamonds with spacing and thinks, "Here is a real hard pattern to cut out." At the same time, he looks at a wrap around, unbroken pattern without the ribbon and classifies this as a snap to checker. Just the opposite is true.

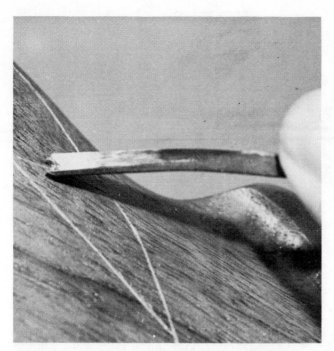

The author uses a small V gouge to cut the two base lines of pattern, which has been outlined previously.

The hardest thing to do with a checkering tool is to keep a straight unbroken line. When it rounds a corner, such as rolling around a forearm, the difficulty increases ten times over. The pattern with the ribbon running through the middle breaks the line. The more falderal in the pattern, the shorter will be the lines and the easier it will be to keep them straight. At the same time, extra care must be taken to stop the cutter dead on the ribbon edge, for any run over cannot be hidden.

If you are using a pattern that ends in a diamond, do not mark the outline permanently. Lines have a way of wandering slightly off course as you go and the chances of carrying a line for four or more inches around a curved surface to a pin-point are pretty slight. It is best to sketch these diamond-shaped pattern ends in with a pencil in the approximate finish position. The pattern may work out close to your desired point, but why take a chance? Should you miss, you have a problem if the point has been cut in permanently. With the point just pencilled in, the pattern can be worked out. Who is going to measure the points with a micrometer?

The beginner should take every opportunity to examine patterns, both factory and individual creations, as a source of idea and methods of checkering. Be critical of every pattern, look for the bad points as well as the good, and try to learn from them.

Some of the factory pressed-in or pressed-out type of "checkering" can be improved by recutting the lines and bringing the diamonds to a point. But, before you start, take a close look at the lines to see whether they are running straight. Many are not, as their diamonds are arranged for looks and are on a curve. These cannot be recut. A lot of the old type factory checkering can be improved with a single cutter. Every stock that comes under your hand should be checked to see if the checkering can be improved. The practice is worth the effort and the more types of patterns you trace, the more checkering knowledge

will be recorded in your think tank.

As your knowledge of checkering grows, you will want to begin designing your own patterns and will need a few instruments. These will include such items as a flexible rule, a protractor for laying out angles, dividers, outside calipers, French curve, and a lot of inserts. These inserts are the little falderals, such as acorns, leaves, and the old checkering favorite, the fleur-de-lis, of various sizes. The final need will be a few plastic diamonds for establishing base lines. Lay these out one inch wide and 3½ inches long for the small size and double this — 2 by 7 inches for the larger size. While you are at it, make two extra of each size. Split one directly across the width and the other directly down the center of the length. You will find these useful.

When you begin to design your patterns, work them out roughly on paper, but remember you are drawing on a flat surface while the stock is a rounded surface; you will have to make adjustments to compensate. There are two ways to get your pattern on the stock. The first is to draw it on free-hand with the use of a grease pencil or a child's crayon. This allows you to erase the line and redraw it until you have it worked out right. When it looks good, stop, set the stock to one side, then later look at your creation again. Does it follow and blend with the lines of the stock? Will the pattern compliment the stock or make the stock compliment it? Is it too small or too large?

Work the frills in after you have the basic lines established. These should be laid in with the grease pencil also, so they can be adjusted if need be. The guide lines are worked out with the plastic diamond, but don't forget to align them with the points of the pattern if you use points. If you will try the narrow plastic tapes to lay out guide lines, you will skip the flexible rule. That tape is hard to beat!

The forearm can be worked out the same way, laying out the basic outline on paper and working it in on the forearm with the grease pencil. However, the second method I spoke of will work out best for the beginner, especially on the side of the forearm. This is called "splitting the pattern." The forearm is the best to explain the process.

First, draw in the lines that will run parallel with the barrel channel and just below the edges of the forearm.

The first way is to use a pair of dividers. With the barrel removed and the forearm flat on the table belly up, place one leg at the point where the stock touches the table and draw the parallel lines on the stock with the other leg. The other way is to use a small adjustable combination square. Most of these lines will be from a minimum of ¼-inch to a maximum of ¾-inch down from the edge of the forearm. Let's use a halfway measurement ½-inch for our example. Set the blade on the square at ½-inch and lock it in place. Now, place the flat of the square across both sides of the barrel channel with the blade up on the side of the forearm. With a pencil at the end of the blade, draw the parallel line as you move the square down the length of the forearm. Switch over to the other side of the forearm and repeat the process. You will have two lines, one on each side of the stock, exactly ½-inch down on the stock regardless of the thickness of the forearm.

Next, tape a piece of typewriter paper onto the stock with one long edge of the paper exactly on one of these lines. The line you have drawn should be longer than the paper. Now wrap the paper around the stock and pull it tight. Smooth it out so there are no bulges and make a small mark on the paper right on the line on the opposite side from the other line. Mark both ends. Remove the paper from the stock, connect your two dots with a ruler and draw a line connecting them. Cut the paper exactly on this

Using homemade tracing tool that has been fashioned from a common triangular file with front end bent and cut off, the old pattern on a stock is being traced.

As explained in text, traced copy is transferred to foil, pattern cut out. Wrapped around replacement forearm it is traced with sharp tool, in this case, around outside.

drawn line. Carefully fold the paper exactly in half and run your finger up and down the fold, until you make a crease in the paper. You had best square up the folded ends; the angle doesn't matter so long as both ends are the same.

Finally, put the paper back on the forend with the edge of both sides exactly on its matching line on the stock and tack it in place with a couple of pieces of tape. To mark the center of the stock, make a small mark on both ends of the crease in the paper, remove the paper and connect the two marks.

Smooth out your paper and draw in your pattern as you wish on the paper; even the guide lines. When finished, put the paper back on the stock; it should match perfectly the three lines you drew on the stock. You can even work out the pattern on half the paper, fold it and copy it exactly on the other half by holding it against a window pane. The same can be done with a pistol grip pattern, working out one side pattern on paper, locating it on the grip, and taking a few measurements with the divider. Then find the location with the divider on the other side and trace the pattern over there. If you miss it a little, it doesn't matter. No one can look at the grip pattern on both sides at the same time, so just get it as close as possible.

After you have traced a few patterns and rebuilt a couplé more, it will be perfectly clear that if the stock wiggles, the lines in the pattern will wiggle. The stock must be held firmly if any quality checkering is to be done. Otherwise the lines will look like the work of a drunk chicken dragging a broken toenail across the wood. Holding the stock firm can be jury-rigged in many ways. Some people get away with holding the stock by hand. I know of one particularly strong-wristed cuss who simply clamps one of his paws down on the stock and saws away.

A regular swivel vise is a fair arrangement, with one end

of the stock held in padded vise jaws and the other end resting on the work bench. A forearm can be attached to a large wooden dowel and one end of the dowel held in the vise. Pistol grips are secured through their screw holes to a board, which is clamped in the vise. The only thing wrong is that the stock is firmly held and cannot be moved. The wrist of the hand holding the checkering tool must be bent to follow the line as it curves over the stock. This is not the

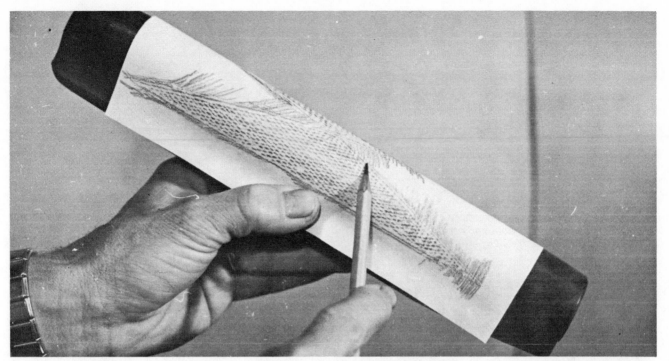

To copy checkering from old stock, a piece of typing paper is placed on pattern and rubbed with soft lead pencil. Paper will bend into the grooves, showing up as white against the darker background of diamonds.

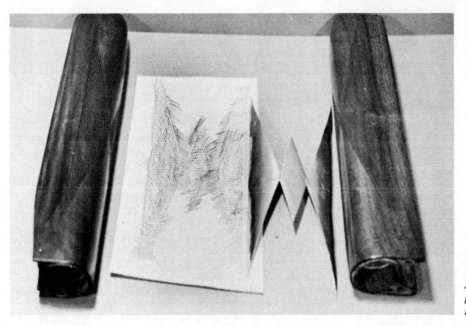

At left is old damaged forearm, with paper tracing, the foil pattern and new forearm carrying copied pattern.

best way to keep a line straight and the chances of a run-out are good. The average person can control the straightness of a line much easier if the stock is turned to meet the tool cutting the line. This way, the wrist stays on the same plane at all times and the wrist, fingers and arm are locked with the pressure to push the tool coming from the elbow and upper arm muscle.

By far the best answer to the problem is a checkering cradle, a support that holds the stock firmly, yet permits it to be turned to meet the tool. Gunsmith supply houses sell them for prices ranging from about six bucks for a simple version, to a fancy rig running over thirty dollars. With a little ingenuity, you can turn a few scraps into an equally functional cradle. It doesn't have to be fancy, just firm. The dean of stock makers and a master at checkering, Alvin

Linden, used one made of pieces of an old cream separator with a section of old rubber boot to hold the butt stock.

The main part of a cradle is the base which must be sturdy enough to hold the stock and the other components of the cradle without flexing. Anything with about the stiffness of a 2X4 will do, and the old 2X4 itself has been the base of a lot of cradles. You can yank a pine wall stud out of the outhouse, but you will be better off buying a good hardboard 2X4, as it has less tendency to split or warp.

Whatever the base is made of, it should be about forty-eight inches long for the average stock with a little longer base needed for Mannlicher stocks. The next components are the uprights that hold the stock up from the base. These should be at least five inches high with one fixed perma-

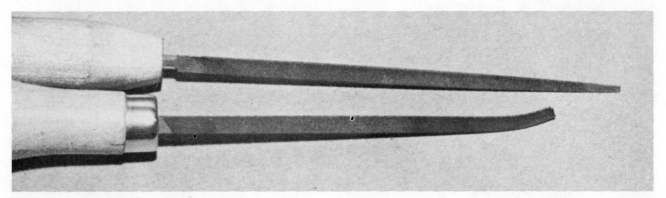

Homemade tracing tool beneath is simply a common file of triangular shape with the front end bent and cut off. The file above shows how it looks before the alternation.

Below: Modern DemBart checkering tool has replaceable cutter with pin that locks cutter to handle.

nently to one end of the base, and the other adjustable up and down the base to fit the different stock lengths. The final components are the rigs that hold the stock to the uprights and allow the stock to rotate. That's it! You can hold the cradle in the vise as most folks do or rig up a bench to hold it with you straddling the bench "hoss fashion."

To see how quickly and inexpensively a checkering cradle could be made, I constructed one especially for this chapter. The total cost of materials was less than two dollars and the construction time around two hours. The dimensions given are not iron-clad and can be adjusted to work with any material you have on hand. Checkering cradles can be made of almost anything. You will notice in one of the photographs that my friend, the professor, is using a homemade rig with a couple of shelf braces as the uprights and 2X4 base. Two connecting rods from a small gasoline engine can be used for uprights; run a pipe through the large ends and a threaded rod through the small ends. The threaded rod can be held in place with a nut on each side of the connecting rod. Any junk yard will yield material to make a dozen different variations at a cost of less than a box of shotgun shells.

Correct lighting can play a mighty important part in your checkering. Regardless of the type of general lighting you have in your work area, you will need a small desk lamp with a flexible neck. This should be equipped with a 60 to 75-watt frosted bulb and placed to one side slightly above and behind you and your work. This will throw the lines and diamonds into shadows making them stand out more plainly. Good daylight can be utilized, but avoid checkering in any bright sunlight, as it is hard on your eyes. Two-power magnification glasses mounted on a headband will ease the strain and make the lines much easier to see, but don't go much above this power. A simple pair of magnification glasses fitted to your individual eyes is the best type.

Make your checkering periods short with about one hour as a maximum. Take a break of the same amount of time and come back to the job. If you try to hang in there like a rusty fish hook, the lines will waver, the quality of the job will suffer and everything will begin to follow Murphy's Law. This law states, "Anything that can mess up, will mess up."

Somewhere along the line you will find a need for some

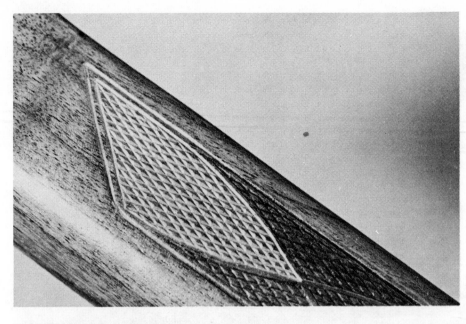

Factory-impressed checkering can be recut, the checkering forming and pointing the diamonds. Not only is the transformation startling, but this is a way for beginner to learn the capabilities of his new tools.

Many of today's stocks are stained birch, made to resemble walnut, and mut be restained after checkering. This photo shows comparison of wood.

As illustration of the type of work that can be done, this is No. 5 pattern by Monte Kennedy, which Walker considers excellent for all bolt action sporters.

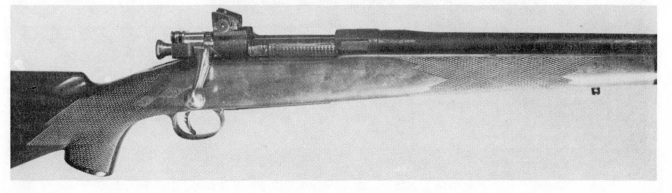

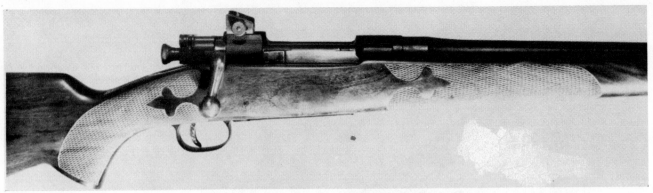

Fleur-de-lis pattern on this Bishop Alaskan walnut stock
is a pattern that fits well on a stock of classic design.

This maple stock from Herter's has a point pattern that
holds well in this type of wood, according to the author.

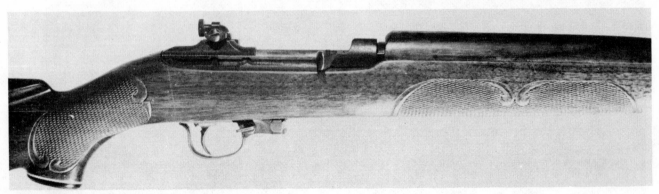

M-1 carbine has Bartlett pattern on
Fajen Mannlicher walnut stock. It
works well on wood lacking quality
required for any intricate carving.

Below: Combination fill-in and point
pattern is simple to do, attractive.

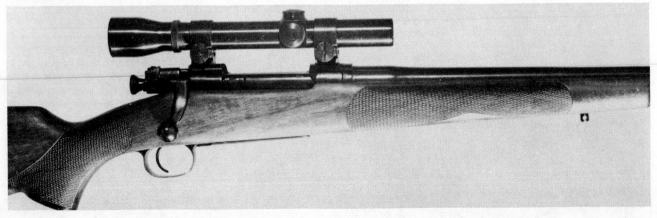

carving. Perhaps it will be in one of the decal checkering patterns around the edges or maybe you just want to fancy up a pattern you have designed. The hobbyist's first reaction to a suggestion that he can do wood carving is one of awe. Even if he has done enough checkering that his work is out of the beginner's class, he still will consider carving beyond his ability.

Checkering is much harder than carving. If he goofs up a line when checkering the mistake is there. If the mistake is in carving, he can alter the lines slightly and who is to know that he did not plan it that way?

Carving is divided basically into two classes. The simple type is incise carving, which is just a fancy name for cutting the background down to make the subject and the surrounding wood stand out. The other type is relief carving and the background is cut away but over a wider area until the subject stands out in relief, the background blending in slowly with the rest of the stock. The tools are simple and can be homemade. In fact, you can get away with nothing more than a sharp pocket knife for a tool.

Instead of jumping right into carving a twenty-point buck jumping over a ten-foot log with a mountain lion riding on his back, let critters alone for a while. They have too many muscles that have to be perfect to be presentable. Stick instead to leaves, acorns, and so on. These have enough variation in form that a mistake can be covered up; a malformed line just adds a rustic appearance.

One of my favorites is an initial carved in the grip cap. This is carving at its simplest, yet is attractive and adds that just-for-you appearance. You can use a letter in script, Gothic or even old English.

First, we have to lay out the border, using a divider set at about ¼-inch. Place one leg on the edge, making the border mark except at the rear, where some caps blend in with the stock and the line will have to be drawn in free-hand.

Pick your letter out of a book or one of these letter sheets that you can buy at the local stationery store. Trace it on a piece of typewriter paper and cut out a small border line around it about equal to your border line in the grip cap. It doesn't have to be a perfect match, as this is to help you line it up on the grip cap. Place a small piece of carbon on the grip cap and your letter on top of this and trace the letter. The first tool needed is a sharp knife. Good knives, like good wives, are hard to come by. A good source of knives is offered by the gunsmith supply houses. Another is the common "Tree Brand" that is available in just about any hardware store. If you choose one of these, buy the model made in Germany instead of the locally brewed one, as the German version has better steel in it. Sharpen this to a razor's edge, especially the point. Your second tool will be a small, flat chisel about 1/8-inch wide. You can buy one, make it out of a ground-down file or even a piece of hacksaw blade. Again, get it razor sharp. The final tool is a common finishing nail.

Grasp the knife as you would a pencil and slowly cut the lines of the letter straight down to a depth of 1/16 of an inch with the point of the knife. Make the cuts even and at the same depth. When finished, switch to the border line you drew and cut this down to the same 1/16-inch depth staying right on the line.

Next is to block out the lines we have cut. Move the knife point out from your cut about 1/16-inch, angle the blade, and cut back to the bottom of the first cut you made. The chip you remove will be triangle-shaped. Do this all the way around the cut lines until the letter and the border stand out in detail. We have created a free zone and border line around our important letter to prevent any cuts

slipping over on them, spoiling the work. All that is left to do is remove the excess wood between the safety cuts.

We can remove this excess wood with the pocket knife alone, but the 1/8-inch-wide chisel that we made will do a better job and do it a lot easier. Make your cuts across the grain instead of with or against the grain and you can keep the removal of the excess wood to an even depth of 1/16-inch without splintering or digging in.

Don't worry if the cut is not smooth all the way, but try to get it as close to an even depth as possible. When you have finished removing the excess wood, the letter and the border will be at the same level with the background 1/16-inch below them. The finishing nail point is used to stipple the background. This is done by tapping the back of the nail lightly with the hammer and allowing the point to just nick the wood. If you let the nail rest lightly between your fingers, it will bounce slightly after hitting the wood surface. Keep tapping and moving the nail over the background until it is a mass of small nicks. Don't try for any kind of pattern, as the more random the nicks, the better. All of the background should be covered.

A good substitute for the nail is a dental burr with a rounded tip. This makes a small star-like mark in the wood. The final step in carving is to round the edges of the letter lightly and the border even more lightly. Finish up by scrubbing in some boiled linseed oil and your initialed grip cap is finished.

Relief carving should be attempted only after you have done several of the initials or other incise type carvings and have the feel of the tools. Relief carving can be described best as giving the visual impression that the subject has been carved out of one piece of wood and glued onto the stock. One or two companies, incidentally, actually offer carved subjects that are glued onto a stock.

Start with something simple like an acorn, a couple of oak leaves and a short section of the stem. This can be as an insert in the checkering pattern or something added to the pattern at the border line.

Keep your relief carving simple, working into the more elaborate patterns as your skill increases. The final step is the pattern where the relief carving becomes the entire stock decoration without support of a checkering background. This usually separates the men with patience. It cannot be hurried.

Relief carving found as the border on many checkering patterns is not elaborate and is well within the ability of anyone who can do checkering. Scrolls and leaves are made to stand out in relief by the use of a small gouge to cut away the center part of the scroll, leaving the edge or rim, high with the background receding. The veins and other decorations also are made to stand out by similar cuts.

One of the best teachers of relief carving is leather carving such as that on belts and billfolds. The same basic cuts, high sections and low sections, will apply to wood carving. Most of the companies specializing in leather carving equipment and material, offer books of patterns for about a dollar each. These are also a source of good carving patterns for your stock as well as showing the use of various tools to gain relief effect. Leather carving requires a specialized stamp tool to depress the leather while the wood carver must use a gouge to remove the wood to the desired depth.

As your skill develops, you will need more help. For this, read and study the book by Monte Kennedy, "Checkering and Carving of Gunstocks." This not only outlines his work, but the thoughts and methods of many other of America's leading professionals, along with patterns by the score.

Chapter 6

A PLACE TO WORK

For Serious Gunsmithing, You Need Room For Tools, Firearms And A Great Deal Of Thought!

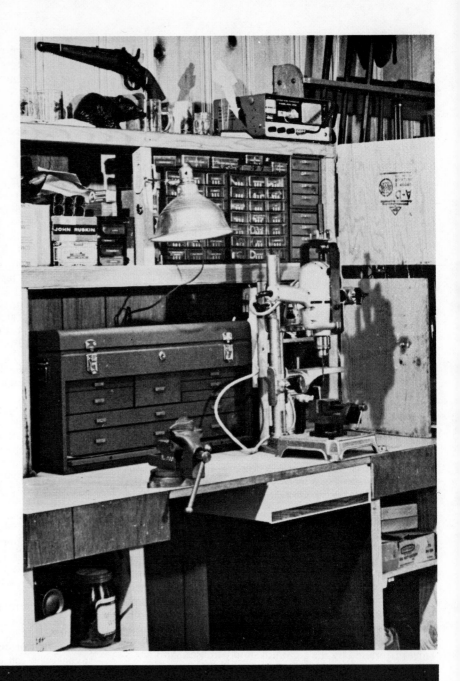

ABOUT THIS TIME, the wife will begin to resent the sawdust, chips and tools lying about the den or kitchen. Your work and tools will end up in a wide assortment of places as the wife goes about her daily task of putting things away. It will become evident that you need to find a place to work with some kind of storage system for your tools. The equipment and tools must be secure from not only the wife's daily cleaning up expeditions, but also from children and borrowing neighbors.

Power tools and equipment are especially dangerous to children. For example, while I was working after hours on a rush job, a customer dropped by and asked permission to come back into the work area of the shop. What I didn't know was that his 5-year-old daughter was with him. I glanced past him and my heart leaped up in my throat at what I saw. His little girl was reaching through the flywheel of the air compressor to touch the pressure gauge! This is the automatic type compressor that jumps on when the

pressure drops to a certain level and this one, like all compressors, leaks down slowly. Dropping my tools, I made one leap and snatched her away, and she promptly let out a squall that would have awakened the dead. Her father was about to say something when the compressor suddenly jumped on. He stopped, looked at it and turned white as a sheet as he realized what would have happened to her hand if I had not snatched her away. He made a bad mistake in bringing a small child into an area full of power equipment, and I made an even more stupid mistake in allowing him to come back into the area without checking. The only time a child should be premitted in such an area is when you are instructing him or have nothing else to do but watch him like a hawk watching a chicken.

Borrowing neighbors will borrow anything from a white elephant to your toothbrush, if you let them. If it's tied down, they will ask to come over to use it. If you lend them tools and equipment, one of two things will happen.

Most will conveniently forget to bring it back and growl if you ask for it back within 30 or 40 days. The rest will return the tools all "buggered up" or allow them to get an inch thick with rust.

Most hobbyists start off with a few simple hand tools in a discarded box and end up with a workshop. While the separate work area or shop is the ideal solution, servicemen, construction workers and apartment dwellers have no other choice but to try to come up with some method of keeping their equipment and work area in the den, kitchen, or other room in the house. Some of the portable shops that these hobbyists build to solve the problem border on genius.

One sergeant worked out a complete arrangement in the form of what appeared to be the cabinet of a hi-fi set when closed up. But when opened, that piece of furniture was an engineering marvel. It contained a work bench top, a sub-miniature lathe, a vise, various power hand tools and drawers galore. The tools rested in individual nests of their own, safe and completely secure when the cabinet was moved. He had a large piece of plastic sheeting to cover the floor to catch chips and filings. He even has a complete shotgun reloading tool and a metallic reloading press in that thing. It does illustrate what can be done with a limited area.

An apartment dweller solved the shop location problem by converting an old roll top desk into a work bench that, when closed, looked right at home with the other antique furniture. But when opened up, the desk was strictly modern inside with a beautiful set of tools.

The simplest of tool containers is the tool roll. This is a piece of heavy cloth folded three-fourths of the way back over itself with the sides sewn together. Individual pockets for the tools are made by sewing seams parallel with the sides. These are spaced so that they accept and hold each tool separate from the others and snugly in place. With the tools in their individual pockets, the top flap is folded down over the pockets and the cloth and tools rolled up and tied with an attached cord. The rolled package is compact as well as protective, yet the tools are readily available for use. These rolls can be stored in a small box or drawer. Canvas or similar material will make the best roll while cloth-backed plastic should be avoided. It has a

tendency to make the tools sweat and rust. Any canvas or awning shop should have a bunch of scraps left over from regular jobs and will sew up a couple of tool rolls for you at a small charge.

You can add more protection to the tools by spraying the inside of each pouch with a rust preventative. Tool rolls are ideal for items with delicate edges such as chisels, even if you have a regular shop. However, sharp chisels will cut through the canvas if extra protection is not used. Heavy corrugated cardboard can be used by folding it back over the chisel in the form of a holster and pushing it down into the pocket. Or a piece of heavy leather can be sewn on the canvas where the chisel points touch it. Don't forget to give the cardboard or leather a shot of rust preventative.

A tool chest of some description is a life saver for one who has no separate room or shop, as well as for those who do have a permanent work area. These can be made of wood, but if any amount of tools or other heavy parts are to be stored in them, the wood version will require some heavy bracketing on the edges and bottom.

The steel chest is far superior, as it offers maximum protection and can be moved or picked up without damage. In most instances, it will house more tools and equipment than a similar homemade rig. The simplest form of these is the mechanic's tool box which consists of just a large box with two or less removable trays. Next is the cantilever box with a series of hinged trays and a large storage area below the trays. These will hold a lot of goodies with just a little planning. I lugged one of these around for about 15 years covering thousands of miles, and it survived every kind of shipping you can name and protected the tools 100 percent all the way. It is still in everyday use and with the exception of a few dents, is as good as new.

The machinist's chest, as the name implies, is more a chest than a tool box. It usually consists of one large top section and eight or more drawers on the sides with the drawers lined with felt to cushion the tools. The machinist's chest is the finest way a hobbyist can store his tools. These last two types are far from being cheap in price, but are insurance for the man who moves about. With a sound lock they will keep the tools safe from prying hands and borrowing neighbors.

Your small parts, accessories and gauges, are stored best in a separate parts cabinet. One of the best is the cabinet with the plastic drawers you can see through. These come in a wide range of sizes and styles, with the outside case available in either plastic or steel. The plastic cabinet will tend to warp or crack, while the metal will remain stable and offer more protection. The price difference between the two usually is small.

Most of these cabinet drawers will have movable partitions that can be adjusted to fit your needs with stick-on tags for identification of contents. Pick one you like and stick with that same size and style, since most are made to stack on top of each other with aligning identifications to hold the top cabinet in place on the bottom one. If you do not have a separate shop and must move the cabinet around for storage, a good trick is to save the cardboard box in which the cabinet was shipped. Lay the cardboard box on its side and insert the cabinet with the drawers facing the solid bottom of the box. You will have a storage for your parts cabinet that will prevent the drawers from sliding out and spilling the contents, if the cabinet is moved about.

Another good storage cabinet for small parts is an empty cigar box. A gun salesman once told me that of all the gun shops he had ever visited, he had never failed to find cigar boxes being used in one way or another. The best are the all-wood boxes, but these are in short supply. Some cigar

Shelf bracket supports are simple but effective. Need for 12 inches between shelves to hold individual parts cabinets and cigar boxes containing parts is evident.

boxes use wood on the sides, but most are all heavy pressed cardboard. Pick one common brand and stick to it, or a box of the same dimensions, as boxes of the same size are a lot easier to stack and store than a conglomeration. You can add partitions in the boxes by gluing the side sections of other dismantled boxes in them. Cigar boxes with the lids removed are just the ticket for temporary storage of gun parts, when you are disassembling a gun for cleaning or repair. It's easier to toss the parts in the cigar box than hunt for them when they roll off the bench. For some strange reason, a gun part can roll off the bench, hit the floor, bounce a dozen times with each bounce in a different direction and roll twenty feet to get under the biggest pile of junk you have in the shop.

One of the worst things that you can use for storage of parts or tools is a glass jar. True, you see a lot of them advertised for just this, with all kinds of fancy revolving tops for holding the jars. It looks good and, at first, seems a good idea. But all you have to do to be convinced they are not is to let one drop to the floor and break. Now try to pick the parts out of the glass fragments without splitting your fingers to the bone. An inexpensive substitute is the empty shortening and coffee cans from the kitchen with the plastic snap tops. Tobacco cans of one pound or larger also serve as good parts containers. Any ardent pipe smoker can empty a pound can a week and will gladly give the cans away. Whatever type can you choose, don't forget to spray a shot or two of rust preventative into the can, especially if you live in a humid area.

Any table can be converted into a work bench without marring the top if you make a special work top. A section of 1/2-inch exterior grade plywood is cut to match the dimensions of the table top and a piece of heavy cloth such as felt is glued to the bottom of the plywood. A couple of C-clamps on each end will hold the work top in place without any wiggling, yet allow it to be removed in seconds and stored while the table resumes its normal occupation. If the weather is good you can use the work top out of doors by clamping it to the top of the picnic table. If you want to attach a small vise to it permanently, use a section of 2X6 with the vise bolted to it and the bolt heads recessed into the 2X6. This, in turn, is nailed or screwed to the work top. A final touch is the nailing of a small one-inch strip of wood around the edges of the work top to prevent small parts from rolling off when the work top is used on a table that is not level. If the top is to match no specific table, then the work top with dimensions about two feet wide and three or four feet long will prove sufficient for hobby needs.

The day will dawn when the hobbyist tires of having to stop part way through a project, gather up his equipment and tools, clean up the area and store the material only to have to set it all back up again in a short time. The solution is to find a place to set up and maintain a permanent work area or shop.

The place to work need not be large or elaborate but it should be separated from other household storage and work areas. This separation must have a wall with a door that can be locked, and for a good reason. The shop area must be for work. You must keep out that household junk. Besides, you will need all of the room to store important things like broken gun stocks, old military sights, bent barrels and other rare gun parts.

Places like a spare room, a basement or even a section of the attic can be put to good service. A basement workshop is the old favorite for most types of building hobbies, but it must be dry enough for gun work. If moisture is a problem, check with local construction supply house for a sealer for

The bottom of a bench that is seldom used has been closed in with 3/8-inch plywood doors for storage. Note that the parts cabinets are built in permanently just above.

This is a view from the front with the drawer removed to show the simple flat drawer runners now installed.

the walls. Most of these sealers are made from refined cement and, when mixed with water and painted on the walls, the moisture problem will be eliminated.

If the floor is of cement, a couple coats of a good decking paint usually does the trick. Most spare rooms need only to have the necessary benches and cabinets added to turn them into good work shops. Be sure to check the wiring to see that it is heavy enough for the power equipment you will be using.

Attics can be utilized if you have enough room to stand up and move about without rattling your brains on a rafter every time you turn. Ventilation will be the biggest problem, as most attics get so hot in the summertime. A used air conditioner or a large window fan will be your best bet. Heat for the winter can come from any of several inexpensive portable electric heaters.

If you are stuck with one of the modern, split level cracker boxes, the location for a shop becomes a problem. Probably the least used part of a modern home is the attic. Most of these are entered via a small access hole that a greasy snake can just squeeze through. If the attic is large

The workbench is attached to the wall with metal strap. Drawer has been left open to show how it fits, while the 2X4 mounted on end of bench is to hold cleaning rods.

enough, the tiny access hole can be enlarged and a disappearing stairway installed. The area may necessitate a work shop that is only four or five feet wide but quite long.

The second place to look is the utility room that often is hooked onto the carport and holds the hot water heater, et al., or is just filled with junk. Look around for a place to build the bench. It need not be extra long, but should be long enough for an assembled rifle or shotgun. Extra bench room can be gained by an extension across the end, forming a bench in the shape of an L. Cabinets or shelves on the wall will provide needed storage space. The bench itself can be built with a series of drawers and shelves underneath to hold tools and material. A friend of mine has such a shop, and he has more equipment jammed into that small space than most people can get into a shop twice the size. His secret in accomplishing this is to keep the tools portable. such as grinders. They are stored in a cabinet when not in use. Also every tool is utilized to the fullest by interchanging wheels, grinders, and so on. He has turned out some remarkable gun work in this tiny shop.

If there is absolutely no possible room for a shop any-

where in the house itself, look for a separate building of some description. Just about anything can be worked over into a shop. If you have an old separate garage, the building can be converted into a shop while the car is housed in a new metal carport attached to your house. Anything from an ex-chicken house to an old coal house can be used. I have even seen a shop made of the body of an old school bus. The wheels were removed, the front end cut off, then it was rebuilt, painted and flowers planted around it with an awning on front and sides.

If no space can be found, the way out is to build a shop. Few families are blessed with more storage space than they need and the new building can serve a dual role by being divided into two areas. One for the shop and other for the household storage. A separate building need not be an insurmountable task financially nor need it be an eyesore in the yard. Construction can match that of the house but a simple material such as exterior plywood can be made presentable with a good paint job. You can save a bit of money by doing most of the trim and inside work yourself. However, it is usually best to hire a carpenter to do the framing and roof if you are not familiar with carpentry.

The walls will go up fast, if you use 4X8 plywood sheets with furring strips covering the joints. Plywood in exterior grade is both strong and inexpensive with a long life span. It can be used for the decking on the roof with the roofing shingles nailed to it and also, for the floor of the building. If heavy winters are predominant in your area, the inside will have to be insulated and sealed, but insulation can be had in foil rolls that are just pressed between the wall studs. You can use sheets of interior 1/4-inch plywood to seal the rolls of insulation in place and serve as the inside walls of the shop. Use inexpensive sheets of paneling if you want things on the fancy side. The ceiling also can be of plywood instead of the usual sheet rock. I keep stressing the use of plywood, for just about anyone with enough brains to work on something as complicated as a gun will have little trouble in putting it up, and it does get a big area covered fast.

If you live in a mild climate, the inside can be left unsealed and the area between the wall studs for shelves. It is best to leave all wiring to a professional in order to comply with building codes, but you can save by having him show you where to bore all the holes for the wiring and access plates. With the heavy work done, an electrician can wire a regular shop in a couple of hours.

Concrete blocks are fast and economical. Basically all that is needed is a good concrete floor-foundation, the walls and the roof. All expensive carpentry work of wall studs, floor joists and so forth is eliminated. You can save in many ways with a concrete block shop, using seconds. These are regular blocks with a corner or edge chipped off, but structurally as strong as a first grade block. They usually cost about 40 percent less than a first grade block. Any brickmason can lay a wall of blocks in short order or you can do it yourself if you have the time. Best bet is to look around your area and find a construction job that involves blocks. Spend a few hours or so watching how they are laid and kept straight. You will find that it is not all that complicated — just hard work. My present shop is of block construction. A block sealer inside and out will eliminate any sweating or moisture problem. It is easily heated or cooled and has a built-in bonus of being virtually fireproof.

Several manufacturers have small metal buildings that can be erected by anyone with a few hand tools. Most are of galvanized steel prepainted with all holes drilled, and the project a sort of king-size erector set. The floor is included with the knocked-down building and all you need is a few concrete blocks as a foundation. These buildings presently available range in size from a small 6X6-foot job for under $100 to a garage-size building 12X12 feet priced around $500. There is an almost limitless choice of floor plans, windows, doors, walls, ad infinitum. If the building will be a permanent one, you can eliminate the floor normally included and use the savings to pay for a concrete slab. The building then is bolted down to the slab. If the cost of the building appears high, remember that you are saving the construction cost, which will more than offset the initial price. Many of these buildings can be purchased in units; you can erect one unit, and later on buy a second unit to attach to the first one. This is done by removing one wall, bolting on the second unit and reinstalling the old wall at the new location.

Similar buildings, already assembled, can be moved and installed on your property by the manufacturer. This, I understand, originated with the need of small office buildings at construction sites. They are available stripped or completely finished on the inside with wiring, floors, walls, etc. Home workshop models with benches in place and ready for you to start work an hour or so after it is installed also are available. Naturally, the price of these finished units is higher than the do-it-yourself versions.

Quite often, good usable buildings can be had from completed large construction jobs. Others can come from old houses being torn down for new homes, etc. Most of these buildings from old house sites are built with the old type lumber and may be better constructed than a similar modern building. Most of the old homes had a variety of small outside buildings such as the coal house I mentioned or garages, storage houses, and such. If you buy them on

the spot and take the responsibility of moving them, the price is dirt cheap. A large flat-bodied truck and the help of a few strong-backed friends will take care of the moving. If need be, you can dismantle the house, keeping walls intact, buy a few extra planks to replace any broken ones and move the building with a pick-up truck or trailer.

The main piece of furniture in any shop is the work bench and should be planned carefully before construction of the bench begins. Pick one solid wall for the main bench and, if possible, add an L extension to one end. The main bench should run the length of the longest wall of the building. It is best to leave the rest of the floor space open until you have worked in the shop and ascertained your future needs. Too often, hobbyists in their zeal for building work benches, fill the shop with them on every available wall. At a later date, there is no room for some piece of machinery, such as a floor drill press. One long bench with the L extension at one or both ends usually will be more bench than you will need. If a window is available, be sure to mount your work area in front of it for natural lighting.

Every book I have ever seen on any type of shop construction carries a drawing of a bench that decrees it must be made out of timbers just short of railroad cross ties in size so that it will be "solid." This may be correct, if you are going to be working on steamship engines and I suspect the idea originated from such shop benches. My present benches are made from 2X4s with one-inch plywood tops and I have yet to find any fault with them. They are braced well and tied to the cement block wall with lag bolts.

If you build your own benches, check with the house wreckers in your area for used lumber. Most of the wood that went into these old homes stands over the modern

This is the small basement gunsmithing shop of Garnett Stancil II. Workbench was parts cabinet converted by installing 2X4s on the top. It has several doors that open to good storage space that is separated by shelves.

lumber like steak over sardines. The grain is close and, after forty or more years, it has dried to the point that a nail can hardly be driven into it. The price is a lot cheaper if you haul it away yourself. Pick straight 2X4s that are knot free with no nails broken off in them. If the lumber is dressed, so much the better. If not, your local cabinet maker can plane them for you.

After you have sawed and nailed some of this wood, you will see why I recommend it over the present type No. 5 wood — which derives its name from being planted the first day, allowed to grow two days, cut and sawed on the fourth day, and delivered on the fifth day. If you nail a plank of Number 5 on one end, it will warp before you can walk to the other end.

Another beef I have with most bench designers is their designation of exactly X number of inches for height. If all of the human animals were poured from the same mold, it would be fine, but a bench that is comfortable for a short man will be a back breaker for a six-footer. Consequently, the bench for the six-foot critter will require old shorty to work while standing on tippy-toe. Build the bench to a height that is comfortable for you and the devil with the designers. A height about three inches below your belt level will be somewhere close to what you will need...that is, if you can still find your belt under the overhang.

To arrive at a correct height, try the kitchen cabinet. Place a gun on the cabinet and turn a screw on the gun. If it is too high, you have to raise your elbows above normal level. On the other hand, if it is too low, you have to bend over to work and your back will feel like somebody hit it with a sledgehammer after a short work period.

You can adjust the height of the kitchen cabinet temporarily by placing a couple of bricks on it and a piece of plywood on top of the bricks. Try working on a gun with the height increased to see if this height feels better to you. You can adjust the height back and forth until you arrive at a height that feels just right. When you find it measure the distance from the floor. This is the height to make your work bench.

You can buy bench legs at hardware stores in sets of two for a 24-inch long bench. Additional sets of legs can be joined together for a longer bench with the steel bracing that comes with the legs. While both hardwood and steel factory legs can be had, it is best to stick with steel legs as the wooden ones are a bit on the shaky side. You can adjust the height of these ready-made legs by mounting them on pieces of 2X4 runners on the floor. A complete factory bench can be had, but the price is respectable.

For a lot less money you can build your own bench, legs and all, out of 2X4s and one-inch exterior plywood for the top. Select good straight 2X4s that are free of knots and defects for the bench. Hardwood is ideal but expensive and not absolutely essential if good quality pine is available. The bench top is half of a 4x8-foot sheet of one-inch plywood. The 24-inch wide bench top, as shown, will be wide enough for any need, and if you cut a sheet of plywood right down the middle, you will have enough for a total of sixteen feet of bench length. Be sure to specify exterior grade plywood, for the interior grade will not stand up under the water and oil that will get on it while working. Plywood is graded by the quality of knot-free surface, A, B, C, D, etc. A sheet of A-D grade will have one knot free side, which will be used for the top work surface. The D side will have open knots but this will be on the bottom and will not

Author feels that one must keep his working area in a state of orderliness if any work is to be accomplished. His bench was not cleaned up especially for this photo.

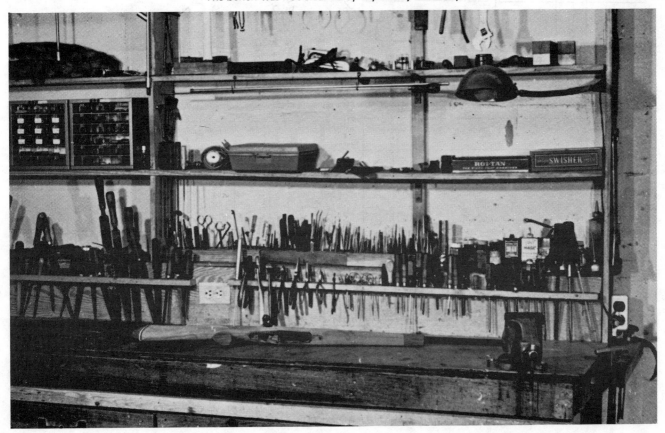

65

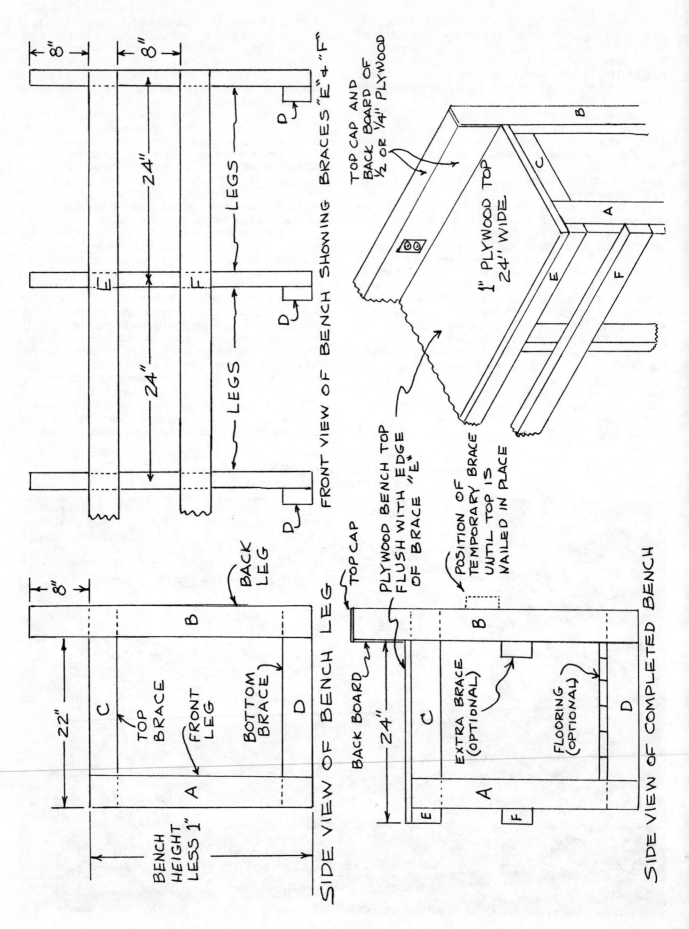

8"   8"

24"

24"

E

F

LEGS

LEGS

LEGS

D

D

D

FRONT VIEW OF BENCH SHOWING BRACES "E" & "F"

TOP CAP AND
BACK BOARD OF
½ OR ¼" PLYWOOD

1" PLYWOOD TOP
24" WIDE

B

C

A

E

F

POSITION OF
TEMPORARY BRACE
UNTIL TOP IS
NAILED IN PLACE

PLYWOOD BENCH TOP
FLUSH WITH EDGE
OF BRACE "E"

TOP CAP

8"

22"

C

TOP
BRACE

A   FRONT LEG

BOTTOM
BRACE

B

BACK LEG

D

BENCH
HEIGHT
LESS 1"

SIDE VIEW OF BENCH LEG

TOP CAP

BACK BOARD

24"

C

A

B

D

E

F

EXTRA BRACE
(OPTIONAL)

FLOORING
(OPTIONAL)

SIDE VIEW OF COMPLETED BENCH

With holes of correct size drilled through the support timber, it makes an ideal rack to hang cleaning rods.

This photo illustrates the shelf supports described in the text, as well as showing special strip to hold tools.

matter.

For an eight-foot bench you will need five sets of legs. This will give a spacing of two feet between the legs providing good support for the top and allowing large two-foot-wide drawers to be built below the bench. The front leg (A) is cut from a 2X4 to a length that is your predetermined bench height less one inch. The one inch is to allow for the plywood top. The back leg (B) for the bench now is cut eight inches longer to allow for the back rest of the bench. Next, measure the width of one of your 2X4s for an exact measure. Most of these are less than 4 inches, but we will use the full 4 inches in the drawings for simplicity. When you do cut the parts for the bench, go by your measurement to prevent any discrepancy. The top brace for the legs will be flush with the front of leg (A) and flush with back of leg (B). This will be 22 inches plus the thickness of the back leg (4 inches) for a total of 26 inches. Cut two pieces this length. One for brace (C) and one for brace (B) on the bottom.

Nail the top brace (C) and the bottom brace (D) in place, being sure they are square with the two legs. The braces should go to the left side of the legs on four of the leg sets. On the fifth leg set, nail the braces on the right side. If you study the drawing and look at the two end leg sets, you will see the reason for this. A short 2X4 fill-in is nailed between the insides of the front and rear legs to support the ends of the plywood top. When you have completed the five leg sets, check to be sure all are square with their braces and that all are of matching height.

You will now need two 2X4s eight feet long for the front tie braces (E and F). These should be your best 2X4s and as straight as possible. You can nail these to the front legs better if the leg sets are lying on their backs with leg (A) up in the air. Nail the leg that will be the left end of the bench to the end of the top tie brace (E). This is the one with the top brace (C) and the bottom brace (D) on the right side of the legs, opposite the other four legs. Now, nail one of the other leg sets to the opposite end of the eight foot top tie-brace (E). When this is completed, nail the bottom tie-brace (F) in place with its top eight inches below the bottom of the top tie-brace (E). This is to allow for an eight-inch deep drawer. Now, measure to the exact center of the eight-foot front tie braces (E and F) for the center leg set. Mark the location and nail the center leg set in place. The other two leg sets go between the center leg set and the outside leg sets, exactly halfway.

When all five leg sets are nailed to the two front tie-braces, stand the whole affair up straight. To hold the back legs in place you will have to nail a temporary brace across the back of the five leg sets. Don't nail this all the way down, as it will be removed after the top is in place. Be sure all legs are square and straight. Then cut the two end fill-in 2X4s and nail them in place as shown in the drawing. When completed, lay the one-inch plywood top in place with a grade A side facing up. Push it back until it is butting against the back 2X4 (B). Check to see that everything is square and matching, and then nail the top down to the leg top braces (C) of all five leg sets and across the front into the top tie-brace (E). These should be finishing nails countersunk below the top of the plywood with a punch to prevent the top of the nails from scratching a gun laid on the work top.

The next step is to close off the back rest of the bench. This back board (see drawing) can be made from anything, but 1/4 or 1/2-inch plywood is ideal. Cut it to fit flush against the bench top to prevent pins, screws, and so on, from getting stuck under it. The width of the board will be eight inches and just flush with the tops of the back leg (B). The main purpose of this back board is to hold the electrical outlets that you will be needing. It is hard to get too many electrical outlets on a bench. One outlet about every two feet along the bench is not excessive, but be sure that the wiring and fusing is of sufficient size to handle all electrical appliances which may be running at the same time.

After you have the backboard nailed in place, leave the top open so the electrician can run the wiring. Specify three prong outlets for the bench to assure that all motors and appliances are grounded. Be certain heavy wiring is used. Don't argue if the electrician wants to use electrical conduit to run the wire in, as this virtually eliminates fire hazards behind the bench. You will need switches, etc., for the motors and will be enticed to use the small, inexpensive toggle type. These will last only a short while before burning out. The best bet is to use regular wall type switches which can be built right into the bench backboard or mounted on the tool in a fully enclosed box.

With the backboard wired and in place, the top cap can be nailed down. This is a four-inch-wide plank or piece of plywood that will also serve as the bottom shelf. The bench is now ready to be mounted in place. Before you push it against the wall, remove the temporary back brace you nailed on the back legs. If you are going to tie the bench to the wall and floor, no additional braces will be needed. But, if the bench is going to just stand in place, it will be best to nail an additional 2X4 across the back legs (B). This can be directly across the inside, opposite either the brace (E) or (F). Another way is to floor the bottom of the bench by nailing planks across the bottom braces (D) as shown in the drawing. This will keep your special rare junk off the floor as well as tying the bench together. The decision as to which additional brace is best, is decided by your shop requirements and your own personal preference. If the bench is tied to the wall, the flooring can be used also.

The space between the electrical outlets can be used in two different ways. One is to cut into the plywood backboard and make a series of small drawers to hold screws, pins, gun parts and other small items. I usually have enough large drawers to hold more stuff than I can use and I prefer to use the space to make a tool rack. You can buy a little item from the gunsmith supply houses known as 3-in-1 holder. These cost about a dime each and consist of a piece of bent spring steel with a screw for attaching it to the backboard. Each will hold three items like screwdrivers, chisels, etc. Another tool holder can be made by drilling holes spaced 1½ inches apart down the middle of a 1X2-inch furring strip. The holes can be of varying sizes to fit different tools, such as screwdrivers, files, pliers, and so on. The furring strip should be attached about an inch below the top of the plywood back. Several of these furring strip tool holders can be seen in the photographs of the bench.

Drawer space under the bench is second in importance only to the top itself. The drawers should be deep and wide, running almost the full depth of the bench. The space between the leg sets and the front tier braces will allow you to make a drawer about eight inches deep, two feet wide and 22 to 23 inches long. There are several ways to make a drawer and the runners to hold it in place. Bottom runners are simple to make. Their only drawback is that they do not align the drawer well, as it is pushed back in place. The second type has the runners on the sides and work better as these align the drawer with no binding. The photographs show the method of attaching the runners to the sides of the drawer and to the bench legs. Also commercial drawer runners are available and are not too expensive. The front of the drawers can be of dressed plank or plywood, but it is best to stick to dressed planks for the sides. The bottom of the drawer can be of plywood or masonite.

I have not given any exact dimensions on the drawers as you will have to build them, one by one, to match the space under the bench. From past experience, if you build five drawers to match the bench, each of them will have just slightly different dimensions to prevent interchangability. Measure the space available and build them as close fitting as you can. Screws or ribbed boat nails should be used to attach the front and back to the sides. The bottoms are best nailed on with large-head, short nails to prevent the bottom from pulling off under the weight of all the tools and stuff you will cram into the drawers. You can make the drawers slide in and out easily by rubbing common soap on the runners. Finally, put a good solid handle on the front of the drawers. I don't mean those little teeny-tiny screen door handles or the kitchen cabinet variety. Put a handle on them big enough for lifting an elephant, if you could get

Punch block is a piece of 2X6-inch pine with spacing laid out in checkerboard pattern. Holes are drilled at intersections of lines with 3/8-inch drill, with several half-inch holes included for larger punches.

Complete punch block has punches and other items in place. Top has been sanded, masonite nailed to bottom.

the screws into his hide.

You can divide the inside of the drawers any way you wish or leave them wide open. Racks to hold your stock chisels can be made from furring strips attached to the sides and notched to hold the chisels. The same can be made to hold your files also. Trays and divisions to hold parts, tools, jigs, etc., can be built into the drawers. Good temporary partitions can be had by cutting the tops off cigar boxes of different sizes and arrangement, provide a variety of containers. I use one such set-up to hold test fire ammunition of different gauges and calibers.

It's okay to run drawers down to the floor on one end of the bench where the top space of the bench is not in steady use. But if you do this where you spend most of your time, the old knee caps and shin bones will take a beating. One big drawer under this area to hold tools and equipment, with the space below left open for big feet and knotty knees, will prove hard to beat. This open space is a good place to store large tool boxes, junk boxes and so on. You can close the open space with cabinet doors and use the space behind to store parts or whole guns as it will be relatively dust-free.

A cleaning rod holder for the bench is made by drilling several holes in a piece of 2X4 and nailing it to the end of

Author has found this type of drawer works well for him. Runners are attached to the upper sides of the drawer with a matching single runner on bench sides.

This drawer has been divided to hold cigar boxes with the lids torn off and offers a storage place for test loads. Similar divisions can be used for tool storage.

the bench. If your vise is on the same end of the bench, this arrangement is about perfect with the cleaning rods where you need them. Add a cigar box to hold the patches and bore brushes. Tear the top off another cigar box to hold bore cleaner, oil and rust remover. Finally, drive a good finishing nail in one of the bench legs and hang a brush for cleaning the bench top.

A practical use for the wall is to build shelves to hold the thousand and one things looking for a resting place. The first thing to settle is the width of the shelves. I've tried 6, 8 and 12-inch shelves at one time or another. The six-inch is on the skimpy side while the wide 12-inch invites a bunch of junk building up at the back. The eight-inch wide shelf seems to fill the bill best for me.

If you have a regular eight-foot ceiling, three shelves, 12 inches apart, will work out best. More shelves can be put up, but this will mean less distance between them and a lot of things like parts cabinets will not fit. Select the boards for the shelves personally to assure straightness and as few knots as possible.

If you are working with an eight-foot bench, try to buy boards in 12-foot lengths since you will need the extra four feet for bracing. Usually, four planks 12 feet long will be all you will need. One will be cut in half for the end uprights,

with other three used for the shelves. The middle bracing will require three 12-inch pieces. Any leftover boards will come in handy for the drawers.

The shelves will have to be tied to the wall in some manner. If your shop is not ceilinged, you can run the end uprights up and tie them to the ceiling joists with the bottom ends nailed to the top of the bench. If the shop is ceilinged, you can use metal angle brackets to tie the uprights and the shelves to the wall.

If you are using cement blocks for shop construction, the brackets can be tied to the wall with either cement nails or toggle bolts. The cement nails are a bit hard to use and, if struck a glancing blow with the hammer, they will take off like a bullet fully capable of perforating the plumbing of any ignorant bystander. The toggle bolts are best, but require that a hole be drilled into the hollow center of the concrete block for the special winged nut to pass through. You can buy a special cement drill for the hand drill or use a star drill and hammer to punch the hole through.

If the shelves are attached to the end uprights with just a couple of nails, they soon will separate under the weight of material on the shelves. This problem is solved with the use of a small piece of furring strip or ripped plank, two inches wide and as long as the width of the shelf. This is nailed across the end upright on the inside, the end of the shelf rests on the strip and is nailed to both the strip brace and the upright. On an eight-foot shelf, the center support is all that is needed to support most of the weight that will be put on the shelf, unless you are planning on crawling up on one to take a nap. Locate the center of the shelf, cut a 12-inch-long board, slip it under the first shelf and nail it in place, down through the shelf. A couple of finishing nails can be toe-nailed to hold the bottom in place. The next shelf up is braced the same way. Some hobbyists like a small board nailed across the end of the shelf to prevent items from rolling off. This will work, but also will collect enough dust and dirt to grow a small garden.

Nails can be driven into the edges of the shelves to hold hammers, dividers, hacksaws and other items that you will be using constantly. Another handy little rig is the punch block. The longer you work on guns, the more pin punches you will accumulate. If these are stored in a box, a lot of time is spent pawing through them to find a specific size. A much more handy storage system can be had by drilling a series of parallel holes through a short piece of 2X4 or 2X6 scrap lumber. A checkerboard spacing with the lines crossing at about 3/4 inch apart and a 3/8-inch drill works out about right. You can stop short of drilling all the way through, but I have found that this will not hold the punches upright. Drill all the way through and tack a piece of masonite or 1/4-inch plywood on the bottom. The punch block can be set flat on a shelf or mounted in an angled position to the shelf, with the back resting on the wall. These little holding blocks can be used to separate and hold small grindstones, dental burrs, polishing arbors and drills. It is a good idea to spray a little rust preventative in the holes and, if you use one for drills, be sure they are stored with points up.

Another approach to the shelf problem is available at your local hardware store in the form of steel shelf supports and shelf brackets. These consist of a heavy-duty upright bolted to the wall that has slots cut in it at regular intervals. The shelf brackets are inserted into the slots, pulled down and locked into place. The steel uprights and brackets allow a wide selection of distance between the shelves. The shelf itself is a wooden plank simply laid on top of the brackets. The cost of these steel shelf uprights and brackets is a bit high but they go up fast and are strong.

A third system for filling up the wall behind the bench is to use pegboard or, as it sometimes is called, hanger board. One 4X8 sheet of it is all that's needed for the eight-foot bench. There are two sizes of pegboard; one is 1/8-inch thick with the holes 1/8 inch and is used for light duty. The other, more preferred for heavy duty, is the 1/4-inch-thick version with 1/4-inch holes. To mount pegboard you must first nail a framework of furring strips to the wall. This appears somewhat similar to a picture frame. Run an extra piece across the width to separate the framework into two 4X4-foot sections. This framing will provide a space behind the pegboard and allow the hangers to be placed through the holes. Nail the pegboard firmly to the framing with large head short nails. You can add an outside frame to the pegboard if you like things to look neat. The hanging fixtures themselves come in every form and shape imaginable. Some are plain hooks, while others are made for a specific purpose such as screwdriver holders, shelf holders, and even gun holders. One thing that pegboard offers is that the arrangement of the tools can be changed as needed.

Few of us know how to choose and install the best lighting for work. Usually, we end up with a conglomeration of assorted lights and tired eyes. When I built my present shop, I went straight to a specialist for the answers. A good friend who is a gun buff and an electrical contractor, after a little arm twisting, designed my present lighting system. It has worked out well and I spend eight to ten hours per day, week after week, under lights.

This lighting consists of long fluorescent tubes mounted directly over the bench, in units of two tubes per eight feet. One of the amazing things about flourescent lighting is the length of time the bulbs will burn without replacement. At present, we have twenty of these eight-foot bulbs in the shop area (just counted them) and, believe it or not, eighteen of them have been burning ten hours per day for over five years. Of two that were replaced, one burned out and the other was the victim of a magazine tube spring that got away. If, for no other reason than the saving in bulb replacement, choose fluorescent lights.

There are two basic types of bulbs, one a warm light which gives sort of a rose color to the light and casts everything in a soft light. The other is cool light which casts a sort of bluish tone to the work for more sharp definition. After trying them both, I prefer the warm light for general work, but this is a personal choice and either will do a good job. If, for some reason you cannot install a permanent lighting system, you can arrive at the same thing by using two banks of plug-in fixtures four feet long. These are hung from the ceiling with a short length of chain and should be positioned about two feet above your head.

While the fluorescent lights will be all you'll need for fully 90 percent of your work, there does come a time when you need as much light as possible to see down into the innards of some gun action. For this, a regular machinist's lamp with a standard 100-watt bulb will be all that is necessary. These clamp to the shelf and have a flexible neck, allowing the light to be moved to the exact spot you need. You can use a flexible neck desk lamp if nothing else is available. I have a homemade rig made from the remains of a desk lamp with the flexible neck brazed to a piece of electrical conduit. The conduit, in turn, is brazed to an old door hinge which is screwed to one of the shelf uprights. It looks like an appendix operation sewn up with a tow chain, but it works. It can be swung out of the way or placed in any needed position in seconds. I have tried the small high intensity lamps, but personally prefer a regular 100-watt bulb.

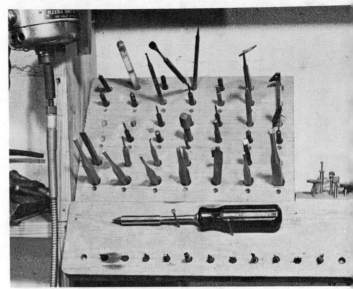

This punch block is mounted at angle. The screwdriver is Brownell Magna-Tip with individual screwdriver points held in drilled recesses below the body of the tool.

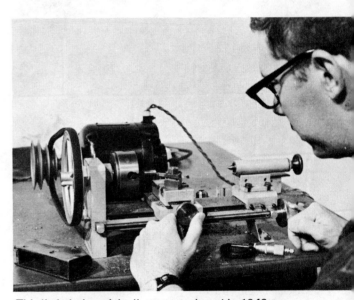

This little lathe originally was purchased in 1940 to turn model railroad engine parts. There is no background on manufacturer. Here a screw is machined for a Martini.

Two other lights I have found most useful are a good flashlight and a bore light. The flashlight need not be a 20-cell floodlight that will blind a mole at a thousand yards. One of the small two-cell versions that take C batteries will be all you need. In a tight spot if you need both hands, you can cradle it between your neck and shoulder sort of on the same order as holding a telephone to free both hands. There are times when nothing else will get the job done. The bore light, like a paper clip, is one of those little things in this world that border on sheer genius. It is nothing but a small penlight with a spark plug rubber cap on the bulb end, and a piece of bent plastic inserted into the rubber cap. Nothing beats it for lighting the bore of a gun. You will find most of them made somewhat hastily with a jagged end on the plastic. Give the plastic ends a couple of strokes with your files, then rub them across some No. 400 grit sandpaper. Don't polish the ends too much or you will have too bright a light. You want the ends smooth and opaque for best results and a soft, but even, light. A dentist's mirror is also a handy rig for seeing behind action parts, etc. You can buy a type of penlight that has both a straight plastic rod and the regular bore light bent rod with an inspection mirror, that attaches to the rods providing light right behind the part that is giving you all the trouble.

A source of water around a shop is almost a dire necessity. It will be needed every day for stock work, quenching and tempering parts, and washing your hands a dozen or more times. If your shop is in part of your home, there is little problem, for you can use some of the household appliances. However, if your shop is away from the house in a separate building, you will have to keep a jug or other container full, or pipe the water to the shop. Regular plumbing can get to be quite expensive, but there is an easier way out.

Plastic cold water pipe is usually available for about $6 per 100 feet and is much easier to use than regular metal water pipe. With a little plumbing, you can attach a T to an existing outside outlet and connect the plastic pipe to the T with little trouble. The pipe can be left lying on top of the ground, but a little spade work will get it down below the freeze level. Run it out to your shop, add an elbow and it can be brought into the shop or left outside, as you prefer. Used sinks are cheap at the local junk yard and with a simple wooden frame it can be used either inside or outside your shop. A metal sink will stand up under hard gun shop use better than the regular bathroom type. An old laundry tub will work out fine. The drain for the sink need not present a problem, if your building codes are not too strict.

Use inexpensive plastic drain pipe and run it underground away from the shop about ten feet or so. At the end of the pipe, dig a hole about two feet square and deep. Fill the hole with rocks and cover with at least six inches of top soil. This will take care of most drainage, but if you will be using a lot of water or have soil a little on the hard side, double the size of the hole. I've been using one like this for quite a while with no trouble.

A short shelf above the sink will hold soap, sponges and other needs. If you have never tried the special cleaner that automotive garages use, I suggest you give it a try. Sold under a dozen different names, most of it comes in a gallon can for a couple of bucks and looks somewhat like soft grease. Most of these contain lanolin and keep your hands from cracking. As for cleaning, a spoonful rubbed in good would make an old wild piney-woods hog look like a new born kitten. After breaking the second regular paper towel rack, I drilled a hole through two wooden blocks, inserted a piece of electrical conduit and nailed it to the wall. The paper towel rack problem was solved.

Ventilation in a shop is important when you consider the amount of fumes, odor and dust that is generated in gun work. One of the small, but important things that you run into, is the use of silver solder and the fumes that are released. If inhaled, it can make you pretty sick. Paint stripper, polyurethane and other fumes must be vented in the interest of health. A large window fan is ideal, but a small portable fan can be used. Any time these fumes are present, be sure you have a cross ventilation air current going. Consider putting them into a good window air conditioner and go first class.

If you find yourself trying to checker a stock while wearing an overcoat, try a portable electric heater with a small fan blowing behind it. A couple of these usually will

This photo illustrates the use of a 1X2 inch strip with holes drilled in it to keep screwdrivers and other tools at hand where the gunsmith can have them in easy reach.

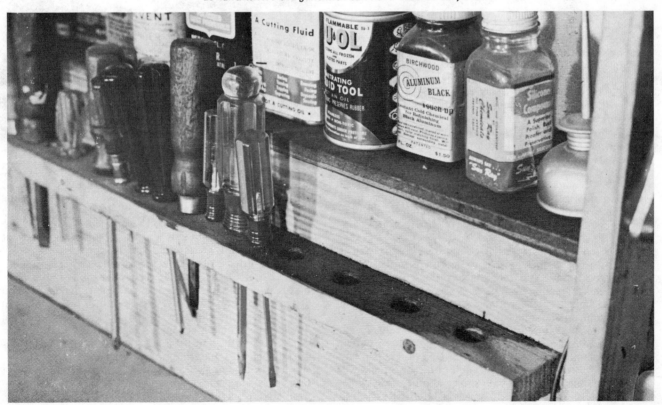

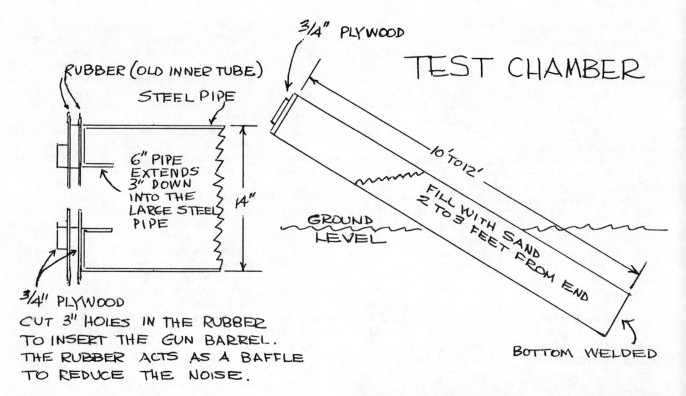

RUBBER (OLD INNER TUBE)

STEEL PIPE

3/4" PLYWOOD

TEST CHAMBER

6" PIPE EXTENDS 3" DOWN INTO THE LARGE STEEL PIPE

14"

GROUND LEVEL

10' TO 12'

FILL WITH SAND 2 TO 3 FEET FROM END

BOTTOM WELDED

3/4" PLYWOOD
CUT 3" HOLES IN THE RUBBER TO INSERT THE GUN BARREL. THE RUBBER ACTS AS A BAFFLE TO REDUCE THE NOISE.

The wooden washer in the test fire chamber allows the rubber barrel protector to be changed periodically. Rubber flap folded back is flipped over to keep out the weather. Rifle is .303 SMLE sporter built up by the author.

provide enough heat in a small shop, even if no regular heating system is being used.

While these will work, a better solution for the small outside shop is a house trailer size butane bottle placed outside the shop. The bottle never should be brought inside for health and safety reasons. These bottles are relatively inexpensive and usually a bottle and regulator can be found easily at any trailer park. A length of copper tubing and a hole through the wall will bring the gas inside. Small gas heaters are not expensive, and if you will settle for one with a cracked grate or a dent or two, you can buy one for peanuts at a junk yard. The only trouble with these small heaters is the lack of moisture in a small shop, but a can of water in front of the heater will add enough moisture to the air for comfort, without any danger of rust to your equipment.

If the end of the pipe that comes through the wall is fitted with a T connection, the extra outlet can be put to several good uses. You can attach a Bunsen burner for heating and tempering small parts. A special butane torch is available, similar to the portable propane torch, that will run on your butane outlet. It is cheap but will not put out quite as much heat as a propane torch. If you reload, you can make a lead melting pot right with the Bunsen burner under a plumber's pot, that will melt lead faster than any expensive electrical pot made. A full bottle of butane will last a long time for heating your shop and other uses.

Regardless of the type of repairs a hobbyist gunsmith

makes on a gun, it should be test-fired for safety and assurance of correct function. Even if just a cleaning job is involved, it should be test fired. It takes only one hunting trip, a good target and a loud "click" for a non-functioning gun to drive the point home. The problem is where to fire the gun? The solution is in the word "test fire", for what we are primarily interested in is correct mechanical function, instead of accuracy performance. This is a different barrel of snakes! All we have to do is find a place that is safe and where the noise is not objectionable. If you live in the country and have a spare hill or high bank, you have no problem. However, if you are a city or residential dweller, the problem becomes a big one. The first thing to do is check with your local lawmen. Most of these fellows are familiar with guns and not only understand your problem, but will go out of their way to help you solve it. Don't take a chance and bypass them or you may end up wondering what kind of steel was used in the cell door bars.

Rack is built from 1X12 with short pieces nailed between spaces to provide holders for butt stocks. Dowels are driven into drilled holes to keep the barrels separated.

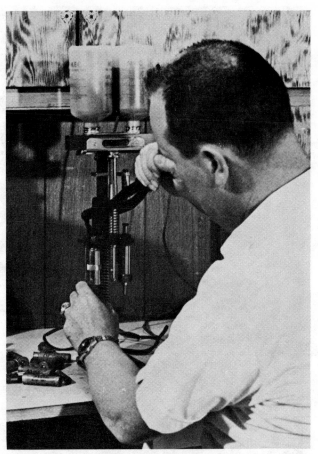

Work cabinet has been converted into reloading bench in this work area belonging to Air Force Major Gerald McDonald. The tool is secured to bench with wing nuts.

I solved the problem with a large 13-inch steel pipe 10 feet long. Both the safety factor and the noise problem are eliminated. I have included here self-explanatory photos of the construction for those who wish to build one. I started off with just the open pipe stuck in the ground about 3/4 of the way at a 30-degree angle. It worked fine for a while, with just a cap placed over the exposed end each night to keep out the rain. One day, I removed the cap, placed the muzzle of a .30/06 in the pipe and touched it off. I was immediately covered from head to tummy with mud and water! Excavating the pipe revealed that worms and bugs had tunneled to the pipe and, after a rain, their tunnels allowed water to flood the pipe, turning it into a small well. Why they went to so much trouble to tunnel to such a noisy neighborhood is beyond me.

To eliminate the water entering the pipe, I welded a steel plate to the end that was buried in the ground making it water tight. To prevent bullets from bouncing back up the tube and interrupting my train of thought, I filled the bottom two feet of the tube with clean dry sand free of stones. To cut down on the noise and back-blast from the gas, I welded another piece of sheet steel to the business end of the tube. Next, a six-inch diameter hole was cut in the sheet steel. A piece of six-inch pipe three inches long then was welded in the hole. This extends down into the tube and traps a lot of blow-back gas on the sides. Well pleased with the results, I then bolted a piece of one-inch plywood with a three-inch diameter hole over the cap to protect the gun muzzle. To add more protection, I fitted a double layer of old truck innertube over the plywood with just a slit in it to poke the muzzle through. The whole thing worked like a charm. Muzzle report was almost non-existent and more like a loud "thump" than a blast. Gas back-blast was almost eliminated. Even shooting big bore elephant magnum rifles in the chamber fails to damage it. Although I can stand in my shop door and throw a rock through several neighboring house windows, I have yet to hear a complaint from a neighbor. I do make it a point, however, to invite any newcomer over to the shop and show him how the test chamber works. Most say something like, "Boy, you could shoot a cannon in that thing and be safe, couldn't you?"

Maybe not a cannon, but it does solve the safety problem. As added safety to your eyes and ears, wear safety glasses and ear protectors while testing any gun, test chamber or not.

The final part of your shop and its basic equipment is some way to keep it clean. If this is bypassed, in a short while the dirt, paper and, general mess will fill it up until you have to shovel your way to the bench. A trashy floor, a spark, and you have to start building a shop all over again. Big garbage cans outside, several trash baskets inside, and a good broom and dust pan are essential to a clean shop. An industrial vacuum cleaner will be a big help, but you can get by with a regular house-type vacuum. The old gun shops with the dirt floor covered with walnut shavings and trash may be picturesque, but they are also about like working in a pig pen.

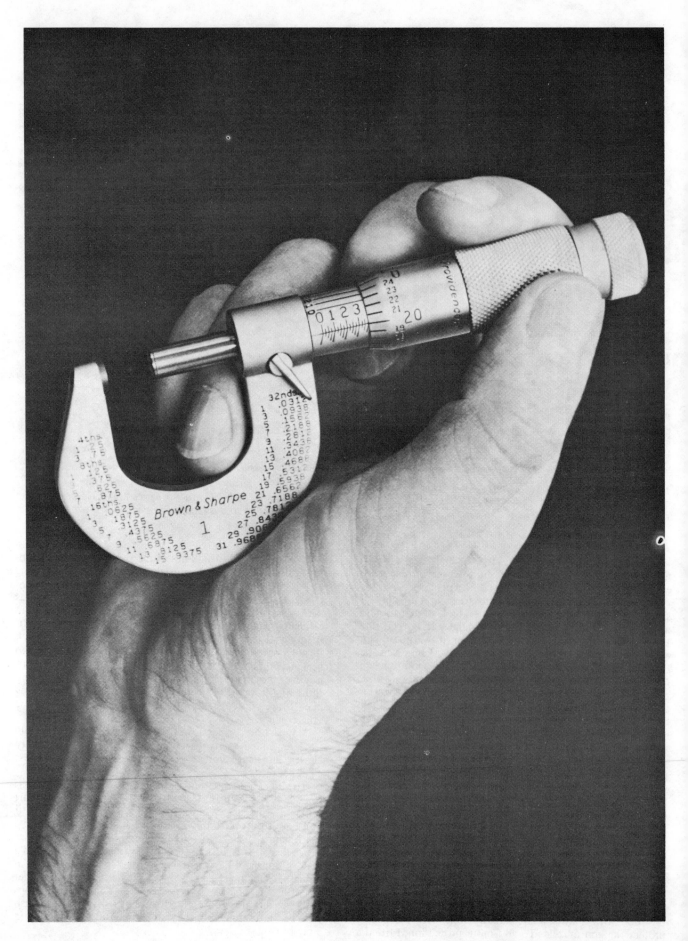

Chapter 7

HAND TOOLS & MEASUREMENTS

These Basic Items Are Musts If You Are To Make Everything Meet Where It Should!

THE TOOLS A HOBBYIST can accumulate are virtually without end. Some will be used constantly while others gather dust between the times they are put to use. It depends a great deal on what type and to what extent gunsmithing is being done. For instance, one hobbyist may prefer to work with wood and compile a full set of stock chisels, while another may like to work with metal and the set of chisels would spend most of their life in a drawer.

Too often, a beginner, filled with enthusiasm, writes out an impressive list of gunsmithing tools. When he totals the prices, he takes a deep breath, thinks it over and takes up something like golf.

Some type of guide is needed in buying tools and instruments to help the beginner avoid expensive mistakes. It must be remembered, however, that the following list of tools is not all needed for hobby gunsmithing. Quite often, the hobbyist can make other common tools perform the work of specialized tools and, if the need arises sit down and make a tool to do the special job.

As your need arises, refer to this list with its descriptions and stick to that simple rule of always buying the best quality tools you can afford. Learn to use the tool correctly and give it the protection and care a fine tool deserves. The way a gunsmith takes care of his tools is a direct indication of whether he is a sloppy workman or a craftsman who does precision work.

A few years back, one of the gun magazines carried a story of the manufacture of copies of British guns in the mountains of India. One photograph depicted a gunmaker seated on a dirt floor with one foot securely pinning a gun barrel to a log while he filed away with both hands. The hobbyist can follow this example, but the position leaves a bit to be desired in efficiency as well as in dignity. Perhaps if man had three hands the problem would be simplified. However, the available choice of vise type, design, and manufacture leaves a few gaps. The majority can be used in gunsmithing, but a few will prove more practical than the others.

The first type to eliminate is the clamp-on vise, since even the largest and best made are too small to hold work securely. Their use should be confined to temporary set-ups or where no permanent vise is to be had. Next on the elimination list is the bench vise with the screw exposed. Grease from the screw can ruin a stock in short order. Another damning factor is that filings, dust, et al., falling on the open screw, soon ruin any precision built into the vise. The third and final elimination candidate is the wood vise. At first glance, it appears just the ticket for stock

work, but after you use one for a while, you will find they actually are clumsy to use and limit stock positions.

By far the best all around choice for wood or metal is the regular machinist's vise of 4-inch width with covered screw. The majority have the desirable feature of a swivel base that allows the vise to be pivoted to the best work angle. I would not own a vise that did not have a swivel base. Machinist's vises are made in a wide range of sizes and most gunsmithing books recommend a massive vise about the size of King Kong's head with jaws opening as wide as an alligator's. I used a 4-inch machinist's vise for years and never found a need for a larger vise for metal or wood. Buy a vise that has a small anvil at the rear as this little addition will prove to be of many uses, such as straightening pins, parts and hammer forging tools.

A recent arrival on the vise market is the Versa-Vise; I use one, since they offer some decided advantages in gun work. The jaws are of sufficient size and there is even the little useful anvil at the rear. The vise swivels in a full circle and locks in position when the jaws are tightened on anything; its unique construction allows it to be mounted either in a standard vertical position or in a horizontal position. Due to the locking system of the Versa-Vise, it works best with metal rather than wood.

Before you start bolting down the vise, disassemble it. This may sound like strange advice, but most are made on mass production assembly lines and are a bit rough. Check the screw for burrs and, with a file, smooth up the threads, adding a dab of grease before you reassemble it.

While you have it disassembled, check the swivel mechanism also for burrs and give it the same smoothing-up and grease treatment. The next step is to find a location and this should receive some careful treatment. If at all possible, put the vise out on the end corner of the bench. This will provide walking space and allow you to attack different problems from the best angle. If circumstances prevent this choice, the next best place is right in the center of the bench length. Tie the vise down good with bolts or lag screws, being sure to include a lock washer on each of them to prevent the vise working loose.

With the vise tied down, run the movable jaw fully in and out a dozen or so times to work the grease in good on the screw. With the jaws together, note their junction to see if one jaw is higher on the side than its opposite matching jaw. If so, mark the high side with a felt pen and run the jaw in and out several more times. Tighten it again and see if the uneven jaw is still in the same position. If so, drawfile the tops of the vise jaws until they match evenly, but be sure the jaw tops are kept level all the way across.

This small alteration will make using the vise and holding small items at a specific depth lots easier. While you have the file out, check the anvil at the rear to be sure it is smooth and give it a stroke or two, if not. To keep the vise working smoothly, disassemble it periodically, wash the screw and nut in mineral spirits or kerosene and regrease them.

The rough jaws of the vise will prove useful in holding items that will be filed down or polished later. Remember, they will mar any metal or wood and a finished gun part should not be put between the naked jaws. Protective jaws can be made in a dozen different ways. Perhaps one of the simplest is to make a set of jaws out of sheet brass.

First, cut a pattern out of paper that extends down the full depth of the jaw, goes over the back and partially laps under to hold the jaw in position. The end should match the length of the vise jaw. Next, cut the brass to match the paper template, put one in the vise and hammer it over the back, molding it to fit. Repeat the procedure with the other jaw. These brass jaws will prove useful where maximum holding power is needed and will eliminate the marring of the gun part.

Another easy-to-make set is shaped in the form of the capital letter H with the top part of the H solid and the bottom legs fitted over the screw beam. These can be cut out of scrap 1/4-inch plywood and used as is, or with a piece of leather glued to the solid top part. The wood/leather protective jaws probably will be used more than any other, as they hold firmly, yet will not mar the finished gun part. Check to be sure no metal filings are embedded in the leather before you clamp a stock between them. The best way to avoid this is to make two sets, one for steel and one for wood.

A handy accessory for your regular vise is a miniature vise that can be held in the hand or clamped in the regular vise. This goes by several names: hand vise, spring vise or pin vise. Its primary purpose is to hold items that would be too small for the regular vise — such as pins, small screws and parts. You will find other uses, such as holding a screw while grinding it down. The cost is only a couple of bucks and its value to you is worth many times this amount.

A good vise will be one of the most used items in your shop. Treat it with respect, avoid hammering on the movable jaw, give it a cleaning every now and then and your grandchildren will still be using it when you are but a memory.

The file is the only hand tool that can duplicate itself, then manufacture other tools that, in turn, can produce any machinery known. In the hands of a master filer, its capabilities are almost limitless. Many of the oldtime gunsmiths could take a handful of files, a pile of steel and literally file a gun out of the raw metal. But filing is becoming a lost art. Complicated machinery, the pressure of time and the high cost of hand labor have pushed the art more and more into the background. For the man with patience to learn the art and a good set of files available, virtually any gun part can be filed out of stock steel. This part will equal the best of machine produced versions.

All files fall into one of two basic categories. The first is the single cut that has a series of parallel teeth running at about a 45-degree angle to the length of the file. The other is the double cut that has the same series of parallel lines but also has a second series running directly opposite the first series. The main purpose of the single cut is to remove a lot of metal in a hurry, while the double cut generally is used to give a smooth cut with a finer finish. At least, that is what the text book says.

Maybe it's my Confederate ancestry, but I'm a rebel and

Small machinist's vise has wood/leather protective jaws. Beside vise (at right) are brass protective jaws also used; small slip in screw is vise's swivel base lock.

This small hand vise is available in several models and designs; this particular one is British military.

go against the book, in that I use the single cut fully 75 percent of the time. It cuts rapidly and, with a bit of careful handling, a single cut file will produce just as smooth a finished surface as a double cut file. One part of the secret is in the size of the single cut file used. Start with a large file and work down to a smaller one. My largest is a big 16-inch (a regular hand milling machine), and my smallest only three inches long.

There are good files and cheap files, but I have never seen a good, cheap file. The best are those hand cut in Switzerland and surrounding countries, but these are not readily available and are expensive. Good American machine-made files are just about as good and more readily available at a much more attractive price. Those advertised in the gunsmith supply houses catalogs can be depended on for good quality.

If you need others, walk into the biggest hardware store you can find and ask to see the most expensive brand they carry. The higher priced files will prove to have several times the usable life of the cheapies and produce a better

This close-up photo illustrates a single cut file (left) compared with the more complex double cut file on right.

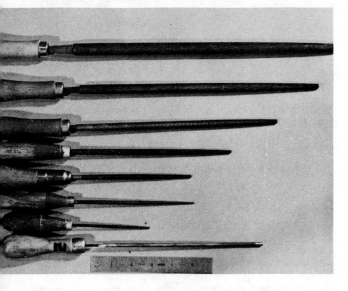

Single cut files range from big magnum at top to small four-inch model near bottom. The author says that these are the work horses of his collection of files.

cut. Use a file card to keep the files clean, for metal shavings imbedded in the teeth will cut big scars across your work, as well as making your filing twice as hard. An old trick is to run chalk over the file. This prevents squeaking and filling of the grooves with metal chips to some extent. When a file becomes worn, don't try to make it last. Instead, toss it in the junk box to be used for some other purpose or use it on wood.

For some odd reason, one of the common single cut files is named mill bastard, and the following story actually happened in the presence of a hardware salesman friend of mine. Seems an old country boy walked into a local hardware store to buy a file for the farm. There was a lady behind the counter, and he asked to see some files. She picked up one and said, "Well, here's a nice six-inch mill bastard," to which he replied, "Now you're talking my kinda language, lady, lemme see that big SOB over there."

Anyway, I have listed below a good set of files that will fill most gunsmithing needs:

Mill bastard, 8, 6, and 4-inch; double cut, 6-inch; triangular, 6 and 4-inch; round, 6-inch (a chain saw file is a good one); square, 6-inch; pillow files, set of three 8 inch-fine, medium, and coarse; screwhead, set of three-narrow, medium, and wide; clockfile, No. 5 cut; sight dovetail, 6-inch; metal checkering, 6-inch, 20 lines per inch; needle file, standard set.

This may sound like a lot of files, but if you do much metal work, all will be used constantly.

Pliers also should be of the finest quality you can afford. Actually, you can get by with just two pair, an 8-inch slip joint and 6-inch needlenose. The term, "needlenose," can be somewhat confusing as the different manufacturers do not use the same nomenclature. What you want is a long pair with serrated jaws. The next pair to buy in addition to these two, is the useful parallel jaw pliers. These are actually a hand-operated vise as the jaws are kept parallel to each other, regardless of the distance between them. Diagonal cutters are also useful pliers whose primary gun shop purpose is to cut small screws, pins and springs. Finally, pick up a pair of vise-grip pliers, as they will prove to be almost a third hand at times.

When you have accumulated the common pliers, start picking up some of the less used ones such as the curved needlenose and water pump pliers. The water pump pliers are useful for those times when a large item must be held or turned. I have found that many of the pump and automatic shotgun magazine tube caps are hard to unscrew by hand, but if a small piece of leather is wrapped arround them for protection and the water pump pliers used, they easily can be removed without damage to the cap. Miniature pliers will prove of value at times, but don't go overboard with them, even if they are cute.

For the final addition, go down to the five and dime store and buy a cheap pair of needlenose pliers. A lot of times you will need to hold small items as they are being heated or soldered. These cheap pliers will do the job and prevent your good pliers from being ruined by the heat.

If you have a good dentist or doctor friend, con him out of a pair of forceps. This is a little pair of thin, longnose pliers that he uses to pick splinters out of your hide or to hold the needle while sewing your innards back in place. There are a few copies on the market, but those that I have seen are not of medical tool quality. The common one is about five inches long with scissor like finger loops and the jaws about one inch long. A version just a bit smaller has curved jaws. In gun work they are to be highly prized, for their small jaws will reach down into the most inaccessible places that would be too small for regular needlenose pliers. As they are capable of being locked with a small item between their jaws, they make installing tiny springs and pins a lot easier. There are precision instruments, beautifully made, and should be treated as such, with the heavy work left to the regular needlenose pliers.

Pin punches used to be a big headache to anyone working on guns. I remember spending hours turning them out of drill rod on the lathe, heat treating, etc., only to have them bend on some balky pin. Then came the introduction of special gun-size punches. There are several brands on the market, usually consisting of five or six punches of various point diameters, a center punch and a starting punch. Cost of most sets run around $15. Later, add a set of standard hardware store punches that start where the special gun punches leave off in diameter.

A few special punches can be made easily. One that I have found useful is a regular nail set punch with the point ground down and used to start large size pins that the

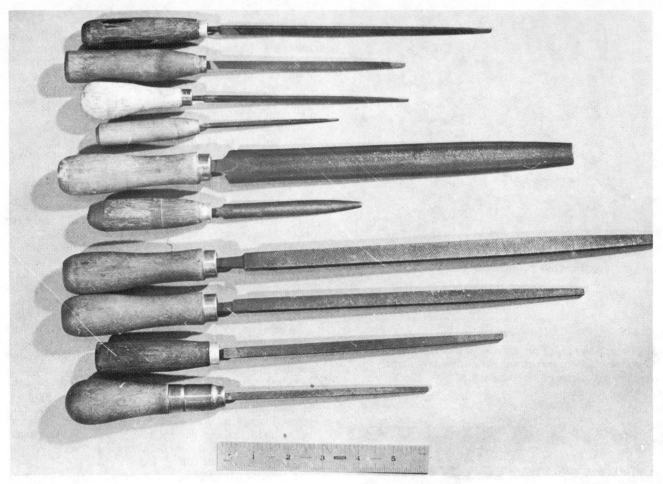

regular starter punch cannot handle. Brass, copper and even aluminum punches can be turned down from large rods for use where force is necessary, but it is of primary interest not to mar the pin finish. Keep these points as short as possible to prevent bending. A square end punch of one of these metals is just about ideal for removing dovetail sights without marring them. The point will become battered but can be straightened up with a few strokes of the file. You can buy a special nylon punch for this same purpose, but frankly, I find that they bounce too much. Many broken firing pins can be reground or altered for punch use, as can short sections of drill rod, etc. If you need a large punch, it's hard to beat an old automobile valve stem, ground down to shape.

For some reason, people have a hard time removing pins from guns, as evidenced by the many battered examples wandering around. The first thing to look for is the new serrated pins. One end will have tiny serrations on it to lock the pin in place. Woe is the gunsmith who tries to drive one of these pins by hitting on the serrated end. If he succeeds in getting it past the outside part, it will surely lock on an inside part. These must be driven out from the smooth end only. The whole secret of using a pin punch is to first use the starter punch to get the thing moving. This is the short, tapered, flat nose punch. It has all the beef you need. Hold it firmly and squarely on the pin and give it a quick tap with the hammer. If it resists, give it a more healthy lick. Once it is started, select a punch with a diameter just a shade smaller than the pin your are removing. A punch too small will bend or mar the pin. Once a pin is removed, make it a habit to wipe it clean and add a drop of oil before reinstalling it.

Hammers should consist of 4 or 6-ounce ball peen, a small brass hammer and a rawhide mallet. The ball peen will do most of the work, while the brass hammer will be used where the surface being hit must be protected against marring. The rawhide mallet will find daily use as it allows you to whale the daylights out of something without battering it. The rawhide mallet will be needed to tap the backs of chisels when removing large chunks of wood in stock work. I also like a big "magnum" ball peen hammer around the shop as there are times when you will need it on balky machinery. But don't use it on guns.

We now come to the bugaboo of all gun tools, the screwdriver. No other tool is responsible for so many ruined gun screws as an ill-fitting screwdriver. The chief cause of the battered screws is that they have machine screw slots. That is, the sides of the slot are straight and parallel with the body of the screw. On the other hand, wood screws have sides that are larger at the top than at the bottom of the slot. Screwdriver manufacturers decided long ago that only the tapered wood screw slot was loose on the American continent and they make their screwdriver blades tapered to match these slots. When one of these tapered blades is

This special file is used for cutting sight dovetails. It has a safe side on two of the three sides, giving control over the area where the metal is to be removed.

This special screw slot file has a cutting edge only. The sides of the file are smooth or safe. Note that the screw is held between protective wood/leather vise jaws.

placed in a machine screw parallel sided slot, the blade will be touching only at the top of the slot. When the screwdriver is turned, the force tends to twist the blade out of the slot in a camming action. The result is a marred screw.

The blade can be ground to fit the machine screw's parallel sides, of course, but the manufacturers are not to be outdone and have an ace up their sleeves. Most modern screwdrivers are advertised as vanadium this or that. This is true, but the tough vanadium is only skin deep, with the rest of the metal being made from something similar to melted down nails and horseshoes. The moment you grind through the vanadium skin, you have a piece of steel underneath about as tough as warm butter. Put any amount of pressure on the screwdriver and the ground blade will outtwist a pretzel.

If you want the best buy in a gun screwdriver, you will find it listed in the catalog of Brownell's Inc., under the trade name, "Magna-Tip." The screwdriver consists of a shockproof handle with a magnetized socket. The blades or bits are inserted into the magnetized socket quickly and are held in place. They can be removed in a second with the finger tips, allowing instant change if the need presents itself. The tips are the same as those used in industrial power impact tools. The whole shebang, the handle with twenty-four tips, costs less than fifteen dollars, which works out to just a shade over 50 cents per screwdriver. The set will answer 90 percent of the gun screw needs and, if a special-size blade is needed, it can be ground from any tip without loss of metal strength. Grace Products and Bonanza also make special gun screwdrivers that will fit the parallel sides of the screws. These sets are ground for specific gun screws and allow a wide choice of blade tip sizes.

Of course, you can break the best of screwdrivers, if you are of the opinion that all it takes to move a stubborn screw is a stubborn gunsmith and brute strength. The trick is to outsmart the screw. If you encounter one, first try unscrewing with firm pressure only. If this fails, try tightening the screw. Stupid as this may sound, sometimes it will give just a cat's hair movement of the screw and break its "set." If it does, work the screw back and forth, gaining more and more each turn. If this fails, the next trick is to whack the back of the screwdriver with the rawhide mallet. This jarring blow will break a lot of them loose, especially if you add a quick snap to the attempt to unscrew it.

The next method of attack is to try to get some type of fluid down on the threads. I have found two that work better than anything else I have tried. The first is Du-Ol, a rust remover. If any rust is suspected, use this, flooding the top of the screw, and allow it to stand for a few seconds to soak down into the threads. If rust is the culprit holding the screw, this usually turns the trick. If the screw is just plain stuck, try flooding it with Tap-Magic. This is an instant refrigerant that is the best thing possible to use on taps and also fine for other machining operations. It will penetrate the smallest of cracks. The use of one of these fluids plus the tapping of the screwdriver, and a quick snap will break 75 percent of troublesome screws loose.

The next thing is heat. Use a torch to bring the metal around the screw to a heat that you cannot touch with your hand. This will not affect the bluing, if the torch is kept moving and not held too close. The heat expands the surrounding metal away from the screw. True, the screw will get hot, but not to the same extent of the surrounding metal if you use the torch right.

While the metal is still hot, insert the screwdriver and give it a whack on the back and a quick snap. This moves a lot of them. If it is still there, unbudged, you are going to have to damage the screw to remove it.

Select your smallest starter punch and place its tips on the outside of the screw slot side and tap it lightly to start it. This tapping pressure on the outside of the slot puts a lot of torque on the screw and solves the problem in all but the most stubborn of cases. It is surprising how many screws that have to be removed this way can be rebuilt. When you get the screw out, oil the threads and reinsert it in the hole. Now, with a large tip punch, place it on the top of the marred side and lightly and rapidly tap the punch. This forces the metal back down in place. Touch up the sides of the slots with a clock file and with a drop of touch-up blue the screw usually will look as good as new.

If it still won't come out, place a center punch directly in the center of the screw and make a deep mark. Chuck a lathe center drill in your drill press and, holding everything tight, drill straight down. Now, switch to a drill that is smaller in size than the body diameter of the screw and drill down about 3/4 of the depth of the screw body. Remove the drill and use a screw remover to get the stubborn screw out. This last method naturally requires a new replacement screw.

Regular right-hand screws, as you know, are tightened by turning them to the right and loosened by turning to the left. A screw remover is a high tensile strength tool that tapers to a point, and on it are heavy, fast advance left hand threads. When it is placed in the hole drilled in a screw and turned to the left, the heavy threads bite into the sides of the hole. As it is turned deeper, the tighter it pulls itself down into the hole, until it is firmly locked to the screw. Continued turning to the left while tightening the screw remover will unscrew the stubborn screw and remove it. These screw removers come in about any size you want, but only those for screws up to about 1/4 inch will be needed and as one size covers a lot of screw sizes, about four will fill all your needs.

The last thing needed in a gun workshop is a cheap, flimsy hacksaw frame. By all means, pick a good sturdy frame with a large hand-filling handle. While the 12-inch hacksaw blade is recommended by many, I prefer the shorter 10-inch blade. The short length is more sturdy and will cut straighter. Hacksaw blades come in teeth 14 to the inch up to blades with 32 teeth to the inch. The rule of thumb is the softer the material being cut, the fewer the teeth and vise versa. The 24 teeth per inch blade is a good compromise.

Give the average person a hacksaw, a piece of metal, and he goes at it like his pants were on fire, elbows flying and the blade smoking. Very little is accomplished by the speed demon except a warped blade, a crooked cut and a pooped operator. Take slow, steady strokes with pressure on the forward stroke only. The back stroke does not cut and heavy pressure will only dull the blade. A good trick often used by professional gunsmiths is to turn the hacksaw into a poor man's milling machine. This is done by installing two or more blades together on the frame. Each stroke removes a wide slot of metal. This trick is particularly useful in rough cutting dovetail sight slots.

While a few Allen-type screws are used on guns themselves, you will find quite a few sights and scope mounts do use them. A small set of Allen wrenches is inexpensive and will be needed from time to time.

A pin block is just a smooth chunk of steel with a series of holes drilled in it. It is used to support a part, while a punch is used to remove a pin. The pin drops through one of the holes. They are available commercially in several sizes, with different diameter holes. You can make one out of any good size block of steel or use something else to get the job done. I have used an old damaged V-block for this purpose for years.

Tweezers come in handy if for no other reason than picking splinters of steel and wood out of your fingers daily. Some of the long blade versions will come in handy for reaching down into actions to recover dropped screws and pins. One of the self-closing soldering tweezers will be useful in holding pins and small springs during assembly of guns.

The average hobbyist will have little need for letter and number steel stamps, but they are handy for marking jigs, fixtures and tools. If you do any rebarreling or chamber and choke alterations, they will be needed to stamp the new designation on the barrel. A set of the 3/32-inch size will be all you should need. Most users try to stamp the letters or numbers just as they write, from left to right. This can be done, but you will find it a lot easier to stamp backwards. Write the numbers or letters out on a piece of paper and lay the appropriate stamps out in sequence. Now start with the last digit. For example, "Cal. 30/06" would require the 6 to be stamped first, then moving from right to left, the "0," the "/," another "0," then the "3."

The reason for using this system is that your hand will not be covering the letters you already have stamped and you can judge spacing better. Another good trick is to draw a line with a felt pen and use it to keep your stamping in

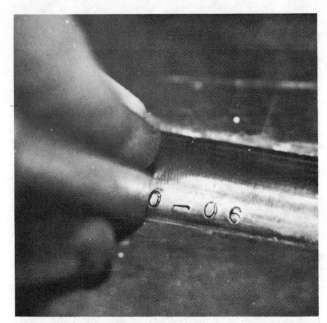

Using the metal number stamps, the caliber — .30/06 — is being stamped from right to left for sake of the gunsmith's visibility, as he places numbers.

Greatly enlarged, this is a standard set of taps. From left, they are starting tap, the plug and bottom tap.

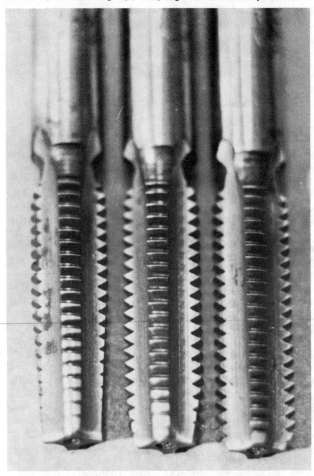

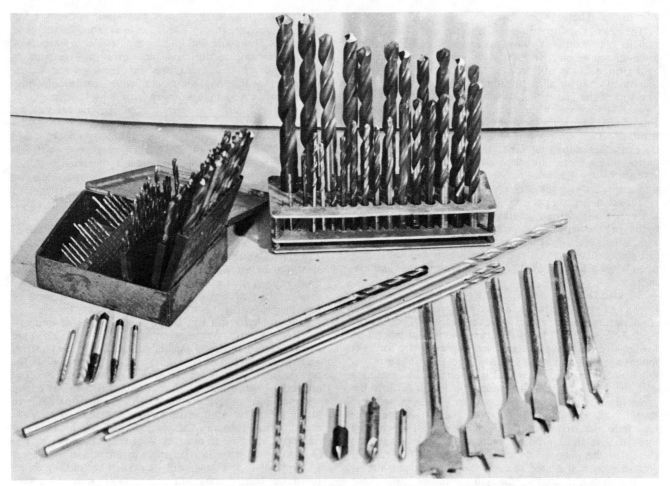

The box contains set of 1 to 60 wire gauge and the stand a set of fraction drills. To the left of the wire gauge box is a set of screw extractors. The long drills are for deep holes; three at bottom center, a carbide, two cobalt drills; next, a chamfer and two center-drills, while those in flat tipped set are for drilling wood.

line. Stamp by hitting the butt of the stamp with just one solid lick to avoid blurred numbers and letters.

While a full set of mechanic's open-end and box-end wrenches are nice tools to own, there will be little need for them around a gunshop except for working on machinery. I keep a little 4-inch adjustable-end wrench in the rack near the pliers and find it handy for a multitude of uses. It will serve as a small spring vise or clamp for bending magazine lips straight and for other uses. A larger wrench of the same type around 8 to 12 inches will come in handy to keep machinery bolts tight, etc. These two wrenches, plus your vise-grip pliers, will answer most of your wrench needs

You will need at least two oil cans, one filled with cutting oil, the other with lubricating oil. The old flat bottom thumb-pumping can is cheap, but one of the newer trigger-actuated cans works a lot easier. The 6-ounce size is about right for general use. Dark cutting oil and regular 20 to 30 weight motor oil will be needed more than any other type of lubricant, except the gun oils.

Drills can be one of the most confusing tools to the beginner, yet he will need them in virtually every gunsmithing project. Let's see if we can clear up some of the confusion! There are three types of drill size designations which we will term as sets. These are the wire gauge set, the fraction set and the letter set.

The wire gauge set runs from number 1 to number 80 and is the set you will need most in gun work. As the drill numbers get larger, the drill diameter gets smaller and vice

versa. Drills from number 61 through number 80 are perfect for drilling holes for shoe laces for ants and flies, but of little practical use in the gunshop and can be ignored. The best thing a beginner can do is take a deep breath, open up the pocketbook, and after the moths have flown out, buy a set of wire gauge drills in a case. These are put up in a compact metal case with drills from number one (.2280) to number sixty (.0400). This set will prove to be one of the best possible investments the serious hobbyist can make. Individual replacements can be bought if you break or bend a drill.

The fraction set runs from 1/64 inch (.0156) usually up to 1/2 inch (.5000) in units of 1/64 inch. You will notice that this set overlaps and passes the wire gauge set. The whole set is useful but expensive and can be thinned down to the following most used sizes: 1/16, 1/8, 3/16, 1/4, 5/16, 3/8, 7/16, and 1/2 inch.

The letter set runs from size A (.2340) to size Z (.4130) and takes up where the wire gauge set leaves off, but overlaps the fraction sizes. They are needed in machine work, but not to a great extent in hobby gunsmithing and can be ignored until the need arises for a particular size.

Now we come to the second specification in drills and this is the type of steel from which the drills are made. The cheapest is the regular carbon drill that is all right for soft metal and wood but about useless in drilling high carbon tool steel. The standard of the industry is the HSS (Hi-Speed Steel) drills and you are money ahead to keep all of your drill purchases in this class.

The next grade up brings you into the special need class and the cobalt drills. You will need sizes No. 28 for drilling for 8-40 screws and No. 31 for drilling for 6-48 screws in hard steel, such as rifle receivers and the like. I stick with the cobalt drill for all sight drilling to be on the safe side. The top of the pile is the carbide drill and again, only the 28 and 31 sizes will be needed. A good thing too, for they cost about $5 each! They will drill right through a file without getting up a sweat, but must not be used in soft steel or other soft metal. When the cobalt drill just sits up on top of the metal and spins without making a dent, you will gladly pay the price for one of those carbide drills as they can really save the bacon.

Taps and dies can get expensive in a hurry! A full set can run over $200 without breathing hard. You can fudge a bit by buying the taps only, as most gun needs will be drilling and tapping holes, not cutting threads on screws. The dies can be purchased as you need them, which will not be too often if you keep a good selection of screws around the shop.

Stick to the common carbon taps for regular use, but a few of the more expensive hi-speed taps will be needed. A good starting minimum set of carbon taps will consist of: 3-48, 3-56, 4-40, 6-32, and 8-32 and should run around $6 for the five. In high speed taps you will need two for sight mounting, 6-48 and 8-40, which will cost about as much as the five carbon taps. These will be enough for a beginning with the other sizes added as needed. You will run into the problem of which of the three kinds of taps to buy: starting, taper, plug, or bottoming. The starting or taper taps have the first five or six threads ground down to a taper to give the tap an easy bite in the hole. Next, you switch to the plug which has a couple of the first threads ground away and is used to carry the threads down almost to the bottom; finally, the job is finished with the bottoming tap. The correct way is to use all three but, if economy is necessary, then buy the plug type, as it will have enough of the first few threads ground down to serve as the starter tap. Taps become worn and broken and, with the damaged ends ground away, the old taps will provide all the bottoming taps you need. When all of the threads are gone on 6-48 and 8-40 taps, grind the tip of the tap down to a point. This is a handy tool, as it can be set in the hole of a scope mount and used to mark the exact center of the hole with a light tap on the end.

Be sure to buy a good T-tap wrench of the plain type.

The ratchet type looks like a good deal, but it is a tap breaker supreme, in my hands, at least. I prefer the plain type as it gives more feel and control. Grasp the handle of the wrench and let the cross piece press into the palm of your hand while you reach as far down on the tap as possible. The fingers guide the tap while the palm provides the pressure. Any time you tap a hole by hand, the item being tapped must be securely locked! Anything less means a broken tap.

Press down on the tap wrench and make a quarter turn and stop. Now release the tap wrench, twist your wrist, and take a grip on the opposite side of the wrench. Make another quarter turn and then back up the tap to clear the chips and repeat the tapping procedure. A quarter turn cutting threads, a half turn backwards to clear the chips, and a steady hand is all that is needed.

Now comes the use of the finest addition to the thread cutting business in a long time, namely, a fluid known as Tap Magic. And magic it is, for the tap will go through most steel like butter with this stuff. Don't put it on the metal until you get the tap started with at least a half turn, then a drop or two as you go will make the whole business of tapping a lot easier.

The hobbyist will run across several types of stones — artificial, Washita, Arkansas, and India. The last three are natural stones and are a bit high-priced in the bench sizes. The Washita and India stones are dark and coarse, while the fine cutting Arkansas appears similar to white marble. The artificial stones come in a variety of cuts with the coarse and medium the most common. All have their particularly individual assets and cutting characteristics. Inexpensive artificial bench stones of six or eight inches in medium and fine grit, will answer most of your sharpening needs. The hard Arkansas stone in triangular, square and other shapes, a couple of inches long, will be needed for putting a fine finish on trigger sears and a few tools. India stones of similar size are used generally for putting the finishing touches on reamers.

An excellent way to store taps, author has discovered, is to use plastic cabinet, taps separated by dividers.

Using the one-hand method described in the text, this shotgun barrel is tapped for a new sight. Notice the handy can of cutting oil that is kept close at hand.

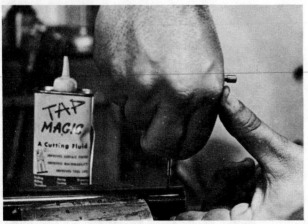

Stones are broken easily and need extra care. An easily constructed holder for the bench stone is made by laying the stone on a piece of 2X4 wood and drawing around the edge.

Inlet this down for about a half inch, until the stone fits in the recess. These holders can be made out of one-inch thick scrap boards if no 2X4 is available. The holder keeps the stone out of the dirt and protects the edges. Artificial stones always should be used with oil. Each time I get a new stone I soak it overnight in a pan filled with 30 weight motor oil, remove it, wipe it clean and put it in the wood holder. Each time you use the stone add a few drops of oil before you start. The oil prevents the slivers of steel removed in sharpening a tool, from working their way down into the pores of the stone. Oil protects the delicate edge of the blade being sharpened from overheating. When you finish, wipe the stone clean with a rag to remove the old oil. You can further clean one of these stones by wiping with a rag soaked in kerosene or mineral spirits, then re-oiling.

Modern disposable blades and the electric razor have turned the straight razor into an antique. Even the barbers have gone to disposable blades. But there are still plenty of good razor stones floating around, even bench-size Arkansas stones, that can be bought for a fraction of the cost of a new stone. If they are in somewhat rough shape, they can be brought back to usefulness with an old but effective method. This consists of finding a cast iron block with a flat and true surface. Oil and silicon carbide are mixed together in a paste and smeared all over the surface. The stone is firmly rubbed back and forth until the surface is true. They will put just as good an edge on your chisels as they did on the old throat-cutting straight razor.

The regular rip or cross-cut wood handsaw will find some use around the shop. Handsaws are designated as so many points or teeth to the inch; the more points, the finer the resulting cut. If you select one, be sure it has eight to 10½ points to the inch for best stock work. A better choice is a back or miter saw with eleven points to the inch. These will fill most needs in the average hobby gunshop and can be made even more useful by adding a miter box. The best are made of metal which can be adjusted for any angle, but a simple, inexpensive wooden miter box with both 45 and 90-degree saw slots will serve. They will be just the thing you need for cutting rifle forends for the installation of contrasting wood tips. Keyhole saws are of little use in my experience around the shop, and the same can be said for the small bench or dovetail saw. The coping saw will be needed occasionally for cutting out pistol grips and a few related projects. All of these latter saws are inexpensive and can be added to your tool kit if desired.

I always advise the new hobby gunsmith to start with wood, rather than metal, in gun work. Wood is much easier to work with and the tools are less expensive. My grandfather used an absolute minimum of tools and was one of the most unorthodox stock makers I have ever known. He used a section of an old cross-cut saw that he had made into a short handsaw with the teeth cut and set by hand. To this, he added a short, razor-sharp hatchet, a good pocket knife, and the rest of that old cross-cut saw was made into stock scrapers and chisels.

When he started into a stocking job, it looked like a big old master beaver had gone mad. Chips flew everywhere, followed by huge chunks of excess wood. To the professional eye, fully half of the things he did were wrong. Yet he could turn out a first class gunstock rapidly that any-

A good assortment of sharpening and polishing stones is a requirement of every gunshop. Note that the larger ones have been set into wood blocks to give them stability.

SCREW SLOT SHAPES IN WOOD AND MACHINE SCREWS

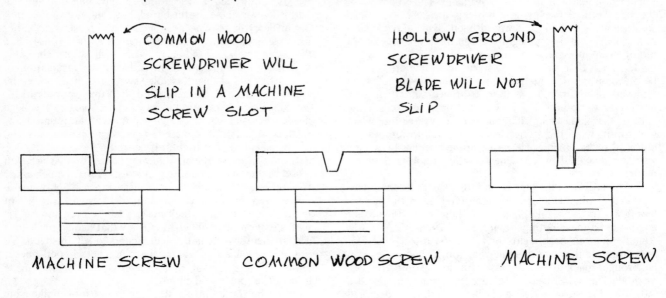

COMMON WOOD SCREWDRIVER WILL SLIP IN A MACHINE SCREW SLOT

HOLLOW GROUND SCREWDRIVER BLADE WILL NOT SLIP

MACHINE SCREW

COMMON WOOD SCREW

MACHINE SCREW

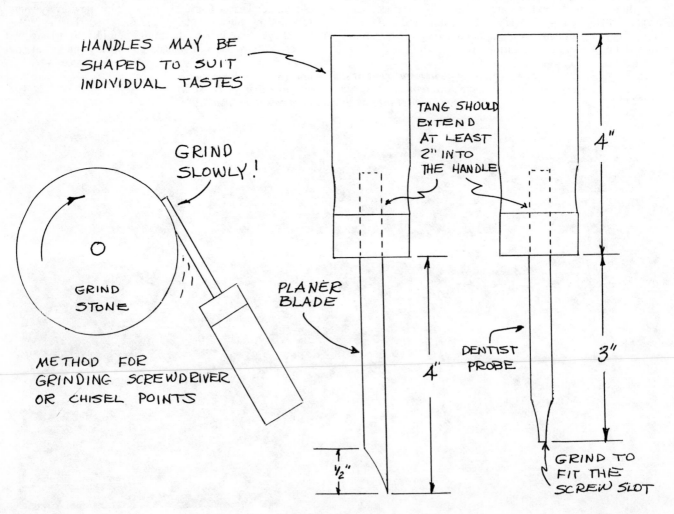

HANDLES MAY BE SHAPED TO SUIT INDIVIDUAL TASTES

GRIND SLOWLY!

GRIND STONE

METHOD FOR GRINDING SCREWDRIVER OR CHISEL POINTS

TANG SHOULD EXTEND AT LEAST 2" INTO THE HANDLE

PLANER BLADE

DENTIST PROBE

4"

4"

3"

½"

GRIND TO FIT THE SCREW SLOT

body would be proud to own. The standard methods, as well as tools, are not the only way a stock can be made. His tools were the result of necessity being the mother of invention and method, the result of a lot of trial and error.

The hobbyist can avoid learning things the hard way and be literally years ahead in his training by purchasing a good set of stock tools from one of the gunsmith supply houses. This can range from a simple starter set to a full complement of stock tools. There are many brands of stock chisels, most made from quality steel. I advise you to stick entirely to first grade chisels, even if you have to buy one at a time. The whole set is not necessary, as you can do a good job with just a few basic tools. A good stock chisel tool kit should consist of, at least:

> 1/8" wide straight chisel
> 1/4" wide straight chisel
> 1/2" wide straight chisel
> 1" wide straight chisel
> 1/8" "V" veiner tool
> 1/8" "U" straight gouge
> A barrel channel rasp
> 3/4" bent "U" scraper
> 1/4" square scraper
> 3/4" square scraper
> 1/4" "U" straight gouge
> 1/2" "U" straight gouge

This is a good working set but can be cut down considerably. The only trouble with cutting down on the number of tools is that you have to make one do the job of two and, any time you do this, you lose efficiency. One correct chisel can do the job in a couple of minutes while the wrong chisel can take three to four times as long and will not do as good a job!

Your chisel edges should be treated with care and protected from hitting any hard object as the edges must be razor sharp at all times. Trying to work with dull stock tools will make you pull your hair and want to wrap the whole mess around a telephone pole. A sharp chisel cuts the wood. A dull chisel splinters it.

These are just the most common hand tools and you will add more.

MEASURING INSTRUMENTS

Whether you buy them all at one time or work up gradually, one thing you can be certain of: you will eventually own just about this whole list of instruments if you continue working on guns. The hobby gunsmith usually is a combination machinist and cabinet maker and, as such, his measuring instruments will have to cover both fields.

On the carpenter and cabinet maker's side is the large carpenter's square which will be of somewhat limited use to the gunsmith. The combination square will be valuable in many ways. The 12-inch standard model is the one to choose. With the beam removed, it is a steel 12-inch rule. With the beam in place, you have both a 90 and a 45-degree angle guide, plus a built-in level. This tool will find itself being used both in stock and in metal work. For instance, many rifles do not have a flat on the top to use in leveling, but will have a flat receiver. The combination square can be pressed against the side and the beam, with the built-in level used to correctly level the rifle for sight work. Its use includes such things as finding the exact center of the stock, aiding in drawing a long and continuous line down the center of the stock, and other uses.

A rich brother to this tool is the machinist's combination square. It looks the same but is more precise in construction and has a center head and protractor, as well as the regular beam. The center head is used mainly for

The Mauser bolt release (left) with regular ear cut off, is customized by having end checkered. This is done by laying out lines with file next to it. Lines are then deepened, diamond points cut with the triangular type.

This special set of files is (from top): clock file; three screw slot files; sight dovetail; three pillow files of different cuts; knife edge type and a warding file. File card at bottom is used to clean the teeth of metal clogging. Small pack contains needle file set.

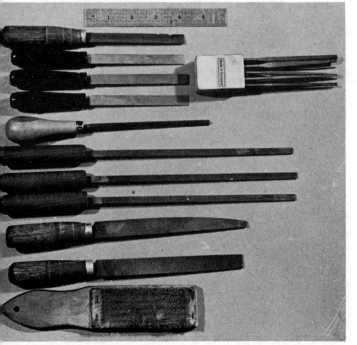

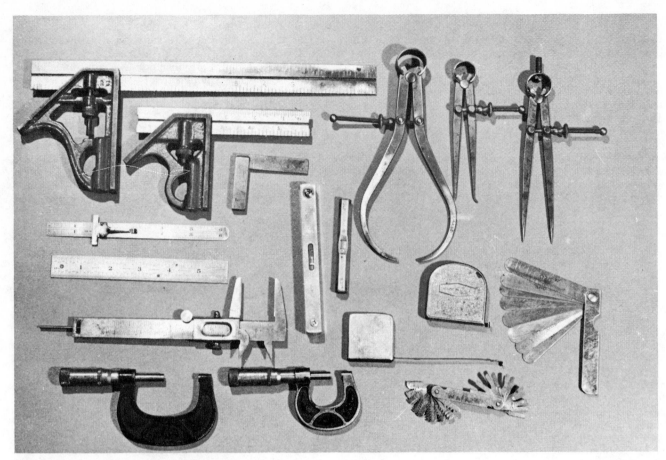

Collection constitutes most of the measuring instruments, all of them probably familiar to those without knowledge of gunsmithing, needed to carry out most uncomplicated jobs.

finding the exact center of a round stock for such needs as preparation for center drilling on a lathe. The protractor is for laying out various angles. Costing about ten times as much as the regular combination square, its purchase should be delayed until the hobbyist has a direct need for it.

A first cousin to both of these squares is the little machinist's square. This may be the solid type two or three inches long or the adjustable and more expensive type that is usually four inches. These are precision ground and will serve many uses where accuracy is important.

A six-inch machinist's steel rule with graduations in 10ths and 100ths on one side and 32nds and 64ths on the opposite, will be the one needed most. A 12-inch version will prove useful but if you have a combination square, the need is filled by removing the square's beam. A three-foot yardstick usually can be obtained free at any paint or lumber store and can be used in several ways.

A small flexible steel tape will prove useful in checking barrel lengths and other quick measurements. While the commercial model is made only in six-foot lengths and longer, a small three-foot version about the size of a book of paper matches is used as an advertising gimmick. Try to pick one of these up and keep it handy. I usually carry one of these in my pocket, as my work constantly requires checking barrel lengths for customers. Another useful item is the small six-inch rule with a sliding pocket clip on it. The clip slides up and down the rule and acts as a small depth gauge.

A set of four or six-inch calipers and dividers is relatively inexpensive and will be needed constantly in both wood and metal gun work. The outside and inside calipers will be needed in stock and metal work, checking and comparing dimensions. The dividers also will be needed on virtually every stock and metal job. The manufacture of replacement parts is almost impossible without them. Buy these with the adjusting screw in as fine a thread as possible, to allow more accurate adjustment. The fine adjusting model is more expensive than the coarser threaded version, but the difference is well worth the price. Smaller versions of the dividers in two and three-inch sizes can be added later.

The vernier caliper is a marriage of inside and outside calipers, depth gauge and a micrometer. They vary somewhat in construction, but most consist of a fixed beam and a movable jaw. The jaw or jaws, as the case may be, will take both inside and outside measurements. When the jaw is adjusted to fit the work, the user reads the measurements from graduations on the beam. Most have a rod down at the opposite end that is connected to the movable jaw and is used as a depth gauge. A more modern version has a dial gauge mounted on the movable jaw and makes reading a setting easier. These instruments range in price from an inexpensive, imported five-inch model costing around $2 to a four-foot version made by Brown & Sharpe costing $350. The original vernier caliper, by the way, was invented by one J.R. Brown way back in 1851. Accuracy has a lot to do with the cost, as does the type of metal from which the caliper is made.

The inexpensive ones are usually accurate to 1/100 inch while the more precision versions are accurate to 1/1000 inch. A vernier caliper will solve many problems in accurate

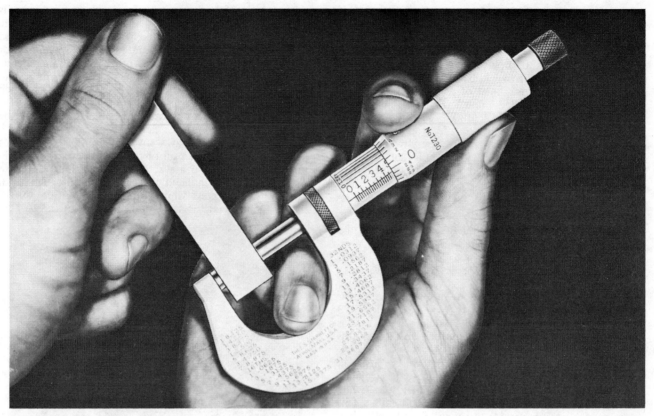

The micrometer is made by an number of firms, but the basic premise of reading it for measurement remains the same. The system is outlined fully by author in the text.

Author utilizes a thread gauge to determine the number of threads per inch on this particular bolt. Measurement is read in turns per inch; 24 in this case.

measurements that cannot be solved in any other way, especially in dimensions in excess of two inches. One of the six or seven-inch models will prove about all that is necessary for the average hobby shop.

The micrometer has been called the machinist's eyes. Without it, he loses all potential for fine and accurate work. While several variations are available, let's concentrate on the one most used, the O to 1 inch standard outside micrometer. Once you understand its use, the others are a cinch.

There are many models and manufacturers and, as in all cases, price is a fairly good guide to quality. You can count on an accurate micrometer costing at least $20, with anything lower priced, sloppily made, or made from inferior material. There are quite a few imported micrometers, some good and some plain junk. I would suggest that you stick to three good American manufacturers: Starrett, Brown & Sharp, and Reed. You also can count on any micrometer offered by the gunsmith supply houses to be of top quality.

In use, the micrometer is placed over the work and the thimble turned until the piece of work is between the fixed anvil and the movable spindle. This should be just a lightly-firm fit. Never use force or the accuracy of the micrometer will be impaired. Now, look on the sleeve (sometimes called the barrel) for a series of numbers from 0 to 9. In between these numbers will be three lines. On the thimble you see a series of numbers running from 0 to 24. To read the micrometer, assume that the frame is the decimal point (.). Now, suppose the largest number we can see on the sleeve is the number 2; this is the first number to be counted after the decimal point (.2). Also, suppose that the thimble is in a position with the zero mark on it right on the line that runs the whole length of the sleeve. Count the number of lines that you can see that are past the number 2. These lines are divisions with each representing (.025). If our example is on the second line we will have (2 x .025 or .050). Add this to the reading you already have (.2 plus .050 for a total of .250).

That's simple enough, but what if the thimble number is not zero and the line is on 5? Well that 5 is simply added to our total for (.2 plus .050 plus .005 for a total of .255). If it is on number 23, this would be done the same way (.2 plus .050 plus .023 for a total of .273). In decimal language, the point is called "unit," the first number is "tenths," the second "hundredths," and the third is "thousandths." If your number is .273, you express it in terms of the last whole number; in this case, "two hundred-seventy-three thousandths." If the number is .250, the zero is dropped and the number expressed as "twenty-five hundredths of an inch." If the number should be .200, again, the zeros are dropped and the number given as "two tenths of an inch."

Some micrometers have a form of vernier scale on the sleeve in the form of ten numbered lines. To use it, determine which of the lines exactly coincides with a line on the thimble and note the number. This is the ten thousandths of an inch scale. If our sample above was on such a micrometer and the line matching was 4, this would be .0004. This would be added to our total (.2 plus .050 plus .023 plus .0004 for a total of .2734) and would be expressed as "two thousand, seven hundred, thirty-four ten thousandths of an inch."

The ten thousandths reading seldom will be used in hobby gunsmithing, but it is good to have it available. Expensive micrometers also have two other worthwhile additions. The most useful is a ratchet on the thimble. This eliminates the need for trying to get the right "feel" when measuring the work. By turning the ratchet, this "feel" is accomplished and no more pressure is exerted, for the ratchet will simply slip and hold the micrometer right on the correct "feel."

The other worthwhile addition is a little lock nut built into the frame. When the reading has been set, the nut is turned and locks it in place, allowing the micrometer to be removed and read at leisure. A twist in the opposite direction and the spindle is free. If you do not like all of this adding of digits, you can buy a micrometer that reads direct in numbers on the thimble, all the adding being done by the mike.

Micrometers are delicate, precision-made instruments and therefore must be treated with respect. Using it for a C-clamp, trying to read revolving pins, or dropping it on the floor will put an end to its accuracy in a hurry. With just a little care and a drop of oil once or twice a year, it gives years of accurate service. It can be adjusted to bring its accuracy right back on the peg. I have an old Reed micrometer that has been with me for over twenty years and, though a bit worn, it is still right on dead zero.

In addition to the one-inch micrometer, the hobbyist will have an occasional need for the 1 to 2-inch micrometer. This is usually not enough to warrant the purchase of a two inch micrometer which is just as expensive as the smaller one, if not more. This is where your vernier caliper comes in handy for the few times readings in excess of one inch are needed. There are also many other kinds of micrometers, such as the depth mike, which works the same way as the common outside micrometer, except that it measures the distance the spindle protrudes past the frame, and the numbers on the sleeves are in reverse order. These will be needed for rebarreling, chambering, and so on, but can be disregarded with the other special micrometers until a definite need presents itself.

Although only one hobbyist out of a thousand will get involved in choke work on shotgun barrels, there is one

other most useful micrometer. This is the bore mike that is a long tube with three balls on the end, actuated by a long tapered rod that is attached to the thimble. Price is around $150, but a lot of choke jobs and it will more than pay for itself. It is in the same class as other special micrometers such as those used to measure threads, tubing walls, and so on. The average hobbyist will need only the O to 1-inch outside micrometer.

We have already discussed the thread gauge in the chapter on checkering. Just don't try to cut corners, buy a good one with thread leaves covering from 6 to 60 threads per inch. This will cover all of the gun screw sizes you will run across. While you are at it, pick up a thickness gauge also. This comes in handy, especially setting the depth gauge on a drill press while drilling holes in a receiver for sights. Radius gauges also come in handy, but can be con-

This shotgun sight is being installed with a collet sight holder, one of several methods of installation that are available to the do-it-yourself gun owner.

This close-up is of Walker's old Reed micrometer, which he has used for years. This setting would read .3652.

sidered a luxury item on your list.

There is a little gauge-gadget called a Screw-Check'r that is available through most supply houses. It is a card made of steel with a series of threaded holes through it. By trying a screw in the various holes, its size and threads per inch can be rapidly determined. It also gives the diameter, tap drill and clearance drill sizes. It serves a secondary purpose as a thread chaser to straighten out lightly battered threads. you can cut screws with a special cold chisel included.

A couple of levels will be needed. Perhaps the most useful is a four-inch precision-made machinist's level. A substitute and less expensive variation is a small pocket level, but check the bottom of these to be sure they are machined true, since some are rough and thus useless. Another handy little level is the circular type, which is just a holder with a one-inch round clear cap. By centering the bubble in the circle printed on the cap, the item being checked is leveled in all directions at one time. There is also a protractor level that will determine the exact angle of any item on which the protractor foot is placed. These come in handy for checking sight dovetails and other parts of the gun that are at an angle to the bore.

There are several other common tools, such as a draw-knife, C-clamps, strap wrench, et al., for which the hobbyist will find eventual need. Add these as the need presents itself.

In addition to manufactured tools, quite a few can be made by the hobbyist at a large saving. In addition to the money saved, tool manufacture is, in itself, a rewarding

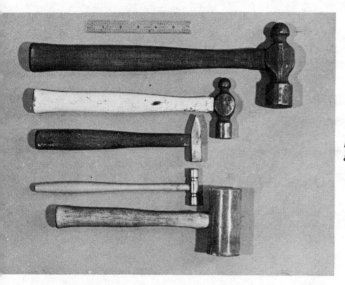

From top: Magnum ball peen hammer; six-ounce ball peen; a homemade hammer; a small brass hammer; rawhide mallet.

Left column, from top: side cutters, end nippers; parallel jaw; slip joint. Middle column: slip joint ignition pliers; Miniature needle nose; cheap needle nose for holding work while heating, standard needle nose. Right column: three medical forceps, with water pump pliers below.

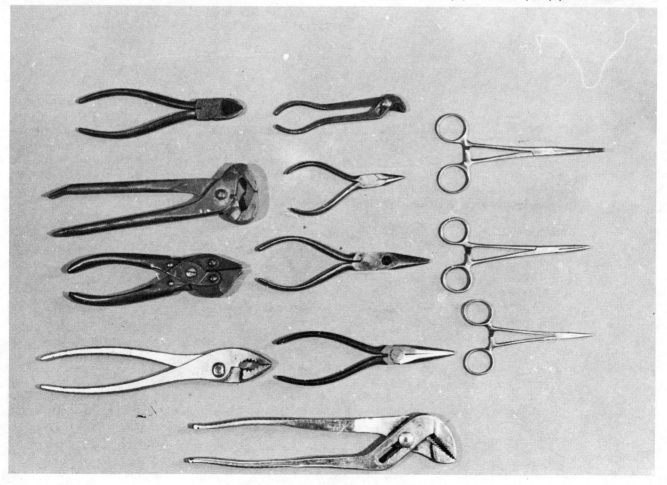

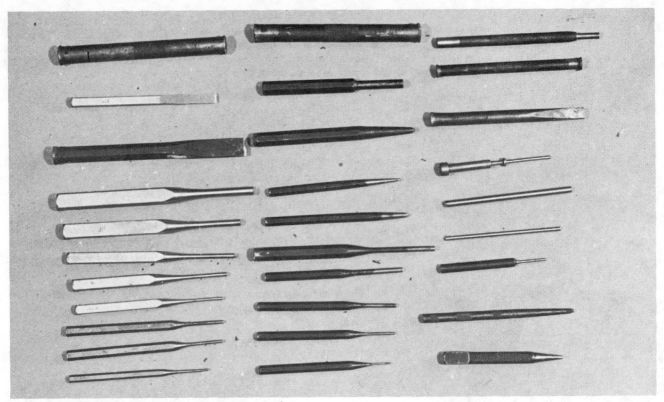

In this large collection of punches, some are standard
hardware, while others are special gunsmith punches.
Some are of brass or copper, others from old firing pins.

As there are endless needs for screwdrivers in the art
of gunsmithing, there are countless instruments to fill
that need. This variety is factory as well as homemade.

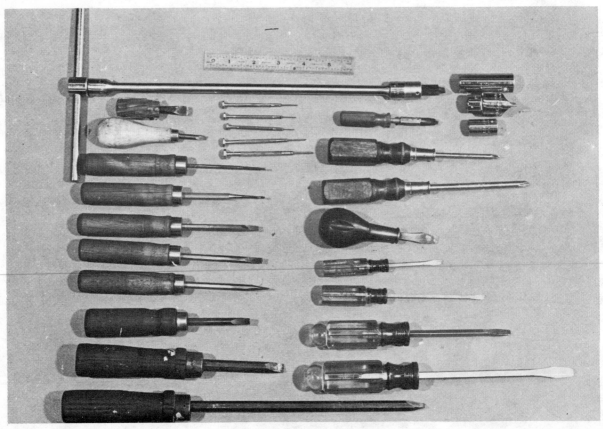

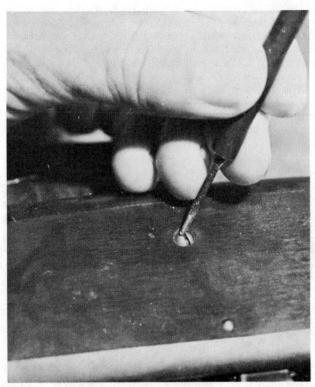

Stubborn screw is started by placing a punch at outer edge and hitting it with a hammer. This usually will start the screw turning, when standard methods fail.

A single hacksaw blade made the cut at right, while the broader cut was made by four blades on a single frame.

project and a source of pride. Such tools, if correctly made out of top grade material, will quite often prove not only the equal of a manufactured tool, but will surpass them. Many of the tools and special jigs needed in gunsmithing work are simply not available commercially, and will have to be manufactured from scratch by the hobbyist. Tools intended for one purpose can be altered or modified to fill the gunsmith's needs. For instance, I have and use a machine that was designed originally to install rivets in automobile brake linings, before the days of the bonded liner. Rescuing it from the junk yard for the sum of $3.00 and building a part here and there, I turned it into a very efficient shotgun barrel straightener.

I never could find a hammer just like I wanted with the right feel and balance. I must have tried a dozen or so from time to time. One day while digging through the junk box for something, I came across a rusty old cold chisel. Suddenly I got the bright idea of making a hammer just like I had always wanted. I buffed the rust off and then, with the torch, heated the chisel to a dull red and allowed it to cool. After cooling, I measured off 2-1/2 inches from the pointed end and cut it off with a hacksaw. The piece was then filed to remove all rust pits and the large end shaped similar to a ball peen hammer. Next, I drilled three 1/4-inch holes in line through the center for the handle with the three holes just touching each other. The excess metal was then filed away until the holes were combined into a rectangle. This was then fitted with a new ball peen handle for a close fit and the handle altered to fit my hand. I then removed the hammer head, heated the metal back to a dull red and quickly quenched it in 30 weight motor oil to reharden it. The handle was reinserted and a small wedge driven in the end to lock it to the head already in place.

The original model has seen about four years of daily use

and it is just as good as the day I made it. The weight is just right for most of my work and the chisel point end is handy for forming and shaping metal, for a lot of gun parts become worn and loose in use and replacement parts are simply not available. And many of these worn parts tightened by careful shaping and extruding the metal. This must be done only where the metal so altered is not under pressure when the gun is fired. A lot of people have admired the little hammer and asked where I bought it. When I reply that I made it, they look at me as if suddenly I had two heads. For some reason people are not surprised at other handmade tools, but a handmade hammer?

You can make your own screwdrivers to fit the flat side-grooves of gun screws and grind each to fit a specific screw. The best steel I have found for screwdrivers is octagon chisel stock, but this is a bit hard to find. I have several screwdrivers made from this steel that are around 15 years old, and they are still on the job. Drill rod is a good substitute and is usually available at any machine steel supply house as well as the several gunsmith supply houses. If you choose it, ask for the manufacturer's specifications on the hardening process for screwdrivers and similar tools and follow those specifications to the letter.

A good cheap source of tool steel for screwdriver manufacture is to be found in the dentist's discarded hand tools. They come in all sizes and shapes with some mighty weird looking twisted ends on them. Pick out a few with straight points and grind them for spring holders, pushers, and scribes. The ones with the wild and exotic twisted ends are your candidates for screwdrivers.

Start by grinding the ends off all the way back to the octagon shank and, when doing so, watch the sparks that fly off the metal. If they are many and sparkling white, you have a good piece of high quality steel that will make a good screwdriver. If the sparks are few and dull red in color, you have an alloy steel that is best discarded. I have found that dentist's tools with the name White on them are about the best to make up into screwdrivers.

With the end squared up, lay one end against the revolving grindstone so it is cutting one of the octagon flats in a half moon arc extending about 3/4 inch back on the shank. Press it against the wheel and when you have cut a ways, stop, quench it in water to keep the temperature down, switch to the octagon on the opposite side and cut a half moon arc on it too. Keep switching back and forth, keeping the cuts equal on both sides. This will bring the end down to a hollow ground screwdriver blade with the forward sides parallel. Try the tip in the screw you are making the screwdriver for, and when the blade goes most of the way into the slot, stop and make the final cut on a polishing wheel.

To harden and temper the blade, first heat the forward 1/3 of the shank to a dull red and quickly quench it in a pan of lightweight motor oil. The steel will be very hard and brittle. To temper it to prevent breaking of the tip, first polish the metal and hold the torch about one inch from

the tip. Rotate the blade to keep the heat even. The metal will first turn a light straw color followed by a brown shade, these colors will form and "run" to the thinner tip. Just as you pass the light blue color and the screwdriver tip starts into the blue-purple color, plunge it into oil and rotate it.

This is usually the best color for screwdrivers made from this steel, but you will get a little variation from different manufacturers. If the screwdriver tip breaks, you have it too brittle and need to carry the tempering color into the purple color before quenching. If, on the other hand, the

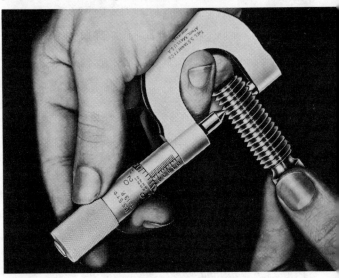

This micrometer is made by Starrett and is used to determine the depth of threads and for use in similar specialized measuring jobs of this particular nature.

This assortment includes strap wrench, allen wrenches, offset screwdrivers, scrapers and probes, tweezers, pin block, sight installers, muzzleloading nipple wrench, open end adjustable wrenches and vise grips, all of which can be important for special gunsmithing needs.

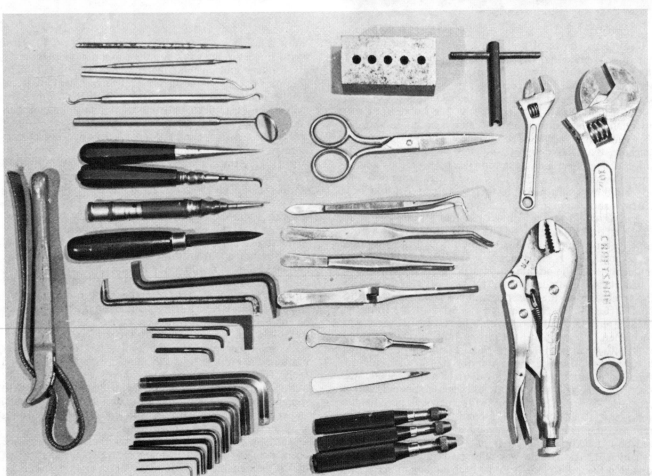

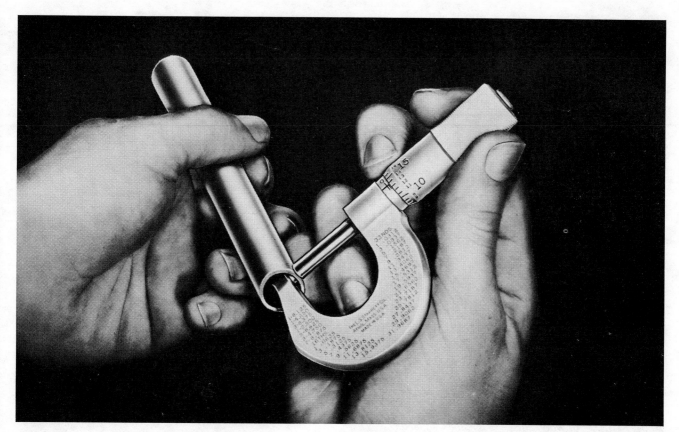

This particular type of micrometer is specifically designed for such measuring jobs as the one illustrated.

This is an assortment of stones that should fill about every requirement in the average hobby gunsmith's shop.

tip twists and bends, the tip is too soft and you should go back and quench at the beginning straw color. The trick is to find a happy halfway mark between being too brittle and too soft. If your screwdriver is still too soft, discard the oil and quench in water, which will harden the steel more. This will just have to be by trial and error, but I think you will find the blue-purple color about right for most screwdrivers of dentist-steel manufacture.

Handles for the screwdrivers can be purchased or made from hardwood dowel stock or even from large broom handles. Commercial handles usually are called file handles and you want the cheap one with just a ferrule on it and a small hole. The hole will have to be drilled larger to accept the screwdriver shank. I have some handles made from remains of a large broom. They were turned to size and a piece of old 20-gauge shotgun barrel used for the ferrules. I never throw anything away.

To assemble the screwdriver shank to the handle, first clamp it in your vise to the depth you want the handle. Now put a drop of oil in top of the shank to make it go in easier. This also tends to swell the wood and make the shank secure to the wood. Set the handle on top of the shank and lightly tap it down until it touches the vise and you have it at the exact length you want. You can cut a couple of longitudinal grooves in the handle for a better grip. As the metal used in the screwdrivers is yours free and you can scrounge the wood and ferrule, a whole set of screwdrivers to fit individual screws will only be a matter of a little time and sweat.

Stock chisels can be made from drill rod and such a set has been part of my tool set of a good many years and is still being used daily. The drill rod is heated to a dull red and flattened on the end with a large hammer. After cooling, the flattened end is filed and ground to the shape you want. Gouges are made by using a simple jig. This is just a block of metal with a groove filed in it. The heated shank is laid over the groove and, with a small rod being

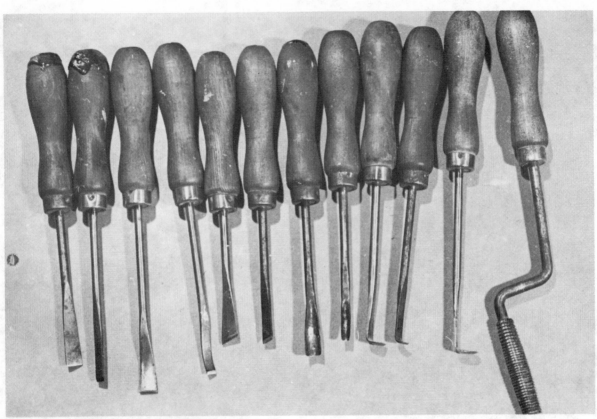

Above: This set of wood chisels was made by Walker from drill rod. Material on the butts of those at left is glass bedding material to reinforce wood, when the mallet is used. Barrel rasp at right also is homemade.

This set of wood chisels, featuring handles made in Walker's shop, was made from planer blades in the manner which the author describes fully in the text.

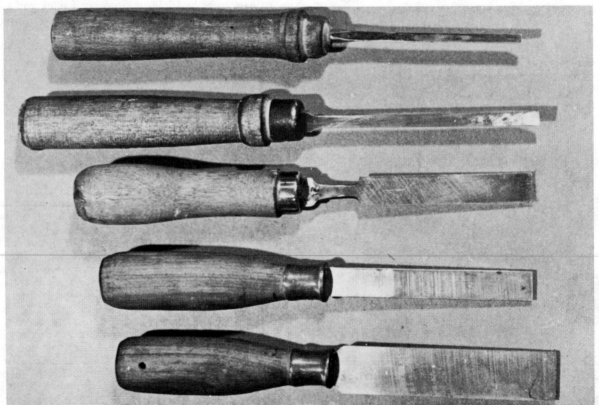

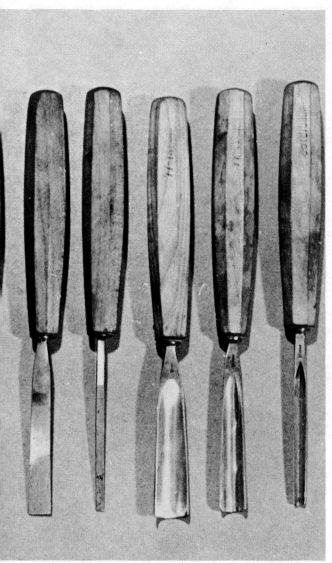

Author says this set of wood chisels, made by J.A. Henckel under the Tree Brand, constitutes an excellent start for the would-be gunsmith, who is starting to assemble tools.

They usually can be bought for pennies.

The blades can be annealed, worked and rehardened, but this is a lot of trouble and not necessary. All you need to turn them into chisels is a good grindstone, a can of water and patience. The secret of working the tool without annealing is to grind the blade and not allow it to get hot enough to alter the temper. The water prevents the steel from burning. You can do the same thing by dipping the steel in water after each quick pass against the wheel.

First, block the blade out into a piece one inch wide and six inches long. Take your time and do it right, but never stop or you will burn the steel. Keep the blade moving at all times. When you have finished blocking it out, begin grinding down one end for the tang. This should be about two inches long and 3/8 inch wide to leave a chisel blade length of four inches. Strange as it may seem, the next step is to install the handle. The reason for this is that the handle will give you better control as you hold the steel against the wheel to cut the tip.

With the handle in place, hold the tip of the steel against the revolving grindstone just as you did the screwdrivers to hollow grind them. All grinding is on one side only, the other side being left flat. When finished, a few strokes on a good stone will bring the chisel to razor sharpness. This chisel literally will slice its way through the toughest wood. It dulls slowly and always can be resharpened with just a few strokes on the stone. All high carbon steel is somewhat brittle, so don't use the planer blade chisels as a crowbar.

With the one-inch chisel completed, grind similar ones in widths of 3/4, 1/2, 1/4 and 1/8 inches for a full set. A skew chisel in 1/2-inch width is the next tool and is made the same way except that the blade is cut back to a 45-degree angle and hollow ground on both sides for a knife-like edge. They are perfect when you need a slicing cut in wood. Another good tool is a scraper made from a planer blade. This is blocked out just like the one-inch chisel, only about eight inches long. A shank is ground on both ends and two handles are installed. Then the blade is ground the full length on one edge rather than on the end, as a chisel. Turn the blade over and grind the other edge for an edge on both sides of the scraper. This grinding should be a quicker taper than that on the chisel. It will prove invaluable when shaping long sections of a stock, such as a rifle forend.

A small draw knife also can be made from a planer blade. It is blocked out just like the scraper except the tang is up on one edge, rather than the middle. You cannot bend a planer blade, so the shanks that hold the handles will have to be silver soldered onto the blade shanks you ground. These are just two 1/4 inch bolts. The wooden handle is slipped on the bolt and secured by a nut on the end to prevent the handles from pulling off. Look at a commercial draw knife and copy it. Oh yes, when silver soldering the bolts, be sure to protect the blade by packing it in wet cloth and keeping the heat on the shanks only. This little draw knife with its four-inch blade with hollow ground edge will shave a frog and not scrape his skin.

You can also make stock bottoming files out of sections of discarded metal files. Grind the section down to shape and silver solder it to a piece of rod, which is then driven into a wooden handle. The file teeth can be protected by making a paste of lime and water and applying it to the teeth before silver soldering. The bottoming files can be made up in round, half round, flat, and any other shape that strikes your fancy.

These are but a few of the many tools you can make and you will find extra pleasure and pride in working with tools you have constructed. Making tools is not preparation for gunsmithing, it is a constant part of that hobby.

tapped on top of the shank, the drill rod is forced down into the groove. The groove forms the outside of the gouge, while the tapped rod forms the inside of the gouge. After the forging, the gouge is filed and polished smooth. The regular chisels are just filed and ground to shape from the flattened drill rod. Scrapers, both square and round, are made the same way, then heated and bent to shape. The drill rod is hardened the same way as the screwdrivers, but the tempering should be done when you reach the straw color. The opposite end of the tool shank should be heated and hammered square to prevent the tool twisting after the handle is installed.

Every cabinet shop or large woodworking firm uses a power planer which consists of a rotating drum, with long cutter blades fitted to it. These blades can be sharpened only to a certain point, then must be discarded. These discards, ranging from four inches up the big four-foot lengths, contain some of the finest steel possible for chisels.

POWER TOOLS & HOW TO USE THEM

Gunsmithing Doesn't Require A Machine Shop; Just Knowing What You're Doing With What You Have!

Chapter 8

THE AVERAGE PERSON associates fine workmanship in a gun strictly with hand tools. Mention power equipment and he immediately associates this with sloppily-fitting parts and mass production. This is wrong. Power equipment, thought mechanized is as much a tool as a file. Workmanship depends on one thing only: the skill of the person using the tool, be it a screwdriver or milling machine. In many instances, it is impossible to do a job without power equipment and, in others, the power tool enables the user to do a job better, faster or both.

If a hobbyist should ask what power tool I consider the most versatile and the most useful in any gunshop, hobby or professional, the answer would be simple: the Moto-Tool manufactured by the Dremel Company of Racine, Wisconsin. I use this tool more than all the other power equipment in the shop. I bought my first one back in 1947 and even then the Moto-Tool had been on the market some thirteen years. I cannot remember how many of them I have owned, but right now we have five in the shop for four gunsmiths. These range in size from the small 260 model, used for delicate inletting of stocks, up to the big 280 model that is my work horse.

This little powerhouse was designed back in the early 1930s and was an immediate success. I've tried several imitators and some are pretty good, but I always seem to drift back to the original Moto-Tool. The old standard version was a little buzz bomb turning up an impressive 27,000 rpm and capable of doing a multitude of jobs. It did have a few drawbacks, such as a loss of torque when it encountered a heavy load. A few years back, Dremel completely redesigned it, using the most modern motor developments. The most important change is a permanent

Power head, with grindstone attached, is used to hollow grind a screwdriver. Don't forget protective glasses whenever this unit is being used, regardless of the job.

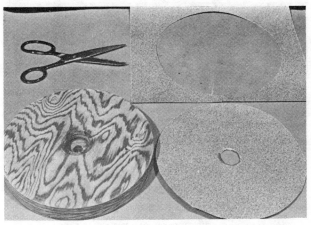

This homemade sanding disk fashioned from plywood uses a circular piece of sandpaper cut from a standard sheet.

Sandpaper disk has been glued to plywood and mounted on power head. Locking nut is recessed. Final sanding of disk's edges is done in place to assure its balance.

magnet field instead of the old wire unicoil. This means the new version has constant torque, regardless of speed of the shaft. Where the old tool would stall at around three ounce-inches of torque, the new 280 keeps going, up to over sixteen ounce-inches of torque. This may sound like Greek to the average person, but it is amply clarified if you first try one of the old tools, then switch to the new version that winds up to 30,000 rpm.

There are three sizes of the new version of the Moto-Tool. The smallest, the 260, is a compact and versatile tool, at its best in delicate work. The middle size is similar in size and power to the old tool except for that added torque. The top is the new 280 with ball bearings and is my personal choice. It is designed for industrial use, and one is ahead to invest the extra ten bucks over the middle size 270 model. The best way to buy one of these tools is in the kit form with molded storage case and thirty-four accompanying accessories. The accessories and some of their uses are:

Chucks: Four of them come with the kit and will handle the accessories and drills from 1/8-inch to the tiny number 80. The collet form of the chucks provides perfect alignment, which is important with that high speed, and earns its worth drilling those small holes, in those out of the way places impossible to get at with regular drills.

Grinding Stones: I use these more than any other accessory. In addition to the general selection that comes with the kit, I have a dozen or so more, ranging in size from one inch in diameter down to 1/8 and including odd shapes such as round, knife edge, cup and tapered shapes. Also included in the kit is the dressing stone to keep the grinding stones shaped up.

With the Moto-Tool wound up, the mounted stone is pressed against the dressing stone and is brought to perfect balance immediately. With the dressing stone, you can alter a standard mounted stone to any special shape you need. I use these mounted stones for literally hundreds of different jobs on a gun, like shaping weld build-up on worn parts, dressing down a new bolt handle, shaping the guide rails on a receiver to handle a new cartridge and so on. Due to their small size and the high rpm, they allow you to get jobs done in tight places.

Cut-Off Wheel: This is a 7/8-inch diameter, narrow, emery cutting wheel that works similar to large industrial abrasive cutting disks. They will slice through a gun pin or screw in seconds. I find them particularly useful when making a replacement pin. With the pin installed in the gun, its correct length is marked with a scribe and the pin driven part way out of the gun. A few seconds with the cut-off wheel and the pin is the correct length and ready to be driven back in place without having to disassemble the gun. The cut-off wheel also will find a lot of use in shaping new parts and truing up the slots in screws. They are tough but break occasionally; however, this is no strain on the pocketbook, as replacements cost less than a nickel.

Emery Polishing Wheels and Points: A rough gun action is a pain in the neck, but a thorough going over with the polishing wheels and points puts an end to the trouble. This

This loose muslin polishing wheel consists of two half-inch wheels mounted together. A pair of large masonite washers are incorporated so wheel will hold its shape.

A narrow pillow file is used in turning a screw, which is mounted in Jacobs chuck. Many parts can be shaped or even made from scratch with this simple arrangement.

Rubber sanding disk furnished with many hand drill kits is used to cut recoil pad to proper shape. This works well, but plywood disk is more firm, without flexion.

is especially true with military actions being converted to sporters. Many times a binding section on a gun's action will prevent correct functioning; the wheels and points can correct the trouble faster and better than any hand polishing.

Cloth Polishing Wheels and Tips: These work about the same as the emery version except being made of cloth and felt, their cutting action is obtained by impregnating them with different grit abrasives. If you do any polishing for rebluing or plating, they are almost indispensable for getting into close places the regular polishing wheel will not reach. A trick for putting the abrasive on is to turn the motor on, then off and quickly push the wheel or tip against the abrasive, allowing it to stop the rotation of the accessory. This fills it full and prevents throw-off, which would occur if the wheel or tip was allowed to rotate while the abrasive is being impregnated.

Sanding Drums and Disks: These names are a bit misleading, for they are used on both steel and wood. Perhaps the one most useful thing a sanding drum can do is to bring the inside of a trigger guard into correct shape and smoothness. However, you will find hundreds of uses for them in shaping and polishing. The disks, due to their thinness, will allow you to reach into tiny cracks for polishing and smoothing.

Bristle Brushes: These are handy for cleaning close places, but I use them least. Every once in awhile, nothing else will get the job done.

Cutters: I saved these until last as they are the stockmaker's best friend, for with them, stock inletting sure comes a lot easier. About the best description I can give of what they can do is to say that they turn a Moto-Tool into a hand-held wood milling machine. They will also cut steel if you take a little care and don't try to hog off a pound of metal at a lick. There are some forty sizes and shapes made of tool steel for regular work. More expensive are the tough carbide cutters designed for cutting tool steel. The carbide cutter makes the Moto-Tool a light hand milling machine, since it will cut steel rapidly, without chatter, in tight spots.

There are a couple of other major accessories at extra cost that make the Moto-Tool more versatile. Those 30,000 rpm come in handy and you normally use the tool at full speed. There does come a time when the speed will work against you and the answer is simple: get the foot rheostat. This little gizmo hooks up between the tool and your power outlet and the switch on the tool is turned on. The rheostat controls the tool completely, increasing or decreasing the speed as the dial is turned through seven speeds.

The tool post holder takes the place of the regular lathe tool holder and turns the Moto-Tool into a small internal and external tool post grinder for your lathe. It has hundreds of uses and I once used it to grind the ears off a 1917 Enfield receiver. I don't recommend this method, but at the time, I had no other choice.

The router attachment makes the Moto-Tool into a small wood router or depth grinder. For inletting stocks, it is at its best on side lock recesses, like that found on the L. C. Smith shotgun stock, and inletting for the receiver tang. Removing the wood to accept the metal in a shotgun forend assembly is time consuming, but accomplished quickly with the router attachment. Another use is to inlet the side of a rifle stock to accept a side scope mount. Regular cutters can be used, but the new router bits cut faster and cleaner in wood. There also is a drill press and a universal stand that holds the Moto-Tool in position on a bench, but to be perfectly honest, I've never tried either of them.

Miniature cutters are available from Dremel, but you can get them free if you put the old squeeze play on your dentist. His little enamel perforators must be perfectly sharp to work on a customer's mouth ivory, and when they become dull, he throws them in the trash can. Give him a cigar box and ask that he toss his discards in this and save them for you. What do you do with them? Okay, suppose you break a screw off down in a hole and are faced with how to get it out. You can drill and use a screw remover, but the dentist's burr is faster. Just cut a slot across the exposed end of the screw and back it out with a screwdriver. Anytime you need to remove a minute particle of metal or shape a small part, the dental burr will be needed. If you burn one up, throw it away and pick up another one. Save the burned-out burrs with the long shafts, for they do make good gun pins.

The Moto-Tool should be the hobbyist's first power equipment without reservation. After awhile he will find that he simply cannot get along without one.

The selection of the second most useful piece of power equipment is open to debate but, after thinking it over, I would vote for the drill press. There are always 10 holes that must be drilled, to say nothing of its need in sight and scope mounting. The cheapest way out is an adapter for your hand drill which clamps this drill to an upright movable bracket and turns it into a bench drill of sorts. It leaves a lot to be desired in sturdiness and accuracy, and should be chosen only when financial embarrassment prohibits the purchase of a standard drill press.

Drill presses are basically all the same with some variation and refinements in the more expensive models. All are alike in that they have a base, a support column, a drill table and the powered spindle. The only difference between a bench and floor version is the length of the support column, each having advantages and disadvantages. Most floor-mounted press owners make the mistake of just standing it up somewhere and not tying the base to the floor. The result is that the press is about as steady as a drunk at Saturday midnight. Securing the base to the floor presents little problem, provided the floor is of wood; a cement floor requires a bit more work. Holes to secure the base can be drilled into the cement with a masonry drill in a hand drill or cut by hand with a star drill. A lead expansion plug then is inserted into the hole to accept a screw and locks the base securely to the floor.

The floor-mounted press, with its long support column, will accept long work and, if your gunsmithing talents are on the woodworking side, it will be the better choice.

The bench model has a shorter support column than the floor press and is mounted on a bench to give the correct

Inexpensive flexible shaft with Dremel cutter is used to shape target pistol grips. Cutter can save many hours of filing, sanding. Flex shaft doubles power head's potential.

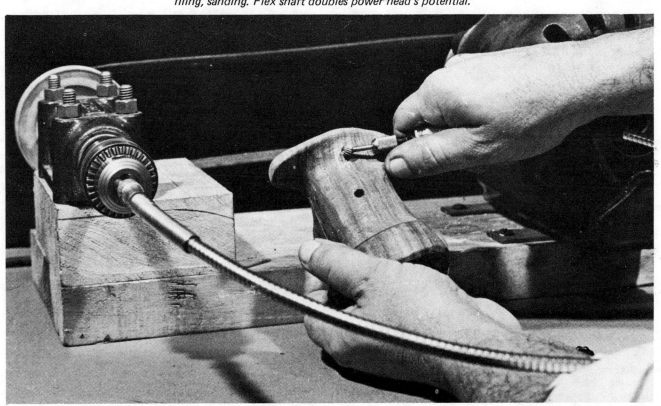

Walker feels that the power head, with the inexpensive tools illustrated here, covers many gunsmithing needs.

working height. This shortness of the column, while restricting the size of the work, is a lot sturdier and more vibration-free. If you work on metal more than you do wood, the bench mount will do a better job on things like scope mounting and precision drilling. If you run across a bargain and it is the wrong kind for your needs, in most cases, all it takes is shortening or lengthening the support column.

All but the cheapest presses will have a variable pulley arrangement that provides a choice of spindle speeds from somewhere around 400 to 4,000 rpm for different needs. Some of the higher priced models offer a third variable pulley to bring the spindle speed down as low as 200 rpm and up as high as 8,000 rpm. Most drilling can be done with standard speeds and if needed the extra pulley arrangement can be added later. There are two types of drill tables. The more common version slides up and down the support column and is locked in place by a split ring and lock screw arrangement. The other type is geared and the table lowers or raises by turning a hand wheel. Also the common version will have a table that is permanent 90 degrees from the spindle while the more expensive presses are equipped with a table that will slant right or left about 45 degrees for angle drilling. Just about all the tables will have a clearance hole in the middle and slots on the sides of the hole to accept one of the several types of drill vises.

Some form of drill press vise is a dire necessity in the gun shop, as metal should never be drilled while being in the hands only. The drill will bind, snatch the metal out of your hand, make a round, and whale the daylights out of your knuckles on the backstroke. The least expensive vise is adjustable only to tighten the work and can be attached to

the drill table with a C-clamp or secured with a bolt through one of the holes in the table. A more refined version of this vise is the angle model, similar in appearance, but capable of being tilted up to 90 degrees for angle drilling. There are dozens of variations, some with a swivel base, and so on.

The best choice of all is the compound vise that is bolted permanently to the drill table and is adjustable in or out as well as left or right. Most are square, but there are round rotary table versions available, too. The adjustments are accomplished by cross feed screws with graduated dial adjustment collars for pinpoint movement in thousandths of an inch. Prices range just as high as your pocketbook is fat, but a good, moderately priced 16-inch compound vise is available from Atlas. I've used one of these for quite a few years and it still is accurate, being equipped with an adjustment arrangement to take up all slack and wear.

The compound vise is composed of three sections. The bottom section moves the upper parts toward and away from the support column of the press in a fixed line, since it is attached to the drill press' own table. On the Atlas, this in and out adjustment is five inches. The top section, which is attached to the bottom section, can be rotated to any desired angle and, when at 90 degrees to the bottom section of the Atlas, will provide six inches of adjustment. The final part is the actual vise that is installed to the top section's table with T-bolts and can be adjusted the length and breadth of the table, providing even more adjustment variations. If you intend to do any amount of precision drilling and tapping, especially scope mounting, the compound vise will soon pay for itself in time and accuracy.

A compound vise with a sharp router bit in the chuck can be used to do light inletting on a stock. But remember that a drill press is designed primarily for its bearings to take vertical, rather than side thrust, so take it easy on feeding of the stock. Metal milling is too much for a drill press and it is best to forget it. You may get away with it for a short while, but each time the press will be damaged. There are several other accessories for a drill press that will increase its use in the gun shop, such as hole saws, planer attachments, sanding disks and so on.

Occasionally you can pick up a good used drill press, but watch out for a few things. One of the best tests is just to listen to the thing run. If it hums on medium speed, chances are good that it will be okay on the other speeds. A small amount of vibration at top speed is to be expected in any press, new or used. The second major test is with the machine shut off and the spindle fully exposed, push and pull on the spindle. Any slackness indicates worn bearings or shaft. If you prefer to buy a new press, those made by South Bend, Atlas and Rockwell are worth inspection.

Some form of bench grinder will be the third most important power tool for the hobbyist. In all gun work — small, large, complicated or simple — there seems to be a never ending need for a bench grinder. It is used not only to grind and shape gun parts, but in the necessary manufacture of tools and jigs for the the many specialized needs of gun work. With it, the hobbyist can manufacture his own screwdrivers, his own chisels, his own scrapers and on and on.

Selection of the correct type is not complicated but a matter of personal choice as to size and manufacture. There are many types that are attractive moneywise, but for gun use they are of little practical value. By this, I mean those grinders you often see at the economy stores offered for about twenty dollars or less and those grinders that are on the order of a polishing head powered via a belt. Forget them! They simply will not keep the grinding wheels turning at high speed without wobble. Invariably they are made with bronze bushings and the power shaft will slip a small amount from side to side. Accurate grinding is impossible.

In selecting a grinder, look first for the all important specification of being equipped with permanently sealed lubricated ball bearings. Next, grasp the grinding wheel and try to push the shaft in and out. It should not budge even a fraction of an inch. If there is any side play whatsoever, this is not the grinder for you. Without side play, the grinding wheels will be steady and you can grind and shape with the utmost precision. A large grinder is not a necessity, as either a quarter or third horsepower motor is all that is needed for gun work. A six-inch grinding wheel diameter will be all that is needed. Such a grinder should cost in the neighborhood of fifty dollars.

Grinding wheels themselves should consist of one fine cut and one medium cut, with a grinding wheel dresser used to true the wheels to perfect roundness for smooth function. Any time you start to get vibration of the grinder, either one or both of the wheels are out of round. Check that the wheels you buy are rated for the revolutions per

The big Dremel ball-bearing Moto-Tool kit, with foot rheostat, lathe tool post holder and router, constitutes the most used power equipment found in average gun shop.

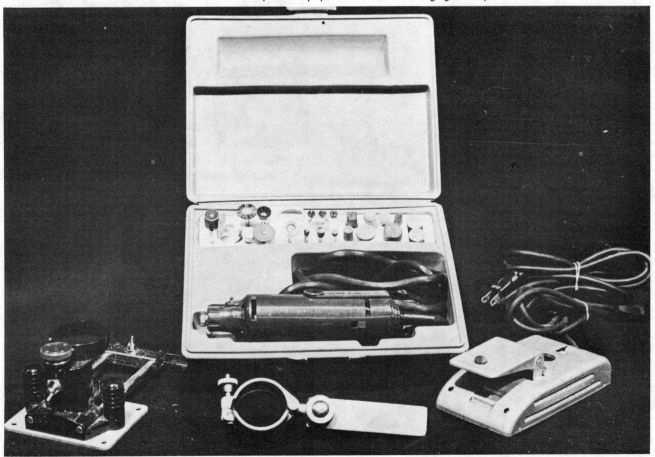

minute speed of your grinder which will probably be 3,450 rpm.

If you buy a good grinder, the machine probably will be equipped with a shatter-proof glass view shield. If it has a piece of bent plastic for an eye shield, pass it by. A pair of safety glasses always should be worn, even when the machine's shatter-proof shield is in position, because quite often you must look to one side of the grinder and place your face out of the range of protection of the shield.

A small container of water close to the grinder can help keep the part cool while you are grinding. This is necessary not only for your fingers, but also to prevent overheating or burning of the metal. Don't wait until it is almost glowing red hot. Instead, dip it often into the water to maintain as near normal temperature as possible.

There are several types of power saws, but for gun work most are as useful as horns on a rabbit. Electric hand saws are at the top of the useless list except for constructing benches or such. The saber saw can be used to some extent to rough out stock blanks.

I got the idea once this would be the ticket for cutting off butt stocks for recoil pads and spent a good number of hours constructing an elaborate vise and jig to hold the stocks. But I couldn't find a way to keep the cut straight and it splintered stocks like mad. After trying every kind of blade down to a ground off section of a hacksaw blade, I gave up. Now I keep the saber saw around for building shelves and benches. A radial arm saw is a fine tool for the carpenter and cabinet maker, but its only practical use around a gun shop is cutting off stocks for pads. It does this extremely well, but the tool is entirely too expensive and too large for just this one use. The jig saw, especially the larger ones, will prove convenient to have around for cutting out pistol grips and anything else up to about one-inch thick.

The most useful of all the power saws for gun work is the band saw. There must be over eleven-dozen different makes, models, and sizes ranging in price from $60 for a small three-wheel model to over ten times that amount for one of the variable speed rigs. A lot of things influence the price of a band saw and it gets a bit confusing. A good standard version that will meet most of the hobbyist's needs will run about $125. This is a two-wheel, ball bearing-equipped, wood cutting bench model. One of this size with about 10 to 12-inch wheels and a 1/3 hp motor will take up to six-inch thick wood, but it's better to stay around a four-inch thickness maximum. Blade speed will be around 2,000 to 3,000 feet per minute for wood, and at this speed it will cut clean and fast with little or no splintering. With a sliding stock holder, butt stocks can be cut rapidly for recoil pads. A wide blade should be used for straight cuts and a narrow blade for curving cuts.

For cutting metal with the band saw, it is necessary to drop the blade speed down to about 200 feet per minute or less, depending on the size and type of metal being cut. This can be accomplished by a series of different size pulleys or a geared speed reducer.

A band saw set up for metal cutting will save a lot of time in cutting out blanks for gun parts, cutting off barrels and so forth. It also can be used for cutting wood at this speed. While not an absolute necessity for a gun shop, the band saw is a nice tool to have around. One final word of caution: the band saw must be used with care and extra efforts made to keep the blade away from your hands. Keep your mind on what you are doing or don't turn the saw on!

The belt sander is a tool that can do a lot of fast, fine work, if the operator knows how to use it. It can be one of

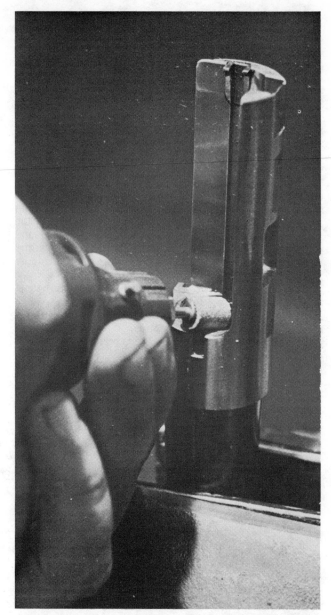

Moto-Tool with grindstone mounted is used to shape barrel extension of old model Browning chambered for 2-9/16-inch shells. Stones cut clean, but are followed with polishing point, which is necessary to remove all grinding marks.

the hand-made models or the bench type, with the latter the most useful. Its primary purpose is to sand along stretches of wood and a lot of places on a gunstock meet this qualification. It also can be used to install recoil pads.

A disk sander is the most useful of all the bench-powered sanders and ideal for recoil pad installation. It will precision-sand any wood and, with an aluminum oxide disk, will cut not only wood but steel also, if too much pressure is not exerted against it. Any flat surface that needs to be ground and sanded true usually can be done with the disk sander. Quite often, a disk sander will come with a belt sander attached on the same frame, combining two useful tools in one. The diameter of the wheel has a lot to do with the disk's efficiency as a 12-inch wheel will cut faster and the disk last longer than a six-inch wheel.

Milling machines come in both vertical and horizontal, but few hobbyists ever have a need for one of the big

Narrow emery cutting wheel slices through a hard gun pin. These wheels provide a cut much smoother than is possible with hacksaw, in author's wide experience.

Dremel tool is used to polish feed ramp on the barrel of a jamming Model 1911 .45 auto. This is almost always a necessity with lead bullets, especially wadcutter loads.

machines. The machine does work that seems almost impossible, but require good training to operate, to say nothing of the $700 to $1,000 price tag for even a small bench model. Most of the hobbyist's milling needs can be met with a milling attachment for the lathe. If you decide to buy one, the vertical miller is the most useful of the two, since it will do double duty as a precision drill.

If a lot of metal is to be cut off, the power hacksaw is a back and muscle saver supreme, but for the small hobby gunsmith shop it is of limited use. A good hand hacksaw and muscle will duplicate its function. There are two types of power hacksaws. One uses a continuous band similar to a band saw with the wheels sort of lying down on the job, being horizontal, the blade held in position by rollers. The second and least expensive is the reciprocating type that uses a blade similar to your hand hacksaw. Its motion is also similar to hand motion. The motor, operating through an eccentric cam, pushes the blade back and forth to make

the cut. If you consider one a necessity, the reciprocating type designed to use common blades will fulfill all of your needs.

These are just a few of the power tools that can be used in one way or another in the hobby gunshop. The ones you will need depends, to a great extent, on how much money you have to spend, how much you have in your shop and how involved in gunsmithing you want to become. The average hobbyist will have a Moto-Tool and probably a drill press and the usual hand tools. With a little work and a lot of imagination, the hobbyist can build one of the most useful machine tools in a shop. It is simply a combination of several power units that the professional gunsmith uses. The only difference is that the hobbyist has time to change the set-up of his one power unit for a variety of work while the professional, to whom time is money, has a separate unit for each set-up. These go by several names, but to avoid confusion we call it a "power head."

The heart of the power head is a single end ball bearing saw mandrel, which is just a one-piece housing holding two sets of ball bearings with a shaft running through them. One end of the shaft has a flat to accept and secure a pulley, while the opposite end is threaded to accept the accessory and hold it to the mandrel with a nut. Screw holes through the housing allow it to be attached to the bench. Price for such a mandrel will average about ten dollars. There are two other possible mandrels that can be used, but they have their limitations. The cheapest, commonly called a polishing head, is similar in appearance to the saw mandrel but has bronze sleeve bearings which limit its accuracy and life span. Besides, it is not much cheaper than the saw mandrel and bronze bearings allow too much end play. Ball bearings cost a little more, regardless of what tools you are buying, but will outlast a bronze sleeve bearing ten times over.

The second type is the ball bearing pillow block which is a ball bearing assembly, housed in an individual block. Two will be required, plus the connecting shaft and spacers. These can be used as a substitute for the saw mandrel, but the pillow blocks must be in perfect alignment to work right. This is a bit hard for the average hobbyist to accomplish and the saw mandrel with the two sets of bearings in a single housing will cost about the same as the pillow blocks. Besides, there are no alignment problems with the single unit saw mandrel.

Saw mandrels come in several shaft sizes, but the one you want is the ½-inch size. This may be a larger shaft with the end turned down to ½ inch which is all right as long as the threaded end is ½ inch with 20 right hand threads to the inch. The ½ x 20 thread is a common size and you will find a lot of matching accessories with this thread size.

With the mandrel purchased, the next item on the agenda is some kind of motor to drive it, which should be a minimum of 1/4 hp with a 1/3 hp even better. The motor should be a standard 1,725 rpm. You can buy a new motor or a rebuilt one for around twenty to twenty-five dollars, but there is a cheaper way.

Any appliance store usually has a few old washing machines that have been traded in and are not worth repairing. The motors in them usually are in perfect shape, and the stores sell them for about five dollars, if you remove them from the machine. Junk yards are another good source of these motors with about the same price and deal. Half of the motors in my shop served originally in washing machines or other appliances. I try to select the ones that are enclosed totally to keep out the dust. Some have odd-size tie downs and I buy the two dollar motor mounts that fit all of the newer motors around the shaft

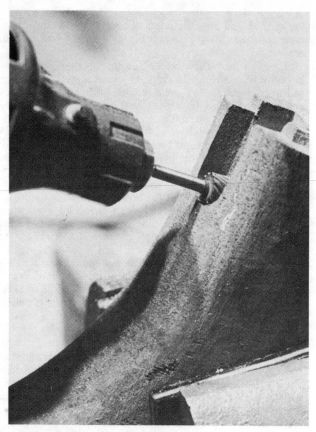

One of many cutters available speeds inletting of stock. Cutters allow control of amount of wood removed, without splintering. Light brush stroke allows for tight fitting.

Router attachment, router cutters are used to fit metal assembly to factory forend. Router has a depth control that gives smooth bottom to the cut, eliminates chisels.

housing. Sorting out the wires is fairly easy, but if you have any trouble, your local electric motor shop can do it in a second or two for you.

Next, we need a couple of pulleys and a V belt to connect them. You can use two single pulleys of the same size and drive the power head at 1,725 rpms as a pulley of the same size on the power head and motor will keep the speed constant. A better bet is to utilize two of the three step-type pulleys. These look like three pulleys of different diameter made together and that is exactly what they are. There are four and five-step pulleys, but the three-step will be sufficient. The diameters of the three steps should be two inches, three inches and the largest four inches. Install one of the pulleys on the motor with the largest step against the motor and the small step toward the end of the motor shaft. Now, install the other pulley on the saw mandrel with the small step in toward the mandrel and the larger step out toward the shaft end. Pulleys can be reversed from the setting I gave, just so both are reversed and the pulley diameters remain opposite.

All of this is for a purpose — to provide three speeds to the business end of the mandrel. To accomplish this, the ratio of the pulleys is varied. The rule of pulley ratio to speed is as follows: first, multiply the speed of the motor by the diameter of the pulley on it, divide the resulting figure by the diameter of the pulley on the mandrel being driven. With our two pulleys installed, suppose we have the belt in the four-inch pulley on the motor and the two-inch pulley on the mandrel. The speed of your motor is 1,725 rpms, so we find that our mandrel speed will be four times, 1,725 for 6,900. This is then divided by two, the pulley on the mandrel for a speed of 3,450 rpm on the mandrel end.

We have doubled the speed of the motor's output to 3,450 for high speed needs.

Next, suppose we drop our belt back to the two middle pulley steps. Both the pulley on the motor and the pulley on the mandrel are three inches in size, so there is no change in the mandrel speed and it remains the same as that of the motor: 1,725 rpm. Finally, we put the belt on the remaining two pulleys, which are the two-inch on the motor and four-inch on the mandrel. Using our formula (2 times 1,725 for 3,400 divided by 4 equals 862), we find the mandrel turning at the reduced speed of 862 rpm.

In selecting which of the three available speeds to use, remember that the more you increase the speed on the mandrel the more power you lose and the mandrel will stall easier. At the opposite end, slower speed will give more power and it will not bog down as fast. All three speeds will be needed and the use of the variable pulleys will give you the equivalent of three different motors.

The next step in the construction of the power head is to get the mandrel and the motor mounted on some kind of platform. Just about anything will do, but perhaps a section of 2X8 hardwood plank will be the easiest. Length will depend somewhat on the belt you are using, but 18 inches should be about what you need. Also, cut a short piece of 2X4 the same length of the body of the mandrel. It must be just long enough to allow the mounting holes to be drilled into it, but not long enough to interfere with the pulley or the accessory on the mandrel end. Center the 2X4 flat across the very end of the 2X8, also flat, and drill the holes through both pieces for the mounting screws; four 3/8-inch bolts about six inches long. Recess the holes for the bolt heads on the bottom so the platform will lie flat, and install

Carbide cutters are available in five shapes, turning Moto-Tool into hand-held milling machine. This allows one to cut hard steel without any additional polishing.

the nuts on top of the mandrel. You can spread some glue between the two pieces of wood if you wish, but this is not necessary. Check to be sure the mandrel is fully seated and exactly square across the length of its base.

With the mandrel secure, the next thing to do is tie the motor down. The best arrangement is a rocking mount in which the motor is attached to a bar on the side mounted next to the mandrel. The bar fits into a mounting rail and, with the belt in position on the pulleys, the weight of the motor will keep the belt tight, yet allow it to be changed from pulley to pulley as needed for a speed change. Before you tie the motor down, turn it on and note the direction of rotation. The pulley must be on your left, and the direction of rotation of the motor's shaft must be from the back, over the top and toward you. With the belt attached, the mandrel, whose pulley is also on the left as you face the end of the board, will rotate over the top and toward you. This is essential to make all of the accessories work correctly. If your motor should run "backwards," you will

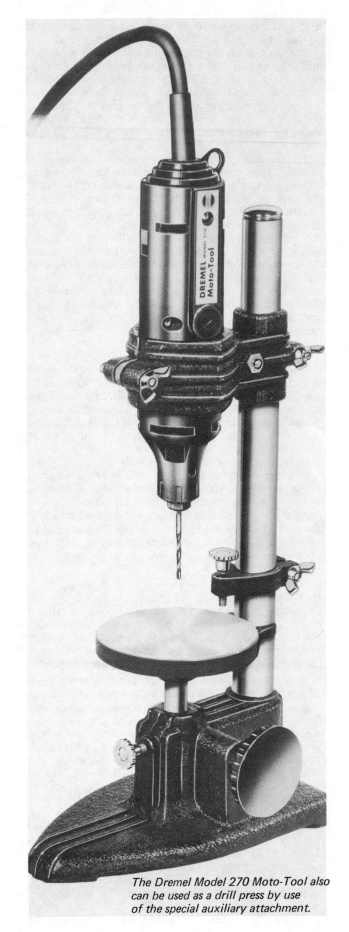

The Dremel Model 270 Moto-Tool also can be used as a drill press by use of the special auxiliary attachment.

have to reverse its rotation. Any electrical motor shop can do this for you and the cost is about a dollar.

Put the belt on the pulleys and stretch it by pushing the motor backwards. Use a C-clamp to hold the motor mount temporarily in place and check for correct belt alignment. If you have a yardstick, lay it against the sides of both pulleys. Each pulley should be flush against the yardstick, if the belt is aligned correctly. Rotate the belt by hand to assure it is turning true. Drill the necessary holes and mount the motor.

If you have a standard motor mount instead of the rocking type, push the motor back as far as you can to tighten the belt and drill the holes. Then drill the holes at the back of the slots in the motor mount to allow for tightening, as the belt wears and loosens up. You can still change pulley selections by pushing the belt over the rim of the pulley. A final item is the installation of a good 25 amp-rated or better switch between the motor and the electrical outlet. The small toggle switches do not last long under continued use and a regular wall switch will do a better job. The platform can be mounted permanently to your bench by bolts or left loose and secured when in use with a couple of C-clamps. The number of ways a power head can be used is almost unlimited, but here are a few attachments.

Wire scratch wheels slip on the threaded end of the mandrel and are secured by the lock nut. They are available in fine or coarse, about 1/2-inch wide. Use two of each to provide a working surface one inch wide. By doubling the wheels, they will hold their shape longer and more than double their effective life span. You will use the fine wheels more than the coarse, so if money is scarce and you cannot afford both sets, buy the fine wheels. Most people use a scratch wheel incorrectly by applying too much pressure against the wheel, resulting in a quickly worn wheel. Just lightly touch the wheel to the metal and give it time; the wheel will get the job done and last a lot longer.

One word of caution. The individual wires are locked to the center rim, but after use they will become loose and the wheel will throw them out occasionally. They will stick in your clothes without harm, but one in the eye can cost your sight.

Any time you are using a wire scratch wheel, use protective glasses. I recommend that you buy a full face shield as it offers more protection and costs about the same as a pair of glasses. The shield is of plastic and made to tilt up, out of your way or back down in place, at a touch of your finger tips. When using the wire scratch wheels, the mandrel speed should be set on the 1,725 rpm middle pulleys.

While it is best to own a bench grinding wheel, the cost of a good one is fairly high and the power head can be used. Again, never use a grinder without glasses or the face shield. These grinding wheels come in several grit sizes, but for average use, a number 60 grit in a six-inch wheel will serve your needs. These slip on the mandrel and are held in place by the lock nut. Be sure to check the rated rpm of the wheel stamped on the side of the wheel. Most will be rated around 4,000 rpm and will be safe on your power head with the pulleys set up to turn the mandrel at 3,450 rpm. Be careful grinding on the side of a wheel, as excess pressure can throw it out of balance and it is possible for the wheel to completely disintegrate. You can rig a tool brace for the grinding wheel with a bracket attached to your base or just put a loose piece of 2X4 in front of the wheel to brace the tool against. An accessory that should be purchased along with the grinding wheel is a wheel dresser which sells for about two dollars. This has a series of carbide cutter-washers that, when pressed against the wheel,

The tool post holder is used to hold the Moto-Tool for precision grinding of a pin in the Atlas 6 lathe. This, in effect, makes a tool post grinder out of the Moto-Tool. As illustrated in both photos, it is capable of fine precision grinding and will do large jobs, if one takes it easy, with a small cut at a time. Lathe bed is wiped constantly of grindstone dust or is foil-covered.

cut off the out-of-round sections to bring the wheel back in balance. Out-of-round wheels will cause vibrations that can shake your bench from one end to another and cause the stone to cut erratically. Be sure to use the face shield when you use the dresser for protection from the small flying chips, as it dresses the stone. Abrasive cut-off wheels should not be used on the mandrel. These wheels are very thin and, while rated for high speed, require side bracing and safety guards.

Sanding disks are almost a necessity, if much wood work is to be done. You will find many uses for a sanding disk and can either buy one or build one for the power head. Ones made to fit the 1/2 x 20 thread of the mandrel can be found as an accessory for converting radial arm saws and bench saws into grinders. Screw the nut onto the mandrel and follow with the disk until the end of the shaft is flush with the disk; then use the nut to lock it in this position.

The disks for the sander are simply glued to the wheel,

Unimat, in drill position, has vertical rod in place, spacer bar, tailstock removed for more room. Face plate is used as drill pad. Plate also acts as sanding disk.

The unit is used to drill hole in shotgun rib for front sight. Chamber end of barrel is supported by wooden block.

usually with disk cement. I prefer to glue a sheet in place with regular white glue as the disk cement will allow the disk to slip if much pressure is applied. Regular white glue makes removal of the worn paper harder, but the secure holding job is worth the extra trouble. Sanding disks made for the ten and twelve-inch wheels cost around a buck apiece. Regular sheets of sandpaper sell for about ten to twenty-five cents each in 9X12 size. If you will buy your disk nine inches in diameter, you can lay the disk on the sheet of sandpaper and mark the outline and hole position with a pencil. Then with a pair of old scissors, cut out the sanding disk, glue it on the metal plate and save seventy-five cents or better on each disk. They work just as well as the pre-cut one and, if using aluminum oxide sheets, you will get a longer service life.

Instead of buying a sanding disk, you can make one of two round pieces of 1/2-inch plywood. The back piece needs a 1/2-inch hole through it to align the plywood disk

on the mandrel, while the front piece needs a one-inch hole to recess the nut. Cut the round pieces of plywood and glue them together with epoxy. When dry, install the assembled plywood disks on the mandrel with a lock nut at the rear to hold it in place. Turn the motor on and use a rasp and file against the outer edge of the plywood disk to bring it into perfect roundness and finish up with sandpaper for smoothness on both the rim and the surface. Since the plywood disks are inexpensive to build, you can make several of them, each with different grits of paper glued on it for fast switching to another grit.

A removable sanding table can be made out of several pieces of 2X8 stacked high enough to bring the table up so the work centers on the sanding disk. The table should be positioned as close to the disk as possible and can be locked in place several different ways. It should not be made permanent, as it will be in the way when other accessories are used.

A sanding drum is used to shape stocks and, while not as useful as a sanding disk, is handy to have around. Sears-Roebuck sells one 2-1/4 inches in diameter, three inches long, and threaded to take the 1/2 x 20 mandrel. It is made of rubber which expands to hold the sanding sleeves in place.

If any work is done on metal, some form of polishing or buffing wheel is an absolute necessity. There are three common types found in gunshops. The least expensive is the loose muslin wheel for light buffing. If used for heavy buffing, they will flex and round the edges of work as well as put waves in the surface. For light buffing and removing the scratch marks resulting from the other firm wheels, they are just the ticket!

The next, going up the price ladder is the stitched muslin wheel. These will do medium buffing and can be substituted for the more expensive felt wheels in the hobby shop. The most expensive and most efficient is the felt wheel, available in soft, medium and hard. For maintaining a true surface and getting the work done quickly, nothing beats them. The soft wheels are used for the quick-cutting 150 and 240 grit; the medium wheels are used with 400 grit, and the hard wheels are most useful on 555 grit for finish polishing. About the best set-up for the hobbyist is a 240 soft felt wheel or a medium felt wheel for 400 and 555 hard felt wheel for that mirror finish. The muslin wheels for the same grits will put the finishing touches on the polish job.

These buffing wheels should be supported on their sides to hold flexing to a minimum. Cut large washers from a piece of masonite so their edges will be about one inch from the edge of the buffing wheel. Drill the 1/2-inch mounting hole and, with the two washers locked on the mandrel, turn the motor on and hold a file against their edges to cut them to perfect roundness. Mount one washer on each side of the buffing wheel with the rough side next to the wheel.

Six-inch buffing wheels are inexpensive, will do good work and the hobbyist will sacrifice time only. The eight-inch buffing wheels cost more, but due to their large

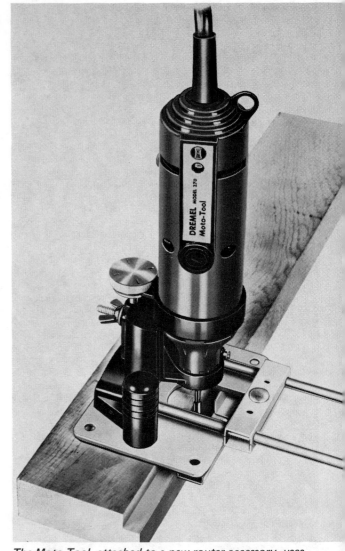

The Moto-Tool, attached to a new router accessory, uses special router bits. Author has found his handy for inletting shotgun side locks in stock, forearm inletting.

The Unimat can be utilized in a variety of configurations. In this instance, the bench saw attachment has been installed for ready use.

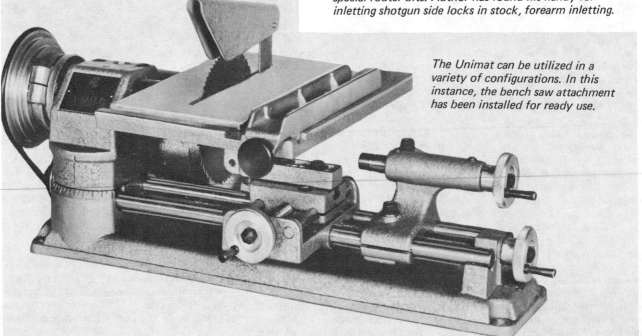

This Hamilton vertical milling machine is about right in size for most gunwork, doing duty both as a milling machine and as a precision drill press, when required.

The Unimat SL also can be equipped with the jig saw attachment. This can be used for sawing out small items in the gun shop, such as pistol grips, grip caps, et al.

circumference, cut work time considerably. As you will be changing the wheels to use other attachments, mark the direction of rotation on the side of the buffing wheel with a felt pen and reinstall them each time with the direction of rotation the same. You must have one buffing wheel for each grit, as they cannot be changed from one grit to another. The mandrel's rpm should be 1,725 for the 240 and 400 grit six-inch buffing wheels, and 3,450 rpm for 555 wheels.

A Jacobs chuck can be purchased for around $7.50 and about double the usefulness of the power head. Be sure to get one with the 1/2X20 threads to match your mandrel thread without an adapter. Adapters do work but leave something to be desired in true turning. A wide assortment of grinding bobs, wheels, brushes, and so on, can be mounted in the chuck and used for shaping and grinding surfaces. These are especially handy for reaching down into close spots that the large regular buffing wheels cannot reach; the inside of a trigger guard is an example. If you do not use a regular sanding disk, you can chuck one of the rubber sanding disk made for hand drills into your Jacobs chuck. These are inexpensive and will work almost as well as a regular sanding disk.

The Jacobs chuck can be used as a small lathe by turning pins, screws and other small items held in it while using a file to cut and shape. This takes a little practice, but most of the professional gunsmiths in the country have made screws and pins this way. One old gentleman I know still makes small pins by holding them in a hand drill chucked in a vise. He turns the hand drill with his left hand and files the pins with his right. I have a one-track mind and never could get the hang of doing this. Screws can be made by turning the shank down to size and using a die to cut the threads. The head is filed to shape and cut off with a hacksaw. The shank is inserted in the chuck and the end of the head filed smooth with the slot cut in later.

The Jacobs chuck should have a capacity of ½ inch. This will handle lots of gun parts and do some unusual work reserved normally for a lathe. For instance, to clean a shotgun barrel of leading and light rust, chuck a three-foot 3/8-inch diameter wooden dowel in the Jacobs chuck and wind a bob of four-ought steel wool on the other end. Turn the motor on and, by pushing the shotgun barrel onto the steel wool bob and moving it back and forth over the bob, it will clean and polish the bore to a mirror finish easily without any damage. Rough and pitted shotgun bores can be cleaned up by cutting a slot in the end of another dowel, inserting a strip of aluminum oxide cloth into the slot and backing it with sponge rubber. The rubber makes a tight fit in the bore and holds the aluminum oxide strip against the barrel's inside. Turn the motor on and run the rod up and down the bore to remove the rust and pitting. Turn the mandrel at 862 rpm when using the steel wool or aluminum oxide and do not stop the motor while the bob is inside the bore.

Flexible shafts are rather inexpensive and made to use with hand drills and drill presses, but will work perfectly with your Jacobs chuck mounted on the mandrel. The flexible shaft has a small chuck on its end to accept small grindstones, cutters, burrs, and so on. Usually maximum rpm will be needed, but some of the cutters will work better at a slower speed. The flexible shaft will prove invaluable and allow you to put a small powered cutter or grinder right where you need it.

The power head will more than double your work potential. The complete sample shown in this chapter totaled less than $30 and the price can be lowered by shopping around. Many other accessories can be used on the power head. I know one hobbyist who mounted another non-powered mandrel on a longer platform and used the two combined for a small lathe. Build a platform over the top of the mandrel, mount a saw blade on it to come through the platform, and you have a table saw. You can even make a drill press out of the power head by mounting it vertically and building a drill table to move up to the mandrel. Use your imagination and you will find a dozen more things it can be used for.

Unimat is a trade name abbreviation of "Universal Machine Tool," marketed by American-Edelstaal, Inc. I would call it a machine shop in a suitcase, for it comes in a wooden suitcase. Unlike most machines, it comes ready to go to work with motor, Jacobs chuck, centers, tool holder, cutting bit and other accessories for the base price of about $150. For the hobbyist limited on space or who moves about, it is one of the handiest little tricks you can own, even if you have a large lathe.

The unit starts as a small precision lathe, converts quickly to a polisher-grinder, then to a drill press, to a vertical milling machine, and finally, to a surface grinder — just as it comes out of that wooden suitcase. With extra attachments you can convert it to a jigsaw, small circular saw, cut-off tool, sanding disk, indexing and gear cutter, and even to a watchmaker's lathe.

Naturally, being this size, you cannot expect it to machine a 26-inch barrel for your .458 elephant duster. You will find, however, that a large part of gunsmithing consists of machining small parts and accessories and this is where the Unimat shines. Here are its basic specifications — Distance between centers: 6-9/10". Horizontal swing over bed: 3"; Headstock rotation: 360 degrees. Bore 1/4": In the vertical position, the distance from spindle nose to cross slide: 6-1/4" and capable of drilling to the center of the 6-1/8" circle. It is equipped with a special 1/10 hp motor and pulleys to deliver 11 speeds to the spindle from 900 to 7,200 rpm. Accuracy is to .0005 spindle runout. Dimensions are 14-1/2 X 4 X 5 inches with a weight of 30 pounds.

The things it will do within its limitations are governed only by the skill of the operator and his imagination. To give you some idea, here are some of the things that can be done with it.

As a lathe: A couple of things take some time getting used to on the Unimat, such as the headstock spindle having the same thread and being the same size as the tailstock spindle. This allows each component to be used in several ways. For instance, all the chucks can be used on both the headstock spindle, the tailstock spindle, and with a special adapter, mounted on the cross slide assembly to serve as a vise. Next, all of the conversions require the use of just one tool; a long Allen wrench which eliminates time being spent hunting the right wrench. (An idea some of the large tool manufacturers should copy.) The three jaw universal chuck and the four jaw independent chuck are extra, just as in the larger lathes, but each is priced below $25 which is less than one-third the cost of large chucks. These are about the highest priced of the multitude of accessories available, with most accessories costing two to ten dollars. For instance, the lathe, as it comes in the box, will handle work up to a three-inch swing over the bed. But, with a two dollar accessory raising block, the swing is increased to 4½ inches.

Both cross and longitudinal feed is by hand, but you can buy a power feed attachment that will give a feed of .0008 per spindle revolution. The lathe is not equipped for cutting threads as it comes out of the box, but an accessory can be purchased to do this. I don't advise the average hobbyist to

This operating rod from an old Model 97 Winchester has been built up by welding new lug to compensate for wear. Lug is milled down to shape, using the Unimat.

The M1911 slide is surface ground with the cup stone. The slide was bent, but careful heating and bending put it back in shape, after grinding, polishing, rebluing.

buy this, as most of your threading needs can be accomplished with dies and the money is better spent on some of the other accessories. The tool's minimum speed of 900 rpm will fill most needs, but a slow speed attachment will drop this down to 750 and 330 rpm and an electronic speed control is available.

Set up as a lathe, the Unimat will machine firing pins, make screws, turn pins all day, and do just about anything desired up to a length of 6-9/10 inches, which will include some pistol barrels. One unusual feature of the machine as a lathe is the 5/8-inch headstock spindle feed which is mighty handy and absent on nearly all large lathes. Most lathes hold the work in the headstock chuck, with the drill in the Jacobs chuck on the tailstock. The work is turning and the drill is not, but is fed into the work.

With the Unimat, you can install the Jacobs chuck on the headstock, hold odd size work on the cross slide fitted with the headstock chuck and use the headstock spindle feed to drill holes in the work. This is quite an accomplish-

The Unimat, mentioned extensively in the text, is a tool of many uses to the gunsmith. In this instance, the power head has been swung aside, allowing for the grindstone to be mounted, complete with its guard unit.

The Unimat SL power unit has been removed from its bed and is used, in this instance, as a hand drill during mounting of a recoil pad. Standard drill is easier.

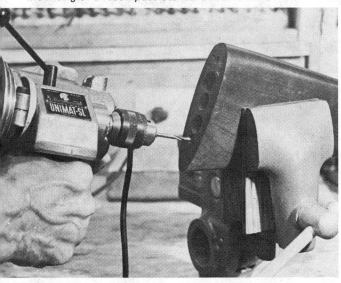

Flexible shaft on Unimat is utilized in grinding a bolt handle to clear a scope. The Jacobs chuck is attached.

This is what Walker refers to as a machine shop in a suitcase. Unimat and accessories all fit into the case.

ment and solves some tricky problems. The Jacobs chuck will hold drills down to the tiny No. 80 size. The usual lathe operations, precision boring, taper turning, and reaming can all be done with the Unimat set up as a lathe. With the steady rest installed and the tailstock removed, you can turn long rods and even squeeze out longer pistol barrels by turning six inches, reversing the barrel, and turning the opposite end.

To change the machine from its horizontal lathe position to a vertical position and convert to a drill press requires only removing the tapered headstock screw and pulling one alignment pin. The entire power unit then is lifted from the lathe bed. In its place goes a steel rod that is locked in place with the tapered screw. The power unit is attached to the vertical steel rod and the Unimat is a drill press. Major adjustment for height is accomplished by sliding the power unit up and down the steel rod and locking it in position. The headstock spindle feed of 5/8 inches is used for the drilling. If the headstock raising block is used, this will add 3/4 inches more to the distance between the drill and the vertical rod.

Vises to hold the work are numerous. The adapter that mounts the headstock chucks to the cross feed can be used to convert the chucks to vises. This allows all sorts of special positions to be worked out to hold odd-shaped parts for drilling. I would suggest you add the machine vise which takes the place of the tool holder on the cross feed, and in essence, gives you a compound vise arrangement with the cross and longitudinal feeds. It will handle regular square work or round rods up to 1-1/8 inches, but you can hedge a bit by removing the stationary jaw to double the vise capacity.

Although it takes a bit of barnyard rigging, you can drill and tap a high power rifle receiver for scope mounts. This is done by using the B-Square jig mounted in the machine vise or the milling table with its hold-down clamps that allows all kinds of odd shaped items to be held securely. If you drill a hole in the bottom of the B-Square bottom plate and use a T-lock bolt to secure it to the milling table, you will have a more solid set up. Side receiver sights and side scope mounts, as well as regular sight holes in the barrels, can be drilled with the Unimat. An added feature is that the power head will rotate out of vertical alignment for drilling holes at an angle.

With the Unimat in drill position and the Jacobs chuck

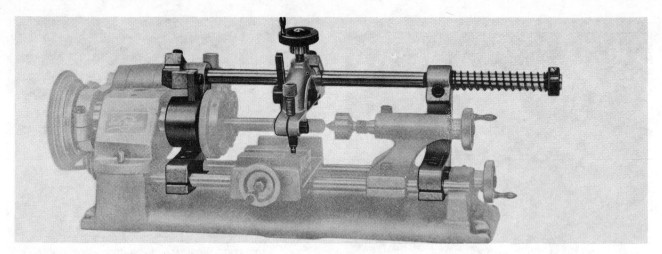

Unimat with threading attachment has tracing system to use collar behind chuck on which the thread is engraved to guide threading cutter attached to guide bar.

or one of the regular chucks on the headstock spindle, you have a small vertical milling machine that will amaze you by its versatility. Milling cutters of various sizes and types can be held securely in the chuck and the work attached to the milling table on the cross feed. Take it easy and the Unimat will allow you to do milling that otherwise would require the use of an expensive machine. Pistol work, such as accurizing, requires some careful filing and turning, but this can be speeded up with the vertical milling ability. Dovetail sight slots are a snap with a special milling cutter available from the gunsmith supply houses.

As a surface grinder, this is accomplished the same as the milling setup, except that a cup wheel grindstone is used instead of the milling cutter. To a gunsmith, the most practical use for this feature is in the truing of flat surfaces, as in the manufacture of a replacement part. It also is useful

with a round grinding bob to undercut sight ramps to fit snugly on barrels and with other bobs to aid in altering actions.

The Unimat can be used as a grinder-polisher with the power unit in regular position mounted on the lathe bed or in the vertical drill position. Grinding wheels mount on a special spindle. As the power unit can be rotated 360 degrees in the normal or vertical positions, you can swing it around until the headstock spindle is opposite its regular position for more clearance to handle larger grinding and polishing jobs. In the horizontal position, but reversed, you have an efficient small bench grinder. This grinding arrangement will solve a lot of problems. For instance, to sharpen lathe bits, rotate the power unit to normal lathe position, adjust the tool holder with bit to the correct angle, then feed the tool into the rotating stone to sharpen or shape the

Equipment described in this chapter can be utilized in jeweling bolts as well as other decorative works. More on this subject is described in detail in Chapter 16.

Machining the end of bronze rod for use as a one-piece cleaning rod. These rods are available in various diameters at welding equipment shops, as they are only brazing rod. Other end will be fitted with file handle.

tool bit!

To enlarge the Unimat's polishing ability, turn a longer adapter on the lathe and drill a hole in it to accept the tap for that common spindle thread. With the power unit in the vertical position and rotated to one side, large buffing wheels can be used. In fact, you can polish an entire gun for rebluing this way, as well as using a large scratch wheel for cleaning or matting.

All you have to do is remove the power unit from the lathe bed and you have a first class portable hand drill with eleven speeds at your disposal!

The first time I saw the Unimat's power unit removed, I immediately thought, "Here is an ideal tool post grinder for a big lathe!" All you need is an adapter plate to fit it to your big lathe's compound cross feed. You can make a steel rod similar to the drill column and mount the Unimat over the work on your big lathe for special grinding and polishing. As a tool post grinder, it will do both external and internal grinding as well as providing a superfine polish on a barrel mounted between the big lathe's centers.

The flexible shaft is ball-bearing equipped and will handle speeds up to 3750 rpm. It attaches directly to the power unit headstock spindle and is locked in place. The business end has that same special spindle thread and will accept any of the Unimat accessories. The Jacobs chuck will be used normally and, as it will handle very small drills, all of the regular hand grinder dentist burrs and cutters can be used. This allows the Unimat to get in on stockmaking and a lot of other things, like grinding a bolt handle to clear a scope with the grinder attachment mounted on the shaft. The flexible shaft will increase the workability of the machine.

I AM AMAZED AT THE number of hobbyists who own a lathe. Those who don't invariably are eager to own one. A lathe is not a necessity in a hobby gun shop, because a lot of quality work is done every day, even professionally, without one. A lathe does, however, open up a large and fascinating phase of gun work that is impossible to do without one.

The largest obstacle is that a brand new, fully equipped production lathe can cost more than a new automobile.

Used lathes are a good possibility and you can pass the word around hardware stores, garages and other repair shops that you are in the market for a used lathe — any kind of lathe. One hobbyist picked up a badly worn armature lathe for under fifty bucks. A little help from a sympathetic machinist and a lot of work converted it into a good working gunsmith's lathe. Another hobbyist found a lathe in the junk yard. It was probably in use when grandpappy was wearing three cornered pants, but a lot of sweat and elbow grease put it back in running shape. It will not turn metal toothpicks for a mosquito, but it will do average size work.

A lot of the older lathes are gathering dust and rusting. Modern machines have replaced them and owners cannot find a buyer or bring themselves to consign the old lathes to the junk heap. At this moment, I know the location of three old lathes, the highest asking price $75. Most of those found will be the small headstock bore type, designed for the old overhead belt drive. The small headstock bore is a problem, but not as much as you would think for a hobbyist's needs. The belt drive design is no problem, as the flat belts can be driven with a regular electric motor mounted on a platform to the rear of the lathe.

LATHE LORE

While A Lathe May Not Be An Absolute Necessity For Gunsmithing, Many Consider It As Such. Here Are Notes On How To Acquire, Repair And Use Them!

Chapter 9

The most common fault with the old lathe is wear in the bed and cross-feed mechanism. Many can be tightened up with the adjustments built into the lathe, others by shimming at critical points. Machine shop production lathes are a far cry from a shiny new punch card electronic wonder, costing as much as some people make in a year's salary. Most will be worn, loose and seemingly ready for the scrap heap, yet the machinist has learned the traits of the machine and works around its shortcomings.

The second common difficulty in buying one of these old lathes is a broken gear. Most of them will be the hand-change gear type with a big pile of loose gears and sometimes you can just substitute another gear and get back into business. Seldom will you find one of these lathes equipped with a quick-change gear box. If your first line of attack on the problem fails, try to find a replacement gear. Most of these gears are fairly common and a substitute should be found at a used equipment firm. Finally, a good machinist can manufacture the needed gear at a reasonable price.

Rust and neglect are common diseases of these old lathes, but most can be cleaned up, provided you supply the elbow grease. First, flood the thing with Du-Ol, wait for it to soak in well, then attack it like a mad bumblebee with steel wool and sweat. When you can see the steel again, start disassembling the thing. Make notes and sketches of where all the bolts and parts go as you take it down. Disassembling a lathe is actually not as hard as disassembling some guns; the parts are large and everything bolts and slides together. With the parts scattered around you like a giant jigsaw puzzle, start cleaning each part carefully, removing every speck of dirt, old grease and rust you can see. Any stubborn part can be cleaned by allowing it to soak for a day or so in mineral spirits. Regardless of the value of your lathe, the prime enemy of any piece of machinery is rust and grime. Oil and dirt together equal valve grinding compounds and, when present between two moving pieces of metal, you soon have a wornout piece of equipment.

While you have the lathe apart, check the headstock bearings. Some types can be tightened slightly if loose, but others require complete replacement. If the slackness is so great as to require replacement, it is time to do some checking on price. If the spindle can be turned down slightly and a larger bearing installed at a reasonable price, it's worth it, but if the price is too high, the best thing to do is abandon the project and start over.

The bearings on the lead screw are usually of the bronze type and a replacement can be poured or turned out of bar stock at a very low price. The cross-feed may be loose and wiggling from side to side. To correct this, look on each side of the dovetail cuts for an adjustment bar and screws.

Tightening the screws should take up the slack, but if not, try some careful filing and make a new, thicker slide adjustment bar. The next problem with the cross feed is too much slack back and forth across the bed. This is controlled by just a long screw riding in a bronze or brass nut. A trick that occasionally works on some brands is to turn the nut around. If the screw, or more likely the nut, is badly worn, any machinist can manufacture a new one for you at a reasonable cost.

A worn tailstock will be evident by the two centers not joining vertically. This can be corrected easily with shims. A worn lathe bed is the toughest to overcome, but looks can be deceiving. Most will have nicks right under the chuck that are the result of somebody dropping the chuck on his fingers, cussing and allowing the chuck to hit the bed. If the nicks are right under the chuck there is no problem, as the cross-feed assembly will not be affected. In fact, several lathes are made with this part of the bed cut away to handle large diameter work. The nicks in the bed where the compound rest rides are important; these nicks should be carefully filed to remove rough edges. Don't get carried away with the file; just remove the rim of the nicks and not the base metal of the bed.

When everything possible has been done, start reassembling the lathe, referring to your notes to assure correct placement of each part. Use grease lavishly. Try turning the lathe by hand when it is all back together before you switch on

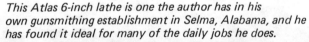

This Atlas 6-inch lathe is one the author has in his own gunsmithing establishment in Selma, Alabama, and he has found it ideal for many of the daily jobs he does.

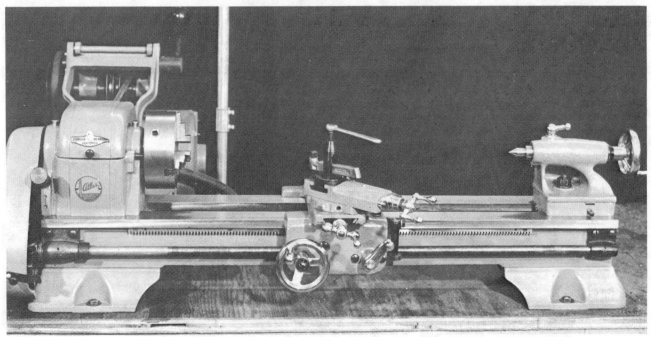

the power. When it is running and purring like a kitten, give the old gal a new paint job and be proud that you have literally brought a lathe back from the grave. She probably has a lot of life left in her and will give you many hours of pleasure.

Purchasing a lathe from an individual is the best bet, because you usually get a better deal and the owner can brief you on any shortcomings and defects. Or shop at the used machine equipment companies. You will find the smaller lathes scarce as hen's teeth, while the large sizes are plentiful. These can be a good buy if you have the room, but be sure to check on the completeness of the lathe. Chucks for big types can cost well over $100 for a used one. It doesn't take many of these missing items to turn the bargain into a money-grubbing hog.

If the chucks are all there, check the jaws for slack and wear. If the gripping section of the chuck jaws are battered, sometimes they can be corrected with careful filing, especially on a four-jaw chuck. A worn three-jaw chuck is expensive to repair and best left alone. If you have to spend money on a chuck, by all means spend it on the four-jaw, for this is the most versatile type. If you should be lucky enough to get a set of collets for the chuck, all of the problems of accurate turning of small items, such as firing pins, is ended. Centers, face plates, lathe dogs, and other such items are relatively inexpensive.

All in all, the used lathe offers a good possibility for the hobbyist with a yen to have his own lathe. While accuracy may not be that of a new one, this can help the operator learn the individuality of the lathe and enable him to turn out good work on it. For some unexplainable reason, lathes seem to have personalities of their own. You can take two brand new lathes, let two good machinists work on them

The top gear guard on Atlas 6 is open to show back gears that reduce spindle speed, when engaged, providing power for heavy cuts, threading. Small plunger to left of the spindle engages 60 indexing holes in the bull gear.

The 6-inch lathe is used to thread, while a steadying rest is used to support the barrel, which is .44 magnum.

for a month, then switch lathes without their knowledge, yet they will spot the change in an instant. The beginner will make mistakes on the lathes and it's better to make them on a used lathe than on a new one.

The new lathe market is about as confusing as income tax. Prices given are for the basic machine and can be somewhat misleading. Necessities such as chucks, tool post holders, steady rests and other accessories — even the motor to drive the critter — are considered extras! The extras can equal or even surpass the initial cost of the basic machine, if the beginner is not well versed in what is needed and what can be considered a luxury.

You can divide lathes into roughly three classifications. First are those costing in excess of $2,000 which will do everything except cook biscuits! These are for top professional gunsmiths or production machinists. The next class is the $1,000 to $2,000 lathe normally found in most professional gunshops. These are rugged, accurate machines designed to produce, day in and day out, to close tolerances. Good examples of these machines are the South Bend, Clausing, Rockwell, Sheldon and Standard, to mention a few.

For the hobbyist who wants to get into detailed gun work, his lathe choice should come from within this classification. However, many hobbyists may not have the money to pour into a lathe in this price range. The final class is the machine under the magic mark of $1,000 and here things get a bit scarce. Only a few machines capable of good accurate work will be found in this class. Some are designed to be used in classrooms to teach basic lathe and milling techniques.

Some will be found with a milling attachment combined with the lathe, such as the Maximat and the Hamilton Lathe Miller. These machines are built to take rough punishment from students and will give good service. Their only shortcomings are length of distance between centers and absence of some of the refinements found on most lathes.

One of the best buys in the under-$1,000 market, and about the only full size machine in this class with the normal refinements, is the Atlas 12-inch bench lathe. Priced under-$600 for the bench version with 36 inches between centers, it is a good buy for the hobbyist who wants a lathe that will be large enough to do all types of gun work.

Surprisingly enough, this price even includes a quick-change gear box with reversible power cross and longitudinal feeds which you would not expect on a lathe of this price. Add $50 for a good four-jaw chuck with another $50 for the accessories you will need and you are still under $700 for the outfit. If you set the total to be spent at $750, you can equip the lathe with just about every accessory you will ever need.

To the best of my knowledge, there is not another lathe of this size and quality on the market. About the closest is an English import, the Myford ML-7 and Super 7. These are available both with and without the quick-change gear box and also a choice of a standard 20 inches between centers or a long bed version of 31 inches between centers. This is a

In this facing operation, the three-jaw chuck is used. This is the beginning of a special bushing which will be used in removing bulge in expensive shotgun barrel.

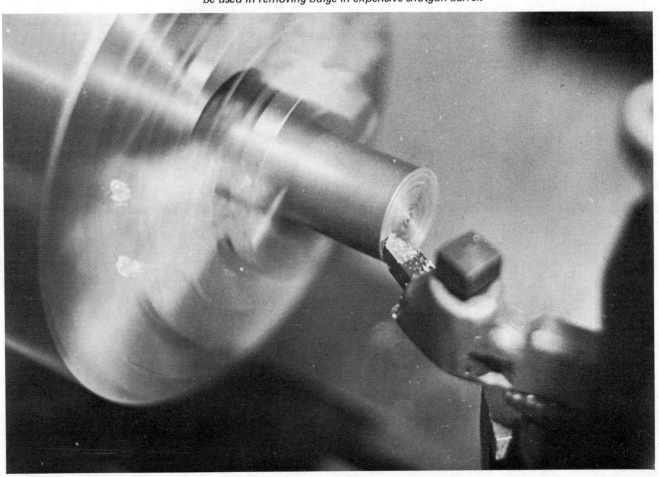

Pl. XLVIII.

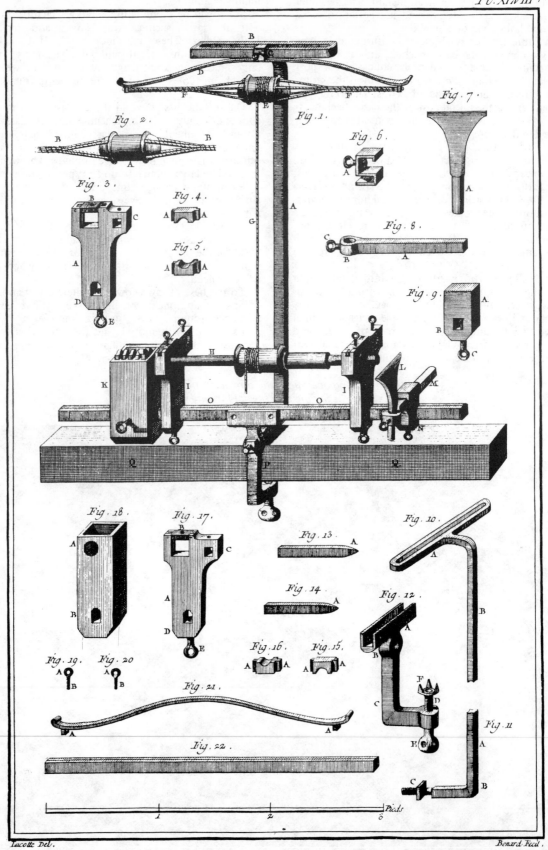

Fig. 1.
Fig. 2.
Fig. 3.
Fig. 4.
Fig. 5.
Fig. 6.
Fig. 7.
Fig. 8.
Fig. 9.
Fig. 10.
Fig. 11.
Fig. 12.
Fig. 13.
Fig. 14.
Fig. 15.
Fig. 16.
Fig. 17.
Fig. 18.
Fig. 19.
Fig. 20.
Fig. 21.
Fig. 22.

Lucotte Del.

Benard Fecit.

Piéds

quality machine and the standard home craftsman lathe in
England. Price in the United States runs from about $312
for the 20-inch standard ML-7 to $545 for the Super 7 with
quick-change gear box. All are seven-inch lathes.

The best lathe choice for the average hobby gunsmith is
reasonable in size, will fit into just about the smallest of
shops and leave room for other equipment. It is capable of
doing fully 90 percent of all of lathe work the hobbyist will
need with accuracy that leaves nothing to be desired, at
about $250 for the basic lathe. The machine has been on
the market for about 35 years with all the production bugs
worked out, plus the fact that it is used for a wide variety
of purposes. Just about any garage or electrical repair shop
has an Atlas armature lathe, which is the same as their
standard lathe but with special equipment. Add the
thousands that are in regular machine shops as a second
lathe, plus the home shops and it adds up to the fact that
the more you produce of anything, the cheaper you can sell
it. The Atlas six-inch lathe is a prime example.

I have seen this Atlas lathe in a lot of strange places.
When I was stationed in Formosa as a smallarms advisor,
there was one in a small back section of the arsenal. A little
five-foot machinist, with a wrinkled face that looked like a
road map, operated it. When the Japanese held Formosa
before World War II, this little fellow was right there in the
same corner turning out special items on that same lathe.
How it got there in the first place is unknown, but it was
his pride and joy, sparkling like a diamond from his continuous wiping. I have one of these fine little machines in
addition to my large lathe, as its size makes it ideal for
working on small items such as firing pins and screws. I use
it for a lot of my work simply because on some items, it is
easier to work with than the large lathe.

The ideal setup for a professional shop is to have one of
these little jewels close by for all of the thousand and one
things that have to be turned, a second lathe with a big bore
through the headstock and 36 inches between centers. For
the hobbyist, this is too much equipment, to say nothing of
the price. He needs a compact lathe with a price tag to

match his pocketbook and the six-inch Atlas is the answer.

The bed ways are ground to align within 1/1000 inch
and the headstock spindle turns on two Timken tapered
roller bearings for radial and thrust loads. The design of the
lathe has been kept simple, a plus factor for the beginner in
that it is easier to learn to operate than some of the larger,
expensive machines. Once you know basic lathe procedure,
you can operate virtually any lathe, but it's easier to learn
on a standard lathe. A quick-change gear box is conspicuous
by its absence, which in itself, represents a savings of well
over a hundred bucks. Changing gears by hand is not as fast
as shifting a couple of levers as in a quick-change box, but it
is just as effective and can be done quickly with practice.
Besides, you learn quickly what makes a gear train work,
something you wouldn't learn on a quick-change equipped
lathe.

The six-inch Atlas is just a fraction under 34 inches
overall in total length and 24 inches wide, which allows it
to be installed just about anywhere in a small shop. Swing
over the bed is six inches with 18 inches between centers.
As it is a back geared lathe, you have a spindle speed range
of eight speeds in back gear from 54 to 481 rpm and eight
more speeds in direct drive from 365 to 3225 rpm. This
covers most needs and the threading dial simplifies the cutting of threads by showing the exact time to engage the half
nut for each succesive cut. Thread cutting range is from
eight to 96 standard right or left. The longitudinal power
feed is reversible with feeds from .0078 to .0024 inch.
Headstock specifications are: 17/32 inch hole through
spindle; 9/32 inch collect capacity; 1 inch diameter spindle;
10 NS threads with a nose taper of No. 2 NT. The tailstock
has a 3/4 inch diameter spindle bored for a No. 1 MT with a
travel of 1-1/4 and 9/16 inch set over capacity. Only a 1/4
or 1/3 hp motor is needed, which saves a chunk of money
over the expensive motors normally needed for a lathe. This
should be the reversible type motor, of course.

There are a lot of little things built into the Atlas lathe
that seem insignificant, until you get into lathe work. For
instance, there is a 60-hole indexing system built into the
headstock for dividing operations. The gunsmith can use
this system for making reamers or damasking bolts for
rifles. Another is the wide variety of accessories available
for the lathe, such as a steady rest, follower, all kinds of
chucks and milling attachments.

Some of these specifications may be meaningless to the
hobbyist with little or no lathe training — which bears out
the need for this chapter. It would be impossible to cover
all aspects of lathe operations in these few pages, but we
can give a basic understanding of what is involved. I recommend that after finishing this chapter, you buy some good
books on lathe operation. One is "Manual of Lathe Operations and Machinist's Tables" available from the Atlas Press
Co., another "How to Run a Lathe" available from South
Bend Lathe Co., and "Volume 2 (Machine Shop) of the
Machinist Library" from Theo. Audel & Co. There are
several others, but these three books are written to cover
the subject in simple terms.

The screw cutting lathe has been called the king of all
machine tools, as more different types of operations can be
performed on it than on any other machine. It is the oldest
of machine tools and all other machine tools were
developed from it. A common lathe, with work revolving
between two supports, was known and used in ancient
times, with the modern wood lathe similar in function. The
modern screw cutting lathe was built in France around
1740.

An Englishman, Henry Maudslay, built the first screw
cutting lathe in 1789 around the principles we now know.

*A bushing is center-drilled in preparation for the job
of drilling it out completely, once center is started.*

This was followed rapidly with refinements, eventually evolving into the modern lathe. The most modern addition is the use of computers with punch cards directing the operation of the lathe automatically. The machinist is left with little more to do than drop in the right card, load the machine and punch a button.

The lathe is composed of four basic parts: bed, headstock, carriage and tailstock.

The bed is the long horizontal part that looks like railroad tracks and on which everything fits. It not only must be rigid to avoid twisting, but must be machined and ground to the finest possible tolerance, for the accuracy of the entire lathe depends on it. The top surface of the bed is called the "ways" and upon it rides the carriage and the tailstock. The term "bed length" is the length of the bed from end to end. Beds are either standard or flame-hardened, with the more expensive flame-hardened ways more resistant to abrasion and wear.

The headstock is a series of components working together to turn the work and is on the left as you face the lathe. The main part is the spindle, a hollow shaft supported on each end with bearings and turned by pulleys and gears built around it. The business end, facing the ways of the bed, supports the chuck and is bored to receive a tapered center. The size of the hole through the spindle is given in inches or fractions of an inch and called the "headstock bore."

The second component is the gears built around the spindle, behind it, and below it. Those behind are the back gears and, when engaged, reduce the speed of the spindle by disconnecting the regular drive and redirecting the power through reduction gears. On the left end of the spindle, as you face the lathe, is a gear that transmits part of the power to the gear train below it. The gear train determines the speed at which the lead screw turns. The lead screw runs almost the full length of the bed and can be seen just under the front edge of the bed. In turn, the lead screw furnishes power to the carriage. The headstock, as the heart of the lathe, is attached securely to the bed to assure perfect alignment.

The carriage is the business part of the metal lathe and the component that separates it from a common wood lathe. It positions the cutting bit and maintains the setting to assure constant pressure against the work and the removal of unwanted stock. It is composed of several smaller components.

The "saddle" is the part that rides on the bed ways and aligns the carriage precisely with the headstock and tailstock of the lathe. The "apron" hangs down on the front side of the carriage and is attached at its top to the saddle. It contains all of the levers, dials and controls that engage and disengage the gears from the lead screw to move the carriage up and down the ways or across the bed of the lathe.

The "compound rest" is mounted on the saddle and composed of two units working together. The bottom section moves the cutting tool across the bed ways at a 90-degree angle. The top section is normally kept at a 45-degree angle to the bottom section, but can be adjusted to any angle. On top of these two components is the "tool post" which secures the "tool holder" and allows its adjustment up or down, for centering the cutting tool on the work, or right and left for special cuts.

The tailstock is the part mounted on the end of the bed opposite the headstock, its primary purpose being to hold the other end of work. It has a small spindle mounted in it with a hole to accept a tapered center and is adjusted back and forth a couple of inches with a hand wheel on the rear. The tailstock is clamped to the bed of the lathe, but may be positioned anywhere up and down its length to correspond with the length of the work being turned. In addition to holding one end of the work, it accepts a Jacobs chuck for

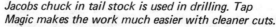

Jacobs chuck in tail stock is used in drilling. Tap Magic makes the work much easier with cleaner cuts.

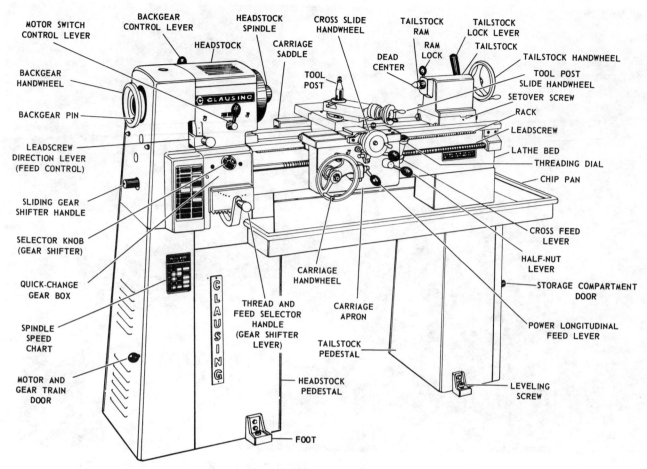

Insofar as lathes are concerned, one can expend a lot of money for rigs such as this. Drawing, however, does afford an excellent layout to understand various parts.

holding drills, reamers, et al. These are fed into the work with the adjustment actuated by the hand wheel. By adjusting two screws on each side of the tailstock, it can be shifted right or left. This puts it off-center and, when work is mounted between centers with such a setting, the work will be turned with a taper to match the amount of off-set. There are several other accessories that can be mounted in the tailstock for special purposes.

These are the basic components found in one form or another in all lathes, whether small and simple or electronic wonders. A few more sub-components are universal, but most begin to vary with the individual manufacturer or with the size and purpose of the lathe. Chucks run a wide variation and it would be quite a task to list them by name, describing them and their uses. As most others will be as interesting to the hobbyist as the wing span of a Mongolian butterfly, let's stick to those on the average lathe. As design and function of lathes vary quite a bit, we will stick to the six-inch Atlas as our example, for its function is elementary to all lathes.

The four-jaw chuck is the most useful of all the chucks the hobbyist will work with and the most versatile, as it will hold both round and odd-shaped work. It has a round base to which are attached four individually adjusted jaws that grip the work. The jaws are moved in and out with a captive screw secured to the base and hollow at the outside end to accept a removable wrench that adjusts it. On the face of the chuck are a series of concentric rings that aid the operator in adjusting work equally between the individual

jaws. The outside of the jaws appear as stairsteps, but actually are used to grip the inside of tubing with the jaws, exerting pressure outward. In turn, the jaws may be removed, reversed and the steps used to grip work that would be too large to hold between the jaws in the normal way. This ability enables the lathe operator to hold work that, at first, would appear impossible to secure in the chuck for machining.

The independent adjustment of each of the four jaws is ideal for odd-shaped work, but an important factor is often overlooked by the average beginner: the four-jaw chuck is the only type to hold round stock absolutely accurate. By loosening one jaw and tightening on the opposing jaw, the work is shifted until trueness of the work is achieved in the lathe. The three-jaw chuck appears more ideal for holding round work to the beginner, but they lose absolute trueness in time, unless careful steps are taken to prevent springing of the jaws.

Hand a machinist a half-inch piece of round stock and ask him to machine the front end down to a specific size that will be concentric with the original diameter. Disregarding the use of collets, which the average hobbyist will not own anyway, the machinist invariably will select the four-jaw chuck. He cleans the threads on the headstock spindle and those inside the chuck, then adds a drop or two of oil. This, by the way should be done every time a chuck is installed on a lathe.

The chuck is fitted carefully onto the threads of the spindle and turned until it is securely in place. Next, he

This high speed photo illustrates turning of the final outside diameter with the tailstock center supporting the rear of the bushing for the expensive shotgun barrel.

adjusts the individual jaws of the chuck until they are approximately the same distance from the center and the opening, about a half inch. The concentric rings aid in this process.

The machinist inserts the round stock and adjusts the jaws to bear equally on it, still using the rings as a guide. Finally, he turns on the lathe and allows the chuck to spin slowly. He picks up a piece of common chalk and inches it toward the work, until it just touches and makes a mark on the work. The lathe is turned off and the results noted.

The side of the work that is nearest the operator will have the chalk mark on it, but the opposite side will not be marked, if the work is not exactly centered. The machinist unscrews the jaw opposite the mark and tightens the jaw nearest the chalk mark, shifting the work more toward the center. The chalk mark is wiped off, the lathe turned on and the chalk used again. This time the chalk mark will be almost all the way around the work and the amount of shifting will be small. The process is repeated until the chalk mark makes a full circle to indicate that the work is perfectly centered in the chuck. The cut now can be made.

For more accurate adjustment of the four-jaw chuck, a dial indicator is used instead of the chalk. This instrument normally is fitted to a special holder and secured in the tool holder. The main component is a dial on the indicator that registers plus or minus. On the rear, or side of the dial, is a pointer that is pressed against the work. The headstock is revolved by hand and the amount of off-center alignment is indicated on the dial. The side of the work nearest the operator will press in more on the pointer, while the opposite side will register as a minus. The independent jaws of the four-jaw chuck then are adjusted in or out, until the dial remains on the zero for a full revolution of the work. When this is accomplished, the dial indicator is removed

and the cutting tool reinstalled.

The four-jaw chuck's ability to hold odd size and oddly shaped work allows the lathe to be used to bring a surface to accurate dimensions, an operation normally requiring the use of a milling machine or shaper. If you ever have to decide between a three-jaw universal chuck and the independent four-jaw chuck, by all means, select the four-jaw.

The three-jaw chuck is the beginner's friend and the speed chuck for round work! It too can be used for a multitude of purposes, but not as many as the four-jaw chuck. It also has a main round holder to which three jaws are fitted, actuated by turning a wrench on the edge of the chuck. The big difference is that this turning affects all three jaws, moving them in or out equally by means of a special gear inside the chuck. The jaws have stairstep notches for holding large work, but unlike the four-jaw chuck's jaws, they cannot be reversed. For holding work with pressure outward, a separate set of jaws is supplied.

Most three-jaw chucks lose their accuracy because people seem to think they must apply ape-like pressure on the wrench to tighten the jaws and stop only short of crushing the work. This springs the jaws and, with a little dirt and grease to grind on the gears, a determined individual can ruin a chuck in a short time. Dropping the chuck on the jaws helps speed up the process. If a little hammering is done on work being held in the jaws, the chuck ruiner can do a good job of destroying accuracy.

By simply changing to the cutting tool, the bushing is cut cleanly and precisely, leaving minimum of handwork.

Face plates appear as a steel disk with holes through their middles. Threads inside allow them to be screwed onto the threaded spindles. A closer inspection shows that four or more slots are cut into each one and sometimes a few holes here and there.

The holes and slots are there to accept and hold odd-shaped work that cannot be held by any other method. Other odd shaped work can be attached to the face plate by drilling holes in the work and bolting it to the face plate. Special fly cutters also can be bolted to the face plate for milling operations. An even more careful look at the face plate will reveal that one of the slots continues toward the edge and through it, creating a notch. This notch is to hold the end of the lathe dog for turning work between centers.

The lathe dog looks sort of like someone bent the tang of a round oar lock at a 90-degree angle to the round hole. The bent tang fits into the notch in the face plate and the work goes through the hole in the lathe dog and is secured to it by a set screw. A special hole is drilled in the end of the work and a lathe center engaged in the hole. The opposite end of the work also is drilled with the center hole and a center in the tailstock is used to support this end. This is known as "turning work between centers" and is the best way to turn work of any length to absolute trueness. Normally, all gun barrels are turned this way. A special lathe dog known as a "clamp dog" is used to secure square and other non-round work between centers but can also be used on large diameter round stock.

The headstock chuck is a special hollow Jacobs chuck that screws onto the headstock spindle and is used for quick centering of small round work. It will be more accurate usually than the universal three-jaw chuck, is less expensive than a set of collets and can be used as a substitute for collets for most work.

Collets are the most accurate way to chuck small round work items in a lathe, but also the most expensive. The collet holder consists of a long hollow draw bar inserted through the spindle hole in the lathe's headstock with a hand wheel on the back end and internal threads on the opposite end. A special tapered collet holder is inserted into the spindle hole from the front and the hollow draw bar goes through this. The individual collets have an external thread on their rear to engage the draw bar's threads and are pulled into the tapered holder by turning the hand-wheel. As they are pulled inward, the tapered collet holder exerts pressure and closes its slit jaws, thus gripping and holding the work. The hole in the collet dictates the size of the stock that can be held, but little variation is allowable; in fact, work should be no larger than .001, nor smaller than .001 of the designated collet size. The average hobbyist simply does not need this type of chucking and at about seven to fifteen bucks per collet, the price alone will dissuade purchase.

The steady rest is an attachment used to steady and support long work as it is being turned or threaded, but it has other special uses for the gunsmith. The steady rest may be placed between the carriage and the headstock, or between the carriage and the tailstock as needed. With the work supported on each end, the steady rest is clamped to the ways of the lathe and the top section swung over and locked in place. Next, the three bronze jaws are adjusted equally to form a set of bearings for the work to turn against. A trick in setting the bronze jaws of the steady rest for correct pressure is to insert a piece of cellophane between the work and the jaw, tighten until it is firm, remove the cellophane and duplicate the process on the other two jaws. The surface of the work at the bearing point must be smooth, with plenty of lubricant to prevent binding. I've tried a lot of lubricants, but nothing beats the thick petroleum additive for automobiles sold under such brand names as Moto-Honey and STP. I use it on both the bearing point of the steady rest and the lathe centers.

The hobby gunsmith will find the steady rest almost a necessity in barrel work. It prevents chatter of the barrel when it is being turned as well as assuring a smooth cut. With the chamber end of the barrel supported by the steady rest, the barrel threads can be cut on barrels too large to go through the headstock spindle hole. It is needed under the same circumstances for chambering. It definitely should be added to the hobbyist's lathe accessories at the earliest possible time.

The follower rest looks somewhat like the steady rest, except only two bronze bearing points are provided with the cutting bit acting as the third bearing point. It mounts on the saddle of the carriage and follows the carriage up and down the ways, supporting the work as it goes. It can be used in conjunction with the steady rest on slim, long work. A follower rest is not an absolute necessity, but it is handy when turning small diameter work and preventing the work from bending away from the cutting tool.

A carriage stop and cross slide stop are nice little accessories that clamp to the ways and carriage slide, to limit the amount of travel. Their primary use is to duplicate the amount of cut on repeat operations, but have limited use in gun work.

Centers are used in both the headstock and tailstock to support work. The one in the tailstock can be "live" or "dead." To explain, a regular center is placed in the tailstock, the work mounted on its point, a drop of lubricant added and the lathe turned on. The work spins on the point of the center with the two bearing surfaces protected by the film of lubricant, but the center is motionless or "dead."

The "live" center is composed of three separate parts. The rear is a tapered shank, the same as the other center, but immediately ahead of it is a set of roller bearings. Fitted to the bearings is the third part, the point of the center. As the work turns, the point of the center turns on the ball bearings while the rear part remains stationary. The live center will cut down on a lot of problems, such as squeaking and preventing the work from heating up, as happens when a dead center is used. Centers are usually designated as No. 1 Morse taper, No. 2 Morse taper and so on.

A tailstock chuck is a Jacobs chuck fitted to a special Morse tapered holder. It mounts into the tailstock, similar to a center. It is an absolute necessity for gunsmithing work. The tailstock chuck will be needed for center drilling in preparation for turning work between centers, regular drilling and reaming. Buy the best one you can afford, preferably a chuck capable of holding as small a drill as a No. 70 and up to a ½-inch drill. The six-inch Atlas has a special headstock chuck that will mount on an adapter and can also be used as a tailstock chuck.

There are three basic types of tool holders: straight, left-hand, and right-hand. All will be needed in lathe operation at one time or another. As they are relatively inexpensive, I recommend the purchase of the set of three. If you can afford only one, it should be the left-hand as this one is used most. The tool holder mounts in the tool post and is locked in place with a set screw through the top. A rocker under the tool holder allows the tool bit to be positioned on the center line of the work for turning.

Ramp front sight is made with milling attachment on the carriage. This doubles versatility of lathe, turning it into milling machine capable of doing many types of work.

Bolt mounted on an adapter and using the 60-point index to position the circles around the bolt, the lathe can be used for jewelling. Actual jewelling is done with a regular jewelling brush mounted in Moto-Tool.

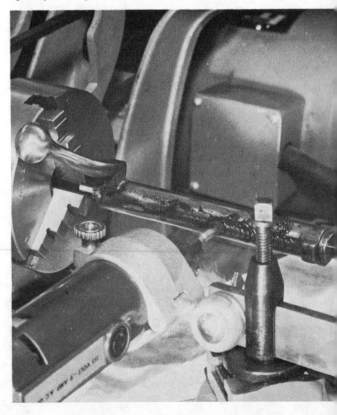

Damaged magazine plug for a Model 12 Winchester shotgun is cleaned up. The plug is being held in the versatile four-jaw chuck. This chuck can hold any shape or form.

Cutting bits usually come in 3/8, 1/4 and 3/16 inch square for different size lathes, with the smaller being used in the six-inch Atlas. I would advise the beginner to purchase a set of pre-ground bits at the beginning and study them carefully. The correct grinding of bits is extremely important and no amount of words or diagrams can convey the angles like an example in your hand. Unground bits are cheaper and several should be kept on hand for special needs that cannot be accomplished with a standard bit.

For cutting threads, a tool bit can be V ground to specifications, but a special threading tool holds a half round blade that saves a lot of time and the pre-ground V-shaped blade presents a perfect 60-degree cutting edge at all times. When the point becomes dull, it is simply ground down a small amount, reset, and is ready for more work. While a hacksaw can be used to cut-off work, the special cut-off tool with a knife-like blade will do a faster and more precise job. A kurling tool is another useful accessory, but should be considered only after the other, more necessary, tools, are purchased. The kurling tool imprints diamonds into the steel via two-special-cut wheels that turn against the work. A boring tool will be needed for cutting internally, to enlarge holes, and such, as well as a modified version for cutting internal threads.

A milling attachment literally turns the lathe into a small milling machine, thereby doubling its usefulness. A milling machine seldom is found in a hobby gun shop and not too often found in even a small or medium size professional gun shop, due to the cost. Most gun shops, professional and otherwise, use the lathe with a milling attachment, since it is easy to use, quickly mounted and capable of fulfilling just about all of the gunsmith's milling needs.

The top section of the compound rest on the carriage of most lathes is secured in place by a couple of Allen screws and is removed completely to install the milling attachment, with the lower cross feed left in place. The milling attachment is mounted on the cross feed and secured by two similar Allen screws. It is moved across the lathe bed by the bottom part of the lathe's compound rest. Just as the top part of the regular compound rest can be adjusted through any setting up to 90 degrees, the milling attachment can be swiveled to any angle. The vise part is mounted on a vertical part of the attachment and can also be swung through a wide arc. These two adjustments allow work to be mounted and moved across the cutter bit for a wide multitude of cuts, both vertical and horizontal.

The milling cutters themselves are held in regular headstock chucks on some lathes, but this is a somewhat slipshod arrangement. A regular milling cutter holder consists of a tapered sleeve that looks like a center with a hole in the front to receive the cutter, which is locked in place with a set screw. On the rear of the holder is a threaded hole into which a draw bar fits, inserted through the spindle hole from the rear. When the draw bar is tightened with its attached hand wheel, it pulls the tapered cutter holder firmly into the tapered hole of the headstock spindle and locks it there. Bushings to fit the holder allow any size milling cutter to be used.

Milling cutters come in about as many sizes and shapes as women's hats, but the hobbyist will need only a few, at a cost of around $5 each. The work horse is the end mill which is used for all general milling, such as slotting, facing,

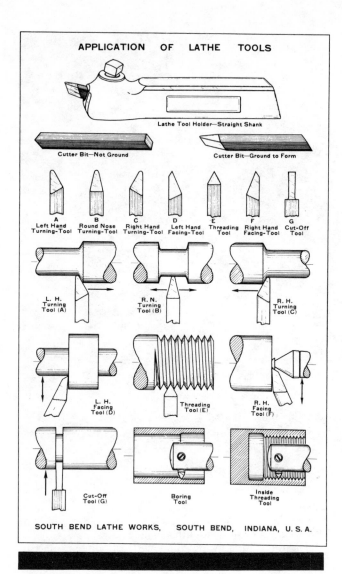

APPLICATION OF LATHE TOOLS

Lathe Tool Holder—Straight Shank

Cutter Bit—Not Ground

Cutter Bit—Ground to Form

A Left Hand Turning-Tool

B Round Nose Turning-Tool

C Right Hand Turning-Tool

D Left Hand Facing-Tool

E Threading Tool

F Right Hand Facing-Tool

G Cut-Off Tool

L. H. Turning Tool (A)

R. N. Turning Tool (B)

R. H. Turning Tool (C)

L. H. Facing Tool (D)

Threading Tool (E)

R. H. Facing Tool (F)

Cut-Off Tool (G)

Boring Tool

Inside Threading Tool

SOUTH BEND LATHE WORKS,   SOUTH BEND,   INDIANA, U. S. A.

check into the use of the Unimat as a tool post grinder, as described in a prior chapter. The large Dremel Moto-Tool also may be used as a small tool post grinder.

If you want a regular grinder, why not make one? All they consist of is a ball bearing or roller bearing-equipped small mandrel, with a pulley on one end and the grinding wheel on the other. A small high-speed electric motor turning up around 3,000 rpms will be needed to power it. All of this is hooked up together and mounted in the slot normally occupied by the tool post holder.

By now you should have a general knowledge of lathes, their accessories and what will be needed in a hobby gun shop. The question of how to learn to operate the lathe is next, followed by exactly what use the lathe will be in gun work.

Most people associate the operation of a lathe with being a machinist and being a machinist the end result of years and years of training and study. Anybody with common mechanical knowledge can learn to operate a lathe efficiently in a short while without formal training, if he studies one or more of the books I have recommended. The best way to learn is to attend a course in lathe operation at a trade school, most of which offer night classes. Here you will learn the same thing that you would in the books, but faster and in more detail.

Learning to operate the lathe is not the main thing. Most important is learning to set the machine up to do a specific job. This can be learned as you go along, but the schools and books or both, will speed up this knowledge. Keep your early projects on the lathe simple, like making a pin or screw, and graduate up to the more complicated jobs as your ability increases.

Suppose you have a single-barrel shotgun with the stock bolt broken or damaged beyond repair. The first thing to do is make a detailed sketch of the proposed new bolt using the old one to provide measurements and shape. Measure the length of the shank of the old one and determine its diameter at the unthreaded part and mark these dimensions on the drawing. Next, determine the diameter of the head of the bolt, plus its thickness and record this. The final measurement is the diameter, length and number of threads per inch on the threaded part. Let's say you found that the stock bolt is six inches long, 1/4 inch in diameter, with 1/4-20 threads per inch. The head is 1/2 inch in diameter and 3/8 inch thick.

For this, we need a piece of steel 1/2 inch in diameter and about eight inches long. Cold roll steel rods are inexpensive and available at most machine shops or you can use a piece of scrap rod larger than 1/2 inch in diameter. I keep such goodies in a scrap box for future needs.

First, we must set the lathe up to give the correct spindle speed to properly match the machining quality of the metal. The ability of steel to be machined varies and it actually takes the manufacturer's specifications to find the exact data, but you can find a listing for most steels in one of the lathe manuals recommended. Too fast a speed will burn the cutting tool, while too slow a speed will take a lot of unnecessary time. Around 500 rpms will be about right for most of the work of the type we are doing here, although you have to speed up the lathe if you are working on a very much smaller diameter.

If you want to be technical about it, go by the book and use the following formula: 3.82 times the rated surface machine-ability of the steel, divided by the diameter of the work. Cold roll steel usually is rated 100 machine-ability which, when used with the formula above, works out to 685 rpms with 1/2-inch stock. Quarter-inch stock would naturally be double this speed. But to avoid confusion, just

squaring, and routing. The following diameters will fill most needs: 1/4, 3/8 and 1/2 inch. The next most useful, and you will need only one, is the angular cutter, which will cut any angle less than 90 degrees, but can be used for face milling also. Woodruff keyway cutters, as the name suggests, are used to cut slots in shafts for keys but will find other uses, such as milling grooves and T-slots, in special tools and jigs which are always needed around the shop. Dovetail sight milling cutters are available from most gunsmith supply houses and will be invaluable to the gunsmith for cutting sight dovetails in new barrels, installing target sights and so on.

What to all of these milling accessories cost? The Atlas, the milling attachment, cutter holder with drawbar, and bushings will run about $55. Compare that to around $500 for the smallest and cheapest regular milling machine on the market and you will understand the popularity of the milling attachment in the lathe.

A tool post grinder is a luxury in a hobby gunshop and the $100-plus cost for a good one is out of reach for most small lathe owners. Their main use is in grinding down the ears on Enfield actions, reshaping other actions to sporting lines, grinding barrels to contour, ad infinitum. With a special quill, they can be used to open up the face of bolts for magnum cases.

The average hobbyist who wants one, will do well to

Replaced by modern lathe, this relic needs an owner with patience and a cleaning rag. With a little work, the machine was back in action in gun shop. Cost was $50!

stick to speeds from 500 to 700 rpms, until you gain more experience.

If you are using the six-inch Atlas and want to set it up for the cold roll rod stock mentioned, this would be with the belt in the small pulley on the motor and the large pulley on the countershaft. Drive from the countershaft to the headstock spindle would be with the belt in the second smallest pulley on the countershaft and the second largest pulley on the spindle. The lathe is left in direct drive. The resulting speed would be 540 rpm. The lathe you are using should have a manual with it showing how to set up the belts to get the speed you want, but if by chance your manual came up among the list of missing items, a letter to the manufacturer will solve the problem.

With your belts set up to provide the correct spindle speed, check to see if the carriage is moving from the tailstock toward the headstock when the half nut is engaged. If not, refer to the manual for correct setting of the gear train. While you are at it, check the feed of carriage with power. I personally prefer a rather slow speed.

When everything is set, insert the 1/2-inch cold roll rod into the chuck with about 1/2 inch of it protruding toward the tailstock. Face the end of the rod square. If you are using the four-jaw chuck be sure the work is centered. Now install the Jacobs chuck in the tailstock and install a centered drill in it. Move the tailstock up toward the headstock until the center drill lacks just a fraction of touching the end of the rod. Lock the tailstock in position. Turn the lathe on and move the center drill forward and into the end of the rod by turning the hand wheel at the rear of the tailstock. The center drill's front section should fully enter the rod and part of the shoulder of the drill start to cut the rod. Unlock the tailstock, move it back a ways, then substitute a center for the Jacobs chuck.

With the lathe turned off, unlock the chuck, and move the rod out a good eight inches from the chuck and retighten the jaws. If you are using a dead center, be sure to lubricate the end of the center before inserting it into the hole you drilled in the rod. With a live center no lubricant is necessary. The reason for using a center to support the end of the rod is to prevent its bending from the presence of the cutting bit and making the cut tapered instead of straight. When the center is bearing firmly, lock the tailstock in place. You could turn the rod between centers, but with the chuck on one end and a center on the other, the accuracy will be close enough.

With the work set up and ready to be turned, insert a cutting bit in the tool holder and get it right on the center line of the work. The bit should be the general turning one that comes in your set. The last thing to do before starting the cut is to mark the end of the cut where the bolt head will be. But remember, you drilled the end where the center is and you will have to allow enough on the rod for this to be cut off when finished. This stop point can be marked with a sharp pointed instrument or nicked with the cutting tool.

Move the carriage down toward the tailstock, being sure the cutter has enough room to clear the end of the rod, and begin the cut. Turn the motor on, and with the work revolving, move the bit forward until it touches, then note the setting on the cross feed dial. Right here you need to know if the cross-feed dial is direct or indirect reading. The difference is, on a direct dial, when turned to one-thousandth of an inch, the bit will be moved forward only one-half that distance. This one-half-thousandth will remove a half-thousandth from each side of the rod for a total overall diameter reduction of the rod, one-thousandth. The indirect, on the other hand, moves the bit forward the full thousandth and will remove two-thousandths from the diameter of the rod. Most modern lathes have the direct dial, but check to be sure.

You can start the first cut with a pretty heavy setting, as all you will be doing is getting rid of excess metal. A cut of about .10 inch should be about maximum, but if the lathe starts to slow down or stall, decrease the amount of cut. The half nut is engaged to feed the carriage toward the headstock and disengaged just before it reaches the stop point.

Finish the last small amount with hand feed. Reverse the carriage and make the second cut. Set the next cut and keep repeating the roughing cuts until you are down to about .350 diameter. Make the finishing cuts lighter, checking with the micrometer after each cut until the diameter is an exact .250 inch. You can just note the setting on the dial when you begin these cuts and work from this, or set the dial back to zero by loosening and tightening the lock screw on it. When the rod is at a quarter inch diameter, switch the cutting tool to a facing one and cut the head of the bolt square with the rod. Next comes the business of cutting the threads.

I normally use the lazy cuss rule-of-thumb, in that any diameter of a quarter-inch or less, has the threads cut with a regular die. This is just a lot faster and on most small diameter rods, cutting threads with the lathe can be time-consuming.

If you use a die, turn the headstock by hand, pulling on the belt with the die supported on its rear by the center, for proper alignment with the rod. As the die feeds up on the work, turn the hand wheel of the tailstock to keep the pressure against the die from the center. If the arms of the die wrench are too long to clear the ways of the bed, cut them off until they will clear. If the rod is center drilled as our sample is, the rod should again be centered to support its end and prevent any bending. Lock the headstock spindle by engaging the back gears without pulling the pin that locks the spindle to the usual pulleys surrounding it. Care must be taken that the lathe is not turned when this is done. Probably the most that would happen if the lathe did turn, is that the belt would slip, but there is a small chance that the gears might be damaged. I usually disengage the counter-shaft when the headstock is locked. Now, turn the die holder until the threads are cut as desired. Remove the die, unlock the headstock and the threading operation is done.

Since this is a teaching project, let's turn the threads in the lathe. The first step is to set the lathe up with the gears to cut the threads. If you are using a lathe with a quick-change gear box, this consists of only engaging the back gears and setting two levers on the box. On a standard hand-change gear box, such as the six-inch Atlas, this will involve setting the gears up by substitution.

Open the gear box cover and look on the inside for the gear chart. It is not as complicated as it looks, if you will study the manual and the gear chart closely. For example, on the six-inch Atlas, the set-up for 20 threads per inch requires only two gears, the 64-tooth idler gear and the number 40-B gear on the screw stud.

Set the gears in place and put a piece of brown wrapping

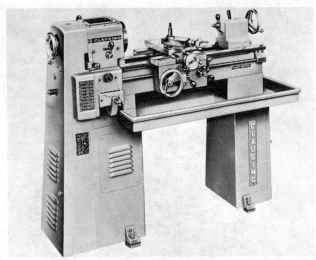

Big, permanently installed units such as this are found in large gunshops and, because of their versatility, can do much to increase efficiency. (Below): Atlas 12-inch lathe also is found in many professional shops, but both of these models are more expensive than hobbyists may need.

paper between them for proper gear clearance setting. Remove the paper and add a dab of gear grease or heavy oil. Set the lathe in back gear. This consists of pulling out the lock pin in the big bull gear on the front of the lathe spindle, then pulling the lever to engage the back gears. All you are doing is disengaging the spindle two-piece setup that has been locked in place with the pin that locks the two together as one.

When this pin is removed, the spindle will not turn if the motor is turned on, but the back part will. The back gears come forward, engaging the small gear on the spindle with a gear on the arbor. On the other end of the arbor is another gear that engages the bull gear. The power then is transmitted through the small gear, through the gear on the arbor. This, in turn, rotates the gear on its other end. This gear being engaged with the bull gear turns the spindle and rotates the work. When the back gears are engaged, the spindle speed is reduced at a six-to-one ratio.

Install the threading tool in the tool post holder and, with a center gauge, set the point exactly 90 degrees from the work, with the cutting tip on the center line of the work. Move the threading tool down into position. The final thing to do is engage the threading dial on the carriage. Normally, this is swung out of engagement with the lead screw, since leaving it engaged will only wear the gears.

You will notice a series of lines on the threading dial. The rule is, if you are cutting threads with even numbers, you can use two of the lines, making sure they are directly opposite each other. On odd threads you must re-engage the half nut when the index is on the same line each time. Forget this and pick one line on the dial and stick with it

*The Atlas 6-inch lathe, with basic attachments, tools
and gears, is not an overly expensive package and can be
the item that puts one in the semi-professional bracket.*

for all threading to avoid mistakes. Without the tool doing any cutting, make a couple of dry runs with the motor on, to get the feel of engaging the half nut when the dial line coincides with the index on the side of the dial. Also, check to be sure the carriage feed is from the tailstock toward the headstock.

After some practice you are ready to make the first threading cut. Wind the tool bit in .005 for the first cut. This must be with the point of the tool between the work and the center in the free space. Watch the dial, and when your line comes up, engage the half nut. Watch the tool cut the first part of the thread and when you reach the stop point, disengage the half nut. The tool will cut a full circle where the nut was disengaged. Back the tool out, reverse the carriage with the hand wheel to the free space. Set the tool to cut the next .005 inch, watch for your line to come up on the threading dial and engage the half nut.

Just keep repeating the process, but reduce your depth of cut making the last one .001 inch. A final trip through the threads without any tool advance after the final cut, will clean up any roughness of the threads. If you are using an old lathe with slack in the feed, you have to hold your hand against the front of the carriage, pushing toward the tailstock to begin each cut. After it is started, the pressure against the tool will hold the tool point in the proper position.

This trick is one of those I spoke of that machinists use in shops with worn equipment. Some operators simply reverse the lathe after the end of each cut, let the lathe run back to the free space, stop and make the next tool advancement for the forward cut. This will work on a new

lathe, but will ruin threads on an old lathe.

When the threads have been cut, set the lathe back up in direct drive and install the cut-off tool. Cut the new screw off at the head to a thickness just slightly over 3/8 inch. When this has been completed, reinstall the facing tool and insert the new screw with the threads in the chuck and the head exposed outside. Face the head of the screw off flush. Now comes a trick. Lock the headstock, but don't forget to keep the motor turned off. Swing the tool post around until the sharp end of the facing tool is directly across the end of the screw and right on center. Move the end of the tool across the face of the screw head and the tool tip will scribe a straight line. This will mark the screwdriver slot which will be cut in later with a hacksaw or file.

Unlock the back gears, reverse the new bolt until the threaded end is protruding, and cut off that part with the center drilled hole. Touch the front of the threads lightly with a file when the work is revolving to aid in getting the screw started when it is engaged with the gun's threads.

That's all there is to it and it can be done faster than the time it required you to read this. Don't forget to clean up the lathe when you are finished!

Manufacturing a new screw on the lathe is just one of hundreds of things that can be done on a lathe, but one quite often required in gun work. Special pins, bushings, studs, sights, what have you, all can be made. With a milling attachment, the number of gun parts and accessories that can be manufactured is more than doubled. Special tools, jigs and aids can be made that will prove invaluable in your work. It all depends on your increasing skill and ability to set work up for the lathe to do.

SOLDERING AND WELDING

FROM THE DAYS OF a cave man attaching a stone to a stick with a leather thong, to modern welding of complicated alloys with a laser beam, man has been troubled with the problem of joining things together. The hobby gunsmith must have a good working knowledge of how to solve the problem. With wood it is usually a matter of glue, screws and occasionally, a pin. With metal the use of bolts, rivets and pins is somewhat limited and the processes of soldering, brazing and welding become necessary. With a little knowledge, patience and practice, the hobbyist can soon master these skills to his needs.

Even some of the professional gunsmiths do not fully understand exactly what makes a good bond in these processes; instead, they blunder around until they hit on a workable method that keeps things together, after a fashion. The average Joe Barrelbender, just starting out, usually grabs an electric soldering iron, acid core solder and daubs batch after batch on the joint, only to watch it ball up and run off onto the floor. It's actually easier to do it right! Suppose we take each of these processes, explain them and build on the knowledge as we go.

Soldering usually is subdivided into "soft" and "hard" solder, with the dividing line somewhat hazy and confusing, even the so-called experts disagreeing. All soft solder is basically a composition of tin and lead, the ratio determining the temperature at which the solder melts and also the hardness of the joint. This ratio usually is given as two sets of numbers, such as 40-60, meaning that 40 percent of the solder is tin and 60 percent of it is lead. Other additives are thrown in occasionally for good or bad measure, and generally more for advertising than anything else. Stick to the pure stuff and forget all the fancy additives. These ratios, their melting point, and Brinell hardness are as follows:

Tin — Lead	Melting Point Fahrenheit	Brinell Hardness
0 – 100	618.8	3.7
10 – 90	577.4	10.1
20 – 80	532.4	12.6
30 – 70	491.0	14.5

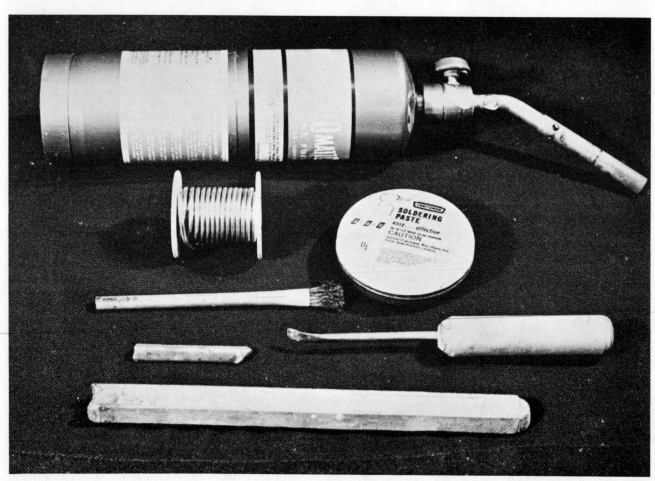

40 – 60	446.0	15.8
50 – 50	401.0	15.0
60 – 40	368.6	14.6
70 – 30	365.0	15.8
80 – 20	388.4	15.2
90 – 10	419.0	13.3
100 – 0	450.0	4.1

You can see by the scale, as the ratio of the tin is increased and the lead decreased, the melting point is lowered until the tin reaches 80 percent. Such ratios heavily in favor of one of the metals is of little practical use to the hobbyist. The most common ratios are 40-60, known as "plumber's solder" and 50-50, known as "tinner's solder." The plumber's solder is more "filling" than bonding, while tinner's solder is designed for close joints and will provide the better bond, in addition to being more useful where gunsmithing is concerned.

By itself, solder is structurally weak and as a gluing agent between two pieces of metal, leaves a lot to be desired. But properly used, the results are just short of amazing. The basic principle is that the melted solder alloys with the metal being soldered; the surface of the metal chemically dissolves and fuses, or alloys with the solder at a temperature much lower than the melting point of the metal. The joint then becomes an alloy of steel, tin and lead with a strength many times greater than that of the solder by itself. This is half the secret of a good solder joint with the second part of the secret accomplishing the alloying.

The first order of business in getting the proper alloying is in the preparation of the metal. Here the key word is cleanliness. Rust, grease, dirt and anything else except naked metal is the enemy of a good joint and must be removed completely. Remember: The better you do this job, the more complete the alloying and the strength of the joint will be.

Another enemy is oxidation, which starts to occur the moment the bare metal is exposed. When heat is applied, oxidation is speeded up rapidly and a good joint becomes less and less a possibility. Something is needed to cover the metal and keep out the air, thus preventing oxidation until the solder melts. To accomplish this, a flux is used which can be in either liquid or paste form. When the solder melts, the flux flows off, scrubbing and cleaning the metal as it

The outfit needed for silver soldering consists of good propane torch, stainless steel brush, flux and silver solder wire in two sizes and also in a flat ribbon form.

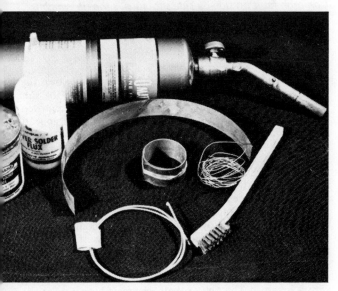

goes and floating away any impurities.

Equally important is the way the heat is applied. This can be done in many ways, but whatever method is used, one thing is important: apply the heat to the metal and not to the solder itself. As the temperature of the metal rises, it will melt the solder and correctly alloy with it, but the metal must be at the melting temperature of the solder exactly at the time the solder melts.

If you heat the solder, it will melt before the metal reaches an equal temperature and you will end up with a "cold" solder joint about as strong in holding ability as butter. If possible, the heat should be applied either behind or to one side of the joint to prevent burning of the flux. If this is impossible, raise the heat slowly until the metal reaches the correct temperature.

That's it, but you would be surprised at the workmen who ignore one or more of these points and end up with a poor joint.

To illustrate the incorrect use of incorrect equipment, I recall a sawmill owner who had a fine little L. C. Smith 20 gauge with the top rib loose for about four inches. He asked around as to who could repair it for him. However, he balked at the price and decided to take matters into his own hands.

He removed the barrels, set them up in a vise he had at the sawmill shop — you can imagine the type of vise — and called in a mill worker. This worker was on the order of a mule walking upright; strong and loyal, but not overly endowed with brains. Not having a regular welding torch, the mill owner utilized a cutting torch he had on hand. With a bar of the plumber's solder big enough to club a bull in one hand, the torch in the other, he went up and down the length of the barrel at full blast. The ribs started coming apart from the heat and in panic, he yelled at the helper, "tighten up on it, you damn fool, tighten up on it!"

The worker quickly tightened up on it — two complete circles of the vise handle. The barrels? I leave that to your imagination. The mill owner sadly turned to my friend who was observing, "what in the world am I gonna do now?" Said friend replied, "Damned if I know, ol' buddy. Damned if I know."

The first thing we need is the right solder, 50-50 tinner's solder in the solid state. Hollow solder with the flux inside is about useless around a gun shop and can, for all practical purposes, be ignored.

Solid solder comes in wire form or in short sticks and bars, with the wire more practical for gun use. A couple of small bars around the place is a good idea as it will be needed occasionally for some of the big soldering jobs. The wire can be had in several sizes and the hobbyist should have some of the thin diameter, as well as a spool of the regular 1/4-inch diameter. Flat 50-50 solder will be needed sometimes, but I have yet to find a source. When needed, I do the simple thing and pound out a piece of the wire until it is flat. If you do this, be sure to scrape the flattened solder when finished to remove the crust on the surface.

The selection of a flux opens up a barrel of snakes. Home-grown versions abound everywhere, with formulas more involved than Einstein's theory of relativity. Personally, I mistrust anything that foams and smokes, except a good cold beer. Forget all the homemade stuff and go buy a good commercial flux. Muriatic acid is a common one used by the automobile radiator boys. In my early days, I bought a bottle (it foams and smokes; hence, my present mistrust) and swabbed a paint brush full on the end of a barrel in preparation to sweat-soldering a sight on. After I had the gun reblued where the acid had eaten the bluing away, the sight stayed on. It sure does eat the bluing off though, plus a hole in you, or the cat if he is under the works.

Three of the best flux I have used for solder are: a paste put out by Sears Roebuck; Farsol Paste by Farelloy Company of Philadelphia; and Blitz by the Force Chemical Company, also of Philadelphia. These have given less trouble and better results than anything that I have used. However, there are probably many more brands just as good.

The paste or the liquid will work with equal ease, and it makes little difference which you choose. Just be sure to read the label to see if it is designated for steel, iron, etc., rather than a special flux for brass, copper, or other metals. While you are at the store, pick up a couple of soldering brushes, which are cheap and about double the size of a pencil. They will prove a handy item for brushing on flux in the right place and spreading solder in tinning operations. When dipped in flux and moved rapidly, the soldering brushes will pull the molten solder over the surface about like a paint brush. Naturally, some of the bristles are damaged, but they will last a long time as long as you remember to keep the torch flame away from them. I buy them by the dozen.

Now to the heat source, which can be either by iron or flame. The so-called iron is really a big chunk of copper on the end of a steel rod with a wooden handle. The idea is to heat the copper which retains the heat, apply it to the metal to be soldered and allow a heat transfer. Also you can tin the copper with a coat of solder and transfer both the solder and the heat to the metal. Some people are a whiz at this and can solder two wildcat tails together without trouble. I never could use the things and quite frankly, doubt their need in a modern gunshop. I prefer the heat to be a flame that I can direct right where needed and also control the amount of flame.

As to type of flame, I've tried them all. The old gasoline blow torch was once the only thing we had, but is about as safe as a drunk woman driver. It's best to make a flower pot out of the thing, if you have one around. Oxyacetylene can be used, but the heat is hard to control as it is too hot for most jobs. The acetylene-only rigs just don't work out, as the acetylene mixes with the metal and prevents a good "wetting" of the surface with melted solder.

I've heard a lot of discussion on this and tried several variations. I think the problem is that the acetylene does not burn completely and the resulting sooty carbon contaminates the flux and metal surface. Butane and air, or butane with pressurized oxygen works fairly well, but the torch doesn't seem to put out sufficient heat. I bought one of these rigs and had high hopes for it, but abandoned it after failure followed failure in good bonding. The price is not cheap and the equipment is too bulky.

The best flame I have found for soft solder is the inexpensive, common hand-held propane torch with disposable bottle. It can be purchased in kit form with paint burner tip and torch lighter, which are somewhat useless around a shop. The lighter, I either lose or forget to buy flints for, and always end up lighting the torch with a match or cigarette lighter. Buy just the torch and bottle and save about half the cost of the kit.

I have owned a half-dozen torches and some brands work better than others. I compare any new hot shot model by timing it on heating the end of an old shotgun barrel red hot, then comparing it with the torch I use. The fastest one I have found is the Bernz-O-Matic Jet Torch. It puts out more heat and keeps percolating in more odd angles than any of the others; it also has a pilot setting to conserve fuel.

Your first soldering project should be something simple, like two pieces of plain metal rather than a gun itself. Mess-ups can be discarded with little loss, which is not the case

with a goof on a gun. A couple of pieces of cold roll key stock about three inches long make a good practice project. First, wash the two pieces of steel in some solvent, such as mineral spirits, or you can use lighter fluid, if you remember to put out your cigarette first. If you forget, they will be trying to put you out!

Scrub all the grease and grime from the samples, finishing up by wiping thoroughly with a clean cloth, Next, clamp the sample in a vise and file one of the surfaces smooth, removing all of the outer coating down to the bare metal. Be sure your file is clean before you start and, once the surface is down to bare metal, do not touch this part with your fingers or you will ruin the prepared surface. Repeat the process with the second piece of key stock.

With one piece held by one end in the vise, apply the flux to the clean surface, spreading it with the solder brush. Now apply the heat to the rear of the metal, not to the front, and move it over the whole section, heating all parts equally. Touch the solder to the cleaned surface and, when the metal is hot enough, the solder will melt and flow over the surface, "wetting" it. A painting motion with the solder

Common fault on side-by-side shotguns is the rib which is loose, having become unsoldered. First step is to raise rib with light force to area where solder still holds.

brush dipped in flux will help spread it completely over the prepared surface. When this occurs, quickly wipe the surface with a dry cloth. All the excess solder will be removed and the surface will be bright and shiny giving the appearance of being nickel plated. The surface is now tinned. Repeat the tinning operation with the second piece of metal.

The two pieces can be joined now, but I prefer to coat each lightly with a little flux for faster bonding. Press the two tinned surfaces together and apply the heat equally to each. When the metal reaches the melting temperature of the solder, the two alloyed surfaces will be bonded tightly together. Allow the metal to cool naturally. If you apply water, the solder alloy will crystallize and weaken the strength of the bond. The strength of this joint will amaze you and to be convinced, try pulling them apart or tapping with a hammer. The tighter they are pressed together at the moment of melting temperature and the closer the fit, the stronger the bond. In gun work, tinning can be put to many uses, such as sight mounting, shotgun barrel ribs being resoldered, and others. One of its uses, often overlooked, is rejoining a broken part to serve as a pattern for a new part. Whenever possible, the tinning method of soldering should be used.

Sometimes tinning cannot be used for various reasons, such as not being able to get to the parts, etc. For this, the process is modified to what is called a capillary joint. This means soldering by capillary action. In gun work, a good example is a shotgun with a short section of a rib loose, about like that sawmill operator's gun. A loose shotgun rib can get a bit involved, as a lot of things enter the problem, such as the length of the loose section, how rusty the rib

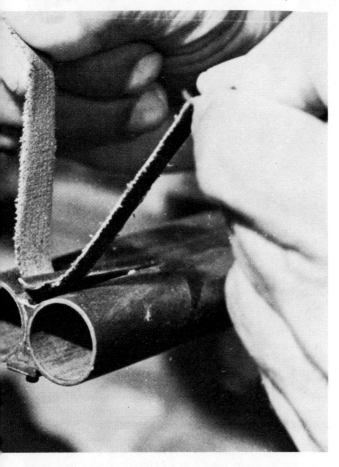

With a thin strip of abrasive cloth — the grit side up — shine the under side of the rib, using shoe shine action. This should clear it of old solder, rust and any residue.

and barrel are, and other factors. The only correct way to do the job is to remove the rib completely, clean the rib and barrel of all old solder and rust, re-tin each, then put the whole thing back together again. But such an operation should be undertaken only after a lot of soldering experience and with the help of a jig to hold the barrels in alignment. Providing the rib and barrel are relatively free of rust and the remainder of the rib is attached securely, the loose end can be put back with a capillary joint.

With a small screwdriver, pry up the loose end of the rib carefully, just a fraction of an inch. Don't get carried away and rip the whole thing loose. Slip a half-inch strip of

aluminum oxide cloth — about 140 grit — under the rib with the grit side up, behind the screwdriver. Seesaw it back and forth to polish the underside of the rib and remove as much of the old solder as possible. Next, with a new strip of the cloth and the grit down toward the barrel in place, remove the screwdriver. Press the rib down on the cloth, hold both ends up and repeat the seesawing motion.

Take care to hold the strip ends up tightly and not scratch the sides of the barrel. You want to work on just the surface that will touch the rib. This usually cleans the rib and barrel smooth enough, but you can use a scraper or a dental burr in a Moto-Tool for stubborn jobs. Try to get through the old solder and down to the bare metal since the more old solder removed, the better. If you have compressed air, give it a good blasting out. Don't try to flush it with any kind of liquid, as most of the time you only contaminate the surface you have just cleaned.

With the cleaning operation complete, press the rib back down in place tight. With a No. 2 pencil, coat the sides of the barrel by rubbing the pencil point back and forth along the edge of the junction and out on the barrel itself. Use the pencil on the sides and top of the rib also, getting a good coat over the whole surface. The reason for this is that the graphite in the pencil lead will coat the barrel, preventing the flux from getting on the blue to damage it and also preventing the solder from sticking to the barrel where you don't want it. Simple as this trick may seem, it works like magic and can be used with all types of solder. The marking chalk which welders use can be utilized, but it doesn't seem to work quite as well.

Now pry the rib back up with the screwdriver and clamp a C-clamp, with strips of brass or aluminum protecting the rib and barrel, back on the solid section of the rib to protect it from tearing loose. Next, coat the bare surface with flux, via the soldering brush, being sure to cover all surfaces. Remove the screwdriver. Place a couple of strips of aluminum or brass on the jaws of your vise for protection and tighten the barrels in the vise with one jaw on each barrel. These should be held with just mild pressure with the loose rib up. You will need a jig to hold the other rib in place and the loose rib securely to the barrels. This can be a short piece of 1/4-inch rod on the bottom curved rib, a flat piece of aluminum on the top rib and a C-clamp holding them in place. Again, use only mild pressure.

Light the torch and adjust it for a medium flame, since you want to bring the barrel temperature up slowly. Apply the torch to the top of the barrel, holding it in a position that will keep the tip of the flame about an inch from the surface. Get too close and you will ruin the bluing on the barrels. Move the torch constantly to heat all the surfaces equally. Try touching the tip of the solder wire to the barrel to determine when melting temperature has been reached.

When the solder melts, switch the flame over to one side of the rib, playing it up and down the full length of the loose section. Press the tip of the solder to the opposite side of the rib at the junction. The solder will melt, flow toward the heat into the seam, and under the barrel by capillary action. Don't forget to keep the torch constantly moving to distribute the heat evenly. If you stop in one section, you will overheat it and burn the flux, preventing a good bond; this also allows the other section to become too cool.

Remember that the metal must be kept just at the melting temperature of the solder. When you have covered the loose section thoroughly, quickly switch sides with the torch and solder, and repeat the capillary action on the other side of the rib. This fills the junction of the barrel and rib thoroughly, covering all the cleaned surfaces.

The barrel also must be cleaned where the rib will press against it. This can be done with a file, but a long shank dental burr in a Moto-Tool will do it more easily.

Some of the solder may flow out from under the rib and toward the torch, but don't worry about it. Look at the rib junction and a new, fine hairline of solder should be showing all the way up and down the section of the rib on each side. Shut the torch off and quickly and, with a clean dry cloth, thoroughly wipe each side of the rib to remove any excess solder. You can clean away the excess this way as long as you do it quickly, while the solder is still molten.

Don't try to cool the barrel by pouring water on it or blowing it with air. Just let it cool in its own good time for the strongest bond. When cool, use the screwdriver and see if you can pry the rib back up when the C-clamp is removed. If you have done it right, the joint will be solid and the rib will stay put. If not, the trouble is a poorly prepared surface; you say a nasty word or two and start over again.

Scrape the new hairline of solder with the blunt edge of a knife to remove any excess solder that the cloth missed. The pencil marks and excess solder can be wiped away and the blue should be unharmed. Chances are, you will have a hole at the muzzle and where the ribs and barrels join. Reclamp the 1/4-inch rod and flat aluminum, but with each ending flush with the muzzle. The barrels should be held muzzle up in the padded vise. A light heating with the torch and application of the solder should fill the gap. A section of flattened copper can be used to smooth it up. When cool, a couple of strokes with a file will flush the solder with the muzzle. Solder black can now be applied to the hairline on the rib and to the muzzle end to hide any trace of new solder.

This is just one example of how solder can be used around a shop. Another good use is to hold a part to another when you are drilling. Scope blocks, sight ramps, and so on that are screw-attached usually require a jig to align the holes. A good trick is to tack them in place with a tinning solder joint. Check for correct alignment. If it is off, all you have to do is reheat and move it over. When it's right, the solder will hold it in place without wiggling and

without bulky clamps while you drill and tap. The one thing to remember is to watch out for aluminum and pot metal parts.

Hard solder can be as confusing as a straight answer from a politician and there are about as many definitions of it as his answers to cutting taxes. Some people include silver soldering in this category, adding to the general confusion. We will cover silver soldering later in this chapter. Silver soldering is much closer to brazing with "silver-brazing" a more apt name. Hard solder generally contains some amounts of silver, but with working characteristics more along the line of regular soft solder.

Hard solder sometimes is referred to as jeweler's solder and variations are used quite extensively in this line of work. As far as gun work is concerned, the jeweler's brands of hard solder are not too efficient. The whole idea behind hard solder is to obtain a solder that melts at a temperature near regular soft solder but with a higher tensile strength.

Quite a few brands with varying elements are available, but those capable of good use on guns are somewhat limited. About the best one I have run across is Force 44, available from most gunsmith supply houses. It works, for all practical purposes, like soft solder, but has about five times the tensile strength. Melting at around 400 degrees Fahrenheit, which is about the same as regular 50-50 solder, it has a shear strength of a whopping 14,000 pounds per square inch. After using it to some extent, I, for one, have switched to it for just about all my soft soldering needs. It even resists hot bluing if a little care is taken with temperature and time, something that most soft solders fail to do. It contains no lead but is, instead, a composition of tin and silver. The only objection is the price, around six bucks per

Barrel and rib are fluxed, pressed together in C-clamp. Note short rod atop rib to exert pressure over the entire length of the barrel to be soldered. Flame is directed from rear to muzzle. Opposite will melt solder still holding. Solder is fed into crack on both sides of rib.

pound, but then, when did you ever find anything good that was cheap? Force 44 should be used only with its matching flux, Blitz, which is marketed by the same company.

A final type of solder that is useful around a gun shop is Fusion solder, which is in paste form with the solder and matching flux mixed together. I would not recommend these for all soldering needs, but their paste form allows use in tiny cracks and crevices that prevent the use of regular solder. There are several different versions that cover the entire field of soldering needs. They usually come in a small jar and are applied with a toothpick or similar instrument, but be sure the surface is good and clean just like any other soldering job. Perhaps their greatest use is to provide trouble-free soldering joints on special metals, such as pewter, stainless steel, copper and so on.

Silver solder is a composition with silver as the base and copper, brass, or zinc added in various ratios to match the needs of specific types of metal. It is without a doubt the gunsmith's best soldering friend, as the strength of silver solder approaches that of brazing and welding. The propane torch can be used for silver soldering, but it takes a bit of time to get the metal up to the proper temperature, which is 1100 to 1500 degrees. An oxyacetylene torch will do the

job quicker and is preferred, if one is available. If you do not have an oxyacetylene rig, you can speed up the process of reaching the desired temperature as well as silver soldering large items quite simply. Just use two propane torches at the same time!

The only thing you have to watch out for is selecting the right type of silver solder, for this can get you in a peck of trouble in a hurry. An example comes to mind involving one of my more absentminded moments. I was as busy as a bee in a flower garden one day, installing the adapter for a Cutts Compensator on a shotgun barrel.

About half way through the job, I suddenly discovered that I was completely out of silver solder. A friend was standing by, watching the operation and immediately offered the use of some silver solder he had in his truck. He was in the air-conditioning business. I kept the metal hot and, without thinking, quickly used the piece he offered on his return. I almost ruined the barrel, because the stuff would not flow right and blend with the other silver solder. The barrel had to be cut off behind the adapter and everything done all over again later. The trouble was that he had given me a piece of silver solder designed to be used on copper pipes. This taught me a good lesson, for the results could have been much worse. It's poor economy to use just any kind of solder without knowing exactly what it is for and running the risk of damaging a valuable gun.

It is best to stick with a silver solder offered by the gunsmith supply houses, such as Silvaloy or Marquette No. 1175, both of which are designed specifically for iron and steel. Stay with the matching flux for best results. Silver solder is available in flat ribbon or wire, and both should be on hand, with the wire in 3/32 and 1/32 diameters. The ribbon has a thousand and one uses, since it can be easily cut to any shape with a pair of common scissors.

Common borax can be used as a flux for silver solder, but why go to all this trouble and chance for poor results, when a small inexpensive jar of commercial flux will last for years? These are available in either paste or a water tube version. I prefer the paste version which come in a wide neck jar. You can apply it with just about anything, but a regular flat-type toothpick is hard to beat. It gives absolute control of amount and point of application and one box will last indefinitely. After some use, the paste may harden in the jar, but a few drops of water and stirring will bring it back into shape. I threw the liquid tube as far as I possibly could after the first job, as it ran down into every nook and cranny. Removing the flux from this job was harder than the soldering itself.

Not only does the flux prevent oxidation of the metal surface, but it also serves as a working thermometer for the silver solder. The moment it turns to a maple syrup appearance, the temperature of the metal is correct and the solder will melt and flow like water. But too much heat and the flux will burn and darken in color, preventing a good bond. When hardened after applying heat, silver solder flux is difficult to remove and will take the bluing with it. Use the pencil trick described under soft solder to coat the surfaces to which you do not want the flux to stick. A final aid in preventing excess flux from sticking is to wipe away all of the unwanted flux while it is still in the liquid state, with a bore patch held in tweezers. The cloth will scorch, but will remove the extra flux and also excess silver solder, if this is done quickly and with firm pressure.

Now a warning: some forms of silver solder contain cadmium, the fumes of which can cause serious illness or even death, if breathed in large quantities. The amount used by gunsmiths — hobbyists or professionals — would hardly be enough for you to climb the wall over, but I always have made it a practice to have good ventilation to remove the fumes just to be on the safe side. A small portable fan blowing a light breeze across the work is sufficient. Personally, I make it a point to have this light breeze flowing while I am soft soldering, silver soldering, brazing or welding.

The uses for silver solder are almost endless and, for the hobbyist, it will allow work to be accomplished that, at first glance, would seem to require welding. Many broken parts that are not under strain from the working pressure of the cartridge or shell can be put back together with silver solder. This can save many hours of tedious work in manufacturing new parts. Some of the finest antique guns in collections have parts that have been restored with silver solder.

A beautifully engraved duelling pistol was brought in by a customer for cleaning. Someone had replaced a broken hammer with a hammer from a common rabbit-eared shotgun. I asked the owner whether he still had the original broken hammer and, as luck would have it, he had both of the parts with him. A little careful work with a fine silver solder joint and the old hammer was like new, except for a faint line at the joint. The joining of two such broken parts actually is not nearly as hard as it looks and any workman can duplicate it with a little care and patience.

Let's take, for example, the hammer spur on a single-barrel shotgun that has been broken off. The break is clean and the two parts seem to fit back together without trouble. The first idea that occurs to most people is to file everything smooth. This is a mistake. Let the jagged break remain to be used as an alignment guide. Besides, the closer the fit, the stronger the joint.

Clean the break with a good solvent, coat the sides of the hammer with the pencil, and apply a small amount of flux to each of the jagged ends. A dab of flux on the silver solder wire will help also.

Set the torch on a soft neutral flame, as an extra hot torch is not needed. Hold one of the broken parts in a vise with as much of the part exposed as possible. The vise will absorb all of your heat if you grip the part too closely. Start heating the part below the break and watch for the flux to turn to that maple syrup appearance. The moment it does, touch the end of the silver solder wire to the jagged tip and the solder will melt and flow quickly over the surface. You want a thin layer of silver solder, about as thick as a gnat's wing.

Remove the part and duplicate the process on the second part. Remember to wrap the sear with a damp cloth to protect it. Both broken ends should appear to be brass coated. If the solder balls up and runs off, you simply have not cleaned the part well enough.

Now sit down, rest awhile, scratch all itching places and take a deep breath before you join the two parts together. Hold the largest part in the vise and grip the small part with a cheap pair of needle nose pliers. Apply just a dab of flux to both parts, touch the parts together and check for alignment. Apply the heat to both parts equally, bringing the temperature up slowly. Don't jam the flame tip right on the joint, but hold it off about an inch.

When the right temperature is reached, the silver solder will melt and the jagged ends will ease together and can be felt when this happens. If you, by chance, have a friend standing around, have him watch for correct alignment. If the parts are not aligned, reapply the heat and keep trying until you get it right. Ninety-nine times out of one hundred, the simple eyeball method is superior to all the fancy aligning jigs you can rig up.

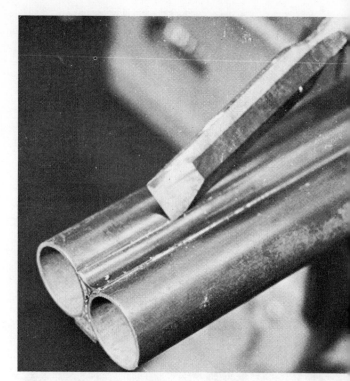

After the rib has been soldered back into position, an old wood chisel, which has been ground to an exceedingly sharp edge, is used to cut away all of the excess solder.

Solder blackener on cotton swab is used on solder joint as a final step. It should be an almost invisible repair, if cleaning, soldering and blackening are done right.

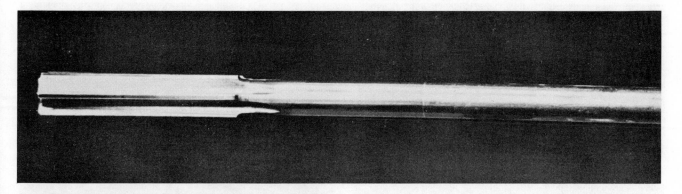

An example of silver solder joint where maximum strength is needed is special reamer used to rechoke .410 gauge barrels from full to modified. Short shank was silver soldered to a longer rod which is of cold rolled steel.

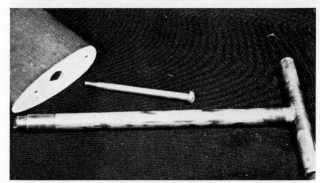

Stock bolt screwdriver is made from electrical conduit and round scrap of steel filed into the screwdriver blade. All joints were made with silver solder which held up even under the greatest pressure author applied.

Silver solder also is useful in the manufacture of new parts. Many times, a part with complicated milling cuts can be made as two parts and joined together with silver solder. I remember a fine old Marlin pump shotgun in perfect shape except that the cam on the operating hand was sheared off. A new part could not be found and it seemed that the gun was headed for the rack as a curio. But a new cam was made from drill rod, both parts tinned with silver solder and joined. Just after the silver solder flowed together, I quenched it in water to harden the new piece. After polishing, the cam worked perfectly.

Repairing screws is another silver solder job that comes in handy. Many times a screw from a gun will have perfect threads, but the head is battered from people using the wrong screwdrivers. To repair it, cut the screw in half and throw away the battered head. Next, cut a new screw of the same body size in half and throw the screw's wrong-sized threaded end away. Now, sweat silver solder both ends together for a screw with a new head and the old thread. A good example of this is in the Savage-Stevens shotguns with plastic stocks that were made just after World War II. When hot, these stocks would melt and smell like a dead wet dog with two year's growth of mange. Savage makes a wooden replacement stock with a special replacement stock bolt, but these bolts are not always available. As the new standard stock will fit, all you need to do is use the threaded end of the old bolt silver soldered to a longer bolt head, and you are in business. To protect the threads while working on screws, coat them with a paste made from lime and water.

You can also use silver solder to build up worn parts as long as they do not involve moving parts. Silver solder will not stand wear as well as steel, but there are many places in a gun with wear from use or neglect that can be repaired with silver solder. Several times I have found shotgun receivers with the stock draw bolt hole worn out from cross threading, etc. These are drilled out to a slightly larger size and silver solder flowed down into the hole. The correct diameter hole is then drilled and tapped to take the stock bolt.

Sometimes you will run across some odd ball thread size and find yourself without a tap of matching size. If you can turn the old thread off in the lathe and replace it with a common size, so much the better. If this is impossible, you can fudge a bit by filing two flats on the sides of a new bolt, turned and threaded in the lathe to match the old bolt, removing the thread from these flats. The altered bolt then becomes a two-sided tap and, with a little patience, you can use it to cut the odd threads in a silver solder-repaired hole to accept the old bolt.

The hobbyist will find silver solder useful in the manufacture of tools and jigs in addition to work on guns. A stock screwdriver to reach down into those deep dark holes in butt stocks is a good example. If you fail to line the blade up just right, you can rip through the side of the stock, but the hardest part is trying to get the blade in the slot. You can make a screwdriver out of a couple of pieces of 3/4-inch electrical conduit and a scrap piece of steel that will automatically line the blade up with the slot. The diameter of the conduit is just about right for most stock holes and all you have to do is drop the screwdriver in, twirl it around and it will slip right into the slot. Its size is also an advantage, because the long handle allows plenty of leverage. With the gun in a vise and pressure against the screwdriver holding it in place, something has to give.

To make the screwdriver mentioned, cut a piece of conduit about eight or ten inches long for the handle and a piece about eighteen inches long for the shank. File a half-moon circle in one end of the shank to match the diameter of the handle piece, as the two will be joined in the form of the letter T. File the galvanized coating away under the half circle for about two inches. Do the same at the middle of the handle also. Silver solder will not stick to the galvanized coating and its fumes, if burned off, can be an irritation. If you wish, you can file it all off and blue or plate the screwdriver afterwards. When everything is ready, flux both parts well where they will be joined. Place the handle in position, apply the heat and watch for that maple syrup appearance of the flux. When it appears, apply liberal portions of the silver solder wire and see that it flows under the joint in a

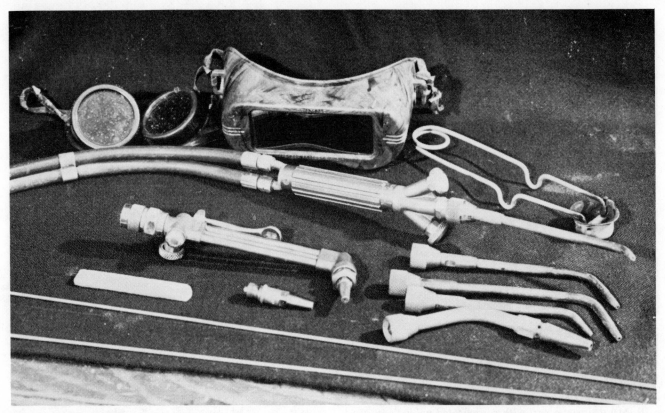

good capillary joint, just like a soft solder joint. It is important that this joint be as strong as possible, because a lot of pressure will be put on it. The opposite end of the shank then is cleaned inside the tube and a piece of round steel found or turned to fit flush inside. The steel rod should extend up in the shank about one inch and protrude about one inch. This toe is fluxed and a capillary silver solder joint used to lock it in position.

When finished, clean up all excess flux and clamp the shank in the vise with the exposed steel rod just above the vise jaws. To shape the screwdriver blade, first hacksaw away the excess metal, then file the blade to shape. The blade should be shaped in the form of a wood screwdriver bit for a good reason — the width of screw slots in butt stock screws vary quite a bit. Unless the tapered-type blade is used, you will have to make several screwdriver blades of varying widths to match the slots. Leave the blade un-tempered, and when it becomes battered, just a few strokes with the file will bring it back in shape.

The Remington stock bolts are much wider and closer to the butt plate than the others, so you will have to make up a special screwdriver for the Remington's. The holes are larger and one-inch diameter conduit will have to be used for the shank, but you can use the 3/4-inch size conduit for the handle. For those butt stock screws that use a nut instead of a slotted screw, a special nut-driver can be made. This consists of silver soldering a socket of correct size to the end of the screwdriver shank instead of making a blade. These are but a few of the special tools that can be made by using silver solder.

Sight ramps have been a problem to gunsmiths since the day of their invention, getting them lined up right, and most of all, getting them to stay on. On high power rifles soft solder is about useless but can be used on .22 rimfires. Long ago I abandoned soft solder and used silver solder almost exclusively. Most workmen, when they try silver solder for ramp attachment, make the mistake of using enough silver solder to join two battleships. For the average

ramp, only a long sliver about 3/4 the length of the ramp is needed. This should be the flat-type silver solder, but you can tin the bottom of the ramp and sweat it on if you wish. Heat the ramp slowly, and you will have very little scale form, if any.

The more you use silver solder, the more you will come to rely on it and the more uses you will find for it. Remember to clean thoroughly, use as little silver solder as possible and apply heat slowly without excess. While I have a complete oxyacetylene welding rig plus an arc welder, I use silver solder twice as much as I use welding. I'd sure hate to try making a living working on guns without silver solder.

I cannot remember ever using brazing on a gun. Any time I have a need along this line, I use silver solder. However, there is a definite place for brazing in the gun shop, provided you have oxyacetylene welding equipment. This is almost a necessity, as brazing requires a much higher temperature than silver solder, actually approaching that of welding. This is out of the range of propane torches except on very thin material.

Brazing rod is generally a composition of somewhere around 50 percent copper, 40 percent zinc, with the remaining 10 percent tin and lead. But there are dozens of special types, including bronze, manganese, nickel et al. Don't waste your time trying to learn all the different variations, since the most you will ever use brazing for is in the construction of jigs, etc. For this, the common brazing rod available at any welding supply house will suffice. The only advantage it has over silver solder, as far as the gunsmith is concerned, is the cost. Brazing rods are somewhere around 1/4 the cost of a similar solder rod. This can

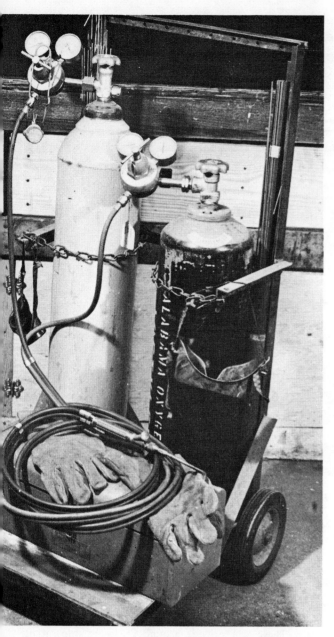

Author's Marquette-made Aero Jet torch assembly is on a homemade dolly made from bed railing, wheels from an old lawn mower. The rod holders are pieces of two-inch pipe.

represent quite a savings on large jig construction or tool repair.

In use, the metal to be heated is brought to a dull red, the brazing rod is touched to the heated surface and melted to flow over the surface. Unlike silver solder, the metal is not fluxed, but the rod itself is lightly heated and dipped into a powdered flux which adheres to the heated rod.

About the best way to explain the process of welding necessitates first going back to how iron and steel are made. As you probably know, metal is extracted from ore and heated until it is in liquid form and then poured into a mold or cooled under a series of rollers. The rollers shape it into bars, flats and such, which are machined later into a part. Then comes the day when you are faced with joining two of these parts together!

Welding consists of heating the ends of these two pieces, until they again change to a liquid form and flow together, uniting into one single piece. In welding talk, this is known as "fusing the parent metals." In flowing together, the two pieces have bridged a gap and the metal necessary to fill this gap lowers the surface dimensions of the parent metals, forming a small dip or valley. Additional metal, also in liquid form, is flowed into the valley until the surface is even, or, in most cases until the valley has become a hill.

This is where the welding or filler rod comes into the game. The principle is simple, but the actual application is a bit more involved. The key is that for the strongest weld, the two parent metals should flow together and the welding rod be used only to fill the hollow or valley. It is possible, of course, to use a welding rod to make a bridge connecting the two parts without their flowing together. But the joint is only as strong as the welding rod and not so strong as when the two parent metals are fused together.

The exception to this explanation is hammer or forge welding. This is accomplished by heating the two metals almost to the point where they are liquified, then rapidly pounding them with a hammer, forcing the molecules of the metal together. The heating is accomplished with a forge and not with a torch of any type. It is seldom practiced today, but at one time it was used daily. Damascus barrels are a good example; consisting of a series of steel and iron wire heated, twisted and hammer-welded together into a flat ribbon.

The ribbon then was heated and wound around a steel mandrel with the edges of the ribbon joined together by hammer welding. The mandrel then was removed and the barrel bored and ground to finish dimensions. The trouble with hammer welding is that the slag also is pounded down into the metal, greatly weakening it. This lack of structural strength, plus time, neglect, and rust, are the reasons for the warnings on shotgun shell boxes against using modern ammunition in Damascus or twist barrels.

For a hobbyist, welding can present something of a problem, unless he has enough of the old green stuff around to buy a welding outfit. I would recommend that, at first, the hobbyist should farm out his welding to a professional gunsmith or to a welding firm. If the welder is not a gunsmith, be sure he understands the safety requirements. Most of these boys are capable of doing just about anything with a welding rig that you may want done. Some will rent the use of a welding rig and also give you good advice with down to earth training, if you show an interest and a desire to learn. Time spent watching a professional welder is time well spent, and you will learn techniques that will not be found in books.

Should you decide to take the big step and do your own welding, you have three choices in learning how to weld. The best way is to take a course at a good trade school. They usually offer night classes, which are inexpensive, not too lengthy and offer doing-while-you-learn knowledge that generally turns out a first class welder.

The second choice is to study a couple of good books on welding and obtain the help of a professional with your problems. Two of the best books on the subject are Metals and How to Weld Them, which is primarily on electric arc welding and the Oxyacetylene Welder's Handbook. A third choice is just to blunder along, learning the hard way through expensive mistakes. Welding is not too difficult to learn and requires only a lot of practice. The more welding you do, the better you weld.

You have a choice of two types of welding rigs, oxyacetylene and electric arc welding. Each has its advantages and

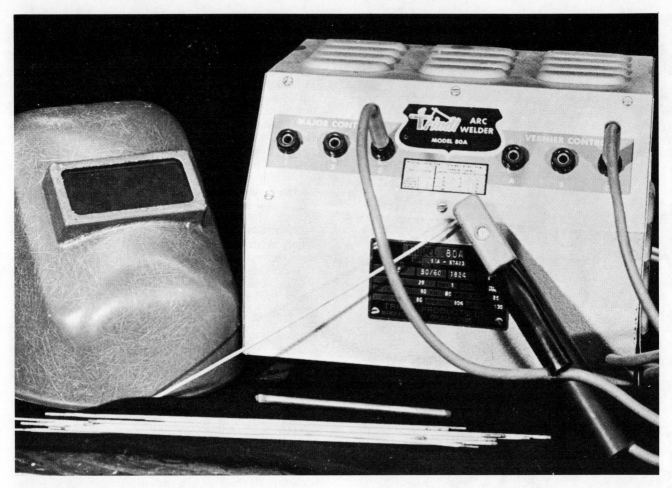

This inexpensive 110-volt arc welder is manufactured by Trindl and will handle any requirement in gunsmithing. It is a portable unit operating off any standard outlet.

also its disadvantages in gun work welding, with some gunsmiths swearing by one, while others choose just the opposite. I guess the best solution is to own both types, but this is out of the question for most hobbyists with limited welding needs, to say nothing of limited finances. Moneywise, the arc welding outfit is probably the cheapest while oxyacetylene is the most versatile.

In electric arc welding, the heat to melt the two parent metals is provided by a low voltage, but high amperage electric current, bridging the distance between the carbon or metal electrode and the metal that is being welded. This arc melts the parent metals, flowing them together and, at the same time, melts the electrode to fill the valley. The current is provided by a transformer with one wire hooked to the metal and the other to the electrode. Welding temperature can reach as high as 7,000 degrees Fahrenheit, but most welds are made at a temperature well below this. The electrode is usually coated, with the coating providing an oxidation shield as it melts off.

Another type of arc welding consists of two carbon electrodes held at a fixed distance, with the arc being performed between them instead of between the electrodes and the metal. These are available as an accessory to most welders and, in special cases, are very practical to a gunsmith. But, it is also the type that you see offered in the Sunday supplement for $19.95, promising to weld, braze, solder, and walk the dog. This is one to shy away from, if you intend to do any serious welding. There are several other types of arc welding, such as spot welding, and inert gas shielded arc welding.

For the gun shop, a large expensive arc welder is not necessary, as a small machine going up to around 175 amps

will be all you will ever need for gun work. Small arc welders in this range usually cost from $80 to about $150, are compact and trouble free. The main choice is in voltage. The light units, running off standard 115-volt house current, require only a common 30 amp fuse and good wiring. These will provide around 75 to 90 amps at the electrode. With a 3/32 rod, most will weld metal up to about 1/4 inch thickness but will handle even thicker metal with a little "know-how." Low cost plus the convenience of plugging it into any correctly fused outlet makes this small unit about as versatile as you can get. I have a Trindl Model 80A that is a 115-volt outfit and with an 80 amp capacity for gun work and I like it because it can be moved about in the shop and plugged in where needed. It is simple to operate and capable of first class work.

The 220-volt machines will handle a larger rod and weld thicker metal with a single pass. With a 5/32 rod, it will weld 1/2-inch diameter metal with ease. The market is wide open in 220-volt machines, but for a gun shop, I would suggest you check the Trindl Model 125A and the Marquette Model 180, either of which will fill most needs.

The main problem with a 220 outfit is the cost of the wiring for 220 volts, plus the fact that the welder is usually tied to one spot, limiting its flexibility. This was the deciding factor as far as I was concerned, but everyone's needs are not the same.

In using the arc welder, the correct rod to match the

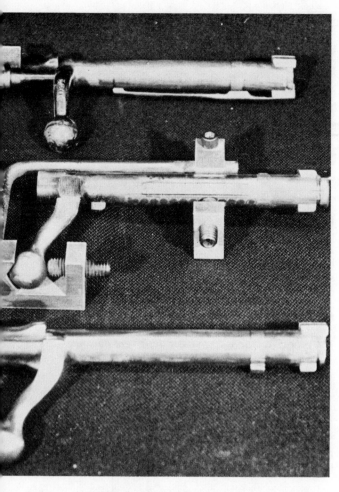

From top: This sequence shows before, during and after in welding new sporter type bolt handle to military bolt, in this case a Mauser. Top is unaltered. Center is new bolt being held in Brownell bolt welding rig. Old handle has been cut off and stub ground. Result is at bottom.

ease with which it can be learned. During World War II the demand for arc welders was high and housewives were trained by the thousands for war production, so this should give you some idea of the ease of learning.

Little or no preheating is required and the area of the metal heated to welding temperature is limited. This can be a tremendous advantage when welding close to tempered or hardened gun parts. It is also an advantage in building up parts which are close to silver or soft-solder parts. For example, many of the old shotguns become quite loose at the breech due to wearing of the barrel lug. Building up on the front of the lug with the arc welder can be done without turning loose the lug, which is silver soldered to the barrels. The weld then is cut down to shape and the barrel is again snug against the receiver.

On the minus side, perhaps the greatest factor is that the welder is committed constantly, and thus limited in his latitude of heat adjustment and control, as compared to oxyacetylene welding. The need for dark eye protection causes somewhat of a blind man's approach to the beginning of an arc weld, and pinpoint accuracy is hard to attain. The arc cannot be viewed with the naked eye for even a second without eye damage. Even the reflection of the arc must be guarded against. I remember once a trailer hitch came loose on my car and necessitated immediate repair. A small shop was found, but the welder's helper was off fishing and I offered to help. The welder and I crawled under the car and, while holding the hitch in place, I turned my face away from the arc and close to one of the tires. A few hours later my eyes felt as though someone had tossed a shovelfull of mixed sand and pepper in each eye. The arc reflection against the tire had caused it. Each time you use an arc welder, remember to guard yourself against the rays and protect bystanders, many of whom are not aware of the danger.

As for oxyacetylene welding, an old welder once explained the difference between the two systems this way: "Arc welding is a construction welding, while oxyacetylene welding is a building welding." This makes a lot of sense once you understand the two types and have used both. Arc welding is almost unbeatable when joining two pieces of metal, especially large diameter work. Oxyacetylene will not give the same depth penetration without a large area being heated, but it is much more versatile in rebuilding, making pinpoint welds and general heating requirements other than welding. The gunsmith is faced with close precision welding needs, as well as building up worn parts and wide heating needs for shaping and silver soldering. For this reason, the majority of gunsmiths use the oxyacetylene system probably ten times more than they use an arc welder.

Oxyacetylene is the controlled burning of acetylene gas with oxygen added to boost the rate of gas consumption, thereby intensifying the flame. Acetylene gas is a form of carbide gas, familiar to all in the old carbide lantern with water dripping on carbide stones to produce the gas. By itself, acetylene gas is consumed only partially during burning and is quite smoky. But when sufficient oxygen is fed into the flame, the acetylene is completely consumed at an extremely high temperature. This temperature varies between 4,000 and 6,000 degrees Fahrenheit. The arc welder uses a setting on the machine to determine the amperage and heat, while the oxyacetylene welder uses the pressure of the gas fed to the tip and size of the tip opening, to govern the depth of the weld and the type of welding.

There are quite a few manufacturers of oxyacetylene equipment and just about any standard make can be depended on to give good service in the gun shop. I use a

metal composition is chosen, and the machine is set then for the thickness of the metal and type of welding joint. This usually is explained fully in the instruction book that comes with most welders, so we won't go into it here. The rod is clamped in an insulated holder connected to the machine. A second wire is clamped to the work itself. The rod is lowered into position just above the work, but not close enough to make an arc, the protective helmet then is lowered to shield the eyes from the rays and the rod continued downward.

An arc then is struck by tapping the work and raising the electrode just above the work. The current will arc across the gap, melting the parent metal and the tip of the rod simultaneously. The rod is pulled across the work with the rod held slightly tilted toward the metal just deposited. The rod must be lowered constantly to compensate for its loss in length from melting, so as to maintain the arc distance at all times. If the tip gets too close, it will stick to the metal and, if too far away, the arc will stop. When the rod is consumed, the weld is momentarily stopped until a new rod can be inserted in the holder and the welding process continued with a new arc.

On the plus side, arc welding has several attractive features, such as the simplicity of the operation and the small unit manufactured by Marquette and designated the Aero-Jet model, which I believe is now called the Lite-Jet model. The present torch is some six years old and still giving perfect service without any repair whatsoever during this period. This is what you buy with a good product — trouble free service. So, pick any standard make and pay the price for quality. Don't bargain hunt on this type of equipment! When you make your selection, buy it as a kit with all gauges, handles, hoses and tips.

The missing elements in your purchase are the tanks of acetylene and oxygen and here you have to make a decision. There are two ways to go about acquiring the tanks; one is to rent them and other is to buy them. Tanks can be of standard size or the C-O size regardless of the torch size. You can buy the C-O size (company-owned) tanks for about thirty-five dollars each. Renting them will cost about a nickel a day per tank. This is just the tanks themselves in both cases, and does not include the gas. If you figure this out, 365 days times two tanks times five cents per tank works out to $36.50. In other words, two years of rental will equal the cost of the two tanks if you buy them outright. Maintenance on the rental tanks is paid by the supplier, while you must maintain your own tanks. This can be ignored, however, as most of the suppliers switch tanks each time for full ones. Personally, I bought my own tanks.

The tanks can be mounted on almost anything, but a dolly of some kind with wheels will come in handy when you need the unit at different locations. You can make the dolly out of a set of old lawnmower wheels and some pipe or angle iron. Get the supplier to hook up your gauges the first time and note how he does it. You can't hook them up wrong, since the threads on the acetylene side are left-handed and the ones on the oxygen are right-handed, with the acetylene hoses in red, oxygen in green color. Also, ask the supplier to show you how to work the gauge settings, using the manufacturer's instructions as to pressure and tip size for material being welded. The manufacturer has gone to a lot of trouble running tests and his recommendations usually will be right.

With the gauges set to match the tip, crack the acetylene valve and light the torch. The acetylene will burn with a sooty dull red flame. Now, turn the valve about a quarter turn and the soot and smoke will almost disappear. Crack the oxygen valve and you will note a feathery cone appears way out in the flame. Keep increasing the oxygen flow and the feather will recede toward the tip. When the feathery flame matches the blue cone just in front of the tip, stop the oxygen increase. This is a neutral flame and the one you will be doing most of your welding with.

There are three types of flame. The acetylene or carburizing flame is obtained when the oxygen is lessened and the feather flame is in front of the blue cone. The carburizing flame feeds excess carbon into the metal and is used only occasionally with brazing. The neutral flame has been described, but if the oxygen is further increased, the blue cone will shorten and you will have an oxidizing flame. This should be avoided, for it burns the metal and fills the weld with slag.

With the neutral flame established, the torch is lowered toward the metal and stopped just before the blue cone touches the metal. The hottest part of the flame is not in the cone, but just slightly in front of it. Keep the torch rotating in a circular pattern to heat the metal evenly and prevent burning in one spot. This motion during welding also tends to flow the metal together more evenly, and wash any slag over to one side. The metal will start to melt, and as the two sides flow together a slight valley will appear. Into this valley the filled rod is fed to keep the

Action and bolt at left are from an unaltered '93 Mauser. Converted action (right) has been cut and finger slot section removed to shorten action by more than an inch. Halves were clamped together, using a discarded bolt as alignment jig. After welding, the weld was filed, ground to match contour of action. Bolt was shortened, with the firing pin and the extractor, to fire the .44 magnum. The other alterations from basic design are obvious.

Mauser trigger has been modified with two small screws, two nuts and two short springs. As described fully in the text, two-stage military trigger pull is eliminated.

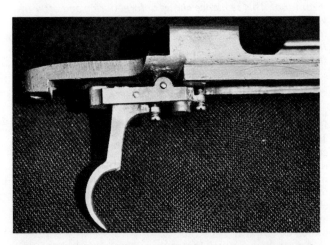

surface level. The filler rod should not be brought right under the flame, but the molten metal should be used to melt the filler rod with the circular motion of the torch blending it in with the parent metal. A slight tipping of the torch to one side will allow the gas pressure to put pressure on the molten metal and, with a little experience, you can flow it right where you want it.

Preparation of the weld joint involves two things. First, all excess paint, grease and foreign matter should be removed to avoid contamination of the molten metal. Second, the depth of penetration of the molten metal is not very deep and, if a thick piece of metal is to be welded, it is necessary to bring the two edges down into a V shape to

Above: On converted M1917 Enfield, ears were sliced off with cutting torch, ground to match front of receiver. Rear of receiver was reshaped, floor plate cut off and rewelded; bolt knob was cut off, turned over and more metal welded for reshaping. Old bolt release was replaced by Mauser bolt release in a simple operation. (Below) Close-up of rear of shotgun barrels shows the intricate matching of metals, soldering required.

torch is caused by excess heat, with the tip getting so hot the gases are ignited up in the tip, instead of in front of it.

Always wear welding glasses and not some cheap sun glasses. Welding glasses have a hardened surface or an extra lens to protect your eyes from spatter of metal. You can keep a good flame by making a habit of drawing the tip end across a piece of 400 grit aluminum oxide cloth before you begin a weld, or in the process of welding if the job is a long one. This removes the spatter from the tip and keeps a clean exit hole. A small set of wire-tip cleaners can be used to clean the hole. Another trick is to shoot a blast of gas through each valve before you ignite the torch. This clears away any dust. But make the blasts short in duration and volume, for safety's sake. Also be sure no grease or oil come in contact with the unit, especially the oxygen side, as grease and oxygen will cause an explosion.

The cutting torch is equally important to the gunsmith as the welding torch. This assembly screws into the torch handle in place of the welding tip and has an extra oxygen valve, as well as an oxygen trigger. The tip section consists of a series of holes drilled around the edge with one large hole in the center. When the metal is heated by gas mixture flowing through the series of holes, the trigger is depressed, releasing a blast of oxygen through the central hole to do the cutting.

Oxygen is absorbed constantly by metal and, at regular temperatures, is noted as rust. When the temperature is increased, the metal absorbs more and more oxygen. When the temperature is sufficient, the metal rapidly absorbs oxygen, forming oxides which disintegrate the metal and burn it. When the blast of oxygen is released, it rapidly speeds up this disintegrating process, burns the metal and blows it away from the rest of the metal. This metal removal creates a gap or cut and with little practice you can make the edge almost as clean as a hacksaw cut. Set the gauges to manufacturer's specifications for the cutting torch. Too little oxygen and the disintegrating process is ragged, but too much oxygen can actually cool the metal and also provide a ragged cut. Slant your torch backwards for the cleanest cutting. Oddly enough, most people slant it forward, blowing the slag right into the puddle where they will be cutting.

In addition to welding and cutting operations, the oxyacetylene unit is about perfect for brazing and silver soldering. However, in my experience, I have found it lacking for soft soldering as the temperature is usually much too hot and hard to control. As a heat source for bending, shaping and tempering metal, it is extremely useful. A can of case-hardening powder will allow you to make surface hardened tools out of mild grade steel with the torch providing the heat.

In addition to protecting your eyes, make sure you take a few minutes to examine your welding area. This should be free of any grease or combustible materials. This includes not only cloth, cotton, bore patches, etc., but also steel wool and filing shavings. When steel is thin enough, such as steel wool, a spark can set it on fire and you will have an incendiary bomb on your hand — hard to extinguish. It must be remembered, regardless of the system of welding, that all welds on a gun must be done with extreme care. No weld should ever be made on any part that will be under pressure from the shell or cartridge, when it is fired. Remember the incorrect use of a welding unit can make the safest firearm completely unsafe to fire with even the lightest of loads. Go slow and confine your welding to non-essential parts. If you are ever undecided about a weld weakening a gun, stop and check with a professional gunsmith before making the weld.

allow the torch to penetrate to the bottom. This can be done by grinding or filing. The bottom of the V is welded first and the sides melted and flowed together, with the filler rod supplying the extra metal to fill up the V as the full depth is welded. Selection of the right welding rod is also important. A rod too large will cool the molten puddle, and a rod too small necessitates holding the torch in one place too long with resulting metal burn. Common welding rod can be used for nonessential joints, but for gun parts, I strongly recommend the use of 3.5 nickel steel rod. This costs more, but is worth every cent because it will eliminate most blow-hole trouble and slag, as well as providing a stronger joint. Another cause of blow-holes is putting the cone of the flame directly into the puddle. Popping of the

SIGHTS TO BEHOLD

Chapter 11

A GOOD GUN SHOULD BE a composite of a stock that fits, an action that functions smoothly and efficiently, a quality barrel and, last but not least, proper sighting equipment. Each is as important as the other and like a chain, the whole is only as good as the weakest link.

Good sighting equipment can bring out the best in the poorest of guns, but bad sighting equipment prevents any gun from delivering its best. Selecting correct sighting equipment is not the hazard it once was, as most manufacturers now provide detailed information and charts covering almost any make and model. You can seldom go wrong selecting sights manufactured by any of the old line American companies, but the imports are another story. Some are first rate and compare to the best American-made products, while others are outright junk.

Once the sights are selected, mounting is a story in itself; often a tale of woe. Sometimes the sights seem to literally fall in place, while others seem to be possessed of the devil and nothing goes right, especially when you are working with converted military rifles. However, if you are using correct mounting procedure, the chances of failure are less and you should have enough adjustment at your disposal to bring the sights into alignment. Each type of gun has its own sighting problems, so let's take them one by one.

Gather any five sportsmen together, start a discussion about the correct sights for a shotgun and invariably one will say that sights on a shotgun are useless, since he never sees them. I don't doubt that some trick shot artists and sportsmen with 100 percent coordination, perfect eyesight, and a radar/computer brain are able to just look at a target and hit it without sight reference. However, most of us average mortals are not that gifted and need all the help we can get to connect with a scatter gun.

Perhaps the biggest reason for the don't-need-shotgun-sights following is that those people simply do not understand the problems involved in shotgun sighting. It's not the same as sighting with a rifle, which most people tend to think of when you mention sights. With a rifle the problem of a hit deals in an inch or so, while the shotgun hit can be anywhere within a 30-inch circle. With a rifle the sighting is done with care and precision, but a shotgun is an instinct weapon rapidly aimed. For these reasons and more, the sighting problems and needs are totally different between the two.

All sighting takes into consideration the loss of velocity and the pull of gravity on the projectile or projectiles, as the case may be. In a rifle, this is compensated for by adjusting the sights to elevate the muzzle with the head forced down by the rear sight to align the front sight with the target.

With a shotgun, the shot will drop on the average about a foot at forty yards and the barrel is bent to compensate for this. As stated in the chapter on recoil pads, the shooter's eye is the rear sight on a shotgun; consequently, the gun must be placed in the same position with relation to the shooter's eye each time for accurate shooting. It's a lot simpler that it sounds. Correct stock fit and shooter's stance are of the utmost importance. But suppose this is all correct, what other sighting factors are involved with the shotgun?

Using the average shotgun not equipped with a rib, the shooter must see the forward one-third of the barrel for correct vertical alignment of the barrel with the target. The eye follows the lines of the barrel terminating at the muzzle but the end of the barrel is quite large and difficult to align correctly. The sight on the end of the barrel serves as a final focal point for the eye. Regardless of what may be said, every shotgun shooter does see the sights on a shotgun and uses them.

You can illustrate this yourself by using two identical shotguns with the sight removed from one of them. Pick up the one with the sight and swing on an imaginary target or point. Now, switch to the gun without a sight and repeat the same swing or aim. You will find yourself hesitating, as the eye wanders from right to left, looking for the sight. It has lost its focal point on the end of the barrel, hence the hesitation.

In order to remove a broken shotgun bead from barrel, it is necessary — in this instance — to cut a screwdriver slot across the stub, using dental burr in a Moto-Tool.

A too large sight tends to disturb the eye and confuse it, while one too small can cause those with less than perfect eyesight to hesitate, searching for it. The best way to select bead size is simple. Try several sizes and settle on the one that feels right.

Unquestionably, the greatest aid to shotgun sighting is a rib on the barrel. Personally, I would not own a shotgun without a rib, as my shooting would suffer at least 25 percent. As an example, pick up a common yardstick and sight down the flatside at the target. Now turn the yardstick and sight down the edge of the same target. The edge, being narrower than the flat, looks longer and aligning it with the target is much easier than with the flat side. The rib on the barrel is narrower than the barrel and you have the same effect.

Another example is to stand in the center of a modern highway and note how the centerline seems to lead your eye right down the road. The rib could be called an eye guide, for in addition to being narrower, it gives the impression that the barrel is about 1/4-inch wide instead of its actual width. A second asset of the rib involves that forward one-third of the barrel that you are supposed to see. Seeing this forward one-third is no easy matter and each shot is a sort of compromise toward the correct amount. With a rib, you have a straight line from the receiver to the muzzle to look down and getting the shotgun in the correct vertical position is easier and much more accurate.

Several companies specialize in installing ribs; the two best known are Simmons and Poly-Choke. The Simmons rib is of steel and consists of studs silver soldered to the barrel, the rib itself fitted on top of the studs. This, of course, necessitates the gun barrel being reblued.

The Poly-Choke rib is of aluminum alloy, consisting actually of two ribs with the studs between. The bottom rib is ground to fit perfectly the contour of the barrel and is attached to the barrel with a patented process. The installation of the Poly-Choke does not necessitate rebluing the barrel, but the rib does have to be removed if the barrel is blued at a later date, due to its aluminum alloy composition. The factories install each of these ribs, but the Poly-Choke rib also can be installed by the local distributor. A third manufacturer, Herter's, has a rib somewhat on the same order as the Simmons rib.

The hobbyist will be faced with replacing broken or bent shotgun sights, which is well within the ability of even the beginner. The bead is the most common shotgun sight and the one that usually suffers most. If the bead is completely gone, the problem is simplified. All that is necessary in most cases is selecting the right bead, cleaning the threads out and installing the bead.

If the threads are damaged, they can be freshed-out or the hole drilled and tapped to accept a larger thread size bead. Determining the correct thread size can be done by trying different size taps in the hole or trying a screw in the hole. There are exceptions, but the three most common thread sizes for shotgun beads are 3-56, 6-48 and 3-48. The 3-56 is found on Browning and Winchester, the 6-48 on Ithaca and guns equipped with a Poly-Choke or Cutts Compensator. You will find size 3-48 on Simmons ribs, Savage, Stevens, Springfield, Remington, and Marlin shotguns. If the Remington gun is fitted with a factory rib, chances are that the thread size will be 8-40. But this is just a guide, so check each sight hole to be sure.

Occasionally you will find a gun equipped with a pressed-in sight, which is best replaced by drilling and

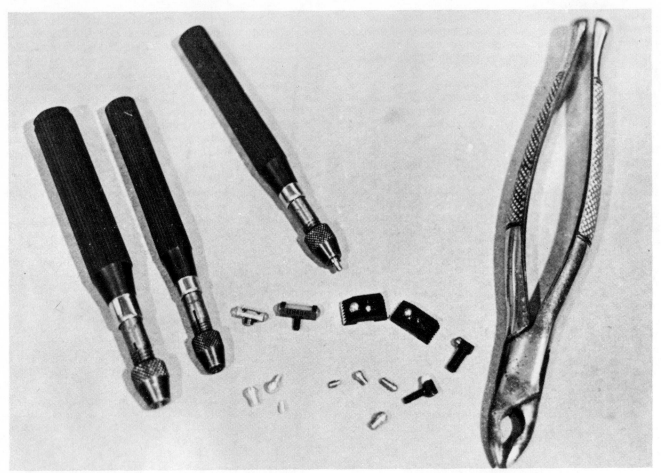

The three tools at left are commercially made sight installers that are available from most gunsmith supply houses, pliers were made from old dental puller. Sights include an Ithaca Raybar and Simmons Glowworm type at far left, two Bev-L-Blocks and Bradley type at right.

tapping for a regular bead, if the old bead is damaged. I never could see the reasoning behind the pressed-in sights.

The hobbyist often will find a bead that has been sheared off with the threaded shank still remaining in the barrel. This appears a tough problem, but in most cases it is a snap to remove. First, try pressing the point of a sharp scribe into one edge of the sight and rotating it to unscrew it. About half of them will come out without the least bit of trouble. It this fails, a second way is almost as easy, but requires the use of a Dremel tool.

Chuck a dental burr in the tool and cut a screw slot directly across the exposed end of the shank. All in all, most of the sights can be removed by using one of these two methods.

For a stubborn one, there is a third method. With the dental burr drill straight through the middle of the shank, enlarge the hole as much as possible without hitting the threads. Now, grind a screwdriver or allen wrench to a point with the sides square and sharp. Press this into the hole, tap the back with a hammer to allow the edges to bite into the shank and even the most stubborn ones will come out.

Once the hole is clear, flush it out with a degreasing agent and check to be sure all dirt and grease is removed. Put in a drop of Loc-Tite, and you are ready to screw the new bead into the hole. Getting one of these in without marring the bead presents an interesting problem, for no matter how carefully you hold it with pliers, the soft bead will be marred.

The best way is to use a sight installer marketed by Brownell's and available in three sizes. These are, in essence, pin vises with the vise part ground to exactly match the contour of the ball part of the bead to provide a firm, non-marring grip. If you install only a couple of beads every

once in a while and do not want to go to the expense of buying a set of installers, try to obtain a pair of old tooth pulling pliers from your dentist friend. These have a small hollow ground between the two tips and, with a little polishing, can be modified into a first rate sight bead installer. After installing a bead sight, look up into the muzzle to be sure that the shank of the sight is not protruding down into the bore. If it is, use a small sharp edged tool, such as a screwdriver or a chisel, to mark the shank right where it is flush with the bore. Now, remove the sight and file or grind the unwanted part off, going a mouse whisker further than the marked section to make it flush with the bore.

You can buy the beads one at a time or, for a small outlay, get an assortment of them to fit almost any need. These usually come in gold (brass) or white (aluminum), but Marble, Lyman and a couple of other companies offer them in about any color.

In addition to the beads, there are several special shotgun sights that you will need to replace occasionally. One style consists of a long piece of colored plastic or glass, held in a metal mounting bracket with a screw shank on the bottom. One of these is the Ithaca Raybar with the Simmons variation somewhat on the same order. The glass or plastic gathers light and stands out like a lantern on the end of the barrel. The Bradley type sight is a cross between

Poly-Choke rib jig is in position. By pushing one side, pulling on the other, jig is tightened against sides of rib and center hole is positioned exactly in center.

Center of the rib is determined with a piece of foil, as outlined in text. Pointer is on last fold and is used to mark rib for center-punching prior to drilling.

these and a bead, as it is a bead mounted on the end of a rod with the threaded shank attached to the side of the rod.

All of these have a special base that eases the installation, but is a bit tricky to get lined up. The secret is to use Loc-Tite in the hole and begin turning the sight in, stopping when the sight first becomes tight. Sometimes you may go too far and the sight is crossways of the barrel. The bottom of the shank will give somewhat, but even this is not enough in some cases. If this happens, all you can do is file the bottom of the sight until it will turn enough to align it with the barrel.

The Poly-Choke Bev-L-Block sight is used mainly with this manufacturer's chokes, but is useful as a substitute sight on Browning, Remington, Savage and other makes that use a ramp sight. The Bev-L-Block sight also can be used on a gun that is shooting too high with the factory sight.

Instead of bending the barrel down or taking other drastic measures, a Bev-L-Block high sight is installed. This forces the barrel down due to the increased sight height, thereby lowering the pattern. Bev-L-Block sights are equipped with a single 6-48 screw to pull the contoured bottom of the sight snug against the barrel, using a drop of Loc-Tite in the hole for added insurance.

Installing a shotgun sight to replace a defective one requires no special tooling other than those I've mentioned and possibly the use of a tap to clean out the old threads. It seems that a good portion of shotgun shooters are engaged in blowing the muzzle off with dirt in the barrel, while another portion is having the barrel cut back for one reason or another. In each case, it becomes necessary to locate a new sight position, drill it, and tap the hole to accept the new sight.

If you have a drill press equipped with a good vise, chuck the barrel in the vise, making sure it's level both ways, then bring the end of the barrel under the chuck. You will need a pointer, which can be made out of an old dental burr with the end ground to a point. Move the chuck down until the pointer is just touching the barrel, then eyeball the barrel from the muzzle, moving it back and forth until you have it centered. Substitute the correct drill for the pointer without moving the barrel and drill and tap the hole.

With care this method will do, but a special, inexpensive sight jig makes it easier. There is a jig known as Top Dead-Center Punch Jig that consists of a V-block with a built-in level and center punch. This is placed on top of the cross-leveled barrel in the position you want the hole, the jig leveled via the built-in level and the center punch tapped on top to mark the position for the hole. There is a little built-in hook that can be used to locate the correct distance from the muzzle. The jig then is removed and the hole drilled where the center punch mark is. This sells for just under nine dollars at present.

Another type is the B-Square Front Sight Jig, but the name is not exactly correct, for it can be used to locate a sight hole anywhere up and down the full length of most barrels. This consists of a V-block with a hardened drill guide bushing for a No. 31 drill and a U-bolt.

In use, the jig is positioned on the cross-leveled barrel where desired and tightened in place with the nuts on top of the U-bolt, which protrudes through the V-block. The jig is leveled and the bushing used to guide the drill and keep it straight during the drilling. After drilling, the jig is removed and the hole tapped in the usual manner. Should you need a smaller hole than the No. 31, you still can use the jig with the No. 31 drill to spot the mark, remove the jig and drill with the desired size drill.

In a pinch, you can use a hand drill or a portable electric hand drill with the B-square jig, but a regular drill press will work much better. This jig will set you back about seven dollars. If you intend to do any amount of shotgun sight mounting which will involve locating new holes, purchase one of these jigs. The cost is small when compared to the price of a new barrel to replace the one you ruin drilling a sight off-center.

One of the hardest shotgun sights to install correctly is the small back bead on a rib-equipped barrel. They have to be mounted exactly in the center of the rib. This is no small task, as any amount of error is quickly apparent. If the rib is of the ventilated type, it must be positioned over one of the studs. And, if this isn't enough, the hole must be drilled exactly the correct depth, as the sight depends on the depth of the hole to position it vertically.

A good example of how not to mount one of these beads was on a Winchester M-101 that the president of a hardware store sent to me not long ago. In his letter, which almost had tear stains on it, he described how a local gunsmith had attempted the job, only to have the tap break off in the hole. This poor cuss appeared to have made a career out of doing it wrong! He drilled the hole off-center, behind a stud, completely through the rib and, to top it all off, the hole was too small for the tap.

I removed the broken tap, drilled the hole out and tapped it to receive a plug. The top of the plug then was engraved to match the cross hatching of the rib and colored to match the rib. Finally, I installed the sight correctly and returned the gun.

To locate the center of the rib, there are two ways to go about this with the simplest of tools. You can use a divider with the points sharpened to a needle point. These dividers are adjusted and tried, then adjusted again until the center of the rib is found. A magnifying glass is a handy accessory when using the dividers. After the center is found, the divider point is pressed in to mark the location and the mark deepened with a center punch to provide a guide hole for the drill.

The other method is to use a piece of heavy foil or just plain paper. The foil should be about an inch square and laid across the rib, pressed down and two creases put in the foil by running the finger tip up and down the edges of the rib. Remove the foil and carefully fold it in half until the two creases match exactly, then crease the middle part also.

Now unfold the foil, lay it back on the barrel with the two side creases matching the sides of the rib. The center crease will mark the exact center of the rib. All that is needed is a scribe pressed down through the center crease to mark the barrel. Remove the foil and deepen the mark with a center punch. Poly-Choke makes a special jig for locating the center of their ribs and will do a first class job as well as provide a drill guide bushing.

When drilling for these sights, depth is important, as it must be just deep enough for the sight to protrude the right amount when it is fully flush with the bottom. You can make a simple depth gauge out of a common finishing nail, which has a diameter larger than the hole you will drill. File the end of the nail square and turn down a short section to a diameter that will just enter the hole you will drill for the sight. You can determine this with a micrometer or by drilling a hole in a piece of scrap and turning the nail down until it will enter the hole.

Cut the same end off the same length you want the hole to be deep. Drill a short way into the rib, try your depth gauge and drill until the larger diameter of the nail is flush with the rib.

If you goof and drill too deep, you still can limit the depth that you tap the hole. If this is not your day and you tap the hole too deep, drop a No. 9 shot into the hole and use this as a depth limit for the sight. Be sure to add a drop of Loc-Tite to keep the sight in place after you have gone to all this trouble.

Barrels that have been damaged on the end often are cut off and made into slug barrels, which necessitates special rifle-type sights. With regular open sights you have a problem, because the barrel is too thin to cut a dovetail or to drill and tap. The easy way out is to use a Marble false base No. 72 or 73 in the sweat-on model and solder it to the barrel to hold the rear sight. A folding leaf type sight, such as the Marble 69W or 69H then is installed in the dovetail on the false base and adjusted for elevation and windage. For the front sight a sweat-on ramp such as the Williams or the Christy will end the problem. This arrangement permits the rear sight to be folded and the barrel used in a pinch for bird shooting, although the pattern will be a bit low due to the height of the front ramp.

Receiver sights to fit a shotgun are available from several

B-Square is used to guide No. 31 drill into barrel that has been sawed off. Vise holding barrel is part of Atlas compound drill vise with plywood-padded jaws.

companies and are generally of the detachable type. A small mounting bar is fitted to the side of the receiver and the sights mounted on this. The sight then is easy to remove and the shotgun can be used in the normal way for scatter-gun targets. A receiver sight should be used only when the barrel-to-receiver fit is close and no slack exists between the two. If there is slack and the barrel can be moved from side to side, it is better to mount the set of sights out on the barrel.

A scope-sighted shotgun is naturally more accurate for slug shooting and most of the scope companies offer both mounts and special scopes for shotguns. An excellent example of a shotgun mount is the one offered by Weaver which consists of a special shotgun plate that is attached to the side of the receiver to accept their standard side mount and rings. The mount and scope can be removed in seconds

This is homemade barrel leveler. By supporting heavy end of barrel, less pressure is needed in the vise. It is adjustable and a near necessity for drilling barrels.

Micro front sight has been silver soldered to engraved slide of Model 1911 Colt. Sight has not been cleared of excess solder, but careful soldering, as illustrated in this instance, will do no harm to the engraving on slide.

by loosening two screws, leaving only the mounting plate on the receiver. This is fast, allows the scope to be removed and the gun converted back to regular shotgun use.

For best results the scope power should be no more than 1½X, which is all you need for effective shooting with shotgun slugs is a 100-yard maximum affair. You want a scope with a wide field of view and a good heavy set of crosshairs. Better yet is a large dot in the center of the crosshairs or a tapered post. Again, check for a good tight barrel-to-receiver fit for best results.

Mounting rifle sights on a double barrel shotgun can be done, but presents special problems, chief of which is getting the two barrels regulated to shoot at the same point of aim. This requires both barrels to be loosened from their ribs and adjusted until the two points of impact coincide. The ribs then are reattached to the barrels. This time-consuming process is the main reason for the high cost of double barrel shotgun. However, there is a simple way to do it. That is to regulate one barrel which can be accomplished easily by regulating the sight itself. The "off" barrel then is used with shot. Such an arrangement, with a slug in one

barrel and buckshot in the other, is potent deer medicine.

Getting the sights on the double barrel will have to be done by modifying other sights. Dovetails can be cut in the barrel top rib for installation of open sights or you can modify one of the flat scope bases to fit on the rib. An acquaintance has such a rig that I built with open sights zeroed for slug use on one barrel, and No. 1 buckshot in the off barrel, which has claimed three deer at last count.

Most of the new model revolvers have good factory sights, but the older models usually have a razor blade front sight and a rear sight that looks like a crack in a mosquito's elbow. For practical shooting these sights can be changed to the more modern type.

If the revolver will be used for target work, pot shots at tin cans or perhaps for hunting purposes, then a set of target-type sights is in order. But if the revolver is to be used for self-defense or for police work, the sights must be designed for ease of carrying above any other consideration. This doesn't mean that the sights cannot be useful for accurate shooting; however, the main objective is that the sights not catch in one's clothing or snag on the holster.

Barrel length is always a big factor in this type of handgun, as revolvers for self-defense are usually of the short barrel type. Older revolvers with long barrels and thin sights can be converted to shorter barrels and the sights modified to match the modern ones. A modern revolver with a long barrel and new-type sights also can be converted to a snubnose. On Colts, length of the barrel presents little problem, as it simply can be cut to the desired length and the sights reinstalled. Smith and Wesson's barrel lug limits the amount of barrel that can be cut off. The barrel can be cut behind the lug, but this destroys the tight lock up of the cylinder pin, both fore and aft. It is a good idea to cut the Smith and Wesson revolver barrels no closer than within 1/4 inch of the lug.

Before you get happy with the hacksaw, regardless of the make of any revolver, take a few measurements of the sights. The front sight is higher on a long barrel revolver to compensate for the upward whip of the barrel as it is fired, but this height is constant and can be put to good use. Lay a straight edge, such as a ruler, with the edge in the rear sight notch and also touching the top of the front sight. Now measure from the straight edge down to the barrel at the point it will be cut and note the measurement. This can be done with a pair of dividers. This measurement will be close to the new sight height, but add 1/16 inch to allow for adjustment.

After the barrel is cut to desired length, the matter of sight selection can be simple or complicated. The simple way is to use the blade sight in the discarded barrel and to make the new sight. To get it off the end, make a cut across the barrel just behind the sight down into the bore, and a similar cut of a similar depth, directly in front of the sight. Next, make the cut on the side of the sight connecting the front and rear cut. Make a similar cut on the opposite side to allow the sight to be completely removed as a unit.

Remove the sight and mount it upside down in the vise. With a half-round file, cut the barrel section away until you are down to the sight base. The sight then is mounted on the barrel by soldering, but naturally it will be too high. Use the dividers to mark the correct height you arrived at with the straight edge and file the sight down to this mark. Most of these blades are tapered, so the new low sight will be much wider, which is exactly what you want.

Shape the front sight to the shape of the new snub-nose sights and switch to the rear sight. This can be modified quickly to conform to the new sight width by enlarging the notch with a needle file. The notch should be just wide enough that, as the revolver is held at arm's length, a tiny sliver of light will show on each side of the front sight when it is centered in the notch. Such a sight change is simple yet attractive and, if correctly done, will provide the desired accuracy.

The more complicated way is to make a full ramp front sight which can be a modified rifle ramp cut down or you can go the full route and whack one out of bar stock. If you use a rifle ramp, half of the work has already been done. The ramp will probably be too long, but you will need to cut the dovetail section away regardless.

Place the ramp on the barrel and note the fit of the ramp to the barrel contour, which probably will be off where the barrel joins the frame. This can be shaped with a file, but a Dremel tool and grindstone will do it faster. When the barrel is flush with the ramp from front to rear, mark the overhang of the ramp and hacksaw this off. Next, file the end of the ramp until it is about 1/8 inch shorter than the barrel. You can shape the ramp while it is held in a vise, but it is a lot easier to work on with the ramp attached to the barrel. Silver solder will provide the strongest joint.

When the ramp is in place, cut down on each side about half the depth of the ramp at the front to form the blade, which should be on the order of a ramp itself, to avoid snagging when drawn from a pocket or holster. A new snub-nose revolver will serve as a good pattern for your sights.

The ramp can be made from bar stock; the easiest to work is the stock available at most machine shops. If you have a milling machine or milling attachment for a lathe, the ramp manufacture is relatively simple. Even without these, you still can make an attractive ramp with hand files. Start by laying out the angle for the ramp, making sure it is a good half-inch longer that the finished ramp will be. Cut the blank out of the key stock with a hacksaw and rough file it to shape. Now with the ramp belly-up in the vise, locate the exact center with dividers and draw a line down the full length of the ramp. With a triangular file, notch each end of the line about 1/16 inch deep and 1/4 inch long. This is your starting mark.

Switch to your hacksaw and make a cut right on the line connecting the two end notches to a depth of about 1/8 inch. Go back to the triangular file and widen the notch until you have a wide V to the full depth of the hacksaw cut. Switch to a round or half round file and widen the V to a U with a contour to match the barrel. Finally, fit the ramp to the barrel and proceed as described for the modified rifle ramp. I have advised the use of silver solder to attach the ramp. Soft solder does not require as much heat, but sights attached with it on a large caliber revolver have the habit of flying off into the brush. With silver solder the joint is solid and, by concentrating the heat more on the ramp than on the barrel, the rifling will not be damaged.

Usually the existing rear notch can be widened sufficiently to serve, but on a few revolvers it will be necessary to make a new sight. About the simplest way is to file a flat where the old sight notch is, and on it silver solder a piece of metal large enough to be shaped into a new sight. Edges and corners should be rounded to prevent snagging on clothing. If you want a larger rear sight or one that can be adjusted, go to a full set of target sights. Micro makes a good set of sights for revolvers, if maximum accuracy is desired. Another way is to modify a set of Smith and Wesson or Colt adjustable sights to the revolver, but this gets involved and usually necessitates the use of a milling machine.

The automatic — or to be more correct, the semi-automatic — pistol presents quite a different problem for improved sights. The small automatics, for the most part, are made for self-defense, sights designed to aim the pistol in the general direction of the target. If you are willing to go to a lot of trouble, it is possible to improve the accuracy of these guns greatly. I remember an Air Force captain who came into the shop with a .25 automatic Browning that he wanted accurized with a good set of sights. Having served as an instructor in a survival school and with orders to report to Vietnam, he had definite ideas on what kind of gun to carry. I did everything possible to tighten the little pea shooter up and assure smooth function, which is no small thing with any .25 automatic. For a set of sights, the top of the slide was filed smooth, removing any trace of the old sights and presenting a flat surface to work with. Next, a piece of key stock was cut to the general overall length and a rib-sight affair filed out. This was a full-length rib with front sight attached and a dovetail slot at the rear to accept an equally small rear sight.

This was silver soldered in place on the prepared slide and, with careful shooting, the little pistol was delivering surprising accuracy with a two-hand hold at 20 yards, which was about its maximum range. The whole thing, with a couple of extra clips, occupied about the space of a pack

Smith & Wesson revolver sight has been installed on the M1911 for target use. Original sight is filed flush with side, slot milled or filed the length of rear of slide to accept tang, with screw at front, headless screw at rear.

Ruler, dividers are used to determine overall height of a new sight, before barrel of S&W revolver is shortened.

of king-size cigarettes and was easily stored in a flight suit. In the hand of a good shot it would provide a man with enough game to survive on, which was the whole idea in the first place.

Since then, I have remodeled several of the small automatics this way and have found it best to simply file the top of the slide flat and start all over with sight construction. Trying to make the original sights perform is a lost cause from the start.

Most sight work on automatics will be installation of target sights, such as on an M-1911 .45 automatic. If you are installing these sights, is should always be remembered the gun itself must deliver the desired accuracy, so the sights should be a part of a general tightening up or accurizing process. All of the large automatics will present similar problems and installation of the sights will follow approximately the same procedure. Two of the best known target sight manufacturers are Micro and Bo-Mar. Choice between them is a matter of personal preference rather than performance difference. Any sight desired, from a fixed rear to a full-length rib incorporating both sights, is available. Also target sights on some of the new revolvers and automatic pistols can be converted or modified to work on other makes and models.

Colt Single Action has a square notch cut as rear sight instead of standard V, matching new square front sight.

For the .45 automatic there is a choice of four basic types of sights. The simple one consists of a target front sight and a fixed non-adjustable rear sight to match the front one. This is a good choice for the man who wants the wide target-type sights, but is not interested in a fully adjustable rear sight. The front blade is installed the same way as' the other versions, but the rear sight is simply installed in place of the original sight, with little or no modification to the rear dovetail slot. Windage adjustment is made by shifting the rear sight in the dovetail, while any elevation adjustment must be made by filing of either the front or rear, but this seldom is needed. The second and most popular type consists of the same sight as the first one on the front, but the rear sight is fully adjustable for both windage and elevation. The rear sight is designed to slip into the standard dovetail slot without any major recutting of the dovetail.

The third type is the low profile sight, similar in appearance to the standard adjustable model but presenting a lower mounted sight, both front and rear. This sight requires enlarging the dovetail slot, as well as cutting away a small portion of the slide directly behind the dovetail. This cut is made best with a milling cutter, but can be done with files.

The fourth type is the rib model which consists of a full-length rib with the front and rear sights incorporated into it. In some models, this includes the rib extending past the muzzle of the pistol for added sighting radius. The hobbyist, unless he is a confirmed target shooter, seldom will find a need for this type.

I prefer to install the rear sight first and use it as a reference to get the front sight aligned correctly, but it can be done either way. On the first two types described, remove the old sight from the dovetail and be sure the slot is clear of all dirt, grease and grime before starting to pound in the new sight. With the fingers only, see if the sight dovetail will enter the slot at all. Chances are it will go in with little trouble, but some will need a little help. If the sight will not enter the dovetail slot, use a three-cornered file with two sides ground safe to widen the slot slightly on the right side of the receiver. This is with the gun pointed away from you.

Now try the sight in the slot again. When it will enter the slot easily, tap it lightly until it goes all the way in, relieving and widening the slot as needed. The sight should be firm against the slot and not movable with finger pressure. Most of the adjustable sights have a small lock screw incorporated into the sight, to lock the sight in position in the dovetail slot.

The best for this is a "sight file," a three-cornered type with the sides parallel instead of tapered and a cutting edge on one side only. When tapping the sight into place, prevent battering the sides by using a plastic hammer or a piece of plastic held against the side of the sight.

For installing the low profile rear sights — type three alone — a milling machine or milling attachment for the lathe with end mills and a sight mill are quickest and best. But it can be done with files, the quality of the job in direct proportion to your patience.

The first step is to cut down the rear of the slide behind the dovetail to clear the rear portion of the sight. Measure the distance from the bottom of the sight dovetail to the sight itself on the front. This front part must be just touching the top of the slide. With this figure, compare it to your dovetail slot distance from the bottom of the slot to the top of the slide. If the slot is not deep enough, it will have to be deepened, but hold off on this for the present, as all you want at this point is some idea of how deep you will have to cut. Now, measure the amount you will have to cut the rear of the slide down. To do this, lay your six-inch rule along the side of the sight, covering up the dovetail and you will see a gap. This tells you how much the rear of the slide will have to be cut down.

Another way is to parallel the edge of the rule with the bottom of the sight in front of the dovetail, covering up the top part of the sight, and note the difference between the edge of the rule and the bottom edge of the sight at the rear of the dovetail. Either way, use a divider to measure the distance.

The Bo-Mar sight is measured this way, but for the Micro rear sight of the low profile type, there is no front overhang to speak of and measuring is harder. Since there are several variations of these low profile sights, common sense has to be used in checking to see how much metal has to be removed from where. But these measuring methods will work and also give you a good understanding of what is required.

After determining how much metal to remove behind the dovetail, check how wide the dovetail must be re-cut to accept the low profile dovetail. This will vary among models, some requiring considerable metal removal while others need only a couple of strokes of the file.

Finally, begin cutting down on the rear of the slide behind the dovetail about 3/4 of your measured distance, leaving the final 1/4 for final fitting. Now, widen the dovetail in the slot and note how much additional metal must be removed to get the sight down far enough. In most cases, this can be done by holding the sight in position with the finger and making an eyeball calibration. Take your time and cut a little, measure, cut a little and measure again.

Finally, the sight will be fitted as far as depth is concerned and all that's left is the widening of the slot if necessary. In most cases this should be done by cutting the front part of the slot rather than the rear. Cutting the rear will move the sight backward and may interfere with the function of the hammer or the ease of cocking it. The low profile sight is more trouble than the first two types, but worth the effort if the pistol is to be carried in a holster. The fourth type of target sight, the full-length rib, is installed on top of the slide and attached by drilling and tapping holes to receive the mounting screws.

The front sight on the first three types presents a problem. The first thing that must be done is remove the original sight which is staked in place. The simplest way is to file it off flush with the top of the slide. When you get to this point, switch from the file to a 1/32-inch punch and a hammer. Place the end of the punch halfway of the remaining stub of the front sight and give it a quick whack with a hammer. The stub should punch right through the slide, coming out to carry with it a couple of small slivers on each side of the stub. You will be left with a slightly rectangular hole in the slide and a small recess that retained the old blade. Now, take a good look at the target front sight. You will see that a small stub extends down from the bottom of the sight. This stub is supposed to go through the hole in the slide where the old sight was, but the hole will have to be enlarged slightly to accept it. This can be accomplished with careful filing, using needle files, or done quickly with a dental burr and the Dremel tool. The hole should be just large enough to provide a snug fit on the sight stud with the bottom of the sight blade snug against the top of the slide.

The sight can be held in place by shortening the stub and staking it in place from underneath. This leaves a bit to be desired, as the big blade presents a good target for a side blow which will loosen it. The staking can be in conjunction with soft solder for a more permanent arrangement. Either of these methods can be used, if the slide is not to be reblued and both will do a good job. The best bet

Dovetail for a loose front sight has been center-punched on the bottom of the slot. This helps to tighten sight.

Homemade sight punch, the end filed to match contour of sight base, is used to remove or install dovetail sights.

is to silver solder the blade in place. This requires that the slide be reblued, as it is difficult to silver solder the sight on without messing up the bluing or having some the silver solder run and require dressing with a file. If the slide is not to be reblued, use the staking or the solder and staking combined. If you use the silver solder, I guarantee the sight will stay put.

To do this, clean the stud of all grease, grime or bluing right down to the bare metal and apply a tiny amount of flux to the stud. Flow a thin coat of silver solder on the stud, the thinner the better. Next, carefully coat the hole with flux and tap the sight stud down in place. With the torch on low heat, insert the nozzle or tip up inside of the slide to apply the heat from underneath. Watch closely and the silver solder will flow down into the hole. Remove the torch and allow the slide to cool. Getting the sight exactly vertical while you are doing this is the problem I mentioned and the reason I install the rear sight first.

Have someone eyeball the front blade while you are busy with the torch. If the sight is not vertical, just reheat

Williams front sight pusher is in operation. It can be used to remove, install sights in ramp without damage.

To rebuild sight bead, shank is filed so it will accept piece of brazing rod, which is soft soldered, shaped.

the sight from underneath and straighten it again. Be sure to check that the sides of the blade are parallel with the sides of the slide.

With the blade attached in the correct position, cut any of the stub that protrudes through the slide and interferes with the barrel bushing. You can file or grind it off with a small mounted grinder in the Dremel tool. Switch to a polishing wheel in the Dremel tool and polish the fills and grind marks off. Try the barrel bushing to be sure it is working correctly and your sight installation is complete.

Most of the old target handguns can be worked over by installing the new Micro or Bo-Mar sights similar to those described. Odd-ball automatics, for which no specific model is made, can have a new set of target sights by adapting sights designed for one of the standard models. About the easiest are those automatics with the same basic configuration as the M1911, such as the Radom, Tokarev and others. Usually you can adapt the M1911 sights to these guns. Another source of target sights for odd-balls is to adapt a revolver sight as, for example, from a Smith & Wesson.

This also can be adapted for the M1911, but it requires the use of a milling machine or a wizard with a file.

Open rifle sights, that is, those with a V or U notch on an upright leaf attached to the rear of the barrel and a front sight of some sort will be encountered more than other types, simply because these are the most common, due to their low cost. It seems that half of the open sight owners are involved in losing the rear sight elevator, while the other half are busy knocking off the front sight or bending it. From my experience, these are the two most common faults, with a worn dovetail slot running a close third. The dovetail slots get most of their wear from the owner moving the sight back and forth trying to "get her dead center."

How all the sight elevators get lost is a mystery, but it is a common problem, which makes evident that every manufacture seems to have his own ideas as to length, width, and number of steps. The best solution is to secure a duplicate of the original, which sometimes is hard to do, since the manufacturers require each new vice-president to design a new sight elevator which adds to the merriment. If a duplicate elevator is not available, it sometimes is possible to modify another breed by thinning the sides, shortening it, and so on.

If all else fails, manufacture a replacement, as all that is needed is a file or two and a piece of scrap metal. The metal selected should fit snugly in the sight slot with smooth sides.

Cut off a tapered sliver just a little longer than the finished elevator will be and chuck it in the vise. File both edges smooth and square up the back side. The elevating notches should not be cut exactly parallel with the bottom of the elevator, but should slope slightly toward the large end of the elevator to hold the sight blade in place.

When the steps have been cut with the file, try your new elevator in the sight and file and adjust until it is working properly. Finish up by coloring the new elevator with touch-up blue or heating it until it turns blue and quickly quenching it in oil. Most of the sights will be in good shape, but occasionally the upright leaf will be bent and require straightening. It is best to heat the blade when you do this. Some of the V or U notches will be worn or battered and will require recutting with a needle file.

Bent front sights can sometimes be straightened by heating with a propane torch and bending with a pair of pliers. Broken sights, on the other hand, are best removed by punching out from left to right and substituting a new sight. Sometimes this is not possible and the sight must be repaired. If the blade is broken all the way or halfway off, it is best to file off the remaining stub flush with the sight base or at least down to an even horizontal line. A new sight or stub is sweat silver soldered back on the original stub and filed to the desired shape. If this is done right, only a thin line of solder will show. This, by the way, is a good trick with some of the M-1 carbines that shoot too high and require a higher front sight than is available.

If only the bead part of the sight is damaged or sheared off, you can make another bead from brass rod. File the top of the stub straight horizontally, then with a needle file cut out a shallow trench the length of the top of the stub. Tin this with soft solder, removing any excess. Now tin a short section of brass rod — brazing rod works fine — the diameter you wish the bead to be. Place it in the prepared trench and sweat solder it in place. Finish up by removing any soft solder that is showing, use touch-up blue and polish the sighting end of the rod.

Our final problem of the three is the battered and worn dovetail slots which can be repaired usually with a few deft strokes of the hammer and punch. With the sight removed and a center punch in hand, place the tip of the punch on the bottom of the dovetail slot and give the punch a whack with the hammer. A small pimple of metal will be raised around the punch mark. A couple of these punch marks usually will extrude enough metal to tighten the sight in the dovetail slot. You also can peen the top of the dovetail slot lightly, forcing the overhang downwards to give added security to the sight being held in place.

Another method involves the use of the electric arc welder. Use a short stub of rod with your hand braced against some support. The rod is positioned over the dovetail just out of arc range and the machine turned on. Slowly lower the rod, pull the helmet down to protect your eyes and quickly peck the bottom of the dovetail with the rod. Remove the rod the instant you get an arc and inspect your work. Just a couple of pecks will do the trick. Try the sight in place and usually you will find it tightened up with the slot requiring only a little filing to remove the excess rod deposited. Finally, if all else fails, position the sight, mark the correct place and solder it on!

Cutting a new dovetail slot is not too difficult and can be done with either an end mill made for such purposes or filed to shape. Dovetail sight milling cutters are available from most gunsmith supply houses. Should you need only an occasional dovetail slot or if you do not have milling facilities, you can do a good job with a few files and a hacksaw. Lay out the sight dovetail position on the barrel and mark the narrow part of the dovetail slot with two lines across the barrel.

The hacksaw is used first, cutting down to about 75 percent of the depth with a cut made on each of the lines across the barrel. Additional cuts are made between the two lines with the hacksaw to remove as much metal as possible. Several hacksaw blades can be combined on the hacksaw frame to make a poor man's milling machine and rapidly remove the excess metal. After the initial excess metal is removed, use a square file or the edge of a regular file, to square up the cut.

Now switch to a sight file or a triangular file with two safe sides. Cut out from the edges to form the dovetail slot being careful not to deepen the slot any more. When the slot is about 75 percent done, insert the edge of the sight (right to left) and note how much wider the slot must be filed and whether it must be carried any deeper. If the slot must be deepened more, do this first and widen the slot later, for to do the opposite will enlarge the slot too much. The slot must be tapered lightly from right to left to hold the sight securely. It is all just a matter of cut-and-try from here.

In addition to the dovetail rear sight, there are several others that will be of interest to the hobbyist, especially when working with military barrels or barrels without a dovetail slot. Perhaps one of the best on the present market is the Williams Guide Open Sight that provides both elevation and windage adjustment. It is attached to the barrel with two 6-48 screws. Installing one of these sights requires that two holes be drilled and tapped, and naturally, a drill jig will do the job best. For those without a drill jig, the job can be done fairly easily with a little patience.

Start by removing the sight blade and the elevation slide from the base. The base then is positioned on the barrel and cross leveled to match the cross leveled barrel and finally clamped in position with a C-clamp. Use the front hole, as it is the longest and will guide the drill or punch straighter than the shallow rear hole.

I never have favored the use of a spotting drill or the use of a sight base as a drill guide bushing; invariably the drill will chew out a chunk of the base hole and make a sloppy

To install receiver sight without jig, action is leveled, sight cross-leveled and held with padded C-clamp. Punch is in hole to mark screw position for drilling, tapping.

fit. A much better system is to use a special little homemade spotting punch, which is made by using the stub of a broken tap which, in this case, would be a 6-48 or any No. 6 tap. Grind away any remains of the thread, then grind a point on the end. To be sure this point is exactly in the center of your little punch, chuck the punch in the drill press and the grindstone in a hand drill. Both are turned on and the stone held against the revolving punch to grind the point exactly centered.

When finished, the homemade tap-punch is inserted in the front of the sight base and a hammer used to provide a mark on the barrel. The punch should fit in the screw hole without any wobbling. Remove the sight base; then drill and tap the hole. Now turn the sight base backwards and use the short screw through the deep screw hole in the base to mark the spot for the second hole; remove the sight and drill and tap for the second screw. Reinstall the sight correctly and screw it in place.

Another good rear sight is the folding leaf offered by Marble and Lyman. These are good sights to substitute for the original sight on a rifle if a scope is installed. Folded flat against the barrel, they are out of the way but are flipped back up easily, if the need arises. If the barrel does not have a dovetail slot, you can attach one of the false bases to the barrel and put the folding leaf sight in the false base's dovetail slot. These bases are available in either screw-on or sweat-on models.

Another method of getting a base on the barrel is to use a barrel band with a dovetail slot cut on top of the band. Kesselring makes a wide assortment of these bands in

For his own use, the author favors this brush hunting combination of open sights, scope in Weaver pivot mount.

sweat-on version. Marble, Lyman, Redfield, Christy, Rex and several other companies offer ramps of various models and styles providing the hobbyist with a selection to fit any need.

There have always been two followings in ramp installation: those who favor the sweat-on method and those who favor the screw-on. If I have the choice, I choose the screw-on method. Any heat applied to a blued barrel always runs the chance of discoloring the bluing around the ramp and requires the utmost care to prevent bore damage. Fifty-fifty solder, if used correctly in a good sweat joint, will hold a ramp, but Force-44 will provide a better joint at about the same temperature.

On a high-powered rifle with heavy barrel whip, sweat soldered ramps have been known to turn loose and go flying off into the wild blue. Silver solder will lock a ramp down tight, but the necessary heat is pretty high and can cause scale in the barrel. This almost always requires that the barrel be reblued. The screwed-on ramp can be attached to a barrel with the finest of blue, requires no heat and is secure. If you object to the sight of screws in the ramp, Lyman makes a ramp attached to a band that can be slipped over the end of a barrel. This requires no solder and no screws. Christy also makes a long ramp with the screw under the dovetail, hidden from view.

There is a wide variety of beads and blade sights to insert in the ramp's dovetail, in height and shape, as well as size. The height of the ramp and blade must be matched to the height of the rear sight. Charts to determine this, plus recommended combinations, are available and should be consulted before the sights are selected. Installing the blade in the ramp's dovetail must be done carefully, as a heavy hand can damage both the ramp and the blade. Check the fit carefully and, if the blade will not start in the slot, do a little careful filing, but keep a snug fit. Usually, if you use a blade of the same manufacture as the ramp, little or no trouble will be encountered.

When installing the blade in the dovetail, use a short section of nylon rod or a dense piece of wood to tap it in place, and at the same time, the ramp should be pressed against a firm object to keep it from being knocked out of line. Williams makes a little gadget called a front sight pusher that eliminates this problem.

Receiver sights — sometimes incorrectly called peep sights — are the more accurate of the two types of iron sights. You would think after exposure to military receiver sights, plus advertising, that anyone would be familiar with their function. But it is amazing the number of butchered modifications of receiver sights, such as those on the M-1 Carbine, made by people who don't understand. People say they have a hard time finding the center of the hole!

The principle of the receiver sight is based on two well known facts. First is that it is optically impossible for the eye to focus on three objects at three different distances at the same time. With open sights, either the rear sight is blurred and the front sight and target clean, or the target is blurred and the front and rear sights are in sharp focus.

The second fact is that any time the eye looks through a small hole, the eye automatically centers that hole, for that is where it finds the most light. The correct way to use a receiver sight is to look through it and forget it is even there, as the eye centers it automatically. For fast snap shooting, a large aperture, or just the sight hole with the aperture removed, is far superior to open sights; while for precision shooting, the small aperture stands over open sights like a dollar over a dime.

The choice of receiver sight will depend on the use of the rifle, plus the personal preference of the shooter.

various sizes and shapes. If you want to get fancy, make a base to house two of the folding sights, then use one such as the Marble 69W for the low and 69WH for the high to provide two ranges. These sights, by the way, have a small amount of windage adjustment in them, in addition to shifting them in the dovetail slot for major windage correction.

Ramp front sights offer a means of correcting many sight problems, as well as giving the barrel a racy line, as opposed to the bobtail appearance of a dovetail front sight. One of the handiest ramps on the market is the Williams Shorty that accepts a standard sight blade in its own dovetail. These ramps can be mounted to a barrel with a dovetail slot by an ingenious little wedge. The wedge has a hole threaded to accept the ramp attaching screw.

The wedge is inserted in the barrel dovetail slot, adjusted to the center and the ramp simply attached by the screw going through the ramp into the threaded wedge hole, hiding the barrel's original dovetail completely. Only a screwdriver is needed to install it.

For barrels without a dovetail slot, the wedge is discarded and a hole drilled in the barrel to accept the ramp attaching screw. For added security the ramp can be sweat soldered on with the screw pulled down tight, while the solder still is molten. The shorty ramp also can be attached by sweat soldering, only without using the screw, except in the lowest height model, which has the screw hole behind the ramp's dovetail slot.

A longer version of the Williams Shorty is offered in the Streamlined model and is available in either screw-on or

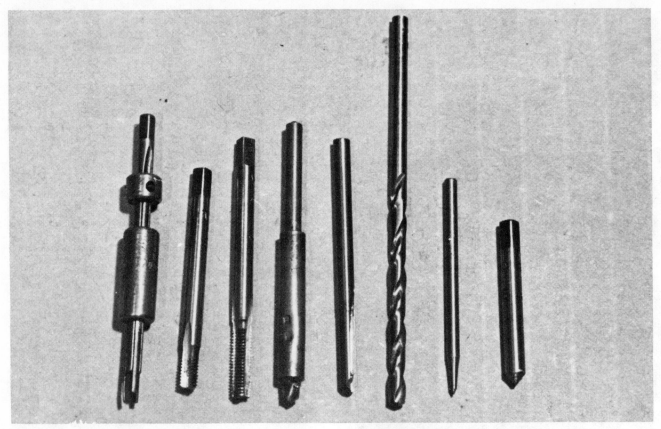

From left, 6-48 broken tap extractor, a pair of 6-48 high speed taps, No. 31 carbide drill, No. 31 cobalt drill are all commercially produced. Center locator and center punch at right were ground from broken tap and long dental burr.

Lyman, Redfield and Williams offer a wide selection, ranging from target styles to a standard hunting type. Usually, the target version will have large, easily turned adjusting knobs, while the hunting model has a small knob or just a keyed slot.

If the rifle already is drilled and tapped for a receiver sight, the installation is simple. Generally, such a rifle will have the screw holes covered with a short plug screw. Remove the plug screw, check to be sure the threads are clear and flush the hole with a cleaning fluid. Try the sight in position and, if everything looks right, put a drop of Loc-Tite in each hole and install the screws. A trick in getting the screws as tight as possible is to tap the rear of the screwdriver and turn that extra little bit until the screw is jam tight. Check that the screws are not protruding into the action to bind any part.

For the hobbyist, the big problem in installing receiver sights will come on converted military rifles. The designer and manufacturer were preoccupied with the idea of building a military rifle and the conversion of said rifle into a slick sporter was the farthest thing from their minds.

For this reason, you often find slight variations in a receiver from one model to another. Never take anything for granted when installing sights on a military receiver. Assuming the receiver is smooth and even on the side on which the sight will be mounted, the next thing on the agenda is getting the sight in the right position, exactly parallel to the center line of the bore.

The best way is with the use of a receiver sight drill jig. B-Square makes one that is attached to the receiver to align the holes exactly and is adjustable for the Springfield, Enfield, Mauser, and Jap rifles. Rex also offers a drill jig that clamps to the receiver. Both have hardened drill guide bushings. The hobbyist will have to decide for himself whether he will be drilling and tapping enough receiver sight holes to warrant the expenditure for the jig. It is

possible to mount a receiver sight without the use of a jig, but it takes time and patience, for measurement is critical.

There is more than one way to set up a receiver sight for drilling without the use of a jig. The receiver sight has a fairly large range of adjustment and usually you can adjust it enough to compensate for a small goof. Mount the front sight first and have it centered before tackling the receiver sight.

The rifle is then stripped down to its naked receiver and barrel before mounting in a vise. Cross level the rifle and pick out some object about 50 yards away that is prominent enough to be used as a bore sighting target. Adjust the rifle until this target is smack-kadab in the center of the bore. If you do much sight work and no such object is available, it is not much trouble to mount a circular disk on a pole and place it where it is needed as a sighting target.

Position the assembled receiver sight on the side of the rifle with the windage on the halfway mark and the slide just slightly elevated. Clamp it in position with a large C-clamp and adjust the sight to get it right on target to match the bore sighting. Drill a couple of holes in the receiver, tap them, and attach it with screws.

Most receiver sights will have one attaching hole to the side of the slide and the other under the slide. Your C-clamp should be attached in such a way as to clear the hole to the side of the slide. Use the homemade tap-punch through this hole to mark the receiver for the first hole. Remove the sight, enlarge the punched mark, and drill the hole.

Author feels collimator for zeroing rifles is the best friend gunsmith can have, as it reduces benchrest testing.

After the hole has been tapped, reinstall the sight, locking it in place as tightly as possible with this one screw. Again, bore sight the rifle and adjust the sight until it aligns with the target, but make this adjustment by shifting the sight itself, not by adjusting the knobs. Without disturbing the sight alignment, remove the slide to expose the attaching hole under it. Again, use the homemade tap-punch to mark the position of this hole, remove the sight and drill and tap the hole.

The sight installed, the receiver is checked inside to be sure the screws are not protruding into the action. Drill the holes one at a time, for to center punch both at the same time invites trouble. The main cause is not that you may not mark correctly, but you will be drilling without a guide bushing and the drill may wander. If it does, you can correct this by marking the second hole to coincide with the same amount of drill wander. If you had marked both holes and drilled them at the same time, the two holes in the receiver may not match the two holes in the receiver sight base. You also can cut down on the chance of drill wander by starting the hole with a center drill.

As the receiver sight is superior to the open sight, the telescopic sight is superior to both of them. There just isn't any contest with the target enlarged, seen clearly; crosshair superimposed on the image requiring the eye to focus on only one distance. Scope technical advances in the last few years seem almost a miracle to those who remember the high mounted, small field of view scopes. Not only have rifle scopes made tremendous advances, but now we even have special scopes mounted on shotguns and pistols.

The modern shotgun with an undersized bore, designed to fit a rifled slug snugly, is capable of surprising accuracy. With a scope of 2½ power or less, the shotgun becomes a deadly big bore rifle, somewhat on the order of the old British express rifles. A deer hit with a 12-gauge slug will drop in his tracks if the slug is placed right and the scope provides the sighting capability.

Several scope companies offer special shotgun scopes with all kinds of reticles and mounts to attach them to just about any make and model shotgun. These usually are mounted on the side of the receiver and can be removed to allow the shotgun to be used on other purposes. There is no special shotgun scope mount drill jig on the market, but the hobbyist can mount one accurately with a little care.

A standard shotgun barrel cut off to be made into a slug barrel is not capable of delivering the slug accurately enough to warrant a scope. The bore is larger than the slug, and the slug wobbles down the tube, exiting in various stages of stabilization. Most such barrels will not keep three slugs inside of a wash tub at 50 yards.

It is better to leave the choke in and try to work from here, mounting the scope only if the barrel proves capable of delivering some kind of accuracy. If you are going to the trouble to mount an expensive scope on a shotgun, drive miles and miles to get a shot at game, it makes good sense to spend a few dollars more and get a barrel designed for slugs. Slug barrels have no choke but are bored undersize to fit the slug tightly and assure its leaving the barrel stabilized in a straight line. Most slug barrels are capable of putting three shots in a six-inch circle at 50 yards and some will do it at 100. This kind of accuracy warrants the trouble and expense of a scope!

To mount a scope on your gun, line up the iron sights on a target and lock the shotgun in a vise. Hold the scope in its mount against the side of the receiver and jiggle it until it lines up with the target. C-clamp it in position.

Now use our homemade tap-punch to mark one of the end holes in the mount, remove the sight, drill and tap the holes. Remount the scope using the one screw hole to pull the sight up snugly, juggling it until it again coincides with the iron sight on the target. Center punch the hole in the opposite end of the sight base, remove the scope and drill and tap this hole. The scope is reinstalled and if everything is okay, the additional holes in the scope base are centered punched, drilled, and tapped, but this time with the base in place.

There is a reason for doing it this way. If you goof on the second hole, one of the other holes can be used for the second aligning hole. The off hole is filled with a plug, and the hole redrilled in the correct position, although this seldom happens. The mount is kept in place for the third hole to assure that the mount and holes line up, even if the mount is out a bit with the drill. The iron sights can be left on the barrel or removed, if in the way of the scope.

Scoped pistols arrived on the scene some ten years ago, and since that time the fad has settled down to some good scopes and good mounts. The special long eye relief scope allows the pistol to be held at arm's length in the normal position and remain clear. As the mounts are made specifically for each make and model, the mounting sequence will vary. Each will have a complete set of installation instructions designed for the person with limited facilities. Just read the instructions before you start installing. Most pistol scope trouble stems from the big bore recoil calibers, so use Loc-Tite and pull the screws up tight.

There is so much demand for scope sights today that few new rifles are made without mounting holes drilled and tapped in the receiver. Installing scopes on these is as simple as installing receiver sights on similar factory drilled and tapped rifles. All you have to do is buy the right base and follow the directions.

Most modern .22 rimfire rifles have a special long dovetail cut into the top of the receiver to accept a clamp-on scope mount. The mount and rings usually are part of the scope assembly and are purchased together. Loosen the clamp screws, slide the mount over the dovetail cuts until it is in the correct position, then lock it in place with the clamp screws.

If the scope is positioned correctly, you should be able to shoulder the rifle with the sight then in focus without moving your head back and forth. If it is not in focus, loosen the clamp screws and adjust the scope forward or backward as needed.

When this is accomplished, the next thing is to be sure the vertical crosshairs are actually vertical with the rifle. You can do this by picking some object, such as a telephone pole or the side of a building, for your vertical target. Clamp the rifle in a vise and cross level it. Compare the vertical crosshair with your vertical target. If they do not align, loosen the scope lock screws and twist the scope until they do align, relocking the screws afterwards. The final adjustment is to adjust the scope for clarity, which is done by unlocking the retaining ring at the rear and screwing the rear lens cap inward or outward to obtain the clearest view. The lens then is relocked in place by the retaining ring.

Some recent .22s such as the Marlin M-39A do not have the dovetail cuts on the receiver, but use a special dovetailed adapter plate, which is secured to the receiver with screws. The mounting of the scope on the adapter plate is done the same way as for the dovetailed receivers. For older model rifles, a special adapter plate must be fitted to the rifle's receiver to accept the scope mount. Several of these are offered by Redfield, Brownell and others. Installation consists of leveling the rifle, then leveling the adapter plate; marking the holes to be drilled similar to mounting the side plate on a shotgun and following the same basic procedure. These adapter plates have a couple of holes fore and aft and sometimes two in between. There is no reason to drill for all of the holes, as they are only there to accommodate the variations in the receivers of different models. In addition to the regular 3/4-inch diameter scopes designed for .22s, you can get a special one-inch set of rings for adapting a large one-inch scope to fit the dovetailed receivers or adapter plates.

A mistake often made by beginners is to mount a scope and bore sight it without first checking that the scope cross-

Lack of knowledge is reflected in fact that owner of this carbine attempted to make open sight from standard carbine receiver sight. It is too close to eye to work.

Author's sight tools include Forster jig, B-Square jigs, Williams sight pusher, Poly-Choke rib jig, the collimator as well as broad array of drills and taps.

hairs are on halfway adjustment. By halfway adjustment, I mean that the reticle of the scope is on mid-center zero with just as much adjustment one way as the other. Scope adjustments have a fascination for people and few can resist turning the knobs a couple of turns. If the scope is left this way and mounted, then it is mounted incorrectly and you will have adjustment only one way. To avoid this, run the scope adjustment all the way to one side. Note the scale on the adjustment or count the clicks necessary to go all the way to the other side. Centering the reticle requires only that you run it back half the amount of adjustment you just counted. Don't forget to check both the vertical and windage adjustment to center the reticle exactly halfway.

One of the most useful items to come on the market in recent years is the collimator. There are several offered, but all work on the same basic principle. A precision-ground stud is inserted into the muzzle of the rifle and held in place by a tension spring. An optical instrument with a

Tapping for sight is done with tap held in drill chuck. Chuck is turned by pulling on motor belt, after making sure it is unplugged. This way, tap is inserted in hole immediately after hole is drilled, assuring alignment.

built-in white background and a set of crosshairs going from the lower corners to the top is clamped onto the stud to form an X or, in some models, a grid.

It is a refined optical version of bore sighting. Instead of first looking through the bore at a target then through the sights at the same target to see if they coincide, you see the bore target in the form of the X with the sights being aligned on the X.

To align a set of sights, it first is necessary to get the scope or sights exactly parallel with the bore and make the necessary bullet drop compensation.

Here is a simple explanation: Imagine a thread stretched right down the exact center of the bore of the rifle from end to end. Imagine a similar thread stretched exactly through the center line of the telescopic sight. We now adjust the sights until these two threads, as viewed from the side, are exactly parallel. Looking down from the top of the scope and rifle, we adjust the windage until the two threads

appear as one.

We now have the scope line of sight and the bore line parallel for elevation and perfectly aligned for windage. The collimator can be imagined as a right angle upward bend of the thread at the muzzle, until it blends with the thread through the scope, then another exact right angle until the two threads are one. In other words, the collimator bends this imaginary bore line upward and presents it as the X in the optical instrument attached to the stud in the muzzle.

When the crosshairs are matched exactly to the center of the X, you have the same perfect vertical and windage alignment as the two threads. To zero the rifle, it is necessary only to compute the drop of the bullet at the desired distance and adjust the scope this amount plus the distance from the X in the instrument to the center of the bore. A collimator, when used correctly, is accurate to one minute of angle, or one inch at one hundred yards.

A full set of instructions comes with a collimator when

you buy it and using one is quite easy. The hobbyist will find this one of the best tools at his disposal, not only for zeroing in all types of sights, but for several other uses.

For instance, say you have a favorite rifle and shoot both heavy bullets for deer, and light ones for varmints. Zero the rifle with, say the light bullets, insert the collimator and count the number of clicks to bring the crosshair back to a perfect match with the collimator's X and write this number down. To reset the scope for this bullet after you have been shooting heavy bullets, it is necessary only to match the crosshair with the X, then adjust the scope the number of clicks you wrote down for the light bullet.

Suppose a rifle is throwing bullets all over the target, and you suspect the stock is exerting pressure on the barrel from one side. Insert the collimator and match the scope crosshairs with the X. Remove the stock and look through the scope. If the stock is exerting pressure, the crosshair and the X will no longer be matched. If it moved the X to the right, this indicates that the stock is exerting pressure on the barrel, pushing it to the left. Relieve stock pressure, repeat the process, and you can eliminate any side pressure.

If you like pressure — say two pounds or so pushing up on the barrel, as some people do — you can arrive at an exact figure easily. Remove the gun from the stock, mount it upside down in a vise and insert the collimator also upside down. Now hang a two-pound weight out on the barrel where the forearm will be touching it. Match the crosshairs to the collimator's X. Remove the weight and mount the rifle in the stock. All you have to do is inlet the stock until the crosshair and the X again coincide to have two pounds of pressure on the barrel at the forend.

This trick also can be used to find how much upward pressure you have on a barrel. Match the crosshair and the X with the barrel in the stock. Remove it and mount the barrel upside down in a vise. Hook a fish scale to the barrel at the forearm point and pull down until the crosshair and the X coincide, then read the amount of pressure from the fish scale.

Drilling and tapping high power rifles for scopes, according to some arm chair experts, is as easy as scratching your backside. Some go to great lengths describing how the home hole borer can use his $1.98 eggbeater to puncture the hide of the receiver and, with a few quick twists of the tap, the job is done. I'm not saying that it is impossible to do it, any more than I am saying that you couldn't train a termite to inlet a stock, but the odds are against success.

If you need a scope mounted only once in awhile, then have a professional gunsmith do the job. I have just seen too many messed-up attempts and good rifles ruined. If you want to mount scopes, get a good drill jig, a good drill press, good drills and taps, or forget it. All of your careful stock work, metal work and loving care is for naught if the scope mounting job is not right.

The drill jig is almost a dire necessity in the mounting of scopes, especially the two-piece base version. It is possible to mount a one-piece base, such as a Redfield, without a jig if you have a solid drill press and a good vise and patience. These bases have built-in adjustments for windage to compensate if you have the base on slightly crooked, but the two-piece bases are another story. The two best drill jigs are the B-Square and the Forster. The Forster is the more expensive but also the more versatile. With it you can drill a hole exactly on center line anywhere from the muzzle to the tang screw in the receiver. Turn the rifle on its side and you can drill and tap for a receiver sight. This is accomplished by mounting the barrel and receiver in a fairly long jig with the barrel held between two precision-ground V-blocks.

Tap wrench is held at rear by a small center in chuck. Wrench is turned with one hand, while the other provides the downward pressure that's needed on drill quill handle.

The B-Square works on a different principle by attaching itself to the receiver and being held in position by a round bar taking the place of the regular rifle bolt. Fitted to this special bolt is a flat plate, two extension studs and a top plate containing a series of holes spaced to match the scope base holes. It will provide correct spacing for both Weaver and Redfield mounts, but it will not work out on the barrel or for receiver sights. Either choice will serve you well.

A new jig on the market is the Billy Best and could be called an elongated and refined Forster, but it is more versatile and simplifies the job.

A complete set of detailed instructions come with each of the scope jigs. Like all directions, however, there are "ifs" hidden between the lines. Perhaps the greatest mistake beginners make with drill jigs is not with the jig itself or in positioning it correctly in relation to the gun or drill press. It is in the actual mechanics of drilling and tapping the holes. There is no set of rules that you can follow to the

If you have unlimited funds and a yen for mechanization, you could use this Milite vertical milling machine with sight dovetail cutter to enlarge the rear slot for sight.

last digit, for some new problem seems to be just around the corner every time you drill a receiver. A few basic rules will help, along with a good dose of horse sense. About the best advice anyone can give is: don't get in a hurry! Take your time and if a problem comes up, stop and think before you bull ahead.

Most of your drilling will be for the 6-48 thread size and the No. 31 drill is used for this size. The best medicine is a good high speed drill as the foundation of your special equipment, since a good portion of the holes can be drilled with one of these. A much better bet is a good cobalt drill, which is relatively inexpensive and will last for a long time with a little careful use. Personally, I use a cobalt drill on all high powered rifle receivers, regardless. Occasionally you will run across a receiver harder than a loan shark's heart. The high speed drill will just polish the surface and the cobalt drill just spins without penetrating. When this happens, you have to go to a carbide drill. These are not cheap, but they will drill through a file.

The reason your regular high speed drill and your cobalt drill will not penetrate the hard receiver is a thin skin of super-hard surface metal. Once the hard skin is penetrated, the underneath is relatively soft and usually can be drilled with either of the regular drills. In using the carbide drill, bear in mind that its primary use is to penetrate this hard skin only, not to drill all the way with it. Doing so invites having the carbide drill bind in the softer metal and break. You probably will run into another thin skin of hard surface on the bottom and I have found it good sense not to push your luck, but to stop. You usually will have enough

depth for several threads, which will hold the scope base securely. If you do not have a carbide drill, you can sometimes substitutes an 1/8-inch lathe center drill which is pretty close to a size 31 drill.

Once the hole has been drilled and the chips blown out, comes the job of getting some threads down in there. It is also the beginning of many hand wringing and cussin' sessions. Sometimes it seems almost impossible to get the doggone tap started in the hole, but if you use taps in a set of three — starting, (taper) plug, and bottoming — the task is made much easier. You also can use the center drill to chamfer the edge of the hole, which aids in getting the tap started, especially on the tough skin receivers. A good high speed tap will cut about a dozen holes before dulling and requiring grinding back of the front. Keep this in mind and you can grind your worn starting and plug taps into bottoming taps.

There are two ways to go about tapping the hole. One is to use a tap wrench to hold the tap and do the cutting by hand. However, use this only if you have a steady hand. The second way is to use the drill press to aid in keeping the tap and wrench steady. This can be done by using the regular wrench with a chucked center punch bearing on its rear. The pressure is maintained by keeping the drill press handle pulled down while you turn the wrench handle. B-Square makes a special wrench for this.

I have used several tap wrenches, but prefer to chuck the tap directly in the drill press and pull down on the handle with my right hand, rotating the tap with my left hand by turning the drill press belt. It is a good idea to unplug the motor to keep your pinkies from being squashed, if you hit the switch accidentally. If you use this system, turn the belt for about a quarter of the tap, then back the belt to unscrew the tap a half turn to clear the chips. Keep repeating this procedure until the threads have been cut to full depth.

Special drilling and tapping fluids will help in these operations and there are several good ones on the market. Regular cutting oil can be used, if nothing else is available, but the best I have found is Tap-Magic, both for drilling and tapping. This is a thin fluid that works on a different principle from regular cutting oil. It is an instant refrigerant and, by cooling both the metal and the drill or tap, it prevents heat build-up and binding of the two metals by expansion. I use it in operations involving any drilling and tapping. It is also handy to get a superfine finish on metal being turned in the lathe.

After the holes have been drilled and tapped, you usually will find a small, raised bit of metal around the hole. If this is not removed, the base will not fit snugly against the receiver. If you are working with a rifle that will be reblued, there is little problem, for a few quick swipes across the polishing wheel will remove the edge. If the rifle is blued already, the edge can be removed with a small grindstone or a file without damaging the bluing, if you are careful.

Getting a barrel in the drill press vise and keeping it level while you drill with one end hanging out in the air can be frustrating! It seems to slide down, no matter how tight you clamp the vise. A little jig can be made that will eliminate this trouble. These can be adjusted to fit the parts and scrap that you have available. In use, the top support system is rotated, which rotates the screw and raises the top section of the jig, until it touches and supports the overhang of the barrel. This is just the ticket for leveling up a barrel with one end clamped lightly in the vise, the level on the barrel, turning the jig rod until the bubble centers.

Repairing and installing new sights is one of the main jobs in any type gun shop. Select the correct sights, install them correctly and you will bring out the best in any gun.

THE PRIMARY CAUSES of firearm malfunction and wear are three closely related and interlocking factors: misuse, lack of cleaning, and improper lubrication. Remove these three factors, and it is almost impossible to wear out a good gun during a lifetime of average shooting. Parts do break from fatigue, of course, but in about half the cases of parts breakage, the cause can be traced directly back to one or more of the above causes.

Little can be said about misuse except not to do it.

an erring dog.

Only recently, a fellow came into the shop with a nice little 20-gauge shotgun with a shattered butt stock and cracked trigger housing. He shot a squirrel out of a tree. The squirrel fell on the ground and started running, so instead of shooting again, he hit the squirrel over the head with the gun and got himself a $40 repair bill. Closely related to these groups are the reloaders, who put in a little extra powder to "kill 'em way out yonder." And don't

THE CLEAN SCENE *Disassembly,*

Lubrication And Cleanliness Are Basic But Nonetheless

Critical In All Phases Of Gunsmithing! Chapter 12

Warnings against misuse generally fall on deaf ears, as it seems some souls are blessed with the ability to tear up a steel ball bearing with a rubber hammer. They will spend a couple of hundred dollars for a good gun, walk out to a pickup truck, toss it in the back and pile six dogs on top of it. Others delight in using a gun to press down the top strand of the barbed wire fence they are crossing. To some, a gun is an ideal club to finish off wounded game or punish

forget those who bang away without checking the bore of a gun after a bad fall to be sure it is clear of obstructions. In just about every case of gun misuse, the owner not only is damaging the gun but putting life and limb in jeopardy.

A large number of guns are worn out each year from the fact that they are not kept clean. If you have ever watched a mechanic lap an automobile engine valve in place, you probably noted that he placed a greasy-gritty substance

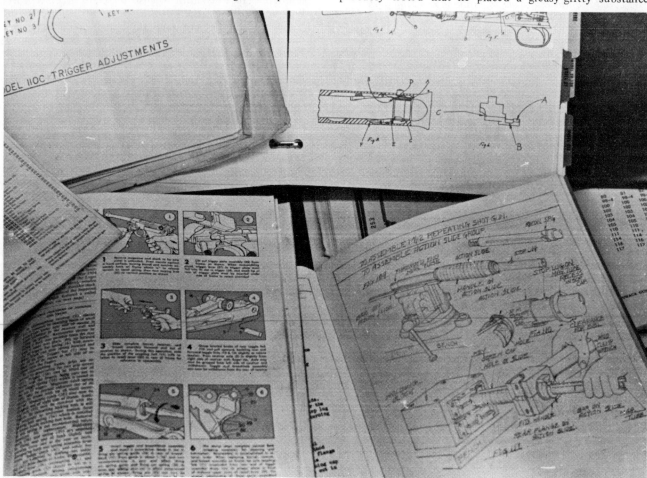

between the valve and the engine block. This is called valve compound and is a composition of grease and grinding compound. Repeated turning of the valve grinds the surface of the valve and the block down because of the cutting compound in the grease. A gun full of old grease, oil, dirt and powder residue has about the same thing as valve grinding compound to wear parts and the action assembly down just about as quickly. It doesn't take much of this for the parts to become so worn that they are loose and out of alignment. This results in jamming and binding of the action until the gun fails to function.

When it comes to lubrication, there seems to be two lines of incorrect thought. Some gun owners have absolutely no use for lubricants of any kind, while their cohorts deem it necessary to dump a full quart of any greasy substance handy into the gun. Let a gun just think about malfunctioning and this last crowd really swings into action, gleefully pumping oil into every available hole, crack and crevice.

If you really want a gun jammed, look for the fellow who is oil happy and, at the same time, never bothers to clean a gun; he just dumps in more oil.

The king of all of them is the gentleman with the above habits who also uses the gun for everything from a boat paddle to a pry bar. The gun manufacturers have a steady customer in this fellow. Hardly a day goes by that some gun, suffering from oil-itis, doesn't find its way into the shop and quite often the cure is a simple cleaning job to remove the half gallon of oil. The bone-dry boys build up so much friction that the heat expands the metal in the parts and binds the action to cause malfunction. Obviously, the ideal is somewhere between these two extremes.

A large part of the hobbyist's gun work will consist of

This screw, badly enough burred to be unslightly, is the result of someone using incorrectly fitting screwdriver.

the disassembly, cleaning, and lubrication of guns brought in by friends; guns he has purchased to rebuild or repair, and the normal care of his regular guns. These guns of friends seem as if by magic to find their way into any hobbyist's shop with a variety of excuses. The more different models you disassemble and reassemble, the more your knowledge grows. The knowledge of how a gun comes apart and how it goes together again is the key to determining why this gun is malfunctioning. Each part of the gun has a function, that is part of the overall operation of the gun interlocking with other parts, performing their own function in sequence.

Once you know where each part fits into the gun, its function and where in the operational sequence the function takes place, then finding a malfunction is simple. All that is necessary is to trace the operation sequence step by step, checking whether each part is performing its function fully and in correct sequence. The malfunctioning part will stand out like a sore thumb.

When you disassemble a gun for cleaning and reassemble it, never treat the parts as something only to be reinstalled in a certain sequence like part of a jigsaw puzzle. Instead, look at each part, try to figure out its function and how it ties into the operation sequence. You soon will see that most guns follow a general basic plan or sequence, with individual variations. After all, an extractor is an extractor, be it in a cheapie or a work of art. As your knowledge grows, the easier it becomes to tackle an unknown model, for you will be working from a solid background.

Most professional gunsmiths have a working knowledge of the disassembling of a hundred or more models of the more common firearms. Then along comes a customer with an uncommon model and the professional is faced with the same problem of the hobbyist; how in the devil to get the thing apart and back together again. The hobbyist, in most cases, will leap right in and start taking the gun apart lickety-split with little thought of the consequences. The professional, having stuck his neck out before, is a little shy. He goes to his working library and looks the gun up in one of the many available sources of data. The best friend in such cases for both the hobbyist and the professional, is a good manual or at least, an exploded-view of the gun. If the hobbyist intends to work on guns to any extent, then a library is necessity. This is not a library in the usual sense, but includes books, manuals, exploded-views and catalogs, plus any other data and information he can gather.

The National Rifle Association publishes two of the best books on the market on disassembly and assembly. Firearm Assembly Handbook, Volume I, covers 77 models of rifles, pistols, and shotguns, while Volume II covers another 89 models. Each step is carefully explained in full detail plus an exploded-drawing of each model is given.

The American Rifleman magazine itself is a good source of material, often covering odd models. All such articles are easily found, as the twelve issues are cross indexed each year in the December issue of the magazine. It is a wise hobbyist, or professional indeed, who has a collection of the Rifleman at his disposal.

The largest and most complete manual available is Bob Brownell's The Encyclopedia of Modern Firearms, Parts and Assembly, a large, thick book compiled and published in 1959. It contains a wealth of material, such as the illustrations and parts list of hundreds of current and out-of-date models, gunsmith manuals released by some of the manufacturers, some of which are no longer available elsewhere. It also contains the Department of the Army Technical Manuals, plus dozens of pages of specifications on pins, screws, springs, etc., for hundreds of models. These

This barrel was blown up because of dirt plugging the bore. Usually the barrel of a shotgun will simply split, but in this instance, fragments could have resulted in serious injury to shooter or anyone standing nearby.

three books should be the foundation of the hobbyist's working library.

Other good sources of material are the parts catalogs available from gun manufacturers. These generally contain a detailed exploded-view of each model which locates the exact position of each part, thus answering a lot of "where does it go?" questions. The factory name for each part is also a big help, for it usually indicates the part's function. Try to get as complete a collection of these catalogs as possible, and be sure to save the old, out-of-date ones.

I remember an imported .22 rifle that a customer brought into the shop with magazine feed trouble. After disassembling the gun, I checked it completely and could find absolutely nothing wrong with the parts, yet when reassembled, it refused to feed the cartridges.

I dug out an old parts sheet on the gun, and after going over the feed system in the exploded-drawing, I discovered that a small steel ball bearing should be on top of the cartridge cut-off spring. Someone had disassembled the gun and left the ball bearing out, thereby allowing the spring to move forward and jam the cartridges. A small ball bearing from an automobile carburetor check valve proved a good substitute and the gun functioned correctly. This is but one of the many times that an exploded view of a gun has solved a malfunction problem for me and the reason that I save every such catalog and drawing I can find to my own working library.

Some manufacturers publish service manuals that detail complete and full disassembly and reassembly of their products, plus repair procedures for various malfunctions. These are the best source of information available. About the most complete is the Remington Field Service Manual, which consists of two large loose leaf binders. These cover every presently manufactured Remington model, plus a lot of the old discontinued models, like the Model 11. Your initial payment of $15 carries an extra dividend in that all new models brought out by the manufacturer will be covered free of charge in inserts to be added to the manual. Not only does the manual cover disassembly and reassembly, but the complete operation sequence of each model, step by step, which helps spot malfunctions.

Suggested repair procedures are outlined step by step.

Winchester follows a somewhat different approach in their gunsmith manuals, which are available from the factory for about a dollar each. Each model is covered in a different manual. The old ones, on such models as the M-12 and the M-94, are works of art, going into the smallest detail of assembly and disassembly, plus repair procedures and instructions for the building of some special tools. The more modern manuals are not so complete but are sufficient for general purposes.

Savage is releasing a gunsmith manual in a loose leaf binder on all their models. It is well written and illustrated. Intended for the professional, they go into close detail on repair procedures, parts illustration, special tools and how to make them, and even some of the problems encountered on disassembly and reassembly.

Ithaca publishes an excellent combination parts catalog and service manual. It covers their present models and some of the old ones. Browning published an excellent manual years ago, but it has been discontinued. However, a copy of the manual is included in Brownell's big encyclopedia. Most other companies publish an owner's manual, which goes into disassembly details only to the extent needed for general maintenance.

The most common mistake beginners make in the disassembly of an unfamiliar gun is to immediately remove every visible screw and punch out any pin in sight. This usually succeeds in turning all the internal parts loose in a mass of confusion which quite often prevents disassembly without breaking or damaging the gun and its parts. In other models, this haphazard procedure jams some of the screws and pins by putting pressure on them to the extent that it is impossible to remove them without damage.

Other beginners attempt to disassemble the gun by starting on the wrong part of the gun, which sometimes results in the entire gun being jammed and regular disassembly impossible without damage. A case in point is the Savage/Stevens pump shotgun. The stock on this gun is held to the trigger assembly housing instead of to the receiver; the draw bolt pulls the stock up hard against the receiver, thereby putting pressure on the trigger assembly screw and

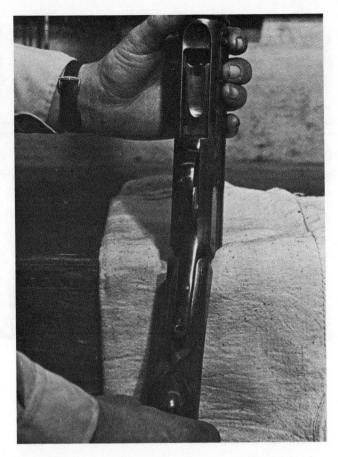

With Browning automatic, the stock bolt is removed, the edge of a bench padded, then the gun brought down with a light blow. This removes butt stock without any damage.

pin. Most beginners try to remove the trigger assembly first by unscrewing the side screw and removing the side pin, resulting in a buggered up screw and a battered pin. They just cannot be removed as long as that draw bolt is pulling back on the trigger assembly, while it is being pulled hard against the receiver.

If you remove the draw bolt, which relieves the pressure, you can almost remove the screw with your fingernail. This is just an example of what a manual can mean, not only in solving problems, but in prevention of damage through improper disassembly procedure.

Sometimes you will be faced with the problem of disassembling a model for which there is no manual available. The best thing to do in such a case is secure the help of a professional gunsmith as chances are, he will have encountered the model before. If not, he is still better equipped from past experience to tackle it than the hobbyist. But if a professional is not available, a letter to the National Rifle Association usually will bring an answer. Only where there is absolutely no other course left open should you attempt to disassemble the gun. When you find yourself in this situation, remember two simple things: proceed slowly and think your way through every step, seeking alternate steps and deciding on the most logical.

You are going to be putting the thing back together again after cleaning or repairing it, so don't rely on memory alone. Instead, write down each step you take in disassembly; this will be invaluable when you start to reassemble. Make sketches of how and where the parts fit. A good

trick is to replace the part immediately, remove it, then replace it again. Doing this a couple of times locks it in your memory.

Be sure your screwdriver fits the screws you are removing without any part of the blade hanging over to scratch the surrounding surface. This circling scratch around a screw is always a sure sign of a beginner's work. Place the screwdriver in the slot and tap the back of the handle with a hammer to fully seat the tip into the slot. This also jars the screw, breaking the surface tension on the threads, enabling you to remove tight screws that would break or bend the screwdriver tip or screw slot if pressure alone was applied. This little trick will save a lot of time and sweat if you make it a habit each time you start to remove a screw.

Your punches should be used in sets, a short shank punch to get the pin moving and a long shank punch to remove the pin from the part. It takes a little practice to develop the knack of hitting the punch with the right amount of force. Too much and you batter the end of the pin, while too little will result in a battered pin also. Try to develop a quick, sharp rap on the punch, as this gets things moving in a hurry. Watch out for the new pins with a serrated surface on one end to hold the pin in place. A close look at both sides of the pin will reveal which end is serrated; the pin must be removed from the opposite side. The new roll or split pins require a close fitting punch, for too small a diameter will just enter the hollow part of the pin. There is a special set of punches for these pins.

There are dozens of disassembly tricks you can pick up by watching others or just stumbling along, learning from your own blunders. You will learn to watch out for springs suddenly released from pressure flying off into the dark reaches of your shop. I learned the hard way always to remove the little cap washer that holds the magazine spring in place on most pump and semi-automatic shotguns. The first one took off like a rocket, smashing an overhead fluorescent light. The one that really drove it home to me was one that came loose and creased my skull, narrowly missing an eye. I learned in hurry to keep that magazine end pointed in a safe direction. Never take anything for granted when it comes to guns. For instance, I always quickly take a gun from the hands of a customer and check to be sure it is not loaded. Most customers appreciate this thought and will agree with you. Make it a practice and don't break it!

A long-time law enforcement officer came into the shop with an M-1 carbine on which he wanted the sights adjusted. He placed it on the counter and we talked a while. A couple of other customers came in and he left the shop, leaving the carbine where it was. Luckily, one of my men walked up and removed the carbine before someone could pick it up. After everyone had gone, he called me into the back and said, "Catch!" Moving the slide lever, he pumped thirty cartridges out of the magazine at my feet. This was embarrasing, to say the least, as I constantly tell all of my gunsmiths to check each gun that comes into the shop.

Keep your mind on what you are doing when you are disassembling a gun, watching for defects and breakage in the parts. Especially keep your mind on what you are doing when you reassemble, for a mistake can mean anything from a broken part to a blown-up gun. About 90 percent of all accidents occur when someone's mind wanders off the project at hand. Becoming tired and keeping right on going can do the same thing. I try to take periodic breaks, talking and swapping hunting lies with a customer or just resting. A few minutes of this, and I'm fresh again and ready to go.

Getting a butt stock off on the five-shot Browning design automatic can be a task. First, remove the tang screw, leaving the stock free to be removed. Lay a pad of cloth on the edge of your bench. Hold the gun by the frame with your left hand, while your right hand grasps the pistol grip and you are looking at the belly of the gun.

Bring both hands downward and hit the hump of the receiver on the back against the pad on the bench. The receiver will stop, of course, but the downward motion of the stock, plus your right-hand pressure, will pull the stock off with no damage to receiver or stock. This trick works with several models of guns and is far better than pounding on the back of the receiver with a leather hammer.

Getting the stock off a rifle if it is glass bedded is no easy trick. The fit is closer than a size ten foot in a size eight shoe. Remove the stock screws all the way but for the last couple of threads. Rap the top of the screws with a rawhide or padded hammer, first on one stock screw, then the other. This will break the hold and the screws can be removed completely and the stock disassembled from the barrel and receiver.

This same trick of partially removing a screw works well on the revolver grips also. Here, the two grips are held to the gun with a single screw, but the fit is tight in most cases. Remove the screw to all but those last few threads. Tap on the head of the screw and you will push the opposite grip out free of the frame. Remove the screw and grip will come completely off, exposing the other grip which can be removed by tapping on the inside.

When everything is disassembled, you will have quite a pile of parts, all of which seem to delight in rolling off on the floor. A box or container for the parts will save a lot of scrubbed knees, dirty hands and time wasted looking for parts on the floor. Cigar boxes make good ones, as do cans, but a metal box of some description will do a better job and not be affected by oil or solvents. A baking pan about a foot long, six or eight inches wide and at least a couple of inches deep work well. If you must delay the reassembly of the gun, put the small parts in a bag and the large ones in a good box. The packing boxes that new guns come in are about perfect. Most hardware and sporting goods dealers throw these away. It doesn't matter if you put the parts in your socks, just so long as you keep them together in some kind of container. Disregard this, and you will come up missing a part of two everytime when you start putting the gun back together.

With the gun disassembled, your next step is to get all the accumulated dirt, grease, powder residue, leaves, sticks, bird feathers and what-not out of the gun. I have seen about anything you can think of in them, including half of a woman's stocking jammed in the action. That must have been an interesting story!

The ultimate goal is to clean the parts right down to the bare metal. The closer to the bare metal the better, for even the smallest amount of residue left on the gun will wear the parts. Too often, the beginner gives up the task and settles for something less than perfection.

There are dozens of ways to get the gun clean and any that gets the job done safely is acceptable. What is needed is something to get down under the dirt, break it loose and lift it up from the surface, dissolving the packed grease at the same time. Once this is accomplished, the final step is to get all the mess out of the action and off the parts.

Back in my army days as smallarms advisor to the Chinese Nationalists, we were faced with the task of rebuilding M-1 Garands, carbines and '03 Springfields. These arrived at the arsenal packed in cosmoline from all over the Pacific. Now, if you have ever been faced with the task of getting cosmoline out of a gun, you can appreciate the problem. Most of these had been in storage since the end of

This pan was made from a one-gallon can to hold mineral spirits with which the parts of a gun are being cleaned.

This heavily gummed trigger assembly is being sprayed with WD-40 before it is washed with mineral spirits.

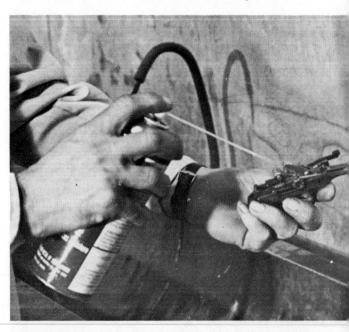

World War II and the climate had turned the cosmoline to the consistency of concrete. Regular cleaning methods drew a blank. The problem was solved by building a "carbontetracine devaporizer." This was a large metal tank about six feet square and about six feet deep. Running around the tank about a third of the way from the top was a water jacket and underneath was a series of electrical heaters.

The guns were placed on a wire platform and lowered into the tank, stopping about a foot above the liquid. Next, ice cold water was circulated through the water jacket in a

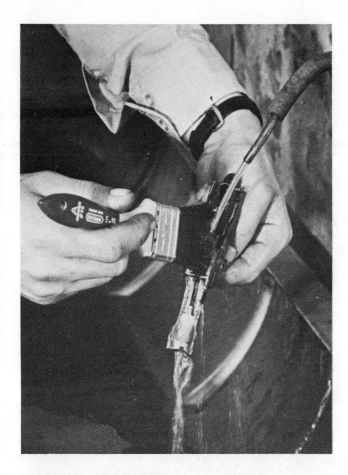

Mineral spirits are pumped from recycling tank, with the stream directed over the part to wash away particles of residue that are being removed by gunsmith with brush.

constant flow. Once the water was going good, the heat was slowly turned up. The heat quickly vaporized the liquid and the vapor surrounded the guns as it rose toward the top of the tank. On reaching the layer of cold air created by the ice water jacket, the liquid condensed and fell back on the guns as droplets. The guns were catching it, going up and coming down. About fifteen minutes of this and the heat was turned off and the tank allowed to cool before the guns were withdrawn. Even the linseed oil in the stocks was removed. This, to the best of my knowledge, is the most efficient way of getting grease out of a gun, but it is like killing a fly with a sledge hammer as far as even a professional gun shop is concerned. It is also about as dangerous as fooling around with a karate instructor's wife. The vapor can kill and is dangerous to use under any but the most carefully controlled conditions.

Carbon tetrachloride at first seems to be the ideal cleaning fluid, but it should be avoided like the plague. Continuous exposure to it will kill you. You don't even have to breathe the fumes, for it can get into your innards via absorption through the pores of your skin and attacks your liver. Leave this stuff strictly alone!

Gasoline will clean a gun, but no matter how careful you are with cigarettes, pipes, and the like, two pieces of steel striking together can create a spark and up you go! While the danger of fire is vastly less than that of gas, the main objection is that kerosene leaves a film on the metal after cleaning. Diesel fuel is in the same league.

The cleaning fluid I use is mineral spirits. This has a low

flash point and almost zero residue, plus the fact that it does a good job. I tested it carefully when I first considered using it, pouring some in an open container out in the yard and tossing lighted cigarettes and matches into it from a safe distance. It just put them out like water. Mineral spirits will burn, but slowly and with a large volume of smoke. This doesn't mean that you can go swimming in the stuff, floating on an inner tube and smoking three cigarettes. Treat it just as carefully as you would if it were gasoline, keeping all sparks, cigarettes and flame away from it. I have used it for quite a few years without a bit of trouble.

The main fault with mineral spirits is that it dissolves any oil, including the oil in your skin. When you first start using it barehanded, your hands turn chalky white and dry, the skin cracking until your hands become quite rough. Regular rubber gloves are useless, as the mineral spirits will dissolve them in about a week's time and the gloves just fall apart. The gloves to use are those made from neoprene for the ladies to use in strong detergent.

I clean perhaps a minimum of four or five guns each day, and do not use rubber gloves, but I would recommend that the hobbyist use them for awhile. My hands have become used to it, but I never fail to wash them in a commercial hand cleaner each time. The cleaner I use goes under the name of Go-Jo, but there are several brands just as good. Just be sure that it contains lanolin to replace the oil lost in your hands.

To wash the parts, pick up a couple of oblong one-gallon cans, the kind with a handle on the end and a capped pouring spout. Stay away from those that contained paint, insecticides or such, as plenty are available that have contained everything non-toxic from orange juice to motor oil.

Lay the can on its wide side with the spout on the end up. With your hacksaw, make a cut along the seam across the can at one end down to where the rounded edge begins. Repeat the cut to the same depth at the other end.

The next step is to cut along the seam across the can at one end down to where the rounded edge begins. Repeat the cut to the same depth at the other end.

The next step is to cut along the rounded edge, connecting your two hacksaw cuts. Repeat this on the opposite side and lift the section you have cut from the can. You can cut the can in several ways, with a knife, chisel or even a can opener, but once the top is lifted off, you will have a slightly jagged edge.

To prevent the jagged edge from slicing into your hand, turn the edges outward and bend them over with a pair of pliers. Finish up by hammering the edge down good to leave a nice rolled edge. You now have a nice parts cleaning can with a handle for moving the can about when cleaning parts. Several of these on hand will hold parts that you need to soak, and they also serve as good containers for assemblies during disassembly or for storage. The mineral spirits need not be thrown away after cleaning parts. Instead, let the can stand overnight and the residue will settle on the bottom, allowing the clean fluid to be poured off the top.

If you really want a cleaning tank supreme, one can be made quite easily from scrap found in most junk yards. The tank itself is made from a 25 gallon drum that is cut in half lengthwise. The two open ends are joined by brazing, to form one long tank. Fill the tank with water and watch for any leak along the joint, closing any that occur. Next, a stand must be made to hold the tank, and an inexpensive way is to use common bed railing as the material. This is an angle iron looking piece of high carbon steel about seven feet long, and used to join the headboard to the footboard of a bed. Most junk yards sell them for about twenty-five

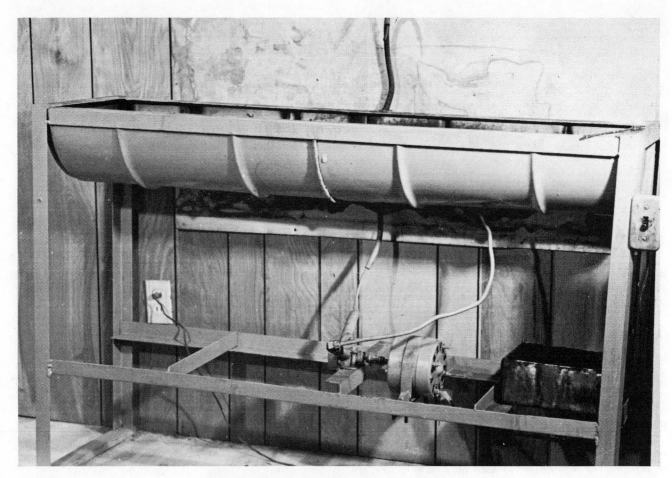

*This big cleaning tank in author's shop is built from a
25-gallon drum cut in half, joined at open ends, Legs,
supports are from common bed railing, pump from an old
washing machine and motor from a discarded electric fan.*

cents each, which is a devil of a lot cheaper than regular angle iron. A rectangular box is made out of the bed railings for the tank to just fit into, and the edges of the tank are brazed to the edges of the box. Four legs are fitted onto the box ends, one to each corner to bring the tank edge height up to just below waist level. Add cross bracing underneath The tank now can be filled about three or four inches deep with mineral spirits, and the barrel and action can be submerged to soak while you scrub the other parts. The length of the tank is sufficient to allow a full length gun to soak.

The tank can be used as is, but a good addition is a steady stream of the fluid to be directed right where you need it. This is a big help. The constant flow washes away the residue the brush scrapes away. A recycling pump is the answer, but the price of one to handle mineral spirits is around thirty bucks. You need only visit the junk yard to obtain a substitute for about a dollar. The pump from a household washing machine will work fine, but it takes a special type. Many of the impellers in these pumps are of rubber and will be deteriorated by the mineral spirits. You want one with a metal impeller, so take along a screwdriver and a couple of wrenches to disassemble the pumps until you find one with a metal impeller. Next, you will need a small electric motor to power the pump. This can be any size you can find. I have used one out of an electric fan for about five years with no trouble. Finally, you will need some copper tubing and two reducing connectors to match the tubing to the intake and exhaust tubes of the pump.

To fit the pump to the tank, drill a hole in the bottom of the tank and run the copper tubing up through the hole leaving about an inch sticking above the bottom of the tank to keep your intake out of the sludge. You can either solder it in place, or use a connector to attach it to the tank. The other end goes down to the intake side of the pump and is attached via the reducer. Some pumps have threads inside the intake and exhaust tubes, but others will have to be threaded to take the adapter.

A copper tube is attached to the exhaust side of the pump via the reducer and the other end run up and over the tank about a foot above the sides, then bent to pour into the center of the tank. The pump is bolted to one of the cross braces underneath the tank. To power the pump, your electric motor is attached to another cross brace opposite the pump. A piece of rubber between the base and the cross brace will cut down on noise. The power shaft of both the motor and the pump should be as level as possible, but a little variation is all right. The two spindles need not be of the same diameter, for they are joined together by pushing a short piece of air compressor hose onto each shaft. A couple pieces of wire, twisted around the hose, will hold it securely to the shafts. This flexible coupling eliminates vibration and compensates for any misalignment. The tank now is filled and the motor turned on. The liquid flows down the hole in the bottom of the tank and fills the pump, which pushes it up the tubing and over into the tank in a steady stream. The same fluid is recycled again and again through the pump and over into the tank. The steady

Connection between pump and motor on the cleaning tank is a piece of air compressor hose, which allows for any misalignment or difference in shaft diameter of the two.

On the underside of the large cleaning tank is the drain plug at far right. Aluminum behind deflects any splashing.

stream directed into the action of a gun, or on a part, is far superior to just dipping.

An added luxury is a cleaning valve, which is just a common off-and-on valve, soldered to the bottom of the tank at one end. When you need to clean the tank, just tip it up and open the valve to allow the dirty fluid to drain into a container. For convenience, I keep a one-inch board under the end opposite the valve and the tank drains itself when the valve is opened. Dirt, bugs and the gunk from the guns sometimes will clog the pump, but just hold your finger over the end of the exhaust tubing and allow the

pump to build up pressure. Release your finger and the sudden surge will clean the pump and tubing every time.

To clear out all the sludge in the pump, empty the tank and allow the pump to empty itself. Now, run in some clear fluid and turn the pump on. This will clean it pretty well, but you can direct a blast of air through the tubing to clear it of any heavy sludge. I had thought about adding a filter to the contraption, but it gives little trouble as is. You can empty the tank when you have finished, or make a top to keep out the bugs, and so on. The mineral spirits will evaporate some, so don't leave it open if you are not using it.

Brushes of various types will prove handy in washing any part. Baby bottle brushes, tooth brushes and similar shapes are needed, but the most useful is a regular cheap one-inch paint brush. To get out jammed-in dirt that the brushes will not touch, an old screwdriver, plus a couple of pieces of wire with one end flattened and filed in the form of a chisel, will do the job. Little or no scrubbing will be needed if the parts are allowed to soak before you start cleaning them.

Nothing beats compressed air for blowing the parts clean. Use a regular air blow gun with a push button. You can make it a little more efficient by soldering or brazing a small piece of 1/8-inch tubing about three inches long into the holes in the end of the blower. This lets you get the air right down into the action of the gun where you need it. About 50 pounds of pressure is sufficient.

WD-40 is used normally to remove rust and crud, but can be used also to cut your cleaning time in half. With the mechanism disassembled, squirt the part full of WD-40 and allow it to soak for a couple of minutes. Run the part through the mineral spirits bath in the usual way and the dirt, grease and powder residue will flow off without any scrubbing. If you do not have a mineral spirits bath, WD-40 will do a pretty good job of cleaning by itself, especially if you have air pressure handy. The WD-40 seems to work as a sort of detergent, loosening the dirt and dissolving the grease, while the mineral spirits finish the dissolving and float the gunk off. The air pressure blows the whole mess out of the gun and onto the walls and floor of the shop.

If you decide not to use mineral spirits or WD-40 and still want to do a good job, you can use dish detergent. Put half a coffee cup into a gallon of water, and boil the mixture while the parts are submerged in it. Then scrub the parts and wash clean with hot water. Allow the parts to dry, then oil them thoroughly to prevent rusting. If you have bluing facilities, the unit's regular cleaning tank will get the parts clean, but will require regular replacement of cleaning solution for bluing. You can build a separate tank of sheet metal or purchase one of the inexpensive chicken trough-type bluing tanks and add a heating unit under it. Oakite, Dacron 44, Blu-Blak cleaner, Dicro Clean 909, or any other similar bluing cleaner will do fine when heated to a rolling boil and the parts immersed for about ten minutes. Lye often is used in home-grown bluing rigs to clean the metal, but it should not be used on just a cleaning job.

After the parts have been cleaned thoroughly — whatever the method — check to see that no grime has been left on them. This can be brushed off with a stiff, cheap paint brush or with a stainless steel brush, in tough cases. Sometimes the grime will stain parts, such as the bolt, but these can be cleaned quite quickly with a loose polishing wheel and No. 400 compound. This sort of adds to the finishing touch. If you find any rust on a part, WD-40 will get most of it off, but the best stuff I have ever seen for this job is Du-ol. It is completely harmless, water soluble, easy to use and a rust remover supreme. Flood the part with Du-ol and allow it to soak for about a minute before rubbing it off. It will not harm the finest of bluing. If a lot of rust is present, use No. 0000 steel wool, rubbing lightly to remove the rust. For high quality bluing with only light rust, you can use a piece of rough towel or similar cloth to scrub the rust off. Repeat the process until a clean patch wiped over the surface comes up clean.

If you run across deep heavy rust that the steel wool will not get off, switch to a soft wire scratch wheel. I buy Du-ol by the gallon and use it every time I see rust, and it hasn't failed me yet. It's also good on rusty bores when used prior to the regular solvents.

While wood has been covered in another chapter, you usually will have to clean dirt and grime from the stock. A good soapy rag, not too wet, is hard to beat and does not harm the finish of the wood. Avoid hard detergents. Wipe the wood thoroughly with the soapy rag and follow with a lightly dampened cloth, followed by a dry one. Don't forget the butt plate, for often dirt is packed into the grooves of the plate. Remove the butt plate screws and check for dirt and rust.

If you are cleaning a scope-equipped rifle, check the lens for dirt and fingerprints. If these are present, you have to be careful cleaning the lens, this is about like wiping the nose of a rattlesnake. The best way to remove dust is with a camera lens blower and brush. This is a little squeeze bottle with a camel hair brush on the end, and is available for about a buck at most camera shops. Don't use your air compressor with its high pressure or the lens may become scratched. Once the dust is gone, the fingerprints are removed best with lens cleaning fluid, also available at camera shops from an optometry shop. Just wipe lightly, using a lens tissue only, not your handkerchief or bench rag.

For rifled barrels, cleaning can be a simple job or a major undertaking, depending on what kind of fodder has been fed through it. If the ammunition is modern non-corrosize, the job will not take long. But, if you have been shooting some of the World War I stuff, you have a job on your hands. For normal jobs, my long-time favorite has always been Hoppe's No. 9, although most other brands of bore solvent will work about as well. Don't hesitate to try them all to find your favorite.

A handgun, if the barrel can be removed, will present little problem. A revolver takes a little more time, as you will have to clean all cylinder chambers in addition to the bore. Remove the cylinder from the frame, if possible, because it is easier to handle and the barrel easier to get at. Clean the front of the cylinder and the edge of the rear of the barrel, for a lot of powder residue generally builds up here. The semi-automatic will present little problem if the barrel can be removed, but, with some, the barrel is attached to the frame and the bore must be cleaned from the muzzle to the rear.

If at all possible, always clean from the chamber toward the muzzle. Primarily, this is to prevent wear to the bore at the muzzle from the cleaning rod. This last fraction of an inch of a rifled barrel is all important, as any wear will detract from accuracy. The sceond reason is that if you clean from the muzzle to the chamber, you will push all that gunk out of the bore and right into the action, making additional cleaning necessary. If circumstances prohibit cleaning from the chamber, then try to catch the gunk as it comes out of the bore by placing a cleaning patch under the chamber. Also, be especially careful of side pressure of the cleaning rod against the muzzle.

Saturate a patch with bore solvent and push it through the barrel, removing it at the other end. This patch usually

contains the majority of the loose residue and, if you pull it back through the barrel on a backstroke, you will just redeposit some of it back in the bore. Follow the first saturated patch with a couple more just like it, then switch to dry patches. Keep pushing these through the bore, until they come out clean. If the patches are not clean after the fourth and fifth one or if the bore looks dark, then switch to a bore brush of the correct caliber. Dip this in bore solvent and run it back and forth through the bore a half dozen times. Remove the brush and switch back to the dry

Lightly pitted chamber is cleaned with 20mm bore brush that is soldered to rod and turned by an electric drill, it also removes light rust left by plastic shotshells.

Regular nozzle of air gun has been removed and a threaded plug inserted. Piece of eighth-inch tubing is soldered in place to direct air flow in blasting away any residue.

patches. On simple jobs this is about all that is necessary, as the bore brush will loosen all the residue from the metal.

For the final touch, saturate another patch with bore solvent and run it through the bore. Now switch to J-B compound and saturate a patch with it. Run this back and forth through the bore a couple of times, then go back to two or three clean patches. Follow up with another bore solvent patch and a couple of dry ones. The bore should shine like new money.

You can clean a bore to your heart's content the usual way with any bore solvent on the market and old J-B compound still will cut more residue out of the bore. It is not a cure-all by itself, however, for it works best when used in conjunction with regular bore solvent as described. For .22 caliber rifles, it is just the ticket, since it really gets the leading out of the bore. You would think something this good would wear the bore, but it doesn't. Even the finest benchrest barrels are helped and the bench shooters swear by it.

For the bore that looks like a sewer pipe: full of rust, rat nests and what-not, you need patience and a lot of elbow grease. It helps first to give the bore an overnight soaking with bore solvent before any regular cleaning methods are employed. The soaking will loosen a lot of that foreign material and make your work easier. Plug the bore and fill to the brim with bore solvent or Du-ol, and let it stand on end all night. Next day, remove the plug and pour out the solvent. Go right to the bore brush, scrubbing the barrel thoroughly, before you even think of running a patch through it. The bore brush, in conjunction with the

soaking, will get the job done normally and a regular cleaning after that is all that's necessary. If you run into a tough one, go back to the soaking and repeat it at least three times. Just have patience and it is amazing how well many of these sewer pipes can be cleaned up.

If all your efforts fail and the bore is still dark, there is one final approach: Lap the bore. Before you rush into this, the rifle should be shot for accuracy, as sometimes a dark bore means little when hunting accuracy is all you seek. This is especially true where only jacketed bullets will be used. But if lead bullets only will be used, such as in a revolver, then lapping may be the answer.

Lapping is the systematic removal of metal inside the bore, down past any defect to bare metal. But it is metal removal inside the bore and, as such, the bore is enlarged. Therefore, lapping should be the last step before replacing the barrel. Practice on a discarded barrel until you get the hang of it, as it is easy for the beginner to ruin a bore.

Suppose you have one of the military barrels of .30 caliber and wish to use it instead of rebarreling. You need a cleaning rod, some lead, cutting oil, twine and some 500 grit compound. A regular one-piece GI cleaning rod can be used, but for some of the other calibers you will have to make up a rod, which is not hard to do. The end of the homemade rods will have to be squared, or holes drilled in it, to secure the lead lap to it. Start your job by pushing the rod toward the muzzle and out about three inches. Before you do this, be sure the barrel is free of any oil. Now back to our lap. Wrap the twine around the rod down about two inches from the end, leaving those last two lines bare. This

Skil variable speed drill allows one to control speed, when it is used with bore brushes, including those that are wrapped with steel wool. The last also will remove leading buildup from shotgun bores without damage.

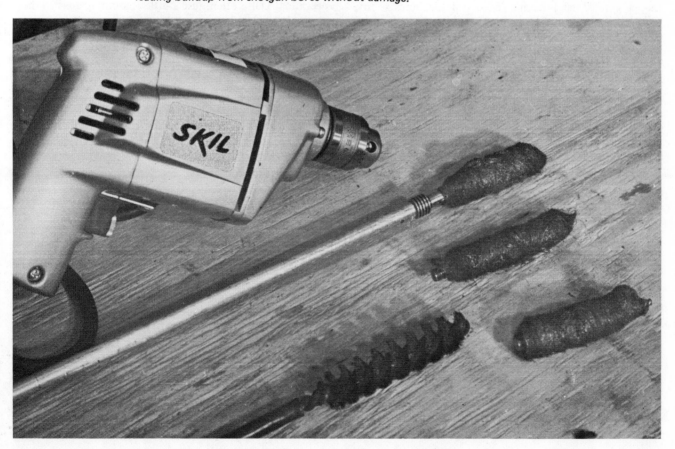

Rusty barrel is being cleaned with Du-ol and four-ought steel wool. With light strokes, the rust can be taken off completely, author says, without damage to bluing.

wrapping must be just enough to seal the bore, so try pulling it back down into the bore, until you have the right amount.

When it is just snug, pull the rod back down into the bore, but leave about a half-inch protruding from the muzzle. Heat your lead until it melts and pour the molten lead around the rod until the bore is full, the lead even with the muzzle. Allow the lead to cool completely before you go any farther, as the lead, in cooling, will shrink just enough to allow the lead slug to be moved.

When it is cool, push the rod up slightly, until you can see some of the rifling marks on it. With a knife, cut around the slug and remove the top portion down to the rifling marks. Push the rod up still farther, but keep the last half-inch in the bore. Remember, the slug never must be pushed completely out of the bore. If this does happen accidentally, melt the slug off and start again.

Make up a paste with 500 grit compound and cutting oil, keeping it a bit on the thick side. Wipe this paste around the exposed section of the slug. When it is completely covered, pull the rod back down the bore the full distance, but not drawing it completely into the chamber. This may be a little hard to do, but keep steady pressure on the handle of the rod, tapping it if necessary with a rawhide hammer. Run the slug back and forth through the bore a half dozen times, then push it all the way out the muzzle. A propane torch will melt the slug quickly and the cleaning rod can be pulled back through the bore. Once the rod is removed from the bore, wipe the bore with several saturated patches and the usual dry one.

Check the bore thoroughly to see whether your lapping operation has been successful. If it is still on the dark side, conduct more accuracy firing before you repeat the lapping operation. Quite often, just a little smoothing up is all that is needed. One lapping operation will not affect bore dimensions materially, but if you have to repeat the process more than twice, you may start getting bore wear to the extent that accuracy will be lost completely. So do a good test firing job each time and use as little lapping as possible. After all, what good is a shiny bore if you can't put two shots into an elephant at three yards?

While most people take relatively good care of a rifle barrel, when it comes to a shotgun bore, the general consensus is that if you can see through it, no sweat!

When cleaning a shotgun bore you must take into consideration the chamber, the bore and the choke; each with its own little problems. Every third gun that comes into my shop for repair suffers from a rusty chamber, which also is the cause of broken extractors and other ills. There may be two dozen explanations as to the cause, but I think most gunsmiths agree that this problem came most sharply with the common use of the new plastic shotgun shells.

Back in the days of the paper shotgun shells, the shells were wax impregnated and, when fired, some of this wax was melted, resulting in a slight wax coating in the chamber. This coating protected the steel from oxidation.

Plastic shells have no wax coating. When fired, they simply heat up the chamber with each shot, adding to the temperature. After firing, the metal cools rapidly and moisture condenses inside the chamber. This alone would rust the chamber, but when added to powder residue, it really does a jam-up job. A simple cleaning and oiling of the chambers after firing will prevent rusting, but most people are lazy and forget about the bores. Next day, they have a nice coat of rust and an even better coat, if the gun is left

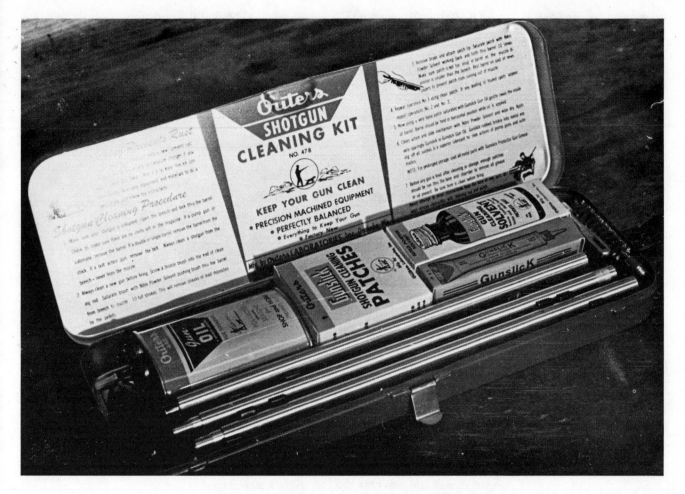

Several firms package shotgun cleaning kits that can do much to relieve problems that otherwise must go to a gunsmith. Outers kit is considered among today's best.

unattended in a high humidity room.

The best way to clean this out is with the use of a surplus 20mm bore brush. If the gun is a double barrel, the brush can be chucked right into the drill. If you will be cleaning barrels other than a double, then an extension must be added to the brush shank to get it down into the chamber past barrel extensions. A rod with a piece of tubing is all that is needed. Chuck this into your electric drill and run the brush back and forth in the chamber a half dozen or so times. This usually will cut all of the rust, plastic residue and what-not loose and allow the chamber to be cleaned with bore solvent and a tight patch.

For easy operation, keep the drill running as you insert and remove the big brush. On 20-gauge chambers, the fit is rather tight, so keep the drill running and don't stop; to do so may jam the brush and make removal difficult.

For a heavily pitted chamber, the only solution is to lightly hone the chamber with a bore and chamber hone from Brownell's. Use plenty of cutting oil and remove as little metal from the chamber as possible. If you cannot get your eager little hands on a 20mm bore bursh, you can wind some double ought steel wool around a regular bore brush as a substitute.

The bore itself usually gets streaked up with lead, plastic residue from shot protectors and anything else that wanders up it. These can be cleaned out with a bore brush saturated in solvent the same as for a rifled bore, even using J-B

Compound. For commercial work, I remove the handle from a one-piece shotgun rod and use it in a 3/8-inch variable speed hand drill. The hand drill with variable speed and the reversing switch is about the best one I've found for this work. A regular bore brush with some four ought steel wool wound around it is screwed into the opposite end of the rod. The quick way to get the wool in place is to stretch a piece of it out flat on the table, lay the brush on the left end and turn on the drill switch. The steel wool will wrap itself tightly around the brush and stay in place.

I run this up and down the bore a couple of times from chamber to halfway out of the muzzle. The steel wool does not harm the bore in any way; it only polishes it. Make up these cleaners in different gauges and stamp the gauge number on the brush shank. I have used this system personally for about four years on an over and under and the bore micrometer registers the same as the day I bought the gun. The bore is as slick and clean as a greased eel.

The choke of a shotgun will close up slowly after repeated shooting, due to leading and plastic residue build-up. If neglected, the pattern will be drastically affected and, in extreme cases, the end of the barrel can rupture from this excess constriction. Getting this build-up out of the choke can be done with solvent and J-B Compound, but the steel wool-wrapped bore brush will clean it a lot slicker and faster. If the choke is rust pitted, it can be honed, but take care. Anytime you lap or hone the choke, you are altering the pattern. So do so only if the rust is affecting the pattern and not just for appearance sake.

There is no shortage of gun oil. Everybody and his grandmother has some on the market, ranging from pure lard to the finest modern chemical concoctions. Strange as it may seem, about 99 percent of them will prevent rust and make parts work better together with less friction. That other one-tenth of one percent includes the sewing machine oil that lists a mile of uses and ends up saying "and guns." This is the only one to avoid, as it is a dirt attracter

Probably the oldest of the gun oils is sperm oil, which, as the name implies, is taken from the sperm whale and highly refined. Being an animal oil, it avoids some of the pitfalls of petroleum-based oils, like gumming. It is used in the most delicate of instruments for lubrication and does a supreme job. But, it has two faults. First, it smells like a three-week old dead fish. Second, it is not a good rust preventer where perspiration is involved. So it's best used on the internal parts of a gun. Many of the oldtime quality guns, when disassembled, will reveal sperm oil in the lock parts, still

This heavily engraved Winchester Model 21 was put in the rack without cleaning. It rusted badly, as is evidenced by lower photo. Rust was removed with 20mm bore brush, then the pits honed out. Gun later was refinished completely and reblued.

supreme! The hobbyist can have his choice of a dozen or more individual brands, just so long as it is designed primarily for gun use.

There is little point in long technical discussions of viscosity, flash point, and so on for little such information and data is available from manufacturers. Most are close-mouthed about such facts. It is best to buy a bottle of the super-duper wonder oil and try it on an old junk gun, running your own rust tests and forgetting the fancy advertising. I have seen some that promised the moon, but wouldn't keep stainless steel from rusting.

doing a first class lubricating job after years of use. I have used it for years in my personal guns and consider it one of the best lubricants available.

Perhaps the most common gun oil is that with a petroleum base. Usually, these have a thinner added to lower the viscosity (thickness or flowing ability), plus other ingredients, to resist rust and neutralize the salt and acid in perspiration. Every company has its own formula and, as I said, about all of them work. One of the best in this class that I have found is Sheath, manufactured by the Casey Chemical Company and available in the regular pinch can or

A few light strokes on the 555 grit buffing wheel can be
used to remove light rust, pits or stains from gun parts.

pressure spray can. The latter is the one I use in the shop
for commercial work. Good oils along this line include
Hoppe's SRP-2, Outers, Browning, and many others. A
good petroleum-based oil available for peanuts is the military general purpose oil found in the small olive drab can
that is so familiar to anyone who has been in the service.
The government goes to great extremes to get the best available oil, but most shooters turn their noses up at it just
because it doesn't contain ingredient X.

Silicon-based gun oils are hard to tie down, since many
of the petroleum-based oils use it as one of their ingredients. It usually is found in wipe cloths, but you may buy
the straight stuff and make your own wipe cloths. It's
expensive, about a hundred dollars per gallon, but only a
small amount is needed.

Graphite is widely known and found in general use for
locks, which, in my opinion, is where it should stay. I
despise getting a gun in the shop, after the owner has
crammed it full of this stuff since it is a nightmare to
remove. There are several secret "oils" on the market that
use graphite as a base, most with nothing but plain mineral
oil added to dilute the stuff and pass it off as an oil.

The final type is the pure synthetic oil, which few of us
know much about, except that those designed for gun use

do a good job. The top of the list of synthetic gun oils is
Anderol, which lubricates, prevents rust and has an unusual
temperature range from 50 below to over 300 degrees
above Fahrenheit. It sticks to a gun and does not wipe or
wear off easily.

Important is the application of the oil to the gun. Too
little oil and you have friction problems, while too much oil
gums up the action to prevent correct functioning. Use the
minimum amount of oil needed and put it where it is
needed. Every bearing point should have a thin film of oil.
A trick to get it in the right place is to use a thin piece of
wire which is dipped into the oil. Turn it sideways to hold
the oil on the wire, then up-ended it to allow it to drop
right at the point you want it.

As to the outside of the gun, you have three methods.
The pressurized cans will spray it in the general direction of
the gun and some will even get on the gun. The rest goes
flying off to the sides, lubricating and preserving such
things as bystanders, the chair, the cat, the bench and even
your cup of coffee. Another way is to put a few drops up
and down the gun and rub them in with a patch. I've always
leaned to putting oil on the patch first, then wiping it
where I want it. Just get it all over the outside in a thin,
even film and down into the cracks and crevices, keeping it
off the wood.

GENERAL REPAIR TECHNIQUES

...Or The Do's And The Don'ts Of How-To-Do-It!

Chapter 13

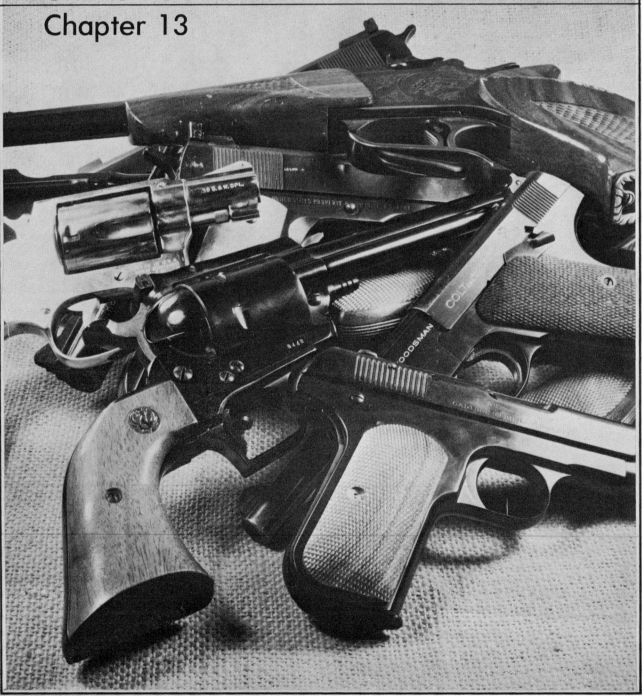

THE AVERAGE SPORTSMAN'S mental picture of gun repair is one of a poorly paid old gentlemen hunched over a dimly lighted vise, carefully filing a replacement part out of bar steel.

This was once true, but the modern day professional gunsmith is a far cry from this classic portrayal. His shop is modern, well lighted and filled with good machine tools to do the work in the shortest length of time. As for pay, the professional gunsmith charges about the same rate as a machinist.

While this may shatter some romantic dreams, most professionals work under a basic rule: When a part is beyond minor adjustment, it is replaced with a new factory part if such a part is available. Only as a last resort will a professional manufacture a part.

There are several reasons, but perhaps the two most important are cost and quality. Why should he set up his lathe to manufacture a replacement screw, when he can use a factory screw that costs less than fifty cents? No gunsmith or machinist can compete with mass production cost-wise in turning out replacement parts.

As to quality, usually the factory part is made to close tolerance and heat control. The gunsmith is hard pressed to duplicate this tolerance and heat control, while it is almost impossible for the small professional shop or the hobbyist. This does not mean that the professional just tosses in new parts by the score. He does everything in his power to repair the existing part and, more often than not, is successful, but such repair is usually a simple adjustment. With obsolete guns he is forced to manufacture a part and the customer understands that such hand and machine work must be charged for on an hourly basis. It is hard to justify

a $4 charge for a hand-made screw, when a factory replacement costs only fifty cents or less!

Most hobbyists feel they can take as much time as needed to manufacture a needed part. While this is true, hobbyists should use factory parts whenever possible, even if a long delay awaiting shipment is involved. Many people have been injured from gun parts made from scrap or cold rolled steel, such as a firing pin out of a nail or some other such potential disaster. You just cannot pick up any old piece of metal lying around and make a gun part of it. Gun parts are made predominantly from good tool steel, carefully heat-treated and tempered.

I once was asked why someone didn't write a book listing all the different malfunctions of guns and how to repair them. It would be a monumental task and it would have to be in looseleaf form to allow for all the new things that crop up. Each model has its own peculiarities and it just takes time and experience to become thoroughly familiar with all of them. Just when you are feeling confident, something new pops up to make you scratch your head. But, regardless of the type of gun or the model, there are similar components in all of them that suffer from similar ills. The hobbyist, with a good working knowledge of these, at least knows where to get started, what to look for, and what to do basically in making corrections.

Failure to extract the fired case is probably the most common malfunction in firearms. It can stem from a dozen different causes, some simple and others complex, but all fairly easily corrected. The various makes and models treat the extraction function slightly differently, but all have the primary purpose of extracting a case from the chamber. This is done through a hook that catches on the rim or extraction groove of the case, holding the case securely to the face of the bolt until the case is withdrawn. All models have the primary extractor attached to the bolt next to the ejection port in the receiver, but some models will have a secondary extractor mounted on the opposite side of the bolt. The function of the primary extractor is to withdraw the shell, but the function of the secondary extractor is more to hold the case firmly against the primary extractor

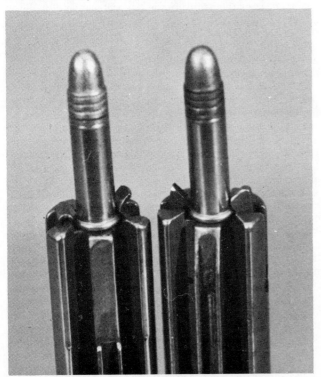

Of two Savage .22 rimfire rifle bolts, one on right has machined extractor, while one on left utilizes a stamped spring. The groove in the bolt actuates the feed mechanism, when it is worked back and forth.

Various types of extractors include (bottom left) shotgun type held under pressure by spring at its rear. Bottom right is common stamped type; spring and plunger at center left. Center right, .22 rifle extractor; the long M1911 Colt extractor is from solid spring steel.

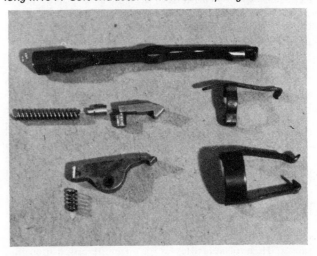

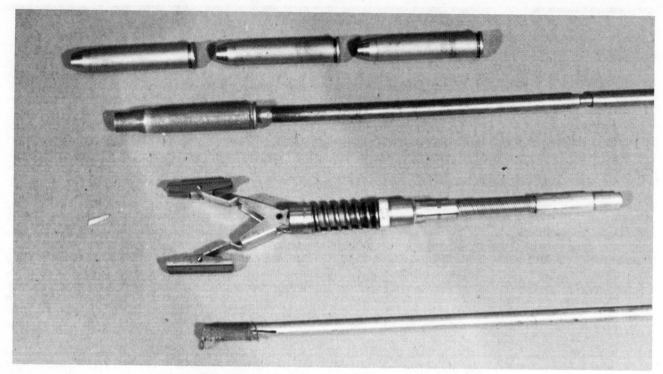

To polish rusty or pitted chamber, small bottom rod is a piece of .22 cleaning rod split with hacksaw, piece of 400 grit aluminum-oxide cloth around it. Center hone cleans up shotgun chambers. Top rod is a fired case soft-soldered to rod, then covered with a mixture of 600 grit aluminum oxide dust, cutting oil. Inserted in rough chamber it is rotated with hand drill, then chamber should be checked during polishing with headspace gauges shown.

than to do any real extraction.

Quite often, the secondary extractor will break off and the primary still will extract the case; but seldom can the secondary extractor remove the case, if the primary is broken. A good example of this system is found in the Browning five-shot automatic shotgun. One of the first things to check in an unfamiliar model gun is whether it has a defective secondary extractor when the primary extractor is in good shape.

Undoubtedly, one of the most common causes of extraction problems lies in the chamber of the gun rather than the extractor itself. Get some light up in the chamber and look for rust, deep pits, rings and fouling of any kind. Any of these can prevent the fired case from being extracted. When a cartridge or shotgun shell is fired, the gas exerts several tons of pressure against the inner walls of the case, pressing it against the sides of the chamber. This pressure causes the case to flow into any crack, pit or crevice in the walls of the chamber.

Once the pressure subsides, the case will spring back toward its original shape and dimensions. If the chamber is smooth, the difference in the chamber and case dimensions is enough for the case to be out of hard contact and it is withdrawn by the extractor with little or no trouble. But, should any pits, rings, or so on be present, the case will have "flowed" into them and will retain some of the shape of the pit, resulting in a case stuck against the wall of the chamber which will not extract. The deeper the defect, or the more the fouling, the worse it gets.

With a shotgun, a hone can be used to polish the chamber and cut a tiny amount of metal out to prevent case sticking. This enlarges the chamber size, but if not overdone, the slight change will not affect performance or safety. High power rifles are a different proposition and

great care must be taken in polishing the chamber. A trick I have used is to take a fired case, remove the primer and solder a small rod in its place. The case is coated with cutting oil and sprinkled with No. 600 grit aluminum oxide dust. The rod is inserted in the hand drill and case into the chamber. Turn the handle of the egg beater type drill about a dozen times, pressing the case firmly against the chamber, then remove it. Clean the chamber of all residue and inspect it under a strong light. Usually, one trip is all that is necessary to clean up light defects, but you may have to do it a couple or more times on the tough ones.

If the gun is a rimless case model, check it with head-space gauges as you polish, to be sure the gun is safe. Rim-fire chambers can be cleaned up with a small piece of 500 grit cloth on a split rod that is turned in a drill. These methods will remove light pitting, rings and such defects in perfect safety, if a little care is taken and you go slowly. Light rust and fouling can be cleared with just a good cleaning job.

If the chamber is clean and smooth, the next most common cause of extraction malfunction is a dirty extractor. This is particularly true of a .22 rimfire, as it requires a good extractor yet it is plagued with dirt. A combination of grease, dirt and powder residue slowly builds up around the extractor, pushing it out of line and preventing the hook of the extractor from grasping the rim, or extraction groove, of the case. You can do a fair cleaning job with the extractor in place, but for a thorough job, it is best to remove the extractor and its sub-components from the bolt and clean each carefully, as well as the extractor recess. Reinstall the assembly with a drop of oil to make things work better.

A broken extractor can range from it being snapped off at the nub to a small chip out of one edge of the hook.

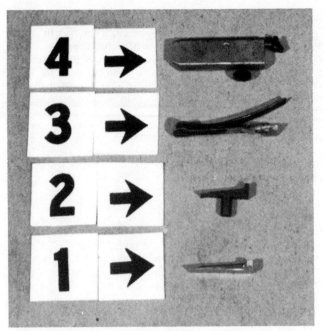

Of fixed ejectors, (1) is silver soldered to the barrel extension; (2) is fitted in hole in extension, end bradded in place; (3) snaps into side of receiver, is held against bolt by spring; (4) is held to receiver by screw in side.

Author calls this good example of spring-loaded ejector held in face of bolt; here, two ejector pins are used. Extractor is becoming more common on newer models; in this case bolt is from a Winchester Model 100 rifle.

Look at the hook carefully under a good light from several angles. No matter how tiny the chip, it will cause an uneven grip on the case and possibly allow the extractor to slip off. Sometimes you can do a little careful filing and stoning to even out the edge of the hook, but in most cases it will be necessary to replace the extractor. But give it a try with the file and stone first, as you have nothing to lose and you might get lucky. However, settle only for perfect function.

The worn extractor is a hard one to spot. Sometimes just the edge of the hook will be worn or the angle worn slightly, but both are impaired enough to allow the hook to slip off the case rim or groove. If you have another gun of the same model or a new extractor available, you can compare the two, but otherwise it is hard to detect wear.

Try slipping a case under the extractor and pulling the case straight away from the breech bolt. If the extractor is working right, it should be extremely difficult, even impossible, to pull it straight out of the grasp of the hook. If the extractor is worn, the case will come out easily. You sometimes can recut the claw angle to allow the extractor to grip the case rim firmly. The underside of the extractor bears against the side of the bolt and is positioned by it. A worn extractor can be reworked occasionally by cutting it slightly on the underside to allow the extractor to move farther toward the center of the bolt. This, with reshaping the hook, saves a lot of extractors that would otherwise be replaced.

On .22 rimfires, be careful about cutting away the under-side of the extractor, for if it goes in too far, it acts as a firing pin by hitting the rim of the case, especially in semi-automatic models. This happened to me once, and I had a full automatic on my hands until the clip was empty!

Some extractors, such as that found on the M1911 Colt Automatic, are a spring or, rather, a part of a spring. Others have a spring either under or behind them, but all need a spring of some description. This spring action keep the extractor pressed against the case, yet allows it to move over and release the case when the ejector hits the case on the other side. Quite a few extraction malfunctions stem from broken or weakened springs.

About the best test is to again try pulling a case directly out of the claw of the extractor, or if you are familiar with this particular model, you can test it by pulling on it with your finger tip. If the spring is weak, little will be gained by stretching it out, since the fault is in the spring to stay and would require re-tempering. It is best to just replace the spring.

Another common extractor failure is found in some models that use a plunger between the spring and extractor. This is a small pin that, in some versions, is square on both ends. Others have a section cut away to exert pressure in a certain way against the side of the extractor. The cut-away models sometimes get turned sideways or completely over to jam the extractor. Dirt and powder residue, along with nicks and burrs, can cause the plunger to jam and, in the process, jam the extractor. Take a close look at the plunger when you are checking the spring for these and, at the same time, be sure the plunger is not somebody's homemade idea of what the pin should be rather than a factory pin.

Some extractors are pinned to the bolt, while others are just a snap fit. On the pinned versions, check to see if the pin is broken. This is a hard one to detect and often is overlooked in the search for extractor failure. Use a factory replacement pin if possible, as the pin must be quite strong to resist the pressure put on it. If a replacement pin is not available, drill rod can be turned to make one.

An odd-ball cause of extraction failure may be found in some semi-automatic rifles and shotguns, especially the gas-operated types. Excess gas is bled to the gas piston; this works the action prematurely, causing the gun to unlock before the pressure has dropped completely in the chamber. This is not soon enough to cause case rupture, but soon enough to seal the case to the chamber; the extractor just snaps over the case rim without extracting it. This can be spotted by a tear in the case rim and double checked by working a live round by hand through the chamber.

If the live round extracts, insert a fired case and again work the action by hand. If the case is extracted, your problem is one of action timing and not extractor trouble. The long, recoil-operated shotguns, such as the Browning or M-11 Remington, have a similar problem, if the bronze friction brake is not working correctly and the action is slammed to the rear too quickly.

The opposite is true of the short cycle. The action does not recoil far enough to the rear to allow the case to be pulled from the chamber; it just recloses and rechambers the empty shell. This usually is quite obvious in most models, as the gun will not be recocked. Double check by working the action by hand with a fired shell and, if it functions correctly, you can be sure of a short cycle.

In gas-operated guns, it means that insufficient gas is being metered to the piston, usually due to a build-up of carbon around the gas vent hole. In the long recoil guns, it is due either to the bronze friction ring being set on high power and using a low power shell, a rough outer magazine surface or the shooter failing to put the gun fully to his shoulder.

A short cycle in a straight blow-back gun, such as the common .22 semi-automatic or some of the small hand-guns, usually is due to the recoil spring being too heavy for the round used. Regardless of cause, the short cycle is quite common and one of the chief malfunctions in extraction.

Repeated firing of .22 short ammunition in a .22 long rifle chamber will burn the chamber just in front of the short case. This attracts moisture and rust results to eat away the surface of the chamber. When a long rifle cartridge is fired, the case swells into this rust-ring and the case fails to extract. The gun then has to be rebarreled or lined to shoot the long rifle cartridge without extraction trouble. Of course, you can stick to the shorts only, and most guns

with this problem will still function.

This erosion of the chamber sometimes occurs in semi-automatic pistols, where the chamber is oversize and there is some gas leakage. The gas burns the front of the chamber, similar to the short in the long rifle chamber, with the case swelling to the point that it is larger at the front than the rear, and the case will not extract. In such cases, you can only replace the barrel.

Always remember when dealing with extraction problems, that the cause of the malfunction often is a combination of defects, so make a thorough check. Take nothing for granted until you check it out. After a little practice, you can run complete extractor checks faster than you can read this.

Once you have the case extracted from the chamber, something must toss it out of the way to clear the action for the next loaded cartridge.

This is the job for the ejector and, obvious as it may seem, a lot of sportsmen and gun owners get the two names mixed up. So when someone asks your help and says that his gun is not ejecting, he may mean it's not extracting — or vice-versa.

The extractor and the ejector work as a team, so the two must be checked out together, the extractor getting the first check. Every manufacturer has his own idea of what an ejector should be, but all fall into one of three categories.

The most common is the fixed ejector, which consists of a stud or projection attached to the side of the receiver or the barrel extension. When the bolt is drawn rearward, the side of the case strikes this projection and pivots the fired case out of the grip of the extractor and out of the action.

The next is the spring-loaded ejector made in two styles. The more modern version is a stud or pin, built into the face of the breech bolt with the pin being forced forward

Multi-purpose ejector from Winchester 290 rifle is in relative position. Curved extractor is powered by same spring as firing pin. Hammer strikes firing pin at step 1. This drives firing pin forward to fire. Bolt is pushed to rear by gas pressure, extracting fired case. Bolt reaches rear of receiver; point 2 of firing pin strikes the back, then pushes it forward to act as the ejector.

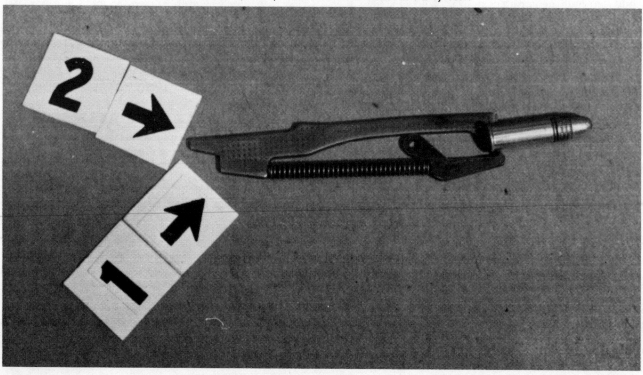

by a spring attached to its rear. This stud keeps constant pressure on the base of the case and, as soon as it is in the correct position to be ejected, the fired case is pivoted out of the action.

A slight variation uses the stud with the spring behind the ejector, but the ejector is fastened to the receiver instead of the bolt. A good example of this type is the Winchester Model 12 shotgun.

The final type is the multi-purpose ejector, which is used for more than one function, such as also being the firing pin. This is an old design and a good one. About the most modern example that comes to mind is the Winchester M-190-290 series of rimfire rifles. In this, the firing pin functions normally, but when the bolt recoils to the rear, its back strikes a plate in the receiver, pushing the firing pin forward to act as the ejector.

A broken ejector is the most common cause of ejector problems and a quick check is all that is necessary to spot it, if you know what the one in this particular model is supposed to look like. Sometimes one of these looks perfectly all right, but actually is broken or chipped. The best check is to work the action slowly by hand and see whether the ejector is striking the case correctly. A broken or weak spring in the spring-loaded type will present a problem occasionally, this it pays to check the spring while you are looking the ejector over. The multi-purpose type can be spotted in a second, for usually, their failure includes their other task as well as ejection. About all you can do in most cases is replace the ejector, but you may be able to do a

good welding job with 3.5 nickel steel rod and reshape the broken ejector.

Worn ejectors are not common on new guns, but will sometimes be found on a gun that has seen a lot of hard service. On some guns the ejector is at a 90-degree angle to the bore line, but on others it is angled so there is no fixed explanation of what to look for. Spotting a worn ejector requires prior knowledge of what one looks like when new, but working the action by hand and closely examining the contact against the case base is the best check. Repair is exactly the same as that for a broken ejector; replace or build up with welding and recut. I weld only when absolutely necessary.

The stud or projection-type ejector is usually welded, silver soldered or screwed to the receiver or barrel extension. These work loose after prolonged firing and, in the case of the screwed-on type, you sometimes can solve the problem by using Loc-Tite on the screw or staking it in place. The welded or silver-soldered type also work loose, but can be repaired by flowing in a small amount of silver solder to lock it securely in place.

On the ejectors fitted to the barrel extension or the frame, the correct function depends on the bolt riding solidly against the ejector with just enough clearance to prevent binding. Sloppy manufacture or wear will leave a gap that can cause erratic ejection which is hard to spot. On some models, you can peen the end of the ejector enough to make it move out for a close fit, but some will require manufacture of an oversize ejector to fill the gap.

In ejector system from single barrel Stevens 94 shotgun, No. 1 is ejector powered by spring at its rear. Small notch in front of the arrow is caught by sear (2), powered by same spring. Assembly is held in place under barrel by cross pin (note arrow on the barrel.)

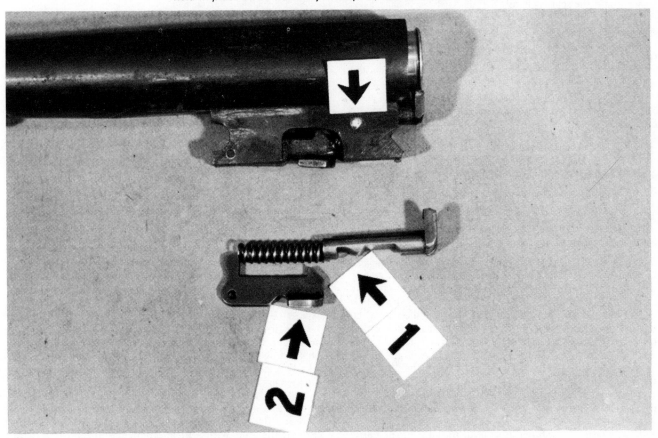

The spring-loaded type sometimes can be bent enough to fill the gap or you may be successful by installing a stiffer spring.

Dirt and grime can cause ejection failure except on those ejectors that are spring-loaded. Looking for dirt and grime around and under any malfunctioning part should become routine.

The worst possible ejectors are those on cheap bolt action shotguns. These consist of a piece of bent spring wire that sticks up in the way of the case. The spring wire becomes bent, loses its strength and other troubles occur. Sometimes one can solve the problem by rebending the wire with a pair of needle-nose pliers, but most of the time you will have to replace the wire.

Automatic ejectors are meant to clear the gun rapidly of fired shells in preparation for new loaded rounds during fast shooting. They are found on double barrel guns, both side-by-side and over-and-under, in the above-average price range. When the gun is unbreeched without being fired, the extractors pull the shells from the chamber enough for them to be removed with the fingers. But, when one barrel is fired and the gun is unbreeched, the fired case is ejected clear of the gun, while the unfired case remains in the gun. Automatic ejectors are of little use in slow precision shooting, but when the shooting becomes fast and furious, they are important.

The ejection system works slightly different on various models, but all consist of two additional tiny actions built into the gun to work the ejectors, one to each barrel. When the gun is prepared for firing, the ejector is pushed into a cocked position and held there by a sear.

When the gun is fired, a rod is moved in the frame to a position that will trip the sear on the ejector when the gun is opened and the quick stroke throws the shell clear of the barrels. If the gun is not fired, the detents are not moved forward and the sear remains cocked.

One time they will eject without the gun being fired, sometimes not eject at all, and other times eject prematurely, before the barrels have moved down far enough for the fired cases to clear the edge of the receiver. Correcting these troubles is far from simple and I would recommend the help of a professional gunsmith.

If you decide to work on the automatic ejectors yourself, understand that you must check the ejection system one barrel at a time, and not try to work on both at the same time. Get one ejector working perfectly, then go to the other if need be.

If the ejector fails to work, usually the sear is not releasing or the detent is not moving out far enough to trip the sear. Check the sear first by tripping it by hand and, if it is found to be in good condition, the solution lies in getting the detent to move out as far as needed. Dirt and grime can jam the sear, so check for this as well as nicks or chips on both sear surfaces.

If the ejector is firing prematurely or every time the gun is opened, check the angle of the "electrol" sears as well as their engagement with each other. Wear is corrected by substitution or recutting. Sometimes, the detent will be moving too far forward and not clear the sear when the gun is opened without firing. In this case, it is either broken, dirt has formed around it to jam it forward or the limit stop for the detent is not working. Anyone of the three will cause the ejector to work without the gun being fired.

Working on automatic ejectors is not the place to get heavy handed, so go slowly, checking and double checking your findings before you go whacking away. When the ejector is correct, it should hold until the edge of the barrel

With automatic ejectors on Savage 444 over/under, bottom barrel has been fired, but ejector is releasing too soon. Fired case strikes edge of receiver, requiring adjustment of timing of ejector. Loaded shell is extracted from gun.

Grease, dirt, powder residue on bolt prevent extractor from doing its job. Also, extractor on left has a small chip out of lower edge, preventing complete grip on rim.

is elevated enough to allow the fired case to clear the receiver when the gun is fired. It should hold securely when the gun is not fired, even when you strike the side of the barrels with the palm of your hand, simulating an accidental blow to the gun.

The firing springs behind automatic ejectors are, for the most part, stiff and the cases go zooming off into the brush. This is fine for the field hunter, but a big problem for the reloader, as he has to scramble around in the grass hunting for his empties. The springs can be weakened by cutting off a couple of coils, but it is better to purchase an extra set of springs to alter, saving the originals for hunting. Cut off one loop at a time, until the ejector is just kicking the fired case clear of the gun. With a little practice, you can catch them

This .30-30 case was fired in rough chamber. Extractor nearly tore off the rim of cartridge case completely.

This is factory replacement trigger with rough sear requiring honing up.

Hammer has badly worn sear that the author says could slip on slight jar.

Browning trigger, hammer in position with trigger return spring. Hammer rear sear is engaged by rear trigger sear, as when held for first shot. If the rear sear fails, gun fires fully automatic.

Common trigger, sear and hammer illustrate firing sequence. Trigger is pulled (1) to rotate pin forward in direction of (2). Lever on front of trigger pushes sear down to disengage from hammer sear (3). Hammer, powered by the hammer spring, plunger (4), pushes up to strike firing pin (5). This, in turn, strikes the primer of round.

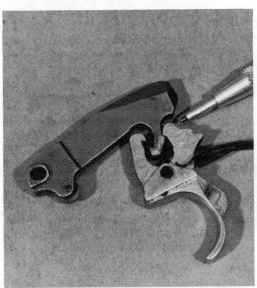

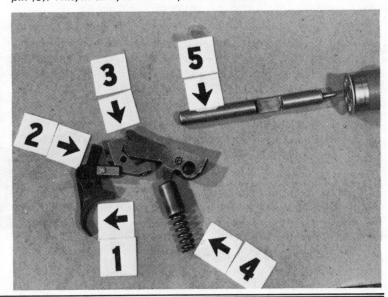

in your hand.

Single-barrel guns have a type of automatic ejector in most models that works much like the double barrel, except that both fired and unfired cases are ejected. The ejector compresses a sear and a spring when the gun is closed. When opened, a stud on the side of the extractor housing catches on the side of the receiver and trips the sear, thus ejecting the shell. The sears become worn, and dirt and grime get under the spring, causing most of the trouble. If the sear does not catch, the ejector will ride up and down, acting as an extractor instead of an ejector. The rod to which the extractor is fitted will become worn and, in ejecting, it rides up too much and presses the shell against the side of the chamber, preventing ejection. This can be corrected only by installing a new extractor.

Failure to fire can be constant or erratic and it is maddening to have a gun snap just when you have the game in your sights. A defective firing pin can be a source of danger, particularly one broken in several pieces, as the pieces can jam and cause the gun to fire when the breech is closed. Never chamber a cartridge or shell in a gun with a broken firing pin or the results may be disastrous. Always disassemble the gun and repair the firing pin first, then test fire it.

There are two basic designs of firing mechanisms: firing pins, which are struck by a hammer, and strikers, which are firing pins with a spring behind them to provide the inertia necessary to fire the primer. Malfunctions are similar on the

two in some ways, but different in most cases.

Dirt is perhaps the greatest cause of firing pin and striker malfunction, building up around and in front of the firing pin and preventing it from going far enough forward to strike a primer fully. On most firing pins and strikers, there is a limit shoulder or notch that stops the forward travel of the firing pin. Dirt and powder residue pack into this shoulder or notch and correct firing pin function is impossible. If the pin or striker is not broken, make your first check for dirt. Chances are this will be the trouble.

Some firing pins have a rebound spring in front of them to move the pin rearward after it strikes the primer. These sometimes become battered or bent; jamming the pin and preventing its rearward or forward movement. While you are checking, see if the end of the spring fits flush on the next coil or whether the end is a sharply cut off replacement. These sharp ends will move up into the firing pin hole and prevent the pin from entering.

On some firing pins, a limit screw goes down through the action and enters a notch in the firing pin to prevent the pin from moving too far to the rear and falling out of the action. Occasionally, you will find such an arrangement with the screw in too far, binding the firing pin. Try loosening about a half turn and moving the firing pin back and forth to assure that it is not binding. The screw then can be staked in position or you can use Loc-Tite to hold it in. This arrangement usually is found on single barrel guns such as the Savage M-94 and some of the combination guns.

A broken firing pin is quite obvious, but sometimes only a portion of the tip will be sheared off; these are hard to detect. On center-fire firing pins, the end of the pin should be a half round, rather like a ball cut in half. If the end is sharp or jagged, a possibility is that this is the cause of the misfiring and also a constant danger, as the pin may pierce a primer. Rimfire firing pins vary in the design of the end, with some square, some rectangular and some round, but all have a flat end. Check the end carefully for breaks or wear.

Pointer indicates projection on trigger which is engaged by safety, when on, to prevent firing Browning auto.

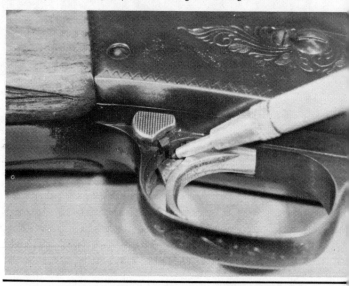

If the misfiring is on a new gun, I have found some with the firing pin too large for the amount of pressure of the hammer, the blow absorbed over too wide an area to fire the primer. These require careful filing, but be certain before you start filing!

On rimfires, look at the base of the misfired cartridge. If the rim is sheared off, the firing pin may be striking too far out on the rim and must be bent back toward the center to fire the cartridge. If there is a big gap between the firing pin blow indentation and the rim of the cartridge, the tip of the pin is not striking far enough out toward the rim and must be bent outward. Finally, check the rimfire firing pin to be sure it is not hitting and sliding off, as occurs when the pin is too loose. These rimfire troubles of not hitting the primer will be found in a few cases involving the center-fire guns, but seldom. If one is found, little can be done, as the barrel is not in alignment with the firing pin and will require the services of a professional gunsmith to correct.

Correct amount of firing pin protrusion is the next thing to check, but this opens up a barrel of snakes. A lot of things can affect this, so don't get carried away with a bunch of figures. Use the dimensions only as a check. Sometimes the amount of protrusion will be well within the minimum and maximum, yet the gun will still fail to fire. The beginner will assume the firing pin is not long enough and take steps to lengthen it, resulting in a punctured primer. The fault will not be in the length of the pin, but rather in the amount of headspace between the case and the face of the breech. If the headspace is excessive enough, even a firing pin beyond the safety length will still not function. Use the minimum and maximum figures only as a check. Standards of minimum and maximum firing pin protrusion vary, but the following is about the average:

CENTER-FIRE Minimum – .060   Maximum – .065
RIMFIRE   Minimum – .044   Maximum – .047

Firing pins of the inertia type, in my opinion, are the safest. A good example is the M1911 Colt pistol. The inertia works on the principle of the firing pin being hit, driven forward and striking the primer. However, unlike a regular firing pin, the inertia pin is shorter than the distance

striking the primer to move it back flush with the breech block. In this type of pin, it is important that the walls of the firing pin hole and the firing pin itself be as smooth as possible and free of any dirt, powder residue, or grime. Even heavy oil will prevent its correct function.

Strikers suffer from most of the maladies of the firing pins, plus a few special ones of their own. One trouble with strikers is binding of the spring that powers it or binding of the pin itself; either of these will absorb the power and deaden it. If both appear to be all right, check the strength of the spring which should be good and strong, but you can double check by trying a substitute spring. On some modern sporting arms, there is a system of adjusting the tension of the spring. Check this to be sure the setting has not slipped. Some of the Mauser bolts have a cam on the front of the striker that can cause misfiring if it becomes battered or full of dirt. The striker cam is supposed to help in camming the striker back when the bolt is rotated to be withdrawn and also to serve as a safety factor. If the bolt is not rotated completely to closed position, the cam will absorb the force of the striker spring and prevent correct firing. Check the end to be sure it is free of burrs. Check also that the bolt is rotated fully, when in the down position. Sometimes, when replacing a broken striker with a new one, the cam will have to be polished to allow correct function.

In all cases of firing pin or striker trouble, wear safety glasses and take safety precautions when test firing. This is

On this trigger block safety the two notches that hold the safety are shown. This one is worn and can be spotted by safety hanging downward, making gun unsafe.

On this single action, hammer is in the safety notch, but it is worn so much that the firing pin is protruding through the frame. Sharp blow on hammer could fire the gun.

from the face of the hammer in full fire position and the base of the primer. On being struck by the hammer, it goes forward, strikes and fires the primer, then rebounds flush with the face of the breech block.

The main cause of trouble with an inertia pin is in the strength ratio between the hammer spring and the rebound spring that moves the inertia pin rearward. If the rebound spring is too strong, it will deaden the force of the hammer blow and prevent sufficient power to strike the primer enough to fire it. The same will occur if the hammer spring is too weak. Some of the inertia pins do not use a rebound spring, but depend on the bounce of the end of the pin

especially true when fitting a new pin. Sometimes a primer will be punctured; when this happens, it sticks vividly in your mind. With proper eye protection and safety precautions, only your pride and undergarments will suffer.

The only completely safe gun is one with the chamber empty. All other forms of safety devices are a compromise falling short of 100 percent reliability. No matter how well designed, built or utilized, a safety can fail. Whenever you are working with a defective safety, do everything in your power to repair it to an effectiveness as close to that 100 percent as possible.

The actual mechanics of a safety involves the placing of

a block of some type within the firing sequence to prevent its function, except when the gun user desires it to function. Two general types are found, although some guns utilize both or variations of both. The most common and the least reliable is a safety to block the pull of the trigger. It is cheap to produce, easy to design into the action and easily operated. A better type is the safety that blocks the firing mechanism itself. Regardless of which type is used, the safety must block the firing sequence and remain in place until removed manually. If it fails in either of these two requirements, repairs are in order.

The most common fault is that a defective safety is not completely blocking the firing sequence and, under certain conditions, allows the gun to fire. There are several tests, which should be made with an unloaded gun.

First, pull as hard as you can on the trigger with the safety in the "on" position. Bump the butt of the gun on the floor several times. If the gun fires in either of these tests, the safety is not doing its job. Associated with these two tests is the safety that is loose and will not stay in position or slips and allows the gun to fire. Check this by the amount of finger pressure required to move the safety from the "on" to the "off" position. The safety should offer a firm opposition to finger pressure, yet work smoothly and without binding. A few will be found that jam in one of the positions and require an elephant to move them.

Wear is another common fault in a defective safety; it can be anywhere in the safety's operation. Most common in the trigger block type involves the hole in which the safety button fits becomes so worn and sloppy that the button is not held securely. This allows the trigger to move and the gun fires. A new safety may solve the problem, but in severe cases, you will have to drill the hole straight but oversize and manufacture a new oversize safety to match the new dimensions. Fit the new safety carefully and check to be sure it works under the most severe tests, then harden it to resist the wear it will get.

Most safeties of these types have a spring-powered plunger that works in two notches. When pushed from one position to another, the plunger is depressed and rides over the "mountain" that separates the two notches. After prolonged use, the "mountain" will become worn and allow the plunger to slip from one notch to the next and render the safety useless. As a last resort before replacing the

safety, try regrinding the two notches a bit deeper to make a new "mountain."

Sometimes this will solve the problem and the safety will work as before. In other cases, the plunger point becomes worn instead of the "mountain" and a new plunger solves the problem. In still others, the spring behind the plunger becomes too weak and has to be replaced. Some safeties use the end of a mousetrap type spring working in the notches and the end will become bent and not exert enough pressure. Bending with needle-nose pliers will usually correct this.

Another point of wear is on the part of the safety that blocks the trigger or maybe the back of the trigger. The gap between the two becomes enlarged which allows the trigger to move too much and the gun fires. A worn sear on the trigger or the hammer can cause a normal gap to become too much for safety. If the amount of sear engagement is too little, even the slightest movement may be too much, so check the sears as well as the safety. It is possible sometimes to do some fine ant-track welding to close the gap, but the repair usually necessitates installation of a new safety, a new trigger or both.

Safeties that block the firing mechanism itself rather than the trigger are found for the most part on rifles, although some pistols employ a variation. Most are made and fitted carefully, hence show little wear and give little trouble. You are more likely to encounter a broken part than wear. But, some of these safeties become inoperative due to wear of other parts in the system and the safety will fail to hold.

For example, in the Mauser system the safety cams the striker back away from engagement with the trigger sear and, even if the trigger is pulled and released, the sear will not become engaged until the safety is moved, allowing the striker sear to move forward for recontact. The striker itself becomes worn and the sear is not moved back when the safety is placed in the on position. Then, if the trigger is pulled, the striker sear moves slightly forward.

If the safety is removed, the striker sear is in front of the trigger sear and cannot re-engage and the gun fires. This fault often is encountered when a new striker or a new safety is installed and the two have not been fitted to work as a team. When installing a low safety for telescope sights, you may encounter this trouble. Always check for this with an empty gun, but check it!

Common firing pins are (1) the rebound type; (2) that with spring that returns to safe position after firing; (3) type that is cammed to rear by mechanical action.

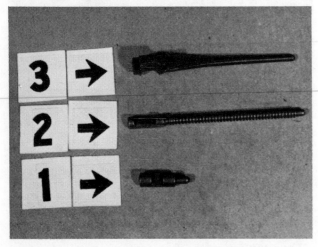

Author contends that this is what the nose of a center-fire firing pin should look like, if it is to be both efficient and safe: it should resembly half round ball.

Few pistols, except the P-38 and a couple more, employ a mechanism safety. In the case of the P-38, the safety moves the firing pin forward out of possible contact with the hammer. There are variations, plus other safeties that involve the positioning of the slide on the receiver, and still others with a block working in a notch in the firing pin. Wear is the main problem here and repair usually involves installing a replacement part.

A jammed safety, either in the "on" or "off" position, indicates something out of line, bent or broken. The gun should be disassembled and each part checked carefully. Sometimes, if you reassemble the safety mechanism, the gun will go back to functioning, but never leave it like this. The correction may be only temporary and the safety probably will fail again. Some jams can be cured by eliminating dirt or other residue causing the jam while others are the result of an intermittent malfunctioning part. Check and recheck until you learn what caused the jam.

The worst possible safety is the type on European drillings and some double barrel shotguns in the form of a trigger block fitted into the stock rather than the action. Being fitted into wood, it is subject to all kinds of warpage and stress from the wood. Little can be done to correct one of these when it decides to quit working except to manufacture an oversize part. You can get a better functioning safety by removing the mechanism, enlarging the hole and glass bedding the original safety back in correct place.

Never get in a hurry when working on a safety, and never settle for make-shift repairs. If you do, you are gambling with the most precious thing on this earth, life and limb. Perhaps your own!

A trigger will give the most trouble in a worn or broken sear, with the wear quite often the result of an attempt to hone the sear. Many a gun owner considers himself qualified to hone a sear for a lighter pull. This is attempted with everything from a brick to fingernail file, often with comical results. The sear ends up rounded, preventing full engagement and slipping off, if you sneeze hard — if it holds at all. Such sears sometimes can be recut, but, if possible, I replace them.

Should you decide to smooth up the pull of a trigger by honing it with a hard Arkansas stone, try to talk yourself out of it until you are thoroughly familiar with sears and what makes them work. Do your first jobs on old discarded sears. Take a good look at the sear under a magnifying glass.

Notice that the angle of the sear is even all the way across. It must be kept at this angle!

If the edges are burred or uneven, there is a chance you can smooth up the pull by careful honing. But, if the edge is as smooth as glass without any burring, you can hone it to a nub and not improve the pull. Your rough trigger pull can be caused by other factors, so double check before you start honing.

Honing should be done only with the trigger firmly anchored in the vise. Grasp the Arkansas stone firmly with both hands, if possible, and brace your hands against the top of the vise to steady them. Make your strokes slow, easy and full length of the sear, taking care to maintain the original sear angle. Make a few strokes, inspect the sear, reassemble the gun and check the pull. A little at a time is the secret of stoning a sear correctly, along with a steady smooth stroke the full length of the sear. When the pull is correct or the sear surface looks like glass, stop, for you can do little more with the stone.

The return spring — the spring that returns the trigger to its normal position once you release it — sometimes will lose its tension and fail to return the trigger. If the trigger fails to return fully, it may not engage the hammer or striker sear completely. This can be a source of danger and should be checked as part of your regular inspection routine. Most return springs are the coil mousetrap type, although older ones and those on expensive models may be the flat spring variety. Replacing a weak trigger return spring is usually quite easy and the springs themselves are not hard to manufacture, if a factory replacement is not available.

Quite often, cause of a rough trigger pull is not in the sear, but in the pin that goes through the trigger or in the hole in the trigger. I remember one shotgun with a pull about like dragging a mule off a cliff backwards by his tail. It must have been a good twenty pounds! Inspection of the sear showed nothing out of the ordinary, except a little roughness. I stoned this and checked the springs, then reassembled the trigger. The pull was down to about 19-3/4 pounds. I disassembled the trigger again and started checking. The pin was lightly engraved with lines running its full length all the way around. Sometime in the past, someone had held the pin in a pair of pliers or perhaps a vise and the lines were pressed into the pin's surface. They were so light that they were almost unnoticeable, but they

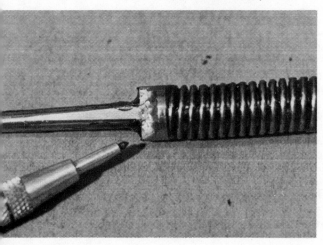

Pointer is directed to grease on the front section of a striker mechanism that can cause misfire in many cases.

Case on left was struck on edge of rim instead of solidly, as was the one in center. Case on right has different type firing pin nose, but light hit makes misfire certain.

were enough to bind in the close-fitting trigger pin hole.

I made a new pin, installed it and the trigger pull was as smooth as a greased eel.

Since that time, I make a point to inspect the trigger pin and pin hole first before looking any further. About 25 percent of the time the pin or the hole is the source of trouble in a rough trigger pull. Check the pin and, if it shows the slightest roughness, polish it and reassemble with a drop of oil.

One occasionally runs into a binding or rough trigger that defies all reason. If everything else checks out, look at the seat for the trigger in the action. Modern production methods get a little sloppy at times and burrs are left on the sides of the recess for the trigger. These will bind the trigger and prevent its correct function, but are removed easily. A few small licks with the file, followed by the stone and crocus cloth will end the trouble.

There are several ways to check the sear engagement, but I use one that is simple and effective. I maintain that a sear should be engaged enough that, if the gun is dropped accidentally, the sear will hold its position and not release the hammer or striker, even if the safety is off. I cock the gun, put the safety off, then whack the butt and muzzle of the gun a couple of times with a rawhide mallet. The mallet does not damage the gun, but the shock is about the equivalent of dropping the gun from waist height.

If the sear lets go, I consider the gun unsafe and go back for a good look at its innards. If there is ever a choice between a safe gun and smooth pull, then somebody is just going to have to end up with a hard pull.

The most common damage to hammers, excepting sears, is a broken hammer spur. Someone always is dropping a gun on the spur or whacking away at it with a hacksaw.

Should a damaged hammer spur come your way, you can file a new spur out of bar stock and silver solder it to the stub provided you take precautions to safeguard the hardness of the sear. This can be done by wrapping the sear in a piece of wet cloth and grasping the cloth and sear together in a vise. The vise will absorb some of the heat.

If a factory replacement hammer is available, use it, unless you want to make some kind of special hammer spur, such as an offset spur for guns with a low mounted scope. Williams makes a hammer extension that fits most guns for low mounted scopes and it is installed easily by just tightening one set screw. If you have an odd-ball hammer for which Williams does not offer an extension, you often can file and alter one to fit. If not, the extension can be silver soldered to the side of the regular spur, taking precautions to safeguard the sear.

Hammer sears suffer about the same ills as trigger sears and the stoning operation is similar. On guns such as the Colt single action, the hot shot fast-draw boys break off the safety and loading notches by the dozen. This is done in an attempt to fan the hammer, but failing to pull the trigger completely to the rear. Consequently, the hammer comes down on top of the trigger sear and shears off any sear notches that happen to be in the way.

You can sometimes recut these, but it is best to replace them with a new factory hammer. Revolver hammers give little trouble except for firing pin breakage on those with a burred pin hole, or the hammer pin itself being burred. On shotguns with an outside hammer, a broken sear or spur will be the most common trouble. Internal hammers are not inviting targets to the experimenters and little, except a broken one, will be found.

The faces of hammers become battered from use and will often prove to be the cause of misfiring. The battered end hits the firing pin off-center and pushes it to one side, rather than straight ahead. The pin drags on the side of the firing pin hole and absorbs some of the energy and, if enough is absorbed, misfire! A few strokes with the file or fine grinding wheel will straighten up the hammer face.

More inexpensive guns may have parts made out of any steel or scrap iron handy and, after prolonged use, the hammer pin hole becomes enlarged. When the hammer spring pushes it forward, the hammer wobbles on the pin and can hit the firing pin off-center or even on the side of the action. In some cases, you can salvage the hammer, but it is best replaced if possible. There are two ways to salvage these hammers, the simplest being to drill the hole straight and install a larger pin through the hammer and the enlarged receiver holes. This is not always possible, and you

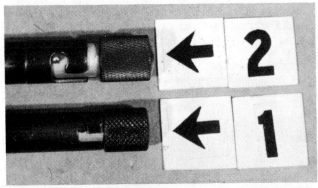

Shotgun feed failure often stems from use of homemade magazine plugs. Correct type of plug is at top, while the twig at bottom has virtually ruined magazine spring.

Failure of .22 rimfire to feed can be traced to ill fit of inner magazine tube. No. 1 shows correct fit, while No. 2 does not maintain correct spring pressure.

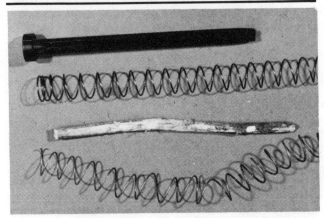

have to go to a bearing arrangement.

I remember a customer who brought in an old odd-ball single barrel shotgun that had belonged to his father. He said to put it back in first class condition, since he wanted it for sentimental reasons. The hammer pin hole was worn out completely and the hammer wobbled up and down. Drilling the frame hole larger was impossible, due to the design of the gun. I drilled the hammer hole out to twice its normal size, turned a bushing to fit into the hole, drilled the bushing to take the original pin and sweat-solder the bushing in place, rehardening the sears at the same time. The hammer worked perfectly.

Dents, gashes and just plain old ordinary bends are the arch enemies of the tubular magazine, be it rimfire rifle, center-fire rifle or shotgun. People are ingenious in getting tubular magazines caught in car doors, dropping things on them and whacking wounded game over the head with them. Even if they fall short of doing a really good job, the small dent usually fouls up the feeding. A severe case will be almost impossible to remedy and you have to substitute a new one, but some of the smaller defects can be repaired.

Rimfire magazines seem to suffer most, due to their small size and light construction. The average outer tube is made from light seamless tubing, but most of the new ones are just thin gauge steel wrapped around a steel mandrel and the mandrel removed, leaving a weak tube. The tubes fit into a recessed hole in the front of the gun's receiver, with the other end being supported by one or more hangers

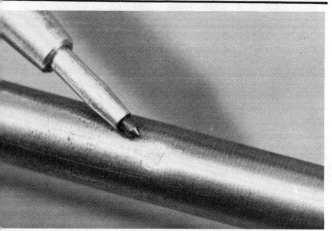

Dents in magazine tube can prevent feeding by binding spring or, in this case, the rim of the cartridges.

Of detachable magazines, No. 1 is for rimfire rifle; No. 8 is for high power rifle; No. 3 fits a pistol, while No. 4 is designed to fit bolt action shotgun.

under the barrel. The end that fits into the receiver will suffer least, because people can't get to them. Often when you remove one, especially on the alloy receivers, it is difficult to get it back into the receiver hole. Lightly taper the outside of the tube right on the very end and it slips in slick as can be. The tube hangers get out of line or loose in their moorings to the barrel, which twists the outer tube off center and can jam or bend the inner magazine assembly.

A lot of trouble arises where the cartridges are loaded and where the inner magazine locks into the outer tube. The cartridges are loaded in a notch cut in the outer tube in the general shape of a cartridge. The edges of these notches sometimes get bent from careless handling and jam the inner magazine or prevent its easy entrance and exit from

the outer tube. Most of the time this can be repaired by turning a plug, inserting it into the outer tubing and pushing it down into place. A few taps on the outside tube with a hammer and that problem is solved.

The most trouble comes on the very end where the inner magazine assembly is locked into the outer tube. The usual locking system involves a pin or the inner assembly fitting into a matching notch in the outer tube. This notch is cut down for a small distance parallel with the tube, then cut at right angles and finally, cut back toward the end of the tube in the form of the letter J. The notch gets worn or is not deep enough on the reverse to lock the inner assembly in place.

Repair is a matter of cutting the notch deeper or straightening out any dents, bulges, burrs and so on. Again, a plug is turned and inserted to act as an anvil, while the dent is hammered out. The very end gets bent sometimes, but can be straightened by inserting a large tapered punch and giving the punch a few taps on the end. Dents up and down the tube can be removed with the same inner anvil rod and careful tapping on the dent, provided the dent is not a heavy gash.

The inner magazine assembly consists of a tube that just slides in the outer tube, an end piece or knob with a pin to lock it to the inner tube, the compression spring and a plunger on the end. The tube gets the same dents, kinks and such that the outer tube gets, plus being scratched from dirt and grit. If the tube slides in roughly, polish it. This, plus a few drops of oil, will make the tube work more easily.

The end caps give little trouble, but the connecting pin gets bent, worn, twisted or whatever, for it is the part that locks into that notch cut like a "J." This is replaced easily by turning a new pin made from spring stock or drill rod. Upset the end that is flush with the outer tube and polish the upset end to assure it will slide up and down inside the outer tube. The springs suffer mostly from moisture trapped in them, but are replaced easily with either a factory replacement or one available from gunsmith supply houses made by Wolff Gunspring Company. The plungers get broken sometimes and you can turn a new one or use a factory replacement, if available. Most of these are reasonably simple and can be turned from bar stock or one from an old scrap assembly may be modified and substituted.

Center-fire tubular magazines will give little trouble as most, such as the one on the M-94 Winchester or M-336 Marlin, do not use an inner magazine assembly and are made from thicker steel. Dents are a bit harder to remove, often requiring some heating, plus the inner round anvil and tapping with the hammer. The main thing to watch is the fit of the tube to the receiver, as any gap will catch the rim and prevent proper feeding. Most of the gap trouble stems from the notch cut in the tube to be locked in place with a cross pin through one of the hangers. The notch often can be cut deeper; or if it is too deep, you can sometimes get by in rotating the tube a half turn and filing a new notch. The tube hanger will hide the old notch from view, but you may have to do some work on the very end of the tube, where it is capped.

There are two kinds of shotgun tubular magazines. The cheap bolt action shotguns use a system similar to the .22 rimfire, especially in the .410 and 20-gauge versions. These suffer similar ills as the rimfire versions. The other type uses the closed system and is found on about everything but bolt actions. These are made from a thick gauge steel, as they often hold the forend in place and, in some cases, the barrel itself. Dents are hard to remove from these tubes due to the thickness and spot-heating often will be needed.

Sometimes trouble results from owners cross-threading

the end magazine cap and repair is difficult. You can file the threads carefully, but great care is needed not to get them undersize or the cap will be blown off during the gun's operation. In severe cases, the tube will have to be replaced. Some of these screw in place and are replaced easily. Others, such as the Remington 11/48, are silver soldered to the receiver and difficult to install. The screw-in models may be difficult to remove, due to rust, dirt and grime, but WD-40, plus a little carefully applied heat, will loosen even the most stubborn ones. Look carefully, however, for a lock screw in the side of the receiver, as some have this.

Some new gas-operated shotguns have a double spring arrangement in the magazine tube. One spring pushes the shells down into the action, while the other spring pushes in the opposite direction toward the muzzle, working against the operating rod to close the action. There is a divider between the two, usually secured with silver solder or center punch staking. While most are firmly anchored in place, the divider sometimes will break loose. If this happens, reposition the divider and lock it back in place with a couple of good licks from the center punch. You can silver solder it, but care must be taken not to warp the tube out of line. Long recoil actions, such as the Browning, Remington M-11 and 11/48, Savage M-750, and the Franchi, depend on a smooth outer surface on the magazine tube for the friction brake to work against. If this surface becomes scored or pitted, the friction brake grabs too hard and the gun will short cycle, for the recoil is not far enough to the rear.

If, on the other hand, the surface is slick, the friction brake slips and does not assist the recoil spring in slowing down the recoiling barrel. Heavy oil will do the same thing. The ideal surface is smooth and free of gouges and dents, but is not glass slick either. A frosted appearance is about ideal. If the surface is rough or too slick, you can get the proper finish by polishing with No. 500 grit cloth or a few careful strokes on the polishing wheel with 400 grit. Regardless of the method, the strokes must be lengthwise on the tube only, not across it.

People cause most of the problems inside shotgun magazine tubes with homemade plugs. For some reason, if the magazine is capable of holding five shells or more, hunters feel cheated if the magazine is plugged. So, they take the plug out later and lose it. Game warden comes into view, hunter cuts a green stick for a plug or jams in a corn

Of magazines for Colt Model 1911 pistol, No. 2 is not damaged, while No. 1 has worn lips and a bent follower. Both faults can prevent correct feeding of cartridges.

stalk to make the gun legal. I have removed everything from knitting needles to electric bus fuses from the tubes. The green stick is about ideal for rusting the spring and jamming the action, aided in its process when the bark peels off. A correct plug should be bone dry and fit the magazine firmly. The ends must be rounded so as not to catch in the coils of the spring. This is one time that plastic is better than wood and I use the new plastic Browning plug whenever I can.

The cap on the end of the spring that pushes against the shells should be free of bulges and dents to work correctly; even a burr will cause malfunction. Check for this and smooth up the surface that fits against the magazine tube. Also, check the inside of the tube to be sure it is free of dirt and rust. A drop of oil helps it work more smoothly.

With detachable magazines — or clips, if you prefer the more common name — when one of these starts malfunctioning, regardless of whether it is for a pistol, rifle or shotgun, the simplest thing is to remove the clip and throw it just as far as you can with your eyes closed. Now, remove the wrapping paper from a new clip and insert the new one in the gun. You have just solved 98 percent of the difficulty in getting cartridges to feed from a detachable magazine.

This is a typical feed system for .22 rifles. Note that, at arrow, cartridge is too high, won't enter chamber.

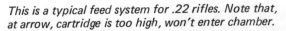

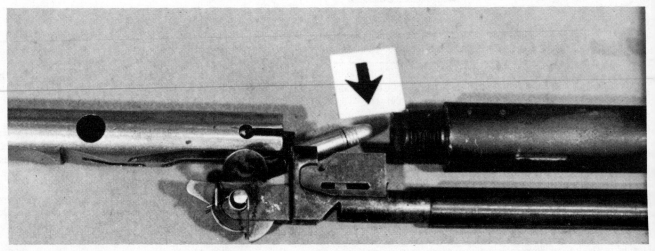

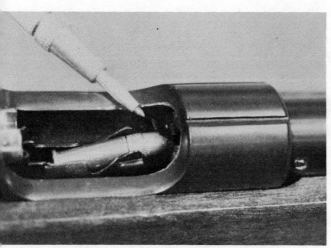

Many .22 rimfire rifles utilize a cartridge guide such as one shown at tip of pointer. This is designed to aid in guiding the nose of the cartridge into the chamber.

If, on the other hand, you are hard-headed, stingy, or cannot obtain a replacement clip and decide to try your hand at repairs, then you are in for an experience. The main trouble will be in the lips of the clip being bent out of alignment. The job looks simple, since all you need is a pair of needle-nose pliers; but it can make you pull your hair. One time the cartridge will feed right, another left, another up, and so on and on, until you are at wit's end. You stand a better chance by turning a metal plug the size of a cartridge rim, inserting it in the top of the clip under the lips and slowly tapping them in line with the hammer, finishing up with a few careful bends with the pliers.

That other two percent of clip failure is in the locking system that holds the clip in correct alignment for feeding. Most of these are spring affairs that enter a notch in the clip to secure it in place. Occasionally, the spring will fail or the manufacturer goofs in positioning the lock assembly. If the lips of the clip seem new and the clip fails to function correctly, check the alignment and looseness of the fit to the receiver. Correction consists of repositioning the spring lock or sometimes, filing the notch in the clip.

A detachable magazine is by far the best feed system for most guns, but when one quits functioning, it should be discarded if possible and replaced, for absolute 100 percent reliability in feeding. Every time I am forced to make repairs on one, I warn the customer that, while I have done everything possible to make corrections, there is always the possibility that it will fail without warning.

Built-in magazines fall into two general types: the vertical feed and the rotary feed, both of which give almost trouble-free service. A good example of the vertical feed is in the Mauser and Springfield rifles, while the rotary feed is probably best known in M-99 Savage lever action and the Mannlicher rifles.

Most of the vertical feeds will be of the staggered cartridge type, although some converted military jobs, such as the Carcano, use an in-line single feed. The Mauser type gives little trouble provided the guide rails are correctly ground or, if altered, the rails are correctly ground to match the new cartridge. The plate that pushes against the cartridges must be free of burrs as well as fitted to the spring underneath. The springs usually are of the flat type, with a couple of folds, and give trouble-free service, except for an occasional one that breaks. Always use a substitute that is made for this particular model and do not try to switch, say from a Mauser to a Springfield spring, as they will give trouble galore. The other end of the spring is often fitted into a notch on the floor plate, although some just press against the plate.

Some newer models use a bent piece of thin metal as the outer magazine box; these tend to hop out of place and cause jams. Every time I work on one of these, customizing a rifle, I always silver solder this box together and lock it down to the floor plate, if possible. This holds it in line and virtually eliminates feed problems. These loose boxes also are a cause of inaccuracy, because they get out of line and prevent the receiver from being pulled down snug to the stock.

The rotary or spool magazine is the best of the lot, as most types are machined to provide a snug bed for the individual cartridges and separates them. Converting to another cartridge involves regrinding this bed, if the two cases are not close in their dimensions. About the only trouble you will encounter with the rotary magazine is in incorrect assembly, especially getting the spring wound the correct number of turns. Check the manufacturer's specifications on this each time you dismantle the spool. Dirt and grime will cause some trouble, but most of these magazines are easily cleaned.

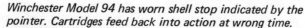

Winchester Model 94 has worn shell stop indicated by the pointer. Cartridges feed back into action at wrong time.

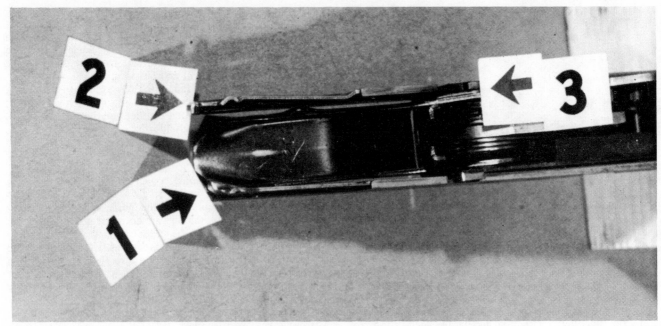

Most shotguns have primary and secondary shell stops. First shell out of magazine is held by stop No. 1; second is held by stop No. 2, as first shell is lifted to position. When lifter returns to bottom position, stop 2 releases shell; it's caught by stop 1 and is ready to be fed onto lifter. Stops are actuated by notches at No. 3.

Ruger has a combination detachable magazine with a spool in their 10-22 that works fine.

When you consider all of the parts and components working back and forth in a repeating gun, plus the accumulated dirt, grease, powder residue, to say nothing of the variations in ammunition dimensions and strength, then it is a small miracle that the gun feeds as well as it does. But, sometimes everything just piles up and it becomes too much for the system and you have a failure to feed.

There is little to any feed mechanism as far as the detachable magazine is concerned, since everything is within the magazine or clip. As long as the magazine is correct and it is positioned correctly, little can go wrong, for the cartridges are simply stripped from the magazine by the bolt. I have seen an occasional bolt with a burred or badly worn end that would prevent feeding from the magazine, but these are few. The built-in magazines, such as that of the Mauser, are relatively trouble-free, with only an occasional broken spring. The rotary spool magazines, if correctly assembled, are equally trouble-free.

Most feed problems will come with the tubular magazines in rifles and shotguns. The mechanism has to function along these lines: after firing, the empty case is extracted and ejected from the gun. At about the same time, a new cartridge has been fed up on the loading ramp or lifter for insertion into the empty chamber. At the same time the other cartridges or shells have been held back in the tube.

Getting all of this timed exactly right in sequence can be a problem but, being a sequence, you can slowly check each component as it works in the sequence and, by process of elimination, arrive at the cause of the malfunction. The feed sequence is actuated by either the bolt itself or the operating rods that are connected to the bolt.

In the .22 rimfire rifles, the feed mechanism usually is a lifter that is cammed up to bring the cartridge in line when actuated by the bolt. This is done by an arm attached to the lifter that bears on the bolt, when the bolt is in the rear position. When the bolt moves forward, the lifter is returned to a position to receive the new cartridge by a return spring. If the end of the arm becomes worn from use, the lifter is no longer raised up far enough for the bolt to push a cartridge out of the feed guides and into the chamber. Replacement is the order of the day if a new lifter is available. If one is not available you sometimes can heat the end of the arm that bears against the bolt and, when it is red hot, hammer the end to extrude the metal enough to compensate for the wear. You can overdo the hammering and have to file it slightly for a correct fit.

On most of these rifles, the end of the lifter is in the form of an arc, which acts as a magazine stop to prevent the other cartridges in the tube from entering the feed guides. This end simply blocks their passage. When it is pulled back down by the return spring, the path is cleared and a new cartridge is fed into the mechanism.

A common fault is a return spring that does not pull the lifter back down to clear this passage and partially blocks it, preventing a new cartridge from being fed into the system. This is checked easily and corrected with a new spring. Sometimes, you can bend the spring enough to add sufficient force to pull the lifter all the way down. The arc end of the lifter sometimes becomes worn and jams the works and is best replaced, but it can be hammered out like the end of the arm to compensate for the wear. All of these problems are relatively simple to spot, if you remove the stock and slowly work the action by hand, watching for the point in the sequence failure occurs.

The feed guide lips often become bent, usually the result of someone prying on a jammed cartridge, while trying to clear the action. Most of the time, the easiest thing to do is just replace the guide, but you often correct this with a little careful bending with needle-nose pliers. Most of these guides are just bent sheet metal, but some models use a stamped or cast alloy guide, which gives better service. When one of these stamped or alloy guides become worn, about all you can do is replace it.

A few of the .22 rifles use a little guide at the top of the action just above the chamber to push the cartridge into the chamber. This guide stops the upward movement of the cartridge. Two models that come to mind are the Savage automatic, which uses a machined guide with a coil spring behind it, and a few of the Marlin bolt actions, which use a a piece of stamped spring as a guide. To replace or repair either of these, you must push out the barrel retaining spring pins and remove the barrel from the receiver, for the guides are retained in a notch cut cross-ways of the barrel.

The .22 rimfire feed systems described are what you will run across most of the time, but there are variations of this basic type, with the same elements present in the more modern, inexpensive models. The older models, such as the Winchester M-61 and 62 and some of the Remington and Savage pump actions, used a mechanism that depended on either a cam slot in the bolt or the action arm to raise and lower the lifter. Little trouble will be encountered with these well built models except in guns that are worn badly. The mechanism is simple, yet ruggedly made.

If you cannot obtain replacement parts, you may have to manufacture a replacement or possibly build up on the lifter with weld and file it back to shape. The cartridge cut-off in most of these older models will be a small cam built into the side of the receiver and operated by the bolt operating rod. If it is not working, in most cases you can heat one of the ends, hammer on it to extrude the metal, then file back to where it will just clear the cartridge in the open position.

I have always considered the butt stock the best place for a tubular magazine, as in the Winchester M-63, Remington M-241, and Browning. The magazine is protected from the usual hazards of denting, nicks and other hazards, as well as dirt and grime — to say nothing of being out of the way of inquisitive owners. In most models, the actual feed mechanism is dependent upon the bolt itself. As it moves back and forth, it actuates cams that cut off the balance of the cartridges in the magazine, allowing one to go past and be fed into the chamber. Only in the case of a badly worn action will they give trouble.

Regardless of the make or model, work the action by hand and watch for the bad part. Look at the system as it works and get the whole function clear in your mind. Don't be surprised if you find some systems where the lifter is raised by a spring and lowered by the bolt, which is the exact opposite of the examples I have outlined. Nor should

Some .22 rimfire rifles utilize a cast cartridge guide system. This can give excellent service, unless it should be broken as is case with one at tip of pointer.

you be surprised at some other method of cartridge cut-off. Look for (1) correct lifter bringing the cartridge up in line to go into the chamber, (2) cartridge cut-off holding the balance of the cartridges back in the tube and (3) the sequence timed correctly.

Center-fire rifles, such as the Winchester M-94 and the

Gas-operated guns can fail to feed, if their gas pistons are allowed to cake up or rust as illustrated on this gun.

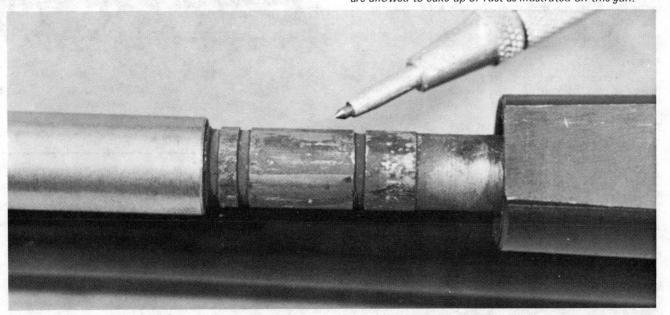

Marlin M-336, use a system on the order of those shotguns, but modified to fit the needs of bottle-necked cartridges. You will encounter few feed problems with these so long as the operator makes a full forward and backward movement of the operating lever. If he jiggles it or stops, backs up, or whatever, then the timing is off and the gun may jam.

In most, the lever is the entire timing mechanism and must be operated smoothly, fully forward and backward.

Little trouble will be encountered with the cartridge cut-off, but the cartridge guides sometimes give a little trouble, especially in the M-94. These are held in place with a screw, which can work loose. The first check is to see that the feed guides are tight and clear of dirt. Damaged parts in these two models are best replaced. Little trouble should be encountered in obtaining the parts as both guns are still being made.

Shotguns seem to give the most feed problems, and seldom does a week go by without a customer coming into the shop complaining that his favorite shell buster isn't working exactly right, as it is putting one in the chamber and one on the ground. You can just picture this poor cuss in the field, game all over the place, the gun loading one shell and hitting him on the toe with the other. Some colorful language really flows on such occasions. While the hobbyist may hesitate to tackle this problem, it is really a simple one and fairly easily corrected, along with any other shotgun feed problems.

All repeating shotguns with tubular feed utilize two shell stops. The primary stop holds the first shell coming out of the magazine, until the bolt and lifter are ready for it to be released. The secondary stop holds the other shells back in the magazine, while the first shell is being loaded. Once it is loaded, the secondary stop releases the other shell, which then is caught by the primary stop. Most of the one-on-the-ground trouble is caused by the secondary shell stop releasing too soon before the primary stop is in position and there is nothing between the shell and the ground but the shooter's toe.

All repeating shotguns can be classified as either fixed barrel or recoiling barrel, with the exception of the Winchester M-50 and 59, which use a recoiling chamber. Most recoiling barrel guns, such as the Browning, Franchi, Remington M-11 and 11/48, use the barrel extension to actuate the primary and secondary shell stops. The others, in which the barrel remains fixed, use the operating arm or arms to actuate the shell stops. There is little difference in the feed mechanisms of pump shotguns and gas-operated models. In fact, the main difference is that one is worked by gas pressure, while the other is actuated by muscle power.

The recoiling barrel guns have a stud from the shell stops that fits into a notch or notches cut into the side of the barrel extension. The Browning system has a secondary stop similar to the others, with the primary stop built on the bolt. However, when the bolt moves to the rear with the barrel, there is a small stop built into the side of the receiver that catches the rim of the shell and holds it there, until the barrel moves back into battery, the bolt being held at the rear. This can be described best as a two-part primary shell stop.

This second part is the one that gives the most trouble. It depends on a stud fitting into a slot in the barrel extension and the stop becomes worn from use, resulting in a malfunction. The best bet is a replacement, but in a pinch, you can heat the stud and bend it to engage the barrel extension more, thus solving the problem.

This same stop often will wear on the backside and return too far, which can cause jams. This can be

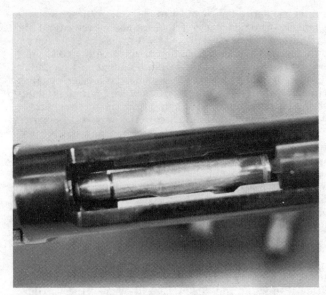

According to author, some feed problems on 94 Winchester are caused by guide rails on each side of the cartridge becoming loose. Tightening will correct most problems.

Incorrect setting of friction ring can cause end of the magazine tube to be stripped off as shown (1). Damaged tube is taken loose (2), new one silver soldered on.

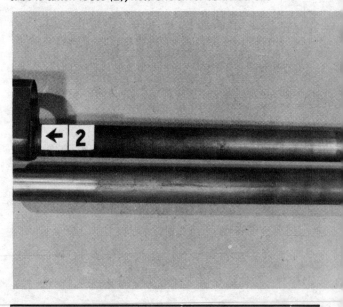

repaired by building up the back with weld or silver solder to reposition it correctly. The secondary stop gives little trouble except for picking up a burr on its edge every once in awhile, but is easily polished and restored.

Fixed barrel guns usually give more trouble. The operating arm or arms, as the case may be, have notches cut into them at an angle to engage the primary and secondary shell stops. The stops have a small extension to be worked by the notches. These notches are placed at strategic positions on the operating arms, which are in turn connected to the bolt.

As the bolt moves rearward, the notches come in contact

Dummy shells should be used for checking feeding. Two on left are factory-made. Center shell has fired primer, rest loaded normally. The .308 also has been reloaded, with fired primer. Rimfire .22 has powder removed, primer nullified by squirting it with oil.

Fired case indicates worn chamber by bulge at rear. The center cartridge is catching on edge of chamber, as shown by dent at rear. Right cartridge has nicked bullet nose; nose is lifted too high, catching on edge of chamber.

with the extensions from the stops and move them in and out to release or catch the shell emerging from the magazine. Trouble here stems from either the extensions or the notches becoming worn, requiring replacement in most cases. Occasionally, the shell stop will work loose in its position on the frame and the extension fails to engage the notch. You can lightly peen the edge of the stop to make it fit more firmly and engage the notch and sometimes you may have to peen the recess or notch in the frame that holds the stop.

The Savage pumps use a system somewhat like the Browning in that the bolt actuates the shell stop. The primary stop is built on the bolt, while the secondary is cammed into position to hold the other shells by the bolt moving to the rear. This secondary stop is long and sometimes becomes bent, but the main problem is the pivot on which it works coming loose.

If it is bent, you can rebend it into position most of the time. But before you start bending, check to be sure it is solidly in position and not loose. The primary stop will cause some trouble if it is not made right or if the lifter is worn, especially in the .410 and 20-gauge models. The shell slips over the top of the stop and under the lifter, allowing the shell to become lodged and preventing the bolt from camming down out of locked position. Correction involves bending the lifter, or sweat soldering a small piece of metal on its bottom to raise it up some, then closing the opening between it and the stop on the bolt.

Shell lifters can become worn or bent and will fail to fully raise the shell. Most of this wear is concentrated on the end opposite the one on which the shells are deposited. There is a little spring-loaded lever on this, known in most models as the "carrier dog." It provides the lifter with a rotating cam for the bolt to act against and catches the devil with the heavy loads. Most of the trouble is caused by burrs that build up from excess battering but these can be stoned off. If this fails to solve the problem, the dog will have to replaced. The springs that work against the dog will break or lose their tension and also cause malfunctions. Some can be stretched or bent to provide the correct amount of pressure again, but usually you will have to replace them.

Again, the best way to spot these troubles is to work the action and watch for the point in the sequence where the malfunction occurs. Dummy shells should be used, since most of the time, the gun will be removed from its stock or some of the mechanism, such as the trigger assembly, will be gone. You can buy some of these cartridges or shells but you will have to make others. A good way to make a cartridge dummy is to file a slot across the body, empty the powder, and pump in a little penetrating oil to kill the primer. Remington makes dummy shotgun shells that are available from some of the supply houses and weigh exactly the same as a loaded shell. If you reload or know someone who does, then dummy shells are not a problem, for the reloader simply leaves the fired primer in position, resizes the shell and fills it with sawdust and shot.

Keep these separated from your test loads. My partner was working on a Marlin .22 once and disassembled the gun twice trying to see what was causing it to fail on firing. Just as he was about to disassemble it for the third time, he noticed that he had been trying to shoot the dummy loads!

Probably the easiest way to work out a malfunction is to borrow a gun of the same model, work its action and watch how it works. Then work the defective model. In most cases, the part that is malfunctioning will stand out like a sore thumb.

There are a lot of low priced guns in pawn shop racks or in the hands of friends that just need a little repair to double their value. The hobbyist who makes a study of gun actions can spot the trouble quickly and build quite an arsenal at chicken feed prices.

Replace the defective part if possible, either with a new item or one from a junk gun of the same model. Whenever possible, avoid manufacture of a new part, but if you have no other choice, be sure you are working with good steel.

A lot of your time as a hobby gunsmith will be occupied with repair, but this will be the thing that moves one up to the status of a semi-professional.

Chapter 14

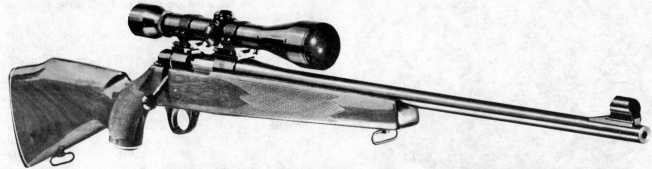

BARRELS NEEDN'T BE A BORE

This Is The Heart Of A Gun's Accuracy And There Are Ways Of Improvement

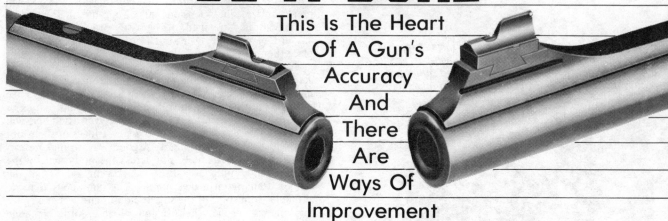

THE HOBBYIST SHOULD undertake barrel repairs, barrel replacement and chambering only when his technical knowledge has advanced to the point that he fully understands what is at stake. To put it about as simply as possible, you can blow your head off, if wrong!

Barrel work requires exactness and quality gunsmithing. Anything less is dangerous.

Breech pressure is the main element involved and unfortunately, most gun enthusiasts and hobbyists read pressure tables without a second glance or thought. To show you what is involved, suppose we take a breech pressure of, say 10,000 psi, and break it down to layman's terms. An automobile weighs about a ton — 2,000 pounds — so we set one automobile on top of another and tie it in place. Now we add another on top of this, another and another until we have five automobiles stacked on top of each other.

To the bottom of the car on the bottom of the stack, we weld a short piece of steel in a vertical position at the balance point. This piece of steel is one inch square.

All of this, when set on a scale, would weigh 10,000 pounds resting on one square inch! If the shell you are firing in a gun exerts 10,000 pounds per square inch,

your gun's chamber would be receiving the same amount of pressure as that one square inch supporting those five automobiles.

This is even more impressive when you consider breech pressure up in the range of 30,000 to 50,000 pounds per square inch. True, this breech pressure lasts for only a split second, but it is still there and must be reckoned with. Now, do you see why I say barrel work must be exact?

There are three matters associated with containing this pressure in a gun. First is the barrel itself, but there is little danger in a modern, well-made barrel. Sufficient steel surrounds the chamber to contain the rated pressure, plus a safety margin of at least 50 percent. Next is the cartridge case which is subjected to the pressure at the rear and around its walls. Cartridge walls are backed up by the chamber walls. The forward end of the cartridge case contains the projectile, which gives way under the pressure and moves down the barrel. The rear of the case seals the end of the chamber but must be supported, since it is not strong enough to contain the pressure itself.

This support is our third factor: the breechbolt, locked into the receiver or an extension of the barrel.

In modern guns, the breech bolt lock-up is of sufficient

strength to contain the pressure, plus a safety margin. But, all three of these factors must work together to contain the pressure. If the receiver and bolt are fitted to a barrel and chamber with more than the maximum tolerance, then the weakest link, the cartridge, is not supported at its rear and the result is a split case and escaping gas pressure. In addition, if you should fit a cartridge rated at 50,000 psi to a receiver rated at only 30,000 psi, you're skating on thin ice, even considering the safety margin.

Thirty thousand pounds of gas pressure suddenly released back into the action of a gun can have disasterous results. Even 5,000 pounds can cause severe damage. Sometimes the receiver explodes like a hand grenade, scattering steel fragments in all directions. At other times, it is the barrel that explodes with equal danger. If the receiver and barrel should hold, the gas can cut the receiver like an oxyacetylene cutting torch. Even if you are lucky and the gas is vented, the stock probably will be shattered, carrying with it the chance of personal injury to hands and eyes, even in the mildest of cases.

Any time you are involved in barrel repair or alterations, know exactly what you are doing or leave it alone and seek the help of a professional gunsmith.

From time to time, one may be faced with the task of clearing an obstruction from the bore. This may include bullets, nails, drills, ball bearings, cleaning rod tips and so on — all of which I have run into at one time or another. Each requires some careful thought and special innovations. The most common thing blocking the bore will be a patch or homemade variation of a patch, about the size of half a bed sheet. Provided you were not the culprit who did it, by the time you get the barrel in your hands, the patch will have been thoroughly pounded and compressed, preventing normal removal. Additional pushing and pounding will only compound the trouble.

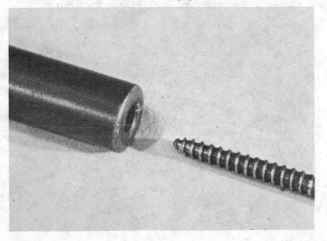

Bullet puller for .22 rimfires is wood screw silver soldered to end of rod. Puller is inserted, when possible, from chamber end of barrel to engage bullet's flat rear.

What is needed is a special puller made from a rod with a wood screw on the end. Select a rod with a diameter slightly less than the diameter of the bore, but small enough for the rod to slide down the bore with ease. The wood screw should be about 3/4 of the diameter of the rod with the head cut off. It is best to drill the end of the rod to accept the screw shank, which then is silver soldered in the hole. If this is not possible, the screw can be butt silver soldered to the end of the rod. Either way, be sure the silver solder joint is as strong as possible, for a lot of pressure is put on the joint during the tool's use.

If you are working on a shotgun bore, you can use a small rod, but you should have a short, large diameter guide on the end to accept the screw. This is to prevent the screw from getting up on the edge of the stuck patch and scoring the bore. The large diameter assures that the screw will stay in the center of the bore. Silver solder a T handle on the other end of the rod.

The most common mistake in using a pull rod is trying to get the screw all the way into the patch to full depth. If this is done, you will find that the rod is stuck and you cannot pull the patch clear. The correct way to use the pull rod is to twist it into the patch a couple of turns and pull. This will tear off a small part of the patch and allow its removal. Just keep nibbling away at the patch and finally, all of it will come clear. If possible, work from both ends of the barrel.

If you reach a dead end and the patch just will not tear any more, it is because the patch has been compressed so much from pounding. You will have to loosen this compression. To do this, fill the bore with water and insert a plug. Turn the barrel around and fill and plug the other end. Allow the barrel to stand for two or three hours to completely soak the patch. This will reduce the compression, but that's not all there is to this trick.

Hold the barrel over a heat source after you have removed the water and get the barrel just hot enough that you cannot hold your finger against it. You will see steam come out of the bore as the soaked patch is heated. The steam will loosen the compression and allow you to nibble away at the stuck patch. There are a few fabrics that will resist water and not be penetrated by it. If you run into such a fabric stuck in the bore, you can loosen the compression by substituting light penetrating oil for water.

For a stuck patch that resists all your efforts with the pull rod, a cutter will have to be made up. Select a short section of any tubing that will just enter the bore, the closer the fit, the better. Solder the tubing to the end of a rod being sure to get a good solid joint. On the business end of the tubing, start to file a series of notches evenly spaced all the way around the edge. Reshape the notches to form teeth about like those on a wood handsaw. Don't worry if the teeth are not all exactly even in size, just so the edge of the tubing is even and the teeth are as sharp as possible.

The patch cutter is now inserted in the bore, pressed firmly against the stuck patch and the rod turned to saw and cut the patch. It is best to do this by hand or with an egg beater drill rather than a power drill, to avoid scoring the bore. I have used these patch cutters a good many times and they have always done the job, except in one or two really bad cases. The final resort is to simply heat the barrel enough for the edges of the cloth patch to burn, thereby reducing its diameter and allowing it to be pushed out of the bore. Quite a bit of heat is necessary for this and you will probably have to refinish the barrel.

refinish the barrel.

Occasionally, you will inherit the job of getting a stuck bore brush or part of a broken cleaning rod out of a bore. Select a rod that will just enter the bore and slide down it. Only this time, you cut a concave hollow in the end of the rod. If possible, harden the end of the rod. The reason for the concave cut is that while the diameter of the rod will prevent it getting hung on the edge of the obstruction, you need the hollow to push any protrusion toward the center of the rod, preventing binding.

Apply a steady pressure on the rod and try to push the obstruction clear of the bore. If this fails, hold the rod steady against the obstruction and give the end of the rod a good whack with the rawhide hammer. If you hold the rod firmly against the obstruction, the rod will not bounce and batter its end or the obstruction. A couple of these whacks usually will get the critter moving, but if it doesn't, soak the obstruction with penetrating oil and try again. As a last resort, heat the barrel slightly to lightly expand it and try. Once you get the thing moving, keep it moving until it is all the way out of the bore.

Bullets jammed in the bore are usually the result of an old or weakly loaded cartridge or sometimes, a light obstruction that prevents the bullet from going down the bore. In most cases, this results in a swell in the barrel that must be dealt with, in addition to removing the stuck bullet.

In either case, there are two rules in removing a stuck bullet. First, push it back the way it came, toward the chamber, as it already will have been sized to fit that part of the bore. Barrels will have slight imperfections or rust pits in them that will make the job tougher if you try to push it out the muzzle.

Second, the end of the rod must be cut to match the contour of the nose of the bullet. If you use a flat rod against the bullet nose, you will just end up pounding the nose flat and wedging it tighter in the bore.

Select a rod that will just slide down the bore, then cut the end to match the bullet nose as near as possible. Press it against the bullet nose, hold it as tightly as possible to prevent any bounce and give it a good solid blow with the rawhide hammer. I have found that the rawhide hammer delivers a softer blow than a metal hammer and the rod has less tendency to bounce or batter the bullet. Whatever the technical reason, one blow usually gets the bullet moving and, if you are pressing hard enough, you can sometimes push the bullet right on out of the bore. Some bullets will require a couple of whacks to get moving, but if this doesn't work, do not keep on pounding. Pour some thin penetrating oil or WD-40 down the bore from the chamber end, allow it to soak for a couple of minutes, then try again.

A solid lead bullet such as a .22 sometimes will resist this method of removal. When this happens, make up a rod with a wood screw or sheet metal screw similar to the patch puller, being sure that the rod fills the bore and insert it from the chamber end and twist into the base of the bullet. With one man pulling on this rod and another tapping on a rod from the front, even the most stubborn bullet will come free. The last ditch stand with stuck bullets is to apply heat at the position where the bullet is stuck. With jacketed bullets, the heat is to expand the barrel enough to loosen the bullet, but with solid lead bullets you may have to apply enough heat to melt the skin of the bullet to get it free. Seldom will the heating method be necessary, if you use the right rod for the job with a little penetrating oil or WD-40 to grease its path.

Right off the top of the deck, the best advice to a hobbyist with a case stuck in a barrel is to take it to a professional who invariably is better equipped to do the job. But, if this is impossible, there are methods.

Some years ago it was quite common for cartridge cases to rupture and stick in chambers. Most of this was due to corrosive primers leaking and weakening the brass of the case. Non-corrosive primers have about eliminated this problem and most ruptured cases nowadays are due to excessive headspace, gun malfunction or poor handloading. Ruptured case extractors were once plentiful, but now are almost as rare as watch fobs and the hobbyist will be faced with the problem of improvising some tool to do the job. Most of the ruptured case removal will involve the .22 rimfire, but the same basic procedure can be used for the center-fire cartridges.

The ruptured .22 rimfire usually means a blown off head

In making special cutter to remove stuck bullet from .45 pistol, thin cutoff blade is used in Moto-Tool to cut the saw teeth. Bullet had been battered in futile removal try.

This is completed tool with cutting edges filed to sharp surfaces. Soldered to rod, it is used with drill brace to cut plug out of center of bullet, then thin lead walls are pushed to the center, collapsing bullet for removal.

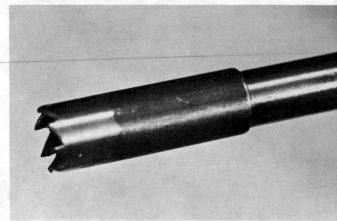

with the case body stuck in the chamber. In semi-automatics, this is caused by either the round firing too soon before the bolt is fully closed, or the bolt weight and spring not being enough to hold the bolt closed and contain the pressure. On bolt and lever action models, it is caused by a poor fitting bolt with excessive headspace or a worn chamber. The .22 rimfire magnum is plagued with this trouble, especially in the inexpensive models that are lacking in the bolt lock-up department.

If the ruptured case is discovered immediately and provided the walls of the chamber are relatively smooth, you sometimes can remove the case by pressing the edge of a knife or sharpened screwdriver into the case and pulling. The real trouble occurs when a loaded cartridge is pushed part way into the jammed chamber before the trouble is discovered. This results in the remains of the case being pushed up into the rifling, where it jams in solid.

Forget about pushing it out from the front, as there is just nothing to push against. Pick up a fired .22 case and cut its head off, leaving the body to serve as your guide in making a shell extractor. Look around your junk box for a sheet metal or wood screw that will just begin to enter the case that you have made into a guide. There is no need for it to be screwed all the way in, as about half a turn will be

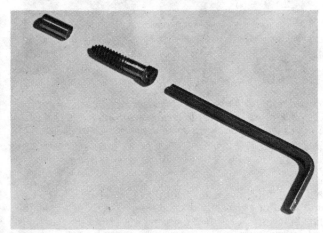

Case remover is made from wood screw. Head of an Allen screw is soldered to its rear. Screw is pushed into the ruptured .22 rimfire case, turned with Allen wrench till it gets bite in case walls. Cleaning rod pushes it out.

Faster than screw and wrench combination is an old tap that is silver soldered to the end of rod, but it can be used only on arms that open at the rear of their actions.

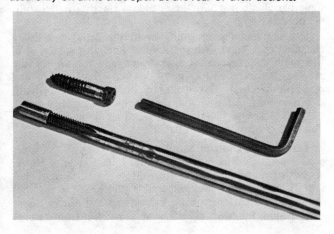

all that you need.

Mark the location on the screw and file off all the threads behind this mark, as these will be too large to enter the case and might damage the chamber. Turn your home-made case remover up into the stuck case, until it catches. With a cleaning rod inserted in the muzzle end, push against the screw and the stuck case should come out with ease. If the end of the screw is filed flat, it will give the rod a better surface to push against, but this is not necessary.

While the screw will work for one or two jobs, it eventually will wear on the threads and become useless. For a more permanent case remover, select an old tap that will just enter your guide case and make about a half turn. A plug tap is perfect, but you can grind the front of a finishing tap down enough to work. To facilitate the use of the tap, solder an extension to the rear and a cross T handle to this. I have used one like this for quite a few years.

On some of the pump and semi-automatics it will be necessary to remove the barrel from the receiver to use the tap. On bolt action rifles this is not necessary as long as the extension will reach the length of the receiver. Once the tap is in place, insert the cleaning rod and tap the end to remove the ruptured case. This same tap procedure can be used on larger cases, if the rear of the case has been blown off.

More common than a ruptured case is the stuck case, especially in center-fire rifles. Shotguns seldom suffer from this, but I have had a few in the shop with this problem. The stuck shotgun case is usually one of the old paper shells that has become swollen or a reloaded case that has not been resized fully or was loaded incorrectly. Stuck rifle cases generally are reloads that the owner has failed to resize to full length for a pump or semi-automatic. These rifles give a little in the receiver and the fired cases need to be resized full length. The bolt action rifle with a stuck reloaded case usually is due to using the case from another chamber without resizing. Seldom will you have this problem in factory cases, except with chambers that are heavily rusted or filled with dirt.

Some of these cases will fail to fully chamber and the bolt will be only half closed, refusing to unlock and extract the case. In others, the firing pin or hammer may fall part way and fail to strike the primer and fire the case, generally as the result of a built-in safety device.

On still others the case will fire, but it is jammed in so tightly that the bolt will not withdraw it from the chamber. Either way, you have a mess on your hands that should be cleared by a professional gunsmith if possible. This is provided you can talk him into it, for most of us would rather not be faced with this particular problem. It is dangerous and the greatest of care must be taken.

I do not advise any hobbyist to attempt to remove a live round that is stuck in the chamber — and any stuck rounds should be considered live unless you are absolutely certain it has been fired. Even if someone swears the cartridge has been fired, I consider it live until I know otherwise. Several times customers have said a stuck round was a fired one, yet the live round was there.

If one can determine that the case has been fired, he can remove it with little danger to himself or the gun. The simple way is to slide a cleaning rod down the bore and lightly touch the cartridge. This cleaning rod, by the way, must be small enough to enter the mouth of a fired case easily. When the rod has bottomed, make a mark on it, withdraw the rod and lay it alongside the barrel. Align the mark with the muzzle of the barrel and note how far the rod reaches down the barrel. Whether the gun is chambered with a fired case or a loaded round is obvious.

If the chamber carries a live round, do not attempt to remove it. This is not a job for a hobbyist and he is facing both personal injury and a damaged gun if he attempts it. It can be removed, of course, but the circumstances vary so much that it is impossible to cover all possibilities in detail. Remember a half-chambered round stuck in a barrel can be as dangerous to remove as trying to defuse a stick of dynamite. One mistake and the case can fire. Being only half-locked, the action will not hold and the case will rupture, showering one with brass and steel fragments. Leave this job to the professional.

However, if your cleaning rod down the bore indicates that the case is empty, the job becomes purely mechanical. To try to loosen the case, insert a cleaning rod that will just enter the case mouth and push it to the bottom of the case. Give the end a good blow with the rawhide hammer. This should loosen the case enough for it to be removed by working the bolt. If not, try pulling on the bolt handle and whacking the cleaning rod at the same time. This usually does the trick and the case should come out with ease. If this fails, fill the bore with penetrating oil, allow it to soak for an hour or so and try again. Seldom will this fail.

Somebody is always changing the looks of gun barrels by driving cars over them, clubbing wounded game, getting them caught in doors, shooting them with obstructions in the barrel. Name it and somebody has done it to a gun barrel.

A slightly bent barrel can be straightened with a minimum amount of special equipment, because the most important precision tool is your eye. Mechanically, all that is needed are two supports for the ends of the barrel, with a third support opposite these to apply pressure at the point of the bend. The idea is to apply the pressure in the form of a short snap, which is released quickly rather than applied constantly. This snap springs the barrel back into line a little at a time. Never should a hammer be used, for this will dent the barrel beyond repair. And never should you attempt to straighten a barrel by jamming one end between a door or under a bench and pulling up on it.

Rifle barrels, because of the thickness of the metal, require a sturdy set-up, but the thinner shotgun barrels require very little. You can use a drill press to provide the pressure where needed, but this puts a strain on the press quill. I use a device that costs less than five dollars to build, yet it works as well as the most expensive barrel straightener. It started life as an automobile brake lining riveting machine and ended up in a junk yard. I rescued it, added a cross bar with two anvils to support the barrel, and a contour pressure lug substituted for the punch. The lug is activated by pressing down on a foot pedal, which leaves both hands free to move the barrel as needed. You may not find an abandoned brake lining riveting machine, but the idea can be adapted to other machines which can be converted to serve the purpose.

In using a barrel straightening machine, first remove the barrel from the receiver, if possible. Next, the bore is cleaned and the outside of the barrel wiped clean. The barrel then is positioned on the two anvils with the bend upward and the pressue lug eased down until it firmly touches the bend. Then a quick snap and release the pressure. Keep at this until the barrel starts to come back in line; look at the barrel lengthwise, whether your efforts are bringing the barrel back in line. Continue the medicine and, when it looks about right, bring it up and use a shadow line for the final checking.

This ability to use a shadow line to check the straightness must be learned through practice and it is best to do your first work on shotgun barrels. Pick out some dark

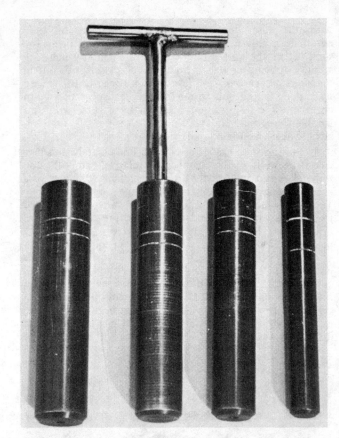

These shotgun chamber depth gauges were made by author to check those too short in chamber for modern 2-3/4 and 3-inch shells. T handle assists in easy removal of gauges.

vertical line such as a telephone pole or an edge of a building. I like to use the light that comes between the edge and jamb of a partially opened door. This is just a shadow line in reverse but is used the same way. Hold the barrel just below eye level and look down the bore. You should see a line extending the full length of the bore, and if the barrel is straight, the line will be like the edge of a ruler running straight and true. If the line is not straight and bends to one side somewhere along the length of the bore, you have a bend in the barrel right at that point. If the line appears broken at any point, the bend is a heavy one, if the bend is to the left, then you must apply pressure from the left at that point, pushing to the right to straighten the line. The bore and not the outside of the barrel must be used, as some barrels do not have the outside perfectly parallel with the bore.

Use the quick snap spring motion a little at a time, checking each time with the shadow line. Just a little at a time with light pressure is all you need, and don't hurry the process, for one lick too heavy can bend the barrel in the opposite direction! The smaller the bore, the more difficult it is to see and interpret the shadow line, so practice on an old junk 12-gauge barrel, bending and straightening it until you have the process down pat.

Test fire the shotgun barrel and see if your efforts have been successful. Fire into a three-foot square sheet of paper at about twenty yards. The short distance will prevent the shot from spreading and will enable you to see where the center of the pattern is. The shooting should not be done rifle fashion, but with a quick snap shot. Shot from a shot-

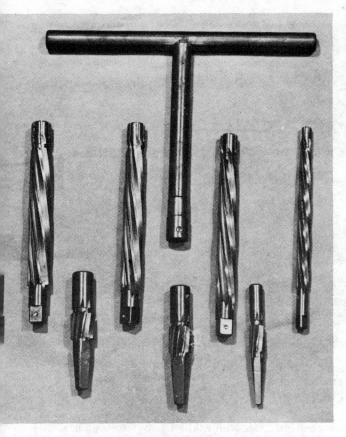

These shotgun chamber reamers and case head reamers are of Italian manufacture for long forcing cones. Spiral fluted types are for hand use. Smaller case head reamers are needed in fitting new extractors to break-open guns.

gun will drop about one foot at forty yards and you may have to give the barrel a slight upward bend to compensate for this. Don't worry about bending the barrel upwards, as this often is necessary with a new barrel right off the assembly line.

Quite often a rifle barrel will be found that is bent out a bit, but shoots beautifully. Leave it alone. During the rifling and contour turning of the barrel, stresses are relieved and others added to move the bore line off-center. The factory straightens the bore line to correct this, but this sometimes leaves the outside contour slightly off. Accuracy is important, not looks, so do some benchrest shooting before you try straightening a rifle barrel. You may be straightening the barrel and bending the bore out of line.

Most gun owners associate a dented barrel and a bulged barrel as the same and think it is possible to completely correct each. They are exactly the opposite in more ways than one and it is important to understand the difference.

A dented barrel is the result of metal that has been moved out of its original position without structural or grain alteration. A bulged barrel is due to pressure building up behind an obstruction or the stretching of weak metal, but in either case the structural results are the same. The bulge can best be compared to a child's balloon in which the rubber has been stretched out of its original shape and remains out of shape. It is impossible to compress the metal back to its original position.

Dents concern metal moved from one position to another unchanged in structure; bulges concern metal that has been stretched and changed in structure. Dents are removed by repositioning the metal to its original position,

while bulges are almost impossible to remove.

In rifle barrels, dents are not encountered often, but bulges are common. Either is impossible to remove. If the barrel is dented, it should not be fired, as the dent will obstruct the passage of the bullet and usually result in a split barrel with possible injury to the shooter. About the only remedy is to cut the barrel off just behind the dent, if the remaining length is within the legal limits. If not, all that can be done is to rebarrel the gun.

However, a slight bulge in a rifle barrel will not present an obstruction to the bullet, and in some cases little or no effect will be noticed in hunting accuracy. If the bulge is severe, it should be treated the same as a dented barrel, but if small, try test firing the gun for accuracy. You may be surprised. A good case in point is a Model 99 Savage-Caliber .250-300 owned by my co-worker, Les Moorer. This is one of the oldtime classic barrels with beautiful flowing lines, but is marred by a slight bulge about four inches from the muzzle. Accuracy tests revealed that the bulge was not affecting the barrel's ability to any great extent, so Les did not rebarrel the rifle. This year he dropped a nice eight-point buck with it!

The hobbyist, faced with a dented shotgun barrel, has three choices of tools with which to remove the dent. The best is a hydraulic tool manufactured in England and imported by Brownell's. Turning an Allen wrench at the rear places hydraulic pressure on a small contoured anvil built into the front end of the tool. The tool is inserted in the barrel and the anvil positioned under the dent. As the anvil is raised by the hydraulic pressure, it is pushed against the dent and slowly moves it back in line. The steady and controlled pressure makes removal of a dent easy, but care must be taken not to go too far, since the anvil is so powerful it may bulge the barrel. I have the set in 20, 16, and 12 gauges. The cost, however, is slightly over $20 per gauge. If the hobbyist wants the best, the hydraulic tool is the answer.

Next are the many variations of expanding plugs, several of which are offered by the various gunsmith supply houses at $5 to $10 per gauge. All of them work on the principle of an undersize metal plug inserted under the dent, then expanded to raise the dent either by turning a screw or tapping a sliding wedge. They are a little slower than the hydraulic tool but capable of doing a first rate job. Most of us cut our teeth on such a tool, and the dents raised with them would cover the moon.

If the hobbyist is equipped with a lathe, he can make his own dent removers. This can be a copy of the sliding wedge, expanding plug or just a series of plugs. The simple method is to turn a plug just under the diameter of the bore, slide this through the bore to partially raise the dent, then make another plug slightly larger to follow it.

This series of plugs will raise the dent, but they are a bit slow and the various bore diameters require a dozen or more plugs. The final plug is turned to where it is a snug sliding fit, then is oiled slightly and pushed past the dent.

When using the solid plugs, if the gun has any choke, the plug cannot be pushed all the way through the barrel. To do so would iron out the choke!

Whatever tool you use, raise the dent slowly and, when you have it about out, tap lightly all around the dent on the outside with a brass hammer. Brass will not dent the barrel whereas a steel hammer will. If the work is done slowly with the light tapping, the dent can be removed completely without any trace.

A bulge in a shotgun barrel, as I said before, is virtually impossible to remove completely, but in some cases it is possible to ease the misery. The first consideration must be

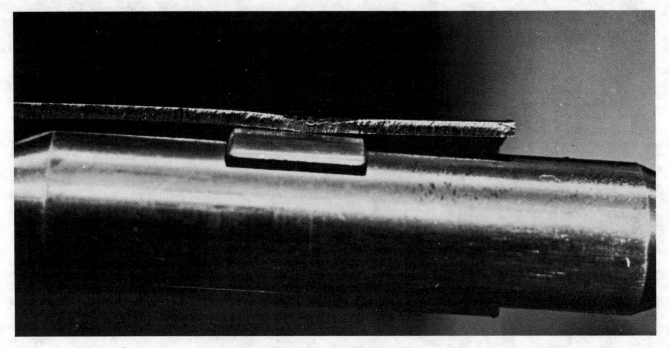

Brownell hydraulic dent remover is shown in cut-away barrel, as dent is raised. It is available for 12, 16 and 20 gauges and author says is the best available.

one of safety. If the bulge is within about a foot of the chamber, it is best to discard the barrel, for the pressure here is still pretty high and there is danger of a blow out.

If the bulge is farther down the barrel, the pressure is less, but it is best to test fire a heavy magnum load through the bore from the end of a long, long string tied to the trigger. If everything is still holding, you can try to ease the pregnant appearance of the barrel. If the barrel lets go, it is better for the fragments to skin up the bark of a tree than your hide and the barrel would have been useless anyway.

A single barrel with a bulge is easier to work on than a double, although the latter can be repaired, if you have the patience and the bulge is not between the barrels. First, turn a plug out of steel that is a snug fit in the bore. Polish this plug so highly that a gnat would slip and break his leg, if he landed on it.

Measure the position of the bulge by laying a rod alongside the barrel, then push your plug down the bore the same distance to right under the bulge. It is a good idea to leave the rod in the bore to maintain the position. You can use a little oil, if you like, but keep it thin. Personally, I prefer the plug to be dry, because it will hold its position better.

With a light hammer, begin to tap all over the bulge, keeping the hammer moving at all times and the tap light. Don't get in a hurry and try to make it one big lick. The hammer must be lightly handled, and each tap should end in a slight bounce of the hammer. When you have the taps right, a stranger passing by would swear that a woodpecker with the palsy was at work.

Just keep at it, and the bulge will slowly begin to disappear. It is possible to heat the barrel and get the job done faster, but I shy away from heat. You will have to accept the fact that you will never get it back exactly as it was originally, but you can improve the appearance. When you have finished, tie the gun down securely and from the end of your string, run a half-dozen buckshot loads through it. Examine the bulge closely and, if it stays put, the gun can

be considered safe with light loads, but not with magnums.

Sometime you may be offered a bargain in a barrel that has been in a fire. While the professional gunsmith often can salvage such a barrel, the hobbyist is better off, if he treats such offers the same as a brother-in-law selling stock in a buggy whip factory.

Some shotgun barrels with severe bulges will be impossible to repair and the only solution is to cut them off behind the bulge. Just remember that the total barrel length must be at least 18 inches to comply with federal law. In a double barrel gun, such a chopping job can provide a quail gun for fast snap-shooting at close range. In my part of the country with heavy undergrowth and quick, close range shooting, many of the oldtime bird hunters swear by a "hacksaw choke." In fact, I have been asked by bird hunters to chop the barrel on a brand new shotgun still in the box. With the plastic shot protectors, a wide open barrel will give a good killing pattern at 25 to 30 yards in a 12-gauge and just a little less in a 20-gauge. Without a shot protector, you get the same pattern about five yards closer.

If the barrel is of the single variety, you have a better choice, as a variable choke device can be fitted to the chopped barrel. It can make an otherwise illegal length barrel into a legal one by adding an inch or so. There are quite a few of these available with the Poly Choke, the Cutts Compensator and the Lyman choke the best known. The Poly Choke will have to be installed by either a factory or an authorized gunshop installer, as the choke devices themselves are not available to the general public. The Cutts Compensator can be installed at the factory as can the Lyman choke, but these are available also to the general public through the gunsmith supply houses.

Complete installation instructions are packed with each of these chokes. The hobbyist with lathe facilities should have little trouble installing them, provided he follows the detailed instructions to the letter. If possible, one should watch a professional install one of these before he tries it himself.

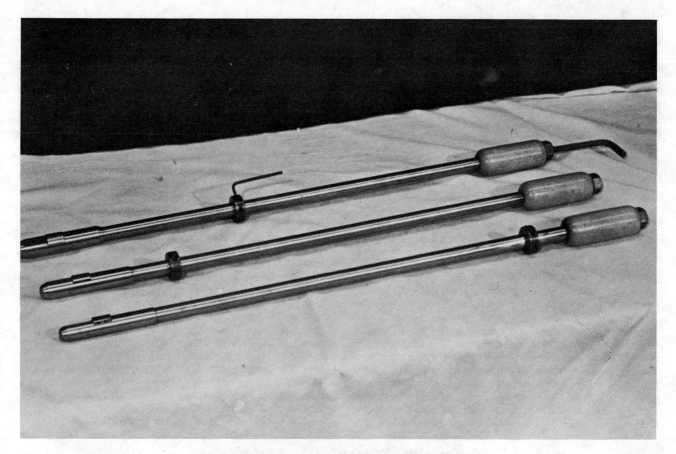

This is the full set of hydraulic dent removers with the handles. Large Allen wrench at rear of top tool exerts pressure by a turning screw that raises anvil on the forward end. Collar spaces tool correctly under the dent.

A device often overlooked is the efficient Lyman Economy choke. The regular Lyman choke consists of an adapter that is silver soldered to the end of the shotgun barrel and an expansion chamber or minnow bucket, as some people call them, screwed to the adapter. The choke tube or, if desired, the variable tube, is screwed into the chamber. The Economy Choke consists of the adapter and the tube only, which is screwed directly into the adapter. Since a good selection of tubes from cylinder to full choke is available, one can have a choke device for less than ten dollars. The Cutts Compensator attaches the same way, via an adapter silver soldered to the barrel, but must be used with the expansion chamber while the Lyman choke can be used without the expansion chamber. I have fitted and patterned the Economy choke and recommend it for performance, as well as an inexpensive solution for a chopped barrel.

Some hobbyists will become interested in reboring regular factory chokes, changing a full choke to a modified and so on. As I more or less specialize in shotguns, this problem of reboring a choke has bugged me for years. There is no simple method of doing it right. To do a first class job, a choke must be cut a little at a time, fired and test patterned; cut a little more, then more test patterns fired until the pattern percentage is correct. Sometimes as little as .001" can mean the difference between a good pattern and an average pattern. There are reamers on the market that are pulled or pushed through the choke, reducing its diameter in their travel, but they have two big drawbacks. They are available in increments of around

.003" per reamer which does not allow enough control; and they are expensive, running fifteen to twenty-five bucks per reamer. When you consider that you need an absolute minimum of ten reamers per gauge you can see how fast this can flatten the wallet.

Just about every gunsmith thinks about using expanding reamers for choke reduction, but it takes only one trial barrel to show why the common one will not work. First, the blades are parallel with the body of the reamer. A straight blade reamer is designed for power use and will chatter if used by hand, yet you cannot do the choke reaming in a lathe for several reasons.

The second drawback is that the expansion reamer expands from one end to the other on a level and you do not have a guide or pilot to prevent the reamer from wandering off and cutting one side more than the other. The old method was to use a flat reamer with a block of wood on the bottom pressing it against the bore and removing a thin sliver at a time. When the cut was made, the wood was removed and a piece of thin paper inserted between the wood and the reamer to give the next cut a bite. Chokes can be reduced this way, but it is an aggravating experience and the results leave much to be desired.

One day I stumbled across a reamer that solved both problems. It had the blades set at an angle to the body of the reamer and gave a nice clean slicing cut rather than a chatter, when used by hand. It is a tapered reamer, smaller at the front than the rear, so it serves as a guide or pilot, automatically keeping the reamer centered with the bore. The expansion range was such that as little as .0005 cut could be made with an adjustment. After considerable experimenting with the reamers and a hone, a system of choke reduction was worked out that was as good as the best hand-cut chokes on the expensive English doubles. Bob and Frank Brownell, of Brownell's, worked with me getting the bugs out of the system, and together, we wrote and photographed the process completely and tied it all up in a booklet. The booklet, the reamers and the hone, plus a choke comparison caliper, are available from Brownell's at about $40. The set will allow precision choke work from 28 to 12 gauge and from full to cylinder choke in these gauges and those between. It also can be used to add a certain amount of choke to a barrel by jug or recess choking, as it is sometimes called.

About once a week on the average, a customer comes into the shop and wants his standard 2-3/4-inch gauge rechambered to take the three-inch magnum shell. Each time, I refuse to do it, for I consider this too much of a radical conversion in the standard 12-gauge gun. The gun will stand the pressure and be safe in most cases, but it is just a matter of time before the terrific pounding from this shell loosens every joint in the gun.

Look at a factory-built gun for the 12-gauge three-inch magnum; the gun has been beefed up in size in certain critical areas to allow the gun to withstand the pounding. Doesn't it just make good sense that, if the manufacturers consider it necessary to enlarge the gun, a standard weight gun will not take the pounding? The hobbyist with similar ideas will do well to consider the possibility that, after about a case of magnum shells goes through his favorite smokepole, he can hold it by the muzzle, shake it and hear every part in it rattle. But, most of all, there are a lot of the older model standard 2-3/4-inch 12 gauges floating around that, if converted, will simply come apart on the first shell.

The 20-gauge three-inch shell is a different matter in some models. Usually the standard 20 gauge is of sufficient sturdiness to make the conversion to the three-inch shell. However, this is not true of all of them, especially the older models. Quite a few of the current models available in the three-inch chamber once were made for the 2-3/4-inch and there has been no change in action size. These can usually be converted to the three inch, but you have to use a little common sense and make the conversion only on guns in strong working order. Break-open guns will present no problems other than the rechambering, but most of the pumps and semi-automatics will be a headache in the feed system, as they are designed and timed for the 2-3/4-inch shell. Personally, I convert only the break-open guns.

Many of the old .410-gauge guns were made with the short 2-1/2-inch chamber and, if in good order, can be rechambered to take the three-inch shell. Few of the pumps and none of the semi-automatics in this gauge will be found with the short chamber.

The 16 gauge has never been made in a three-inch chamber to my knowledge, but the hobbyist will encounter a special problem with some guns in this gauge. The standard European shell length is 2-9/16 inches and many of the older American-made guns are in this chamber length. The current American 16-gauge shell is 2-3/4 inches, a difference of 3/16 inch between the old chamber and the new one. The longer shells will chamber in the short chamber, but when fired, the mouth of the case opens up

Getting bulge out of a barrel is difficult and calls for close fitting mandrel inside bore beneath the bulge, which is slowly tapped back into place with brass hammer.

into the bore of the barrel, forming a bottle neck and raising breech pressure. The barrels normally will take the strain, but the gun will kick like a mule and the pattern suffers from the shot being squeezed through the bottle neck.

On European doubles, look under the barrel and, if you see the designation "16-65mm," the chamber is the short one as 65mm is 2-9/16. The new guns are designated "16-70mm," which is the 2-3/4-inch chamber. Any American-made gun without the 2-3/4-inch designation stamped on the barrel will be chambered for the short 2-9/16-inch shell. With double barrel guns and the single break-opens, all that is required is to rechamber the barrel to take the 2-3/4-inch shell. When rechambered, the recoil will drop and the pattern percentage will improve noticeably. In addition to rechambering, the semi-automatic and pumps with the short chamber will require alteration of the feed system in order to work.

Shotgun chambering reamers are available from the gunsmith supply houses at about $13 to $25 per reamer. These will be in either a standard forcing cone or a long forcing cone. The forcing cone is the point on the reamer, or chamber, where the shell body tapers up to match the bore.

I always have favored the long forcing cone, as I believe there is less distortion of the shot pellets in this, as opposed to the short forcing cone. In several experiments, I have found an average of seven percent pattern density increase when a regular short forcing cone was recut to a long forcing cone. These experiments were conducted on various makes and models, using shells out of the same box both before and after. The conversion is a simple one and is safe

in about 90 percent of the barrels.

Any time you convert a gun, you have to consider each gun separately rather than making a blanket conversion of any certain make or model. I would recommend, if the hobbyist is not well versed in gun action strength, barrel strength, and so on, that he seek the advice of a professional gunsmith on each gun before doing any work. There just isn't any set rule to go by!

One of the most fascinating and economical projects is rebuilding .22 rimfires. Literally hundreds of these line gun shop and pawn shop racks with prices well within the reach of even the tightest pocketbooks. If the hobbyist is careful in his selection, with a little work he can rebuild these into guns he will be proud to own or can use as good trading material.

Those with mechanical problems are offered at a greatly reduced price and the hobbyist in the know can select a gun with only minor parts replacement needed. Usually, the guns offered at the lowest prices will be those with a worn or defective barrel. These you can pick up for a song.

After acquiring the gun, give it a good cleaning, especially the barrel. Next, test fire it for accuracy. If the group is about as big as a bathtub, you have to take some drastic steps with the barrel, but clean the gun again and test fire it a second time. Some guns will surprise you on the second test, as the first firing often cleans out of the bore. If, the group is still scattered, you will have to do something about the barrel.

In the strong sunlight or with a good flashlight, carefully inspect the last inch of rifling at the muzzle. That last inch determines the accuracy. Quite often, this last inch will

Author's homemade shotgun barrel straightner is made from old brake lining tool. It is fitted with bar and a barrel contoured anvil at top. The anvil is activated by a foot lever that exerts proper pressure on barrel.

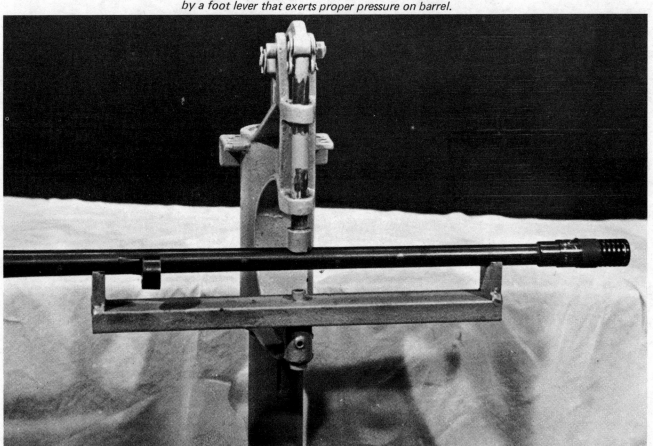

show signs of heavy wear from dirt or a cleaning rod-happy owner, while the balance of the bore is sharp. If you cut the barrel off below the worn section and the section below is sharp, you should get a much better group on the next test fire. It is surprising how many shot-out rifles can be revamped with this simple alteration.

I remember one Remington M-550 semi-automatic that a customer brought in as trade on a new gun. He admitted it would not put two shots within a foot of each other, except by accident, and offered the gun to me for ten bucks as parts. A few days later I started to disassemble the rifle to see what usable parts remained and noted that the bore showed good clean rifling except for the last inch or two at the muzzle. I ended up cutting three inches off and reworking the magazine tube. Afterwards, that little short rifle would stack five shots under a silver dollar at fifty yards. I intended to keep the rifle for myself, but a farmer with a need for a short rifle who had thirty-five dollars changed my mind.

Some rifles with a rough bore midway down the barrel will shoot well so long as that last all-important inch is still sharp, so do some careful checking before you discard a "shot-out" barrel. Unfortunately, the worn end also can be on the chamber end and, if this proves to be your problem, evident from badly bulged or split cases, the barrel cannot be saved. It is possible to ream the chamber out and sweat solder a new chamber insert in, but this is a tough job.

If the barrel is too worn, the obvious answer is a new barrel and, if the rifle is of fairly current manufacture, there is a good chance that you can buy a replacement barrel from the manufacturer. If none is available here, check with the companies that specialize in out-of-date parts, for they generally buy up all of the old factory parts as the manufacturer discontinues carrying parts for a model in his line.

The older model .22s and some of the current ones use a threaded barrel, but most of the current crop lean toward the pinned barrel. From a practical standpoint, the pinned barrel is just as good and a lot easier to work with.

If the barrel is of the pinned variety, you should see one or two steel pins on the bottom of the receiver going crossways. Look at the ends of the pins, as they are usually tapered slightly. Drive them out the way they came in, saving the pins for reuse with the new barrel. Once the pins are removed, you generally can pull the barrel out of the receiver with hand pressure only, but you will run across a stubborn barrel sometimes.

About the easiest way to separate the two is to chuck the receiver in a padded vise and use a short brass rod held against the chamber end to drive the barrel out of the receiver. Even if you intend to replace this same barrel for some reason, the brass rod will not damage the chamber face when used this way. All that remains to be done is to insert the new barrel and put the pins back in place.

If, for some reason, the pin slots in the barrel do not line up exactly with the holes in the receiver, you may have to file the notch slightly. This filing should be on the side of the slot toward the muzzle, if possible, so as to pull the barrel shoulder snugly against the receiver shoulder. Reinstall the bolt and check to see whether the extractor grooves have lined up and if they are cut deeply enough. I always slip in a cartridge and work the bolt by hand to check the extraction before I reinstall the firing pin.

For barrels that screw in, you need some form of barrel vise and receiver wrench to remove it and to reinstall the new barrel. Sometimes a good set of padded vise jaws with the barrel pulled up tight in the vise will suffice. If this fails, for a one-time affair you can make barrel vise blocks out of two pieces of hardwood. File a half-round trough cross-

Of two methods of attaching threadless .22 rimfire barrels, top uses lock screw through receiver into a recess in barrel. Lower method uses two cross pins.

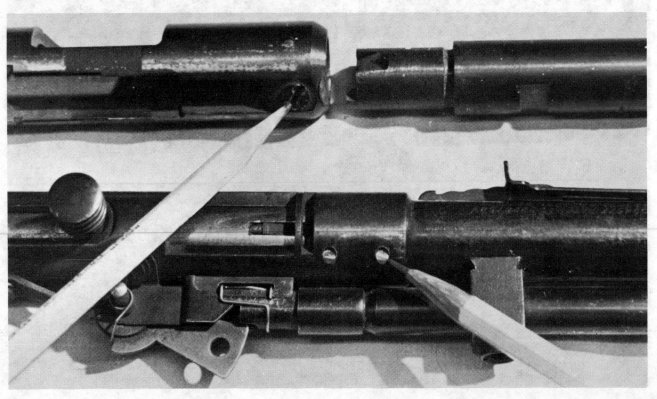

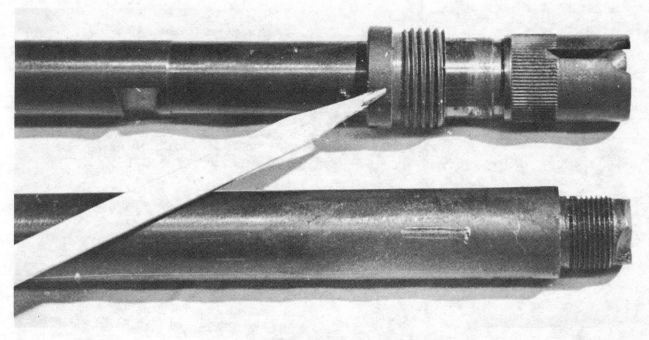

Top barrel is for Winchester Model 190 .22 rimfire and uses a threaded collar to hold it to the receiver. The bottom barrel simply screws into receiver in usual way.

grain of each block, checking it constantly by comparing it with the barrel contour. When the blocks are right, they should fit firmly against the barrel, yet leave about a quarter-inch space between the two blocks of wood. A little rosin sprinkled in the troughs will help hold the barrel more firmly.

The blocks, the barrel between them, are clamped in the vise. The shape of the receiver wrench you will use to turn the receiver will depend on the shape of the receiver. Sometimes you can get lucky and get by with a good strap wrench with rosin sprinkled on it. If not, you will have to improvise a wrench. A big, heavily padded crescent wrench, tightly gripped to the receiver, will work on flat receivers. For round receivers you will have to cut out a set of wood blocks about like the barrel blocks and hold them together with C-clamps to turn the receiver.

Most receivers have a flat on them, as the manufacturer needed the flat to turn the barrel into the receiver in the first place. A V-block and crescent wrench will work, if you have an old worn V-block around, but don't try it with a good one. You can cut out a wooden V-block, but in either case, the "V" goes toward the round section, while the flat of the crescent wrench goes against the receiver flat.

Screwed-in barrels are not put in place by sheer brute strength. Instead, the barrel is turned into place almost with finger pressure, then the installer gives a quick snap motion to lock the two together. To break the snap fit, snap in the opposite direction. If you are using a crescent wrench or a similar wrench with a long handle, all that is needed is a good tap against the end of the wrench with a hammer. Once this is done and the sealing snap is broken, you usually can unscrew the barrel with hand pressure.

The exception will be the barrel with threads that are rusty or gummed up with old oil and dirt. Penetrating oil sometimes will do the trick, as will Tap Magic squirted on the threads and allowed to soak in. For the really tough nuts you may have to heat the receiver, but this should be

only enough heat that you just hold your finger against it for a second. Any hotter and you can damage the receiver, while a slight amount of heat will expand the metal of the receiver and break the rust-gum seal. Do not, under any circumstances, heat a receiver more than this!

Once the old barrel is clear, scrub the receiver threads clean and install the new barrel, tightening with hand pressure only. If it lacks a quarter turn coming up in line, you will have to file the shoulder of the barrel slightly. It should lack about 1/32 inch of coming into line, with this last fraction of an inch pulled up with the "snap" seal just as the manufacturer installed the original barrel. If it doesn't come up exactly right, unlock the barrel with a reverse snap and try seating the barrel again. Sometimes two or more tries are needed to allow the barrel shoulder and receiver shoulder to sort of wear in to one another. Use the file as a last resort!

For getting the gun back into shooting condition, there is a third method if you have lathe facilities. This involves the purchase of a .22 rimfire barrel blank that consists of a rifled barrel with the outside not contoured, the barrel not chambered, no extractor cut made. These are available from a half-dozen sources for five dollars and up.

I would recommend that the hobbyist interested in doing rebarreling work start first on such a .22 rimfire barrel. Copy the old barrel step by step, turning the contour on the outside and any threads if necessary. The barrel can be chambered and fitted to the receiver with any sight slots and other indentations cut after fitting to assure alignment. You will need only a finishing reamer to cut the chamber and a single .22 rimfire reamer will cut dozens of chambers in soft rimfire barrels without loss of accuracy.

For the hobbyist, not yet ready for barrel turning, the logical step, if a new barrel is not available, is to line the old barrel. This is not as tough as it sounds. Liners are made in several ways, but the most common in the .22 rimfire is simply a rifled piece of seamless tubing, costing less than ten dollars. When correctly installed, this liner delivers on a

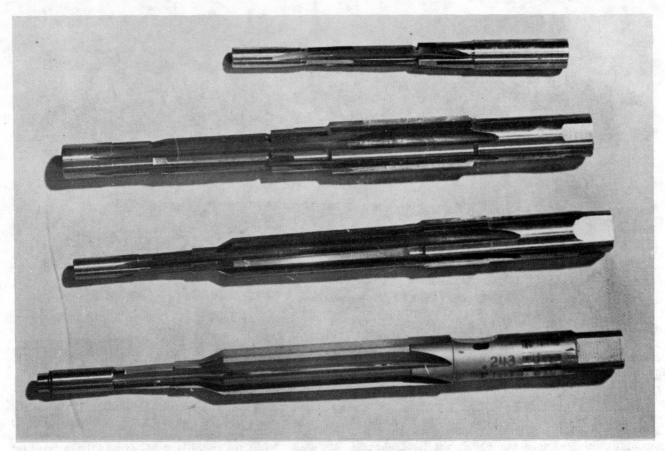

Chamber reamers are (from top) for .22 rimfire; the .44 magnum pistol cartridge; standard rifle reamer; one with special bushing pilot that does a slightly better job.

par or slightly better than a comparative factory barrel.

There are a half-dozen or more ways to install a barrel liner, if you have lathe facilities, but let's do it the hard way and install one without the use of a lathe or fancy drill and reamers. Instead of expensive deep hole drills and pressurized oil lines, we can use two common twist drills of a diameter that matches the liner diameter, usually about a size "P" drill.

First grind a pilot on the end of each drill so the major drill diameter will cut a hole exactly parallel with the bore. This pilot should be about an inch long and a snug fit in the barrel bore. The pilot does no cutting, so the edges should be rounded. The edge that goes from the pilot up to the drill's diameter should be at about a 45-degree angle, but sometimes you have to make this a little less, depending on the barrel. This angle is the cutting edge, so it should be cut equally on both sides and stoned to a clean edge.

When pilots have been ground on both drills, silver solder one of the drills to an extension rod with a butt joint. The rod should be as close a match to the drill body diameter as possible, but slightly less is acceptable. Sweat both the drill and the rod well, then have a friend help in lining up the two for joining.

If you watch from one direction and your friend from the opposite, you should be able to get the drill soldered in perfect alignment, but check by rolling it across a table. Lack of alignment will be obvious and must be corrected. The second drill is left in its original length.

With the barrel removed and locked tightly in the vise, install the short drill in an electric hand drill of the variable speed type. Insert the pilot in the muzzle, press it in until the angle just touches the face of the barrel and goose the drill trigger. The drill should take a bite and start in perfectly straight. Add some cutting oil and drill as far as you can into the barrel.

You will see immediately that the amount of one cut depends on how much chip clearance you have in the drill grooves. If you try to keep going, the drill binds. The drill then must be removed and the chips cleared before you can make another pass. (In a lathe set up with a deep hole drill, the chips are removed by pressurized oil pumped through the hollow drill shank.)

When you are in as far as you can go from the muzzle, switch ends and drill from the chamber end in the same way, as deeply as possible. By using the short drill first, you have made certain the important chamber end and muzzle end of the barrel have been drilled straight.

Switch to the drill with the extension rod and keep drilling, clearing chips and drill some more, until you are about half way down the barrel. Switch ends and drill from the opposite end until the drilled holes meet. Take your time, use plenty of cutting oil, keep the chips cleaned off and you should have little trouble. Watch the chips, and as long as they are coming out clean, the drill is cutting right, but if the drill bogs down, don't hesitate to resharpen the drill. Let the pilot do the guiding and not your eyes, but you can help by looking straight down, keeping the drill and barrel in line. If you have someone watch from the side, and keeping you corrected, it is surprising how fast the drill will cut without binding. All of this can be done much

Headspace gauges in upper left are common type used for rimless cartridges. Three just below are for M-1 carbine. Large gauges are minimum and maximum gauges for shotgun. Beneath are same type, but only for .22 rimfire caliber.

better in the lathe, but it is possible to do adequately with the vise and hand electric drill, if you take your time.

When the hole is all the way through, clean it thoroughly with a bore brush and mineral spirits, since all oil must be removed. The hole may be a bit rough, but so much the better for a good bond between the liner and the barrel. If you were relining a big bore barrel, the hole would be finished, reamed, lapped and polished for a skin-tight fit, but this is not needed with the .22 rimfire.

Try slipping the liner down the hole. It should go in with just heavy hand pressure. If not, you may have to polish the outside of the liner. You can polish any real rough spot in the hole by slitting a rod and inserting a strip of aluminum oxide cloth, with a piece of rubber to back the cloth. This is turned in an electric drill with the rubber backing pressing the cloth against the walls of the hole. When everything fits and the liner will go all the way into the hole, you are ready to bond it into place.

There are two ways to secure the liner; solder and Acraglas. As I began relining barrels quite a few years before the invention of Acraglas, I always have stuck to solder, but the hobbyist probably will find Acraglas a little easier to use. If you choose solder, the liner first is tinned all over. Then, the hole is fluxed well, heated and tinned by pushing molten solder through it on a bore brush. This is not as hard as it sounds, so long as the barrel is kept hot through its full length with a torch.

Start the tinned liner in the hole, moving the torch over both the liner and barrel and keeping the solder at melting temperature. The liner will slip in place like a greased pig. Once you have it all the way through the barrel, let a little

protrude from each end and feed some solder around the junction at each end. Feed in as much as it will take, then let the barrel cool of its own accord. All that is left is cut the ends off, face the ends, chamber the liner, and cut the extractor slots.

Some liners come from the manufacturer already chambered and offer a big savings to the hobbyist concerned with only one barrel, who does not want to purchase a reamer. To correctly position a liner such as this, pull the bullet from a cartridge, dump the powder and pump a little oil in the case to kill the primer. With the barrel fitted to the receiver, remove the extractors from the bolt, install the case in the liner's chamber, push the liner and case firmly against the bolt, then allow it to cool in this position. This will set your headspace right and, after cooling, the barrel can be removed from the receiver and the extractor slots cut as needed.

Acraglas has innumerable uses, including the installation of liners. One company that manufactures liners uses nothing but Acraglas to install them. In use, the hole is thoroughly cleaned of all grease and oil which would prevent the Acraglas from bonding. The liner also must be cleaned carefully. Mix up a batch of Acraglas and push a wad through the hole with a cleaning rod. Coat the outside of the liner with acraglass and install it in the barrel. Allow the glass to set up 24 hours and clean up afterwards. That's all! If you are using a liner with a chamber, don't forget to smear the bolt face and the inside of the receiver with glass release agent to prevent the Acraglass from sticking.

The hobbyist who has fitted a few new barrels to .22 rimfire rifles, plus maybe a liner or two, and if possible turned a barrel from a blank, will have a background in barrel work that will be invaluable when he goes into center-fire barrel work. The basic principles are about the same, yet the .22 does not have the high pressure problem and the hobbyist can make a mistake and live to talk about it. Any barrel job should be test fired with a long string, regardless. Try to do a better job each time and soon your work will start to approach the quality needed for center-fire barrel work.

There has been a fairly recent trend to advertise barrels for center-fire rifles that supposedly are pre-turned, pre-threaded and pre-chambered to fit former military rifles such as the Mauser 98, Springfield '03, and others. According to some of the advertisements, all that you have to do is unscrew your old barrel, screw in the new barrel and go bang away.

It isn't this simple, and can be downright dangerous in the majority of cases. Remember what I said about chamber pressure and the factors involved in containing it safely? Remember that most rifles, and especially military rifles, are not made to an exact tolerance that enables one to screw in a barrel without adjustment. Even the manufacturers cannot do it under the most controlled conditions. How close do you think the dimensions would be between a Mauser M-98 manufactured in, say 1918 at the Mauser Works in Germany and Mauser M-98 produced in occupied Poland in 1943? Obviously there would be considerable variation, yet some advertisers would have the uninitiated believe that one of their barrels would fit either — without adjustment!

Even if your receiver and the barrel are of excellent quality, they must be fitted carefully and headspaced with gauges. A good lathe is a necessity as is a good barrel vise with wrench, chamber reamers and headspace gauges. Few so-called pre-chambered barrels will fit and be within safety limits; if one does, it is pure luck. Not only is expensive equipment needed to fit and install a center-fire barrel, but technical knowledge also is needed. I would advise the

In cutting off a shotgun barrel, the pipe cutter is used only to mark concentric circle around the barrel, not for actual cut. Masking tape prevents the rollers of the pipe cutter from scarring the barrel or even the bluing.

Stevens Favorite .22 has had shot out barrel restored to service by sweating in rifle liner, which is visible.

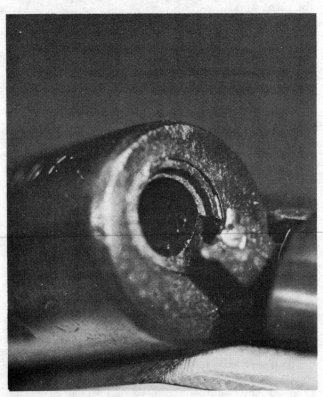

Author's daughter, Kim, with rebuilt Stevens Favorite rifle. It was being used aboard a fishing boat as a protective piece against snakes, when Walker found it!

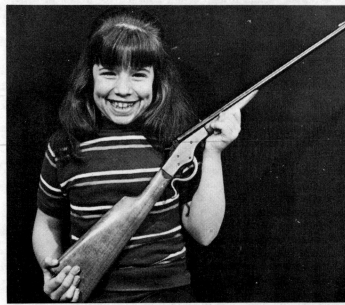

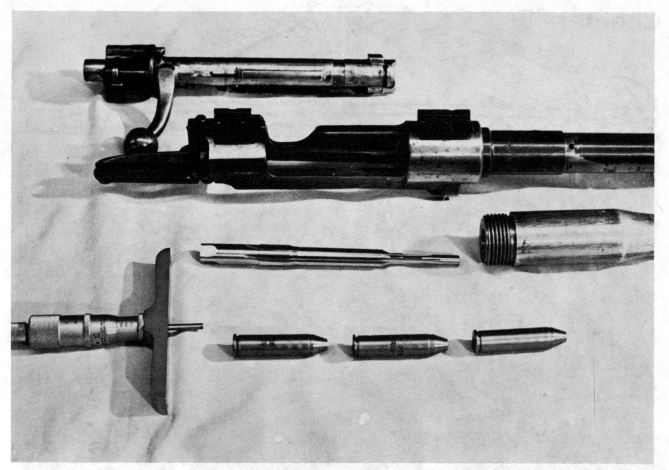

Model 98 Mauser with barrel advertised as ready to screw
into action. But depth micrometer, headspace gauges and
finishing reamer all are needed to handle it correctly.

hobbyist to have his center-fire barrels fitted by a professional until he has had time to increase his technical
knowledge and skill. Only when you reach the status of a
semi-professional, should you attempt this work and then,
only with proper equipment and gauges at hand.

In your gun dealings, you probably will acquire a handgun with a shot-out barrel. The semi-automatics do not
offer much challenge, if the barrel is of the type used in the
M1911 Colt, Browning Hi-Power, or similar models, as
these are removed and reinstalled in the normal course of
cleaning. Some inexpensive pocket automatics, such as the
.25s and .32s, will have barrels that are fitted to the receiver
with a pin, wedge or dovetail joint. Fitting a new barrel to
one of these requires, for the most part, observing how the
old one came out and installing the new in a like manner. A
few will require a small amount of filing, especially those
attached with a dovetail joint.

Some of the semi-automatics like the older Hi-Standards,
the Colt Woodsman, the Ruger, and similar models in .22
rimfire have their barrels screwed into the receiver. These
are a bit harder to remove and install, but the operation is
similar to that of installing a rimfire rifle barrel. The fitting
is quite simple and one should encounter little trouble
except in getting the old barrel out.

Revolver barrel replacement is more common, and while
care must be taken, it is within the capability of the

hobbyist. Replacements are available from the various
manufacturers.

In most cases the fit will be extremely close, requiring
only minimum fitting. Once the new barrel has been fitted
with that snug snap fit and the sights are aligned, the final
fitting is the rear of the barrel to the cylinder. During the
barrel installation, the cylinder should be removed and reinstalled once the barrel is snug in place. Ease the cylinder
back into place and try to turn it by hand. If the cylinder
will make a complete revolution without binding, you are
home free. But, if the cylinder binds at any point, you will
have to lightly file the end of the barrel to gain the needed
clearance. When it is right, you should be able to turn the
cylinder to any position and still see a faint hairline crack
of light between the face of the cylinder and the end of the
barrel. In a few cases, the gap will be excessive and require
that the shoulder of the barrel be faced off in a lathe
enough to allow the barrel to make another complete turn
inward to close the gap.

Barrel work, in general, is not something to rush into
without fully understanding what you are doing. If
possible, seek the advice of a professional in any barrel
work you undertake and, if circumstances permit, watch
him doing barrel work. When you are satisfied that you
know exactly what to do and what precautions to take, go
ahead — slowly and carefully.

There is no such thing in barrel work as too much care!

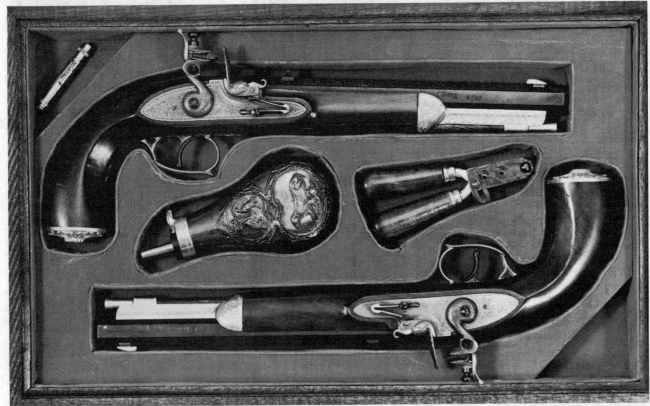

Chapter 15

ANGLES FOR ANTIQUES

Restoration Of Those Priceless Arms Of The Past
Is An Art That Should Not
Be Rushed!

MORE IMPORTANT THAN the "how" of antique restoration is "what to and what not to restore."

Suppose one has acquired a Winchester Model 73 rifle in fair operating condition, most of the original finish gone, a little rust here and there, and the hammer broken. The hobby gunsmith is faced with the problem of what and how to go about restoring the gun.

Should he approach three average collectors and ask what to do about it, chances are he will get three different answers.

One probably will say to leave it exactly as it is; rust, broken part and all. Another would say to clean up the gun, saving as much of the original finish as possible, and replace the broken hammer with one cannibalized from a similar junked model. The third one would agree with the second, but might recommend the complete rebluing and stock refinishing.

Each is correct under certain circumstances, but none is right under all conditions. The only thing that is certain is that each gun must be considered as an individual piece and treated accordingly.

Getting back to the Winchester Model 73, how would the collector who advises, "don't touch it" be right? The answer is a bit involved, but almost invariably concerns the circumstances surrounding the gun or the story behind it.

Suppose our collector has a rifle that was found in the West in a cave along with a skeleton that is pierced with an arrow. The obvious story of the last few minutes of a desperate man with the hammer broken on his defensive weapon would be there for all to see. To refinish the rifle or restore it in any way would destroy the story and the rifle then would become just another example of that particular model. But if left alone, displayed with the arrow and maybe a photo of the original scene, it would be of considerable interest in any collection. Archeologists who deal with history use the term, "In Situ," to describe artifacts found during their digging. The term means, "The situation as uncovered or found." So, a gun found as described should definitely be left "In Situ," so to speak, for herein lies its value and interest.

A well known example of this is the derringer John Wilkes Booth used to assassinate President Lincoln. If you have ever closely examined a photo of this pistol, you probably noticed that the screw that holds the hammer to the lock is missing, while a small chip of wood has been broken off the stock just in front of the lock.

To have repaired these defects would have detracted from the pistol, and thankfully, those in charge of it left it alone. These very defects tell a story of the character of the person involved as one of a political mind, rather than of a professional killer who would have used only a pistol in perfect order.

A less historic example concerns a collection of Luger pistols I saw a year or so ago. It was about as complete as you will find, well documented, and every variation you could think of was displayed, each in almost mint condition. In the center of the collection was a standard BYF (Mauser) model, deeply etched across the side and most of the finish gone. I was confused as to why this particular model of one of the most common variety was displayed with this collection and in such a prominent place.

The owner of the collection had purchased the pistol from a retired major who was with one of the army units that freed the inmates of a Nazi concentration camp during World War II. The German SS colonel in charge of the camp could not face the end of the war, so he committed suicide with this Luger, fell across it and his blood covered the pistol. The major picked it up, but failed to clean the gun. A year later, when he returned home and unpacked it, the blood had etched the gun's surface. He cleaned and oiled the gun but did not try to refinish it. A common model had become an interesting collection piece. Had it been refinished, it would have become only a refinished common model, not worthy of even a poor collection.

The second collector recommended cleaning and restoring. In most cases, this will prove to be the common answer. If the rifle is a good example of that model but without any history or special distinguishing characteristics, it can be restored without loss of value or depreciation of authenticity. Guns in this category are, for the most part, just examples of a particular model showing common use in everyday life.

For every In Situ example, there must be a thousand or more of the common examples of the same model gun. The idea is to keep the gun as authentic as possible, yet preserve it for future generations to enjoy by removing rust and grime. Condition of such guns will run the gauntlet from those that need only an oily rag wiped over them, to those with broken or missing parts, which need major restoration.

What about the third collector who recommended rebluing and complete refinishing? This seems a drastic step and most collectors regard anyone who recommends such a step as some sort of nut!

The answer depends on a good knowledge of gun models, scarcity of this type and condition. The third collector would be right if the serial number of the Model 73 was in the right category. This model was made from 1873 until 1925, and if this particular gun was made in the later years, it would have little value to a collector, unless it was almost mint condition. Careful rebluing and refinishing would neither add to nor detract from the gun's value in this case.

Another set of circumstances might involve a rare model of the Model 73 that some kook had nickel-plated from stem to stern as a showpiece. The gun definitely would be improved by refinishing. I remember a customer bringing in a mechanically perfect Remington .44 percussion revolver that the previous owner had nickel-plated. The new owner had gone over it carefully and discovered that, in addition to being in perfect mechanical condition with good sharp lines, the gun was martially marked, which greatly increased its value.

I removed the plating, carefully reblued it to match the original bluing, then refinished the wood grips that had been coated with cheap varnish. In this case, rebluing and refinishing were necessary to restore the gun to something approximating its original appearance.

The hobbyist not well versed in antique guns should leave the gun as he receives it, until he can be absolutely sure what to do about it. Too often, a hobbyist rushes into the project — sanding, polishing and hammering away at an antique in an honest attempt to restore it — only to discover later that his efforts have destroyed the value of the gun for all time. I could quote story upon story regarding such efforts that the owners have brought to me afterwards; sometimes it is almost heartbreaking to see the sad results. One local customer found a Spencer carbine in an attic of an old house he purchased. He wanted to "clean it up some" and worked it over, metal and all, with emery cloth without even disassembling it! Not only was the bluing destroyed, but he also sanded the stock down a good 1/8 inch overall.

When I saw it, the stock had received a couple of coats of furniture varnish and the owner wanted a bottle of liquid bluing for the metal. I lost a customer when I bluntly informed him that his ignorance had destroyed a fine collector's item. A hobbyist who seeks help in the careful restoration of an antique will be admired by any collector, while those who jump in without thinking will be remembered only for their vast ignorance.

The absolute, unquestionable first step with any antique gun is to find out exactly what it is, the model, its rarity and the accepted standards of collector conditions. Do not even wipe the gun with an oily rag until you have completed this first step.

No single source of information ever should be accepted as gospel. Check and double check. Even the answer of the professional gunsmith should not be taken as unquestionable, as some members of my profession are not versed in antique guns, because they deal in so few of them. I have

Wad puller is large brass wood screw soldered to end
of long rod. Placed in muzzle of barrel as it is, the
tool is of brass to prevent striking sparks on steel.

always offered free appraisal of any antique that a customer cares to bring into the shop and, while I have collected guns for quite a few years, I still get stuck and have to ask for time to do some careful research before I can provide the right answer. Even with a good library, you may come up against a blank wall and have to seek the help of other gunsmiths or collectors. But, neither should you accept the opinion of just one collector. Too often the collectors have only a shallow knowledge of guns beyond those in which he specializes, but may try to bluff his way through a question rather than simply say he doesn't know.

If you are a member of the National Rifle Association, you have about the most unquestionable source of information possible, for only in extreme cases will this organization be stumped at identification. If you seek their advice, be sure to give a full and complete description of the gun, any markings or proof marks and a good clear photograph.

If the gun is out of the ordinary and you want to determine the market value, there are a couple of ways to do this. Advertisements in gun magazines and papers will give you a rough idea of the top price, as will attending gun shows to compare the gun with a similar one displayed. A few professional authorities make a living evaluating and identifying rare guns. Their cost is high for this service, but their word is accepted by most collectors, who usually will purchase a gun on these experts' estimate without question.

Age alone does not determine the value of a gun. Neither does rarity necessarily determine its value, as value is simply a matter of demand. If there is one item and ten people want it, the price will be high; only two want it, the price is invariably less. Some makes, such as Colt, Winchester and U.S. martial guns demand a higher price, because there are more collectors of these guns. A Smith & Wesson, Marlin or European martial gun in identical condition and scarcity will not bring as much, because fewer people collect them. A martially-marked Colt will be in much higher demand as two types of collectors will bid for it: The Colt collector and the U.S. martial collector.

A few years ago, one could buy a good Luger pistol for about forty dollars and there seemed to be an unlimited supply. The number was greater than the demand.

A couple of books were written about the Luger, detailing the variations and that supply of pistols virtually vanished overnight with prices double and triple the old price for even a mismatch-numbered Luger in shooting con-

dition. People started collecting them. The same thing has happened with other makes. Supply and demand are the governing factors in any market and guns are no exception.

Supply and demand also govern the accepted standards of condition in relation to price and acceptance in collections. For example, the Colt Walker and Dragoon models are in high demand because of the larger number of Colt collectors and the limited supply of these models. Therefore, one of these models with poor mechanical condition and finish would be a welcome addition to a collection lacking these models. The price would be more than triple that of a Colt Navy model in perfect condition in a fitted case, while the same gun in poor condition would not be acceptable in most collections. As the model becomes rarer and the demand increases, the acceptable conditions are lowered and the price increases in like ratio.

All of the foregoing has been given to guide the hobbyist in arriving at that all-important question: Should he attempt to restore a certain antique gun in his collection or possesion? More important, is he qualified to do the work

Double barrels of percussion shotgun have been removed from stock. Note retaining wedge at forearm, matching notched lug under the barrel into which the wedge fits. This once beautiful Joseph Manton gun was restored.

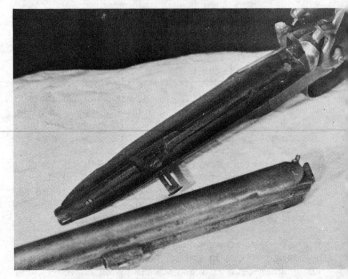

or should he secure the services of a professional gunsmith?

There is no simple, clear-cut answer. If the hobbyist has advanced in his gunsmithing ability to where he feels he can do a good job, perhaps the answer will be yes, if the gun has been identified fully as one of the more common models. If it is anything else, have this work done by one of the professional gunsmiths who specialize in antique restoration. The hobbyist interested in this branch of the gunsmithing field should concentrate his first efforts on guns with little antique value.

Percussion shotguns constitute the best example of an antique gun on which to start. While a few of these are rare guns valued in the hundreds of dollars, more are common and their value, even in tip-top condition, is less than a hundred dollars. Many of the models can be purchased in this condition for less than fifty dollars. Those that are just hanging together can be had for around twenty-five dollars or even less.

The shotgun, during the percussion era, was the most common gun, just as the shotgun is the most common gun today. While there was a high casualty rate from wear, corrosive primers, black powder and lack of care, there are still enough of these common models around that little will be lost if the hobbyist's efforts are not of the highest workmanship. And the one who takes his time seldom will goof up one of these guns behind the ability of a professional to make full repairs. If the just-hanging-together gun is chosen, the hobbyist will learn more, be required to do more handwork and any restoration effort will be on the plus side, regardless of his skill.

The different brand names of the more common models are about as varied as the names in a telephone book, as most of these were made in small shops both in the U.S. and in various European countries. Like all small manufacturing plants, they were more interested in profit than in fame. Consequently, anybody who would come up with an order for several hundred guns could have his name engraved on the lock plates. So, if you run across one with "Plowpoint Arms Corporation" stamped on the locks or the barrel, don't think that this was some huge arms factory, manufacturing guns by the hundreds. Chances are that it was a small wholesale hardware store out in the boondocks, the owners of which never rubbed two pieces of tool steel together, much less manufactured guns.

There are exceptions, however, to bear in mind before passing judgement on a gun. Some of the old quality name guns made in the U.S., and even more of those made in England, still are around, undiscovered. A customer recently walked into my shop with a double barrel percussion shotgun with the name, "Joseph Manton," on the lock plates. Joseph Manton was one of the finest of the old line gunmakers in England and each gun was hand-made with minute details revealing the skill of the craftsmen who put these guns together.

Besides just knowing the names of the quality makes, which often fails even the best of collectors, the hobbyist can spot one of these guns if he knows what to look for. Only the best of material was used in an artistic way that even time and rough use cannot disguise. Look for a fine piece of wood in the butt stock, carefully made thimbles to hold the ramrod, close metal to wood fit and a racy set of lines in the gun's design. Craftsmanship is always there for anyone to see if he looks close enough.

Should you luck out and buy one of these quality name guns from an individual, always ask if any other member of his family owns a similar gun. Quite a few of these guns were identical and used on "pass shooting," with the owner firing one of the brace while a servant or friend loaded the second. You may find that the brace has been split up with two segments of the family receiving a gun. A brace of

Locks have been disassembled from Manton shotgun stock, then connected with cross screw. With trigger guard removed, note hole in stock just above triggers. Sear bars protrude through this to connect trigger sears.

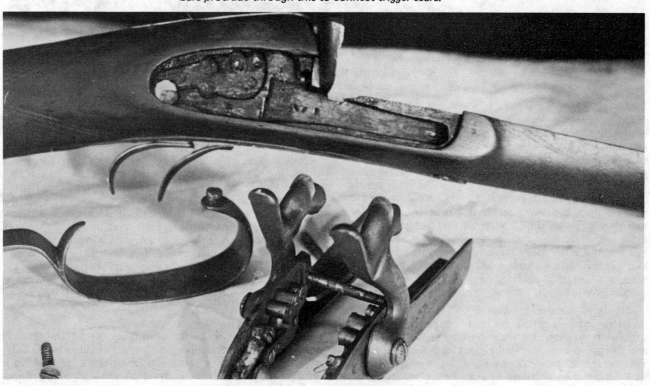

these guns usually brings about twice what the two would sell for on an individual basis.

Assuming you are the proud possessor of a genuine Plowpoint Arms Corporation double barrel percussion shotgun in dire need of repair and restoration, see if the thing is loaded! It is amazing how many antique guns, especially the muzzleloaders, will be found fully loaded, ready for bear.

I consider them all loaded until I check each barrel personally. This is done by sliding the wooden ramrod or a wooden dowel down the bore until it stops, then making a pencil mark on the ramrod at the muzzle. The ramrod is withdrawn and laid beside the barrel with the mark re-aligned with the muzzle. By comparing the other end of the ramrod in relation to the end of the barrel at the breech, you can quickly see whether the barrel is carrying a load.

If loaded, clearing it can be tricky, because black powder is touchy stuff. It may be best to leave this unpleasant job to a professional, but the first idea that will pop into your

the stock with screws. The idea of getting at the charge from the rear is a good one, but for a different reason. Instead of removing the charge, we will neutralize it first, then attack it from the muzzle.

The ideal method is to remove the nipple, pour out as much powder as possible and kill the remainder by pumping in water or oil. The majority of time, the nipple will resist removal, unless extreme pressure is applied. This results in damage to the nipple, possibly firing the gun by a spark. If the nipple will not move, buy a cheap hypodermic needle and syringe. Back at your shop, cock the hammer, fill the syring with water and inject it into the barrel through the hole in the nipple. Pump in as much water as you can, allow it to stand for a half-hour and try to pump in some more. The water will neutralize the black powder and you can work at the load from the muzzle in relative safety.

But never completely trust any critter with teeth or a gun still loaded, water or no water! Keep your body and

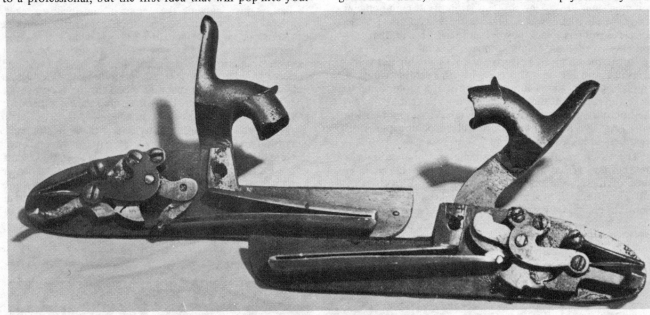

The right lock of the Manton was in perfect condition, while sear notch on left was worn and was recut.

head is to shoot the load out. Forget it! There are just too many possibilities and too many chances of damage to your hide and the gun as well. Sometimes, you will come across a gun that Uncle Stupid owned and he never could remember whether he loaded the gun or not, so he adds another charge, another charge later, and so on. One such gun came into the shop, the owner asking that it be cleaned up for a wall display in his den. I removed four complete charges from one barrel and two from the other! Adding to the merriment are the many things that inquisitive people and kids poke down the barrels, like stones, ball bearings and what not. All this adds up to a burst barrel if you try shooting the load out.

Trying to remove the breech plugs at the rear of the barrel in order to get at the load is impossible with most percussion shotguns, for the barrels are sealed permanently and the gun is attached to the stock with a patent breech. This consists of two male hooks on the rear of the barrels that fit into two openings in a separate plate attached to

head away from the muzzle as you work.

The best tool to remove the charge from a muzzle-loading shotgun is known by the very unlikely name of a "worm." This looks like two cork screws hooked together and fitted to the end of a ramrod. These screws are twisted into the wadding and the ramrod is pulled free of the barrel, bringing the wadding with it. It is quick, efficient and should be one of the special tools in a shop that does any work on muzzleloading shotguns. Original worms are available for less than two dollars from Dixie Gun Works, Union City, Tennessee. These people, by the way, are the source of some of the hardest to find antique gun parts, accessories and muzzleloading odds and ends. If you intend to do any antique restoration at all, write for a copy of their catalog.

The worm works perfectly on shotgun wads and also will work at times on a bullet in a muzzleloading rifle, but a bullet puller does a better job on rifles. A bullet puller is just a large wood screw fitted to the end of a ramrod, similar to the one described in the chapter on barrels.

If you do not have a worm handy, make up a bullet puller using wood screws as large as possible and, by nibbling away at the wadding, you can remove the load. When the wad, shot, powder and other residue finally are removed, flush the barrels with hot water to remove any lingering trace of powder. Once the charge is clear, you can start to work.

First order of the day is to disassemble the gun down to its basic components where you can get a better look at things, then make plans for the necessary repairs. The main thing to keep in mind when disassembling an antique is to take plenty of time and not get in a hurry. Antique restoration must always be a labor of love, with no item too small for your close attention and careful workmanship. The professional restorer makes it a point to examine closely and rework every small detail of the gun; this attention to tiny details is what separates the professional from the amateur.

that engage in matching recesses in the patent breech, which is screwed to the stock. This holds the barrels securely at the rear when the barrels are pivoted down in place. The forward end of the barrel is held to the stock with one or more wedges that connect the barrel to the stock. Look up along the forend for the wedge or wedges, then push them clear of the gun. Some of these are hooked to the stock to prevent loss, so if they will not clear the stock completely, don't worry about it.

Old wood can be as brittle as glass, so be extremely careful when you start to lift the front end of the barrels clear of the stock. A trick to freeing the barrel for the first time is to tap it from one end to the other on top with a rawhide hammer. The tapping frees the age-bond of metal to wood.

Grasp the barrels at the muzzle and lift upward and toward the butt stock. They should pivot upwards and unhook from the patent breech. When the barrels are free, you can concentrate on the locks. These will be held to the

This is right lock of Manton, showing internal parts. Lock was well enough preserved after years of neglect and, with a bit of cleaning and adjustment, worked well.

As you disassemble the gun, keep a notebook close by and jot down the sequence in which the parts are removed, plus helpful notes. For instance, sometimes you will have two screws that looks almost alike, but if reassembled wrong, they will not align correctly and will stand out like a sore thumb. Most screws will have some identifying mark, such as a rust spot, scratch, and so on. This can be noted for future use and will be invaluable in reassembly. These notes can get you out of a lot of tight spots, for it is impossible to remember the location and exact placement of every part in an unfamiliar gun. Even the professionals use notes. Take your time on the disassembly, for here is the place where a lot of guns are severely damaged by the hobbyist, damage that is difficult — if not impossible — to restore.

The barrels are the first component to be disassembled and the task is simple, except on a few of the really old ones made without a patent breech. The barrels with the common patent breech have two male hooks on the rear

stock with one or two screws passing from one lock, through the wood, to the other lock. Select a screwdriver that fits the screw slot perfectly, insert it in the slot and whack the back of the screwdriver with a hammer to jar the screw and loosen the rust and grime that is probably binding the threads. A little squirt of WD-40 or a similar penetrating oil on the thread ends will help. Back the screw almost all the way out, but leave the last couple of threads engaged. If there is a second screw, repeat the same process.

Next, tap the head of the screw with a hammer and this will push the lock plate on the other side clear of the stock. Once it is clear, remove the screw or screws completely and pull the lock plate clear of the stock. The other plate is removed by reaching through the screw hole from the cleared side with a pin punch and pushing the lock plate clear of the stock. Remove the locks carefully to prevent splintering of the wood. Never use a wedge or screwdriver to pry the locks clear.

The patent breech is next and should be easy to remove,

as it is secured to the stock with only one or two screws. Remove these, but don't forget that rap on the back of the screwdriver to shake them clear of any age-bond to the wood. When the screws are out, the patent breech should lift clear with ease, but it is a good idea to tap it a couple of times with the rawhide or plastic hammer to prevent any wood adhering to it and being splintered off.

Trigger guards are secured to the stock in most cases with a couple of wood screws, but some are attached with a couple of pins passing through the side of the stock. Take care in removing the guard as you did with the patent breech. Some guns will have the triggers attached to the trigger guard, while others have the triggers pinned directly to the stock. To further confuse you, still others will have a separate trigger plate screwed to the stock.

Whatever the method, if they are pinned, be sure your drift punch is no longer than the pin you are trying to remove. If it is larger, the hole through the wood will be enlarged by it and the original pin will be too small when you reassemble the gun.

Remove the butt plate also, if it is made of steel. If of horn or similar material, it is best to leave it in place, although the screws should be removed for cleaning off rust. Your gun now should be down to the bare components and a careful examination should reveal any defects.

It really doesn't matter whether you start at the butt plate or the muzzle. Taking the barrels first and working toward the butt plate, check over the nipples, which play a large part in the correct function of the gun and invariably will be the most abused part of the percussion gun. It seems that every soul that picks up a percussion gun feels this fantastic urge to haul back the hammer and snap the gun. This makes short work of the nipples, as the continuous hammer blows batter them completely useless.

If you are going to keep the gun strictly for decoration purposes, some can be filed carefully and reworked back to original shape. If you think that you may get around to doing some shooting with it, the best move is to replace any battered or defective nipple with a new one. If the original nipples look good from the outside, take a careful look at the hole through them. This should be small and not enlarged at the end or in diameter, although some were made with a tapered hole which was quite large on the inside end to get the powder as close to the percussion cap as possible. Replacement nipples are available in many sizes with threads to match the original one, and only in the really rare guns will new nipples be considered a wrong move.

Regardless of whether you keep the original nipples or replace them, the primary problem is to get them out of the barrels where you can clear them and the barrel. This is done best with a nipple wrench that fits the contour of the nipple and the flat sections on its sides. Pliers, wrenches and homemade rigs sometimes will work, but usually they just succeed in ruining the nipple or breaking it off, adding to the problem of getting it out. Nipple wrenches cost around a buck and are cheap insurance to prevent the nipple from being damaged, as well as getting it out.

The nipple wrench should be fitted firmly to the nipple and a quick snap of the wrist will usually free it. If it does not, soak the nipple with penetrating oil and try again. If the nipple is still there, get out your torch and heat the nipple slightly to expand the metal and break it free of the rust. This, of course, is done only on a gun that is definitely known to be free of any powder charge! Several heating and soaking sessions may be necessary on the real stubborn ones.

Once the nipples are free and out of the way, you can get at the bore and do a better job of cleaning it inside. There are dozens of ways to go about this, but it is hard to

Left nipple has been removed, using nipple wrench that is available from most supply houses. A nipple wrench should be used in lieu of pliers to prevent damage.

Top rib was badly battered when gun was discovered in a closet. It was cleaned and reshaped after the author had ground a special punch used to push metal back in place.

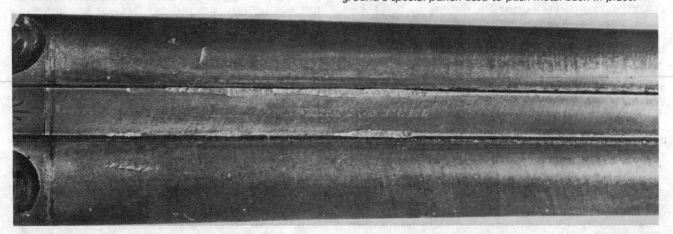

beat the oldtime favorite of plain hot, soapy water as the first cleaning liquid. The water should be hot enough to scald a brick, with half a handful of good strong dish detergent thrown in for good measure. Wrap a strip of cloth around one end of a three-foot wooden dowel until it is a tight fit in the bore of the barrel.

Insert the breech end of the barrels, nipples removed, into a deep pan of the hot soapy water and use the cloth-wrapped dowel as a sort of piston, to suck the water up into the barrel on the back stroke of the rod and expel it through the nipple hole on the downward stroke. This cycle of suction and ejection of the hot soapy water through the bore is continued for about five minutes per bore to break down and flush out any stubborn, caked powder residue in the bore. Switch to plain hot water and repeat the cycle with the dowel and cloth piston to flush away the soapy water. Next, use good commercial powder solvent, such as Hoppe's No. 9, to work the bores over with a brass brush on a cleaning rod, followed by clean patches.

To inspect the bore of a modern gun requires only un-breeching it and peeping through, sometimes with the aid of a bore light. The muzzleloader presents a problem in this department, as the breech is closed, but if the nipples are removed, you can shine enough light up in the hole to get a good look. However, to check the bore with the nipples in place can be a problem. But somewhere in the dim past a delightful soul invented a solution. Take a short stub of a dowel that is close to bore size, but will slide up and down it without jamming. Glue a small piece of a common mirror to one end of the dowel and, when it has dried, grind the mirror edges down until they are flush with the sides of the dowel. Dropped down the bore with a mirror pointing to-

ward the muzzle, it comes to rest against the bottom of the barrels and the mirror will catch and reflect any light in the bore, lighting it from end to end for your inspection. After you have finished, point the muzzle toward the floor and the mirror-dowel slides out. This gadget can be made in any size and used on the smallest muzzleloading rifles or pistols, as well as shotguns.

If your inspection reveals that the bore is lightly pitted, you can clean most of this up with a piece of aluminum oxide cloth wrapped around a dowel which is powered by an electric hand drill. Don't worry if you cannot remove all of the pitting and get the bores shining like a new penny. You can shoot the gun to your heart's delight, but you will just have to clean it thoroughly each time you shoot; but any black powder gun must be cleaned after shooting anyway.

When the bores have been improved as much as possible, turn your attention to the top and bottom ribs between the two barrels. These should be tight, without any springing free at any point along the barrels. If you do have a short loose section, you will have to tack you do have a short loose section, you will have to tack solder it back in place. (See the chapter on soldering for this.)

Once the ribs are secure, check the thimbles that hold the ramrod to the underside of the barrels. These sometimes will be loose or missing completely. If they are just loose, you can resolder them back in place, but if one is missing, you have to get a replacement from one of the suppliers or make it from scrap tubing. Manufacturing a thimble is not too hard, especially if you can copy one of the other ones.

Someone tried to repair this .32 Ford Brothers percussion rifle by building up around the lock with metal putty. Drum to which the nipple is attached has been positioned in angle that is too straight, preventing correct firing.

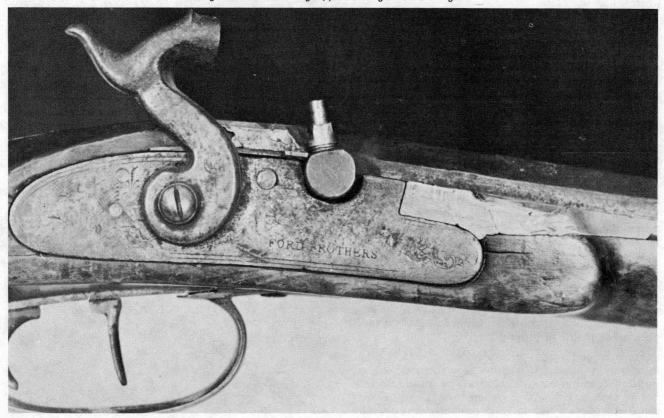

Take a close look at the end of the barrels. These should be square across and not worn or ragged. If they are, a few strokes with the file across them should take care of any defects.

Severely damaged barrels sometimes can be salvaged by cutting them off behind a bulge and dents can be removed with the dent removal tool just like a modern barrel. If the top or bottom rib is completely off or loose for a good part of the way, it is best to have a professional resolder the rib in place for you. It can be done in the home workshop, but it is a tough job, especially on the old guns due to the large amount of rust usually found between the barrels. If the barrels are heavily rust pitted inside, you will be wise to consign this one for use as a display piece only.

Deeply gashed, badly rusted sections or nicks on the outsides of the barrels can be removed only by draw filing the barrels, which will necessitate refinishing them. In addition, this thins the barrels and the safety of the gun becomes doubtful. A burnishing tool can be used to smooth out some mild nicks and it is better to live with a few metal blemishes than attempt refinishing the barrels.

Assuming the barrel work has been completed, check the patent breech for closeness of the fit between the breech and the barrel lugs. The joint should be close fitting, without any appreciable wear either up or down, as well as side to side. A real sloppy fit is hard to overcome, but if it is not too bad, you can correct it by peening the female openings in the breech. This simply means hammering on the edges of the openings to extrude metal inwards toward the opening for a closer fit. This peening should be done with a ball peen hammer on the backside of the breech where it will not show. Keep checking the fit and try to avoid overdoing it and having to file the hole back out larger.

If the openings are large enough for an elephant to walk through, about all you can do is add additional metal inside the opening by welding. Again, keep the repair on the rear where it does not show.

The top tang of the patent breech may be broken or cracked, probably at a screw hole. Repairing this can be a ticklish business, for if the crack is all the way through, even welding or silver soldering may not provide sufficient strength. In addition, any attempt at welding on such a small section will run the risk of blow holes in the metal which will show. Silver soldering can be done, but a hairline of silver solder will show and the strength of the joint is always in question.

The best method of making this repair is to use a bracing patch, which is just a short section of steel about 1/8-inch thick and of the same width as the tang, extending about a half inch to each side of the crack. Clean underneath the tang at the broken section right down to the bare metal, being sure one side of the patch is cleaned likewise. Sweat silver solder the patch in the needed position on the underside of the tang, using a C-clamp to provide the needed pressure.

When the patch has cooled, you can file the sides until they exactly match those of the tang; finish up by drilling a hole in the patch to match the tang screw hole, if the break is at this point. This is a solid repair and will withstand any reasonable pressure. Of course, it will be necessary to inlet the stock slightly to accept the patch, but that's a small price to pay to save the original tang.

For some odd reason, percussion locks seem to be either in beautifully preserved condition or almost total wrecks, with few found in between. Most will be found relatively free of rust, as the oldtime owners seemed to have kept them well oiled. Those in good condition need only be cleaned thoroughly of grime and rust, then reoiled. If the locks are working correctly, it is best to leave them alone and not disassemble them, taking a chance of breaking a spring or encountering a stubborn screw. In other words, don't go looking for trouble!

A damaged lock usually will be suffering from either a loose hammer, a broken or weak mainspring, or damaged sears. The loose hammer will be the most common and there are two main types of these. The hammer is attached to a lock part commonly known as the tumbler. It is at the point of attachment of the two parts that one of the loose hammer problems arises. Most hammers will have a square hole, although some are octagonal.

The square hole fits into a matching square lug on the tumbler. Generally, the lug and the hole are tapered to provide a tight constant fit, but you will find somewhere the lug and hole are not tapered. Either way, after prolong-

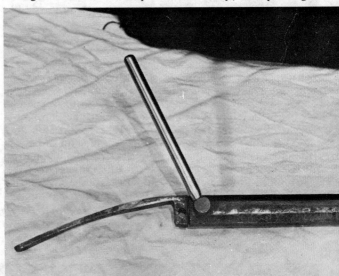

Barrel removed from stock, nipple removed, special tool is used to remove drum. Tool is a rod threaded on one end to screw down into drum and offer handle for removal.

With nipple, drum and breech plug removed from the Ford Brothers rifle, bore can be cleaned. The threaded end of the drum removal tool is better shown in this photograph.

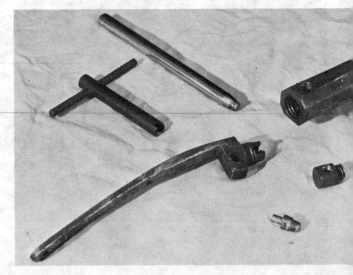

ed use, this fit becomes sloppy and worn from the pressure, and the hammer will no longer line up correctly with the nipple.

One of the oldest remedies in the gunsmithing world is to hold a small cold chisel parallel to the sides of the hole and whack it with a hammer to extrude metal inward toward the sloppy hole. After this is done all the way around the hole, enough metal will have been extruded to tighten the hammer to the tumbler lug. This always is done on the backside of the hammer where it will not show. For really heavily-worn hammers, you can first heat the area around the hole and extrude even more metal without affecting the function.

The second type of loose hammer problem is not actually the hammer at fault, but rather a worn, sloppy fit of the tumbler where it comes through a hole in the side of the lock plate. This is a rough one to repair. The best way is to substitute another tumbler that is larger in diameter than the old one; however, this leads to all kinds of complications. Seldom will the other parts fit the new replacement and recutting and modifying will be necessary. About the best way to repair the fit, if the old tumbler is used, consists of extruding metal inward just as you did with the hammer hole. However, instead of using the cold chisel, a

Rear of lock for Ford rifle shows that it has been badly abused. It was cleaned and two screws made to replace those that were too worn to correctly align parts that turned on them. Note similarity to Manton shotgun locks.

Simplicity of the set triggers for the Ford Brothers rifle is visible. They have been removed for cleaning.

round steel tube, slightly larger in diameter than the hole, is placed over the hole which has been heated red hot, the metal extruded with a blow on the other end of the tube. But move just a little metal inward at a time to avoid any need for filing or reboring.

An associated hammer problem involves the large head screw that goes into the end of the tumbler lug and holds the hammer in place, preventing its working off the lug. These suffer all types of ills and often will be found broken off flush with the end of the lug or missing completely. Those that have been broken off will have to have the stub removed and a replacement screw found. We already have gone through the procedure for removing a broken screw.

Once it is out, you will be faced with the problem of a replacement. The perfect solution is to find an exact duplicate of the original, of course, but this is pure luck. Even if you find a screw with the right thread size, seldom will it match the one on the other side. In addition, the threads in the hole usually are much the worse for wear, rust or cross threading, so about the simplest way is to drill the hole larger and retap it. Do the same on the other side, even if the screw is still functional, and make two new screws to match. Quite often, all that is necessary is to chuck a large headed modern screw in the portable hand drill and file the head to the contour that you want. If none are available, they always can be made from scratch on the lathe.

A broken mainspring is a problem supreme, any way you want to look at it. If you are contemplating the purchase of a percussion gun and it has a broken mainspring, pass it by. If you already are stuck with it, try to find a duplicate spring in an old junk lock. Many of the common makes have locks that were more or less standard, regardless of the name on the plate, for they were made on sub-contract with the same lock used on dozens of makes. Sometimes a little careful grinding will alter a spring enough to make it work, but don't forget that the strength of the spring is important; make your alterations a matter of length and width rather than thickness. If all avenues lead to a dead end, the only way left is to sit down and make the spring or have a professional make it for you. For the hobbyist, the best way is to have a professional make the spring, for it requires some special knowledge and is best learned by watching rather than trying to read it out of a book. After you watch the procedure, you should be able to make your own springs.

Often the mainspring will be weak, without sufficient power to deliver the hammer blow needed to fire the per-

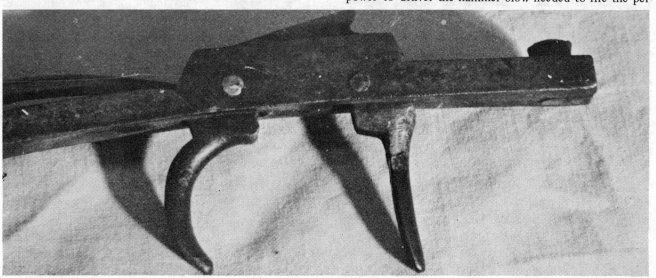

cussion cap. This appears a problem on the same par as the broken mainspring to one unfamiliar with springs. It is easier to solve in most cases, however, as all that is necessary is to retemper the spring. Remove the spring from the lock and also remove its brother from the lock on the other side. Heat the weak spring to a dull red and bend it out to match the other spring exactly.

While it is still a dull red, quickly plunge it into a container of oil. The best oil to use is linseed, but you can with 30 weight non-detergent motor oil. Water should not be used, because it will make the spring too brittle.

After the spring has cooled, it must be drawn to prevent breakage. There are two ways to do this, both accomplishing the same thing. Flashing is one way and amounts to dipping the spring into the oil, igniting the oil with the torch and allowing it to burn completely. This is repeated three times and plunged back into the oil for a final cooling. The other way consists of placing the spring in a container about the size of a quart jar lid, pouring it full of oil until the spring is covered, and setting the oil on fire. The oil is allowed to burn completely out and the spring then cools by itself. Your spring should be retempered just like new and, if it isn't, then you have a piece of scrap metal on your hands without the needed properties and no

for a pie. At the time, he owned a beautiful double barrel muzzleloader in perfect condition, except for a hair trigger on the left lock. He always intended to repair it, but like the old story of the shoemaker's children not having any shoes, he kept putting it off to work on someone else's gun.

I loaded the gun with a heavy load in each barrel and Injun styled it down to a tree that was literally overrun with black birds. I intended to let go with one barrel at them in the tree, then take advantage of their habit of sweeping back toward their perch by having a go at them with the remaining barrel on their return trip.

When I was in range for the first shot, I made the mistake of cocking both hammers, easing up on one knee and firing the right barrel. The left sear slipped and both barrels went off at the same time. I ended up on my backside with a bruised shoulder and a long remembered knowledge of the pitfalls of a slipping sear. But, if memory serves, there were over thirty birds on the ground — with assorted tree limbs and bits of bark.

If the trouble is in the sear notches on the tumbler, you probably can stone these enough to reshape the notches, but it may be in a worn sear bar. This is a short piece of steel, shaped in the form of the letter L, with the upper part of the letter fitting into the notches of the tumbler

Among the antiques brought to him for repair, Walker noted this rifle which has the ramrod thimble fashioned from a cartridge case that then was soldered to barrel.

one can temper it. Simple as these methods sound, they are old techniques, and if correctly done the resulting spring should equal one made in the fanciest of furnaces.

I forgot to mention one important fact. That is never to release the compression of a spring suddenly, for to do so invites a broken spring. The longer the spring has been compressed, the more danger there can be. A spring vise is a dire necessity. These are available from gunsmith supply houses or you can use a pair of vise grip pliers, provided the jaws are not serrated and the spring is not protected. Compress the spring with your vise, remove it from its position and slowly ease up and allow the spring to move out to its normal shape. The same goes for reinstalling the spring. Use the spring vise each time you compress or decompress the mainspring when it is out of its position in the lock.

Some locks will show up with a worn sear that simply will not hold, slipping out of engagement at inopportune moments. This was brought home to me once in a way that I have never forgotten.

My grandfather had talked repeatedly about the delicacy of black bird pie and, as the local woods seemed to be over-run with them, one day I voluntered to go get enough

sears. It is attached to the side of the lock with a screw and, when the trigger bar is pressed against the lower foot of the L, the upper part is pivoted out of the sear notch to release the hammer.

The end of the sear bar that engages the notches should be inspected carefully to determine if it engages the notches fully and has not been rounded off or a chip broken from its engagement surfaces. Reshape this with the stone if necessary.

Most locks have a small separate spring pressing against the sear bar, but some will utilize the other end of the mainspring. Either way, the pressure must be enough to return the sear bar each time and force it into the notches on the tumbler.

Besides a weak spring, about the only trouble you may encounter is a worn screw hole, if the spring is attached to the side of the lock plate with a screw. This usually involves drilling and retapping the hole for a new screw. Some of these springs have a little tit on one side to hold them in place on the lock plate; this can give some trouble, if the recess in the lock plate is worn. Get out the small cold chisel and extrude metal into the recess to tighten the fit.

About the only remaining part of the lock that we have

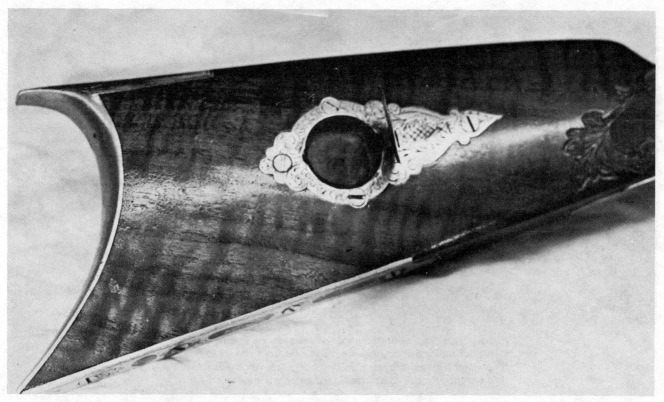

This antique percussion rifle has been restocked, but the original patch box has been inset in the wood.

not covered is the bridle or, as it sometimes is called, the yoke. This is a flat piece of metal that goes across the tumbler to support it on the end opposite the end entering the hole in the lock plate. This seldom causes trouble, but occasionally you may find one with a crack in it or one of the screw holes washed out. These are not much of a problem to make, as they can be cut from a piece of thin sheet steel, filed and drilled to shape. If any screw on the inside of the lock is worn or loose in its seat, it should be replaced with a larger substitute or a new one manufactured that will take up the slack.

The lock described is a simple one with the basic components only. There are exceptions to the rule and you may run across a lock, the innards of which are slightly different, even including a few parts that I have not mentioned. But there is little in a lock that cannot be repaired or a replacement made in even the smallest shop. The smoother the lock works, the better the gun's action will be, so be on the watch for anything that will inhibit this smoothness — particularly rust, burrs and grime.

The trigger system on most double barrel shotguns is a simple arrangement on even the most expensive versions. The cheap ones have the two triggers attached to the stock with a cross pin through the wood. No matter how fancy the gun on the outside, it is the inside that matters and this is the poorest arrangement possible. These get out of order fast as the triggers are used and the fit gets sloppier. You can drill a hole through the stock and the triggers for a larger pin, but a much better remedy is to glass bed the holes in the stock to form a seat for the pin. This is done by drilling a large hole about half-way through from each side and inserting a special long pin that is of the correct diameter, which has been covered with release agent.

The holes then are filled with glass bedding and allowed to harden before the long pin is removed. The regular pin and the triggers are reinstalled and the problem is solved.

You can use epoxy glue, if you do not have glass bedding material. A few triggers are fitted to a special plate and others right to the trigger guard. These give little trouble, but wear can enlarge the holes in the trigger and, if this is the problem, you can drill for a larger pin to take up the wear and reposition the triggers correctly. If the trigger guard is broken where it is attached to the stock with screws, repair it with a bracing patch as outlined for the patent breech tang. If the guard is broken elsewhere, you probably will have to resort to welding.

About half of the percussion shotguns — and the rifles too — will come into your possession minus the ramrod. As easy as it looks to make a new ramrod, most homemade jobs look like an abomination from the back woods. The best approach is to secure a good factory replacement if possible, but one can be made with a little patience. First, find a good long hardwood dowel that will slide tightly through the thimbles. Push it all the way into the ramrod thimbles and up into the hole cut in the front of the forearm to receive it. Check that this hole in the forearm is not filled with trash before you start the project or you can end up with a ramrod that is too short. Once the channel is clean and the dowel fully seated, mark it where it is flush with the end of the muzzle. The ramrod is pulled out and cut off at this mark. A metal button will be needed for the business end of the ramrod, and these can be purchased from one of the antique parts suppliers or turned out of brass or similar material on the lathe. The end of the dowel is inserted into the recess in the button and either glued in place, or secured there with a cross pin.

The final length of the ramrod may require a bit of trimming, but the button should be about a quarter of an inch behind the end of the muzzle. This may appear too short if the ramrod is placed in an empty barrel, but remember that you will not be using it on an empty chamber. The barrel will have a load of powder in it first,

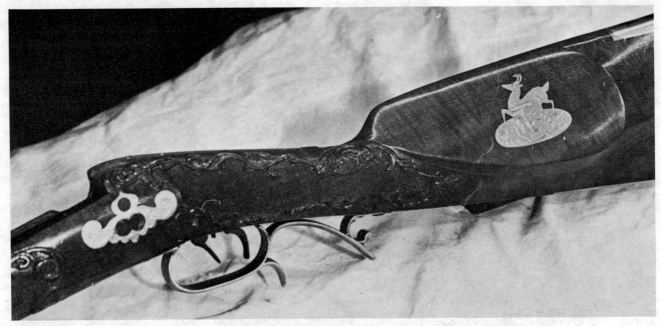

Here is an outstanding example of what can be accomplished by way of saving a good old percussion rifle from the scrap heap. The original triggers, trigger guard and butt plate were re-used, as the gunsmith, Brooks Coats, fashioned an ornate new stock for it.

and you will be using the ramrod to push a wad down on top of this, which will take up the length.

The spiral markings on the ramrod can be applied in several different ways. The old armchair gunsmith story is that you soak a string in gasoline and wind it around the ramrod and set it on fire. If you try this, you'll find, like I did, that the string will burn in two at some point and the rest falls off.

The easiest way is to set your propane hand torch on the bench and cut the flame down to a small pinpoint. Slowly twirl the rod between your fingers and move it from one end to the other past the flame. This will create a perfect spiral with the burnt wood carefully controlled. Try this first on a scrap dowel and you should pick up the knack in a few seconds. Lightly sand the dowel, rub it down with steel wool and apply a coat or two of stock finish. If the wood is white or near white, you can stain it lightly with a good walnut stain to a light walnut or dark oak color to blend in with the gunstock before applying the stock finish.

Of the chapter on stock repair and refinishing, about 99 percent will apply to an antique stock. A lot of stocks will have a rotten white section right under the nipples. That is the result of using corrosive primers and the flash of the percussion cap. Little can be done to correct this other than cutting away the affected part and splicing in a new piece of wood. If the lock plate recesses in the stock are worn or battered, you have to splice in new wood or repair it with glass bedding material to position the locks correctly.

If your restoration has been done carefully and provided the gun has a good set of barrels, there is no reason why you shouldn't enjoy shooting it. The first three or four shots from each barrel should be done as a test fire, using a ten percent overload with the gun secured and the firing done with a long string. You can use an old automobile tire for your test stand, the butt stock pushed down inside where the tube should be, the forearm resting on the outside of the tire across from it.

As for the charge, first determine the gauge with a bore micrometer, bore calipers, or make a close comparison with a breech loading shotgun. Before the advent of smokeless powder, all shotgun shells were loaded with black powder and the load was given as "3 drams 1 ounce," meaning three drams of black powder and one ounce of shot. When smokeless powder came along, it was loaded in so many grains, which was pure Greek to the average hunter.

To provide a method of designations, the new smokeless powder loads then came out as "3 dram equivalent and 1 ounce shot." The percussion shotgun owner can put this little gem of knowledge to work for him by simply dropping the word "equivalent" and using the common load for his gauge.

But never, under any circumstances, should anything but black powder be used in the percussion shotgun. Try the lightest load in the gauge and slowly work up to the medium loads, settling on the one that produces the results you desire. Seldom will the real heavy load do as good a job as the medium or light loads.

The repair and restoration of percussion rifles is similar to that of the percussion shotgun except that you are dealing with one rifled barrel and only one lock. One other difference is in the value, for fewer percussion rifles survive; hence the value is usually about double that of a percussion shotgun of the same quality and condition. The hobbyist must take this fact into consideration in his decision as to whether or not he should attempt the restoration himself.

The barrel will be our primary concern, especially the bore itself. The first step is the same as that of the percussion shotgun; that is, seeing if the critter has a load in it and, if so, removing it safely. About the only change is that the rifle may have a single ball load rather than a shot charge and will require the use of the special ball pulling screw to remove it.

After the load has been removed and the barrel is clear, remove the barrel from the stock by pushing out the barrel

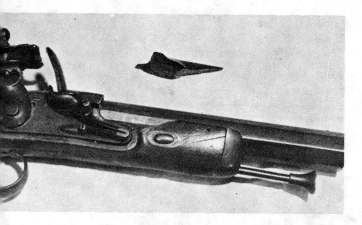

This flintlock pistol suffers from a chipped stock.

retaining wedges or pins up along the forearm, and removing the tang screw. The trick of tapping the barrel along its full length with a rawhide or plastic hammer will be needed to free the barrel from the stock without wood damage, as dirt, rust and grime probably have it stuck. Lift the barrel straight up out of the stock without rotation.

A percussion rifle barrel is much like a modern rifle barrel, except that where the chamber normally would be, a threaded section accepts the threaded breech plug. The breech plug, in turn, is built onto the tang. Getting the plug out can be a bit tricky. The plug and barrel must be held securely or the gun can be scarred and ruined.

The rear of the plug is attached to a lug on the order of a rectangular teardrop with the larger part at the top. Do not try to remove this with a vise or a common wrench. Instead, a special breech plug wrench must be made to exactly fit this tapered shape.

Remove the cardboard backing from a couple of bank checkbooks for use as a template for making the wrench. Through trial and error, cut the side of one of the pieces of cardboard until it is shaped exactly like half of the tapered plug. Lay this on the other piece of cardboard and mark the cut-out section on the second piece. Cut this out and lay the two halves, one on each side, on the breech plug and trim each piece of cardboard until you have a perfect fit around the breech plug.

Finish by taping two pieces of cardboard together for the full template of your wrench. The cardboard then is placed on a piece of good flat steel, preferably 3/8 inch thick, and a line is scribed on the inside of the cut-out section. Remove the template and drill the excess metal in several spots inside the scribed line, finishing up by filing up to the line but leaving a red cat hair of metal inside the line for final fitting. Through filing and trying, filing and trying, cut this final metal to a perfect snug fit around the breech tang plug.

Leave a good one inch of metal all around the hole in the wrench for strength and also about a foot of handle. There simply is no other way to get that plug out without damaging the plug or the barrel.

Squirt some type of penetrating oil down the bore and all around the joint of the breech plug and the barrel, allowing it to soak in for about ten minutes. Now secure the octagon barrel in a padded vise, and fit your breech plug wrench snugly: "snugly in place and hit the end of the wrench handle with a hammer." The breech plug should break free, allowing its removal by hand pressure with the wrench. If not, soak it some more and repeat the blow. Do not keep pounding if this fails the second time, as you will only damage the plug and your wrench.

Instead, heat the plug with your torch until you cannot

hold your finger against it, allow it to cool completely then heat the barrel surrounding the plug to the same approximate temperature. Do not get the barrel hot enough to damage the finish. While the barrel is still hot, install the wrench and hit its end with the hammer. On rare occasions, you will have to repeat the heating and cooling process a couple of times to free the plug. The heating expands the metal and breaks it free of the rust and grime.

When the plug is free, clean its threads on the wire scratch wheel, then clean the internal threads of the barrel. Add a drop or two of oil on each and wipe the excess oil away with a cloth. Reinstall the plug and, using the wrench, bring it up as snug as you can with hand pressure. If the plug is in good order, it should stop about 1/8 of an inch out of alignment and will require a light tap on the end of the wrench with a hammer to bring it into alignment with the barrel.

This fit must be tight to prevent gas from escaping at the joint when the gun is fired. If the fit is too loose and the plug goes past the alignment with hand pressure, you will have to use a washer to fill the gap. Many oldtime gunsmiths preferred a washer of lead between the plug and the barrel, but lead will work only if the plug is allowed to remain in position and not removed repeatedly. I prefer one cut out of sheet brass. Either way, cut the washer to fit the plug closely and thin it until the breech plug comes up in correct alignment with that tap on the end of the wrench.

Once you have the breech plug problem solved, you can turn your attention to the bore. With the breech plug removed, clean the bore of all rust and caked powder residue. If you are lucky, the rifling will come up clean and sharp. Even if there is a little pitting here and there, the barrel still may prove to be accurate enough, if shooting is your ultimate reason for restoring the gun. The main part of the barrel to watch is the last inch or so at the muzzle, for the continued use of the ramrod may have ruined the barrel's potential accuracy.

Determine the caliber of the barrel which seldom is designated on the barrel. Select a round, pure lead ball that will just start in the muzzle and carefully push it the full length of the bore. Measure across the bullet land diameter (which will be the groove diameter of the bore) with a micrometer, taking several readings. Let's say, for the sake of argument, that this comes out .45 caliber (hundredths of an inch). We must allow for the thickness of the patch which will surround the bullet, as it is pushed down the bore during loading. This will depend a great deal on the depth of the grooves and the thickness of the material you are using for a patch.

If the material is thin, try subtracting one caliber (.01) from your measurement and use a .44 caliber round ball for the first test. With a patch laid across the muzzle of the barrel, press the round .44 caliber ball down into the bore with your thumb or a short section of hardwood dowel until the ball is flush with the muzzle. Cut away the excess patch material and use the ramrod to push the bullet through the bore and out the open rear, the breech plug having been removed.

If your patch-and-ball diameter is correct, you should be able to push the ball the full length with firm hand pressure only. If you must pound on the ramrod with a hammer to get it through, then the ball diameter is too large or the patch material is too thick. For fast loading, many oldtimers used the rule of "two calibers for the patch" and you may have to go to this diameter ball which would be .43 caliber in our example. Usually, the thinner the patch the better the accuracy, but the bore gets a bit fouled during repeated shooting and a real tight fitting patch and

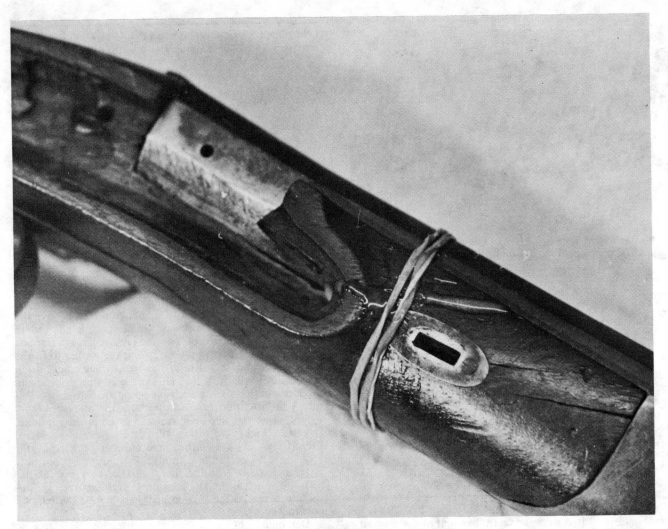

Lock removed, chipped portion of the stock reglued in position with epoxy and held until dry with a rubber band, the flintlock pistol already looks different. The other cracks were not repaired at the owner's request.

ball may necessitate cleaning after several shots.

If the patch is lubricated, the ball can be rammed home much easier. Plain old spit was the mountain man's favorite, but if you prefer the sanitary route, try sperm oil or Crisco. A lubricated patch also helps to keep the bore clean.

Round ball moulds are available from several sources. Lyman makes a whole swarm of such moulds in about any caliber while similar moulds are available from Dixie Gun Works, SAECO or Hensley and Gibbs.

If you want to make your own, you will need two thick sections of brass and a few other fittings. The two sections are hinged together and a cross pin put through up in one corner. The pin is removed, cut off, and staked into one side with the protruding end rounded off so it will enter the other side of the mould. This acts as an alignment along with the hinge which is screwed to the two sections.

Lay a steel BB on one side right in the center, fold the other half carefully down on the BB and hit the other half lightly with a hammer. This will mark each side of the mould and give you a reference point. All that is needed is to cut out the brass you don't want. It is simple, if you will drill a pouring hole down from the top, half on each side,

and drill out a little of the excess where the bullet cavity will be. All that remains is to get out the Dremel Moto Tool and cut away some of the brass on each side, attempting to keep it equal. When it looks about right but still small, cast a bullet or two and measure it all the way around with the micrometer. Your mistakes will be evident. If you do not get in a hurry, it is possible to make a first class mould this way. Back in my younger days, I made about a half dozen moulds this way. But an easier way, if you have lathe and milling facilities, is to cut a round cherry of correct bullet diameter out of drill rod and mill some cutting flutes on it. The cherry is hardened and used to remove the excess brass to form the bullet cavity. Once the cavity is correct, add the handles by attaching them to the sides of the mould with screws and finish with wooden handles.

If the rifling is worn badly in your barrel and your test shots leave a lot to be desired, you have to decide whether to leave the rifle as it is or to have the bore "freshed out." This consists of cutting the grooves uniformly deeper and truing the bore to a larger uniform diameter. This is the way it was done in the old days. A rifle many times started out as a .40 caliber and ended up years later as a .45, or even a .50 caliber by repeated "freshing out" when it became worn.

I would recommend this be done by a professional, but many hobbyists who enjoy working with muzzleloaders have made their own rifling and "freshing out" machines which turn out good work. A minister in a nearby town became deeply interested in this and, with the help of his local machinist, constructed a nice rifling machine out of scrap material. The work is slow and painstaking, but it can be done without a large, elaborate set up. The National Muzzle Loading Association publishes a monthly magazine that contains articles on barrel work from time to time. The association is devoted entirely to muzzleloaders and the publication alone is worth the price of membership!

The sights on the barrel may have been lost or damaged, but these are simple affairs and you should have little trouble filing out a replacement. The rear sight is little more than a piece of steel dovetailed into the barrel, a V filed into the top. Front sights usually are of German silver and replacements are offered by Dixie Gun Works and other suppliers in finished or rough cast form. Seldom do these sights have any method of elevation adjustment, for the rifle was built to handle one load perfectly and the sights filed and adjusted on the range until they were zeroed in on the target. Lighter loads were used occasionally, but the shooter allowed for the different amount of drop of the fired ball by changing his sighting.

In severe cases of gun damage, the flats and edges of the octagon barrel may be deeply pitted and nicked. As a gun in this condition, with a few exceptions, will not have full value, you can consider draw filing of the flats of the barrel until all such defects have been removed. First check the value of the gun and do it only where such restoration will not affect the price. Octagon barrels can be recut on the milling machine, but few hobbyists will have such a machine and elbow grease and a flat file can almost duplicate the machine's work. The barrel was draw filed originally and finished by wrapping abrasive cloth around the file for the final strokes. There is no need for a real high polish, because such finishes were found only on display or presentation rifles.

On some rifles the nipple is screwed directly into the barrel, but the majority will be found with a drum screwed into the barrel with the nipple, in turn, screwed into the drum. The nipple is removed with a nipple wrench, but the drum is much more difficult, especially if the gun has seen a lot of hard use. Some drums will be fitted with a flat to facilitate removal, but others have none.

Do not use the nipple as a bearing surface for a wrench in an attempt to remove the drum. Instead, remove the nipple and turn a foot-long section of steel rod for use as a wrench with one end threaded to match the nipple. This is screwed into the drum and tapped on the end to get the

This is the rear view of the lock from the flintlock pistol. There is no great difference insofar as parts are concerned between this and the lock on a percussion.

Remington percussion revolver was damaged by attempt to convert it. Cylinder required welding at rear, cutting and reshaping, as well as thorough test firing before it was back in shape. This work should be left to the pros.

drum moving. In severe cases, go to the heating method to free it.

Once the drum is free, treat it as you did the breech tang, cleaning it thoroughly, even using a washer to realign it if badly worn. If necessary, a new drum can be turned, drilled and threaded by any good machinist or by the hobbyist, if he has access to a lathe. The drum must be a tight seal-fit as does the breech plug, and align the nipple directly under the hammer when the hammer is in the fired position.

Many rifles will have various decorative and useful fittings, called "furniture," inletted into the stock. In most cases, these require only a good cleaning and maybe a re-placement spring for a patch box. A section of the decorative furniture may be broken off, but an entirely new piece can be cut and filed out of sheets of flat German silver or brass. Decorative furniture, such as eagles, stars and such can be added to a stock to cover a bad gouge or defect, so long as it matches the rest of the furniture.

Some rifles will be fitted with set triggers, the rear trigger setting the mechanism and the front trigger releasing it to fire the gun. Surprisingly, most of these will be found in working order, as they are of simple construction and design, and require only thorough cleaning and oiling. If the trigger will not hold the set, look for a small adjustment screw between the two triggers or the hole where it should

be. The screw may be broken off or missing and all that is necessary is to replace it. If this is not the problem, look at the notches and sears, as well as the fit of the cross pins that align the parts.

A little filing or stoning generally will return the trigger to full safe service. Missing or broken parts can be filed out of bar stock, using the old part for a pattern or, in the case of a missing part, through trial and error. On these old guns, usually the original parts were constructed entirely with hand tools in shops little better equipped than a good hobby shop.

The lock mechanism of most rifles is almost identical with that of a percussion shotgun and, in a few cases, some of the parts will interchange. Stocks are either of the half stock, three-quarter stock or full length variety, meaning only the length of the wooden forend. If some nut in the past has cut a full stock back to a half stock, one might consider making a replacement section out of an old matching piece of walnut and splicing it back on. Ramrod thimbles were usually attaced to a rib in the case of the half or three-quarter stock, so if they are attached directly to the barrel, it is a good sign that the stock has been cut off.

Shooting muzzleloading rifles has become a favorite pastime with many gun enthusiasts and since it is a growing sport, there is becoming a scarcity of good rifles. So the only way many hobbyists could own one was to build his own percussion rifle from scratch, using an old lock. New muzzleloading barrels are available from a half dozen sources, as are good used locks and hammers. Dixie Gun Works offers several kits that contain everything you need to build a new muzzleloading rifle. The hobbyist with a hankering for such a rifle needs only patience and time to turn out a good working percussion rifle.

Percussion single-shot pistols can be placed in two basic categories. One is the duelling or horse pistol, which resembles a short percussion rifle with a hammer a bit smaller and a pistol grip instead of a butt stock. The lock, stock and barrel can be treated the same as the percussion rifle, for there is little difference. The main difference will be the ramrod, for on some of these it is hinged to the barrel with a swivel thimble arrangement to prevent loss. Sometimes these have seen hard use and parts will be missing, bent or worn badly. If enough of the hinged thimble remains, one should have little difficulty in filing out replacement and, if the entire assembly is missing, he can copy a new one from a similar gun.

The second type can be loosely termed muff pistols or maybe pocket pistol, if you prefer. The lock part of the frame is similar to that of a modern pistol and may be released by removing one screw. You will find a side plate on most of these that, when removed, will reveal the trigger, sears, mainspring and lower part of the hammer. On most of these, the mainspring serves a dual purpose, powering the trigger as well as the hammer. Because of their concealed lock parts and steel frame construction, these pistols survive in much better condition than the first type. Generally, restoring consists of removing rust and such, plus a little touching up of a worn part here and there. Instead of using a breech plug, these have the barrels screwed into the receiver, or onto a plug fitted to the breech. A wrench must be filed out to fit the barrel about like the one for the percussion rifle breech plug.

Percussion revolvers are becoming as scarce as an honest politician and the price of some of them is about like a down payment on a new Cadillac. For this reason, the hobbyist should check the value of a gun in his possession and honestly ask himself if he is qualified to do the restoration work. If not, the work should be turned over to a professional, with the hobbyist limiting himself to cleaning and oiling such guns.

Disassembling the gun is a task in itself and some models can be badly damaged, if the hobbyist is not familiar with the parts and the takedown sequence. The NRA handbooks recommended in the chapter on disassembly and cleaning contain instructions for disassembly of the more common models, but not the rare ones. Guns such as the Savage, Adams, Cooper and others should be disassembled only by a professional gunsmith. Some of the lock work is strictly Rube Goldberg and just one mistake can ruin the gun.

The high demand for percussion revolvers has resulted in several companies manufacturing replicas. Price for a shooting percussion revolver is well below that of an original and most of the replicas will shoot just as well, some even better! Many replicas are beginning to show up on the used gun market, suffering the usual ills, and one should investigate this possibility. Even on a new one, the parts are seldom as well fitted as the old originals due to the lack of hand work, and the hobbyist with time and patience can gain a lot of knowledge about this type of gun, plus have a lot of fun in the reworking and hand-fitting of the parts. It is good training for the hobbyist who wants to work on antique restoration without running the risk of destroying a valuable gun.

Defining an antique and what is not when it comes to cartridge arms is a tough proposition. It gets a little more complicated when you try to determine what is a collector's item. I once thought that it involved the different models and variations of known guns, but this idea went down the drain when the so-called commemoratives came on the market. These are manufactured rarities purposely limited in number to establish a market.

Quite often, today's common gun becomes tomorrow's hot collector's item as more gun enthusiasts become interested and data is uncovered and published. A friend of mine, George Taylor, became interested in Japanese weapons and bought them right and left when the going price was about five bucks each. He slowly worked up a collection, rebuilding and restoring the odd models even when little or no data was available. The present interest in Japanese weapons is snowballing, and old George is sitting on top of one of the best collections in the country, with rare models galore and the price still going up!

The restoration of guns, such as the Colt Single Action, Lugers, Winchesters and similar ones, is more a matter of determining what is the accepted standard and using this as a guide in how far to go with restoration. The beginner is far better to undertake his first repairs and restorations on guns not in the accepted collector status. But this need not be a thankless or uninteresting task, or there are hundreds of guns that are not normally considered collector items but are unusual and interesting. Few die-hard collectors will fail to note and appreciate an interesting gun that someone has taken the trouble to restore in good taste.

A good example is the little handgun commonly called the "spur trigger" that was made from before the turn of the century and up to the 1930s in various shapes and forms. Inexpensively made, they quickly suffer from harsh use and seldom will be found in good condition. An interesting collection can be made of them, since they sell for practically nothing, even in good condition. As there is no beginning and no end to such a collection, you can stop anywhere along the line you wish.

This is only an example of guns awaiting the hobbyist on which he can practice and practice, increasing his gunsmithing skill and gathering a collection that will be interesting to anyone. When you begin restoring a gun, try to find any information you can on the gun; background data, disassembly procedure, owner's manual or even an exploded view will be of invaluable help. If possible, pick up a junker of the same model to be used for spare parts. Many of these, especially the old ones, are tricky to disassemble, so take your time and think each step through carefully before you move. Watch for hidden springs that can be released and fly off into the wild blue to be lost for all time. Be careful of the screw slots and the stock, taking care not to add another restoration problem to the pile that you already have by ruining it. Once the gun is disassembled, take your time and clean each part as well as possible. Replace or repair any needed part and go slow with each detail.

All of the foregoing has avoided any reference to refinishing an antique. This is a big question and there is no simple answer. On some guns a refinish job will destroy the value, while on others it is acceptable. You just have to treat each gun separately and make your decision based on current acceptance.

Antique restoration is an interesting part of hobby gunsmithing and a lot of gun enthusiasts get into it, even into professional gunsmithing, as a result of it. The main ingredients are common sense, patience, time and a little skill, of course.

But you never gain the skill until you try!

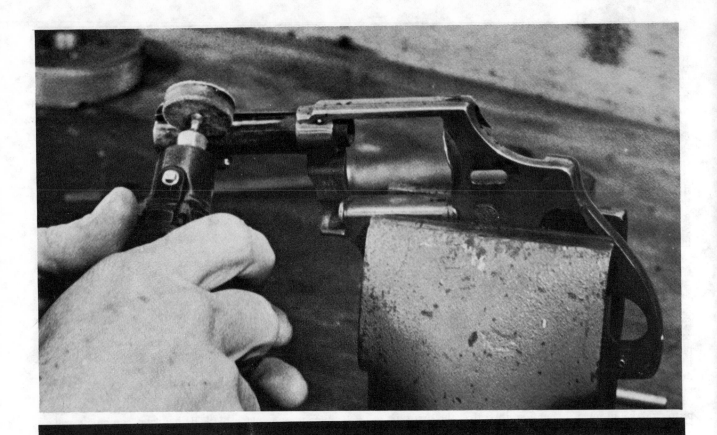

Chapter 16

TO POLISH & JEWEL

Function And Appearance Can Be Parallel Matters; One Often Depends Upon The Other!

POLISHING GUN PARTS is done for two basic reasons: function and appearance. Sometimes the two reasons overlap and one becomes the other, but for our purpose we will try to separate the two, give the reasons for each and describe how each is done. Jewelling usually is thought of as a decoration, yet it has a functional reason and we will get into this.

Most hobbyists think of power buffing when polishing is mentioned and do not attempt it, because they lack the necessary equipment or they think they lack the equipment. Actually, power buffing is a fairly recent development, coming on the gunsmithing scene about the same time as the general availability of household electricity and small electric motors. The arms industry and a few shops had utilized steam and water wheel power for buffing prior to electricity, but not to any great extent, as most of the polishing was done entirely by hand.

One would think that in this Space Age all buffing would be done by power. The British Purdy shotgun is considered by many to be the finest in the world, yet every single piece that goes into this fine gun is polished 100 percent by hand, including the outside surface that is blued.

Even today's fully equipped professional gunsmith often reverts to hand polishing. All that is needed to turn out quality polishing are a few files, some Arkansas stones, aluminum oxide cloth in various grits, crocus cloth and a hand burnishing tool. The final ingredients are your elbow grease and patience.

Functional reasons for polishing can be illustrated best by a simple experiment. Take two pieces of sandpaper, place them face to face and attempt to slide them across each other. You will find that they drag and bind, with movement of one piece over the other difficult, due to their rough surfaces. Now, place two pieces of glass together and slide them across each other. This time they feel like two greased eels with no binding or roughness whatever.

Also, you probably noticed that it required little pressure to slide the two pieces of glass across each other, while quite a bit of pressure was needed with the sandpaper. The reason is the amount of friction involved. A basic rule of physics is that the smoother the surface, the less the amount of friction; the less the amount of friction, the less the pressure needed to move the item.

Every moving part in a gun is affected by friction and

Aluminum oxide cloth wrapped around edge of small file is used to polish slide grooves of M1911 automatic. This eliminates rough spots and allows smoother working.

After slide is smoothed up, hand-held burnishing tool is used to slick up surface for friction-free operation.

Author draw files M1911 slide. Dark areas are hollow depressions yet untouched by file. Note also the position of both thumbs to guide file in forward stroke.

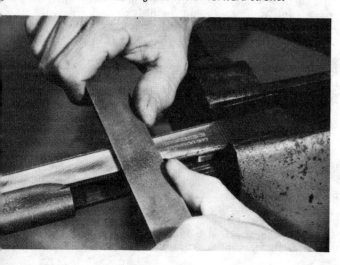

the amount of friction will affect the correct function or be the cause of malfunctions, regardless of the type gun or action. Friction affects the amount of pressure necessary to pull the trigger, the speed of the lock, the opening of the action, the extraction of the fired case, the ejection of the fired case and insertion of another round into the chamber. In the case of repeating arms, it undoubtedly is the source of more malfunctions than any other single cause.

In days of yesteryear, hand labor was relatively cheap and each part of a gun usually was hand polished and hand fitted, resulting in an action that felt as though the parts were made of glass. For each rise in labor wages, the manufacturers have been forced to decrease the amount of hand labor in the construction of a gun and rely more on machine-fitted parts with ever increasing tolerances. The results can be seen in today's guns with their stamped and cast parts fitted loosely together with the resulting jamming and malfunctions. If this appears a manufacturer's neglect or as a desire for profit at the expense of quality, appearances are deceiving.

Recently I talked at great length with the chief engineer of one of the largest firearms manufacturers in the country about this and the possibility of quality workmanship in future guns. We were discussing a .22 rimfire semi-automatic rifle that retailed at just under fifty dollars and I was surprised that the actual cost of manufacturing was about one-fourth of the final cost. The other three-fourths of the price was added after the gun left the assembly line in such things as packaging, shipping, invoicing and, of course, the jobber's and retailer's profits. Keeping this in mind, it is easy to understand why so little expensive hand fitting and polishing is done in present day manufacturing. Hand-fitted and hand-polished guns are available on the American market, but invariably the product is of foreign manufacture, where labor costs are less and the retail price of such guns usually is more than that of our native machine-produced products. The hobbyist without the means of purchasing one of these guns or preferring an American design can improve the operation of one of the machine-produced guns by disassembling the gun and polishing each part by hand.

Before disassembly, the hobbyist should work the action of the gun by hand and note the places that the gun seems to bind, as well as the places where the action is smooth. During disassembly take careful note of the fit of each part in relation to the entire assembly, paying particular attention to the amount of tolerance between parts.

If the fit is sloppy with large tolerances, then there is a possibility that further polishing will increase this tolerance to a degree that the part will be too sloppy to function properly. On such parts you must compromise and, at most, polish only the portion of the part that is rough or burred. In most cases, the fit will be close enough to allow polishing of the entire part without affecting the function of the gun. In a few rare cases you may have to replace an extremely sloppy part, for they can cause binding or will not align correctly due to the sloppy fit. A few times I have found it necessary to fabricate a completely new part, as even the replacements would not function correctly, although usually this is something simple like pins.

Time and experience will quickly teach you the tricks of polishing for function, but let's assume that you never have polished a gun and choose a model that is fairly familiar to all, such as the Model 1911A1 Colt .45 service automatic. The procedure for other models and types is basically the same and little trouble will be encountered once you have mastered the basics.

I once collected U.S. martial handguns and in this collection was a Model 1911 that was produced by Colt about 1920 during the transition period from the M-1911 to the M-1911A1. This was the finest, smoothest handgun I have ever owned and, since that time, I have judged every handgun by its standards. Anyone who has handled one of the commercial Colts manufactured during this period will understand this, for they were literally works of art.

It is possible to take a regular wartime military model and obtain about the same degree of smoothness, but it takes a lot of work, for you will need to do almost a full accurizing job on the gun

With the M-1911, completely disassembled down to the last step, we will need several files, preferably single cut, although a double cut file can be used. These should consist of one six-inch, one eight-inch and a couple of narrow pillar files, plus one small four-inch triangular file. Arkansas stones can be put to good use, but the most useful shape will be the triangular one. Next we will need several sheets of aluminum oxide cloth of 240 grit, 320 grit, and No. 500 grit, plus several sheets of crocus cloth. The final item is a hand burnishing tool which can be obtained from a gunsmith supply house or a jewelry supply house. One last thing before we get started; it is going to take about eight hours of actual work to turn out a first class polishing job.

Our first concern is the fit of the slide to the receiver. To check this, we install the stripped slide onto the matching grooves of the stripped receiver and work it back and forth a couple of times. If the fit is close you will need only to do a good job of polishing the matching surfaces, but chances are that, with a wartime model, the slide will be a sloppy fit, wobbling from side to side. Always remember that our reason for polishing for function is to obtain a good working, friction-free performance; sometimes we must also refit the parts in addition to polishing to obtain this.

For a close fit with a sloppy slide, we will have to close the amount of tolerance between the slide grooves and the matching grooves — a common alteration in an accurizing job on a M-1911A1.

There are two ways to go about this. The simplest is to place the slide in a padded vise top up, and slightly tighten the vise jaws to spring the slide inward to close that sloppy fit. This takes a bit of practice, and it is best to go easy. Tighten the jaws just a teeny, tiny bit, then try the slide on the receiver to see how much more springing of the slide will be necessary to close that tolerance. Keep repeating this until the desired fit is obtained.

The second way is to peen the top guides on the receiver with a hammer to extrude the metal outwards to take up the slack. This is done with a light pecking stroke all the way along the top of the receiver guides. Keep trying the slide on the receiver and be sure to peen each side of the receiver equally. Usually, you will need to file the extruded metal lightly to smooth it up and make it equal on all sides.

I personally prefer to spring the slide inwards with the vise rather than peen the top of the receiver. Use either method you prefer, but go slowly and keep checking the fit of the slide to the receiver.

Once the slide is tight without binding, polish the grooves in both the slide and receiver to a glass-like smoothness. Tear off a strip of the No. 500 grit aluminum oxide cloth and wrap it around the edge of one file that will fit down into the grooves. If necessary, cut a strip of wood about an inch wide and about six inches long that is just thick enough to match the grooves with the aluminum oxide cloth wrapped around its edge. Work this back and

Finger grooves of slide often are battered in misuse, but can be reconditioned easily with three-corner file.

Virtually any round surface from a pin to, as in this case, a barrel can be polished quickly and efficiently with shoe shine action, using aluminum oxide cloth.

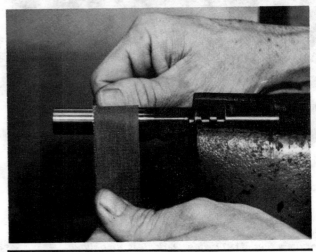

forth the full length of the groove until the bottom and sides of the groove are as slick as possible, then switch to crocus cloth wrapped around the file or wood; repeat the same process until the polished surface is like glass.

For the outside counterpart of the grooves, wrap a piece of 500 grit cloth around one of the flat files and work its flat surface back and forth along the entire length until all burrs are removed and the metal is smooth. Then switch to the crocus cloth, wrapping it around the file the same way, and working back and forth, until you have a glass-like finish.

After all mating surfaces in both parts have been thus polished, the slide — without any oil — should work the full length of the normal movement without even a hint of binding or dragging. The hand burnishing tool is worked hard across the exposed surfaces of the slide to bring the polish to the ultimate smoothness. Press hard with the burnishing tool and, if necessary use both hands on it, for the harder you press and the more vigorously you burnish the metal, the smoother the finish will be. Burnishing metal is an old and honored method of getting the surface to a high polish and an almost unbelievable degree of smoothness, but few gunsmiths ever use the tool.

Next, reinstall the barrel and the barrel bushing along with the recoil spring and lock the barrel in place. Work the slide back and forth, noting the camming action of the barrel lugs into the locking recesses cut in the slide, as well as the fit of the barrel at the bushing. Disassemble the gun and notice the locking lugs on the barrel. Chances are, you will see a few scratches where some uneven surface up in the slide is bearing against them. Wrap the No. 500 grit

Small surfaces such as this pistol hammer are polished by sliding it back and forth across section of aluminum oxide cloth, using fingers to apply downward pressure.

cloth around a file edge and work the barrel locking lugs over, bringing them to a smooth finish both inside and outside.

Now switch your attention to their matching recesses cut into the slide. To get down into these, whittle out a piece of wood to match the thickness of the grooves cut into the slide. Wrap a piece of 500 grit cloth around the wood, and work it back and forth in each groove until they are smooth. To smooth up the top of the recesses in the slide, whittle out a round wooden dowel large enough to go down the slide from the front end with a piece of aluminum oxide cloth wrapped around it. Push this back and forth the full length of the inside of the slide, until this entire surface has been smoothed up. Follow up your polishing with the crocus cloth for the final finish as you did on the slide and receiver grooves.

The final place to polish on the slide is to the rear where the hammer is pressed down, for this must be free of burrs or roughness for easy operation of the slide during recoil. Once you have all this done, turn your attention to the barrel bushing that fits into the end of the slide. The fit of the bushing to the slide should be easy but snug and any roughness must be polished away. The end of the barrel should slide through the bushing easily, but the· fit of the barrel to the barrel bushing is extremely important, for if it

is too slack, the end of the barrel will wobble and accurate shooting will be impossible. If the bushing binds the barrel, it will prevent functioning of the gun and result in a jam, so watch out for both extremes.

If your fit is sloppy, try another bushing, but you may have to go to a Micro-Tite bushing which will have to be installed by a professional, if you do not have lathe facilities. At the rear of the barrel is a small link that operates the barrel up and down into the lug recess in the slide to lock the barrel. The fit of this link is extremely important for accurate shooting. With the gun assembled, the link must push the barrel firmly into the linking recesses in the slide, and no downward play of the barrel should be evident. If there is play, try substituting a longer link to push the barrel lugs more firmly into the recesses in the slide.

To assure flawless function of the link, push out the pin that holds it to the barrel and polish both the pin and the hole in the link, as well as the hole in the barrel. To polish the holes, wrap a small piece of aluminum oxide around a toothpick and push it back and forth through the hole.

You may be wondering when to use the 240 grit cloth that I said would be needed. Use it whenever it is needed, for the cardinal rule of polishing is always to use the finest grit that will get the job done! It is not necessary to use a rough grit to polish a part, if the surface is fairly smooth the No. 500 grit will do. Naturally, if the part is rough or pitted, you would spend many unnecessary hours trying to do the polishing with the 500 grit alone, but if the No. 240 grit is used first to cut away the heavy roughness, the 500 can be used to finish the job quickly. The crocus cloth is much finer than even the 500 and will put a mirror-like finish on any part if you give it time. The files are used bare only where there is a large burr or an exceptionally rough part that even the No. 240 will not smooth up, but the files must be used with care, for improper use can put in more scratches than you had to start with. The burnishing tool is not an absolute necessity, but where it can be used affords the ultimate in polishing. The Arkansas stones will see the least use since they are needed for sear work only or on extremely rough spots where the files will not cut.

By now the .45 pistol slide should operate on the receiver with a minimum of effort and be much like those 1920 products. The job is only half done, however, for we now must concentrate on the internal action parts to make the gun operate without binding at any point. Every part that works against another part must be brought to a smooth finish. The pin that goes through the side of the receiver and through the barrel link should be polished to aid the link in easy operation. To polish this and similar pins in the action, tear off a one-inch wide strip of No. 500 grit cloth about eight inches long. With the pin secured by one end in a vise, polish the pin by "shoe-shining" with the 500 cloth. That is, pull down first one side of the cloth and then the other just as you would shine a pair of shoes, but be sure to do this shoe-shine polishing all the way around the pin. Follow up with the crocus cloth in a similar manner and the pin will be as slick as a politician's brother-in-law. Repeat this on every pin and link in the gun, including the sides of the firing pin, but do not polish the tip of the pin, as you may alter correct ignition of the primer.

To polish the holes through which these pins operate, wrap a toothpick with the aluminum oxide cloth and the crocus cloth. The sides of parts such as the hammer must be polished, as it bears against the side of the receiver and this particular bearing surface must be polished also. You can do this by wrapping the aluminum oxide cloth around the file and pushing it back and forth against the part. An easier

Heavily pitted shotgun barrel is rough polished, using aluminum oxide cloth wrapped around file, pushing it in same motion as draw filing. However, extreme care must be taken not to cut flats into the barrel during work.

way is to lay a piece of the aluminum oxide cloth on a flat hard surface with the grit up. Then lay the part on the cloth and with your thumb pressing down on the part, move the part back and forth rapidly across the cloth. The hard backing assures an even polish job across the entire surface of the part. When one side is smoothed up, flip the part over and repeat the process on the other side. Finish up by substituting a piece of crocus cloth and repeat the procedure.

This same method is used on the sides of the sear, disconnector and so on, until all internal parts are smooth as glass on their sides, as well as in any hole through them. The internal sides of the receiver, against which these parts bear, usually can be polished with the aluminum oxide cloth wrapped around a flat file or a piece of wood cut to fit. The better the job you do on this section, the easier the gun will work, but if you neglect it, all the polishing of the sides of parts, such as the hammer, will have been in vain.

Don't forget to polish the sides of the grip safety and the hole through it, for this is depressed each time the trigger is pulled. Be careful of the end of the safety, for if you change these angles you may ruin the safety feature of the grip safety. If the trigger is sloppy and wobbles from side to side, spring out the arms of the trigger until they ride firmly in their recess in the receiver, but be sure to polish the outside of the arms and the recesses also.

Slack in the trigger before it engages the sear sometimes can be eliminated a little at a time, for if you overdo it, you can create an unsafe gun, with the trigger bar partially disengaging the sear without any pressure from the trigger finger. The hard Arkansas stone is used to touch up the sear edge and the sear notch in the hammer, but go slow and

don't change this angle!

You should have every part of the action polished until you can almost see yourself in the surfaces. Then, and only then, should the job be considered done. Wash the parts thoroughly in mineral spirits and check that all dust from the polishing process has been removed before reassembling the gun. Even without a drop of oil, the action and the entire function of the gun should feel like those two pieces of glass sliding across each other. Add a drop or two of good non-gumming gun oil on the bearing surfaces as the final touch.

All we have done is use the file, the aluminum oxide cloth, the crocus cloth and the burnishing tool to polish the bearing surfaces of all the parts and major components. In doing this, we have reduced the amount of friction between the parts. This requires less pressure for the parts to operate. This same slicking-up process can be used on virtually any gun made, except for some of the parts of modern guns that are nickel plated or made from castings of pot metal. In each gun you must treat every part as important and pay close attention to the smallest detail where two pieces rub against each other.

While all of this can be done entirely by hand, polishing a gun for function can be done faster and easier, with a small hand power tool, such as the Dremel Moto-Tool or a flexible shaft driven by a high speed motor. For actual polishing, you can use small bobs of felt fitted to a mandrel that is chucked in the tool. The bob is coated with polishing compound by pressing the turning bob quickly against the end of a stick of polishing compound. The bob is allowed to rotate; this, in turn, dries the compound quickly and the bob is ready to do its job.

Another method is to use small rubber wheels that have been impregnated with cutting compound by the manufacturer. These are available from several sources in all kinds of grits and sizes, either long or tapered. With a Moto-Tool and a few of these rubber wheels, you can polish a part in less than one-fourth the time it would take with hand polishing and do a better job down in those hard to reach spots.

In preparing to polish a gun for appearance, one first concerns himself with the condition of the surface as to roughness of the metal and amount of pitting present. Most roughness will result from the manufacturer not carrying the polish to a high enough degree and this can be eliminated with additional polishing. Rust is simply the changing of metal into ferrous oxide which, when removed, will reveal a small missing bit of metal — or a "pit," as it commonly is called.

This can be compared somewhat to a cavity in a tooth, but unlike the tooth, the missing metal cannot be replaced by filling up the hole with a substitute. Instead, the pit can be erased only by cutting down the surface of the metal that is surrounding the pit until the surface level is even with the bottom of the pit. To prevent a dished-out appearance that will occur if the polishing is done around the area surrounding the pit, it is necessary to polish down the entire section of metal on which the pit occurs.

For example, if the side of the trigger has a rust pit .001 inches deep on it, then the entire surface of that side of the trigger must be reduced in thickness .001 inch to be level with the bottom of the pit. This must be done evenly over the entire side of the trigger, for to do otherwise will result in either a dished-out look to the trigger or the trigger will lose its lines entirely. Here lies the problem in polishing — getting the surface down evenly without cutting waves in the metal or dishing it out. The manufacturer used a milling cutter and a surface grinder to make this side of the trigger while you must cut the surface down evenly by hand.

Suppose we continued on our M-1911 pistol that we have already worked over for function: polishing it for appearance preparation for rebluing. Our same basic tools will be needed and again, our first step is to disassemble the gun down to the last part and screw.

You can start polishing anywhere on the gun, but the slide usually will have the lion's share of pitting. On the really rough ones it will be necessary to draw file the sides of the slide to get the surface level below the bottom of the pitting. Draw filing is becoming a lost art, yet, correctly done, it is like having a hand milling machine. A skilled draw filer can almost work miracles in getting a surface down fast and accurately. An eight-inch single cut file is about perfect for the work in most cases, although a shorter file can be used.

Place the file flat against the surface of the slide crossways. Grasp the handle of the file with the right hand and the end of the file with the left hand, while the thumbs of both hands are pressed against the edge of the file about two inches apart. When draw filing, don't bear down on the ends of the file or you will bow it in the center, resulting in the file cutting on its edges more than in the center.

With the slide secured in the vise, one side up, slowly push the file across the surface of the slide with an even, steady stroke. You will feel the file bite into the steel and the cut made by the file will be a planing one, resulting in long, thin slivers of metal as the file makes its journey across the length of the slide.

At the end of the stroke, lift the file clear of the slide and reposition it as the start for the second cut. Do not make a back stroke, as the file will not cut this way, and

Dremel Moto-Tool is used with drum sander to polish the inside of trigger guard. With care in operation, the tool can be used on larger, flat surfaces, in crevices.

you will suceed only in clogging up the cutting teeth of the file. Also be sure to keep the teeth of the file clean, for any jagged piece of metal caught in the teeth can deeply scratch your work. Make these full-length steady strokes until the slide is materially reduced about half of the desired amount. Reverse your position and make the rest of the draw filing strokes and work on the slide at the thick ends until the surface is even all over.

At the rear of the slide there is a series of serrations cut into the slide and used to provide a firm grasp on the slide when it is pulled to the rear by hand. Disregard these in your draw filing even though it seems that you are ruining them. Also, disregard the name on the side of the slide if it is necessary to reduce the thickness of the slide to remove deep and heavy pitting and scratches. It is better to cut away the name than to leave the pitting or scratches.

Once you have the side of the slide cut below the pitting, turn the slide over and repeat the same process on the other side. Once the sides are done, tear off a strip of the No. 240 grit aluminum oxide cloth and wrap it the length of the file. Now begin filing the same as before, but with the aluminum oxide cloth doing the cutting instead of the teeth of the file. To prevent deepening of any lengthwise scratches or marks in the slide, make your polishing cuts at a slight angle to the length of the slide instead of straight back and forth. About a 30-degree angle to the length of the slide will be right.

Make these polishing cuts pointing to the top of the slide, then reverse this and make additional strokes with the angle pointing to the bottom of the slide. This cross-polishing, or first one way and then the other, will erase any deep scratches left from the draw filing, as well as the polishing cuts you just finished to smooth up the side of the slide. You can also reverse ends of the slide to further smooth up the surface.

Repeat the same thing on the opposite side of the slide changing the aluminum oxide cloth as it becomes worn. When both sides have been completed, switch to the No. 500 grit aluminum oxide cloth around the file and do the whole business over again until the sides are as smooth as you can get them. Repeat the process for a third time with crocus cloth taking the place of the aluminum oxide cloth.

At the end of all of this polishing, you should have the sides of the slide looking mighty sharp. The finish will be almost mirror-like, but to get it in mirror-like shape, switch to the burnishing tool and rub it as hard as you can over the entire surface of the sides until it is slick as glass. The final step on the side of the slide is to replace the serrated grooves we cut down during the draw filing. This is done with a small three-cornered file, cutting the serrations deeper, until the edges of the serrations are back where they were at first.

For the top of the slide, we draw file if necessary and stop at the No. 240 grit cloth rather than go the entire sequence to a bright finish. The reason is that we do not want light reflected up here to interfere with sighting. If this is done carefully, the top of the slide will give about the same appearance of having been sandblasted lightly.

Repeat the same process at the rear of the slide below the top, where the hammer strikes the firing pin. Up front, the slide slopes away on the bottom and, while this area can be brought to a high polish, it is a hard spot to work and is best left alone after it has been smoothed up with 240 grit.

Because of the shape, you will have to do most of the polishing here with the aluminum oxide cloth wrapped around your finger or thumb, although some polishing can be done using the cloth around the end of a file. Finish up with a few strokes across the muzzle end of the slide ending

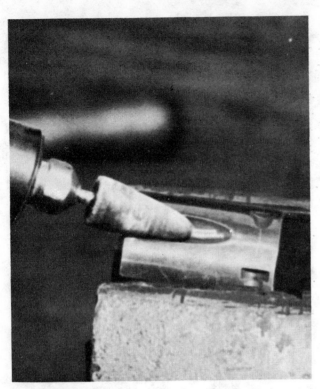

A pointed felt bob is used here to polish the flutes of a revolver cylinder. It is held here in the Dremel tool.

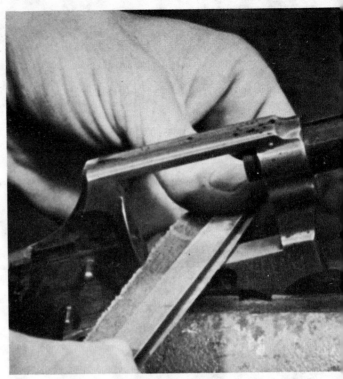

For reaching those inaccessible spots that require that a flat surface be maintained, use aluminum oxide cloth, which is backed up with a flat file or similar tool.

with the 240 grit cloth.

Next, polish the frame itself just as we did the slide, the sides of the frame being brought to the same high polish. You will encounter some difficulty around the pistol grip screw studs, but by working the aluminum oxide cloth up close while it is held tightly around the end of a file, most of the area can be polished to a nice gloss.

Avoid polishing the grooves and rails at the top of the frame, otherwise you will cut away this area and get the slide fitting sloppy again after all of your trouble tightening it up. During all of your polishing on flat areas, try to avoid holding the cloth in the fingers only, as they make a relatively soft backing substance for the cloth, and the cloth will cut unevenly. Keep the cloth around the file or, if needed in close quarter, around a small piece of wood cut and shaped as needed.

Finish up on the sides of the frame with progressively finer grits of aluminum oxide cloth and make your mirror polish with the crocus cloth and burnishing tool. For a firm grip on the gun, most shooters prefer that the front of the frame below the trigger guard is roughed up by stippling. This is nothing but a pattern of small marks made by striking the surface of the frame with the end of a small center punch. Light hammer taps on the back of the punch are all that is necessary. Keep repeating the light punch pricks while moving the punch slowly across the surface of the metal, until all of the area appears pock-marked about like rough sandpaper. The stippling should extend the full length of the front of the frame under the trigger guard and terminate at the sides where the frame turns to meet the grips and at the top at the juncture with the trigger guard.

To polish inside the trigger guard, it is best to wrap the aluminum oxide cloth around a small wooden dowel and cut the surface down with a filing motion, both across the trigger guard and up and down it. Watch out for the serial number on the frame which, in most cases, is just above the trigger guard. To remove the serial number is a federal offense that can put you in the pokey for a prolonged visit at the worst or a healthy fine at the least. Leave the underneath portion of the frame slightly rough, as you did the top of the slide, for best matching appearance of the two components.

The barrel, where it shows through the opening in the slide, should be brought to a mirror finish. This is done by shoe-shining the barrel with one of the finer grits of aluminum oxide cloth and ending up by shoe-shining with crocus cloth. The barrel bushing front should be draw filed across its face, if any dents are evident, and brought to the soft finish appearance with the No. 240 grit cloth.

The arched mainspring housing will be found in several different variations. Some will be cross hatched with cuts similar to checkering, while others have serrations cutting straight up and down the back of the housing. The appearance of either can be enhanced with a little careful filing of the grooved serrations using the small three-cornered file, but don't make the edges sharp enough to cut the palm of your hand when firing the gun. The grip safety also must be polished on the sides and rear and on top, but do not bring it up to a real high polish, stopping instead at the 240 grit aluminum oxide cloth, for it receives a lot of wear.

The other smaller components, such as the safety, must be polished and can be done in the same way as the larger parts, except that you must use a smaller file, if draw filing is necessary. Also use the smaller file to wrap the aluminum oxide cloth around for polishing these parts. The slide lock just over the trigger must be polished and it is a good idea to use the small triangular file to cut the grooves in it a tiny bit deeper for easier operation. The magazine release, the return spring and lock plunger should be removed, and the release placed back in the frame before draw filing or polishing the right side of the frame. This is done to prevent any dished-out appearance around the hole in the frame that accepts the magazine release.

The serrations on the opposite side of the release are

usually in the form of checkering and can be brought up much sharper by a little careful filing with the small triangular file.

If you have already reworked the internal parts of the pistol, you probably have already polished the sides of the hammer and trigger, but if not, be sure to polish these to a high gloss. Also, don't forget to polish the heads of the grip screws or the heads of the pins that show when the gun is assembled. You can spin these in your fingers while pressing a piece of aluminum oxide cloth against their heads.

Check the screw slots for any buggering and recut the slots if necessary, to hide any such blunders. It is surprising how many people polish a gun to a beautiful finish, then overlook such things as the screw slots. Attention to small details is the mark of a craftsman!

Provided you have carried through completely all of the foregoing steps, your gun should be ready for rebluing or plating and should be equal to similar work done by a professional using power equipment. If any length of time will elapse before the gun is blued, spray on a coat of thin protective oil to guard against rusting. Once you have the mirror-like finish, do not touch the metal with your bare hands. Every place you touch will be slightly etched by the salts and acids in your perspiration. The etched spot will be as evident after bluing as a wart on the end of your nose.

Other types of guns can be polished by hand in the same manner, especially on their receivers. For long barrel guns, such as rifles and shotguns, the problem is in getting the barrel polished evenly the entire length. Draw filing can reduce the surface, if it is badly pitted or rough, but make your strokes the length of the barrel and never cross it. Keep rotating the barrels while taking light cuts and do not make a cut in the same place, thus avoiding cutting flats on the surface of the barrel. Draw filing a round surface, such as a barrel, appears hard to the beginner, but once you try it, you will find that it is easy if you keep moving the file over just a bit for each stroke and keep your strokes long and steady.

The draw filing completed, polish by wrapping the aluminum oxide cloth lengthwise on the file and making long strokes on the barrel surface as if you were draw filing. With each stroke, move over a bit to prevent flats. Blend the polishing to erase the draw filing scratches and any flattening of the barrel surface that you goofed on.

Once you have finished the first polishing with the No. 240 aluminum oxide cloth wrapped around the file, tear off a new strip of the same grit, place it cross-ways of the barrel, grasp each end of the cloth and shoe-shine the barrel from one end to the other. Rotate the barrel while you are doing this and also keep the cloth moving up and down the length of the barrel to prevent overpolishing in one place.

Go back to the lengthwise polishing with a strip of No. 500 cloth when you have finished with the 240 grit cloth. After this, shoe-shine the barrel with the 500 grit cloth the same way you did with the 240 grit cloth.

Go back to the lengthwise polishing of the barrel with

Inexpensive power polishing unit is made easily from two ball-bearing pillow blocks and a one-third horse-power motor from a washing machine. This unit has been in use for ten years. The metal cover over the motor keeps out polishing dust.

This special long shaft polishing buffer was built to put final touches to barrels with chrome rouge compound. Ball-bearing mandrels were used for 20 years in cigar making machine, were salvaged from junk yard; total cost was $5.

the No. 500 without it wrapped around the file and just held to the barrel surface with the palm of your hand.

The palm of your hand will wrap around the barrel surface and if any fine scratches are left in the barrel, they will be lengthwise and parallel with the barrel since they will stand out like a beacon in the night if they are cross-ways of the barrel. The crocus cloth is substituted for the 500 grit cloth and again, held against the barrel's surface with the palm of your hand for the lengthwise strokes to bring it to the final polish.

You can remove every scratch in the barrel with the crocus cloth provided you are patient and don't quit too soon. The burnishing tool can be used to aid in removing the final scratches and will provide the mirror-like finish. Many times a softer, more velvet-like finish will be desired on a hunting gun and you can end your polishing with the 240 grit, but be sure that the last polishing is done with the palm of your hand pressing the cloth against the barrel using the lengthwise strokes.

Octagon barrels must be polished by hand alone if you want sharp edges on the flats, for a power wheel will tend to flex around the edges and roll them. Draw file the barrel, paying particular attention to maintaining the original flats and edges, then make your final polish with the 240 grit aluminum oxide cloth wrapped around a flat file length-wise. Do not use the palm of your hand, nor your finger tips when polishing one of these barrels, as you will round the edges the same as the power wheels do. Barrels with much engraving invariably must be polished entirely by hand, with the burnishing tool doing the final polish, for

power wheels will wash out the engraving.

Hand polishing takes time and you will begin to wonder how much power polishing will speed up the job and how far you will have to dip into your pocketbook to buy the equipment.

The speed of polishing will run about neck and neck with the cost and the answer depends on how far you want to go. But regulate this desire to your actual needs for it makes little sense to go whole hog and buy a couple of hundred dollars worth of equipment just to polish two or three guns per year.

Each time I am faced with a decision whether to buy a new piece of equipment, I always ask myself this question: Will the equipment pay for itself in increased proficiency?

A small hand unit such as the Dremel Moto-Tool will handle a wide range of polishing wheels and polishing points that greatly simplify the problem of getting down into those hard-to-reach sections of guns. Felt mounted bobs can be coated with regular polishing compound to reach into the nooks and crannies or you can use the rubber impregnated polishing points and wheels.

The next best power hand tool is a flexible shaft, mounted to a motor that runs up at least 1725 rpm and higher, if possible. These hand power tools will speed the job and most professional shops use them for this purpose, even though they have a full line of regular buffers.

The next step up the ladder of power polishing equipment is the power head described in a previous chapter. This rig, with a few felt and muslin wheels will be a little slow, but will do as fine a job as the most expensive power

Pneumatic wheel holding aluminum oxide bands is mounted on inexpensive polishing stand. Other end is a homemade arrangement that uses half a strip for rough polishing.

Big Baldor buffers are for production work, large wheels speeding job. Barrel is being polished at 45-degree angle, rotated as it is passed across and downward on the wheel.

polishing equipment, provided you can furnish the patience and skill.

You can take an even cheaper route with a used electric motor fitted out with a threaded arbor attached to the shaft of the motor. These are available in hardware stores for a few dollars and are simply shafts threaded on one end and drilled on the other. The drilled end is slipped over the shaft of the motor and locked in position with a set screw, while the polishing wheel is fitted over the threaded end and locked in place with a nut on the end.

You can buy the arbors with either a right or left hand thread, necessary if you use a double-end shaft motor which requires that the gun be held against the wheel at a slight angle in order to clear the motor. If finances are a problem, however, by all means fit out a motor with these threaded arbors.

It may be worthwhile to buy a separate mandrel, like the one I described with the power head. This type will allow the gun to be held flat against the wheel for a much better polishing arrangement, as well as providing you with a selection of different mandrel speeds via the multi-stage pulley. The different speeds will come in handy, especially for the high finish polishing with the fine compounds.

About the nicest arrangement for the home shop is one or more double-end mandrels, although you can get by with only one of them. These allow a felt wheel to be carried on one side and a loose muslin wheel on the other for fast cutting with the felt wheel and a quick switch over to the loose muslin wheel, without all the trouble of changing wheels. If both wheels are charged with the same grit com-

pound, you can work this grit out to its full extent before switching to another set of wheels with a finer grit of compound. There are all sorts of mandrels and most will do a good job, but by far the best and longest lasting will be those equipped with ball bearings instead of sleeve bearings. The mandrel can be of one-piece construction, but these are hard to find, especially one with a multi-stage pulley.

The best choice is a mandrel you make. It consists of two ball bearing pillow blocks with the bearings mounted in rubber instead of metal to allow for flexing. The pillow blocks should be securely mounted at least a foot apart on a non-flexible stand, preferably one made of steel. The shaft is run between the two pillow blocks with the multi-stage pulley on the shaft between them. The shaft is held in place with a shaft lock, which is nothing but a thick washer with a lock screw through it. One of these is placed on each side of each pillow block and locked in position as close to the blocks as possible to eliminate any end play of the shaft.

The shaft must have a right and left-hand thread with the right-hand thread on your right. The reason for this "right hand, left hand" business is that, as the shaft turns, the nuts on the ends holding the wheels in place will be constantly tightened. If you install them backwards, the nut will be unscrewed by the rotation.

Such a mandrel will serve for years, if given only a little care and, for the professional, even with special-built buffing equipment, it serves as a secondary buffer for rush business and for polishing odd stuff that he would not want to polish on his high priced wheels. I have such an arrangement in my own shop as a second buffer and the mandrels are used for everything under the sun, while the big equipment is reserved for rebluing and plating polishing.

The ultimate in polishing equipment is the buffer made especially for the job. This consists of a heavy duty motor with extra long shafts. The motor is ball bearing-equipped and totally enclosed to prevent polishing dust from entering it. There are various makes and models, but perhaps the most popular with professional gunsmiths are those made by Baldor in either the 1/2-horsepower version or better yet, in the one-horsepower model at 1725 rpm.

Mounted on a pedestal to provide the maximum availability of wheel surface, this is the answer to the power polisher's dream. The price runs about $100 for the half-

In second angled pass across wheel, it is at 30-degree angle; sides are switched to form X-pattern of buffing.

After this final vertical pass of barrel, whole process is repeated on loose wheel to erase scratches and to condition the barrel for polishing with the next grit.

horse and $150 for the full horsepower model.

So you have a power buffer, either the threaded arbor mounted on a motor or something else up to the special-built one horsepower buffer. How do you polish a gun on it?

For best results, you need a series of buffing wheels starting with a soft felt wheel for the No. 140 grit compound plus a loose muslin wheel for the same grit. This is followed by a soft or medium felt wheel for the 240 grit plus a matching loose muslin wheel for this grit. Next comes a medium felt wheel and a loose muslin wheel for No. 400 grit, and last, but not least, a hard felt wheel and a matching loose muslin wheel for the high polish fine grit 555 or for chrome rouge, if you prefer this to the 555 grit.

This all adds up to a lot of wheels to keep track of and a good-sized investment, especially in the felt wheels. This series is the best buffing set-up and the one found in most professional shops, in addition to extra special buffing equipment, such as pneumatic wheels to hold sanding or polishing aluminum oxide bands, hand polishing equipment and several other pieces of specialized equipment. All of this equipment is a necessity to the professional faced with the need to do a quality polishing job in the least amount of time; to him time is the difference between profit or loss.

The hobbyist can spend a lot more time on any given project and this expenditure of time can be substituted to a great extent for an expenditure of money. To economize on the power polishing equipment, the hobbyist can use one mandrel and change wheels as they are needed. By substituting time again for speed, he can further diminish the cash outlay by making a finer grit wheel do the work of a faster-cutting coarser grit, eliminating some of the wheels involved.

The No. 140 grit compound is used normally to cut down a rough and pitted surface in a minimum amount of time, but the hobbyist can get the same job done either by draw filing or by spending twice the usual amount of time on the finer 240 grit. If you are interested in getting factory equivalent polishing, there is no need to have finer grits and wheels. The 400 grit compound will give a softer finish than the No. 240 grit and should be included if you want a nicer bluing job on your favorite smoke pole.

Actually, you can draw file a rough pitted gun and finish up with the 400 grit wheel alone, although this requires a considerable amount of time buffing on this one 400 wheel.

The hard felt wheel for the 555 or chrome rouge wheel will be needed only if you are interested in a high mirror polish and even this can be eliminated by using the burnishing tool instead. Only you can decide how much equipment you can afford and what your actual needs will be, but have as many of the wheels and grits as possible.

For a full knowledge of the polishing procedure, let's assume you have all of the wheels and go through the entire procedure from the No. 140 grit to the mirror finish with the 555 grit compound, leaving it up to the individual to determine which of the wheels he can afford and adjust the procedure to match his equipment.

First we need to know which buffing compound to buy as well as how to get the compound on the wheels. Quite a few companies offer their own brand of buffing compounds, but virtually all fall into either the stick compound or the brush-on compound.

The brush-on type is the more economical in several ways, but it also has a couple of serious drawbacks. The brush-on compound is a thick liquid composed of the actual cutting grit and a glue that dries when it is exposed to the air. It can be applied with a heavy brush or wiped on with the finger tips, but either method invariably results in the compound building up heavier on one side of the wheel than on the other, producing a wheel that is out of balance. This requires that the wheel be trued up with an old file or a special truing brick as the wheel rotates after the glue has dried.

The drying time varies from manufacturer to manufacturer, but usually is six hours or more. This time lag can present problems, if any amount of buffing is to be done and usually necessitates two or more wheels with the same grit compound on them to allow replacement as the grit wears off during buffing.

The stick compound looks like a round cylinder, or in some cases, a brick with foil wrapped around it to keep in the moisture, for the compound dries rapidly when exposed to air. The stick compound is also composed of the actual cutting grit and a glue, only drying time is reduced greatly. Application is made best by pressing the stick of compound against the rotating wheel for a uniform coating which is fast drying, if the wheel is allowed to continue rotation.

Drying time becomes a matter of minutes, but the stick compound is not very economical, since it follows the rule of thirds. That is, one third goes on the wheel, one third goes on the wall and ceiling, while the last third goes on you, as the rotating wheel throws off the excess. Even with this annoying habit, most of us rely on the stick compound for speed and ease of application.

The diameter of the wheel and the speed of the rotating shaft to which the wheel is attached have a lot to do with how much compound is thrown off. (This diameter also affects the price of the felt wheels considerably.) The large diameter ten and twelve-inch wheels will cut faster at any given speed, because there is more surface on which to place the compound and because of the surface speed of the larger wheel. The larger wheels tend to sling off compound faster, which follows the rule that you never get something without giving up something. The larger wheels also require a heavier motor to pull them. Felt wheels are available in 12, 10, 8 and 6-inch diameters, although even larger wheels are available if you want to go whole hog.

For the hobbyist, the six-inch felt wheels and similar diameter loose muslin wheels will prove sufficient, as well as being more economical in price and requiring a smaller motor. Should you live close to a manufacturer who uses polishing equipment, check into the possibility of getting his discarded wheels. Usually, they buy the large 10 and 12-inch wheels and discard them when they wear down to about six inches. For the hobbyist's needs, the wheels are sufficient and require only a little truing up, which can be done with a large single cut file. But be careful when truing a wheel with a file as it can sling the file through you or a table, if the wheel catches on the edge of the file. A truing brick is inexpensive and much safer.

Assuming that you have your wheels charged with compound, the gun disassembled and your nerves are steady, let's go through the polishing steps of a 98 Mauser barrel and action.

The old bluing can be polished off, but you are ahead of the game if you remove it with a bluing remover available from any of the gunsmithing supply houses. All grease and dirt as well as the sights, should be removed from the surfaces, if possible. Any action alteration or drilling for scope mounts also should be done prior to polishing, but not the inletting of a new stock, as the polishing process will remove a small amount of metal. This is especially true if you plan to glass bed the barrel. The inletting and glass bedding will scratch the surface a small amount, but this can be removed and the gun brought back to the high gloss finish in a few minutes on the No. 555 wheel.

Grasp the receiver in your right hand and the muzzle end of the barrel in your left, muzzle lower than the receiver and the barrel crossing the revolving wheel at about a 45-degree angle to the wheel. Start at the muzzle, pressing the side of the barrel against the soft felt wheel charged with No. 140 compound.

If you push the barrel toward the floor while maintaining contact with the wheel, you will cut a line the length of the barrel and make a flat surface on the barrel. At the same time, if you rotate the barrel while it is pressed hard against the revolving wheel, you may cut a groove around the barrel. For the beginner it is best to apply only light pressure and rotate the barrel without pushing it up and down across the wheel.

In power polishing, always keep the barrel moving, for if you stop for any reason, you will cut a flat spot on the barrel. Do not try to rotate the barrel a full turn, but instead rotate about a quarter of the way around the barrel and at completion, lift the barrel from the wheel's surface. Rotate the barrel in your hands for a better grip and start the next cut on the wheel at the point you left off on the last cut.

Once you have repeated this and made a full trip around the barrel, move the barrel up toward the receiver for the next series of cuts, blending the second series with the completed cuts for an even polish. Always blend one polishing cut with another, until there is no separating line or any scratches. Repeat these polishing cuts until you have traversed the full length of the barrel. In addition to keeping the barrel moving at all times, do not attempt to do the entire polishing job in one pass, but rather apply only light pressure and cut just a little with each polishing pass. This way you will have less tendency to cut waves or dish-out the surface.

With the first pass completed the full length of the barrel, switch the 45-degree angle to the right instead of the left. That is, raise the muzzle and lower the receiver (exactly opposite the first 45 degrees) until the barrel is crossing the face of the revolving wheel at a 45-degree angle. In doing this, make the second polishing cuts across the former cuts at a 90-degree angle, somewhat in the form of the letter X, which will not only make the polishing more even, but will also erase and polish out the scratches put in the surface on the first polishing cuts.

Again make your rotating quarter turn polishing cuts around the barrel just as you did before, with each series of cuts blended in with the one just completed. Once this is completed the full length of the barrel, examine the surface and see if you have cut away all of the pitting and rough spots. If not, switch your angle back the way it was in the beginning on the first pass and do the whole thing over again this time making your angle about 30 degrees instead of 45 degrees. Another basic rule is to make each polishing cut on a wheel at a different angle from the previous one, for in doing so, you erase any scratches from the former polishing cut, but do not deepen any existing scratches, if you repeated an angle while polishing.

One of the hardest things for a beginner to learn is just how much pressure to exert against the wheel, as hard pressure will cause the barrel to bounce, while too little pressure will, too. You have to practice polishing a little, until you get the feel for the right amount of pressure, but this doesn't take long to learn. With a little practice, you can modify your circular quarter polishing cuts and make the professional stroke. This professional stroke consists of making those circular polishing cuts and at the same time sliding the barrel back and forth across the face of the rotating wheel. This increases the area of your polishing cuts and cuts down on the length of time for polishing, as well as producing a more even polish. Stick to the circular quartering polishing cuts until you get the hang of it, then work on the professional stroke. Once you have it going, you should be able to cover four to six inches of the barrel in one pass.

With the felt wheel work done, switch over to the loose muslin wheel charged with the same 140 grit compound whose primary purpose is to erase the scratch marks left on the metal's surface by the felt wheel and to further polish the surface. This is accomplished by again putting the barrel across the wheel at about a 60-degree angle, following the rule of making each pass at a slightly different angle from the previous ones. Use the professional stroke, if possible, and cover the complete barrel from muzzle to receiver.

When this is finished, switch the angle to the opposite direction as you did with the felt wheel to form our letter

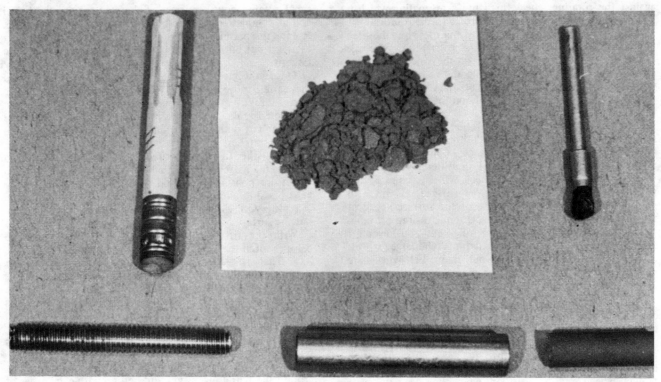

For jeweling, eraser on short pencil (left) is used to make circles as it is rotated in electric drill. Small wire brush (right) can be used in similar manner. Paper contains No. 600 aluminum oxide dust. Mixed with cutting oil, it jewels metal surface. At bottom is more common tool, which is made commercially, featuring rubber polishing rod.

X for the second pass against the muslin wheels. When these two complete passes have been made, all of the scratch marks should be erased, but for the final pass with the No. 140 grit, hold the barrel exactly vertical with the muzzle pointed toward the floor. Make a long pass the full length of the barrel, pressing the barrel lightly against the loose muslin wheel in a sort of brushing stroke and without rotating the barrel. When the first stroke has been completed, remove the barrel from contact with the rotating wheel and shift it enough in your hands so the second vertical pass will blend with the first one. Keep doing this at the end of each stroke until you have gone all the way around the barrel.

This final vertical polishing pass will erase any lingering scratches and any marks that are left from the polishing will be parallel with the barrel and will be less noticeable than if they were going across the barrel or at an angle to the barrel. For a gun that is to be used in hunting and where a high gloss mirror finish is not necessary or desired, you can stop right here. The remaining portion of the barrel will be up along the side of the sight ramp and the receiver, of course.

The part beside the sight ramp can be polished out by pressing the barrel vertically against the loose muslin wheel. The receiver is polished along the top in about the same way that you polished the barrel, using first the felt wheel then the loose muslin wheel to erase the scratch marks. Don't worry too much about that part of the receiver that is below the stock line level, as it usually is quite rough and, if you spend a lot of time on it and return it to an already inletted stock, you probably will have a sloppy fit due to the amount of metal removed.

The floor plate, trigger guard and the other components usually can be polished best on the loose muslin wheel

alone unless they have deep scratches or pitting. Along the line, you will have the interesting experience of the loose muslin wheel grabbing a part and jerking it out of your hands rather suddenly. An edge on the part has been caught by the wheel causing it to dig into the wheel and, because of the rotation of the wheel, be jerked from your grasp.

The secret in preventing this is never to try to polish a part with an edge pointing upward into the rotating wheel, but have the edge on the bottom, making your polishing from the center of the part out to the edge. When you have polished one side of the part, turn it over and start again at the center and blend the second pass with the first one. Be careful, as a part jerked from your hands can be thrown a considerable distance with enough force to cause a painful injury.

Now for some other Do Nots:

First, never hold the barrel horizontal and try to polish it, for you will end up with waves in the barrel. Always keep the barrel at an angle to the wheel or vertical in the case of the final pass on the loose muslin wheel.

Never polish without wearing safety glasses or a safety shield, because the flying pieces of compound thrown off by the wheel can put out an eye. Always wear a respirator when polishing, for the dust from the compound, plus the rust and surface metal being removed, will fill your lungs as you work, which is not conducive to a long and healthy life. The respirator can be of any style, but perhaps the best is the light disposable mask type used by doctors and available from the gunsmith supply houses.

If you want a high polish, you go to the felt and loose muslin wheels charged with No. 240 compound instead of 140 and repeat the entire polishing process over again from start to finish, just as you did with the 140 grit. This time, use a little less pressure against the wheel and make these

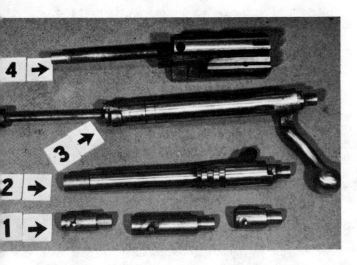

(1) Three adaptors to fit inside rear of rifle bolts.
(2) M1911 barrel with adaptor in chamber, muzzle to hold
it, while barrel under ejection port is jeweled. (3) A
rifle bolt with adaptor in rear, support in firing pin
hole. (4) Adaptor to hold Browning shotgun bolt in jig.

Securely held in place in the jeweling jig,
this bolt is ready to receive the ornate
damascening. Gear at rear turns and locks
in place to ensure that each row of the
overlapping pattern will perfectly line up.

more as polishing passes, rather than the heavier cutting passes employed with the 140 grit wheels. Use the felt wheel first, then the loose muslin wheel to erase the scratches, paying particular attention to keeping the barrel at an angle to the wheel. An even higher polish is attained once this is completed by doing the whole affair over for a third time against a felt and loose muslin wheel charged with the finer 400 grit compound.

A barrel finished off with the No. 400 grit compound will have a soft, velvet finish that, when blued, is appealing to the eye. The mirror-like finish is obtained with either the No. 555 compound or the chrome rouge compound. For the ultimate, use the 555 followed by the chrome rouge. Actually, there is little difference between the 555 and the chrome rouge or the seldom used 500 grit compound for that matter and only a trained eye can detect the difference. In using either of these compounds for a mirror finish, examine every square inch of the polished surface for scratches. Even a tiny scratch will show up against the highly polished surface surrounding it, once the gun has been blued.

All types of guns are polished the same way basically, with modifications as required, such as polishing a shotgun barrel with a ventilated rib. On one of these it will be impossible to polish a full circular pattern as with the rifle barrel, but you still can reach around most of the barrel on the bottom and the sides. Be careful not to touch the sides of the ventilated rib with the wheel, or you will cut a deep gash in it. Switch over to the loose muslin wheel and hold the barrel vertical to polish the area next to the rib.

Large, flat-sided receivers, like those found on the Browning style shotguns, can be polished with little trouble if you make your right and left 45 degree cuts and end up with a good bit of the final polish being done vertically with the muzzle end pointed at the floor. This way, the final strokes are parallel with the receiver and will be less visible than those across the receiver.

Receivers may have pin and screw holes in them and care must be taken in polishing these areas. If you ignore them, the wheels will flex down into the holes, washing them out in a volcanic effect. Keep most of your polishing of these areas confined to the felt wheel, not using the loose muslin wheel except for one final brushing stroke to erase any

scratches.

The same procedure is used on engraved guns, for the loose muslin wheel will wash out the engraving until it loses all resemblance to the original. Watch the edges of the receivers and do not allow the wheel to run around them, for the edges will be ground down and, no matter how fine a job you do in polishing, the gun never will look the same as it did before. Besides, it will show the polisher didn't know his job!

Jewelling sometimes is called "damascening" or "engine turning," but whatever you call it, this consists of a series of overlapping circles laid out in a pattern, each circle overlapping the other about one-third. You are probably familiar with the result, having seen it on such things as breech bolts, hammers, triggers, and other parts of guns where it is used to provide a very striking appearance.

Few people realize that jewelling also has a practical purpose, in that the circles hold oil to the surface better than a slick finish. This not only prevents rust but aids in the smooth function of the part. This is the reason it once was employed so widely on the lock parts of fine guns. As the process is not complicated, it is within the capabilities of even the greenest of beginners.

You can do jewelling with an inexpensive outlay for tooling; in fact, you can do it for practically nothing, as any round item that will cut a circle in the surface of the metal can be utilized. A common wooden pencil can be cut off about an inch from the eraser with the eraser chucked in a power drill and used to cut the circles. Another cheap way is to use a hole puncher made to cut holes in paper for notebooks, but used in our case to cut round plugs out of aluminum oxide paper. The plugs are glued to wooden dowels with the grit down, and the dowel with the plug tip used to cut the circles. All of these will work as will other homemade rigs, but none produces a pattern as nice as those polishing tips made specifically for this purpose.

Most gunsmith supply houses offer jewelling equipment, such as that made by B-Square and Rex, at a reasonable price. All of these use a cylinder-shaped piece of grit-impregnated rubber that is held in a tubular piece of steel or brass which is, in turn, chucked in the drill. To move the rubber from the tube, a small screw is inserted at the rear and, when turned, pushes the rubber out as needed.

No. 600 aluminum oxide grit, cutting oil are smeared on rifle bolt before circles are cut. Here, one row already has been cut, gear rotated a notch, second row begun to overlap the first. This is repeated around the bolt.

Bright Boy offers a small holder that fits a stub piece of grit-impregnated rubber, but when the stub is worn out, it is thrown away and replaced with another piece instead of being pushed farther out. Brownell's offers a small wire brush that is used to cut the circles with aluminum oxide grit and cutting oil placed on the surface, but I have found the regular round rubber and tube holder arrangement the best of all.

In use, the holder is placed in the drill chuck and rotated at a medium speed, while the tip of the rubber is pressed lightly against the surface of the metal. Only a short time is required for the rubber to cut the circle and it will work either dry or with the aluminum oxide dust and oil placed on the metal surface. The fancy "jewelled under oil" advertisements mean nothing but regular jewelling with oil and aluminum oxide dust on the surface. The oil and aluminum oxide dust is of questionable value. Although it does produce a slightly deeper set of circles, it also eats away the end of the rubber much faster than when the rubber is used dry. Samples of finished products with and without the oil and dust paste are hard to tell apart.

The pattern can be laid out free-hand, but the results are not nearly as attractive as a pattern done with a spacing rig. If your drill press is fitted with a compound vise, you can use the vise to provide the correct spacing by the number of turns you make on the side handle to move the part being jewelled.

The next trick will be to space the circles evenly around a bolt which will require some form of indexing equipment. B-Square makes a simple affair that holds the bolt securely on the front and rear with the spacing around the bolt regulated on one end by a series of click-stops provided by a divided wheel. This assembly is placed in the compound vise and the first row of circles made the full length of the bolt with this spacing being accomplished by the vise and, when completed, the divided wheel is turned one click-stop

to rotate the bolt the correct amount for the next row of circles. Rex puts out a similar tool, except that no compound vise is necessary. All spacing, both down the bolt and around the bolt, is done by the tool itself. For those not equipped with a compound vise on their drill press, the Rex tool, while more expensive than the B-Square, is more practical.

You can make your own jewelling jig out of an old gear and a few scraps of flat metal, as illustrated by the one I use. A center holds the bolt at the front by entering the firing pin hole, while the rear is held in a small adapter turned on the lathe to fit snugly into the rear of the stripped bolt. The adapter is fitted into a recessed headstock going through a piece of support metal and attached on the other side to a gear which provides the indexing.

To stop the gear and hold it in place while a line of circles is made down the bolt, all that is needed is a small detent pushed against the gear by a spring. In making the detent, be sure to round its nose to allow the gear to be turned for the next series of circles around the bolt. Many special holders can be made up to hold other items, such as semi-automatic pistol barrels, shotgun breech bolts and hammers.

To get the right pattern, the second circle overlaps the first one by about one-third. The third circle to overlap the second about one-third and so on, until the row is completed. If you are jewelling around a bolt, you want the rows staggered just a bit for the best effect. To do this, make the first circle of the second row just a little forward of where you started on the first circle of the first row. This staggers the second line of circles, but for the third line of circles, go back to the rear the same distance as you did on the first row of circles.

Confused?

Okay, suppose you start one line with the first circle on zero of a rule, then the second line would be started, say a half inch further forward on the rule, while the third row would be brought back to the zero mark and the fourth row put forward on the half-inch mark and the fifth row back to the zero mark, and so forth. This back and forth staggering of the first circle produces the jewelled effect, but be sure to overlap each succeeding circle about one-third of a circle diameter and each row around a bolt should overlap the previous row about one-third.

Jewelling can be used in many uncommon ways to produce a striking effect, such as on the bottom of a rifle floor plate which is jewelled, then blued over the jewelling. You can even jewel an entire gun, if you wish. I bought an old M-1911 pistol once that was so rough that my best efforts at polishing left a lot to be desired.

As a lark, I jewelled the entire side of the pistol, left and right, then blued it. A set of maple grips completed the gun and, to my surprise, it remained in my possession for less than a day before a fellow walked in and bought it on sight. Jewelling can be done on a plated surface provided the plating is thick and you exert only light pressure, but you cannot jewel a gun, then plate over the jewelling, as the plating process will fill up the lines of the circles.

Function-wise, instead of leaving a polished inside part of gun just bright, jewel it. The part will function more smoothly due to the oil holding process of jewelling and I guarantee that anyone seeing the internal parts of a gun jewelled will be impressed.

Polishing, both for function and appearance as well as jewelling, are an important part of gunsmithing and few hobbyists will do much gunsmithing work before they find themselves in need of these skills. As you have learned, expensive equipment is not a dire necessity, but skill and patience are the main ingredients of the processes.

Chapter 17

BLUE, BROWN OR PLATE?

The Requirements For All Three Techniques Are Similar — And Not As Mysterious As You've Been Led To Believe!

THERE HAVE BEEN MORE half-truths, mistruths and outright lies about bluing, browning and plating than any other phase of gunsmithing. Anyone contemplating doing his own browning or bluing will be overwhelmed by the huge volume of formulas, advice and propaganda and end up more confused than before he started.

Most of the information available up until recent years has been the result of individual gunsmiths mixing chemical after chemical, and through trial and error, arriving at a solution that would darken the surface of a gun. With few exceptions, these men were not chemists and any success they achieved was pure, unadulterated luck. A few formulas worked, but many of them would not darken a piece of charcoal, much less blue a gun. Formulas that did work have been modified constantly by writers trying to arrive at their own world-shaking formula with many not even bothering to mix up a batch and try it before recommending it!

Thankfully, the serious hobbyist has at his disposal solutions and processes worked out by professional chemists. For the one who happens to have a chemistry background, there is no shortage of available formulas, but for the other, the answer is to stick to the manufacturer's processes.

There are two main reasons why I am so positive in this

recommendation and opposed to mix-'em-up-yourself plans. Most of the chemicals in these formulas are dangerous in the hands of anyone not familiar with chemistry, for they can — and sometimes do — burn the careless user severely enough to require hospitalization or even result in permanent injury. Some, such as cyanide or bichloride of mercury, are extremely dangerous and can put you six feet under in a hurry.

Even mixing the chemicals in the formula can be a hazard to the uninitiated. For example, most require the mixing of acid and water, so do you pour the water into the acid or the acid into the water? The answer is to pour the acid into the water slowly, for to do the reverse will result in the acid reacting violently and blowing back on you.

The formulas are misleading in several aspects, which the beginner soon will discover. While there are literally hundreds of formulas, without exception they leave out one key factor: the strength of the chemicals! They give the exact ratio of mixture down to the last cc, but never do they give the strength of the base chemical. Now this can be a concentrated 100 percent strength chemical or one diluted down to as little as one percent, and on the commercial market they come in all strengths between, as any pharmacist or chemist will tell you. Walk into any drug store with the formula, ask the pharmacist to mix it for you, and the first question he asks is, "What percent?"

Obviously this omitted fact will determine the difference between success or failure, and the hobbyist can spend time and money trying to solve the percentage riddle.

Another item often overlooked is that many of these formulas were worked out for one grade of steel and will fail completely on another grade. This was part of the secret behind the finish on some of the old quality doubles, such as the L.C. Smith and Parker. A basic formula was used and through trial and error, modified until it worked perfectly on that one model, producing a beautiful finish, but not working at all if used on another make. This is the same reason that many gunsmiths will get a perfect blue on one gun and fail on another with the same formula.

But let's understand exactly what's meant by bluing or browning and how they actually work.

Browning is the oldest of the two processes and consists of nothing more complicated than ferric oxide, (plain old red rust) the same stuff you work like made to keep off your favorite gun. While there is no record of the beginning, perhaps browning began by accident back in the early days simply because a gun was left standing in a damp spot and worked up a coat of rust. The owner discovered this and tried to wipe off the rust with a cloth and succeeded in removing the top layer, but the metal remained permanently stained.

Further handling with sweaty hands, plus standing in the corner some more resulted in another rust coat which was wiped off, leaving an even darker brown stain. Repeating this several times resulted in a gun covered with dark stain. Perhaps the owner noted that the metal was no longer bright and flashing in the light to warn game, so he purposely rusted or "browned" his other guns. The early gunsmiths worked on the simple rusting process, refining it until they could deliver a beautiful uniform dark brown color that, in the case of damascus barrel guns, was a striking sight that still brings approval from those who appreciate fine guns.

By the way, the nickname of the British musket used during our Revolutionary War is the result of this process, plus an abbreviation of the Queen's name, i.e., Brown Bess.

The hobbyist faced with refinishing the barrel of an antique can use several methods to achieve browning. Just about anything that will rust steel can be used, the simplest

Setup shows how pistol to be plated is positioned in relation to anodes. This is exactly as it would appear in tank containing plating solution, except that one anode has been removed to better show position of pistol.

After cleaning and rinsing to clear cleaning solution, pistol parts are etched slightly in mild acid solution to remove grime and condition the surface to receive the plating. This is a dipping operation without any current.

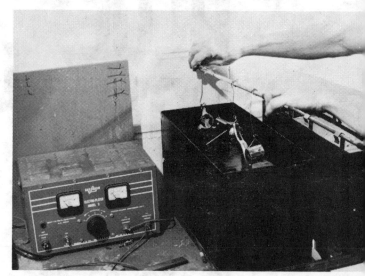

being a solution of plain salt and water, but getting the color the same from one end to the other with this is a different story.

Several good commercial browning solutions do a much better job and do it more safely, being cheaper in the long run than a complicated home brew.

The Casey Chemical Company produces a solution by the name of Plum Brown that is fast acting and produces a nice finish with minimum trouble and skill. It does require that the metal be heated to accelerate the process, but this is simple to accomplish.

The Dixie Gun Works Browning Solution works on the same basic process, but is slower acting and does not re-

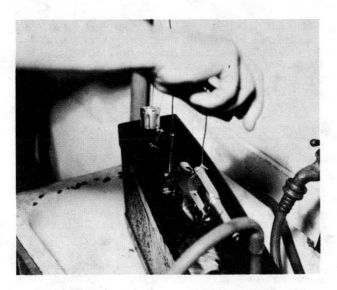

Clean water rinse is between cleaning, pickling tanks. It also is used after pickling, following plating. This is an old auto battery case with partitions removed. It is rigged with copper tubing to assure constant flow of clear, clean water from the bottom of the tank upward.

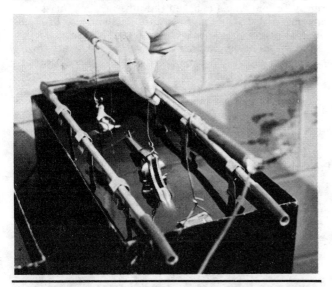

Plated gun is being taken from nickel plating tank. Note single rod and the U-shaped rod. The tank is of metal coated with a non-conductive, acid-resistant material.

quire the metal to be heated, as it is more or less concocted on the old original formulas. There are others that will give equal results, but I am more familiar with the two I have named and would not hesitate to recommend either of them.

About 1820 a modified browning process that resulted in a blackish-blue began to come into common use and the term "bluing" was used to describe it rather than browning, at least in the United States; our British friends still call all of it browning. This was also the beginning of the age of formulas, for every shop seemed to have its own, more often the result of available chemicals and luck than plan.

About the earliest type of bluing consisted of a mixture of nitric acid and hydrochloric acid with steel shavings and nails dumped into it. These were dissolved to form the bluing solution. This mixture has been known by different names, but generally it is known as the "slow rust process."

In use, the metal is polished, then coated with a paste of lime which is allowed to dry hard, then is brushed off, carrying with it any grease present on the surface of the metal. The bluing solution then is swabbed on the metal in long even strokes and the gun placed in a damp place for the solution to react. The next day, the gun will be coated with a deep red rust, but when this is carded off, the surface should be tinted a pale blue.

The surface is swabbed again with the solution, allowed to rust another day, and carded off for a second time to reveal an even deeper shade of blue. The process is repeated until the surface is the desired color. Then it is rinsed in plain water and oiled. Depending on the climate and the time of year, plus the place you put it to rust and the type of steel, the length of time required will be between about ten days and a month. The result is beautiful and some high quality guns still are blued this way, but it is time consuming and getting those strokes to cover the surface evenly requires considerable skill.

This lengthy time requirement forced gunsmiths and gunmakers to seek a faster and easier process. Anyone who has worked with metal soon learns that steel, when heated, will rust more rapidly due to rapid absorption of oxygen which forms ferric oxide or red rust. Obviously, the way to speed up the bluing process, which is only a controlled form of black rusting (ferric oxide) required only that the metal be hot when the solution is applied. Unfortunately, the slow rust formula does not work as well when this is done, so experimentation got in high gear. All of the Joe Blow Blu-'Em-All and Old Blue Tick Hound Bluer formulas can be lumped together under the common name of accelerated bluing. You will run across this process under the term, "20 Minute Process," which undoubtedly refers to the length of time required to disassemble the gun, for the process requires much more time than this. The English normally call it the express method and I am told that in France it is known as the steam process, but regardless of what name is used, the metal temperature is raised either by boiling it in water or placing it in a steam cabinet.

There is nothing wrong with this process and, in my opinion, it is the best one for the hobbyist who will be bluing only an occasional gun and does not wish to invest a bundle of money in equipment. Several manufacturers market the best of these formulas and you are fighting the problem in attempting to mix your own. I have used several of these and all are superior to the best that I concocted myself, as well as those I had prepared by a professional chemist.

You can take the do-it-yourself road if you wish, but having walked every rock-filled foot of it several times, I recommend the prepared solution.

At the turn of the century a so-called black oxide process was patented, but did not gain common use in the firearms industry until the mid-1930s. In this process, the surface of the metal is changed to a black oxide through a high temperature chemical bath or baths, requiring less than two hours for the entire process. Added advantages were that the process worked exceptionally well on a wide variety of steel and was much more economical for mass production. For industry, it had the attractive advantage in that virtually anyone could be trained in a short length of time to operate the equipment. Instead of one gun at a time, the black oxide system was limited only by the size of the tanks and the heating facilities. This is the process used in about every gunshop in the country and the system upon which most gun manufacturers depend.

A cussin' cousin to the black oxide process was used by Smith and Wesson, Colt and a couple of other manufacturers before World War II to produce what is perhaps the finest bluing in the sporting arms industry. Called the Carbonia process, the gun parts were suspended on rods inside a large metal drum partially filled with a special powder. The drum was rotated and heated up to 700 degrees Fahrenheit. As the powder fell on the heated metal surface, it produced a deep lustrous mirror blue that you see on some of the handguns produced during this era. The Carbonia system is complicated, dangerous and expensive, so like all such things, it has slowly gone the way of the passenger pigeon.

The military always has wanted a more durable process than bluing and at the beginning of World War II, they switched to Parkerizing. This system consists of powdered iron and phosphoric acid particles deposited on and being bonded to the surface of the metal to give a gray non-reflecting surface. The finish wears well and is rust resistant, but from a sporting gun standpoint, it leaves a lot desired in appearance. Military surplus guns that come into the hobbyist's possession can be blued directly over the Parkerizing with the black oxide process. The result is not unattractive for a hunting gun that will see a lot of hard use. For the hobbyist, the Parkerizing process is much too complicated and has very little to offer except for restoring military weapons.

If the metal itself cannot be made rustproof, then plating it with a rust proof metal seems to be the obvious answer. It is the answer for many applications in industry, but is limited in the field of firearms and has seen its most useful application on handguns that are to be constantly exposed to the elements, such as a police officer's sidearm. On hunting handguns and target arms, the bright finish is less desirable. As far as long guns are concerned, plating is used seldom with the exception of guns that are intended for display. Nickel plating is the most common, although gold, silver, brass and occasionally chrome are found on guns, the last generally being on European imports. The hobbyist with a yen for plating has a couple of systems which will give good results, yet are not priced out of his reach.

Black nickel plating is often spoken of as the most practical method of gun protection against rust and from a non-glare standpoint, but it is rather involved for even a regular commercial gunsmith shop. The process is available from several plating suppliers, but the hobbyist is far better off to have it done commercially by Marker Machine Company, a firm that specializes in this for firearm application. They do an excellent job of this, as well as chrome plating bores. The black nickel finish has some of the aspects of plating without the bright finish and is on the soft side in general appearance. Stainless steel rifle barrels present a problem for the regular black oxide finish. It will not even stain them, but the black nickel takes well on these barrels and is about the only answer.

By the early 1960s the firearms industry was so hard pressed by the rising cost of labor that one well known manufacturer of a fine pump shotgun was losing ten dollars per gun before it left the factory. The need for machine-produced guns with minimum hand labor was the only solution, but would the American sportsmen buy them?

A careful survey revealed that only 10 percent of the market consisted of sportsmen who appreciated and demanded fine craftsmanship. The other 90 percent were satisfied, so long as the gun was cheap, looked fancy, and fired in the general direction of the target. As a result, gun manufacturers began stamping parts out of empty beer cans, casting them out of plastic and making what formerly were steel castings out of aluminum and pot metal. The stampings were blued or plated, the plastic colored before casting and the aluminum anodized. As these guns came on the market, gunsmiths were faced with the problem of refinishing. As the old bluing tanks dissolved the aluminum and plastics, they were stymied. Anodizing is nothing more than the cleaning of the aluminum surface of all oxide and the metal is then colored with a chemical dye!

The most recent development in metal finish for firearms is Teflon, which is baked onto the surface. This is the same material that pot and pan manufacturers use to keep food from sticking. When used on a gun, it is rust-free, as well as affording an extremely slick surface that cuts down the friction of moving parts. Personally, I do not care for the appearance, but in an environment where rust is a major problem and the gun will see severe hunting conditions, a Teflon-coated gun has much to recommend it. The Teflon process is involved and only a few shops in the country are equipped to do it.

It is only a matter of time before a hobby gunsmith starts experimenting in an attempt to arrive at a nice finish. Probably the first thing he tries is touch-up blue, thinking it

Touch-up blue is for touching up small, marred places, not for an entire gun, author contends. He uses a bit of cotton wrapped around a toothpick as bluing applicator.

Small parts such as screws can be blued with heat. Hold part in old pair of pliers, applying heat evenly. When part is deep blue color, plunge it quickly into oil.

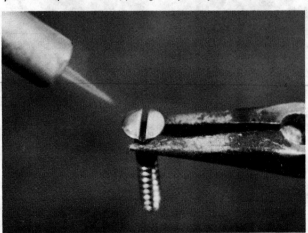

an easy, quick and cheap way to blue a gun. Most people haven't the foggiest idea of what is involved in bluing, even touch-up blue. Recently a customer came into the shop and asked for a bottle of bluing. I placed a bottle of touch-up on the counter and was about to give him a quick lesson in its use, when he floored me with a question, "Haven't you got something in a darker shade of blue?"

Touch-up blue, as the name implies, is designed specifically for touching up the surface of a scratched place or a small spot where the regular bluing has worn off. For a complete blue job, it is a total loss. Most touch-up preparations consist of a mixture of copper sulfate and hypo, with the copper sulfate putting a thin copper wash on the surface of the metal and the hypo blackening the copper. You can usually spot a touch-up blue job by the simple process of smelling the surface. If you can smell copper, the metal has been coated with touch-up blue. Some of the touch-ups have other ingredients added, but they fail to really safe-

Average commercial blue room uses series of tanks for hot bluing. Note exhaust hood to rid room of all fumes.

Polished guns, ready for bluing tank, have rods inserted in barrels, which are attached to chains that allow for control of depth to which barrels are lowered in tank.

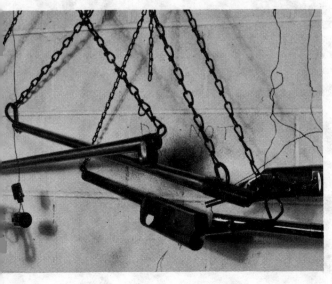

guard the surface if applied over a large area. To touch-up a scratch or burred screw slot they are fine, but should never be used in an attempt to blue an entire gun.

Two brands do work on a form of accelerated process and they can be used as a substitute, but the job will not be as good as the regular solution would produce. One is Minute Man and the other is Numrich's 44-40 brand. Both do an excellent job on touch-up needs, especially if the metal is cleaned thoroughly, then slightly heated. Apply the solution in an even stroke with the chemical applied via a small piece of cotton wound around the end of a tooth pick. Allow the chemical to work for a few minutes, then wipe it clear.

If the touch-up does not perfectly match the color of the original finish, apply another coat after you have reheated the metal. When you arrive at the desired color, swab the area thoroughly with gun oil.

Any steel that is heated will go through a series of color changes as the temperature increases; while this normally is used for tempering, it can be put to good use as a form of bluing also. The color will change slowly from a straw to a brown and then to a shade of light blue turning into even darker blue. All that is required is to quench the part in oil when the deep blue shade is reached and it will remain that color for a considerable length of time. This is most useful on screws, pins and other small parts that are hard to blue by other means, but it never should be applied to a part that will receive stress, such as the bolt or receiver. A form of this bluing once was used mainly on revolver frames, but it has gone the way of many such skills.

There have been thousands of attempts to develop a solution that could be applied cold like a touch-up blue, yet provide sufficient penetration to adequately protect the surface of the metal. About 99.9 percent of them fall flat on their faces when given the critical test of wiping the surface hard with a wad of steel wool.

The only solution I have found to survive the steel wool test is Oxpho-Blue, which is distributed by Brownell. Perhaps there are others, but I have not run across them.

Oxpho-Blue not only survives the steel wool test but is applied with steel wool! The only fault is that the quality of the finish is dependent upon the skill of the person doing the work. The metal is polished first, leaving a soft sheen finish rather than a high polish, then is thoroughly cleaned as per manufacturer's instructions. It will work without cleaning, but like all metal finishes, does better, if applied directly to an immaculate surface.

The first coat is applied with a piece of cotton or cloth, then rubbed with steel wool until the surface takes on a burnished gray appearance. The harder you rub with the steel wool the better, as this prepares the surface for the second coat that actually colors the metal.

The secret of getting a good color with the second coat is to use the absolute minimum amount of solution on a cotton swab. This is applied with long, even strokes, each stroke blending with the others. If you goof, grab the steel wool and go at it again as you did the first time, then try the second coat all over again. It takes practice but you can get a nice finish with Oxpho-Blue. It also is useful as a touch-up, especially on worn surfaces, for you can control the shade of the blue.

The slow rust process appeals to a lot of hobbyists and, if you are willing to spend the time and get in some practice before you try it on a prize gun, it will deliver a beautiful finish with the absolute minimum of equipment. The usually accepted home brew solution consists of 300 cubic centimeters of nitric acid and 250cc of hydrochloric acid. Regarding acid strength, every time I have used it, actual mixing has been done by a pharmacist and I gave him the simple instructions, "Make it as strong as you can."

Dump as many oil-free steel shavings into the mixture as the acid will absorb, and allow the concoction to fume and digest the metal. It is deadly stuff to fool with and my advice is to leave it alone, as you can buy all that you want from Stoeger Arms. They sell it as their Gunsmith Bluer with a complete set of instructions and precautions. Used according to their instructions, the Gunsmith Bluer will turn out first rate slow rust blue with minimum difficulty. You can help the process along by selecting a damp place to store the gun during the time the solution is working on the surface.

Assuming that you do not have the time to make a career of getting one gun blued by the slow rust process, the accelerated process will require some equipment, most of which can be made out of scrap found in the junk yard.

Your first need will be two tanks, one in which to clean the gun in, another for the bluing. Just about any kind of container from a soup kettle to a chicken trough can be used, but if you are going to be doing any amount of bluing, it is far better to purchase these two items or have them made up at your local sheet metal shop. They can be purchased from Herter's, Brownell, Blue-Blak and several other suppliers at a cheaper price than for which you can have them made.

If you do have them made, be sure that galvanized metal is not used, since it will react with the bluing chemicals and cause all sorts of problems. A tank six inches wide, six inches deep and thirty-six inches long should enable one to handle anything from a handgun to a muzzleloader.

For heat you can use the kitchen stove, but spillage will cause the wife to say something smart to you. I advise against it health-wise also, bluing chemicals on the bread you use for toast does not digest well.

A much better solution is to buy scrap burners at the local junk yard and make up a burner and tank-holding rack from scrap angle iron. The burners from a floor furnace will make the best; the jets built into the burners greatly simplifies construction. You can even use a plain length of common pipe with a series of holes drilled its length, but this will require a mixer valve and the hole size must be exact for the type of gas you are using. Brownell offers a pipe burner with the necessary jets at a reasonable price, incidentally.

For best operation, the burner should be mounted under the tanks in a position that will allow the tip of the flame to be about one inch from the bottom of the tank when the flame is at its highest. The flame can touch the tank if you wish, but this has a tendency to smoke up the tanks and build up a deposit of soot under them.

If you are using natural gas, your local gas company can hook the burners up for you in a short while, but if you will use bottled gas instead of natural, the flame will be much hotter and the hook-up is simpler. The small butane tanks used on mobile homes and campers are ideal and the tank takes up little room.

Place one of your bluing tanks at the front of your stand, the other one just behind it with the rims of the two missing each other about two inches, the top of the tanks about waist high or a couple of inches lower. A vertical rod about twelve inches high with the top split into a Y is welded to the frame at the end of each tank. These will support a short piece of electrical conduit that will be directly over the center line of each tank, running full length of the tank. This provides a means of supporting the gun in the solution at a desired depth. Wire hooks and sections of light chain are attached at one end of the gun,

with the other to the overhead rod.

If the bluing tank is up front, you will have more room to work when time is of the essence. For gun cleaning solution, you can get by with a couple of spoonfuls of household lye, but this is messy stuff to use and can burn the hide off you, as well as cause problems on the metal surfaces of the gun. I much prefer Blu-Blak Cleaner or Brownell's Picro-Clean No. 909 which are safer to use and do a much nicer job of cleaning.

The gun, assuming it has been polished, is suspended in this cleaning tank for about five minutes after the solution has been heated to a rolling boil. It then is rinsed in plain water to remove any traces of the cleaning solution. One can put in a third tank to hold clear boiling water and use this instead of the cold water for rinsing. Not actually necessary, it does add to the chances of a good bluing job.

The old saying of cleanliness being next to godliness was never more true than in the case of cleaning a gun that is to be blued. If the metal is clean, the water from the rinse should puddle on the surface instead of running off. The latter is an indication that oil or grease are still present on the surface of the metal. If it runs off, take the gun back to the cleaning tank for another complete cycle and repeat, if necessary, until the metal is absolutely free of oil.

A trick to assure cleanliness of the surface, as well as aid the bluing solution in taking, when it is applied, is to etch the surface of the metal with a 10 percent nitric acid solution. A 10 percent solution is mild and will not even burn your hands, although I don't recommend it as a substitute for coffee.

This solution is swabbed on the surface with a clean white cloth and allowed to work from two or three minutes before rinsing it off with clear water. Rubbing the surface

These small parts, awaiting bluing, are suspended on pieces of wire, while pieces of old spring hold screws, pins.

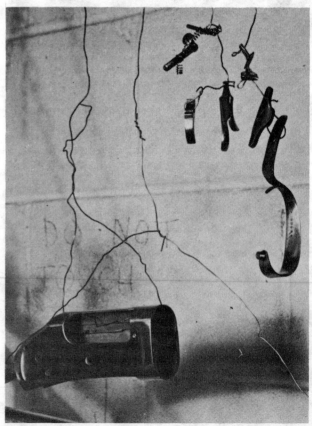

with a wad of clean steel wool (with the oil burned out) while the 10 percent solution is on it will help accelerate the etching and assure even coverage. Many times, when the bluing solution will not bite into the metal or take, you can etch the surface with the 10 percent solution and the bluing will go right to work.

On some occasions you may run across the term, "pickling," which means the same as etching and is different only that in pickling, the metal part is usually suspended in the acid rather than being swabbed with it.

For actual bluing, you need the bluing tank filled with the purest water you can find, quite often failure in the accelerated process can be traced entirely to contaminated water. City water works add chlorine to the water to make it safe to drink, plus other chemicals thrown in for good measure that are supposed to help you keep your teeth, prevent bad breath and help fight the communist conspiracy, all of which play hob with the bluing process.

In the country, water from a well often contains lime, sulphur and iron, plus ingredients from the pig pen, if it is close by. The oldtime gunsmiths swore by rain water and this is still a good source of pure water, provided you do not collect it from the run-off from the roof of your house. Instead, stretch a sheet of plastic over your wife's clothes line and let the rain collect on this and run off into a clean tank or drum. It is a simple and cheap way even though it looks a bit foolish, and your neighbor may think you are some kind of nut. Distilled water is even purer but is expensive in some areas.

Just as the cleanliness of the gun is important, the cleanliness of the water is equally important for you will have eliminated any contamination problem and simplified your procedure. The tanks themselves must have been scrubbed free of grease, dirt and rust.

With the tank filled with water, use a quart glass jar to hold the bluing solution and wrap a piece of wire around the neck of the jar. The jar is suspended into the tank with the mouth of the jar about two inches above the water level and secured in place by wrapping the wire around one of the end uprights. Pour the bluing solution into the jar and turn the heat on under the tank. The suspending of the jar of solution in the water allows it to reach the same temperature of the water and, when applied to the metal, the hot solution will accelerate the bluing even faster than if applied cold. The water is brought to a hard, rolling boil and nothing less will do. When the rolling boil is reached, the gun is lowered into the tank, without touching either the sides or the bottom of the tank.

This really is no big problem, if you will make up a series of hooks connected to a chain. This is connected to that overhead bar and to the gun on the opposite end of the chain.

Many professionals recommend that you grease the bore of a barrel, whittle out wooden plugs, drive the plugs tight-

Barrel is lowered into cleaning solution, one end at a time. This allows any trapped air to be expelled slowly and prevents what can be dangerous solution eruption.

Burst of cold water sprayed into cleaning tank agitates hot cleaning solution for better job. Note that the chains are hooked to S-shaped wires over suspension bars.

Numerous parts can be placed in perforated steel basket and number increased with cross rods through the sides.

ly in the bore and use the extended part of the plug as a handle to which your hooks and suspension chains can be attached. The idea of the grease and plugs is to keep the solution out of the bore to prevent rust. Personally, I consider this about the equivalent of dodging a gnat and swallowing an elephant, for the grease and plug business can create more problems than it solves.

In the first place, you are trapping air in the bore between the plugs and, unless you really drive them in hard, the air that is expanded by the heat can blow out the plugs. It only takes one plug to blow with the accompanying geyser of boiling hot water to convince you that this idea leaves a lot to be desired.

Provided you survive the scalding and still are interested in bluing, you are presented with the problem of the grease in the bore getting out into that clean water that you went to so much trouble to get. If the plugs are not in tightly, the grease will leak out. If you drive them in hard enough, the swelling of the wood submerged in that hot water really creates an interesting problem in getting them out after the job is over.

You have gone to a lot of trouble to get a nice finish on the metal, so pounding on the barrels is not a good idea, and about all you can do is tighten the plug in a vise and pull on the barrels. You either get them out pronto or you get a hernia!

I started out using the plugs, but after one blow-up I considered them something to get by without. True, you will get a little mild rust in the bore, but I have never had any real trouble scrubbing the bore out after the bluing was completed and the bore was none the worse for the ordeal.

To make the barrel holders — no plugs used — I select a piece of steel rod about a quarter inch in diameter and about a foot long, which is heated on one end with the torch and bent back over in a circle about two inches in diameter. Over the curved end, I slip a link of a section of small non-galvanized chain that is long enough to reach the bottom of the tank and still touch the overhead bar. The circle then is closed and the link secured to the bar.

To secure the chain to the overhead bar and allow for adjustment in the length of the chain as needed to suspend the barrel at the correct depth in the water, you will need a wire hanger of some sort. A common curtain hanger will serve. Or you can settle for a couple of discarded coat hangers and make your own hangers by cutting them into four inch lengths and bending them into an S shape with the ends long enough to provide a good hook that will not slip off.

The top part of the S is hooked over the overhead bar and a link of the chain selected to hook over the bottom part of the S that will suspend the gun at the right height from the bottom of the tank.

Do not make the hook through the link permanent, as you will need to adjust this up or down to fit different guns and gun parts. With one of these chain and rod holders in each end of the barrel, you can quickly position the gun in the tank or remove it. Various odd-shaped parts and components can be hung best by cutting and bending short lengths of wire or coat hanger as needed to suspend the part in the water.

While the gun is submerged at the right height, you can get a swab ready to apply the solution to the metal. As you will not enjoy trying to hold a swab saturated with hot bluing solution between your fingers, one can use a clean dry wooden dowel as a handle, with a section of clean cotton cloth wound around it.

With this the cloth may come loose and hang in your way or the pad formed by the cloth will be too firm to mould itself around the contour of the metal being swabbed.

The best solution is surgical cotton that is pulled off the bundle and rolled into wads the size of a golf ball or perhaps a little smaller. To hold the cotton you can use large self-closing tweezers or forceps. The cotton is absorbent and it will mould itself around the contour of the gunpart you are swabbing to get the solution into the tiniest of cracks and crevices. When the cotton becomes dirty or contaminated from use, you drop the ball into the trash can and pick up another clean ball. You use more solution this way, but I will sacrifice a little extra to get a more even coat over the surface of the metal.

Cardinal rule is ignored here, as protective gloves are ignored. The bluing salts can cause bad burns.

Second step is to remove the parts from cleaning tank, holding in hot rinse tank for few seconds to remove any traces of the cleaning solution.

Next, lower parts into bluing tank, again allowing air to escape from barrel. White chemical on tank is normal and requires cleaning over period of time of extended use.

For those close hard-to-reach spots, it is difficult to beat Q-Tips, available at any drug store. The cotton ends are secure to the handle and will not slide off as does a piece of cotton on a tooth pick.

Application of the bluing solution to the surface must be done quickly with even strokes the full length of the barrel to take advantage of the metal's high temperature, when it is removed from the boiling water. The solution will dry almost immediately when first applied, but keep applying it as long as the hot metal will dry the solution. When it stops drying it, stop applying the solution.

Many gunsmiths recommend plunging the part right back into the boiling water, but this doesn't make sense to me, for you will be both diluting the solution on the part and removing it from the atmosphere where it can rust, as the chemical absorbs oxygen.

I personally let it stay out of the tank for about five minutes to allow the solution to react with the metal. When applying the solution to small parts, remember that they cool rapidly, so have the swab ready to apply the solution the moment the part clears the surface of the water and work rapidly.

You will notice about now that the surface of the part you have coated with the solution will be covered with a heavy coat of rust from the chemical action. This rust must be removed completely from the part before it is placed back into the hot water in preparation for the next application. You can use a soft wire scratch wheel, but it must be new or have been cleaned thoroughly by boiling in the cleaner tank.

The simplest and easiest way to remove the rust is to grab a handful of steel wool and rub the metal surfaces as hard as you can. This removes the rust and burnishes the metal for a better appearance. When the ball of clean steel wool becomes clogged with rust, discard it and select another piece, for this is no place to get stingy.

During the time you are applying the solution and removing the rust, you must not touch the metal surface with your bare hand or allow it to come in contact with grease. To violate this rule will result in a spot on the metal that will not react to the chemical solution. The resulting mess sometimes requiring a complete new start, even including repolishing.

Many gunsmiths recommend cotton gloves, but the gloves quickly become soaked and contaminated with rust from the metal surface. I recommend a pair of dishwashing gloves, as these are designed to be worn while working with hot dish water and hard detergent. They are not affected by bluing solution and, being padded inside, you can hold hot chains and hooks while applying the solution. If the outside of the gloves become contaminated with rust, you can wash them while still on your hands. Even though the gloves may be clean, do not touch the actual metal surface with them.

Wash blued parts in cold rinse tank to clear sludge. Part is inspected to assure it is blued evenly. If spot is not covered, it can be returned to the tank again.

After cleaning away the rust from your first application, the metal surface should have taken on a light bluish tint, but the color will be deepened with each application. Put the parts back into the boiling water and give them about five minutes to bring the metal temperature back up equal with the temperature of the boiling water. Remove the parts and swab on the solution as you did the first time and again set the parts aside to work. This is followed by a hard rubbing with steel wool after the rust has formed on the surface. This sequence is repeated until the metal has reached the desired shade of blue-black. On the final sequence, rub as hard as possible with the steel wool to remove every speck of rust you can find, but do not return the part to the boiling water.

Most of the solution will have evaporated or been rubbed off, but a small amount will cling to the surface and keep working, if left there. This adds to the rust that will be created anyways, if the metal is left naked and exposed to the air. To solve both problems and stop the after-rust, the part must be submerged in oil and allowed to remain there for at least fifteen minutes.

As to the oil itself, everything from used motor oil to bear grease has been recommended, but what you really need is a water displacing oil that will not only stop the chemical process of the bluing solution, but also displace any water clinging to the metal surface. Any company that offers bluing solutions will usually offer this oil. For economy, the oil-soaked parts are suspended directly over the oil container and allowed to drip and drain back into the container which will leave only a small amount of the oil remaining on the gun.

If water gets into the container, do not worry about it, for it will do no harm to future guns immersed in it. Allow the oil to remain on the gun overnight, wash the parts in mineral spirits the next day and apply a coat of regular gun oil as you reassemble the gun. When reassembled, the gun should not be stored in a gun case for several days and should be recoated with gun oil, as the oil is absorbed into the pores of the metal surface.

As for what bluing solution to use, there are two ways to go about this business. If you are determined to mix your own, I would suggest that you read Firearm Bluing and Browning by Angier, which is a book literally running over at the brim with the various formulas and it contains a lot of general information as well.

As to the manufactured solutions, there are quite a few on the market, but I have personally used only three to any extent. These are Stoeger's, Herter's Belgium Blue and Brownell's Dicropan IM. All give excellent results, if the manufacturer's instructions are followed. They are not expensive, generally costing somewhere around four dollars for a pint, which will blue a mess of guns. The Stoeger and Herter's solutions follow the old proven basic solutions that have been used for generations. The Dicropan IM was designed originally as a steel blackening chemical for industry, but Orvill Bell, a gunsmith, developed a method of using it for guns and Brownell added it to his line of goods. The process differs slightly from the sequence that I have outlined but instructions are included with each bottle. Used as directed, it produces a deep blue with excellent wearing and appearance qualities.

The cost to set up a bluing operation, including tanks, solutions, oil and burners depends on how much of the material you can scrounge out of the junk yard and how much you buy from the suppliers, plus labor costs, if you have it made up for you instead of doing it yourself. If you buy burners and tanks, having the tank holders made, you can count on spending $50-$75. For one who scrounges his burners and makes up his own tanks and holders, the price can be cut in half.

Bluing is not a cheap operation and you should decide whether you are going to blue more than one gun, for it is cheaper to have one gun done commercially than to set up this whole operation for just one gun. Bluing cannot be accomplished by pouring a magic chemical on the barrel and spreading it out nor can it be learned overnight or by reading a book. Like all forms of craftsmanship, it takes practice.

Most professional shops and advanced hobbyists do not use the accelerated process that I have just described. Instead, they use the black oxide or hot blue, as it sometimes is called, for several reasons. The hot blue is faster and produces more uniform bluing with less trouble. It also cuts out all of the handwork involved in the accelerated process, such as the swabbing of the solution on the surface and carding the rust off. The gunsmith can blue several guns in the same tank simultaneously for greater economy of operation.

Black oxide does have several disadvantages. It is almost impossible to set this process up correctly for less than two hundred dollars for a set of tanks, burners, stands, thermometers and necessary chemicals. You can jury-rig the set-up by making your own tanks and burners, but I do not recommend it; you will have enough problems as it is without creating additional ones.

Another disadvantage is that the bluing room must be separate from the rest of the shop, as the fumes will rust any steel in sight. It also requires that the room be well ventilated, for the fumes — while not toxic — lower blood pressure if inhaled for a prolonged period. The bluing salts will absorb water, so an air tight cover must be provided for the bluing tank. The solution is caustic and can be compared to lye boiling at 285 degrees, so it must be handled with care, not allowed to come in contact with the skin and definitely kept away from the eyes.

Should the operator splash some on himself it is not the end of the world, but it will produce a good burn if not flooded immediately with water and washed in vinegar after the rinse. If dropped on the shoes, it eats a hole through them in a matter of minutes.

Used daily or weekly, as in a commercial shop, the solution will give little trouble for, oddly enough, the more often you use it the better it seems to work. But if left standing and unused for several weeks, it will create problems. The longer the time between the uses, the more the solution gives trouble in bluing.

But for the hobbyist interested in easing into a paying semi-professional status, hot bluing offers him an opportunity to realize a good payment for his labor at a relatively low investment, compared to some of the other aspects of gunsmithing.

One hobbyist set up a hot blue system while attending college and realized enough money out of his moonlighting occupation to pay most of his educational expenses. There are many such basement and garage setups all over the country, and seldom do they go lacking for guns to reblue.

Several companies sell bluing salts and most of them will turn out a good job. Lynx-Line Blu-Blak and Brownell's Oxynate-7 are used in about ninety percent of the professional shops and differ only slightly, with each having its advantages and disadvantages. The firms marketing Blu-Blak and Oxynate-7 offer a complete line of bluing equipment, accessories, needed chemicals and oils. I have used Blu-Blak most and originally chose it, because another local gunsmith wanted to sell the setup. By buying it, I eliminated my competition and acquired a complete bluing rig at a price that was hard to turn down.

Blu-Blak also offers a complete unit which includes a set of tanks with a unit frame to hold them and the burners underneath. The buyer hooks the burners to the gas line, mixes the chemicals and is ready for business in a matter of hours.

Used according to instructions, Blu-Blak produces a deep, attractive bluish-black color with the emphasis on black. There is only one actual bluing tank, but this is sufficient to blue about any type of gun metal that can be blued. It will blue nickel steel, such as that in the receivers of the '03-A4 Springfields at a regular 285 degree temperature, without the use of a second tank at a higher temperature.

With Oxynate-7, no complete unit is offered. Tank holders and frame must be built by the hobbyist or by a local welding shop. Normally, one tank is used for the bluing, but for nickel steel a second tank carrying solution at a higher temperature is recommended. The hobbyist can blue nickel steel with only one solution tank, if he raises the temperature slowly to the level normally used with the second tank. Oxynate-7 produces more of a bluish-blue-black color than Blu-Blak. The color is attractive on a highly polished gun and I added it to my own bluing shop for this reason.

I have used black oxide bluing rigs, ranging from home brew salts made from fertilizer and lye, up to a complete

Next step is to boil the blued parts in stop bath for 30 minutes to neutralize the remaining bluing solution.

arsenal setup. I designed the bluing section of the 44th Arsenal in Formosa, Nationalist China and it was something to behold. Guns were lowered into the six-foot deep tanks via a hydraulic winch, with about fifty rifles to the tank! The salts were mixed at the arsenal and we constantly were running into trouble due to the wide variety of local chemical strengths.

Whenever we accept a gun for rebluing, we give it a visual check and test fire it for correct functioning. Should you ever do bluing on a paid basis, remember that if you disassemble the gun without checking, it is your problem to get it back together after bluing and get it to work.

If the difficulty is brought to the attention of the customer before bluing, you will not get an argument out of him for the extra repair bill. If the gun is yours, it is best to find out a difficulty and repair it before bluing.

When you are sure that it is functioning correctly, disassemble it completely. No springs can be left in the gun as the bluing process will etch them and cause loss of surface smoothness. This results in broken springs, while the high temperature involved can retemper some of the small ones.

All aluminum and pot metal must be removed, as bluing salts will eat these up faster than a cat can swallow a canary. Many of the newer receivers are made from cast powdered iron and bluing salts either will not touch them or turn them every color in the rainbow. Case-hardened receivers such as those found on some double barrel shotguns will not blue in the regular tank. They can be blued, but it involves more time, plus special know-how. Usually we recommend to the customer that the frame just be cleaned unless he is willing to pay a bonus price. Naturally, all wood must be removed. Tom Collard, the former president of Blu-Blak, once told me that one of his customers complained to him that every time he blued a gun it ruined the finish on the stock!

With the gun down to its bare innards, the next problem is to remove all of the old bluing and any rust to the bare metal, leaving it polished to a soft luster, if not a high glow. This can all be done on the polishing wheels, but it is a lot easier to run the gun through a stripping bath before any polishing is done. This is a mild acid solution that dissolves the oxide, be it bluing or just red rust, leaving the metal clean and ready for polishing. In addition to saving hours of polishing, a stripping bath reduces the amount of surface metal that must be removed, plus any oil that is on the

The final step in bluing is immersion in soluble oil, while parts still are hot from the stop bath. This oil now will seep into the tinest cracks in the gun metal.

surface.

After the stripping bath, the gun must be rinsed thoroughly in clean running water to stop the acid. The secret of polishing guns is to remove as little metal as possible, for the more metal you remove via polishing, the easier it is to round the edges and lose the lines of the gun. Commercial stripping bath solutions are recommended over a home mixture. Stripping baths can be mixed if a commercial solution is not available or you are in a tight spot and cannot await delivery.

Nitric acid normally is used, but muriatic acid can be substituted with the percentage running 10 to 20 percent, depending on the strength of the acid used. Starting with 10 percent, run a test strip of blued metal through it, increasing the percentage, if the solution does not work. But take it easy, for a fast acting solution can etch the surface too much and require deep polishing. Do not hesitate to go to the polishing wheels, for the metal is clean and being free of protective oil, it will rust quickly.

After polishing, the gun is hung on the same type of rods

and chains used in the accelerated process, smaller parts suspended by individual wires. Tiny parts can be placed in a perforated steel basket which will be immersed in the bluing bath along with the other parts.

From here on, the metal must not be touched with the bare hands, as a non-blue spot will result wherever you touch it. If a wax base polish such as No. 555 or chrome rouge is used, the wax base must be removed from the gun with mineral spirits or, in a pinch, even lighter fluid. Try to avoid heavy use of petroleum base fluids, not submerging the parts in them, for they tend to leave a hard-to-remove film on the metal surface. Hang up the gun parts and predetermine how many parts you can get into the tank without overcrowding.

Enough time is allowed for the bluing bath temperature to reach 285 degrees. If the bath has not been used for several days, the salts will have settled to the bottom of the tank and must be stirred with a steel rod, breaking up the clumps and allowing them to redissolve.

One key rule when getting a bluing tank to the correct temperature is that the bath is never controlled with the amount of flame under it. If the temperature is too low and will not increase to the required level, the solution is too thin; additional salts must be added or time allowed for the excess water to boil away.

If the temperature rises too high and will not settle back down, the solution is too thick and must be diluted by adding water. Be careful when adding water to a hot bluing tank, for it will spit solution over everything – including you. Sweep the water into the tank with a long handle dipper going below the solution surface in a full-length stroke.

When the bluing solution reaches the correct temperature, allow it to run for awhile at the working temperature. This seems to produce better blue, than if you instantly submerge the parts, when the temperature first reaches the 285-degree mark.

Take this time to light the cleaning and hot rinse tanks, allowing them to come to a good rolling boil before you start the cleaning cycle. The guns are lowered into the cleaning tank, the time they remain there determined by the solution you are using; with Blu-Blak this is five minutes.

The cleaning tank can be used many times, but this is poor economy, for after about the third bath, it will start to fail and the guns will have spots on them after bluing.

After five minutes, the parts are removed, given a good quick swish in the rinse tank to clean them of any lingering cleaning solution, then without delay are placed in the bluing tank. This must be done carefully for any trapped air will rapidly expand from the sudden heat and blow solution over everything, including the operator.

If bluing barrels, insert one end in the solution slowly and ease the barrel down, allowing the trapped air to be pressed out of the bore by the solution as it takes its place. Small parts create no trouble, unless they have a hollow space where air can be trapped. It is extremely important that the parts be suspended in the solution carefully without touching another part or the sides or bottom of the tank; wherever they touch, there will be discoloration in the bluing finish.

If you will be bluing only one batch of guns, the cleaning tank and the hot rinse tanks can be turned off and allowed to cool. To help preserve the cleaning and rinse solutions and – more important – to keep out the trash, cover them with a piece of masonite, exterior plywood or tin.

The neutralizer tank is turned on to allow it to reach a good rolling boil by the time the gun parts are ready to be removed from the bluing tank. By working a time schedule, you can cut down on the amount of gas consumption and lower the cost of bluing. If you will be bluing a second batch of guns, the cleaning and rinse tank flames can be lowered slightly to maintain temperature, being brought back to a rolling boil when needed, but you will conserve gas in the meantime.

For safety in the bluing room, the operator should equip himself with a full-face shield to protect his eyes and skin. Hands should be covered with neoprene gloves designed for bluing work and available from gunsmith suppliers. It is best to wear a long sleeved shirt and a rubber apron. Rubber boots are not necessary, although I would recommend that you wear old shoes, for one drop of solution can ruin them.

Avoid standing directly over the bluing tank for a prolonged period and breathing the fumes. Ventilation, as mentioned, should be an exhaust fan directly over the tanks or the tanks should be placed either outside under a weatherproof shed or in a large, open room. Keep a bottle of boric acid eye solution available and a bottle of common household vinegar for spatters of solution on the skin or clothes. Use these if necessary and, in case of a bad accident, request a doctor to treat as he would for hot lye.

The bluing bath will start to blue the metal in about five minutes and a good surface color is accomplished in about fifteen minutes. For maximum penetration, the parts should remain in the tank for the length of time specified by the manufacturer. After this period ease the parts up one by one and inspect them for even color, watching for defects.

If it appears a part has not taken well, you sometimes can solve this by wiping it with a clean piece of surgical gauze that has been wound around a steel rod and dipped in the solution. After wiping the surface with the pad, place the part back in the bluing tank for about fifteen minutes; the spot usually will disappear, color blending with the rest. Do not try to wipe the part, while holding the gauze in your hands, for you can slip and plunge your hand into the hot bath. This will result in a bad burn, whether or not you have on protective gloves.

If the part looks right, remove it from the bluing to immerse it in the cold rinse tank. This must be done slowly, for you are quenching the part and lowering it back to room temperature. Barrels should be lowered into the rinse tank in the same manner they went into the bluing tank; one end down first, the rest slowly to allow the bore to clear itself.

When the part is in the rinse tank and back to room temperature, inspect it closely for defects. If a red splotch should appear, it sometimes can be cleared up by wiping it with a piece of gauze. Do not use steel wool except in extreme cases, for the bluing is scratched easily at this point.

If the part did not take the blue, rub it thoroughly with the pad and place it back in the bluing tank, being extra careful, for you are changing temperature rapidly again back up to 285 degrees. If the part is right after rubbing with the pad, it can be placed into the neutralizer tank along with the other parts that have been rinsed.

The neutralizer does what its name implies: it neutralizes the bluing salts that may remain on the surface or in tiny crevices. With Blu-Blak, the parts remain in the neutralizer for thirty minutes at a rolling boil, but this may vary with products of other manufacturers. Neutralizing should not be hurried, for if you skip this bath, the salts in the cracks and crevices will keep working and you will see a white bloom-like mar, as the salts work over a period of time.

The final tank is the water soluble oil into which the parts are submerged after removal from the neutralizer tank. They should remain submerged in the oil tank for about ten minutes, then are suspended above the oil tanks to cool completely, as excess oil drains back into the oil tank. I leave the parts suspended until the following day, which gives them ample time to soak oil in the pores of the metal, a further aid to neutralizing the bluing salts.

The parts then are rinsed in mineral spirits and inspected for the final time before reassembly. Be sure to coat each part with oil as you reassemble and do not place the gun in a closed case for a week, reoiling as the oil is absorbed into the metal.

This has been a quick run-through of the method I use with Blu-Blak, but it is basically the procedure for all hot black oxide bluing, regardless of brand name. Each manufacturer provides complete instructions as to the sequence and temperatures, and these should be followed to the letter.

The hot black oxide process is relatively free of problems provided you follow the manufacturer's instructions, but it seems sometimes that the tanks have minds of their own. Everything will be going along fine with batch after batch of gun parts coming out beautifully, until suddenly the whole operation seems to go haywire. The fault usually is operation error or bath contamination. Only time and experience provide the know-how for correcting most of these errors, but it does not take long for the operator to realize that hot bluing is no place to get sloppy with procedure or safety precautions.

I always recommend to a beginner that he start out with the accelerated process and, after he has gained experience and know-how, make the decision about hot blue. Rebluing is fascinating and I can think of nothing that allows the beginner a better opportunity to exhibit his skill and pride of workmanship, for all bluing, regardless of the process, is about 80 percent skill in polishing the metal and handling the equipment, with the rest a matter of solutions.

The primary difference between plating and bluing or browning is that, unlike bluing or browning, which involves the changing of the surface of the metal, plating deposits one metal on top of another metal through chemical or electrical transfer. Naturally, the amount of metal deposited must be controlled rigidly in gun work, for plating too thick results in oversize parts that cannot function in the mechanism. This often is the case when a commercial nongunsmith plating firm plates guns. These firms usually work on things like trophies, automobile components and so on, all of which is done for wear protection with no thought given to close tolerance, as in gun parts. Few long guns are plated completely except for display purposes, so we will concern ourselves with the more common use of plating in gunsmithing, which involves handguns and sub-components such as triggers and hammers.

You probably will run across a gun on which the plating is peeling or some that have only a tiny section of the original plating remaining. Removing nickel plating from a gun can either be done by polishing or by deplating, but polishing, while cheaper and simpler, leaves a lot to be desired in efficiency. Too often the highly polished metal cannot be identified from the remaining traces of nickel plating and the gun, when blued, shows these traces of nickel quite vividly. Deplating can be done in relative safety in any small shop without a mass of equipment. The container to hold the deplating solution must be non-conducive to electricity and, at the same time, acid resistant. Any large glass jar can be used. The solution itself can be of several acids, but probably the easiest for the hobbyist to obtain will be sulphuric acid of 30 percent strength; nitric acid may be substituted, if necessary, in the same strength.

Blued parts are hung from their suspension chains and wires to cool after oil bath, allow excess oil to drain.

Weaker solutions will work less well and more slowly.

Pour the water into the tank first, if mixing your own, and add acid slowly, running it down the side of the container rather than just dumping it in.

The next need is a piece of sheet lead with total area equal to or larger than the surface area of the part to be deplated. This sheet is scrubbed clean of any grease or oxidation on the surface and a hole is punched through one end to receive a copper wire.

Set an automobile battery beside your deplating tank. Run a heavy copper wire from the negative side of the battery to the sheet of lead and hang the sheet in the deplating solution, moving it to a position that allows the solution to be on all sides. Connect the positive pole of the battery to a similar piece of heavy copper wire and, on the other end of the wire attach your gun part, lowering it into the solution when the connection is completed. That is all there is to it.

The nickel is stripped from the gun part and transferred through the acid to the lead plate by the electrical current. The length of time will depend on the thickness of the nickel plate and the amount of surface area it covers, but about fifteen minutes usually will be enough. Watch the parts closely and remove them as soon as all of the nickel plate is gone, for excess time in the tank will etch the surface of the metal.

Wash the part thoroughly in clear water to rinse away remaining traces of the acid, then oil the part if any length of time will occur before the part is polished for bluing or replating. Should you spill acid on your skin or clothing, immediately flood the area with water and apply baking soda to neutralize the acid after rinsing.

There are many long, technical engineering terms for the different types of plating, but I lump them into two general classes: chemical plating and electro-plating. In chemical plating, the molecules of the plating metal are suspended in a chemical solution and deposit themselves on the gun part, when it is submerged for a length of time in the solution. A good example of this is copper sulfate, which quickly deposits a thin skin of copper on metal placed in the solution. This type of plating is simple, but as the plating metal molecules gradually are used up to plate the metal, the solution finally becoming useless. It has little use in gunsmith plating except for a variation which we will discuss.

Electro-plating works the same, but instead of using up the molecules in the solution, a bar of plating metal is suspended in the solution and the solution remains strong as ever, the plating molecules being transferred from the bar to the solution via an electrical current passing through the solution.

This is not a totally correct statement, for after a period of time the solution will weaken and require a booster shot of the concentrated solution.

In plating, the bar that is consumed is referred to as the anode and the metal that will receive the plating is called the cathode. There are a few special plating processes that use the reverse polarity to add to the confusion of a beginner, so stick to the one described above. The speed of metal transfer and the thickness of the deposit is controlled by the amount of electrical current.

A third plating method uses parts of both the chemical and electrical means and is known as brush plating. You have probably seen advertisements for this in automotive parts catalogs, but these should be avoided for gun use. Texas Plater's Supply offers a variation of this especially designed for gunsmithing that works quite well and is economical. The solution, in jelly form, is available in nickel, gold, silver and copper. The jelly is applied to the surface of the gun with a special metal-handled brush that is hooked to a dry cell battery with a wire. The other pole of the battery is hooked to the part to be plated.

The brush is dipped into the jelly and pulled slowly across the surface of the work in a series of strokes not unlike common painting in slow motion. No anode is used and the jelly is consumed in the process, necessitating replacement as the supply is used. When the work is carefully polished, cleaned and the directions followed to the letter, this system will give good results, although the plating is naturally not as good as that by a commercial plater.

The chemical process wherein the part simply is immersed in a solution has much to offer the hobbyist, but it can be tricky and is more complicated than it first appears, for the solution must be exactly right for the metal being plated.

A major metal refinishing firm currently is working the bugs out of a process that uses the chemical plate process for guns. When perfected it should be a boon to the hobbyist not wishing to go the whole electrical plating route. I have seen this system and I think it has great potential even for the professional. The main problem in this chemical system is that it does not have the adhesive power of electrical plating and does have some peeling problems, but this can be overcome partially by pickling the part in a mild acid solution prior to immersion in the plating solution. Pickling prepares the surface of the metal to receive the plate by cleaning it and creating tiny crevices in the surface of the metal to which the plate can bond more firmly.

The electrical type of plating is used by commercial firms, as it is faster, more precise, more economical and produces better plating.

In my shop, the part first is polished as it would be for bluing, except that a soft velvet surface is the stopping point instead of a high gloss finish. The part then is washed thoroughly in clear water to remove any surface dirt or clinging polishing particles. Then it is cleaned thoroughly, for any spot of grease or foreign matter will ruin all of the plating efforts.

At first we used electrical cleaning as done in the large plating plants, using a heated solution and a stainless steel anode. We later switched to cleaning the parts in our regular bluing tank cleaner, as it seemed to do a better job on gun parts than electrical cleaning. After cleaning, the part again is rinsed in clear running water, placed in a pickling solution for several minutes, removed and again rinsed in clear running water.

Many plating firms recommend an underplating of copper on gun parts prior to the deposition of the nickel plate, but in some solutions this step can be eliminated. I have tried it both ways and the solution we use seems to work better if the nickel is deposited directly on the part, but it does require that the part be absolutely clean. Also, the pickling process must be a little on the deep side. Try it both ways, if you go into plating, and use that which produces the best plating job. Whether you are plating copper or nickel, the sequence is about the same and, if you are using an underplate, you simply plate the gun with copper, rinse thoroughly and go right to the nickel plate.

In the plating tank, the part is connected to an overhanging copper rod with bare copper wire and placed in the solution in a position that will assure full circulation of the solution around it. The anodes of the plating metal are rinsed in clear water and placed in a ring around the tank and connected together. All that remains is to connect the wire from the plating machine to the copper bar on which the part is suspended, and a similar wire to the anodes, plus turning the plating machine on, of course.

The voltage and length of time required will depend on the surface area of the part being plated, but one volt and one hour is a good starting point for most large handgun parts. If you get into plating, you will discover that a slow deposit of metal at a low voltage will give the best results on gun parts. A quick check is to ease the gun part up to the surface, increase the voltage and watch for tiny bubbles to form on the part. When these appear, ease back on the voltage until they stop appearing.

If bubbles appear and you are in a hurry, agitate the part to prevent the bubbles from clinging to the surface. Wherever a bubble clings to the surface, the metal is not plated under the bubble and the plating will appear pockmarked. If the machine is set to where the bubbles do not appear, agitation is not necessary and the plate will be even and smooth, but it requires a longer period of time. When the part has a nice plate, turn the machine off, remove the part and rinse it. The plating will have a frosty appearance but is brought to a high luster by polishing with No. 555 or chrome rouge on a soft muslin wheel.

Information on plating guns is almost non-existent, but you can find sufficient data on jewelry plating, which is similar. Shy away from industrial plating, for generally this is designed for wearing qualities and will tend to peel when used on guns, due to heat and metal stress. The size of your operation will determine the cost and this can be from less than a hundred dollars to well over a thousand for the more complicated processes.

The hobbyist who does not specialize in guns should caution the operator that the plate must be thin to coincide with the close tolerance of gun components. Triggers and hammer sears should not be plated for obvious reasons and must be covered with a stop-solution, but the rest of the trigger or hammer can be plated with no ill effects.

Should you decide to go into it yourself, the Hoover Plater is a small machine offered by several firms along with the anodes, solutions, wire, and other necessities. Tanks can be made from any number of common containers, but one that is easy to come by is a pyrex pan intended for cooking meat loaf. Tanks also can be made from wood and covered with fiberglass or marine epoxy paint, to be absolutely water tight.

If you live near a battery manufacturing plant, you sometimes can buy new battery cases and remove the liners for about as nearly perfect a tank as possible, but the case must be new. Covers should be made for all tanks to keep them clean of trash or you can pour the solutions into large glass jugs for storage.

For those who wish a larger setup, I would suggest contacting a commercial plater and talking to his supplier. Most suppliers will bend over backwards to help you get set up and supply you with everything you need, including plating data and procedures. The better the equipment, the better the plating and the more variations of plating you can do, but this should be matched with actual need, for the solutions cannot be left unattended for long stretches of time.

It is only a matter of time before the hobbyist wonders whether he can replace the beautiful color case-hardening on some of the older double barrel shotgun receivers and on some revolvers, such as the Colt single action. This is probably the hardest type of metal refinishing and one that is past the ability not only of most hobbyists, but most professionals as well.

The beautiful color case-hardening is done by immersing the part in a pot of molten cyanide, then quenching it in water. It sounds simple, but cyanide is about as dangerous as putting a filling in a wildcat's tooth. Extreme safeguards must be adhered to rigidly or disaster and death can result. Personally, you could not drag me into a room with cyanide and I leave it strictly alone. There is another way to do color case-hardening, which involves heating the part to a dull red and dropping it into a special solution. The solution is agitated by air bubbles being released through a series of holes at the bottom of the tank. The part will color, but it also is badly warped 99 percent of the time, making the process almost useless for gun work.

Many of the old guns are fake color case-hardened by some torch artist using a small jet oxyacetylene torch, and playing the flame closely over the surface in a pattern duplicating regular color case-hardening. It is relatively easy, but the results are not permanent. Anytime you are contemplating buying an antique gun that has a nice color case-hardened surface, look at the color closely to determine whether the blue lines flow or jump. If they flow in a continuous line, you probably are looking at the work of a torch artist.

Another way to uncover this is to watch for rust pitting under the case hardening. If rust is under the color, the color was put on afterwards and is a fake.

The Alamo Heat Treating Company produces beautiful color case-hardening on any gun sent to them. I recommend that the hobbyist send their needs to these good people who are equipped to do the work. There is a need for a simple and effective system of doing color case-hardening in the small professional shop, and the man who comes up with the answer will have a money-making proposition on his hands.

The hobbyist who becomes interested in metal refinishing will find himself in one of the most fascinating aspects of gunsmithing. Without a doubt, it is the easiest way for a hobbyist to express his artistic ability, for a beautiful job of metal refinishing is admired by any gun enthusiast, be he beginner or professional.

Some of the finest work I have ever seen was done by a hobbyist with absolutely the poorest setup in the business, but he devoted hour after hour of careful handwork on each part, which points out the well known phrase of "perfection is a matter of determination and patience."

Chapter 18

This Partially Done Woodwork Can Reduce Your Problems And Speed That Custom Job!

THE INLETTED STOCK

In 1820, A CONNECTICUT GUNMAKER by the name of Blanchard carried Eli Whitney's new concept of inter-changeable mass-produced gun parts a step farther by producing interchangeable gun stocks, which were manu-factured entirely by machines. Prior to this, all gunstocks were inletted and shaped entirely by hand.

It required seventeen different especially-built lathes to turn out the Blanchard machine-made stocks, but the saving in man-hours was enough to convince the gun manu-facturers for all time. Today, probably no more than one percent of all gunstocks are made entirely by hand, as even the highest priced guns have stocks that have been partially machined. Yet, strangely enough, a hundred years after the birth of the machine-inletted stocks, the independent gun-smith still was whacking away at a plank, making his gun-stocks entirely by hand.

It was not until after the end of World War II that partially machine-inletted stocks became common on the gunsmith market and, even then, they were slow to gain favor. In the twenty-odd years since, the story has changed drastically, for now the semi-inletted stock has taken over the market almost completely and stocks made by hand from scratch are few and far between.

High labor costs have been the main reason for the general acceptance of the semi-inletted stock, as only a few gun enthusiasts are willing to lay down a hundred dollars or more for a full custom-built stock, no matter how much contempt they have for a semi-inletted one. Even a hundred dollars is about a rock bottom price for a custom stock, although a few so-called stockmakers will modify a plow handle and call it a gun stock for less money. The main requirement for quality work done by a craftsman always has been time and time is expensive.

The plain truth of the matter is that starting a stock from scratch seldom is necessary. Most armchair gunsmiths who bemoan the passing of the custom gunstock simply are not familiar with the wide selection of semi-inletted stocks available today, and think only in terms of the 90 percent

When working from a plain plank, plane the surfaces flat and square as a start. Bandsaw is ideal for rough shaping, or it can be done with a handsaw and chisel.

Here, a milling machine with a wood cutter is being used to rough-cut the barrel channel. This can be done by hand but Walker prefers electricity to muscle.

inletted and shaped stocks. A little research into the stock manufacturers' catalogs should clarify this misunderstanding. The trade names for the different types of stocks will vary from manufacturer to manufacturer, so look more at the description of the stock than at the name I have used, although it is the one most commonly accepted.

Planks seldom are seen on the market, but usually consist of a piece of stock wood around three inches thick, 12 inches wide and 36 inches long. Sawmills that specialize in stock planks roughcut this size to allow for trimming poorer sections of wood. While this hardly can be called a semi-inletted stock by any stretch of the imagination, it does point out the key fact that unless the gunsmith hauls himself out into the woods, chops down the tree and saws out the planks by hand personally, then his stock has reached him via the help of a machine. So you see, it really is all just a matter of how much machining has been done on a stock.

Good stock wood is becoming more and more scarce, because of the heavy demand. I know one gentleman who systematically buys every walnut tree he can find. These are dug up, carefully sawed and the choice grain pieces saved, while the common grain pieces are sold to dealers, usually for more than the cost of the whole operation. The select pieces go into what he calls his bank toward the day of his retirement.

A stock blank is the plank rough-sawed into the vague shape of a stock, eliminating the poorer grain sections, while taking advantage of the more fancy or select grain sections. All sides are planed square and the plank is ready to be laid out for inletting and shaping. The hobbyist probably will reach the point in his stockmaking career that he will want to tackle a full custom stock from a plank, but the knowledge of how to do it all correctly must be learned step by step from experience.

The rough inletted blank is the same as the stock blank, except that the rough outline of inletting has been done. In the case of a rifle, the holes for the stock screws have been drilled, excess wood where the receiver will be inletted has been eliminated and a small barrel channel about a quarter of an inch wide has been cut full length. The saving in time is in that all of the basic and necessary lines to start the inletting have been laid out; the gunsmith can concentrate his efforts on completing the inletting and shaping rather than figuring out all of the lines and angles. Because all shaping still has to be done, one still has full freedom of design.

The shaped stock blank has no inletting done, but the general outline of a stock has been established with all of the outside edges rounded and shaped. The top of the blank has been squared to match the lines of the stock for correct inletting by the gunsmith. These stocks are intended for the odd model guns, for which regular semi-inletted stocks are not normally available. Plenty of wood has been left for the gunsmith to shape and model the stock as his little heart desires.

A semi-inletted blank is a sort of combination rough inletted blank and shaped stock blank except that the rough inletting and the general shaping of the stock will be a little closer to a finished stock. These were the first of the semi-inletted stocks on the market and offer perhaps the best choice for the hobbyist who wants to do a lot of stock work, or has some special design in mind. Plenty of wood has been left on the outside for shaping, as well as enough inside for good close hand fitting. If the truth were known, I'd bet a good $300 mule that most of the so-called custom-made stocks sneaked in the back door as a semi-finished blank! There is nothing wrong with this, for only the surplus wood has been removed, saving the gunsmith many hours of work that will not affect the final outcome of the stock one single bit.

With the 90 to 95 percent semi-inletted stock, the percentage depends on who is doing the advertising, but either way, the stock is shaped almost completely on the outside and the inside inletted to within about .008 inch which is almost a press fit. A few careful cuts with a sharp chisel plus a few strokes with the scraper and the action will fit into the stock as snug as a bug in a rug. The barrel channel is cut for a standard weight barrel and will usually have to be opened up a bit, but this can be done quickly with little trouble, unless you have a truck axle screwed onto the receiver.

The amount of work necessary to shape and finish the outside will vary from one manufacturer to another. Some will require sanding only, while others have some extra wood left on for final shaping to the stockmaker's preference before sanding. This 95 percent semi-inletted stock is the type most people think of when they hear the term, "semi-inletted stock." It is the type the hobbyist should select for his first try at stockmaking, as he really has to work hard at goofing up to fail to wind up with a nice stock. Many gunshops keep a supply of these on hand to provide a customer with a good stock at a minimum cost in labor.

The stock manufacturers offer these 95 percent semi-inletted stocks in a wide selection of designs, ranging from those that are identical twins to a factory stock, to some really wild designs. A rather recent addition to this selection are the stocks that duplicate factory originals of antique guns long out of production. This is the answer to the collector who has a good specimen in tip-top shape in the metal department but is saddled with a stock that has come out second best at a termite convention. When completed by a good hobbyist or professional stockmaker, these are very hard to detect from the original stocks.

Most manufacturers offer a fitted stock for those who do not wish to do any inletting or do not know how. In most cases, the fitting is done to a standard action by the manufacturers, which may not be the same in every detail as the purchaser's action. The best way to assure a close fit is for the purchaser to ship his gun to the stockmaker for the fitting. The outside is left the same as the 90-95 percent stock and is sanded and finished by the purchaser.

The ready-for-sanding stock carries the fitted stock a small step farther in that, in addition to completely fitting the metal to the stock, the outside has been shaped and smoothed by the manufacturer to a point that none of the real hard work is left for the purchaser. All that remains to be done by the purchaser is sanding, filling and finishing, plus any checkering or carbing the new owner may care to add.

A finished stock is completely inletted, shaped and sanded, with all the filling and finishing done entirely by the stock manufacturer. All that remains for the purchaser to is to key the bill. This type of stock probably will have little appeal for the hobbyist, unless he is the type who cares nothing for wood work. It is intended for the non-gunsmith who wants his gun stocked by someone other than the gun manufacturer or who wants something a little different. Most of the work done on this type is far above a factory stock, but it is on a semi-mass production line basis and the stocks do not compare with those installed by an independent stockmaker who has a lot of professional skill and can devote more time to the project.

So-called "finished stocks" may also be purchased with checkering, either unfinished or with final finish. Standard checkering patterns are generally available; some stockmakers offer a wide selection to satisfy most tastes. Although not the equal of an individual craftsman doing a one-of-a-kind pattern, the patterns and work are far superior to most factory checkering.

A carved stock is the top of the line for stock manufacturers and the highest priced of all types, costing on the average about twice the price of the finished and checkered stock.

In addition to the wide selection in types, the manufacturer can supply your choice in over a dozen different woods! The eleven different types available in a dozen different woods provide the purchaser with over a hundred possible choices. But this is only the beginning.

A lot of things have a bearing on wood; its color, grain and structure. For example, a tree that grows in the swamps will receive more water and, as a result, will grow much faster than a similar tree clinging to the side of a dry, rocky hill. The faster the tree grows, the more porous the wood. This, in turn, makes filling the pores and finishing more difficult and the checkering different, since a porous wood will not take a delicate pattern without the diamonds in the pattern breaking off.

The hard, dry climate produces a dense piece of wood easily filled and checkered. The composition of the soil will affect the color of the wood, sometimes quite drastically. I remember one customer who brought in a huge plank of wood he had cut back in the 1930s to be used to stock a fine double barrel shotgun. The tree had grown in a heavy lime-iron soil and the color of the plank was a beautiful shade of walnut red that was unlike anything I had ever seen before. How many limbs were on the tree and where they grew also will affect the grain structure and figure, as will the part of the tree from which the stock blank was cut. Even the way the sawmill cuts the stock blank from the tree can affect its appearance.

Walnut has been the choice of stockmakers for many years, but with the dwindling supply of good walnut resulting in higher prices, stockmakers and gun manufacturers are beginning to look to other woods as a source of gunstocks. There are over 1400 different woods available on this old planet and, while most are not well suited for gunstocks, those that are offer an enormous variety of grains, structures, strengths, weights, colors and characteristics. The forests of South America have hardly been touched and, judging from some of the samples I have seen of stocks made from one of their varieties of walnut, we have a pleasant surprise in store for us. To give you an idea of the different woods currently available in semi-inletted stocks and a little information about them, here is a quick description of the most popular.

Walnut, the all-time favorite, comes in a wide selection with several confusing names and advertising descriptions, but for all practical purposes, you can lump them into two basic categories. European walnut is known by many names, such as French, Italian, Spanish, English and Circassian, but it grows in practically every European country in a wide range of colors and textures. Sometimes a tree will be cut in, say Belgium, shaped into stock blanks and shipped to Italy where it is fitted to a gun and sold as Italian walnut!

Generally speaking, European walnut usually is light in color and somewhat dense with close pores which produce a superior stock easily-filled, finished and checkered. American walnut is commonly called Black walnut and varies from the porous wood to a close grain type found in the

Missouri-Kansas area. Generally speaking, American walnut will be somewhat darker than its European counterpart with considerably more figure in the expensive blanks.

A third type, which might be classified as a half-breed, is marketed under several names, but consists simply of grafted European walnut grown in America, generally in the California area. It combines the close grain of the European walnut as well as its lighter color with the figure of the American walnut, due to the grafting of the two varieties. Oddly enough, some of this wood has been exported to Europe, fitted to fancy guns and resold in America as European walnut!

Maple was one of the favorites of the early stockmakers and beautiful examples of their maple stocks will be found on flintlocks and percussion guns of that era. Walnut slowly pushed it out of first place over the years, although maple ranks second today in the semi-inletted stocks. It too goes under a wide variety of names, such as rock maple, sugar maple or hard maple. Maple will consist of either a plain grain with no figure, a birdseye figure which looks like the termination point of dozens of small limbs or eyes or burl maple which consists of swirls and twists of the grain. Any of them will finish up into a strikingly handsome stock, especially if it is stained lightly. When it comes to working maple, you will find that while it weighs about the same as walnut, it is much more dense and requires good tools and a lot of patience. It checkers but carving is another matter, especially on the burl type.

Birch has little to offer in the appearance contest; it is as plain as your old maid aunt with no figure to speak of. It is, however, rapidly taking the place of walnut in the lower-priced, factory-stocked guns and usually is stained to resemble walnut. It is not quite as dense as walnut or maple, but has sufficient strength for light recoil guns. It's biggest attraction to manufacturers seems to be the low price and general availability over a good portion of the United States.

Cherry is another oldtime favorite of stockmakers of the flintlock and percussion period. The wild or "whiskey cherry" is the one used most commonly for gunstocks, for it has quite a dense grain and a reddish-brown color with little or no figure. Cherry stocks seem to have an appealing and attractive appearance of their own and are a good choice for the hobbyist who "wants something a little different" but does not want something exotic. When a good checkering pattern, with perhaps a bit of carving, is added to a cherry stock, the results are sure to bring compliments to the owner.

Myrtlewood, a beautiful native American wood, is found only in northern California and southern Oregon. The wood is extremely close grained, dense and makes up into a stable stock that takes a fine finish and checkers nicely. As to color, it is similar to a golden hue maple, but the wood comes in so many shades that it is hard to tie it to one specific color. Perhaps the most outstanding feature of the wood, besides its density, is the grain structure, which consists of whirls, curls and waves, producing a stock that is quite different and distinctive, since no two pieces of wood are ever alike.

Mahogany is perhaps the most widely distributed hardwood in the world. Mahogany seems to crop up in virtually every country, with just as many variations in color, grain and texture as there are countries. I have seen the color vary from almost a cream white to a deep red-brown; texture varies from something just above balsa wood to almost brick-like hardness. The stock manufacturers select the types that are most like walnut in weight and strength, but generally mahogany will have virtually no figure. In the heavier types it works up into a stable bench target rifle.

Mesquite is a good dense wood from the dry Southwest that has become quite popular in the last few years. In the more inexpensive grades it is mahogany colored with little figure, but in the extra fine grades, the figure is the most striking in appearance of all gunstock woods. The only fly in the ointment is that the more the figure, the more the wood tends to have flaws which must be filled.

Sycamore is an unusual gunstock wood that, only a few years ago, was classed only as a cabinet wood. It is light in weight, but tough enough for most gunstocks except heavy recoiling magnums. The grain is somewhat lace-like with streaks of reddish brown. I received one by mistake in an order a few years ago and was about to return it, when a customer walked in, saw it, and bought it for a rifle he was working on. He used the stock on a .250-3000 rifle for his wife and, after viewing the finished product, I completely changed my mind about sycamore.

The easiest way to describe laminated wood is to compare it to regular plywood. Plywood, as you know, consists of layers of thin sheets of wood glued together to provide a plank which has twice the strength of a regular sawed plank of solid wood. The alternate layers cross each other with the grain at 90-degree angles. Laminated wood is made the same as plywood, except that the grain of each layer runs parallel with the grain of all the other layers and the layers generally are much thicker than those of plywood.

A stock made from such an arrangement of layers avoids the grain stress and strain of regular wood and virtually eliminates warpage. The usual laminated wood stock consists of alternating layers of walnut and maple for an unusual effect. Other woods are used in a similar way to contrast with each other. Some laminations have all of the layers made from the same wood for a more subdued appearance, yet still having the strength and warp-free factors.

There are many other woods floating around that can be made into gunstocks, such as zebra wood, rose wood, vermilion, lace wood and purpleheart. All of these are available from one or more of the stockmakers on special order, but the hobbyist will do well to become better acquainted with the common types before venturing out into the exotic woods.

The final factor in the hobbyist's choice of a semi-

Inletting for the trigger guard with a straight chisel. Note stock is left square.

inletted stock will be the grade of the wood. Grading is not an easy matter, as no two items produced by nature ever are exactly alike. Added to the problem is the manufacturer's desire to sell his product and the dwindling supply of good wood. Each manufacturer has his own standards of grading, and they vary slightly from one another, but their grading of stocks generally fall in the following basic catagories:

Utility is the bottom of the line, but not necessarily a grade to be disregarded, for regardless of the manufacturer, you can be sure that it will be a good serviceable stock. Usually the wood will have minor faults and flaws that will hold it down in classification, such as the presence of white or sap wood, small knot holes or tiny wood cracks that have been filled or repaired. There will be no structural flaws in the wood and, in the hands of a competent stockmaker, utility grade wood can be made into a nice stock. The white wood usually can be darkened by staining and the repaired flaws hidden by bleaching, and varying the amount of finish applied in that section of the stock. Considering the possibility of loss due to inexperience, the utility grade stock is perhaps the best choice for the hobbyist's first attempt at stockmaking.

Standard is the second grade and is a good, plain stock, for it is the one most often encountered by the hobbyist on a dealer's shelf. It consists of a good sound piece of wood with no defects, with a tiny flaw here and there in a few exceptions. These have been repaired and are difficult to detect. Usually, the wood will be straight grain with no white wood or any figure in the grain. Prices in most cases will be around five dollars higher than a stock of the utility grade.

Select sometimes is known as the deluxe or slightly fancy grade, but usually is a dense grade of wood with no structural defects or flaws whatever. The color will be uniform with no white wood and probably will include a small amount of figure in the butt stock.

It is a good selection for the hobbyist who does not want to go into fancy grades, yet wants a stock without flaws or color irregularities. I usually recommend it for a customer who goes to the expense of having a custom rifle built and is more interested in performance than in fancy appearance. The price increase will run about seven dollars above the standard grade, depending on the manufacturer, as some of them break the select grade down into two different grades, according to the amount of figure in the butt section.

There are two fields of thought about stocks. One group maintains that burl, fiddleback and other fancy-grained wood have no place in gunstock, as the structural nature of these will weaken the strength of the stock. This group prefers a good plain straight-grain stock with few pores and uniform color.

The other group prefers stocks with as much figure as they can afford. The fancier the better, and they maintain that, as long as the fancy figure is kept in the butt stock, the material strength of the stock is not affected. I must confess that I side with the second group.

Some manufacturers of stock woods use a series of numbers (No. 4, No. 5, No. 6 grade and so on) to designate the fancy grade while others use letters (A, AA and AAA) for the same purpose. Since the numbers system starts with No. 1 for the utility grade, we will use the A, AA and AAA for our discussion and examples. Prices will vary from one

Here, trigger guard for an M17 Enfield has been cut, straightened and rewelded. It's being tapped into place for fitting, through the use of a non-marring mallet.

An old flare, filled with mineral spirits,
is used to smoke the metal for marking.
Metal surface must be clean, oil-free.
Other materials can be used, as discussed.

Headless stock screws have been installed to
serve as guides. Note marks on wood to show
location of stock holes. Receiver and barrel
have been smoked to show points of contact.

stock manufacturer to another and from blank to blank. For all practical purposes, you can consider a price increase of from five to ten dollars each step up the ladder above the select grade. Extra fancy wood sometimes will exceed even this, with a few special blanks bringing fifty to a hundred dollars above the select grade.

"A" grade stocks have about 50 percent of the butt stock filled with fancy figure grain, the rest of the stock uniform in grain structure and color. The pores of the wood will be small, which means a nice finish with a minimum amount of filling and trouble. The term, "fancy figured grain," can mean virtually any departure from a plain straight grain that is appealing to the eye. The most common are fiddleback, which appears as waves in the stock; feather curl, which is about like fiddleback, except that the waves blend outward in a feathery fashion, and crotch or burl, which resembles a large feathery fan spreading out from some point with different shades of color in the individual feathers that blend and overlap each other.

"AA" grade usually is distinguished from the regular A grade only by the amount of fancy figure in the butt stock which, with most stock manufacturers, will be about 75 percent as opposed to the 50 percent with the A grade.

"AAA" grade is the top of the grading ladder, with each stock an individual blank, especially-selected as the best available from the stock blanks. The fancy figure will be upwards to 100 percent throughout the butt stock and in some cases, a small amount in the forearm which, by the way, should be avoided except in the case of a two-piece stock. The price of the AAA grade varies from blank to blank due to the extremely wide variety of shades, types of figure and location of the figure in the stock.

Most stock manufacturers keep these in the blank form and inlet them to the action specified by the purchaser on receipt of the order. The hobbyist interested in such a stock is far better off to have a gunshop order several of these blanks for eyeball inspection before making the final choice. This can eliminate any misunderstanding as to exactly what is meant by such and such a percent of fancy figure. Most manufacturers require down payment for one blank plus shipping charges both ways, but the money is well spent when you are going up to this grade.

Quite often, one will be the proud possessor of an exceptional piece of wood which he wishes machined into a semi-inletted stock. This is called customer wood. Most stock manufacturers will machine the wood for you to any of their regular designs or to duplicate an existing stock if you can supply the stock to be used as a guide. This is all done at your risk, for if the machining turns up a flaw in the blank it is just "tough luck, Charlie." Price will vary, but usually will be about the same as that for a select grade stock.

Although some of the companies may not offer every one of the types, woods or grades described, they are all available from one or the other. Stock manufacturers offer a wide assortment of designs, ranging from the classic-style stock through the target and semi-target styles, all the way to the real wild designs that look about like something out of Buck Rogers in the 25th century. Mannlicher stocks, pistol grips, racy pistol grips and no grip at all in the English style, plus a variety of butt plates and recoil pads are available. When you add to all this the wide selection of exotic wood forend tips and grip caps available, you have a chance to work out a combination that is quite different from any other stock. The possible choices from all the variations would require a computer to figure. Whatever your taste in design, shape or fittings, the stock manufacturers have it. If this fails to satisfy you, there is always the rough inletted blank with plenty of wood to work out your own ideas.

Get a good selection of catalogs from the stock manufacturers and study them thoroughly before deciding on the exact semi-inletted stock for a project. I would suggest that the hobbyist's first semi-inletted stock be either a utility or standard grade in one of the 90-95 percent types chosen from a manufacturer who machines the wood almost to a ready-to-sand state. The inletting required is minimal with little chance for error. This assures success and acquaints the hobbyist with exactly what is involved in fitting the metal to wood correctly. Once one understands this and gains the feel of the tools, he will be equipped to try his hand at a stock that requires more inletting and shaping.

This is especially true on the outside shaping, as too often the hobbyist will select a stock requiring a lot of shaping, then stop before the job is completed. The end result looks like a club with stock finish on it. As in other phases of gunsmithing, it is best to build your skill and knowledge step by step.

A semi-inletted stock will be a one-piece stock for most rifles, or a two-piece stock for some rifles and most shotguns. Inletting and fitting of metal to wood are basically the same with all stocks, but there is enough difference to cause confusion.

For inletting and shaping a one-piece rifle stock, one needs a few specialized tools along with the common chisels and screwdrivers. It can be done with a pocket knife and a piece of broken glass, but so can an appendectomy!

One of the most useful special tools is a set of headless stock screws for the rifle. These are simply short sections of drill rod threaded on one end to screw into the stock screw holes of the receiver. They are available from most of the stock manufacturers as well as the gunsmith supply houses for about a dollar per set. They act as two guides by sliding down into the stock screw holes in the stock and lining up the receiver and barrel with the stock. In addition to a couple of straight chisels, one needs a barrel channel rasp, a few scrapers and sandpaper, all of which can be bought from the gunsmith supply houses or the stock manufacturers.

To show that the metal is touching the wood, you need some type of dye marker to spread on the metal. This will transfer to the wood when the metal is pressed down against it. Lamp black is perhaps the oldest thing used and is still a good, cheap choice. The smoke and unburned particles cling easily to the metal, provided it has been cleared of all oil and grease, and transfers easily to the wood — yet can be cleaned away rapidly with little effort.

A common candle can be used to provide the lamp black or you can use a regular kerosene lamp, smoke pot or even make one out of a tin can filled with kerosene or mineral spirits and a rag for a wick. There is a special inletting black available from the regular suppliers or the stock manufacturers which consists of an oil black substance that is rubbed on the metal to act as the transfer dip. Prussian Blue is an oil paint available from some art suppliers. This is an old-time favorite because of its bright color, and is applied with either a finger or a small brush. However, Prussian Blue is extremely hard to remove from your hands. Even a little of your wife's lipstick can be used.

The commonly accepted way of getting the metal fitted to the wood is first to inlet and fit the trigger guard to serve as an alignment guide for the barrel and receiver. This is correct when you are going from a blank, but is open to some argument when it comes to fitting a barrel and action to a 90-95 percent semi-inletted stock. I believe most gunsmiths recommend it because it was the way they learned before semi-inletted stocks were available.

To use the trigger-guard-first method, turn the stock belly up and secure it in a padded vise about waist high. If using lamp black to mark the wood, light your smoke pot or candle and hold the trigger guard over the flame where the flame stops and the smoking begins. Coat all of the surface that will come in contact with the wood and, when finished, try to insert the trigger guard into its inletted recess in the stock. Chances are that it will not go all the way in, so tap it with a rawhide mallet lightly, then pull it out.

In the recess in the stock, there should be lamp black everywhere the metal contacted the wood and was stopped by it. With a sharp straight chisel, carefully remove a thin curl of wood at each of the marked points that are colored with the lamp black.

Re-smoke the trigger guard assembly with a new coat of lamp black and try to insert the trigger guard again. Chances are you will have to cut away some more of the marked spots, repeating the process until the trigger guard fits snugly into place at full depth. Take your time and go slowly, removing only a minimum amount of wood each time. It is better to make a dozen tiny cuts than try to do it all at one big whack and end up with a gaping hole where you cut away too much wood.

Once the trigger guard assembly is fitted snugly into its recess, screw the headless stock screws into the receiver, coat the bottom of the receiver with lamp black and slowly ease the action down in place with the headless stock screws going into the stock screw holes and serving as a guide. They should pass through the matching holes in the trigger guard which is left in place once fitted.

Let the receiver touch the wood evenly and tap along the top of the receiver with the rawhide mallet to mark the wood with the lamp black. Ease the receiver out of the stock and you should be able to see where it is binding by the marks left on the wood from the lamp black. With your chisel and a scraper, cut away the marked place, taking only a small amount of wood each time until after repeated fits and cuts the action fits snugly into place. The receiver and barrel must go down into the stock together, so you probably will have to do some scraping up in the barrel channel also. Take your time, for this is the most important part of getting the metal into the stock and no place to try for a speed record.

Keep your cuts and scraping clean and smooth, carrying the lines of the inletting just deeper and wider instead of changing the angles. Too many hobbyists get a little chisel happy and the results look about like a beaver was trapped between receiver and trigger guard and tried to chew his way to freedom. The receiver will bottom on the front at the receiver screw hole and at the rear tang hole, plus up in the barrel channel. The wood should come just about halfway up the barrel and receiver. The top of the magazine box should lack just a red cat's hair coming in contact with the bottom of the receiver. If it bottoms against the receiver, the stock will be too loose and you cannot pull the stock screws up tight for a good snug fit of receiver to wood. The sides, rear and front of the magazine box should not come in contact with the stock, for if they do, they will act as a recoil plate. If they are touching, sand the wood away a small amount to provide clearance all the way around about the thickness of a piece of typewriter paper. The forward recoil lug of the receiver should be touching on its bottom and at its rear only, and the receiver tang should be touching firmly at its rear and bottom. This is the accepted method of fitting the metal to the stock and the one that must be used on all stocks except the 90-95 percent semi-inletted. And it can be used on these, too, if you choose.

A much easier way to get the metal down into the wood is to inlet the barrel and receiver first and the trigger guard last, but only with the 90-95 percent semi-inletted stocks. Install the headless stock screws into the receiver, darken the bottom of the receiver with the lamp black and, using the headless stock screws in the stock screw holes drilled in the stock as your guide, slowly ease the barrel and receiver down evenly until it contacts the wood. Tap the top of the receiver lightly the full length with the rawhide mallet to mark the wood and, when finished, ease the barrel and receiver out of the stock.

It works fine on the 90-95 percent semi-inletted stocks, if everything is where it should be and the trigger guard and screw holes have been inletted in exact alignment with the barrel and action. If not, something has to be adjusted; either the trigger guard or the barrel and action. It is a devil of a lot easier to adjust the position of the trigger guard than it is to try to figure out how to cut the barrel and receiver inletting off to one side when you have a limited supply of wood left on the stock. Gunsmiths who use a lot of 90-95 percent semi-inletted stocks soon figure out that it is easier to inlet the barrel and action down into the wood, first, then inlet the trigger guard. But, since the barrel-and-action-first method can only be used on the 90-95 percent stocks, let's understand both.

With the chisel and scraper, carefully remove the darkened portions of the wood that are keeping the barrel and receiver from going down into place. Several tries probably will have to be made before the receiver slides into position. It should bottom firmly on the inletted portions at the tang and forward locking plate on the receiver. No additional wood should be removed on the bottom where the receiver fits, for it will throw the depth out of kilter.

Next, the trigger guard is inletted, using the headless stock screws in the receiver — which is left in place in the stock — as a guide to keep it straight. It may be necessary to inlet the trigger guard a little deeper for proper alignment and spacing with the receiver. Be sure the magazine box is not serving as a recoil plate and clear it if it is. If the top inletted section is out of alignment with the inletted trigger guard recess, you usually can cut away enough around the trigger guard to get it back in line and fill any gap with glass bedding material.

This is the superior system over the trigger-guard-first method described earlier. Try the barrel-and-receiver method on your first attempt at stock fitting. It is just a lot faster and simpler on the 90-95 percent semi-inletted stocks.

Regardless of which method you choose, the final step is fitting the barrel to the barrel channel in a way that will deliver good accuracy and the fit of barrel to barrel channel is extremely important in this. There are three different ways to fit a barrel. The oldest way, which some stockmakers swear by, is to fit the barrel free of the channel from the receiver out to within about two inches of the end of the forearm. The barrel does not touch the wood the full length of the barrel channel, except at the tip. Here it fits snugly on all sides and the bottom for a firm bearing pressure.

This pressure is usually around two pounds and can be determined in several ways. The simplest is to hold the rifle upside down while it is in the stock and hang a three-pound weight on the barrel at the forend. With this weight pulling down on the barrel, the barrel should not touch the wood nor should it touch when you substitute a 2½-pound weight. But when a two-pound weight is hung on the barrel, the barrel should touch the wood firmly. This all seems a lot of trouble, for the two-pound bearing pressure is just a start and you usually will have to adjust the final pressure through a shoot-and-try method.

The second and easiest way to fit the barrel is simply to free-float the barrel the whole way, relieving the wood until the barrel is not touching the forend at any point. This does not mean to hack away until you have room enough for a snake to crawl under, but leaving enough clearance between the barrel and channel to allow a single piece of typewriter paper to slide under from the end of the forearm back to the receiver.

There has been a lot of controversy about free-floating a barrel, some contending it is the greatest thing since the invention of the wheel, while others term it an idiot's delight. The free-floating barrel, in my opinion, is at its best when used with heavier rather than standard weight barrels, such as a medium weight varminter, target barrel. In a standard weight barrel, the free-floating method will produce excellent results, usually better than the shooter is capable of backing up.

To achieve the free-floating barrel, it is necessary to coat the underside of the barrel with lamp black, install the barrel and receiver into the stock and tap along the top of the barrel with the rawhide hammer to mark the bearing points on the wood. Remove the metal components straight up, taking care not to wiggle the barrel and incorrectly mark the wood. Scrape away all sections of wood in the barrel channel that show the lamp black marks. The scraping can be done with either a round-nose barrel scraper or barrel channel rasp, but keep the lines and curves constant. Keep repeating this until the barrel no longer touches the wood when receiver and barrel are inserted into the stock. Carefully sand the barrel channel from end to end, until you can slip a thicknesses of typewriter paper between the barrel and stock from the forend back to the receiver. Any additional clearance is unnecessary and will only serve as a catch-all for trash, sticks and twigs, as well as looking bad.

Smoked receiver is tapped in place, then it's removed. Transfer or marking pigment shows points of contact, here being scraped clear.

With inletting completed, it's time to commence shaping the stock. It's surprising how effective a good plane can be at removing the excess wood.

The third method — and the one I prefer — is to glass bed the barrel channel from forend tip to receiver. Some stockmakers use glass bedding in the action area only, while others use it in the barrel channel only. Still others recommend glass bedding the entire metal bearing area from tang to tip of forend. I advocate full glass bedding, this opinion based on years of experience with all three methods while trying to satisfy the public. Many so-called experts look down their noses at any gunsmith who uses glass bedding, claiming that it is the tool of a sloppy workman. From talking to these self-styled experts, I have come to the conclusion that 99 percent of them have never fitted even an axe handle, much less a gun stock!

To convince yourself of what glass bedding will do, mix up a small batch and coat one end of a test block of walnut about the size of a common brick, then allow it to set up and cure. Give both ends of the block, both the coated end and the natural end, a good whack with a heavy hammer. On the natural end you will see that the blow has compressed the wood and the ends of the grain gives way under the force, while the glassed end will show no compression at all. Considering that the average high-powered rifle delivers a minimum of twenty-five foot-pounds of recoil, with some of the big magnums delivering much more, it is obvious this repeated pounding from this recoil will compress the unprotected wood in the stock to the point that the fit of metal to wood is loosened or the stock splits or chips.

Next time one of the experts condemns glass bedding, ask him to make a simple test with you and take all of the bets he wishes to make. Place the butt of your fully glass-bedded stock against a tree and fire the gun. If the glass bedding job has been done correctly, the stock will not be affected. Ask the expert to do the same with his pet non-glassed rifle and watch him pick up the splinters and pieces, if he is fool enough to try it.

This is not a recommended procedure with any gun, but it does illustrate the protection and strength of full glass bedding. Most firearm manufacturers now use glass in one way or another, especially on the heavy recoil rifles.

In addition to protecting against recoil compression, glass bedding provides the closest possible fit of wood to metal. The finest stockmakers cannot inlet a stock as close as can be achieved with correct glass bedding. In fact, you can scratch your initials on the bottom of the receiver or barrel and they will be faithfully reproduced in reverse in the glass bedding! A glass bedded stock will be so close and tight that you have to wiggle the metal back and forth to slide it out of the stock, about like a fat lady getting out of a tight girdle. An additional advantage is that the glass seals off the wood completely on the inside from all moisture and oil that can cause warpage. Up in a glass-bedded barrel channel there is perfect contact with equalized pressure on sides and bottom, plus a strengthened forend to resist warpage.

Several types of glass bedding are on the market but most consist of three ingredients: a resin, a hardener and the glass floc. When the resin and hardner are mixed in correct proportion, a chemical reaction takes place that turns both liquids into a hard epoxy plastic. To give the plastic strength, the floc, which is simply specially chopped glass fibers, is added to the mixture before it starts to set up, then becomes bonded within the plastic once it hardens.

The ground glass is used instead of the usual cloth associated with fiberglass to allow the glass bedding to flow into cracks and crevices. The glass cloth has little use in stock work except in a few special instances, such as the forearm of a shotgun for strength. This is used by Reming-

ton in the Model 1100 forend.

The material designed for gun work is far superior to that obtained at boat building companies or auto repair sources. Glass bedding usually starts to set up in less than fifteen minutes and must it be in place prior to the start of the chemical reaction. If the manufacturer specifies 11 minutes, he does not mean 11½ minutes. Any time you are using glass bedding, I strongly urge reading and re-reading the instructions. Completely understand them before you start mixing the ingredients.

Glass bedding material is a type of epoxy and, like epoxy, it will stick to any surface, be it hide, steel or wood So, to prevent bonding of the metal parts of the rifle to the wood, it is necessary to coat the metal with a release agent which prevents the glass from sticking to the metal. Most glass bedding kits include a release agent, but even then you occasionally run short. Regular paste floor wax, heated and applied with a brush, will work as well.

Mixed by themselves, the resin, hardener and glass floc are crystal color. To make it blend in with the wood, a coloring agent must be added to the mixture. This also comes with most kits. When first mixed, the glass bedding has the consistency of thick syrup and will flow into the tiniest cracks; this can serve as a lock, binding metal to wood even though you have coated the metal with release agent. Modeling clay can be pressed into the nooks and cracks to prevent this and removed after the glass bedding has hardened.

To illustrate, a customer walked into the shop one day and asked if I knew anything about glass bedding. He had a small problem in that the metal could not be removed from a stock he had glass bedded. The rifle from the outside looked perfect, but the metal would not budge a fraction of an inch, regardless of where and how much pressure was applied. I asked if he had used the release agent on the metal and plugged all holes with modeling clay. His reply was, "What is release agent?"

His next question was how could he get the wood off the metal. I answered him by asking if he had a good pocket knife and when he said that he did, I gave him the only possible answer. "Start whittling it off."

After you have been glass bedding for a time, you can glass the entire receiver section and barrel channel at one whack, but until you are thoroughly familiar with the process and have your timing down correct, I urge you to make it a two-step operation. Glass bed the receiver first and, when this has set up and cured, glass bed the barrel channel. The key areas in the receiver are behind and under the recoil lug and around and under the rear tang. To assure a good thickness of glass at these key bearing points, cut away a small amount of wood until a piece of cardboard backing off a check book still can be pressed between the metal and the wood when the metal has been pulled up tight with the stock screws.

The holes through the stock for the trigger guard screws can be strengthened by boring them slightly larger, about half depth. When the glass bedding flows down into this enlarged recess and hardens, it forms a sort of glass bushing for the screws. The trigger guard also can be glass bedded if you wish, although this is not necessary. The area around the magazine box can be glass bedded or left free, but if you choose to glass bed it, you must take steps to prevent the magazine from acting as a recoil plate. To do this, remove enough wood around the magazine so that a check book cardboard will pass around it, then wrap two layers of electrician's tape around the magazine box itself and coat with release agent. The tape acts as a spacer and, when removed after the glass has hardened, there will be sufficient clearance between the magazine and the glassed wood.

Final preparation before applying the glass bedding material is to rough-up the wood surface to assure good bonding. This can be done with rough sandpaper, but I use a small dental burr in a Moto-Tool. The burr is pressed into the wood about 1/64th of an inch at all angles, pock-marking the entire wood surface that will receive the glass bedding.

Mix up the glass bedding material exactly to the manufacturer's instructions, paying particular attention to the time element. Stir the recommended time, but do not overdo it, for excess stirring will cause bubbles to form in the material. These appear in the glass bedding material after it has hardened and will result in a sloppy job.

Pour the bedding material into the inletting where desired and push it into all corners and crevices with a small wooden paddle. Now ease the release agent coated metal down into the wood and seat firmly in place. Install the trigger guard and pull the trigger guard screws up relatively tight. The regular trigger guard screws can be used, but the best way is to use stockmaker's hand screws. These are especially-made long stock screws, with a cross T handle for better control and to eliminate the use of a screwdriver. They are available from the stock manufacturers and gunsmith supply houses. But don't forget to coat them with release agent!

When the glass starts to harden, it will generate a small amount of heat and expand slightly, pushing some of the glass out of the stock. Wipe this off with a wooden paddle or similar tool, to prevent it from flowing down on the wood. There is no need to heat the stock in any way, as the glass bedding material cures by chemical action instead of temperature. Wait about half an hour and loosen the trigger guard screws or stockmakers hand screws to be sure they are free, then retighten them. Leave the stock overnight for complete curing of the glass bedding. Next day, remove the stock screws part way and tap on their bottom to break the receiver free of the glass bedding. It also helps to tap the top of the receiver with the rawhide mallet while doing this.

Ease the metal free of the glass bedding, removing the stock screws in the process. A certain amount of rocking back and forth may be necessary to free the receiver completely from its new bed. You probably will have to trim the top of the receiver slightly to remove any overhang of excess glass bedding.

The next step is to glass bed the barrel channel which, with a couple of exceptions, is done exactly the same as glassing the receiver. Be sure the receiver slips in and out of the stock fairly easily before doing anything else. The barrel channel must be relieved enough from the forend tip back to the receiver for a piece of cardboard to slide from one end to the other. Use that same piece of cardboard from the back of your check book or something of the same thickness for a gauge. You can relieve it more than this if you wish, but it is not necessary and just requires more bedding material to fill up the recess.

Rough-up the wood in the barrel channel the same way you did the wood in the receiver to assure good bonding. In addition, to lock the new glass bedding material to that already hardened in the receiver section, rough-up that part of the glass bedding that will come in contact with the new material you will be putting in the barrel channel.

I use the dental burr in the Moto-Tool for this, drilling holes into the hardened glass bedding fairly deeply and regularly over the entire section that will be joined. Don't forget to coat the underside and sides of the barrel with release agent! If your stock has a hole for a sling swivel through it in the barrel channel, it is best to plug this hole with modeling clay for removal of the sling swivel if the need should ever arise. Otherwise the glass will make a cap over it and prevent any future removal without drilling.

Apply glass bedding material to the barrel channel, spreading it evenly full length, then slip the barrel and receiver into place. Pull the receiver up tight with the stockmaker's hand screws and wipe away any excess glass bedding that is pushed out by the barrel, taking its place in the channel. Allow the stock to set overnight before removing the barrel from the new glass bed.

When you have completed the glass bedding, wipe the release agent from the metal and remove the modeling clay that has filled the holes and crannies. Some of the glass undoubtedly will have flowed over the sides and become stuck to the outside of the stock. The overflow must be removed with a metal file!

After you have glass bedded a few rifles, you may choose to do both the receiver and barrel channel at the same time, but this should never be attempted on the first few tries. I am sure that the more you use glass, the more you will be convinced that it is a tool in the stockmaker's trade that can make a good stock even better.

Glass bedding material has 1001 other uses around a shop, such as smearing some on the ends of your stock chisels to prevent the ends from splitting when you are striking them with a mallet; using it to fit a new handle to a

A good stockmaker's rasp takes over when the plane can do no more. Note the center line that has been laid out on top of the stock as a guide.

The cheek piece is laid out with a series of flat and half-round chisels. Home made grip cap is salvaged from an old horn butt plate in this case.

hammer and so on.

On stocks — both new and old — glass bedding material can solve a lot of problems, such as replacing chipped portions inside a stock, retightening loose stocks and reinforcing stocks that have been cracked or split. It works fine as a method of tightening wood screws, for all that is necessary is to coat the screw with release agent, pour in some glass bedding material and push the screw in place. When hard, the glass bedding will have made a perfect female thread for the screw, allowing the screw to be pulled up as tight as desired. Time and need will teach you its many uses.

When inletting has been finished and the stock glass bedded — if you chose glass bedding — you can turn your attention to finishing the outside of the stock. The amount of work necessary will depend on which manufacturer you chose, but there should be little to do except a few careful strokes with the wood rasps and a little scraping here and there. Old metal files that have outlived their usefulness on metal are useful in the final finishing of the outside just before sanding. Several good photos of completed stocks are handy in keeping you straight on which way the lines should flow, and so forth. Take your time and remember to keep the stock lines flowing rather than being blunted off or allowed to wander here and there.

Once final shaping has been completed and all rough chisel and rasp marks removed by scraping and using the old metal files, you can go to the task of sanding the stock.

The complete method of sanding, filling and finishing has been covered in another chapter. But whatever you do, be sure that you have thoroughly and completely sanded the stock until all marks and scratches have been removed. The stock must be as slick as a peeled onion before any filling and finishing is attempted.

Inletting and shaping a two-piece shotgun stock is almost identical in method to work used on a two-piece rifle stock, with variations as needed for the different models. Being in two pieces, the stock is not as strong as a one-piece stock and therefore requires that fitting and inletting be as close as possible to allow the stock and forend to be pulled up tight against the metal. The separate butt stock will be held to the receiver either with a vertical screw from the top tang, through the stock and into the bottom tang or trigger guard or by a butt stock screw running horizontal from the rear of the stock to the back of the receiver, pulling the stock tight against the receiver.

The horizontal butt stock screw is the more common of the two and the easier to fit, as all that is required is to install the screw and start pulling the semi-inletted stock to the receiver by turning the screw. Usually, the rear of the receiver will be recessed to accept the stock and you probably will have to do some light inletting and fitting only to obtain a snug fit. Lamp black on the rear of the receiver will show you where the wood must be relieved. You can use glass bedding material for a better fit by fitting the butt stock, backing off slightly, then lightly coating the end of

A metal scraper works well to give the final shape to the cheek piece. It's also handy for straightening out any waves or dips in surface.

the stock with the glass bedding material. Do not pull the stock up tight; instead, leave a little slack and make the final tight pull-up after the glass bedding has hardened. Don't forget to coat the metal with the release agent! After the glass has cured, shape the outside for a good fit of metal to wood, but it is best to leave just a tiny bit of wood overhang to prevent splitting.

The vertical butt stock screw is a bit more involved in that the hole must be drilled in the exact position to provide a forward push to the stock, when it is pulled up tight by the screw in the hole. Sometimes, after a lot of shooting, one of these holes will become egg-shaped to allow the stock to slide back and forth and no amount of tightening of the vertical screw will solve the problem. The best way to fit the new hole or to repair the old sloppy hole is simply to drill it oversize and use glass bedding material in the hole to form a glass bushing around the screw. Again, be sure to coat all metal with the release agent, especially the screw itself.

With the glass bedding material in place and the screw pulled up tight, use a clamp to push the stock forward against the back of the receiver while the glass bedding material is setting up hard. When cured and the clamp is removed, disassemble the gun and clean away the release agent.

The stock will fit solidly against the back of the receiver, but for added insurance, lightly coat the end of the stock with glass bedding material to prevent compression of the wood during recoil and further prevent loosening of the butt stock.

Perhaps one of the greatest causes of a stock splitting is a rough metal surface on the rear of the receiver where the stock bears. This is especially true in shotgun receivers that are cast and machined, as often a small metal tit is left that bears against the stock and acts exactly like a small chisel. The recoil from firing hammers the action against the chisel and splits the stock. It only takes a small spur of metal in the right place to completely ruin a good butt stock, so check the rear of the receiver every time you install a new stock and file or grind away any such protrusion.

trusion.

Another common fault is with butt stocks that do not bear completely on all points against the metal. This puts pressure on a small section of wood instead of distributing it equally over the entire area. A split stock can be prevented by using lamp black to check the bearing points, then relieving the wood until the stock end is bearing evenly over its entire area. Glass bedding the end of the stock also will eliminate this and prevent wood compression.

Most semi-inletted separate forends are cut to almost a perfect fit without need for additional inletting, but occasionally you encounter one that looks like the workman went to sleep while turning and machining it. Lamp black on metal is the way to assure a good close fit. Most pump and semi-automatic shotgun forends will offer few problems, except on guns where the forend positions the barrel and breech block. This is found in the Browning five-shot automatic and similar guns.

On these, the forend must be inletted just the right amount to position the barrel, breech block and receiver in relation to each other for correct function. If the forend is inletted too long, the barrel is held too far to the rear and the gun will not fire. If it is inletted too short, the barrel and breech block go too far forward to cause extraction and feed problems. The best method is to take a good look at the alignment on a similar gun and cut and inlet the forend to achieve the same relationships. It is a good idea to work the barrel and action by hand several times to be sure the barrel lug is not bearing on one tiny spot and causing an incorrect alignment.

Finally, be sure the forend is fitting against the front of the receiver correctly to prevent any splitting. On pumps, the forend usually is held between two caps on the slide arm and must be trimmed and adjusted to allow the caps to pull up, securing the wood to the slide arm. All that remains is a small amount of shaping and sanding before the forend is ready for the filling and finish.

Semi-inletted pistol grips often are overlooked, as few hobbyists realize that several manufacturers offer semi-

A Dremel Moto-Tool is being used here to cut the bolt handle recess. Again, the metal is smoked to mark contacts for to be inletted.

Metal files such as this one, too worn for use on steel, still work well for finishing touches in shaping the stock without raising splinters.

Sanding is the final step before applying filler
and finish. Wooden blocks of appropriate size
and ever-finer grades of sandpaper are used.

inletted pistol grips in addition to their regular line of semi-inletted rifle and shotgun stocks. Several more specialize in nothing but pistol grips. The small amount of wood needed for a set of pistol grips allows pieces of wood otherwise too small for rifle or shotgun stocks to be put to good use and some of these contain beautiful fancy figure. The semi-inletted pistol grips offer those with even the simplest tools and limited work area an opportunity to build a set of grips to his own ideas. Semi-inletted pistol grips come in three basic types: factory replacement, combat style and full target style.

The factory replacement type usually is closely inletted and almost completely shaped on the outside, with little remaining for the hobbyist to do except for careful rasping and scraping before sanding. Many of the older handguns, such as the cap and ball revolvers, will be found with split grips, are oil soaked or otherwise unserviceable, even as a collector's item. Replacement grips in the factory style provide the answer, since they have just enough wood left to assure a good close fit and contouring to match the variations found in these guns. Modern factory replacement types in the exotic woods can turn a standard handgun into one that will stand out in any crowd with a minimum of labor.

Combat-type semi-inletted grips generally are of the wrap-around style that completely enclose the metal frame of the handgun, with sufficient wood left for shaping to fit the individual hand. Practically no additional inletting will be required inside except for careful scraping. If you are unlucky enough to get a pair that have been inletted too much, coat the metal with release agent, fill the space between the frame with wood and modeling clay and use glass bedding material to get a close fit.

Full target grips are the combat type with more wood left on the outside for shaping. A general outline of a target grip will be machined on the outside, but you have to do the majority of the shaping with rasp and scraper, plus a little chisel and knife work.

The ideal fit of the combat or target grips is to have the wood shaped exactly to the contour of your hand, filling the voids between your palm and fingers. Arriving at this skin-tight contouring is a bit difficult, unless you have a model to go by.

The simplest way is to use the old grips as a model, adding plastic wood on their outsides, grasping the grips in your hand and adding or taking away plastic wood, until the fit is perfect. After the plastic wood has dried, shoot the handgun several times and note any pinching of the hand or any gaps left where the plastic wood has shifted during application. Rasp away the pinching sections and add additional plastic wood where needed, until the fit is absolutely perfect.

Now transfer these dimensions to your semi-inletted grips with the use of outside calipers, cutting away the semi-inletted grips as needed. When the semi-inletted grips are about right, make a final check with your calipers and cut the last fraction of an inch on the grips themselves, until they feel like a part of your hand. All that remains is the final sanding, filling and applying the finish.

Installing semi-inletted stocks — be they for rifle, shotgun or handgun — offers many enjoyable hours with only a small outlay for tools and equipment. The finished stock can turn out to be a modified baseball bat or a thing of beauty, depending entirely on skill, determination and patience.

Chapter 19

A MATTER OF CUSTOM

The Little Things Even The Amateur Can Accomplish Do Much To Make A Gun A Personal Thing!

NO GROUP OF AMERICANS is more freedom-loving or has more rugged individuals than gun enthusiasts, which perhaps explains the tremendous appeal of the custom-built gun. Maybe there are other reasons or explanations, but I do not think they are strong enough by themselves to drive the gun enthusiast to the point that he pays 200 percent or more above the cost of a factory gun to have one custom-built to his own ideas and tastes. Give a gun enthusiast the financial means and it is just a matter of time before he owns a custom-built gun!

The largest hurdle for most enthusiasts to overcome is the expense and they usually attempt to get around this by doing some of the work on the guns themselves. The hobby gunsmith with a modestly equipped gunshop and a lot of determination can custom-build a gun at considerable savings. The actual amount of savings depends, of course, on how much of the work he can do himself and how much he has to farm out to the professional gunsmith. The price also will go up and down like a yo-yo, depending on what type of gun he wants to build and what accessories he wants to add. There are no hard and fast rules on a custom-built gun as, obviously, they are one of a kind. There are, however, certain basic things that must be done and certain basic procedures to follow, so we will concern ourselves with these and leave the frills to the individual taste.

A custom gun can mean a handgun, a shotgun or a rifle, but most hobbyists immediately think of a custom rifle. The Model 98 Mauser has long been a favorite to "customize." Before beginning, let me explain that the two terms, "action" and "receiver," are often used interchangeably. For our purposes in this chapter the term "action" will mean the entire functioning part of the rifle while the term "receiver" will specify only the upper part of the action into which the barrel is screwed.

While a few available 98 Mausers will be the old World War I long barrel rifles, the majority will be the new short barrel version so familiar in World War II, of which there seems to be an inexhaustible supply. I do not have the exact data available, but I can think of half a dozen countries that have manufactured the M98 actions at one time or another.

Most of these actions will be of good quality and gener-

ally can be considered safe for any reasonable conversion. One exception involves the rifles made during the last months of World War II, when the Nazi's had their backs against the wall and the arms were being made almost exclusively by slave labor. If you have any doubt as to the strength of a particular Mauser action, it is best to have it checked by a professional gunsmith who has rebarreled a few and is qualified to pass judgment on the action.

Once the safety of the action has been established, your first decision will be whether to leave the original barrel on the action or rebarrel to another caliber. The M98 action has been made in quite a few calibers, with the 7.9x57mm Mauser cartridge the most common. This is an excellent caliber, both in performance and availability of ammunition, but even the M98's made in relatively unknown calibers often can be utilized for sporting purposes. One will do well to check availability of ammunition in these calibers and also explore the possibility of handloading, for many of these calibers come close in performance to matching the so-called red-hot magnums that the ammunition companies rave about.

Provided you can find available ammunition, the next step is to decide whether the barrel is good enough to deliver accuracy that is acceptable; the best way to do this is to shoot a few groups and examine the results.

If both the availability of ammunition and the accuracy of the barrel are on the plus side, you may decide to use the barrel already on the action and sporterize the appearance. Most Mauser barrels are turned in a series of steps that give the initial impression of being a manufacturing shortcut. Actually, the steps are positioned at certain vibration points of the barrel and act as a damper to lessen the vibrations, thereby stabilizing the barrel and increasing the accuracy. This works exceptionally well in increasing accuracy, but leaves much to be desired in the appearance department.

Almost immediately the hobbyist decides that he can fix this up fine by turning the steps out of the barrel on a lathe and contouring it to match a modern sporter barrel. He soon learns that this just cannot be done, for the steps of the barrel are roughly parallel, making it impossible to completely eliminate them on the lathe. It is possible to cut the steps down somewhat, blending them into the lines of the

At top is author's personal turkey rifle converted from 310 Martini Cadet action. Every part was stoned smooth and the operating handle redesigned. It's in .22 Hornet. Beneath is original Cadet for the sake of comparison.

barrel and making them less apparent when viewed from the side, but it is impossible to turn them out completely. The barrel then can be cut and crowned, sights installed and so forth, for a nice inexpensive sporter.

If, on the other hand, you decide to rebarrel the action to another caliber, you should give this some careful thought. Too often, hobbyists rush into rebarreling without the proper equipment, gauges and knowledge. There is no great secret to the process, but I recommend you have your first one done by a professional gunsmith and ask him to allow you to watch the process. Read everything you can lay your hands on about rebarreling and ask the professional to clarify any point that you do not understand. After you have completed your first job, have it checked by the professional before you test fire it.

The M98 action will accept a wide range of cartridges similar to the original cartridge and many others with certain modifications to the bolt, guide rails and so on. Leave the exotic alterations for a later date, when you are thoroughly familiar with standard rebarreling. Maybe I'm overly safety conscious, but rebarreling involves the containing of pressures that often exceed 50,000 pounds per square inch and that is a formidable task not for the beginner.

With the barrel question settled, the next major item to consider is what sights are to be installed, as this will be a big factor in determining the overall cost of the gun, especially if you are going to a scope. You can leave the old sights in place if you are using the original barrel, but military sights leave a lot to be desired for sporting purposes.

The least expensive new sights will be a set of open sights, such as the Williams Guide Open Sight or perhaps a folding leaf sight on an adapter base and a simple ramp front sight. The next choice is a ramp front sight and a receiver sight. Either of these choices will involve the installation of the sights only and no additional action alterations will be necessary.

If you decide on a scope, the military M98 action has a raised section on the rear bridge that is designed to support the cartridge stripper clip. A few one-piece scope bases are ground to fit over this raised section, but if you are planning on using the less expensive two-piece bases, it will be necessary to grind this raised portion down to provide enough room for the rear base.

The cutting-down operation is best done in a milling machine, but a good job can be done by first rough grinding the excess metal away, then finishing up with careful filing. Pay particular attention to keeping the rear bridge level as you shape it and continue the existing lines of the lower section of the rear bridge.

When you have finished, check the reshaped area with a straight edge to assure that your filing has been smooth, then drill and tap both the front and rear of the receiver for the scope sight bases. Fit the bases to the receiver, level and cross-level the rifle in a vise. Lay the level cross-ways of the rear scope base and check to see if your filing and reshaping have been done correctly.

If the rear base is not level you have goofed, but all is not lost. Notice which side of the base is highest and remove level and base. Now, carefully file away the higher side, taking care to keep your cut level and all on the high side. Re-install the rear base and again check it with the level. In severe cases it will be necessary to repeat this a couple of times before you have the base sitting level and matching the front one.

Once the front and rear bases are level, remove the rear base and notice the portion of the receiver just in front of the rear scope base that served as the lower part of the cartridge guide. This can be left as is, but to add that little final touch to reshaping the rear bridge, hold a file vertically and cut away the little tits of metal in the cartridge guide. Once these are cut away, you will have a square-shaped cut

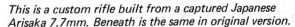

This is a custom rifle built from a captured Japanese Arisaka 7.7mm. Beneath is the same in original version.

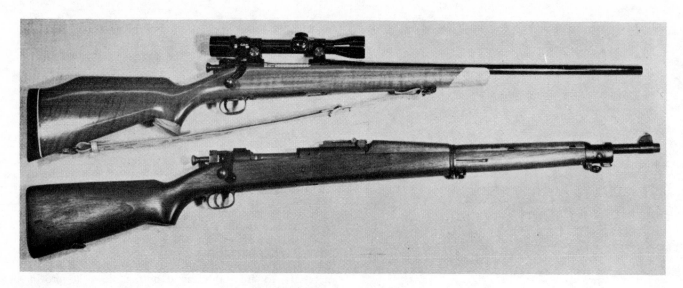

The old familiar Model 1903 Springfield has been taken out of its battle dress and groomed for civilian use.

at the bridge that enhances the appearance of the receiver. Re-install the scope bases, fit the scope mount and attach the scope.

When the scope is in place, ease the bolt forward and you will notice that the bolt handle will not clear the rear eyepiece of the scope. It will be necessary to rehape the bolt handle to provide the needed clearance. If you are in a hurry, you can simply grind away at the bolt until you get the needed clearance, but the results will be about as attractive as a wart on a hog.

A better way is to use a set of forging blocks to reshape the handle. The blocks support the bolt while it is heated and the handle pounded and forged to give the needed clearance and to reshape it to a more pleasing line. The forging blocks are available from most supply houses. I have always disliked this approach, as it requires extensive heat in the bolt handle area, plus a lot of pounding in the forging process. This can damage the bolt, if proper precautions are not taken.

I prefer the graceful lines of a new bolt handle welded onto the bolt to take the place of the old handle. The old handle is hacksawed or ground off approximately 3/8 inch from the bolt body. The new streamlined bolt handles are available from the gunsmith supply houses in plain, knurled or knurled with a hollow knob. You can support the bolt body and new handle on a couple of bricks while you are welding, but this is doing it the hard way. Brownell's offers a simple bolt welding jig that pays for itself on the first job, as it holds everything in perfect alignment while the welding is being done.

Once the new bolt handle has been welded on it is allowed to cool, removed from the jig and ground and shaped with files, with a final pass or two against the polishing wheel to match its smoothness to that of the bolt body. If you have welding facilities, the entire job will take about an hour. In case you do not have these facilities, your local gunshop or even a competent welder can do it, provided you make sure that the welder wraps the bolt locking lugs with wet cloth during the welding. You can save a little on cost if you have the gunsmith or welder leave all of the grinding and shaping to you. Regular welding rod can be used, but I recommend that you buy a small pack of 3.5 percent nickel steel rod instead, as this rod virtually eliminates blow holes in the weld and assures a smooth finish of the welded section.

The original safety will work fine if open or receiver sights are to be installed, but if you choose to go to a scope, it will be necessary to replace the military safety, which will strike the scope before it engages the striker sufficiently to lock it in place. A special safety such as the Buehler must be installed in place of the original. These safeties are designed to engage and lock the striker, while the lever of the safety is still away from the scope body enough to allow it to be manipulated with the thumb. Another way is to install one of the special-built adjustable triggers that includes a built-in safety. The old safety can be left in place or a plug made and soldered in its place. Regardless of the gun, my choice of safeties is always one that locks the striker instead of only blocking the trigger.

The military trigger can be left intact without modification, but it consists of a long, two-stage pull that was designed for safety in a military rifle that would be

It may be difficult to recognize, but this is the British SMLE rifle, which has been rebuilt into a brush gun.

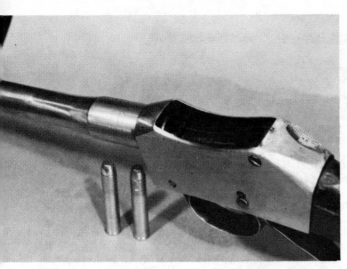

At the time photo was taken, this Big Martini action was being turned into a custom big bore for the .444 Marlin.

subjected to rough treatment. The best solution is to install one of the special-built triggers as a complete replacement to get a clean, crisp adjustable pull. Most will require only removing the original trigger and replacing it with the new trigger without any additional alterations. If you are pressed for cash, you can rework the original trigger, taking out the two-stage pull and providing a trigger stop to eliminate movement of the trigger after the sear has been released.

For this, you will need two small screws, two nuts and two short coil springs. The first nut is silver soldered to the trigger directly in front where there is a small bar. The short coil spring is inserted on the screw and the screw inserted into the nut. Re-install the trigger and bolt assembly. With the gun cocked, tighten the screw until it presses the trigger down enough to fire the gun. Back off two complete turns on the screw and re-cock the gun.

This time, pull the trigger by hand and you should have a nice crisp pull without the two-stage pull. It may be necessary to shorten the screw slightly, as the short coil spring must be under pressure between the head of the screw and the nut in order to maintain the setting of the screw. The second screw is placed in front of the sear bar by silver-soldering the nut to the bar. As the trigger is pulled, the rear of the sear bar moves down while the front of the bar moves up.

By placing the second screw in front of the bar and adjusting it all the way in, trying to pull the trigger, backing off one turn and so on, you will arrive at a setting that allows the trigger to pull enough to release the sear. It also prevents any further backward movement of the trigger and acts as a trigger stop. When these two screws are installled correctly and the sear honed for smoothness, you will have a nice sporter trigger pull, but be sure that the screws are not turned in far enough to limit the amount of sear engagement. I usually check for this by whacking the muzzle of the barrel a couple of times with a rawhide mallet to see if I can jar the sear enough to cause it to release.

There are several other small modifications that can be made on the M98 action to add to appearance or smoother operation. For instance, the cartridge follower is square on the back to engage the face of the bolt when the magazine is empty. This was added to the military rifle to serve notice that the magazine was empty and prevent an excited soldier from working the bolt and assuming that the rifle was loaded in the heat of battle. It is a small nuisance on a

sporting rifle, since it requires depressing the cartridge follower with your finger in order to close the bolt on the empty magazine. You can eliminate this feature by grinding the rear of the cartridge follower to a gentle slope and polishing it to allow the bolt to ride over the follower without need of depressing it with the finger. Any angle from about 45 to 30 degrees can be used, but be sure to polish the new-ground angle, rounding all edges.

Another nice alteration of the receiver is to reshape the bolt release which is found on the left side of the receiver. Remove the release from the receiver and file away the small extended top lip until the release is level on top. Polish the top and the sides. To provide a finger grip on the release, secure it in your vise with the forward end of the release vertical and, with a metal checkering file, checker this end, bringing the metal diamonds up to a point with a three-cornered file. Finish by squaring up the release screw head. It is surprising how this simple modification affects the appearance of the receiver.

Flip the action over and take a good look at the trigger guard and floor plate assembly. This is a section of the action that can be altered easily and reshaped to make the action truly custom. The flat military trigger guard was made to protect the trigger against any and all blows, including pounding the enemy over the head, but it is not very attractive. You can regrind the trigger guard in a teardrop shape similar to the one found on most sporting rifles and finish up by filing and polishing the guard.

If you really want to go whole hog in changing the appearance of the trigger guard, cut the original guard off completely, flush with the bottom and attach a single barrel shotgun trigger guard by welding, silver soldering or a screw. Check with new trigger guard to be sure that it does not touch the trigger in any position.

The floor plate on most military M98 actions is held in place by a simple catch arrangement that releases the floor plate when the catch is depressed with the nose of a bullet and the floor plate pushed forward. To sporterize this, B-Square offers a simple button arrangement that replaces the catch and allows quick removal of the floor plate by thumb pressure on the button. If you wish, you can weld a hinge to the floor plate and trigger guard frame and make the floor plate permanently attached with the release either in the form of a button or lever. Also, there is a cast aluminum floor plate available that is engraved with a game scene that simply replaces the original floor plate or is part of an entire new aluminum trigger guard assembly shaped to sporter lines.

Most M98 actions use a small lock screw in addition to the regular front and rear stock screws that attach the floor plate and trigger guard to the rest of the receiver. This is fine on a rifle for military use, but is of no practical advantage on a sporter rifle and detracts from its appearance. You can eliminate this by welding up the lock screw holes, redrilling the main hole and buying a set of solid-head stock screws. Most who do this go at it the hard way by welding up the hole and filing and reshaping. The easy way is simply to screw the lock screw in place with the half moon cut of the lock screw lined up with the main hole, then just weld the screw in place. This eliminates a lot of grinding and reshaping of the main hole and makes the welding much easier to accomplish with a minimum amount of rod melting to fill the hole. The original stock screws also can be welded on the head, recut to shape in the lathe and a new screwdriver slot cut with a thin edge slot file.

There are a few other modifications that can be made, such as cutting the trigger in two just above the arc where your finger fits, cutting a similar section from an '03

Colt auto has new sights, hand-fitted action, burl maple grips.

Springfield trigger that is grooved and silver soldering it back to the stub of the M98 trigger. This changes the trigger appearance and the grooves give you the firm feel of a trigger shoe.

The bolt release can be discarded and a new slim substitute installed and held in place with a small screw. It is necessary to remove the screw in order to remove the bolt and the only advantage is in appearance. If you are going to use one of the new triggers with a built-in safety, you can buy one of the new commercial bolt end shrouds that does not have a slot for the military type safety. This really changes the appearance, but you will have to do a little fitting to make the streamlined shroud work.

This should complete your action alterations and have the sights and barrel question settled. The next step is to polish the metal from the muzzle to the tang of the receiver, doing everything in your power to eliminate any roughness of the action and get a silk-smooth surface over the entire outside without changing the lines. The inside of the action can be lapped for smoothness and any binding of the bolt operation corrected to assure easy operation. Next select your stock, finish inletting it and shape the outside to your satisfaction, adding exotic wood forend and grip cap if you wish, plus other goodies, such as a trap door butt plate and an initial shield. Finish up by glass bedding the metal into the stock and sanding the stock to perfection. Take your time on each step, doing your very best work, for quality is what distinguishes a good custom rifle from a factory job. The last step is the bluing and jewelling, which should be done only if you have the facilities; otherwise have this done by a good professional shop.

There are other military rifles that can be converted into sporters. Some will be of equal quality with the M98 action and others will not. Generally, the conversion will follow the same basic lines we have discussed, with variations to fit the individual makes and models. Here are a few of them:

Springfield Model 1903: There is an old saying describing the British SMLE, the German Mauser and the American Springfield: "The British build a fighting rifle, the Germans a sporting rifle and the Americans a target rifle." The '03 Springfield barrel takes a back seat to no one in

accuracy and, if you are lucky enough to get a good one on your rifle, you are money ahead to leave it alone rather than rebarreling.

The .30/06 cartridge is perhaps the most versatile cartridge in the world. Give me a good loading tool and I'll hunt everything from elephants to squirrels with the .30/06. You doubt it? Well, for the elephants you need a good solid 220-grain bullet and a knowledge of where to put it. For the squirrels, load three grains of Bullseye pistol powder in the case and press a No. 0 buckshot into the mouth of the case with your thumb. If the buckshot is loose, patch it with a piece of facial tissue. You have to elevate the muzzle of the rifle each time you fire or rather, just before you fire, to seat the powder back on the primer, but this pip-squeak load will give good accuracy out to about fifty yards and will take old bushytail out of the highest tree without excess meat damage.

There is some confusion as to why the name .30/06. Originally, both rifle and cartridge were 1903 with the cartridge being similar to the present 1906 cartridge, except that a round nose 220-grain bullet was used at a velocity of 2,300 feet per second. In 1906, a new cartridge was adopted that used a lighter 150-grain pointed bullet at 2,700 feet per second in a new case that was .107 inch shorter. Hence the name, caliber .30 Model 1906 or the shorter version .30/06.

The original M1903 rifle was the one used during World War I with the straight stock and the rear sight mounted on the barrel directly in front of the receiver. In 1920, the stock was changed from straight to one with a pistol grip and the rifle designated as the Model 1903A1 with no additional changes in the metal componenets. The Model 1903A2 was a stripped barrel and receiver inserted inside a cannon barrel and used for inexpensive practice as a sub-caliber device.

Early in World War II, Remington Arms Company began manufacturing the M1903A1, but in an effort to expedite the manufacture under war-time pressure, several modifications were made. This included a two-groove barrel, a stamped trigger guard, the rear sight moved back to the rear bridge of the receiver and changed to a simple peep sight. This model is designated M1903A3 and was manufactured by both Remington and L.C. Smith-Corona Typewriter Company.

There was a need for a sniper rifle, so the M1903A3 was altered slightly to accept a Weaver 330 four-power scope in a Redfield mount, and the new rifle designated as the M1903A4, the last of the Springfields. Any of these versions will make up into a nice sporter and the owner need only have the rifle headspaced to assure that it is safe before going ahead with the conversion to custom sporter.

The M1903 and 1903A1 rear sight can be removed fairly easily and the barrel will be nicely contoured, with the only fly in the ointment a slight groove in the barrel next to the receiver. This is where the rear sight was retained to the barrel with a longitudinal pin. The M1903A3 and A4 did not have this groove, but the barrels were not turned as nicely and it will be necessary to shape and polish the roughly finished barrel. The A3 sight is removed by simply driving it off the dovetail on the rear receiver bridge. The front sight is attached with a band and the band can be used if you are going to install open sights simply by changing the military blade to a bead sight.

If you want to mount a scope or install a ramp front sight, you can drive the band off, but a slot under the band will resist any effort to blend in the last inch of the barrel to the contour of the rest of the barrel. It is simpler to cut the barrel behind the band, crown it and the problem is solved. The amount of barrel loss is about an inch and usually the cutting and recrowning will result in slightly better accuracy, especially if the muzzle has been worn from repeated cleaning with a metal cleaning rod while the gun was in active military service. If you plan to mount an open rear sight, all that is necessary is to drill and tap for the sight; or you can use a special barrel band to support the rear sight and eliminate the necessity of drilling and tapping the barrel. A receiver sight can be installed, of course, on either the M1903 receiver or the A3 along with a matching ramp front sight. With open sights there will be no need for receiver alterations.

Unlike the M98 Mauser, the Springfield receiver does not have to be altered for either one-piece or two-piece scope bases. Some of the receivers are quite hard and it probably will be necessary to use a special carbide drill or to anneal the location of the screw hole before drilling. Unless you have the correct tools and jigs, drilling and tapping should be left to a professional gunsmith. If a scope is mounted, it will be necessary to alter the bolt handle and safety exactly the same as in the case of the M98 Mauser action that we have already discussed. Also the trigger alterations, trigger, guard and floor plates will require the same alterations as the M98, except for the lock screw holes, which are not present on the Springfield action.

If you are stuck with one of the ugly A3 or A4 stamped guards, it is best to buy an '03 milled trigger guard and floor plate to replace it or you can choose one of the aluminum replacements offered by most gunsmith supply houses. The cartridge follower on the '03 and A1 actions will be milled and can be altered similar to the M98 to allow the bolt to be closed on an empty magazine. The A3 and A4 cartridge follower is stamped and will need to be replaced with the milled type or the cut made and welded where you grind through the stamping.

One of the main differences between the '03 and the M98 actions is the bolt release. On the '03, the designers still were thinking in terms of the old single-shot trap door .45-70, and built a magazine cut-off into the action. The idea was to lock the magazineful of cartridges off from the action and allow it to be fired single shot while the magazine was held in reserve. I doubt whether it ever was used in combat.

The special magazine cut-off affair was incorporated into the bolt release to allow it to work in three positions, (1) magazine on (2) magazine off and (3) magazine in half-way position to allow the bolt to be removed from the action. Most people prefer to simply put the magazine on the feed position and forget about the other setting, turning the cut-off to the No. 3 position when the bolt needs to be removed. If the lever offends your idea of a streamlined receiver, you can make a bar arrangement that is knurled to allow movement and eliminate the magazine off position. This is a lot of trouble and requires some close machining of the replacement on the lathe.

The '03 action will take about any cartridge in the .30/06 class and you can rebarrel it safely to a few even hotter cartridges after having a professional gunsmith check

Model 1903 Springfield has new bolt handle, special scope-clearing safety, jewelled bolt and a variable scope. Author feels model is top conversion choice.

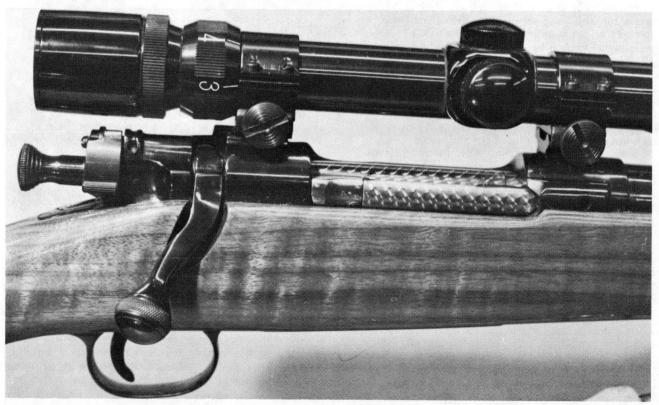

it out. The actions made just after World War I were perhaps the best in smoothness, but there is little doubt that the action made on the old '03A1 pattern by Remington just prior to the A3 modifications, is the strongest of the lot and the most desirable for the hot cartridge conversions.

Receivers manufactured at the Springfield Armory with serial numbers below 800,000 and those made at the Rock Island Arsenal with serial numbers below 285,507 were of the old case-hardened type and should be used only with factory loads in the original .30/06 caliber. This is a commonly known fact and accepted as gospel by most gunsmiths.

When I was smallarms advisor to the Nationalist Chinese 44th Arsenal, I supervised the rebuilding of literally thousands of '03 Springfields. After rebuilding, each rifle was test fired with a heavily overloaded proof cartridge. Many of the low numbered receivers were noted, but out of all the thousands test fired, we had only one action that failed the test and it was an A3!

Investigation revealed that somewhere in the past it had been subjected to a heavy blow on the side of the receiver at the front, near the locking lug recesses. This resulted in a hair-line crack that our inspectors had failed to notice. The barrel and receiver went through the rebuild line including bluing and you could see where the surfaces of the old crack had taken the bluing with just about a quarter of an inch showing the new break. I doubt if the action would have let go with regular cartridges, as the break, even with the heavy proof load, was only about a quarter inch wide, bulging the receiver enough to loosen the barrel and allow gas to escape. There was no other damage to the rifle. Being somewhat of a fanatic when it comes to safety with firearms, I still go along with the rule of limiting low number receivers to the original .30/06 caliber and factory loads only.

Quite often, customers ask if the two-groove barrel commonly found on the A3 rifle is accurate. This has been tested by dozens of people, all of whom agree that the two-groove barrel is more than adequate for hunting, as it delivers top notch accuracy. Quite often these barrels are advertised at give-away prices and can be used not only in the Springfield action but in others as well by rethreading.

The balance of the conversion of the M1903 Springfield into a custom rifle follows the identical path we took with the M98 Mauser, such as stock, accessories and rebluing. Teddy Roosevelt is said to have ordered what could be classed as the first "custom" M1903 Springfield and, even though the actions are becoming more scarce every year, it still remains a favorite of a lot of gun enthusiasts.

Mauser M93 and M95: These were the predecessors of the M98 and differ from it in several ways, mainly in cocking on the forward stroke of the bolt instead of on the initial upward stroke. They were used by quite a few countries, especially the South American nations and were purchased by the boatloads. In the last fifteen years or so, these countries have gone to more modern weapons and the M93 and M95 rifles have flooded the market here. Prices of these rifles and actions are cheap and offer a good possibility for the hobbyist. Most are chambered for the 7x57mm Mauser cartridge, which is a good choice if you can find one with a decent bore and also a good choice of caliber if you have to rebarrel the receiver.

The 7x57mm Mauser cartridge is one of the old favorites often overlooked in our magnum-crazy gun market. With a 150-grain bullet, the factory loads deliver a respectable 2,750 feet per second muzzle velocity, which is adequate for most deer-size animals. If you are determined to chamber for another caliber, you must limit such con-

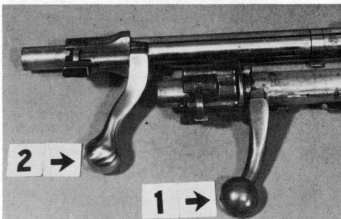

Top photo: (1) is standard 93 Mauser and (2) is the same military model with rear bridge altered to sporter lines, drilled, tapped for scope mounts. Note square guides for cartridge. (Lower photo) Bolt 1 has been heated and forged to sporter style. On 2, bolt handle is replaced.

versions to cartridges that develop no more chamber pressure than 45,00 pounds per square inch, the safe limit on the M93 and the M95 Mauser actions. This will include such cartridges as the .250 Savage, .300 Savage and the .257 Roberts. The .35 Remington also can be used, if you are looking for a cartridge with good brush bucking qualities. Some M93 and M95 actions have converted to the .308 Winchester cartridge and they seem to give no trouble, but the .308 chamber pressure is in excess of 50,000 pounds per square inch and the safety of the conversion is questionable.

The actual conversion of the action will follow that of the M98 action almost exactly, except for the floor plate. These were made in a wide variety, some following the same design of the M98 but others will be found that are hinged and released several ways via a lever or plunger in the forward part of the trigger guard. The hinged floor plate is much to be desired, as it can be altered slightly to form a custom line. It is possible to convert the trigger from the two-stage pull to the single-stage with the two screws, as described in the section on the M98, but one small

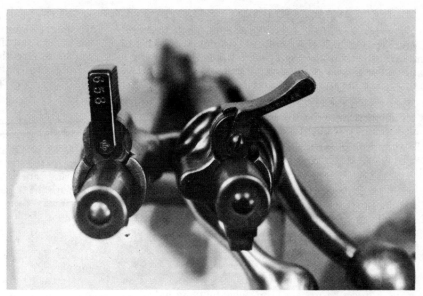

The rear of the bolt handle can be flattened, checkered to provide a better grip.

With original safety lever on left, new low position model on right, the need for a special low position safety to clear the scope sight becomes quite obvious.

alteration must be made before it will work.

There is a small safety stud on the trigger bar that fits into a recess in the bolt. If the bolt is closed full, the stud fits into the recess, allowing the trigger to be pulled. If you install screws, they press the trigger bar up enough to bind the bolt and prevent its going into the receiver. Simply grind off the stud and the conversion will work. There is nothing wrong with this, as the whole idea was deemed unnecessary by Mauser and discarded in the M98 design.

Enfield M1917 and P14: These two actions are almost identical with only one basic difference. The P14 (Pattern 1914) is the original British design made in caliber .303 British and the M1917 is the American modification of the action to caliber .30/06. At the beginning of World War I, our armories simply could not produce enough M1903 Springfields and they turned to the modified British P14 rifle as a substitute standard rifle. The British had turned to America during the early part of the war to manufacture the P14 rifle and three plants already were tooled up to make the Enfield. It was simpler and faster to modify the action slightly, changing the bore diameter and chamber to .30/06, than to convert to the production of M1903 Springfields.

Winchester, Remington and Eddystone turned out 2,202,429 of the M1917 Enfields during the war years. These remained in service for quite a few years, but were sold after the end of World War II and are fairly common on the market. The British P14 was also sold after World War II and quite a few of them are also available.

The M1917 Enfield action is as ugly as a mud fence and requires a ton of modification to turn it into something resembling a sporter, but the action is big enough for virtually any cartridge your heart desires, up to the big .458 Winchester. The P14 actions, made for a rimmed cartridge, are somewhat limited in conversions, but recently they have gained popularity as a good action for the new .444 Marlin cartridge, plus some of the belted cartridges.

One could write a book on Enfield conversions but a couple of basic changes are needed on most of them. The military rear sight is protected by a couple of ears on the rear bridge and it is necessary to remove these ears and reshape the rear bridge before any receiver or scope sight

can be installed. A milling machine is about ideal for this, but you can do a good job on the bench grinder.

The rear bridge can be reground to several shapes, but it is easier to shape it to match the front of the receiver. It is best to cut a half moon template out of sheet metal that exactly matches the contour of the top of the receiver at the front. This will be the template for grinding the rear bridge.

If you have a cutting torch, you can whack most of the metal in the ears off without overheating the receiver, but only use this if you are thoroughly familiar with a cutting torch. If not, crank up the bench grinder and using the coarse wheel, grind off the ears. This is slow, but it will get the job done just as well as a $2,000 milling machine, if you take your time.

Once the rough metal is removed, switch to the finer grit wheel and continue taking the metal down. Check constantly with your template and grind slowly. You also can check with a straight edge, such as a twelve-inch metal ruler, by pressing it against the forward part of the receiver, while the ruler extends back to the rear bridge. If you do not get in a hurry, it is possible to match the front contour perfectly.

Finish up on the polishing wheel. If correctly done, you can use two Weaver No. 11 scope bases for your scope mount; one on the front and one on the reground rear bridge. There will be a hole where the sight has been removed which can be plugged by filing out a piece of steel and silver soldering it in place.

Next is the problem of the pregnant trigger guard and floor plate assembly. This can be corrected two ways. The most common method is either to forge it straight or cut it in two at the front and reweld it flat and even. I personally prefer to cut and reweld.

The second method is to remove the box magazine, cut the trigger guard free of the floor plate housing, round the end and throw the rest of the trigger guard housing and floor plate as far as you can. The stock then is inletted, but the trigger guard section does not go all the way through the stock in the usual way. Instead, the stock is recessed to take the box magazine only, being left solid on the bottom.

The trigger guard then is attached with the rear stock screw in place. In front of the trigger guard, drill a hole to accept a wood screw which goes through the front guard and into the stock to secure the trigger guard front. The front screw is fitted by using an escutcheon inletted into the stock. This is simple and the appearance is rather sporty.

Then comes the broken dog-leg of a bolt handle, which is an abomination. The lower bend of the handle can be straightened by heating and forging to give it more sweep similar to a sporting rifle bolt handle, but the handle will be too long after it has been straightened.

To remedy this, cut the bolt knob off and regrind the stub of a handle until the hollow in the knob will fit on the stub. Tap it up tight and weld it in place. This shortens the handle and, by adding welding rod, you can shape the knob until it flows up into the handle in a teardrop shape. Grind the handle, removing as much excess metal as possible and shaping it to sporter lines.

The bolt release on the left side of the receiver is an eyesore, but can be reshaped somewhat by filing and grinding. If you really dislike it, you can throw it away and fit a M98 Mauser bolt release to the receiver by welding on a hinge. This affords a nicer appearance and is not as much trouble as it would appear, if you are a good welder. The safety on the Enfield is a good one and is about as conveniently placed as a safety can be. This is about the only thing about an Enfield action that you do not have to change!

When you have finished these alterations, grind off every bit of excess metal you can find that does not affect the safety of the action. There is a lot of excess metal on the rear of the bridge and you can eliminate a lot of it and reshape the action to sporter lines. The Enfield action is as bulky as a fat elephant, but still is a work horse of the first order. The cock on the close feature of the bolt is objectionable to some people and, if you want to change it, the easiest and simplest method is to install a speed lock which converts the bolt to cocking on the initial lifting of the bolt handle. Homemade modifications can do this also, but if not done correctly, they can affect the safety of the gun.

Japanese Arisaka: There are two common varieties of these. The earliest is in 6.5mm and the other in 7.7mm. The latter is the one most often encountered. The 6.5mm cartridge (6.5x50mm) was the Japanese service cartridge from 1905 to 1939 and was used in the Model 38 Arisaka rifle in its many varieties. It is a good cartridge, being somewhat on par with the 6.5 Mannlicher-Schoenauer and the 6.5 Mauser cartridges, giving about 2,600 feet per second with a 140-grain bullet. Norma loads this cartridge in sporting loads and it is a good choice of caliber for deer-size game.

In 1939, the Japanese adopted the Model 99 rifle, similar in appearance to the earlier Model 38, but chambered for a new 7.7x58mm, which is about equal in power to the British .303 cartridge. This cartridge also is loaded by Norma and is readily available.

For quite a few years after World War II, there was no sporting ammunition available in these two calibers and attempts to rechamber the rifle were made by numerous gunsmiths. The 7.7mm Model 99 rifles usually were rechambered to take the .30/06 cartridge. This was a bad choice, as the rear of the original 7.7mm cartridge is larger than that of the .30/06 cartridge. This resulted in the .30/06 cases being expanded at the rear, often splitting in the process. A second fault is in the bore diameter, which is .311 for the 7.7mm and the .308 for the .30/06. This results in erratic accuracy as the smaller .308 bullet was fired down the .311 bore of the Model 99 rifle.

The 6.5mm rifles usually were rechambered, using a .257 Roberts reamer, for a wildcat chamber designated as the 6.5

Standard military trigger assembly is altered with two screws to eliminate two-stage military pull and provide a trigger stop. The nut is silver soldered to the front of the trigger to receive a short screw that is held in the correct position by a short coil spring. A similar arrangement is installed on front of the sear as the trigger stop.

Jap-Roberts. The .257 brass was loaded with 6.5 bullets, but it was a reloading matter from beginning to end, as no commercial cartridges ever were made in this mixed caliber.

Today, thankfully, there is no need for such rechambering, as the rifles can be left in their original calibers with plenty of commercial ammunition and reloading components available for the handloader. They can be rebarreled to other calibers, of course, but it is hardly worth the effort.

P.O. Ackley ran a series of extensive tests on all common military actions back in 1950. I assisted in several of these experiments. The rifles were fired in original calibers with the cartridges being loaded progressively higher and higher. In addition, other actions were rebarreled to a common caliber and the cartridges again loaded higher and higher, until something let go!

Surprisingly, the Arisaka actions still were in one piece while Mausers, Springfields, Enfields and assorted other actions lay shattered on the ground. Probably the most extensive test we made on the Arisaka was to ram a cleaning rod down the barrel resting the end against the loaded bullet. On firing, the barrel was stripped clear of its threads and out of the receiver, but the action held!

There is no question in my mind that an Arisaka action in good condition is the strongest military action of them all. One word of warning! Some Arisaka actions were made up as training rifles and intended for firing blank loads only. These never should be used with ball ammunition and can be spotted by the extremely rough appearance of the cast iron receivers.

Captured rifles will have the Japanese national chrysanthemum insignia on the front of the receiver, while those that were surrendered will have this insignia ground off. The Japanese considered the insignia the emperor's property and would not allow it to be disgraced by surrender!

Converting the Japanese Arisaka to a sporter mainly involves altering the bolt handle and the trigger. The Arisaka has a round safety knob on the rear of the bolt that prevents any attempt at alteration, except turning the knob down in size, which does nothing but make it harder to operate.

The bolt handle is an odd appearing thing and is best cut off and a new sporter-shaped bolt handle welded on in its place. The trigger can be replaced with a new sporter type or can be altered with the two screws and nuts as described for the trigger alteration on the Mauser.

Short bevel ground on rear of cartridge follower allows bolt of most military rifles to close sans assistance.

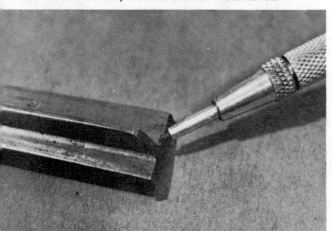

The trigger guard can be reshaped but not to any real nice appearance, so the best thing to do is hacksaw it off and weld on a single barrel shotgun trigger guard as a replacement. About the only other alteration is to shorten the long rear tang and fit a semi-inletted sporter stock, plus other accessories to suit your taste. Sights can be either iron or scope and the barrel, while on the light side, will deliver good accuracy, making the Arisaka a good, inexpensive choice for the hobbyist wanting a light rifle.

SMLE Enfields: The SMLE is an abbreviation for Short Model Lee Enfield, but often is converted to slang and expressed as a "smellie." This is also the opinion of a lot of gunsmiths. Nevertheless, many of these rifles have been converted into sporters and in any British-influenced country, they are as common as the Model 94 .30-30 Winchester is here.

The earlier models will have the rear sight mounted on the barrel and, while this offers a somewhat cleaner receiver, the barrel is thin and whippy. The later models have the rear sight mounted on the receiver and are fitted with a barrel close in contour and weight to a modern sporter barrel.

The best of the lot are the jungle carbine models produced for use in the South Pacific and Indo-China during World War II. All are in the British .303 caliber, which is a good cartridge sufficient for any North American game. It can be converted to other calibers, but the conversion is a nightmare.

Converting any of the SMLE rifles represents a series of interesting problems, centered mainly on the odd-shaped receiver and the two-piece stock. The stock part can be solved by installing one of the many semi-inletted stocks available. The trigger is a simple affair and, with patience, it can be worked over into something resembling a sporter pull.

Putting a scope on an SMLE is quite an experience and you have to do it at least once to understand why grown professional gunsmiths either groan or cuss, when a customer walks in with one and gleefully announces that he wants a 3x or 9x variable scope mounted on it. If you decide on a scope, be sure that you use the mount for that exact model of the SMLE, as they do vary quite a bit in receiver dimensions. The bolt handle and safety are best left alone, as they will not give any trouble even with a scope mounted.

The most elaborate job I ever turned out on an SMLE was for a deputy sheriff who just liked the gun and turned me loose on it with reasonable funds. As it was something of a challenge, I reworked the receiver completely, spending ten times more hours than I charged for; reshaped the barrel, then mounted a set of English-type express folding sights with a matching front ramp. With a nice piece of wood shaped to flowing lines and a shortened magazine, the rifle was an unusual sporter that delivered good accuracy to boot.

Italian Carcano: The best advice I can give to anyone considering converting one of these to a sporter, can be summed up in two simple words: Forget it! The receiver is of the split-bridge type, making mounting of a scope or receiver sight totally impossible. The Italians make beautiful shotguns, but their World War I and II military rifles were the poorest of all countries.

Other Military Actions: There are many other military rifles that have been sold on the American market at one time or another, ranging from the old .41 Swiss to the FN semi-automatic of modern design. All can be sporterized to one degree or another and many can be made into custom rifles. The odd balls, or those like the FN semi-automatic are best left alone, for no amount of work will turn them into an acceptable sporter. You just end up sinking more money into them than you can possibly recoup by selling the end results.

Commercial Actions: The demand for good clean military actions for conversion to custom sporters has created such a lucrative market that many of the import companies and most of the domestic manufacturers have, in recent years, offered either stripped actions or barreled actions to the market. The imports have included such well known actions as the FN, Sako, Husqvarna and the numerous variations of the basic Mauser M98 manufactured in a half-dozen countries under an equal number of trade names.

Virtually every domestic manufacturer has offered high-power rifle models in either a barreled action or the action by itself. These have placed a semi-custom rifle within the reach of anyone who can fit a semi-inletted stock to a barreled action. Many companies offer finished stocks of several designs in addition to the barreled actions in a sort of do-it-yourself kit.

For the hobbyist without metal working facilities, the barreled action offers a good opportunity, for the wide selection of barrel types and calibers leaves little to be desired. Considerable expense is saved, as the actions have been drilled and tapped for scope mountes, the bolt handle made to clear a scope, a scope-type safety is installed, with a sporter trigger on most models. Many of these are available without bluing — referred to as "in the white," or blued. The unblued version should be chosen over the blued one whenever possible, for it is difficult to stock a rifle that has been blued without getting a scratch or two on the metal finish. Also, most blued versions are a bit on the rough side as they are production guns and the manufacturer is doing everything in his power to keep price down. This includes skipping some final steps in polishing before bluing. The hobbyist has the time to hand polish his project to that ultimate degree which is the primary ingredient of a high-quality blue.

For those who have their own idea of what a barrel should look like, the unbarreled actions are a good choice over the regular military actions, provided you can stand the higher price of the commercial model. This price is overcome somewhat by the savings in drilling, tapping and scope modifications. Smoothness of function always has been a big attraction to me and some of the new actions are about as smooth as rubbing two bricks together. Many are churned out too fast with little regard to quality.

On the other hand, there are those such as the Sako that rival the smoothness of the old Krag and early Model 1903s. If you get stuck with one of the rough ones, a few hours of careful honing, stoning and lapping the rough surfaces will achieve a reasonable degree of smoothness.

Special Action Conversions: This covers quite a bit of territory, but in essence, it means special work that must be done to an action to convert it to a caliber other than that for which it was designed. Little is necessary in most cases if the head diameters of the new and original cartridge are the same, and if there is little difference in the case body dimensions. It will be necessary, however, if there is very much difference, especially in the head diameters, case length, or case diameter, as all of these will affect the feed, extraction, and ejection of the fired case. If you have the alterations done at a professional shop, the price can be rather high, for the work involves a lot of time both in measuring and the mechanics of cutting and fitting.

If one has the equipment, the knowledge and the skill, it becomes more of a matter of patience than anything else.

Bolt release on Mauser action is changed to much more attractive lines by cutting off protrusion, checkering end of release as shown on left. At right is the original.

Safety always must be given top priority in any action conversion and there is never any excuse for jeopardizing it. Be doubly sure you are qualified to perform these alterations and modifications correctly before you attempt them, for your safety is at stake!

In some cases, such as converting a standard M98 Mauser to feed a short cartridge like the .243 Winchester, one encounters the problem of the original magazine box being too long for the cartridge. They will feed after a fashion, but the cartridges in the magazine will slip forward on firing, battering their tips and causing feed problems. To correct this, it is necessary to shorten the magazine box and its components. Select a sample cartridge with the longest bullet loaded for this caliber and use this as your gauge of the new length you want for the magazine box.

The easiest solution is a simple rectangular sheet metal or tin box inserted and silver soldered in the magazine box to take up the excess space. You can put the little box at the front or rear of the magazine box, but the back is the best choice, since it places the cartridges closer to the chamber and eliminates a lot of feed problems.

The cartridge follower also will have to be shortened and this is done best by taking the major amount of metal off the rear of the follower and shortening the front of the follower as little as possible. You can shorten the open ends of the magazine spring a good bit, but you cannot shorten the ends more than the total length of the spring, when it is fully compressed. To do so will only result in a jammed spring, as the magazine is loaded and the spring compressed in a shortened box that is too short for its compressed length. This compression length is short enough for most needs, but it probably will be necessary to recut the sides of the spring to allow the shortened ends to slide into the holding recesses on the bottom of the follower and top of the floor plate.

If you are converting the action to some odd-ball caliber that is so short or small that even the altered magazine will not suffice, the answer is to use a special-built magazine. Discard the magazine follower and the magazine spring. In its place fit a new magazine made from scraps or utilize a detachable type magazine from another model rifle. This can be fitted in several ways to assure correct feeding, the most positive being to attach it to the bottom of the receiver with screws or by an adapter plate silver soldered in position. If you choose to use silver solder, be sure that you apply heat to the rear of the receiver or side rails only and then only with the forward end of the receiver wrapped and stuffed with wet rags to protect it from the heat.

The guide rails of the receiver sometimes have to be opened up to assure correct feeding of cartridges larger in body diameter than the original cartridge. As this varies from cartridge to cartridge, about all I can tell you in generalities is to use a Moto-Tool fitted with a mounted grindstone to do the work. Go slowly, cutting an equal amount from each side of the rails and trying the cartridge often for feeding. Note where the cartridge is binding and carefully remove a slight amount of metal, keeping the lines even and smooth. Try the cartridge again and repeat the sequence, until the cartridge feeds correctly. It is easy to remove metal, but difficult to replace it, so go slowly. Be sure to clean all grinding dust from the receiver before you try the cartridge, for this can cause binding and be misleading. For cartridges smaller than the original, it is possible to weld and reshape the rails, but it is better to fit a special detachable box magazine, as excess heat can destroy the safety of the receiver permanently.

If the head diameter of the new cartridge is larger than that of the original, it is necessary to open up the bolt face to accept this new size. If you have steady nerves and

secure the bolt in a vise, it is possible to do this by hand, using a Moto-Tool fitted with a mounted grindstone that has been shaped to offer a true flat surface on both its rim and face. Turn the Moto-Tool on and make one rather rapid pass around the edges of the bolt face and try the cartridge for fit.

The key thing is that you must remove the metal evenly all the way around. It is important to keep the stone moving, for if you hesitate, the cut will be uneven. It is very easy to ruin the bolt this way, so if you have a lathe available, you are better off using it. The end of the bolt is hard and will require a special round carbide cutter mounted in a tool post grind for ideal results. You can also use a regular tool bit holder fitted with a special carbide tool bit to do the job, but I recommend that you buy these from one of the gunsmith supply houses rather than trying to grind one yourself.

Make the cuts light and keep trying the cartridge for fit, which should not be a snap fit but rather an easy fit to compensate for any dust or dirt build-up. You can get the idea of correct fit by inserting an original cartridge and noting the amount of tolerance, then cutting the bolt to fit the new cartridge with the same amount of tolerance.

On a few special conversions, the opposite will be true and it will be necessary to close the front opening of the bolt in order to fit the new cartridge. The only way this can be done successfully is to cut the regular opening out to a very minimum ridge and then solder a tool steel washer in place. The washer then is opened up the correct diameter to fit the head of the new cartridge.

Let's get one thing clear before we go further. By soldering, I am speaking of soft solder only. Soft solder that melts at the lowest possible temperature and, under no circumstances, should silver solder be used, for it requires too much heat which will soften the locking lugs on the bolt.

A set of British three-leaf folding express sights is unbeatable on open sight brush rifles, according to the author. These were cut for impact at 50, 100, 150 yards.

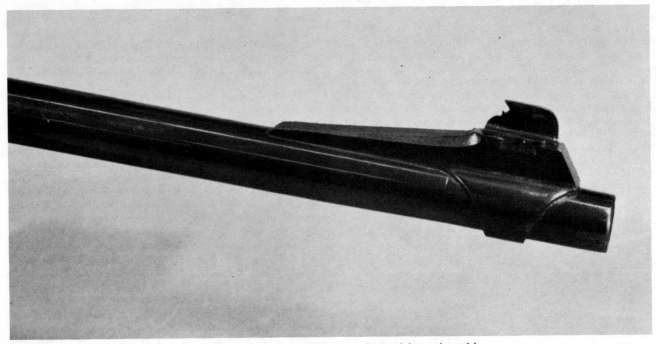

Author feels that a band ramp front sight such as this adds something extra at little expense to custom rifle.

This is a tricky conversion and I recommend that you watch a professional gunsmith do it at least once before you attempt it yourself.

The extractor seldom will present any problem, as about all that is necessary is either to enlarge the cut on the end of the extractor to compensate for larger head diameters or to allow the extractor to go in farther for smaller diameter cartridge heads. This latter conversion is done by cutting down on the support rim that holds the extractor away from the body of the bolt, which allows the extractor to move in closer and grasp the new cartridge. Nine times out of ten, the ejector will work perfectly with just about any cartridge, although it may be necessary to cut some of them back a bit to allow a real long cartridge to clear the action. A new extractor can be quite easily filed out of thin tool steel using the old one as a pattern.

Bolt release bodies also are almost trouble-free, but on short cartridges you may want the bolt to stop its backward movement quicker, as in the case of the shortened magazine box already described. All you need is to silver solder a small block on the forward end of the bolt release which will stop the bolt earlier and, in turn, shorten the amount of bolt movement. Be sure to check the ejection at the same time, for often you must cut out a new ejector that is longer and which will match the new longer bolt release stop that you soldered onto the old one.

Probably the ultimate in special conversions is a shortened action which is a standard action that has been cut in two, a section cut out of it and the two halves welded back together again. About an inch is the maximum you can take out successfully. A mandrel is used to align the two halves which have a deep vee cut on the end to allow the weld to reach to maximum depth. Use 3.5 percent nickel steel rod for the welding, protecting the forward end of the receiver with packed wet rags.

A similar section then is cut from the bolt just forward of the handle, staying as far away from the locking lugs as possible. These two halves are aligned with an inner mandrel and welded with the 3.5 percent nickel steel rod,

while the lugs are wrapped in wet rags to protect them. It is necessary to do the same with the firing pin.

The extractor is cut off at the rear and the old rear stud repositioned and soft soldered to the new short rear end. The magazine work can get a bit involved, so it is best to fit a detachable box magazine from another rifle in the correct caliber. I made one from an old M93 Mauser that was gathering dust in the shop. Fitted with a new barrel and chambered for the .44 magnum cartridge, it makes a dandy short range brush rifle. I would hate to be faced with the proposition of making a living by cutting down an action, for it is extremely time consuming. If, however, you have the time and patience plus the skill and equipment, it makes an interesting project.

Customizing: For those who do not wish to take on the task of building a custom gun or who do not have the necessary funds or equipment, there is another fascinating opportunity to express individual taste. This is in the alteration and modification of regular mass-produced guns. You might term this personalizing instead of customizing, but either way, the gun is changed to reflect the ideas of the individual owner.

The regular stock of a factory gun can, in most cases, be improved greatly by removing the usual sprayed-on plastic finish and refinishing the stock with a good oil finish.

After the old finish is removed, take careful note of the fit of wood to metal, for here is a good place for that personal touch. Mass-produced guns usually leave excess wood to compensate for minimum and maximum tolerances of the metal parts. A little careful hand fitting and sanding for a closer fit will improve the appearance, if excess wood has been left on the factory stock. This is also the ideal time to glass bed the gun for a closer fit.

Recoil pads, special grip caps or exotic wood on the forend with matching wood on the grip cap will add that individual touch and are best installed while the stock is stripped of the old finish. An initial shield inletted in the correct place can personalize a gun at a minimum cost and labor.

Left: Smith & Wesson adjustable sight is fitted to Model 1911 Colt. Original sight was filed flush, recess cut for new sight. (Upper left) Custom grips on Colt auto give it new life. (Above) The top of stippled receiver of 1911 Colt eliminates glare.

Check the stock for fit at comb, length of pull and length of grip, making alterations to the gun as needed for that just-right feel that is so important to good accurate shooting.

If the stock is too dark in color, it can be lightened by bleaching; or if it is too light, it can be dyed to the desired shade. As outlined in the chapter on checkering, if your stock is embellished with some of the new pressed-in checkering, it is possible to recut some of this for a much better appearance. If the stock is not checkered, you have a free hand to add any special pattern of checkering or carving you desire.

With few exceptions, the bluing on factory guns will have a rather dull and flat appearance, because of a poor polishing job. Remove the old blue with a stripper and do a first class job of polishing every part before having the gun reblued. Add a little jewelling to the bolt and other components while you are at it to separate your gun from the thousands of others made at the same time. This is also the ideal time to completely hand-fit the entire action by honing and stoning the bearing surfaces, until they are slick as glass. Engraving will change the entire appearance of the gun, but does require a thorough knowledge of the process and a lot of skill,

Handguns can be customized in many ways, but perhaps the simplest is with a set of special-made grips. They also suffer from a lack of proper buffing before bluing and offer the hobbyist an ideal project, for a high grade polish on a handgun always will attract attention. Good nickel plating with special gold trim on components, such as the trigger and hammer, plus a nice set of grips can give an outstanding look to a regular production model gun. Special sight, hand-fitted action, trigger shoes and other items already discussed in great lengths can be added at a minimum of cost to make your custom handgun.

Shotguns are the most numerous of all guns on the American market, but unlike rifles, they are too often a work horse with little attention given to customizing. The usual refinishing of stock, checkering and rebluing plus a hand-honed action will do as much to personalize them as they do on a rifle. If you have a pump or semi-automatic with a plain barrel, you can add a ventilated rib to change the appearance and greatly increase the performance.

I am a firm believer in a variable choke on such guns, as it provides the shooter with a wide variety of chokes, enabling him to select the proper one for each need. Double guns can be fitted with a beavertail forend, swivels attached and so on, or they can be modified to special purpose guns, such as a close range deer gun. I have made several of these by installing a set of sights front and rear on barrels that have been chopped off to twenty inches. The sights are set for one barrel loaded with a slug while the other is loaded with buckshot. For close range shooting in heavy brush, it is an almost ideal gun.

Chapter 20

ACCESSORIES – CUSTOM & BOLT-ON

There Are Many Small Items Which Adapt A Gun To Fill Individual Needs Better. Here's A Review Of Such Additions In Various Forms!

ABOUT NINETY-FIVE PERCENT of all custom guns consist simply of standard manufactured components combined. True, the wide selection of these components available allows the builder to make many possible combinations, but most items are recognized easily and read like a gunsmith's supply catalog.

For instance, we may have a rifle with a Neider steel butt plate, a Williams bolt handle, a Beuhler safety, Michael swivels and so on in a seemingly never ending variety. The professional gunsmith usually has little or no choice but to use these manufactured components, for he is working under a time-labor price limit imposed by the customer. Not so with the hobbyist, for he has almost unlimited time to devote to one single gun. Yet most follow the same path taken by the professional gunsmith and bolt on item after item of the standard manufactured accessories and components.

Custom-made accessories and components not only add that personal touch to make the gun a one-of-a-kind, but provide the hobbyist with many interesting projects and increase the pleasure of building the gun. Any custom-made accessory, if tastefully done, will increase the dollar value of the gun, to say nothing of the hobbyist's pride in the gun.

A complete machine shop is not necessary to build

Many old butt plates with trade names can be reworked by stippling over the lettering, as is illustrated here. On one, maker's name has been stippled out completely.

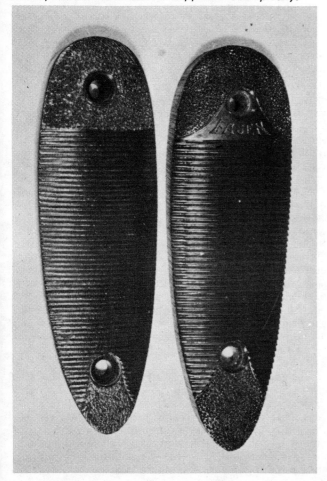

accessories and components, for in most cases they will require more hand work than anything else. The one ingredient that you must have and use is your imagination. Ask yourself, "How can I change this part to make it different? What other material can I make this part of and what material do I have available? Can I modify a part from another model gun to make my gun different?"

The old saying, "One man's junk is another man's treasure," was never more true than in the making of accessories and components, for quite often something that would be considered a discarded piece of junk can be turned into an eye catcher with a little imagination and sweat.

Disregarding recoil pads, we have butt plates available on the market made from several materials. They all offer certain advantages and you will find them used about in the following order: plastic, aluminum, steel and horn. So if you want something a little out of the ordinary, consider one of the butt plates available in horn for your rifle. There is no need to use any of the manufactured butt plates, if one uses a little imagination.

Many of the older guns, such as the early Browning automatic shotguns, have butt plates that are made from horn and are large in size. Just about any gunshop has a big box of these lying around. They have been taken from guns during the installation of recoil pads. Your gunsmith probably will charge no more than a dollar each for these. Some will give you all you can haul away.

Select one of the old horn butt plates that is not broken or split, but do not pay any attention to the design on them, for this will be filed and scraped completely away. Check the overall size against your stock, then cut the old butt plate to the approximate size, leaving about one-sixteenth of an inch excess material all around for final shaping.

If your stock has a flat butt and the old butt plate is curved, all you need to do to straighten the old butt plate out is to soak it for a few minutes in boiling water and lay it on a flat surface. Now place a flat plate on top, adding as much weight as possible and allow the old butt plate to dry and cool. When you remove it, the butt plate will be as flat as a taxpayer's pocket book. You can probably use the original butt plate screw holes, but you may have to drill new holes in your stock if you are not fitting it to a new stock.

After the butt plate is fitted snugly, file and shape the edge for a perfect blend with the sides of the stock. For a design on the butt plate, one must have a clean surface; with a metal file cut away any remaining design and polish with aluminum oxide cloth. You can carve a new design on the butt plate if you are artistic, but if you are not so endowed, there are other choices.

A nice border around the butt plate will be our first step and for this we will need a pair of dividers or a compass. Set these at about 3/16 inch and scribe a line all the way around the edge of the butt plate with one of the legs of the dividers riding on the edge of the butt plate and the other scribing the line. A small V chisel can be used to deepen the border or you can use a dental burr in a Moto-Tool to do the same thing. A checkering cutter also can be used to deepen the border line.

The space inside the border can be used in dozens of ways. Your initials can be spaced down the length of the butt plate. Cut the lines of the letters the same way you did the border and use a sharp punch to stipple the horn out-

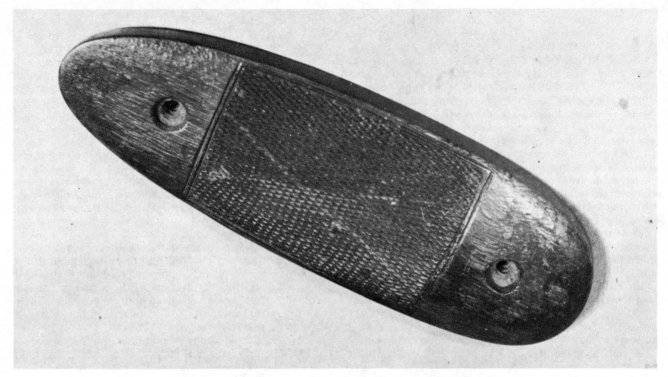

This is an old rosewood butt plate from a custom shotgun.
Almost any exotic wood can be used, but the grain must run
from end to end of the wooden plate for sake of strength.

side of the letter lines all the way to the border line. This will make the initials stand out sharply.

Another design can consist of vertical lines running from the heel of the butt plate to the toe. To lay these out, select the largest metal file you have and hold the edge of the file against the butt plate and pull it the full length of this plate. The edge of the file will scribe the series of parallel lines deep enough to lay out the design.

Now deepen the lines the same way you did the border lines. If you have a metal checkering file, you can use it to do the same thing or you can lay out a checkering pattern on the butt plate to form diamonds just like checkering on the stock. A V chisel or a bent triangular file then is used to deepen and point the diamonds in the pattern. So you see, it is not a hard matter to come up with a one-of-a-kind butt plate made of horn, if you will just use your imagination.

Metal butt plates offer another fascinating possibility and again one does not need one of the factory replacements. Many of the oldtime rifles that are not too well known were equipped with distinctive steel butt plates and these are available on the used parts market. Some can be used as is, but others will require slight alterations. Even some of the inexpensive .22 rimfire rifles had steel butt plates that prove quite attractive on a custom gun. Another often overlooked possibility is the butt plates offered by the antique gun dealers for percussion rifles and shotguns. Many are rough cast and allow the hobbyist to incorporate his own ideas and skill in the finished butt plate.

Military butt plates are about as scarce as rocks and most gun shops will give you an armload for the asking. These can be filed and ground to shape to match your stock with either their original surface left as is or you can file and cut away some of the inner material to form a skeleton butt plate, which is always an eye catcher. Many of these butt plates have a trapdoor built into them that can be utilized on the custom gun with a little fitting and reshaping. A recess is cut into the butt stock under the trap door and

utilized to store and carry spare cartridges, cleaning equipment or a spare sight.

An unusual butt plate can be made from a piece of exotic wood of close grain. This must be chosen carefully for straight grain without knots and large enough to cover the butt of the stock. It also should be about a half-inch thick to avoid splitting. These are best used on butt stocks that do not have a butt stock screw that is removed periodically. But if the wood is dense enough and thick enough, it can be used for these stocks. Permanent gluing to the butt stock is preferable, but the wood butt plate must be run vertical from heel to toe of the stock. Shape, sand and finish the wood butt plate, then checker it or finish by carving it. The English used many of these wooden butt plates on some of their finest guns and I have seen some that were still in good condition even after evidently hard field usage.

Grip caps can be made from about any material that you can make butt plates of, plus an exotic wood to match the forend cap if preferred. If you want something a little different, you can make a grip cap out of one of those military butt plates with a built in trap door, using the space underneath for small items. Many pieces of unusual metal can be filed and shaped to the lines of a grip cap to form an unusual personal touch. Brass, aluminum, plastic, bakelite and many other materials are available at low cost for shaping into special grip caps. The base of a large deer horn can be used to provide an unusual grip cap as well as to exhibit a trophy.

The grip cap is an ideal place for an initial shield which can be inletted and glued into a regular cap. Several current models, such as the Winchester Model 1200 and 1400 shotguns, have a metal grip cap with an insert that can be changed from the original to a custom cap by the simple process of gluing in a new insert. One of these with nothing more complicated than a piece of walnut for the insert will add a surprising amount of custom appearance.

Customizing sling swivels is somewhat limited, but if you give it a little thought, you can come up with something different and special. For instance, most of these consist of a simple round rod used for the sling bows. How about removing the round rods and making new bows out of small octagon rod?

If your gun is real fancy, you might consider having the sling swivels gold or silver plated. Many of the European shotguns are fitted with sling swivels that are almost impossible to remove and if fitted with a sling, it is often in the way after carrying it to the bird field. You can alter these to take a set of Q-D (quick-detachable) swivel bows by drilling out the regular bow recess in the attached swivels. With the Q-D bows a sling can be used to carry the shotgun yet the sling is instantly removeable. If you are building a Mannlicher-type stock, you might copy the original style that used a rod through the forend crossways with the sling bow attached to the ends of the rod.

original trigger off, a wide trigger shoe can be purchased or made and fitted over the regular trigger. Another way is to file out two pieces of metal to match the contour of the trigger and silver solder them to the sides of the trigger to offer a wider surface. Any of these wider triggers should be checkered with a two-row checkering file or stippled with a sharp punch to provide a non-slip surface.

A trigger stop is common on target pistols and rifles, yet few ever are installed on sporter rifles or shotguns. There are various ways to do this, but the simplest consists of a screw through the rear of the trigger guard. It is turned in enough to stop the rearward movement after the trigger has released the sear, then staked in place. On the opposite end, many sporter rifle and shotgun triggers have considerable slack in them before the trigger engages the sear for release. This slack is distracting from accurate shooting and can be

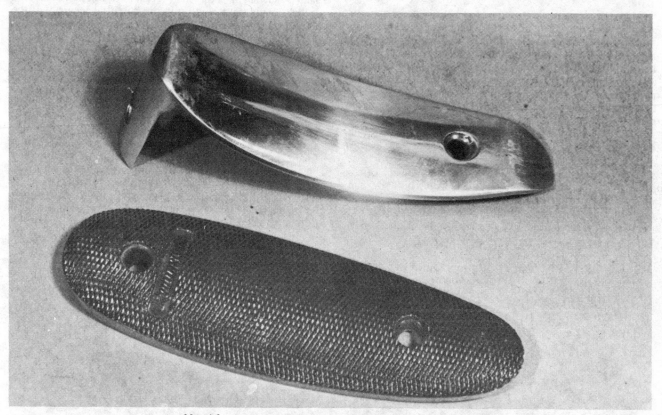

Metal factory butt plates, both old and new, can be worked over to take on all of the outer appearances of custom.

Sling swivels can be attached to rifle barrel bands but are distracting from the accuracy of the rifle due to the pulling down on the barrel and I do not recommend them. However, if the front of the sling is fitted to a hook swivel with the rear to a Q-D swivel, this arrangement can be used for a carry sling and be removed when the rifle is to be fired.

Most triggers are somewhat on the skinny side and offer a slippery surface to the finger. The chapter on custom guns described how to cut off the lower portion of a Mauser trigger and silver solder a Springfield M-1903 serrated lower section to the upper stud. This also can be used on other model guns the same way as long as the sears are protected from the heat. One can achieve the same effect by filing a substitute out of bar stock and attaching it to the cut-off trigger stud in the same way. If you do not want to cut the

eliminated by using a trigger stop in reverse. That is, install a screw to limit the forward movement of the trigger and thus eliminate any slack. This never must be fitted in such a way that it limits full sear engagement or partially pulls the trigger. When the forward limit screw is used in conjunction with a trigger stop, greater control of trigger pull and movement will result which means better accuracy.

Trigger guards can be filed and shaped to sporter lines on a military action and also sometimes altered to more graceful lines on factory actions. Often you can use a trigger guard from another gun to provide an unusual effect. Many of the old rabbit-eared single and double barrel shotguns had beautiful trigger guards on them that can be welded or attached to a modern rifle or shotgun for that different effect. I remember a standard Stevens Model 311 that one of my employees rebuilt for his own use. It was stocked English-style without a pistol grip and fitted with a trigger guard taken from an old junk rabbit-eared shotgun. The guard was quite elaborate with a long figured tang on it. It completely changed the appearance of that Model 311, and with the new stock and rebluing it was an outstanding gun.

Standard floor plate replacements are available, but the hobbyist can alter many other floor plates to change the appearance of a custom rifle. For instance, there are numerous small, carved game heads in silver and gold available from the gunsmith supply houses and jewelry stores that can be utilized for decoration. Many are intended for charm bracelets or tie and cuff links, but can be installed on the floor plates with either jewelry solder or by gluing with epoxy. This, of course, is done after the floor plate has been highly polished and blued. Correctly chosen to match the rifle's use and carefully installed, they greatly enhance the appearance of what otherwise would be a plain floor plate.

Many modern rifles are equipped with either plastic or aluminum floor plates and some are nothing but a piece of stamped tin. These can be improved either by altering a floor plate, such as that from a Mauser or simply by manufacturing a new one out of sheet steel. Many military actions, such as the Japanese Arisaka, have a stamped floor plate that is an abomination, but this can be changed and improved by substitution or manufacture of a new replacement along with a matching trigger guard. These are not too difficult to manufacture; the work consists mainly of filing rather than machining.

Floor plate releases offer another opportunity for that special one-of-a-kind touch. The B-Square Company offers a small button that can be installed easily, but you can make your own out of a piece of rod if you have any kind of system for turning it, even if this is nothing but the rod inserted in a hand drill and filed to shape as the rod is turned.

The end of the release button can be polished, circles turned in it, jewelled or checkered, plus the option of gold or nickel plating. Other systems of release, such as the lever that was quite popular on European rifles of the 1920s, can be fabricated and installed in even the smallest of shops. The release method can be incorporated into the trigger guard with a little work.

Another possibility for personalizing a floor plate is to build a hinge on the front, which can be done by welding and cutting with a file or by soldering a small cabinet hinge to the bottom of the floor plate inside and fitting the other leaf to the magazine well.

With a few exceptions, the hobby gunsmith is better off to stick to factory products when it comes to sights. This does not mean that a custom sight is not possible, but sight manufacture should be attempted only when one has gained sufficient skill in precision work. Obviously, a crudely made sight could ruin the potential accuracy of the custom gun.

Ramp blanks with the bottom part already contoured and the dovetail cut are available from gunsmith supply houses. The hobbyist can cut the slope in the ramp to match his own ideas with perhaps a straight or contoured slope. Finish the ramp by cutting cross-hatch lines across the slope to break the light reflections or, instead of cross hatch lines, you can stipple the ramp slope or use a metal checkering file to checker it. If you want to go the long way, cut an entirely new ramp from bar stock. It is harder to do, but it does allow the hobbyist to make ramp lines blend better with the overall appearance of the rifle.

False bases for folding leaf sights can be made about as easy as a ramp sight. The underside is cut with a half-round file to match the contour of the barrel. Next, shape the top to good flowing lines and cut the dovetail slot to accept the folding leaf sight. These false bases can be attached to the

Bottom row of grip caps came from broken stocks and can be used to dress up other stocks. Top center is made from a scrap of horn butt plate; it's flanked by custom grip caps cut from horn.

barrel either with soft solder or with a couple of screws. If you have a milling machine or a lathe equipped with a milling attachment, the manufacture of ramps or these bases is a simple machining problem, but with time and patience they can be shaped completely by hand.

Auxiliary sights were standard procedure some years ago, but the modern scope sights are so trouble free that little thought is given to them. If any second sights are used on a rifle, they usually are of the ramp front and a folding leaf rear types. Redfield incorporated a small peep sight into some of their bases, and the hobbyist can borrow the idea for other scope bases. It is not a difficult project to make a small peep sight and fit it to the rear of a Weaver scope base or other similar bases where it will be out of the way, yet is readily available if the need arises.

Perhaps one of the easiest accessories to make is the common rifle sling, although these are available commercially in a wide variety of styles in any price range. There are several styles of slings including that abomination known as the military sling, but most shooters prefer a simple type, such as the popular carrying sling. The carrying

sling, while primarily designed for freeing the hands while transporting the gun, also can be used to provide a quick steadying support while shooting. This support is commonly called the hasty sling and consists of slipping the left elbow through the sling between it and the stock while the rifle is in the mounted position. By pulling outward with the left arm, the sling is tightened across the chest and provides a surprising amount of steadying support to the rifle.

The leather for your custom sling can be purchased from your local leather shop or ordered from one of the mail order companies that specialize in leather supplies and tools. Most of these offer pre-cut leather designed to be made into a belt. This, in a one-inch width, is about perfect for a gun sling. The leather can be left plain, stamped with a design, such as basket weave or detailed patterns can be carved into the leather. These companies offer numerous transfer patterns designed for belts, but they can be used also as a pattern for the sling. Tools for the carving or stamping also are available, as well as inexpensive manuals that will teach you how to carve leather in the utmost detail. The process is not difficult to learn and offers many interesting potentials for decoration of leather gun accessories.

To build a custom sling, you will need a standard snap or screw snap for the forward end. The screw snap is the easiest to use for this and consists of a threaded brass stud to match an internally threaded stud. To fit it, punch a hole large enough to admit the brass screw stud in one end of the sling about a half-inch from the end. Now drop back about two inches and punch a second hole of the same diameter. This end of the sling goes through the forward sling swivel bow, the brass screw stud goes through the back hole, while the end of the leather is folded back over the swivel bow. Next, the screw stud goes through the forward hole with the internally threaded stud added to the end of the screw stud to secure the sling in place. While strong, the threaded stud allows the sling to be removed quite easily. Some hobbyists prefer to lace this end of the sling with rawhide, but this is ragged looking and not as neat as the threaded stud.

The rear end of the sling can be fitted the same way and, if you do not wish to adjust the sling, the permanent length

Custom magazine floor plate is achieved on this rifle by polishing the plate, jeweling it, then bluing metal.

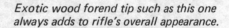

Exotic wood forend tip such as this one always adds to rifle's overall appearance.

can be determined by trial and error before the end of the leather is cut off. A buckle arrangement permits adjusting the sling length for carrying or use as a hasty sling. This buckle is attached to one end of the sling exactly as your belt buckle, with matching holes, if you wish to use the buckle tongue to maintain the sling setting. Personally, I never have liked this arrangement, as it is slow to adjust and a lot of trouble in the field. A buckle can be slipped back and forth easily without a lot of bother. A common harness buckle is made on a slight arc with a bar on each end and the usual tongue in the center. Cut off the end of the buckle tongue, but leave the part that circles the center bar. When this is used, the arc of the buckle will maintain the sling setting due to pressure on the leather, yet once this pressure is relieved, the buckle can be repositioned with two fingers. The final component, the keeper, is optional but one will hold the bottom part of the sling close and greatly improve the appearance.

Rub a coat of neatsfoot oil on the leather as a final finishing touch. There are numerous leather dyes available to color the leather from light tan to jet black. If you mix carving with sections of the background dyed in a contrasting color, the sling can be quite attractive and individualized. An added touch is to add your initials in a shield or scroll cut into the leather. The letters can be carved or stamped with a set of inexpensive stamps available from the leather suppliers. Even if you do not carve the sling, these

A hand-carved rifle sling with owner's initials stamped in leather adds a personal custom touch.

letter stamps will add that special appearance that you are trying to achieve and they require no other skill than positioning them on the leather and whacking the back of the stamp with a mallet.

Custom holsters for handguns require almost no special tools or equipment. These are available in kit form from most leather suppliers in a variety of styles for the common handgun models. Tandy Leather Company publishes an informative booklet for a couple of dollars that describes making a holster in minute detail. This includes not only full size patterns but various carved and stamped designs that can be transferred to your leather to give it that professional appearance. Having made a few holsters myself before running across this booklet, I know how much time and trouble it will save the beginner. Full holster and matching belt rigs, saddle scabbards, gun cases, cartridge belts, cartridge boxes and many other items that will provide interesting and useful projects are shown.

An interesting leather project is the closed, fleece-lined belt holster to protect that special handgun in the field. All one needs is the material, some waxed cord and a couple of leather needles. Simply make a pattern out of paper, trans-

Custom effect can be achieved by leaving the shape of usual grip cap, but contouring it for a new design.

fer it to the leather, cut out the leather, then sew it together. The sewing is no problem but requires a series of holes punched along the edges of the leather that will be closed.

Next, a needle is fitted to each end of a long waxed cord. Insert one needle through both parts of the leather that will be closed, then draw it tight. Insert the other needle in the next hole from right to left and pull it through, bringing the waxed cord with it and taking up the slack. Now insert the needle on the other end of the cord through the same hole but from left to right and pull it up tight. This passing of the cord through both sides makes the stitch. Now go to the next hole up, push the needle in from right to left and pull tight, followed by the other needle on the opposite end of the cord from left to right through the same hole and pull both ends of the cord tight. Keep repeating until the edges have been sewn together. Add a simple snap to the flap, plus a belt loop on the rear and your fleece-lined holster is complete.

A fitted trunk case not only provides a maximum amount of protection for your gun, but display it to the best advantage. I used one of these cases for a personal Beretta shotgun for over five years and the case was subjected to all kinds of abuse, such as dogs sitting on it, riding in the trunk of the car with shell cases on it, etc. Yet when I sold the gun and case, they both had survived the years in excellent condition and the case helped sell the gun for fifty dollars more than it actually was worth. But first decide whether the case will be used primarily for display or for field use, as this will determine the kind of wood to use as well as the method of construction.

For display purposes, you will want a wood with sufficient figure to compliment the gun. A case made from a solid plank in a wood such as walnut, especially with figured grain, will be expensive. The same holds true for many other woods. A less expensive way is to make the case of good plywood and, when finished, veneer it with high-grade figured walnut or other such wood. Veneer is a

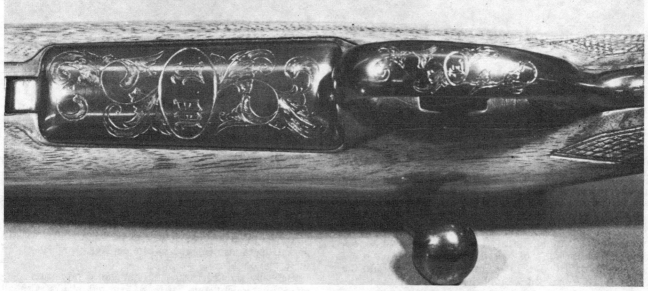

Above: Simple scroll engraving will add that custom touch to any firearm.

Trigger guard of this Japanese Arisaka rifle has been cut off. New one is from an old single-barrel shotgun.

Original trigger guard of this shotgun has been changed by welding long extension to it, fitting gun with straight English-style stock.

thin sheet of wood about 1/26 inch thick that is glued to the surface of the plywood and, if correctly done, will appear as a solid plank. Due to thinness of the veneer, it will match the contour of the wood and, after the glue has dried, actually become a part of the plywood. It is available in hundreds of shades, colors and types of wood which offer a wide selection in as fancy a grain wood as one desires. Constantine's of New York and Minnesota Wood Supply are only two of the companies that offer both the veneer and the inexpensive tools needed to apply it to the plywood. Both companies also offer complete instructions that will answer any question you may have on the process, as well as giving a step by step procedure.

The field case is much more practical and, if well done, can serve as a display case as well. The wood for the case can be either solid plank or a good grade of plywood in exterior type A-A or A-C. Plywood, because it is about twice as strong as regular planks of the same thickness, allows a case to be made that is of minimum dimensions and light in weight. You can leave the plywood bare, sanding and finishing it as you would a stock, or the case can be covered with some material such as Naugahyde for a nicer appearance.

To arrive at the correct dimensions, make a mock case using a cardboard gun box and cardboard partitions. Lay the gun in the mock case in the exact position that you want it in the finished case, moving the components as close together as possible for the most compact overall dimensions. Chances are that your mock gun box will be too large and you will have to shim it up at different points, using cardboard strips. Once you have everything as close together as you can get it, make a rough sketch of the layout and start taking your needed measurements. You must keep one thing in mind at all times when taking these measurements: These are inside dimensions.

All figuring as to the size, how long to cut tops, bottoms, et al., must be computed to allow for thicknesses of these parts. This, of course, is added to the inside dimensions taken from the mock case. Mark each dimension on your sketch and add the initials, ID, to each to avoid confusion and wasted lumber.

There are two ways of building the inside of a case: English casing and French casing. These names must be taken with a grain of salt, for they have nothing to do with present methods of casing but reflect styles originally from these two countries.

Basically, English casing has the gun components separated by straight thin strips of covered planks with all necessary turns in the form of straight angles. Colt used this system back in the percussion days and most gun enthusiasts are familiar with the appearance.

French casing has components separated by a solid form cut to fit the exact contour of each of the components. Both have advantages and disadvantages, but either will accentuate the good points of the gun being cased, provided the workmanship is of high quality.

If you decide on French casing, you must separate the components a bit more than if you had chosen the English style. About one-half inch between the components must be the minimum with a bit more, if the arrangement of the components will allow this. No additional allowances are necessary for arriving at the correct inside dimensions of the case. Should you select the English style of casing, you must allow one-quarter inch for each partition, as you will probably be using quarter-inch plywood for these partitions. To this quarter-inch allowance add the thickness of the cloth you will use to cover the partition and remember there will be one thickness of cloth on each side of the partition.

If you are using something like felt to cover the partition, felt is about one-sixteenth inch thick, so two thicknesses would be two-sixteenths which equals one-eighth inch that must be added to the quarter-inch partition. Adding these two together gives us three-eighths inch, which is

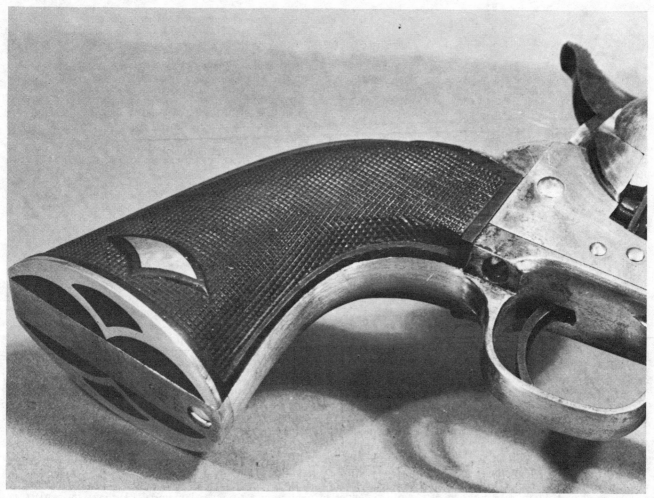

*This Colt single action is set off as something special
by addition of rosewood grips, square checkering, silver.*

added to the inside dimension to allow for the finished partition. You also will be using a thickness of this felt on the inside of the case to hide the sides of the case, so you must allow for this also. This means one-eighth inch for the width and the same for the length.

If you decide to put a dust seal in the case, allow for this, regardless of whether you are using French or English style. A dust seal is nothing but a partition of quarter-inch plywood that is about half an inch deeper in width than the depth of the case. The dust seal is placed around all four sides and, when the cover of the case is closed, the half-inch extends on up into the top of the case to present a block or seal at the joint where the top and bottom of the case come together. If you use a dust seal, the thickness of each partition must be added to those inside dimensions. Finally, you should have all dimensions worked out, but go back over them carefully for the second time to be certain you have not goofed on your addition. This is where the mock case comes in handy, for each partition can be represented with either a short piece of quarter-inch plywood or a piece of cardboard.

Most beginners make the top and bottom segments of a case separately, but this is doing it the hard way, as the two seldom match exactly. It is simpler to make a solid case, then cut it in two, one part serving as the top section of the case, the other as the bottom segment. A case depth of around three inches will be all you will need except in rare cases and for guns such as a Colt M1911 two inches of

depth is sufficient. The thickness of the plywood is up to you, but I have found that a case made with the top and bottom out of quarter-inch plywood and the sides out of three-eighths thickness will be as strong as is necessary. Select a good grade of exterior plywood instead of the cheaper interior grade, as the exterior will not warp or separate, if the case gets wet on a hunting trip.

Nails alone can be used to assemble the case, but you will get a much stronger joint if you will coat all bearing surfaces of the wood with glue. Any glue will do, but white cabinet maker's glue is hard to beat. This is about the same as Elmer's White glue, which will probably be easier to find. For maximum strength, use ribbed boat nails which resist pulling out much better than the common nail. Assembling the case will be easier, if you assemble the sides of the case first, nailing and gluing each joint carefully. Double check to be sure the side sections are exactly square, then allow this assembly to set up overnight, so the glue will thoroughly dry. You can double check your measurements and cut out the top and bottom sections. These are assembled the next day, gluing each joint as you go in addition to careful nailing. Again, allow the glue to set overnight for a good bond.

Before you start to cut the case in two for the top and bottom sections, make a heavy mark on one side. The purpose of this is to match up the two sections of the case after they have been cut. A bench saw is the best way to cut the case into the two sections, but it can be done with a

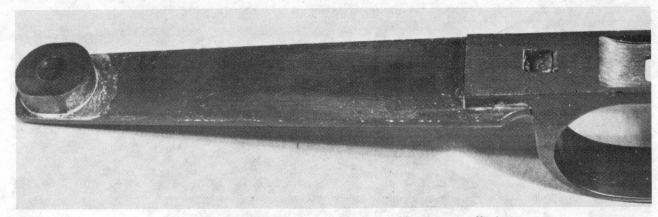

Special floor plate from scrap metal is silver soldered to cut off trigger guard for custom effect. Forward lug to hold the stock screw is soldered on.

good handsaw if you mark a line all the way around the case and follow it closely. Don't forget to allow for the thickness of the top when making this line or setting the bench saw gauge. If you used quarter-inch plywood for the top and want the top section to be one-inch deep inside, the line will have to be drawn 1¼ inches from the outside edge. Carefully sand the sawed edges but do not take off much wood, as you probably will do it unevenly and end up with an ill fitting case.

With the top and bottom sections separate, you are ready to start putting in the partitions if you are using the English style. These quarter-inch partitions can be glued to the bottom and sides then covered, but you will find it easier to cover the sides and tops of the partition first. Leave the bottom bare and put a good coat of glue on this and press into place. Some of your wife's pins or needles can be used to hold the partitions in place until the glue dries.

Once the partitions are secure, cut out a piece of foam rubber to fit down between each partition. Cover the foam rubber on the tops and sides, but leave the bottom bare. A

little glue on the rubber bottom and you are ready to press it into place. Be sure it goes down smoothly with all corners carefully tucked into place. This will finish up the bottom section.

The one-inch-deep top is filled with a piece of one-inch foam rubber covered with lining material and glued into position. If you are going to leave the wood bare or veneer it, you have but to add the hinge and other hardware. If you are making a field case, you must glue the covering such as Naugahyde over the outside, being sure there are no wrinkles. The hinge is best fitted to the rear instead of being mortised. Add a couple of trunk locks, corner protectors and the handle to complete the job.

If you decide on the French style, the top of the case is handled in the same way, using the covered one-inch-thick foam rubber. You can make the filler for the bottom section out of several materials. Perhaps the easiest and cheapest material is styrofoam, which can be obtained at any floral shop. Chisel out a form-fitting recess, if you wish, but it is easier just to cut all the way through the styrofoam leaving a form-fitting hole. This then is covered with your

Custom folding rear sight bases are being made from bar stock. One on left has dovetail slot cut; center base has two dovetails, while one at right is curved to fit the barrel. Ramp front sight can be made from the same materials, with the sight milled into the metal as shown.

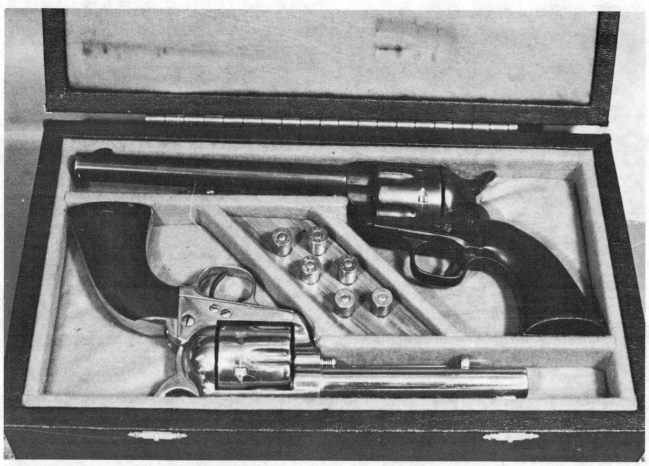

Custom fitted case for arms such as this set of Colt single actions with cartridge-holding divider not only offers an attractive note, but is protective.

Protective corners for heavy gun cases can be fashioned from pieces of scrap brass, then closely fitted to wood.

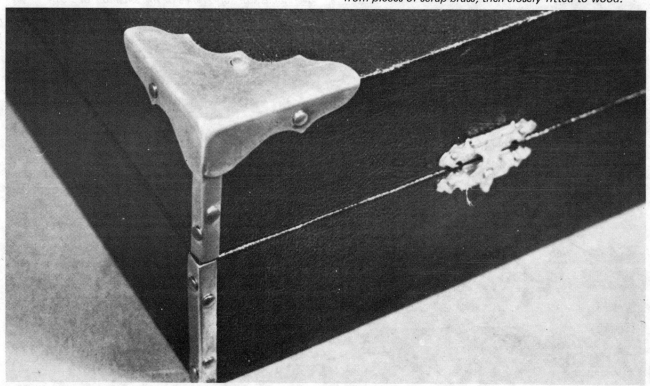

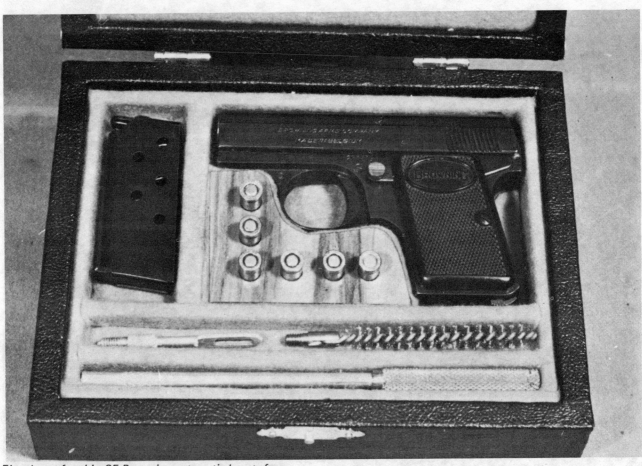

Fitted case for this .25 Browning automatic boasts form-fitting cartridge block, with knurled cleaning rod handle.

Brass corners, with small brass initial plate add to overall custom appearance of this small pistol case.

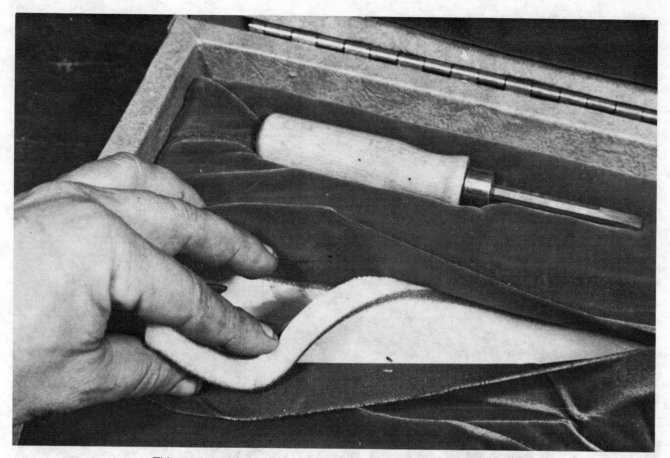

Thin section of foam rubber at bottom and top of the case can be hidden within inside case material. The accessory screwdriver is custom item.

material, gluing it in place on both the top section and around the walls of the form-fitting hole. Now cut out a piece of foam rubber to fit down the hole. Cover it with the material, add some glue on the bottom of the foam rubber and press it down into the contoured hole and allow to dry.

By varying the thickness of the foam rubber, you can use this system for any gun thickness. You may have trouble finding two-inch thick styrofoam to fill up that bottom section, but this is no problem as all you have to do is glue two one-inch thicknesses together, allowing them to dry before cutting the contoured holes.

You can dress up any of the cases by adding items such as cartridge blocks, cleaning rods, cleaning compartments or a screwdriver. Further dressing can be done with a name plate glued to the outside cover of the case. Corner protectors, edge protectors, leather handle, trunk latches, trunk locks, inlays in veneered cases and other items can be added to make a one-of-a-kind fitted gun case.

Before you start to make the case, look at the photographs accompanying this chapter, plus the photographs of gun cases in other books and magazines. Perhaps you know of a cased gun in the hands of a friend or in a local museum which can be inspected to give you ideas. The more you study them, the easier it becomes to make a case to fit any gun you desire.

In addition to gun cases, you will find that a fitted case for some of your tools, such as a micrometer, chisels or reamers not only protect them from damage, but makes them easier to store and use.

Perhaps a pistol case to hold your target guns will be needed. All they require is a little careful study and measuring. The actual assembly, fitting of internal partitions and outside coverings is about the same.

Engraving is the ultimate in personalizing a gun, but I am without a doubt the poorest engraver in the world. I have tried this many times, but even with the finest of tools I simply do not have the artistic talent. If interested, first study some good books on the subject, then invest in a modest set of gravers and keep all first attempts on soft metal such as aluminum or brass. Practice on scrap metal and not on your favorite gun.

Stick to simple scroll work, until you get the feel of the tools. Try figures only if you can draw them in honest proportions and correct lines. Some attempts at game engraving make it difficult to decide whether the engraver was trying to represent a house cat or a grizzly bear.

I am a firm believer in doing the things you do best and leaving your poorest talents alone. Nothing detracts from a fine gun more than some poor soul trying to engrave, when he has about as much talent as I have in this department. I think this lack of talent in engraving stems from the fact that I am a machinist who thinks in terms of absolute straight lines and degrees. The engraver must be an artist and think in terms of beautifully curved and proportioned lines.

Custom accessories and components can prove one of the most rewarding parts of hobby gunsmithing. Too often we get in a hurry and take the easy way out, which often is necessary for the professional. The hobbyist is in the game for the simple, pure pleasure of working on his gun or building a custom gun.

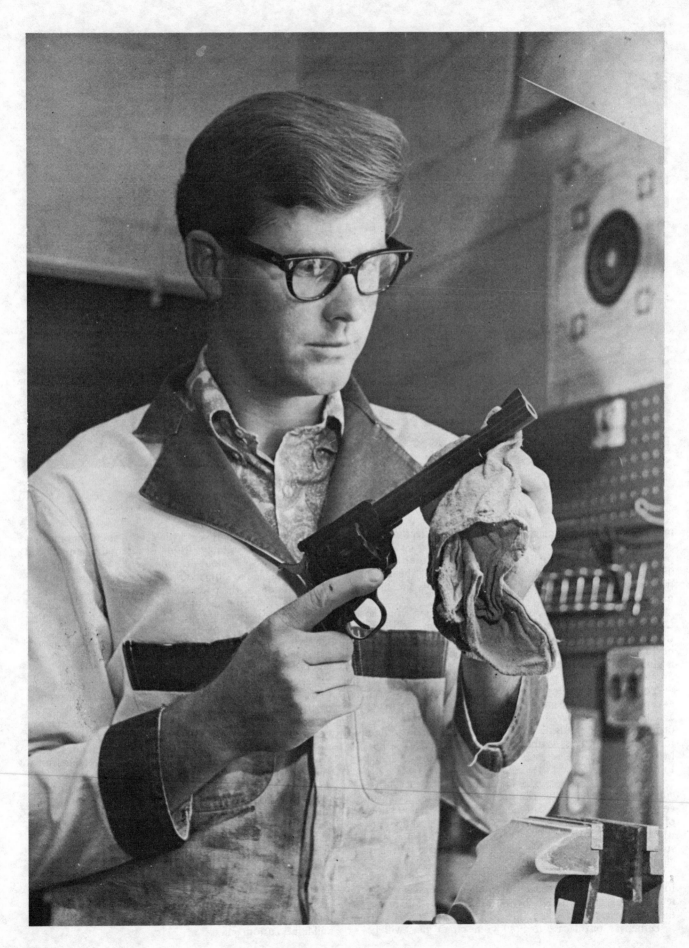

Chapter 21

THE NEXT STEP

Do You Stop Here Or Move On To Professional Status?

Too OFTEN PEOPLE READ ONE BOOK on a subject or arrive at a certain level of proficiency, then simply cease all efforts to learn more or to increase their skills. It is only through practice and study that anyone achieves success. This makes the difference between mastery of a skill or mediocrity.

All the skills of gunsmithing cannot be mastered by everyone, for we are individuals with varying talents. By now you probably have found what talents you possess and in what phase of gunsmithing they can best be applied.

Your skill will improve without help through practice and time, but never will attain its full potential without help. Assuming you have come this far, the question is, where do you go from here? Will you discard what you have learned, enjoy it as a recreational hobby, become a paid semi-professional on a part-time basis or decide to make gunsmithing a full-time career?

Gunsmithing as a career is a wide departure from what most gun enthusiasts and hobby gunsmiths think it is. Most envision it as a life filled with interesting and continuous projects and tend to think in terms of custom gun building as the main cup of tea. I wish this were true, but unfortunately this isn't correct. The quickest and easiest way for a professional gunsmith to go broke is to go into the custom rifle business full-time.

Custom rifles require an enormous amount of time and, if you charge for this time, the total price becomes so high that you have immediately limited your potential market. There will be some of this work, but usually on an inexpensive basis. This forces the gunsmith to stereotype the custom guns and turn them out on a limited production line basis using as many pre-manufactured parts and components as possible.

Occasionally you will have a customer who demands the best of your creative skill and, more important, is willing to pay for it. For the most part, the life of the professional gunsmith is one of general repair, adjusting, cleaning and replacement of parts. Make no mistake about it, this is where the money is, but it is also not very challenging. In the average gunshop, the work will consist of about 75

Earl Sweet, who heads gunsmithing department at Oregon Technical Institute, one of several such schools in the nation, checks lathe work on rifle barrel by student.

Trinidad school offers informal approach to learning gunsmithing trade. Graduates of this school usually experience little difficulty in obtaining positions.

At Colorado School of Trades in Denver, each student is assigned his own work bench and uses it exclusively to complete projects that build knowledge step by step.

Using machinery available in gunsmithing school, pair of students cut a dovetail slot for sight on barrel.

Another gunsmithing student goes through routine of making sure glass bedding project is accomplished with success.

percent of this, with the remaining 25 percent offering opportunity for creative skill. Most gunsmiths are simply specialized repairmen. Only a few professional gunsmiths ever achieve the status of known specialists with the demand for their services great enough that they can abandon regular gun repair.

As to the money that you can make out of it, let me explain it this way. For the most part a professional gunsmith will either be good in metal or good in wood, with a very few good in both fields. The professional who is good in metal usually will be an excellent machinist on the same talent level as a tool and die maker. He can walk out of the gunshop any time he chooses and make from 50 to 100 percent more money working as a full-time machinist or tool and die maker. If he is a good welder, the same holds true for a similar increase in salary.

If wood is his best subject, he can get a job as a cabinetmaker or in a custom furniture factory with that same increase in pay. Some people will probably say we are a little off in the head and I will not argue the point.

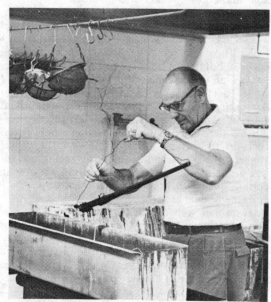

Not all student gunsmiths are teenagers, as evidenced by one who learns bluing.

Left: Projects completed by students.

At Lassen Junior College in California, students are engaged in day to day work on firearms that will serve them at such time as they become professionals.

As for myself, money is important, of course, for I have a family to support, but equally important is the fact that I deeply enjoy my work. My grandfather gave me the following advice long ago: "If you enjoy digging ditches, don't try to be a farmer, but work hard to be the best ditch digger in the business."

I have followed that advice and I enjoy gunsmithing as a career. If you feel the same way and want to try it, be sure you understand what is involved and what to expect.

If you are determined to make gunsmithing a full-time affair, my advice would be to attend one of the gunsmithing schools. To the best of my knowledge there are two colleges that offer courses and a degree in gunsmithing. One is Trinidad State Junior College, located at Trinidad, Colorado; the other is Lassen Junior College, located at Susanville, California. These schools offer well rounded courses in gunsmithing, covering all phases, plus other academic subjects that will be of daily use to the professional gunsmith. Two years are required for each school, which means that you will have to invest a considerable amount of time as well as money.

There are two trade or vocational schools that offer courses in gunsmithing. They are Colorado School of Trades in Denver and Oregon Technical Institute at Klamath Falls. These are somewhat less expensive than the junior colleges, but do not offer the other academic subjects.

Any of these schools will provide a unique and worthwhile background for the person interested in going into gunsmithing full time. They cannot make an instant master gunsmith nor can they assure complete success, but they do provide the student with training that would require many years in the School of Hard Knocks. The graduate who applies his training and continues to seek more knowledge and proficiency has a tremendous advantage over any other person seeking to become professional through a trial and error method on his own.

The other way of gaining the required knowledge and skill is to hire out as an apprentice in a professional gunshop. This, while offering a salary while you learn, often is limited in scope. The small shops simply are not interested in teaching the apprentice, as they are kept quite busy earning a living and have little time to devote to teaching. A few shops are quite large and, as these shops are run on something of an assembly line basis, the apprentice will be taught only one phase of gunsmithing.

In either case, the apprentice probably will be put on some simple job and draw all of the tough and unpleasant duties. However, he will be exposed constantly to gunsmithing and, if he keeps his eyes open and does some studying at the same time, he does have a chance of becoming a good professional gunsmith.

Having trained a few gunsmiths on something resembling an apprenticeship, I do not recommend it to anyone wishing to become a full-time gunsmith. It should only be considered when circumstances or finances prevent attending one of the gunsmithing schools. The pressures of modern business make the apprentice's education a catch as catch can affair and it takes a deeply interested and devoted person to stick with his goal through this period.

If you are interested in gunsmithing as a part-time job to pick up extra money or simply want to keep it as a hobby,

you still need to increase your skill and knowledge. Unless you have both the time and money to invest in one of the schools or can work as a part-time apprentice, your knowledge and skill will have to come from some other source.

There is one correspondence gunsmithing school with

Most gunsmithing schools have ranges on the grounds so that students can test the products of their learning.

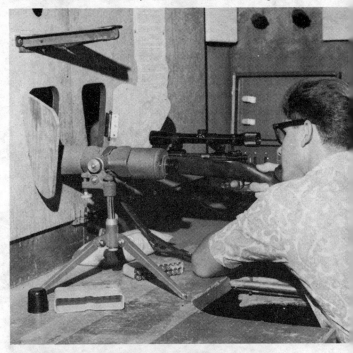

Below: Cut is made to lengthen 8mm Mauser magazine to handle .270 cartridge. (Right) Student at Trinidad State Junior College works on rebarreling.

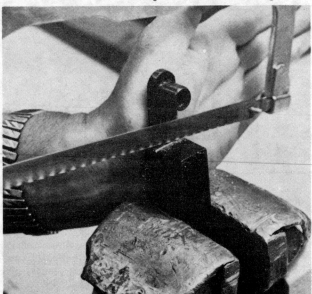

*There is only a handful of bona fide gunsmithing schools
in the nation today. However, those that do exist have
much to offer in the way of equipment, practical work.*

which I am familiar. I have talked to a graduate of this
school and he was quite pleased with the course and seemed
to be fairly proficient on gunsmithing, being engaged in it
on a part-time basis. Whether this is a result of the school or
his determination is a matter of question.

In preparing the background for this chapter, I wrote to
this school and requested a curriculum outline of their
course; after studying it closely, I find it surprisingly complete, well thought out and well written. Total course
consists of 32 lessons with the student setting his own pace
of lesson completion up to a time limit of one month per
lesson. Total cost currently is $480 payable on a per lesson
basis. If you are interested, contact Modern Gun Repair
School, 21st Avenue, Scottsdale, Arizona.

There are quite a few trade schools across the country
that offer many courses in subjects that can be utilized in
gunsmithing. Equally important is that many of these

schools offer night courses and make them available to the hobbyist already working a full eight hours at his regular job.

Most will offer some kind of general shop course and, while it will not be designed for gunsmithing, it will provide valuable information that can be used. A course in machinist training probably will be the most useful, because this will include instruction and practice on virtually every type of power equipment found in a gun shop. Once you understand the basics and gain proficiency in using the machines, it is quite easy to utilize your new skills in gunsmithing requirements.

Welding is another good course useful to the hobbyist or the semi-professional, for it is constantly needed in gunsmithing. In the woodworking department, such courses as cabinet making, furniture making and refinishing, wood carving, etc., are all closely related to stock work and the training and skills acquired will be invaluable. Leather classes are usually quite short in length and the hobbyist will find this skill of use in such things as holster making, sling making, ad infinitum. Check your local trade school, talk with the administrator about your interest and visit some of the classes if possible, to learn which will be of use to you.

Most trade schools are interested in assisting anyone who wants to learn a new trade, regardless of the motives, and usually will allow you to proceed consistent with your available time and even stop short of completion, if you do not need the entire course. Tuition charges are low at most schools and some are even free, except for expended material.

If no trade schools are available in your area, check for night extension courses at the local high school. Some of these classes such as general shop, can be converted to gunsmithing needs. If bluing and plating interest you, a short course in basic chemistry will be most valuable. Even a short class in blueprint reading and sketching will help the hobbyist understand exploded gun drawings, as well as making his own sketches of gun projects. Talk with the administrator and you will find that most educators will go out of their way to help you once they understand what help you need. Your local gunsmith can be a source of help in your education, provided you approach him in the correct manner.

Most gunsmiths, the author included, seldom fail to offer help when a hobbyist says something like, "I am working on a gun of mine and I would appreciate your suggestions as to how to solve a problem." Usually I end up with this fellow back at my bench, showing him step by step how to solve this problem.

If this fellow brings his gun back to have it reblued or for me to do some other work on it, I feel that my time has not been wasted. This is not a mercenary attitude, but there are bills to be paid and a "thank you," while being appreciated, does not help pay them. Bring paying jobs to your gunsmith and he in turn will not mind spending a few minutes giving you instructions on a single problem. Send him a customer and ask that the customer give your name as reference.

Over the years I have gained a lot of friends among hobbyists and they refer their friends to me. Consequently, I never am too busy to help with their problems or offer suggestions on a project, if they ask. It is the old Scottish proverb, "Scratch the back of he who scratches the back of thee."

Regardless of whether you decide on gunsmithing as a full or part-time career or as just a hobby, a good library is an absolute necessity. I said in the beginning that there are several well written and informative gunsmithing books that are available for the semi-professional and the professional gunsmith. Some are excellent and others not quite so good, but having read every one in print that is available, I do not hesitate to state that I have learned something from every one of them. In fact, there is a large section of my personal library crammed with them and I refer to them constantly in my everyday work. Assuming that you have no other publications, except this one, I would recommend that you add the following books in this order:

HOME GUNSMITHING DIGEST by Tommy L. Bish. This is the most recent gunsmithing book and is written in everyday language with the hobbyist in mind. It consists of a series of projects and how-to chapters that will whet your appetite as well as teach you as you work. It is extremely well illustrated with both photographs and sketches that leave little to be desired in clarifying the projects.

GUNSMITHING by Roy F. Dunlap. This is a large volume that covers professional gunsmithing from A to Z, the only criticism being that it assumes the reader is well versed in basic gunsmithing. This book will answer practically every question you will have in the more technical aspects of gunsmithing and deserves to be on your workbench as well as in your library.

PROFESSIONAL GUNSMITHING by Walter Howe. This one preceded Dunlap's book and, while some subjects are repeated, they are from another man's viewpoint, which is important. The main attraction of this book is that it deals quite extensively with setting up a professional gun shop.

GUNSMITHING KINKS by Bob Brownell. This is a fascinating book for both the professional and hobbyist. Actually it is a combination of short articles written by hundreds of gunsmiths, but compiled and blended into one volume. It deals in every phase of gunsmithing, ranging from how-to articles to detailed jigs and fixtures, plus professional methods that enable one to do a better job. Many subjects not covered in the standard gunsmithing tomes are discussed in detail.

THE MODERN GUNSMITH by James V. Howe. This consists of two large volumes that deal with the highly technical aspects of gunsmithing. In fact, it is probably the most technical writing available on the subject. It is definitely for the more advanced gunsmith but should be in your library, for it contains important data and methods that simply are not available elsewhere.

These five books, added to this volume, if carefully studied, will provide you with a well rounded knowledge of gunsmithing. I consider them the best, but this does not mean that you should not read and study the others.

In addition to the books on gunsmithing in general, I would recommend that you read and study those volumes on specific subjects that are of interest to you, such as **CHECKERING AND CARVING OF GUN STOCKS by** Monte Kennedy. Finally, add these books on the type of gun that interests you. Shotguns are my main interest and I have over two dozen books on the subject, adding any new one that I come across.

DIRECTORY OF GUNSMITH SUPPLIERS

CLEANING & REFINISHING SUPPLIES

ADSCO, Box 191, Ft. Kent, Me. 04743 (stock finish)

Allied Products Co., 734 N. Leavitt, Chicago, Ill. 60612 (Cor-O-Dex)

Armite Labs., 1845 Randolph St., Los Angeles, CA 90001 (pen oiler)

Backus Co., 411 W. Water St., Smethport, Pa. 16749 (field gun-cleaner)

Ber Big Enterprises, P.O. Box 291, Huntington, CA 90255 (gunsoap)

Birchwood-Casey Chem. Co., 7900 Fuller Rd., Eden Prairie, Minn. 55343 (Anderol, etc.)

Bisonite Co., Inc., Box 84, Buffalo, N.Y. 14217

Jim Brobst, 299 Poplar St., Hamburg, Pa. 19526 (J-B Compound)

Geo. Brothers, Great Barrington, Mass. 01230 (G-B Linspeed Oil)

Browning Arms, Rt. 4, Box 624-B, Arnold, Mo. 63010

J. M. Bucheimer Co., Airport Rd., Frederick, MD 21701

Bullet Pouch, Box 4285, Long Beach, Cal. 90804 (Mirror Lube)

Burnishine Prod. Co., 8140 N. Ridgeway, Skokie, Ill. 60076 (Stock Glaze)

C & R Distr. Corp., 449 E. 21st So., Salt Lake City, Utah 84115

Cherry Corners Gun Shop, 8010 Lafayette Rd., Rte. 1, Lodi, Ohio 44254 (buffing compound)

Chopie Mfg. Inc., 531 Copeland, La Crosse, Wis. 54601 (Black-Solve)

Clenzoil Co., Box 1226, Sta. C, Canton, O. 44708

Craftsman Wood Serv. Co., 2729 S. Mary, Chicago, Ill. 60608

Custom Industries, 18900 Detroit Ave., Lakewood, O. 44107

Dex-Kleen, Box 509, Des Moines, Ia. 50302 (gun wipers)

J. Dewey Gun Co., Clinton Corners, N.Y. 12514

Dri-Slide, Inc., Industrial Park, Fremont, Mich. 49412

Dry Film Gun Coatings, 1521—43rd St., W. Palm Beach, Fla. 33407

Forty-Five Ranch Enterpr., 119 S. Main St., Miami, Okla. 74354

Garcia Sptg. Arms Corp., 329 Alfred Ave., Teaneck, N.J. 07666

Gun-All Products, Box 244, Dowagiac, Mich. 49047

Percy Harms Corp., 7349 N. Hamlin, Skokie, Ill. 60076

Frank C. Hoppe Div., P.O. Box 97, Parkesburg, Pa. 19365

Hunting World, 247 E. 50th St., N.Y. 10022 (P-H Safari Kit)

J & G Rifle Ranch, Turner, MT 59542

Jet-Aer Corp., 100 Sixth Ave., Paterson, N.J. 07524 (blues & oils)

K.W. Kleinendorst, Taylortown Rd., Montville, N.J. 07045 (rifle clg. rods)

Knox Laboratories, 2335 S. Michigan Ave., Chicago, Ill. 60616

LPS Res. Labs. Inc., 2050 Cotner Ave., Los Angeles, Calif. 90025

Carl Lampert Co., 2639 So. 31st St., Milwaukee, Wis. 53215 (gun bags)

LEM Gun Spec., Box 31, College Park, Ga 30337 (Lewis Lead Remover)

Liquid Wrench, Box 10628, Charlotte, N.C. 28201 (pen oil)

Lynx-Line Gun Products, Box 3985, Detroit, Mich. 48227

Marble Arms Co., 1120 Superior, Gladstone, Mich. 49837

Micro Sight Co., 242 Harbor Blvd., Belmont, Ca. 94002 (bedding)

Mill Run Prod., 1360 W. 9th, Cleveland, O. 44113 (Brite-Bore Kits)

Mint Luster Cleaners, 1102 N. Division, Appleton, Wis. 54911

Mirror-Lube Div., Amer. Spec. Lubricants, Box 4275, Long Beach, CA 90804

Mistic Metal Mover, Inc., R.R. 2, P.O. Box 336, Princeton, Ill. 61356

Mitchell Chemical Co., Wampus Lane, Milford, CT 06460 (Gun Guard)

New Method Mfg. Co., Box 175, Bradford, Pa. 16701 (gun blue)

Numrich Arms Co., West Hurley, N.Y. 12491 (44-40 gun blue)

Nutec, Box 1187, Wilmington, Del. 19899 (Dry-Lube)

Outers Laboratories, Box 37, Onalaska, Wis. 54650 (Gunslick kits)

R.E.I., 101 Wolpers, Park Forest, Ill. 60466 (whale oil lube)

Radiator Spec. Co., Charlotte, N.C. 28201 (liquid wrench)

Realist Inc., N. 93 W. 16288 Megal Dr., Menomonee Falls, Wis. 53051

Reardon Prod., 323 N. Main St., Roanoke, Ill. 61561 (Dry-Lube)

Reese Arms Co., R.R. 1, Colona, IL 61241 (Dry-film lube)

Riel & Fuller, 423 Woodrow Ave., Dunkirk, N.Y. 14048 (anti-rust oil)

Rig Products Co., Box 279, Oregon, Ill. 61061 (Rig Grease)

Rocket Chemical Co., Inc., 5390 Napa St., San Diego, Calif. 92110 (WD-40)

Rusteprufe Labs., 605 Wolcott St., Sparta, Wis. 54656

Saunders Sptg. Gds., 338 Somerset, No. Plainfield, NJ 07060 (Sav-Bore)

Service Armament, 689 Bergen Blvd., Ridgefield, N. J. 07657 (Parker-Hale)

Sheldon's Inc., Box 508, Antigo, Wis. 54409 (shotgun brushes)

Shooter's Serv. & Dewey (SS&D), Clinton Corners, N.Y. 12514

Silicote Corp., Box 359, Oshkosh, Wis. 54901 (Silicone cloths)

A. D. Soucy, Box 191, Ft. Kent, Me. 04743 (ADSCO stock finish)

Southeastern Coatings, Ind., (SECOA), Bldg. 132, P.B.I. Airport, W. Palm Beach, Fla. 33406 (Teflon Coatings)

Sportsmen's Labs., Inc., Box 732, Anoka, Minn. 55303 (Gun Life lube)

Sun Ray Chemicals, 371-30th Ave., San Francisco, Calif. 94121

Surcon, Inc., P.O. Box 277, Zieglerville, Pa. 19492

Taylor & Robbins, Box 164, Rixford, Pa. 16745 (Throat Saver)

Testing Systems, Inc., 2836 Mt. Carmel, Glenside, PA 19038 (gun lube)

Texas Platers Supply Co., 2458 W. Five Mile Parkway, Dallas, TX 75233 (plating kit)

C. S. Van Gorden, 120 Tenth Ave., Eau Claire, Wis. 54701 (Instant Blue)

WD-40 Co., 5390 Napa St., San Diego, Ca 92110
W&W Mfg. Co., Box 365, Belton, Mo. 64012 (shotgun cleaner)
Webber Gage Division, 24500 Detroit Rd., Cleveland, O. 44111 (Luger oil)
West Coast Secoa, Inc., 3915 U.S. Hwy. 98 So., Lakeland, Fla. 33803
Williams Gun Sight, 7389 Lapeer Rd., Davison, Mich. 48423 (finish kit)
Winslow Arms Co., P.O. Box 578, Osprey, Fla. 33595 (refinishing kit)
Wisconsin Platers Supply Co., see: Texas Platers Supply Co.
Woodstream Corp., P.O. Box 327, Lititz, Pa. 17543 (Mask)

CUSTOM GUNSMITHS AND CUSTOM GUN WORK

A & M Rifle Co., Box 1713, Prescott, AZ 86301
Abe-Van Horn, 5124 Huntington Dr., Los Angeles, CA 90032
P. O. Ackley, Inc., 5448 Riley Lane, Salt Lake City, UT 84107
Ed Agramonte, Inc., 41 Riverdale Ave., Yonkers, NY 10701
Ahlman Cust. Gun Shop, R.R. 1, Box 20, Morristown, Minn. 55052
R. E. Anderson, 706 S. 23rd St., Laramie, Wyo. 82070
Andrews' Ammunition & Arms, 7114 So. Albion, Littleton, Colo. 80120
R. J. Anton, 1016 Riehl St., Waterloo, Ia. 50703
Arms Divs., M. R. Co., 968 Radcliffe Rd., Baltimore, Md. 21204
Bacon Creek Gun Shop, Cumberland Falls Rd., Corbin, Ky. 40701
Bain and Davis Sptg. Gds., 599 W. Las Tunas Dr., San Gabriel, Calif. 41776
Joe J. Balickie, 6108 Deerwood Pl., Raleigh, N.C. 27607
Barber's Southpaw Conversions, 26 N.W. 2nd, Portland, Ore. 97209
Barta's, Rte. 1, Box 129-A, Cato, Wis. 54206
Bayer's Gun Shop, 213 S. 2nd, Walla Walla, Wash. 99362
Bennett Gun Works, 561 Delaware Ave., Delmar, N.Y. 12054
Irvin L. Benson, Saganaga Lake, Ontario, Canada
Gordon Bess, 708 River St., Canon City, Colo. 81212
Bruce Betts Gunsmith Co., 26 Rolla Gardens Dr., Rolla, Mo. 65401
John Bivins, Jr., 446 So. Main St., Winston-Salem, N.C. 27101
Edwin T. Blackburn, Jr., 1880A Embarcadero Rd., Palo Alto, CA 94303
Boone Mountain Trading Post, Averyville Rd., St. Marys, Pa. 15857
T. H. Boughton, 410 Stone Rd., Rochester, N.Y. 14616
Kay H. Bowles, Pinedale, Wyo. 82941
Wm. A. Boyle, Box 5-770, College, Alaska 99701
L. H. Brown, Rte. 2, Airport Rd., Kalispell, Mont. 59901
Lenard M. Brownell, Box 6147 Sheridan, WY 82801
George Bunch, 7735 Garrison Rd., Hyattsville, Md. 20784
Tom Burgess, Rte. 3, Kalispell, MT 59901 (metalsmithing only)
Leo Bustani, P.O. Box 8125, W. Palm Beach, Fla. 33407
Gus Butterowe, 2520 W. Mockingbird Lane, Dallas, Tex. 75235
Cameron's Guns, 16690 W. 11th Ave., Golden, Colo. 80401
Dick Campbell, 1445 S. Meade, Denver, Colo. 80219

Carpenter's Gun Works, Gunshop Rd., Box C, Plattekill, N.Y. 12568
Carter Gun Works, 2211 Jefferson Pk. Ave., Charlotteville, Va. 22903
Cassell's Gun Shop, 403 West Lane, Worland, Wyo. 82401
Ray Chalmers, 18 White Clay Dr., Newark, Del. 19711
N. C. Christakos, 2832 N. Austin, Chicago, IL 60634
Kenneth E. Clark, 18738 Highway 99, Madera, Calif. 93637
Cloward's Gun Shop, 2045 Eastlake Ave. E., Seattle, WA 98102
Crest Carving Co., 14849 Dillow St., Westminster, Ca. 92683
Philip R. Crouthamel, 817 E. Baltimore, E. Lansdowne, Pa. 19050
Custom Rifle Shop, 4550 E. Colfax Ave., Denver, Colo. 80220
Jim Cuthbert, 715 S. 5th St., Coos Bay, Ore. 97420
Dahl's Gunshop, Rt. 2, Billings, Mont. 59101
Dave's Gun Shop, 3994 Potters Rd. West, Ionia, Mich. 48846
Dee Davis, 5658 So. Mayfield, Chicago, Ill. 60638
Jack Dever, Box 577, Jackson, Wyo. 83001 (S. S. Work)
J. Dewey Gun Co., Clinton Corners, N.Y. 12514
Joe E. Dillen, 1206 Juanita S.W., Massillon, Ohio 44646
Dominic DiStefano, 4303 Friar Lane, Colorado Springs, CO 80907
Don's Gun Shop, 128 Ruxton Ave., Manitou Springs, Colo. 80829,
Drumbore Gun Shop, 119 Center St., Lehigton, PA 18235
Charles Duffy, Williams Lane, W. Hurley, N.Y. 12491
Gerald D. Eisenhauer, Rte. #3, Twin Falls, Ida. 83301
Bill English, 4411 S. W. 100th, Seattle, Wash. 98146
Ellwood Epps, 80 King St., Clinton, Ont., Canada
Ken Eyster, Heritage Gunsmiths Inc., 6441 Bishop Rd., Centerburg, O. 43011
N. B. Fashingbauer, Box 366, Lac Du Flambeau, Wis. 54538
Ted Fellowes, 9245-16th Ave., S.W., Seattle, Wa. 98106 (muzzle loaders)
Loxley Firth Firearms, 8563 Oswego Rd., R. D. 4, Baldwinsville, N.Y. 13027
Marshall F. Fish, Westport, N.Y. 12993
Jerry Fisher, 1244—4th Ave. West, Kalispell, Mont. 59901
Flagler Gun Clinic, Box 8125, West Palm Beach, Fla. 33407 (Win. 92 & 94 Conv.)
Freeland's Scope Stands, 3737—14th Ave., Rock Island, Ill. 61201
Fred's Gun Shop, Box 725, Juneau, Alaska 99801
Frederick Gun Shop, 10 Elson Drive, Riverside, R.I. 02915
Frontier Arms, Inc., 420 E. Riding Club Rd., Cheyenne, Wyo. 82001
Fuller Gunshop, Cooper Landing, Alas. 99572
Geo. M. Fullmer, 2499 Mavis St., Oakland, Cal. 94501 (metal work)
Georgia Gun & Smith, 222 Jones Shaw Rd., Marietta, GA 30060
Gibbs Rifle Products, Viola, Ida. 83872
Ed Gillman, Upper High Crest Dr., R.F.D. #1, Butler, N.J. 07405
A. R. Goode, R.D. 1, Box 84, Thurmont, MD 21788
E. M. Greashaw, S. Centerville, RR 2, Sturgis, Mich. 49041
Griffin & Howe, 589-8th Ave., New York, N.Y. 10017
Dale M. Guise, Rt. 2, Box 239, Gardners, Pa. 17324 (Rem. left-hand conversions)

H & R Custom Gun Serv., 68 Passaic Dr., Hewitt, N.J. 07421

Paul Haberly, 2364 N. Neva, Chicago, IL 60635

Chas. E. Hammans, Box 788, Stuttgart, AR 72160

Harkrader's Cust. Gun Shop, 111 No. Franklin St., Christiansburg, Va. 24073

Elden Harsh, Rt. 4, London, O. 43140

Rob't W. Hart & Son, 401 Montgomery St., Nescopeck, Pa. 18635 (actions, stocks)

Hal Hartley, Box 147, Blairs Fork Rd., Lenoir, N.C. 28654

Hubert J. Hecht, 55 Rose Mead Circle, Sacramento, CA 95831

Edw. O. Hefti, 300 Fairview, College Sta., Tex. 77840

Iver Henriksen, 1211 So. 2nd, Missoula, Mont. 59801

Wm. Hobaugh, Box 657, Philipsburg, Mont. 59858

Richard Hodgson, 9081 Tahoe Lane, Boulder, Colo. 80301

Hoenig-Rodman, 853 So. Curtis Rd., Boise, ID 83705

Hollis Gun Shop, 917 Rex St., Carlsbad, N.M. 88220

Wm. R. Horvath, 742 S. Scott Dr., Farwell, Mich. 48622

Huckleberry Gun Shop, 10440 Kingsbury Rd., Delton, Mich. 49046 (rust blueing)

Hurst Custom Gunstocks, RFD 1, Box 1000, Exmore, Va. 23350

Hurt's Specialty Gunsmithing, Box 1033, Muskogee, Okla. 74401

Hyper-Single Precision SS Rifles, 520 E. Beaver, Jenks, OK 74037

Independent Machine & Gun Shop, 1416 N. Hayes, Pocatello, Ida. 83201

Jackson's, Box 416, Selman City, TX 75689

Paul Jaeger, 211 Leedom, Jenkintown, Pa. 19046

J. J. Jenkins, 462 Stanford Pl., Santa Barbara, CA 93105

Jerry's Gun Shop, 9220 Ogden Ave., Brookfield, Ill. 60513

Jerry's Gun Shop, 1527 N. Graceland Ave., Appleton, Wis. 54911

Johnson Automatics Assoc., Inc., Box 306, Hope Valley, R.I. 02832

Johnson's Gun Shop, 1326 N. Blackstone, Fresno, Calif. 93703

Johnson's Kenai Rifles, Box 6208, Annex Br., Anchorage, Alaska 99502

Kennedy Gun Shop, Rt. 6, Clarksville, Tenn. 37040

Monte Kennedy, R. D. 2-B, Kalispell, Mont. 59901

Kennon's Custom Rifles, 5408 Biffle, Stone Mtn., Ga. 30083

Kerr Sport Shop, Inc., 9584 Wilshire Blvd., Beverly Hills, Calif. 90212

Kess Arms Co., 12515 W. Lisbon Rd., Brookfield, Wis. 53005

Kesselring Gun Shop, 400 Pacific Hiway 99 No., Burlington, Wash. 98233

Knights Gun Store, Inc., 103 So. Jennings, Ft. Worth, Tex. 76104

Ward Koozer, Box 18, Walterville, Ore. 97489

R. Krieger & Sons, 34923 Gratiot, Mt. Clemens, Mich. 48043

Lacy's Gun Service, 1518A West Blvd., Charlotte, N.C. 28208

Sam Lair, 520 E. Beaver, Jenks, OK 74037

LanDav Custom Guns, 7213 Lee Highway, Falls Church, VA 22046

Harry Lawson Co., 3328 N. Richey Blvd., Tucson, Ariz. 85716

John G. Lawson, 1802 E. Columbia, Tacoma, Wa. 98404

Gene Lechner, 636 Jane N.E., Albuquerque, NM 87123

Ledel, Inc., Main and Commerce Sts., Cheswold, Del. 19936

Art LeFeuvre, 1003 Hazel Ave., Deerfield, Ill. 60015

LeFever Arms Co., R.D. 1, Lee Center, N.Y. 13363

Max J. Lindauer, R.R. 1, Box 114, Washington, Mo. 63090

Robt. L. Lindsay, Box 805, Gaithersburg, Md. 20760 (services only)

Ljutic Ind., Box 2117, Yakima, WA 98902 (Mono-Wads)

Llanerch Gun Shop, 2800 Township Line, Upper Darby, Pa. 19083

McCormick's Gun Bluing Service, 4936 E. Rosecrans Ave., Compton, Calif. 90221

Harry McGowen, Momence, IL 60954

Pat B. McMillan, 1828 E. Campo Bello Dr., Phoenix, Ariz. 85022

R. J. Maberry, 511 So. K, Midland, Tex. 79701

Harold E. MacFarland, Star Route, Box 84, Cottonwood, Ariz. 86326

Maryland Gun Exchange, Rte. 5, Frederick, Md. 21701

Mathews & Son, 10224 S. Paramount Blvd., Downey, Calif. 90241

Maurer Arms, 2366 Frederick Dr., Cuyahoga Falls, Ohio 44221

Middaugh's Nodak, 318 2nd St., Bismarck, N.D. 58501

C.D. Miller Guns, St. Onge, SD 57779

Earl Milliron, 1249 N.E. 166th Ave., Portland, Ore. 97230

Mills (D.H.) Custom Stocks, 401 N. Ellsworth, San Mateo, Calif. 94401 (antique)

Mitchell's Gun Repair, Rt. 1, Perryville, Ark. 72126

Natl. Gun Traders, Inc., 225 S.W. 22nd Ave., Miami, Fla. 33135

Clayton N. Nelson, 1725 Thompson Ave., Enid, Okla. 73701

Newman Gunshop, 119 Miller Rd., Agency, Ia. 52530

Nu-Line Guns, Inc., 3727 Jennings Rd., St. Louis, Mo. 63121

Oak Lawn Gun & Sports, Inc., 9618 Southwest Hwy., Oak Lawn, Ill. 60453

O'Brien Rifle Co., 324 Tropicana No. 128, Las Vegas, Nev. 89109

Pachmayr Gun Works, 1220 S. Grand Ave., Los Angeles, Calif. 90015

Harry Pagett Gun Shop, 125 Water St., Milford, Ohio 45150

Charles J. Parkinson, 116 Wharncliffe Rd. So., London, Ont., Canada

Pendleton Gunshop, 1210 S. W. Haley Ave., Pendleton, Ore. 97801

C. R. Pedersen & Son, Ludington, Mich. 49431

Al Petersen, Box 8, Riverhurst, Sask., Canada

A. W. Peterson Gun Shop, 1693 Old 44 No., Mt. Dora, Fla. 32757 (ML rifles, also)

Gene Phipps, 10 Wood's Gap Rd., Floyd, Va. 24091

Purcell's Gunshop, 915 Main St., Boise, Idaho 83702

Ready Eddie's Gun Shop, 501 Van Spanje Ave., Michigan City, IN 46360

Marion Reed Gun Shop, 1522 Colorado, Bartlesville, Okla. 74003

Fred Renard, Rt. 1, Symsonia, Ky. 42082

Ridge Guncraft, Inc., 234 N. Tulane, Oak Ridge, Tenn. 37830

Riedl Rifles, P.O. Box FR, Azusa, CA 91702

Rifle Shop, Box 657, Philipsburg, Mont. 59858

Riflemen's Hdqs., Rte. 3, RD 550-E, Kendallville, IN 46755

Carl Roth, P.O. Box 2593, Cheyenne, WY 82001

Royal Arms, Inc., 10064 Bert Acosta, Santee, Calif. 92071

M. L. Ruffino, Rt. 2, Milford, ME 04461

Sam's Gun Shop, 25 Squam Rd., Rockport, Mass. 01966

Sanders Custom Gun Serv., 2358 Tyler Lane, Louisville, Ky. 40205

Sandy's Custom Gunshop, Rockport, Ill. 62370
Saratoga Arms Co., R.D. 3, Box 387, Pottstown, Pa. 19464
Roy V. Schaefer, 965 W. Hilliard Lane, Eugene, Ore. 97402
George Schielke, Washington Crossing, Titusville, N.J. 08560
N.H. Schiffman Cust. Gun Serv., P.O. Box 7373, Murray, UT 84107
Schuetzen Gun Works, 1226 Prairie Rd., Colorado Springs, Colo. 80909
Schumaker's Gun Shop, 208 W. 5th Ave., Colville, Wash 99114
Schwab Gun Shop, 1103 E. Bigelow, Findlay, O. 45840
Schwartz Custom Guns, 9621 Coleman Rd., Haslett, Mich. 48840
Schwarz's Gun Shop, 41-15th St., Wellsburg, W. Va. 26070
Jim Scott, Hiway 2-East, Leon, IA 50144
Joseph M. Sellner, 1010 Stelton Rd., Piscataway, N.J. 08854
Shaw's, 1655 S. Euclid Ave., Anaheim, Calif. 92802
Shilen Rifles, Inc., 930 N. Belt Line, Suite 134B, Irving, Tex. 75060
Harold H. Shockley, Box 355, Hanna City, Ill. 65126 (hot bluing & plating)
Shooters Service & Dewey Inc., Clinton Corner, N.Y. 12514
Walter Shultz, R.D. 3, Pottstown, Pa. 19464
The Sight Shop, 1802 E. Columbia Ave., Tacoma, Wa. 98404
Silver Dollar Guns, 7 Balsam St., Keene, NH 03431
Simmons Gun Spec., 700 Rogers Rd., Olathe, Kans. 66061
Simms Hardward Co., 2801 J St., Sacramento, Calif. 95816
Skinner's Gun Shop, Box 30, Juneau, Alaska 98801
Markus Skosples, 1119-35th St., Rock Island, Ill. 61201
Jerome F. Slezak, 1290 Marlowe, Cleveland, O. 44107
John Smith, 912 Lincoln, Carpentersville, Ill. 60110
K. E. Smith, 8766 Los Choches Rd., Lakeside, Calif. 92040
Smitty's Gunshop, 308 S. Washington, Lake City, Minn. 55041
Snapp's Gunshop, 6911 E. Washington Rd., Clare, Mich. 48617
R. Southgate, Rt. 2, Franklin, Tenn. 37064 (new Kentucky rifles)
Sportsman's Den, 1010 Stelton Rd., Piscataway, N.J. 08854
Sportsmens Equip. Co., 915 W. Washington, San Diego, Calif. 92103
Jess L. Stark, 12051 Stroud, Houston, TX 77072
Ikey Starks, 1058 Grand Ave., So. San Francisco, Calif. 94080
Keith Stegall, Box 696, Gunnison, Colo. 81230
Suter's House of Guns, 332 N. Tejon, Colorado Springs, Colo. 80902
Swanson Custom Firearms, 1051 Broadway, Denver, Colo. 80203
A. D. Swenson's 45 Shop, 3223 W. 154th St., Gardena, Calif. 90249
T-P Shop, 212 E. Houghton, West Branch, Mich. 48661
Talmage Ent., 1309 W. 12th St., Long Beach, Calif. 90813
Taylor & Robbins, Box 164, Rixford, Pa. 16745
Daniel Titus, 119 Morlyn Ave., Bryn Mawr, PA 19010
Tom's Gunshop, 600 Albert Pike, Hot Springs, Ark. 71901
Dave Trevallion, 3442 S. Post Rd., Indianapolis, IN 46239

Trinko's Gun Serv., 1406 E. Main, Watertown, Wis. 53094
Herb. G. Troester's Accurizing Serv., Cayuga, ND 58013
C. Hunt Turner, 618 S. Grove, Webster Groves, Mo. 63119 (shotguns only)
Upper Missouri Trading Co., Inc., Crofton, MO 68730
Roy Vail, R. 1, Box 8, Warwick, N.Y. 10990
J. W. Van Patten, Box 145, Foster Hill, Milford, Pa. 18337
Herman Waldron, Box 475, Pomeroy, WN 99437 (metalsmithing)
Walker Arms Co., R. 2, Box 38, Selma, Ala. 36701
Harold Waller, 1288 Camillo Way, El Cajon, Calif. 92021
R. A. Wardrop, Box 245, Mechanicsburg, Pa. 17055
Watertown Shooting Supplies, Box 233 Thomaston Rd., Rte. 6, Watertown, Conn. 06795
Weatherby's, 2781 Firestone Blvd., South Gate, Calif. 90280
Weber Rifle Actions, Box 515, Woodbridge, Calif. 95258
Wells Sport Store, 110 N. Summit St., Prescott, Ariz. 86301
R. A. Wells, 3452 N. 1st, Racine, Wis. 53402
Robert G. West, 6626 S. Lincoln, Littleton, Colo. 80120
Western Stocks & Guns, 2206 E. 11th, Bremerton, Wash. 98310
M. C. Wiest, 234 N. Tulane Ave., Oak Ridge, Tenn. 37830
W. C. Wilber, 400 Lucerne Dr., Spartanburg, SC 29302
Williams Gun Sight Co., 7389 Lapeer Rd., Davison, Mich. 48423
Lou Williamson, 129 Stonegate Ct., Bedford, TX 76021
Wilson Gun Store Inc., R.D. 1, Rte. 225, Dauphin, Pa. 17018
Robert M. Winter, Box 484, Menno, SD 57045
Lester Womack, Box 17210, Tucson, AZ 85710
W. H. Womack, 2124 Meriwether Rd., Shreveport, La. 71108
Russ Zeeryp, 1026 W. Skyline Dr., Morristown, Tenn. 37814

ENGRAVERS, ENGRAVING, TOOLS

E. Averill, Rt. 1, 60 Chestnut St., Cooperstown, N.Y. 13326
Joseph Bayer, Sunset Ave., Sunset Hill, RD 1, Princeton, N.J. 08540
Sid Bell, Box 188, Tully, N.Y. 13159
John T. Bickett, 401 Westmark Ave., Colorado Springs, CO 80906
Weldon Bledsoe, 6812 Park Place Dr., Fort Worth, Tex. 76118
Henry D. Bonham, Box 656 (Main St.), Brownville, Me. 04414
Ray Bossi, 3574 University Ave., San Diego, CA 92104
Max E. Bruehl, 781 No. 9th Ave., Canton, IL 61520
Burgess Vibrocrafters (BVI), Rt. 83, Grayslake, Ill. 60030
Chizar Engr. Serv., 690—12th Ave., San Francisco, Cal. 94118
Carl E. Courts, 2421 E. Anaheim St., Long Beach, Cal. 90804
Creative Carvings Inc., R.D. 2, Tully, N.Y. 13159
Bill Dyer, P.O. Box 75255, Oklahoma City, Okla. 73107
J. M. Evans, Box 1850, Los Gatos, CA 95030
Ken Eyster, Heritage Gunsmiths Inc., 6441 Bishop Rd., Centerburg, O. 43011
Ken Flood, 63 Homestead, Stratford, Conn. 06497

Jos. Fugger, c/o Griffin & Howe, 589-8th Ave., N.Y., N.Y. 10017

Donald Glaser, 1520 West St., Emporia, Kans. 66801

Griffin & Howe, 589-8th Ave., N.Y., N.Y. 10017

F. R. Gurney, Engraving Methods Ltd., #207-10344 Jasper Ave., Edmonton, Alberta, Can.

Neil Hartliep, Box 733, Fairmont, Minn. 56031

Frank E. Hendricks, Rt. 2, Box 189J, San Antonio, Tex. 78228

Bob Izenstark, 101 Wolpers Rd., Park Forest, IL 60466

Jaqua's Sporting Goods, 225 N. Main St., Findlay, O. 45840

Paul Jaeger, 211 Leedom, Jenkintown, Pa. 19046

Robert C. Kain, R.F.D. Rte. 30, Newfane, Vermont 05345

Lance Kelly, P.O. Box 1072, Pompana Beach, Fla. 33061

Kleinguenther's, P.O. Box 1261, Seguin, TX 78155

Lynton S.M. McKenzie, 240 Chartres St., New Orleans, La. 70130 (booklet $3.00)

Wm. H. Mains, 2895 Seneca St., Buffalo, N.Y. 14224

Rudy Marek, Rt. 1, Box 1A, Banks, Ore. 97106

Franz Marktl, c/o Davis Gun Shop, 7211 Lee Hwy., Falls Church, VA 22046

S. A. Miller, Central P.O. Box 619, Naha, Okinawa

Frank Mittermeier, 3577 E. Tremont Ave., New York, N.Y. 10465

Albin Obiltschnig, Ferlach, Austria

Pachmayr Gun Works, Inc., 1220 S. Grand Ave., Los Angeles, Calif. 90015

Hans Pfeiffer, 286 Illinois St., Elmhurst, IL 60126

E. C. Prudhomme, 302 Ward Bldg., Shreveport, La. 71101

R. E. I. Engravings, 101 Wolpers, Park Forest, Ill. 60466

John R. Rohner, Sunshine Canyon, Boulder, Colo. 80302

Robert P. Runge, 94 Grove St., Ilion, N.Y. 13357

Shaw-Leibowitz, Rt. 1, Box 421, New Cumberland, W.Va. 26047 (etchers)

Russell J. Smith, 231 Springdale Rd., Westfield, Mass. 01085

Robt. Swartley, 2800 Pine St., Napa, Calif. 94559

Ray Viramontez, 5258 Robinwood, Dayton, O. 45431

Floyd E. Warren, Rt. 3, Box 87, Cortland, O. 44410

John E. Warren, P.O. Box 72, Eastham, Mass. 02642

A. A. White Engr., Inc., P.O. Box 68, Manchester, Conn. 06040

GUNS & GUN PARTS, REPLICA AND ANTIQUE

Antique Gun Parts, Inc., 569 So. Braddock Ave., Pittsburgh, Pa. 15221 (ML)

Armoury, Rte. 25, New Preston, Conn. 06777

Artistic Arms, Inc., Box 23, Hoagland, IN 46745 (Sharps-Borchardt replica)

Bannerman, F., Box 126, Blue Point, Long Island, N.Y. 11715

Shelley Braverman, Athens, N.Y. 12015 (obsolete parts)

Carter Gun Works, 2211 Jefferson Pk. Ave., Charlottesville, Va. 22903

Cornwall Bridge Gun Shop, Cornwall Bridge, CT 06754 (parts)

R. MacDonald Champlin, Stanyan Hill, Wentworth, N.H. 03282 (replicas)

David E. Cumberland, 3509 Carlson Blvd., El Cerrito, CA 94530 (Replica Gatling guns)

Darr's Rifle Shop, 2309 Black Rd., Joliet, Ill. 60435 (S.S. items)

Dixie Gun Works, Inc., Hwy 51, South, Union City, Tenn. 38261

Ellwood Epps Sporting Goods, 80 King St., Clinton, Ont., Canada

Kindig's Log Cabin Sport Shop, R.D. 1, P.O. Box 275, Lodi, Ohio 44254

Edw. E. Lucas, 32 Garfield Ave., Old Bridge, N.J. 08857 (45-70)

R. M. Marek, Rt. 1, Box 1-A, Banks Ore. 97106 (cannons)

Numrich Arms Co., West Hurley, N.Y. 12491

Replica Models, Inc., 610 Franklin St., Alexandria, VA 22314

Riflemen's Hdqs., Rt. 3, RD 550-E, Kendallville, IN 46755

S&S Firearms, 88-21 Aubrey Ave., Glendale, N.Y. 11227

Rob. Thompson, 1031-5th Ave., N., Clinton, Ia. 52732 (Win. only)

C. H. Weisz, Box 311, Arlington, Va. 22210

Wescombe, 10549 Wilsey, Tujunga, CA 91042 (Rem. R.B. parts)

GUN PARTS, U. S. AND FOREIGN

American Firearms Mfg. Co., Inc., 1200 Warfield, San Antonio, Tex. 78216 (clips)

Badger Shooter's Supply, Owen, Wisc. 54460

Shelley Braverman, Athens, N.Y. 12015

Philip R. Crouthamel, 817 E. Baltimore, E. Lansdowne, Pa. 19050

Charles E. Duffy, Williams Lane, West Hurley, N.Y. 12491

Federal Ordnance Inc., P.O. Box 36032, Los Angeles, Calif. 90036

Greeley Arms Co., Inc., 223 Little Falls Rd., Fairfield, N.J. 07006

Gunner's Armory, 2 Sonoma, San Francisco, Calif. 94133

H&B Gun Corp., 1228 Fort St., Lincoln Park, Mich. 48166

Hunter's Haven, Zero Prince St., Alexandria, Va. 22314

Bob Lovell, Box 675, Roseville, CA 95678

Numrich Arms Co., West Hurley, N.Y. 12491

Pacific Intl. Import Co., 2416-16th St., Sacramento, CA 95818

Potomac Arms Corp. (see Hunter's Haven)

Reed & Co., Shokan, N.Y. 12481

Martin B. Retting, Inc., 11029 Washington, Culver City, Cal. 90230

Ruvel & Co., 3037 N. Clark, Chicago, IL 60614

Santa Barbara of America, Ltd., 930 N. Beltline Rd., 132, Irving, TX 75060 (barrels and barreled actions)

Sarco, Inc., 192 Central, Stirling, N.J. 07980

R. A. Saunders, 3253 Hillcrest Dr., San Antonio, Tex. 78201 (clips)

Sherwood Distr. Inc., 7435 Greenbush Ave., No. Hollywood, CA 91605

Simms, 2801 J St., Sacramento, CA 95816

Clifford L. Smires, R.D., Columbus, N.J. 08022 (Mauser rifles)

Sporting Arms, Inc., 9643 Alpaca St., So. El Monte, CA 91733 (M-1 carb. access.)

N. F. Strebe, 4926 Marlboro Pike, S.E., Washington, D.C. 20027

Triple-K Mfg. Co., 568-6th Ave., San Diego, CA 92101

GUNSMITH SCHOOLS

Colorado School of Trades, 1545 Hoyt, Denver, Colo. 80215

Lassen Community College, Highway 139, Susanville, Calif. 96130

Oregon Technical Institute, Klamath Falls, Ore. 97601

Penn. Gunsmith School, 812 Ohio River Blvd., Avalon, Pittsburgh, Pa. 15202

Trinidad State Junior College, Trinidad, Colo. 81082

GUNSMITH SUPPLIES, TOOLS, SERVICES

Adams & Nelson Co., 4125 W. Fullerton, Chicago, Ill. 60639

Alamo Heat Treating Co., Box 55345, Houston, Tex. 77055

Albright Prod. Co., P.O. Box 695, Bishop, CA 93514 (trap buttplates)

Alley Supply Co., Box 458, Sonora, Calif. 95370

American Edelstaal, Inc., 1 Atwood Ave., Tenafly, NJ 07670

American Firearms Mfg. Co., Inc., 1200 Warfield, San Antonio, Tex. 78216 (45 Conversion Kit)

Anderson & Co., 1203 Broadway, Yakima, Wash. 98902 (tang safe)

Armite Labs., 1845 Randolph St., Los Angeles, Cal. 90001 (pen oiler)

Atlas Arms Inc., 2952 Waukegan Rd., Niles, Ill. 60648

B-Square Co., Box 11281, Ft. Worth, Tex. 76110

Jim Baiar, Rt. 1-B, Box 352, Columbia Falls, Mont. 59912 (hex screws)

Bonanza Sports Mfg. Co., 412 Western Ave., Faribault, Minn. 55021

Brown & Sharpe Mfg. Co., Precision Pk., No. Kingston, R.I. 02852

Bob Brownell's, Main & Third, Montezuma, Ia. 50171

W. E. Brownell, 1852 Alessandro Trail, Vista, Calif. 92083 (checkering tools)

Maynard P. Buehler, Inc., 17 Orinda Hwy., Orinda, Calif. 94563 (Rocol lube)

Burgess Vibrocrafters, Inc. (BVI), Rte. 83, Grayslake, Ill. 60030

M. H. Canjar, 500 E. 45th, Denver, Colo. 80216 (triggers, etc.)

Centerline Prod., Box 14074, Denver, Colo. 80214

Chicago Wheel & Mfg. Co., 1101 W. Monroe St., Chicago, Ill. 60607 (Handee grinders)

Christy Gun Works, 875-57th St., Sacramento, Calif. 95819

Clymer Mfg. Co., 14241 W. 11 Mile Rd., Oak Park, Mich. 48237 (reamers)

Colbert Industries, 10107 Adella, South Gate, Calif. 90280 (Panavise)

A. Constantine & Son, Inc., 2050 Eastchester Rd., Bronx, N.Y. 10461 (wood)

Cougar & Hunter, 6398 W. Pierson Rd., Flushing, Mich. 48433 (scope jigs)

Craft Industries, 719 No. East St., Anaheim, Ca. 92800 (Gunline tools)

Dayton-Traister Co., P.O. Box 93, Oak Harbor, Wa. 98277 (triggers)

Dem-Bart Hand Tool Co., 7749 15th Ave. N.W., Seattle, WA 98107 (checkering tools)

Die Supply Corp., 11700 Harvard Ave., Cleveland, Ohio 44105

Ditto Industries, 527 N. Alexandria, Los Angeles, Cal. 90004 (clamp tool)

Dixie Diamond Tool Co., Inc., 6875 S.W. 81st St., Miami, Fla. 33143 (marking pencils)

Dremel Mfg. Co., P.O. Box 518, Racine, Wis. 53401 (grinders)

Chas. E. Duffy, Williams Lane, West Hurley, N.Y. 12491

Dumore Co., 1300 - 17th St., Racine, Wis. 53403

E-Z Tool Co., P.O. Box 3186, East 14th Street Sta., Des Moines, Ia. 50313 (taper lathe attachment)

Edmund Scientific Co., 101 E. Glouster Pike, Barrington, N.J. 08007

F. K. Elliott, Box 785, Ramona, Calif. 92065 (reamers)

Foredom Elec. Co., Rt. 6, Bethel, Conn. 06801 (power drills)

Forster Appelt Mfg. Co., Inc., 82 E. Lanark Ave., Lanark, Ill. 61046

Keith Francis, Box 343, Talent, Ore. 97540 (reamers)

Frantz Tools, 913 Barbara Ave., Placentia, Cal. 92670

G. R. S. Corp., Box 1157, Boulder, Colo. 80302 (Gravermeister)

Gilmore Pattern Works, 1164 N. Utica, Tulsa, Okla. 74110

Gold Lode, Inc., P.O. Box 31, Addison, Ill. 60101 (gold inlay kit)

Grace Metal Prod., Box 67, Elk Rapids, Mich. 49629 (screw drivers, drifts)

Gopher Shooter's Supply, Box 246, Faribault, Minn. 55021 (screwdrivers, etc.)

The Gun Case, 11035 Maplefield SE., El Monte, Calif. 91733 (triggers)

Gunline Tools (see Craft Ind.)

H. & M. 24062 Orchard Lake Rd., Farmington, Mich. 48024 (reamers)

Half Moon Rifle Shop, Rt. 1B, Box 352, Columbia Falls, MT 59912 (hex screws)

Hartford Reamer Co., Box 134, Lathrup Village, Mich. 48075

O. Iber Co., 626 W. Randolph, Chicago, Ill. 60606

Paul Jaeger Inc., 211 Leedom St., Jenkintown, PA. 19046

Kasenite Co., Inc., 3 King St., Mahwah, N.J. 07430 (surface hrdng. comp.)

LanDav Custom Guns, 7213 Lee Highway, Falls Church, VA 22046

John G. Lawson, 1802 E. Columbia Ave., Tacoma, WA 98404

Lea Mfg. Co., 237 E. Aurora St., Waterbury, Conn. 06720

Lock's Phila. Gun Exch., 6700 Rowland Ave., Philadelphia, Pa. 19149

Marker Machine Co., Box 426, Charleston, Ill. 61920

Michaels of Oregon Co., P.O. Box 13010, Portland, Ore. 97213

Viggo Miller, P.O. Box 4181, Omaha, Neb. 68104 (trigger attachment)

Miller Single Trigger Mfg. Co., Box 69, Millersburg, Pa. 17061

Frank Mittermeier, 3577 E. Tremont, N.Y., N.Y. 10465

Moderntools Corp, Box 407, Dept. GD, Woodside, N.Y. 11377

N&J Sales, Lime Kiln Rd., Northford, Conn. 06472 (screwdrivers)

Karl A. Neise, Inc., 5602 Roosevelt Ave., Woodside, N.Y. 11377

P & S Sales, P.O. Box 45095, Tulsa, OK 74145

Palmgren, 8383 South Chicago Ave., Chicago, Ill. 60167 (vises, etc.)

C. R. Pedersen & Son, Ludington, Mich. 49431

Ponderay Lab., 210 W. Prasch, Yakima, Wash. 98902 (epoxy glass bedding)

Redford Reamer Co., Box 6604, Redford Hts. Sta, Detroit, MI 48240

Richland Arms Co., 321 W. Adrian St., Blissfield, Mich. 49228

Riley's Supply Co., 121 No. Main St., Avilla, Ind. 46710 (Niedner buttplates, caps)

Rob. A. Saunders, (see Amer. Firearms Mfg.)

Ruhr-American Corp., So. Hwy #5, Glenwood, Minn. 56334

A. G. Russell, 1705 Hiway 71N, Springdale, AR 72764 (Arkansas oilstones)

Schaffner Mfg. Co., Emsworth, Pittsburgh, Pa. 15202 (polishing kits)

Schuetzen Gun Works, 1226 Prarie Rd., Colo. Springs, Colo. 80909

Shaw's, 1655 S. Euclid Ave., Anaheim, Calif. 92802

A. D. Soucy Co., Box 191, Fort Kent, Me. 04743 (ADSCO stock finish)

L. S. Starrett Co., Athol, Mass. 01331

Technological Devices, Inc., P.O. Box 3491, Stamford, Conn. 06905 (Accu-Orb circle cutters)

Texas Platers Supply Co., 2458 W. Five Mile Parkway, Dallas, TX 75233 (plating kit)

L.B. Thompson, 568 E. School Ave., Salem, O. 44460 (rust bluing/browning services)

Timney Mfg. Co., 5624 Imperial Hwy., So. Gate, Calif. 90280 (triggers)

Stan de Treville, Box 2446, San Diego, Calif 92112 (checkering patterns)

Twin City Steel Treating Co., Inc., 1114 S. 3rd, Minneapolis, Minn. 55415 (heat treating)

R. G. Walters Co., 3235 Hancock, San Diego, Ca. 92110

Ward Mfg. Co., 500 Ford Blvd., Hamilton, O. 45011

Will-Burt Co., P.O. Box 160, Orrville, O. 44667 (vises)

Williams Gun Sight Co., 7389 Lapeer Rd., Davison, Mich. 48423

Wilson Arms Co., Box 364, Stony Creek, Branford, Conn. 06405

Wilton Tool Corp., 9525 W. Irving Pk. Rd., Schiller Park, Ill. 60176 (vises)

Wisconsin Platers Supply Co., see: Texas Platers

W. C. Wolff Co., Box 232, Ardmore, PA 19003 (springs)

Woodcraft Supply Corp., 313 Montvale, Woburn, MA 01801

LOAD TESTING & CHRONOGRAPHING

Carter Gun Works, 2211 Jefferson Pk. Ave., Charlottesville, Va. 22903

Custom Ballistics' Lab., 3354 Cumberland Dr., San Angelo, Tex. 76901

Horton Ballistics, North Waterford, Me. 04267

Hutton Rifle Ranch, Box 898, Topanga, CA 90290

Jurras Co., Box 163, Shelbyville, Ind. 46176

Kennon's, 5408 Biffle, Stone Mountain, Ga. 30083

Plum City Ballistics Range, RFD 1, Box 128, Plum City, Wis. 54761

Shooters Service & Dewey, Inc., Clinton Corners, N.Y. 12514 (daily fee range also)

Gene West, 137 Baylor, Pueblo, Colo. 81005

H. P. White Lab., Box 331, Bel Air, Md. 21014

METALLIC SIGHTS

B-Square Eng. Co., Box 11281, Ft. Worth, Tex. 76110

Bo-Mar Tool & Mfg. Co., Box 168, Carthage, Tex. 75633

Maynard P. Buehler, Inc., 17 Orinda Highway, Orinda, Calif. 94563

Christy Gun Works, 875 57th St., Sacramento, Calif. 95819

Cornwall Bridge Gun Shop, Cornwall Bridge, CT 06754 (vernier)

E-Z Mount, Ruelle Bros., P.O. Box 114, Ferndale, MT 48220

Firearms Dev. Lab., Box 278, Scotts Valley, Calif. 95060

Freeland's Scope Stands, Inc., 3734-14th Ave., Rock Island, Ill. 61201

P. W. Gray Co., Fairgrounds Rd., Nantucket, Mass. 02554 (shotgun)

Paul T. Haberly, 2364 N. Neva, Chicago, IL 60635

Paul Jaeger, Inc., 211 Leedom St., Jenkintown, PA 19046

Lyman Gun Sight Products, Middlefield, Conn. 06455

Marble Arms Corp., 1120 Superior, Gladstone, Mich. 49837

Merit Gunsight Co., P.O. Box 995, Sequim, Wash. 98382

Micro Sight Co., 242 Harbor Blvd., Belmont, Calif. 94002

Miniature Machine Co., 212 E. Spruce, Deming, N.M. 88030

Oxford Corp., 100 Benbro Dr., Buffalo, N.Y. 14225 (Illum. Sight)

C. R. Pedersen & Son, Ludington, Mich. 49431

Poly Choke Co., Inc., P.O. Box 296, Hartford, CT 06101

Redfield Gun Sight Co., 1315 S. Clarkson St., Denver, Colo. 80210

Ruelle Bros. Co., P.O. Box 114, Ferndale, MI 48220

Schwarz's Gun Shop, 41 - 15th St., Wellsburg, W. Va. 26070

Simmons Gun Specialties, Inc., 700 Rodgers Rd., Olathe, Kans. 66061

Slug Site Co., 3835 University, Des Moines, Ia. 50311

Tradewinds, Inc., Box 1191, Tacoma, WA 98401

Williams Gun Sight Co., 7389 Lapeer Rd., Davison, Mich. 48423

W. H. Womack, 2124 Meriwether Rd., Shreveport. La. 71108

PISTOLSMITHS

Alamo Heat Treating, Box 55345, Houston, Tex. 77055

Allen Assoc., 7448 Limekiln Pike, Philadelphia, Pa. 19138 (speed-cock lever for 45 ACP)

Bain and Davis Sptg. Gds., 559 W. Las Tunas Dr., San Gabriel, Cal. 91776

Bar-Sto Precision Machine, 633 So. Victory Blvd., Burbank, CA 91502 (S.S. bbls. f. 45 Acp)

Behlert & Freed, Inc., 33 Herning Ave., Cranford. N.J. 07016 (short actions)

R. M. Champlin, Stanyan Hill, Wentworth, N.H. 03282

F. Bob Chow, Gun Shop, 3185 Mission, San Francisco, Calif. 94110

J.E. Clark, Rte. 2, Box 22A, Keithville, LA 71047

Custom Gunshop, 33 Herning Ave., Cranford, N.J. 07016

Day Arms Corp., 7515 Stagecoach Lane, San Antonio, Tex. 78227

Alton S. Dinan, Jr., P.O. Box 6674, Canaan, Conn. 06018

Dominic DiStefano, 4303 Friar Lane, Colorado Springs, CO 80907 (accurizing)

Dan Dwyer, 915 W. Washington, San Diego, Calif. 92103

Giles' 45 Shop, Rt. 1, Box 47, Odessa, Fla. 33556

H. H. Harris, 1237 So. State, Chicago, Ill. 60605

Gil Hebard Guns, Box 1, Knoxville, Ill. 61448

Rudy Marent, 9711 Tiltree, Houston, Tex. 77034 (Hammerli)

Maryland Gun Exchange, Inc., Rte. 40 W., RD 5, Frederick, Md. 21701

Match Arms Co., 831 Mary St., Springdale, Pa. 15144

Pachmayr Gun Works, 1220 S. Grand Ave., Los Angeles, Calif. 90015

Geo. E. Sheldon, 7 Balsam St., Keene, N.H. 03431

R. L. Shockey Guns, Inc., 1614 S. Choctaw, E. Reno, Okla. 73036

Silver Dollar Guns, 7 Balsam St., Keene, N.H. 03431 (45 auto only)

Sportsmens Equipmt. Co., 915 W. Washington, San Diego, Calif. 92103

A. D. Swenson's 45 Shop, 3223 W. 145th St., Gardena, Calif. 90249

Dave Woodruff, 116 Stahl Ave., Wilmington Manor, New Castle, DE 19720

REBORING AND RERIFLING

A & M Rifle Co., Box 1713, Prescott, AZ 86301

P.O. Ackley Inc., 5448 Riley Lane, Salt Lake City, UT 84107

Bain & Davis Sptg. Gds., 559 W. Las Tunas Dr., San Gabriel, Calif. 91776

Carpenter's Gun Works, Gunshop Rd., Box C, Plattekill, N.Y. 12568

Fuller Gun Shop, Cooper Landing, Alaska 99572

Ward Koozer, Box 18, Walterville, Ore. 97489

Les' Gun Shop, Box 511, Kalispell, Mont. 59901

Morgan's Cust. Reboring, 707 Union Ave., Grants Pass, OR 97526

Nu-Line Guns, 3727 Jennings Rd., St. Louis, Mo. 63121

Al Petersen, Riverhurst, Saskatchewan, Canada

Schuetzen Gun Works, 1226 Prairie Rd., Colorado Springs, Colo. 80909

Sharon Rifle Barrel Co., P.O. Box 106, Kalispell, Mont. 59901

Siegrist Gun Shop, R.R. #1, Whittemore, MI 48770

Snapp's Gunshop, 6911 E. Washington Rd., Clare, Mich. 48617

R. Southgate, Rt. 2, Franklin, Tenn. 37064 (Muzzleloaders)

J. W. Van Patten, Box 145, Foster Hill, Milford, Pa. 18337

Robt. G. West, 6626 So. Lincoln, Littleton, Colo. 80120

RIFLE BARREL MAKERS

A & M Rifle Co., Box 1713, Prescott, AZ 86301

P.O. Ackley, Inc., 5448 Riley Lane, Salt Lake City, UT 84107

Apex Rifle Co., 7628 San Fernando, Sun Valley, Calif. 91352

Christy Gun Works, 875 57th St., Sacramento, Calif. 95819

Clerke Prods., 2219 Main St., Santa Monica, Calif. 90405

Cuthbert Gun Shop, 715 So. 5th, Coos Bay, Ore. 97420

Darr's Rifle Shop, 2309 Black Rd., Joliet, IL 60435

J. Dewey Gun Co., Clinton Corners, N.Y. 12514

Douglas Barrels, Inc., 5504 Big Tyler Rd., Charleston, W. Va. 25312

Federal Firearms Co., Inc., Box 145, Oakdale, Pa. 15071 (Star bbls., actions)

A. R. Goode, R.D. 1, Box 84, Thurmont, MD 21788

Hart Rifle Barrels, Inc., RD 2, Lafayette, N.Y. 13084

Wm. H. Hobaugh, Box 657, Philipsburg, Mont. 59858

Hoffman Rifle Barrel Co., Bucklin, Kans. 67834

Intern'l Casting Co., 19453 Forrer, Detroit, Mich. 48235

Johnson Automatics, Box 306, Hope Valley, R.I. 02832

Les' Gun Shop, Box 511, Kalispell, Mont. 59901

McGowen Rifle Barrels, Rte. 3, St. Anne, Ill. 60964

D. M. Manley, 295 Main St., Brookville, PA 15825

Nauman Gun Shop, 1048 S. 5th, Douglas, Wyo. 82633

Nu-Line Guns, Inc., 3727 Jennings Rd., St. Louis, Mo. 63121

Numrich Arms, W. Hurley, N.Y. 12491

R. Paris & Son, R.D. 5, Box 61, Gettysburg, Pa. 17325

Rheinmetall (see John Weir)

SS & D, Inc., Clinton Corners, N.Y. 12514 (cold-formed bbls.)

Sanders Cust. Gun Serv., 2358 Tyler Lane, Louisville, Ky. 40205

Sharon Rifle Barrel Co., P.O. Box 106, Kalispell, Mont. 59901

Ed Shilen Rifles, 4510 Harrington Rd., Irving, Tex. 75060

Titus Barrel & Gun Co., Box 151, Heber City, Ut. 84032

John E. Weir, 3304 Norton Ave., Independence, Mo. 64052

Wilson Arms, Box 364, Stony Creek, Branford, Conn. 06405

STOCKS (Commercial and Custom)

Abe-Van Horn, 5124 Huntington Dr., Los Angeles, CA 90032

Ahlman's Inc., R.R. 1, Box 20, Morristown, MN 55052

R. E. Anderson, 706 So. 23rd St., Laramie, Wyo. 82070

Dale P. Andrews, 7114 So. Albion, Littleton, Colo. 80120

R. J. Anton, 1016 Riehl St., Waterloo, Ia. 50703

Jim Baiar, Rt. 1-B, Box 352, Columbia Falls, Mont. 59912

Joe J. Balickie, Custom Stocks, 6108 Deerwood Pl., Raleigh, N.C. 27607

Bartas, Rte. 1, Box 129-A, Cato, Wis. 54206

John Bianchi, 212 W. Foothill Blvd., Monrovia, Calif. 91016 (U. S. carbines)

Al Biesen, West 2039 Sinto Ave., Spokane, Wash. 99201

E. C. Bishop & Son Inc., Box 7, Warsaw, Mo. 65355

Nate Bishop, Box 158, Minturn, CO 81645

Kay H. Bowles, Pinedale, Wyo. 82941

Brown Precision Co., 5869 Indian Ave., San Jose, CA 95123

Lenard M. Brownell, Box 6147, Sheridan, WY 82801

Cadmus Ind. Sporting Arms, Inc., 6311 Yucca St., Hollywood, Calif. 90028 (U. S. carbines)

Calico Hardwoods, Inc., 1648 Airport Blvd., Windsor, Calif. 95492 (blanks)

Dick Campbell, 1445 So. Meade, Denver, Colo. 80219

Cloward's Gun Shop, 2045 Eastlake Ave. E., Seattle, Wa. 98102

Mike Conner, Box 208, Tijeras, NM 87059

Crane Creek Gun Stock Co., Box 268, Waseca, Minn. 56093

Crest Carving Co., 8091 Bolsa Ave., Midway City, CA 92655

Charles De Veto, 1087 Irene Rd., Lyndhurst, O. 44124

Custom Gunstocks, 1445 So. Meade, Denver, Colo. 80219

Reinhart Fajen, Box 338, Warsaw, Mo. 65355

N. B. Fashingbauer, Box 366, Lac Du Flambeau, Wis. 54538

Ted Fellowes, 9245 16th Ave. S. W., Seattle, Wash. 98106

Clyde E. Fischer, Rt. 1, Box 170-M, Victoria, Tex. 77901

Jerry Fisher, 1244-4th Ave., Kalispell, Mont. 59901

Flaig's Lodge, Millvale, Pa. 15209

Horace M. Frantz, Box 128, Farmingdale, N.J. 07727

Freeland's Scope Stands, Inc., 3734 14th Ave., Rock Island, Ill. 61201

Aaron T. Gates, 3229 Felton St., San Diego, Calif. 92104

Dale Goens, Box 224, Cedar Crest, N.M. 87008

Gould's Myrtlewood, 1692 N. Dogwood, Coquille, Ore. 97423 (gun blanks)

Rolf R. Gruning, 315 Busby Dr., San Antonio, Tex. 78209

Gunstocks-Rarewoods, Haleiwa, Hawaii 97612 (blanks)

Gunwoods (N.Z.) Ltd., Box 18505, New Brighton, Christchurch, New Zealand (blanks)

Half Moon Rifle Shop, Rte. 1B, Box 352, Columbia Falls, MT 59912

Hank's Stock Shop, 1078 Alice Ave., Ukiah, Calif. 95482

Harper's Custom Stocks, 928 Lombrano St., San Antonio, Tex. 78207

Harris Gun Stocks, Inc., 12 Lake St., Richfield Springs, N.Y. 13439

Elden Harsh, Rt. 4, London, O. 43140

Hal Hartley, Box 147, Blairsfork Rd., Lenoir, N.C. 28654

Hayes Gunstock Service Co., 914 E. Turner St., Clearwater, Fla. 33516

Hubert J. Hecht, 55 Rose Mead Circle, Sacramento, CA 95831

Edward O. Hefti, 300 Fairview, College Sta., Tex. 77840

Herter's Inc., Waseca, Minn. 56093

Richard Hodgson, 9081 Tahoe Lane, Boulder, CO 80301

Hollis Gun Shop, 917 Rex St., Carlsbad, N.M. 88220

Hurst Custom Gunstocks, RFD. 1, Box 1000, Exmore, Va. 23350

Jackson's, Box 416, Selman City, Tex. 75689 (blanks)

Paul Jaeger, 211 Leedom St., Jenkintown, Pa. 19046

I. D. Johnson, Rt. 1, Strawberry Point, Ia. 52076 (blanks)

Monte Kennedy, R.D. 2B, Kalispell Mont., 59901

Leer's Gun Barn, Rt. 3, Sycamore Hills, Elwood, Ind. 46036

LeFever Arms Co., Inc., R.D. 1, Lee Center, N.Y. 13363

Maryland Gun Exchange, Rte. 5, Frederick, Md. 21701

Maurer Arms, 2366 Frederick Dr., Cuyahoga Falls, O. 44221

Leonard Mews, R.2, Box 242, Hortonville, WI 54944

Robt. U. Milhoan & Son, Rt. 3, Elizabeth, W. Va. 26143

C. D. Miller Guns, St. Onge, S.D. 57779

Mills (D.H.) Custom Stocks, 401 N. Ellsworth Ave., San Mateo, Calif. 94401

Nelsen's Gun Shop, 501 S. Wilson, Olympia, Wash. 98501

Oakley and Merkley, Box 2446, Sacramento, Calif. 95801 (blanks)

Ernest O. Paulsen, Chinook, Mont. 59523 (blanks)

Peterson Mach. Carving, Box 1065, Sun Valley, Calif. 91352

Andrew Redmond, Inc., No. Anson, Me. 04958 (birchwood blanks)

Richards Micro-Fit Stocks, P.O. Box 1066, Sun Valley, CA. 91352 (thumbhole)

Roberts Wood Prod., 1400 Melody Rd., Marysville, Calif. 95901

Carl Roth, Jr., P.O. Box 2593, Cheyenne, Wy. 82001

Royal Arms, Inc., 10064 Bert Acosta Ct., Santee, Calif. 92071

Sanders Cust. Gun Serv., 2358 Tyler Lane, Louisville, Ky. 40205 (blanks)

Santa Barbara of Amer. Ltd., 930 N. Beltline Rd., #32, Irving, Tx. 75060

Saratoga Arms Co., R.D. 3, Box 387, Pottstown, Pa. 19464

Roy Schaefer, 965 W. Hilliard Lane, Eugene, Ore. 97402 (blanks)

Shaw's, 1655 S. Euclid Ave., Anaheim, Calif. 92802

Walter Shultz, R.D. 3, Pottstown, Pa. 19464

Sile Dist., 7 Centre Market Pl., New York, N.Y. 10013

Ed Sowers, 8331 DeCelis Pl., Sepulveda, Calif. 91343

Sportsmen's Equip. Co., 915 W. Washington, San Diego, Calif. 92103 (carbine conversions)

Keith Stegall, Box 696, Gunnison, Colo. 81230

Stinehour Rifles, Box 84, Cragsmoor, N.Y. 12420

J. R. Sundra, 683 Elizabeth St., Bridgeville, Pa. 15017

Swanson Cust. Firearms, 1051 Broadway, Denver, Colo. 80203

V. S. Swenson, Rt. 1, Ettrick, Wis. 54627

Talmage Enterpr., 1309 W. 12 St., Long Beach, CA 90813

D. W. Thomas, Box 184, Vineland, N.J. 08360

Trevallion Gunstocks, 3442 S. Post Rd., Indianapolis, IN 46239

Roy Vail, Rt. 1, Box 8, Warwick, N.Y. 10990

Harold Waller, 1288 Camillo Way, El Cajon, CA 92021

Weatherby's, 2781 Firestone, South Gate, Calif. 90280

Western Stocks & Guns, Inc., 2206 E 11th, Bremerton, Wash. 98311

Joe White, Box 8505, New Brighton, Christchurch, N.Z. (blanks)

Lou Williamson, 129 Stonegate Ct., Bedford, TX 76021

Robert M. Winter, Box 484, Menno, S.D. 57045

Fred Wranic, 6919 Santa Fe, Huntington Park, Calif. 90255 (mesquite)

Paul Wright, 4504 W. Washington Blvd., Los Angeles, Calif. 90016

SURPLUS GUNS, PARTS AND AMMUNITION

Century Arms, Inc., 3-5 Federal St., St. Albans, Vt. 05478

W. H. Craig, Box 927, Selma, Ala. 36701

Cummings Intl. Inc., 41 Riverside Ave., Yonkers, N.Y. 10701

Eastern Firearms Co., 790 S. Arroyo Pkwy., Pasadena, Calif. 91105

Hunter's Lodge, 200 S. Union, Alexandria, Va. 22313

Lever Arms Serv. Ltd., 771 Dunsmuir St., Vancouver 1, B.C., Canada

Mars Equipment Corp., 3318 W. Devon, Chicago, Ill. 60645

National Gun Traders, 225 S.W. 22nd, Miami, Fla. 33135

Pacific Intl. Imp. Co., 2416-16th St., Sacramento, CA. 95818

Plainfield Ordnance Co., Box 447, Dunellen, N.J. 08812

Potomac Arms Corp., Box 35, Alexandria, Va. 22313

Ruvel & Co., 3037 N. Clark St., Chicago, Ill. 60614

Service Armament Co., 689 Bergen Blvd., Ridgefield, N.J. 07657

Sherwood Distrib. Inc., 9470 Santa Monica Blvd., Beverly Hills, CA 90210

Z. M. Military Research Corp., 31 Legion Dr., Bergenfield, NJ 07621

THE TOOLS OF THE TRADE

The gunsmithing tools included in this section are only a sampling of those available through any number of sources, but these, at least, are essential to the success of the hobby gunsmith. For more complete information, we refer you to the listings under the Directory of Gunsmithing Suppliers. Most of them will furnish full information on their products upon request.

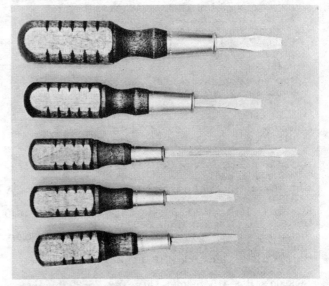

BROWNELL'S BOLT WELDING JIG

This jig employs a different approach to aligning the handle to the bolt; that by use of a protractor supplied with the jig kit. Full and complete instructions are supplied with each jig set. Properly used, this jig assures a perfect bolt handle weld. . . . . Each: $6.75

BROWNELL'S HYDRAULIC DENT RAISER

Removes dents from shotgun barrels hydraulically in a few minutes. A must tool for the man specializing in shotgun repair and maintenance. No hammering or peening of barrel is necessary with this tool. Available in 12, 16 & 20-gauge sets. . . . . Per Set: $22.50

GUN SCREWDRIVERS

Professionally designed screwdrivers for the gun owner are available from BELLCO. The set of five is packed in a plastic pouch, complete with instructions on use and fitting for precision work. The five screwdrivers range in size from 1/8x2 to 5/16x2 . . . . $5.98

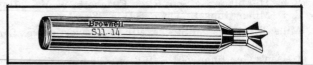

BROWNELL'S SIGHT BASE CUTTER

High speed steel, 60-degree cut, .020" undersize to compensate for milling tolerances. For standard front/rear sight bases. Higher priced than competitive cutters because: 1) Lips of cutter have radial ground relief - 2) Vapor honed for ultimate sharpness - 3) Center relief hole only .052" as compared to others' .082" diameter; thus giving many times more flute strength for longer money-saving life. Engineered for maximum production with least investment.
60-degree Sight Base Cutters . . . . Each: $5.25

BROWNELL'S NYLON/BRASS DRIFT PUNCH

Knurled handle is of high impact steel. Interchangeable nylon tip is steel reinforced to prevent bending or breaking. Interchangeable brass tip is used for more solid impact.
Each drift punch with brass and nylon tip $1.00
Each tips, brass or nylon 25

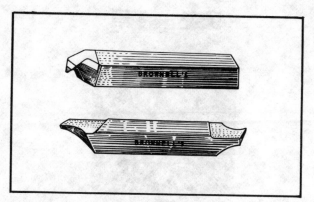

BROWNELL'S BOLT FACING, CROWNING BITS

For the gun worker with a lathe. The bolt facing lathe bit is for opening up bolt faces to magnum dimensions. Each is ground professionally to give best performance on bolt steels. Carbide tip is securely brazed. Barrel crowning bit is professionally ground to give maximum cutter strength and proper clearance as cutter enters bore and shank approaches barrel. Two radii are cut on each bit, one for .210-inch the other for .250-inch radius cut.

1/4-inch square Barrel Crowning Lathe bit $4.20
3/8-inch square Barrel Crowning bit 4.75
1/4-inch square bolt facing lathe bit 4.50
5/16-inch square bolt facing lathe bit 4.95

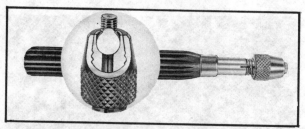

BROWNELL'S SHOTGUN BEAD INSTALLER

For positive, easy installation of aluminum or brass shotgun beads. An instrument with precision holding jaws which are ground and lapped to assure a positive holding surface without marring or defaceing the bead. Available in three sizes for small, medium and large beads.

Each: $2.10
Set of two 3.90
Set of three 5.40

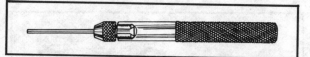

BROWNELL'S REPLACEABLE PUNCH SET

Designed exclusively for the gunsmith with pin punch troubles. The steel punches may be replaced instantly should they become damaged or broken. Available in three sizes: .039 for 3/64; .060 for 1.16; .091 for 3/32. (Special handle is needed for each size.)

Set of three sizes $3.25
2-inch replaceable pins, 6 pins your choice 1.00
2½-inch replaceable pins, 4 pins your choice 1.00

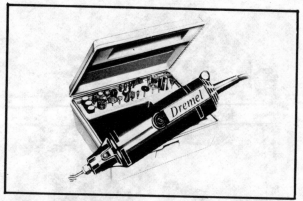

DREMEL MOTO TOOL

This tool is one of the handiest pieces of equipment one can own around a gun or hobby shop. Capable of completing jobs no other tools can master.
Model 270 .... $29.95
Model 280 with bearings 39.95

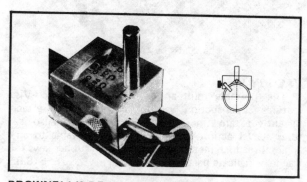

BROWNELL'S DEAD-CENTER PUNCH

A rugged, foolproof tool for finding the dead center of rifle or pistol barrels for purposes of drilling for sight installations. Fitted with bubble level and center punch for exacting work.................... Each: $8.75

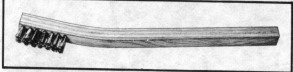

BROWNELL'S GUNSMITH BRUSH

Of special value for cleaning hardened grease and caked dirt from gun mechanisms. Brush is stainless steel, uneffected by bluing solutions or the various cleaning agents used in the gun trade............. Each: $ .90

BROWNELL'S GUNSMITH V-LEVEL

Precision-ground level with heat treated alloy frame. Ideal for barrel and action work where guess work is taboo for a precision job. May be used on drill press for scope and sight mounting jobs. .... Each: $16.00

317

VACUUM VISE

The portable multi-angle, swivel action Vacu-Vise features super-suction vacuum power grip to attach instantly to any smooth, non-porous surface. Also features swivel action to any position, adjustable to any angle, three inch metal jaws with slide-on rubber jaws for fragile or delicate parts $18.95

BROWNELL'S GUNSMITH LEVEL

A magnetic protractor level designed especially for the gunsmith. Assures that gun is absolutely level with drill press table, workbench or surface plate. Ideal for mounting front or rear sights. Will automatically hold position anywhere on barrel or action of steel or cast iron. Easily adjusts for any degree of angle reading.

Each: $3.20

CLAMDOWN TOOL

This handy little bench clamp for holding small parts during soldering or cementing operations can be used for setting small stock and pistol grip inlays.   . Each: $10.50

MINI GRIND-O-FLEX

One-inch diameter Merit Mini Grind-O-Flex wheels are used to remove rust and polish-grind the small opening in trigger housing mechanism prior to bluing. Mini Grind-O-Flex wheels eliminate hand sanding problems and also reach the hard to sand spots. $10.95

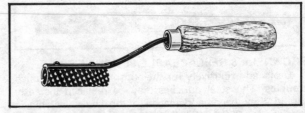

BROWNELL'S QUICKUT INLETTING TOOL

Quickly removes excess wood from barrel channel during inletting operations. Easy to use for both the professional and beginning gunsmith. . . . . . Each: $2.90

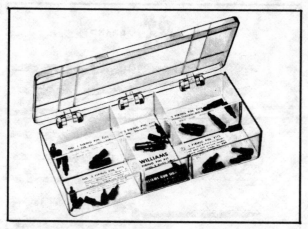

WILLIAM'S FIRING PIN KIT

This kit takes care of ninety-five percent of all single and double barrel shotgun firing pin replacements. Contains 25 numbered firing pins of different styles for such guns as Stevens, Svage, Iver Johnson, Montgomery Ward, Western Field brand, Harrington & Richardson.

Complete kit $18.75

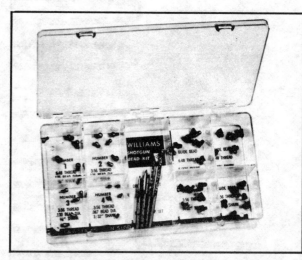

WILLIAM'S SPECIAL SHOTGUN BEAD KIT

Contains a complete assortment of beads in various styles and colors. Will fit any shotgun. Included are two drill and tap sets, the 6-48 and 3-56. There are 48 beads in all in varying sizes.

Complete kit $63.70

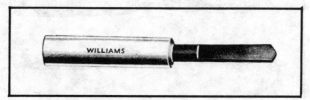

WILLIAMS CARBIDE DRILLS

For drilling hard receivers such as the M/70 Winchester, Springfield and Mauser. In two sizes to cover the majority of scope mounting chores, these carbide drills are available in No. 28 and No. 31. Are capable of cutting through the toughest case hardening.

No. 28 Carbide drill . . . . Each: $8.00

WILLIAM'S SERVICE KIT

This kit contains screws and taps most used by the working gunsmith. The 6-48, 8-40 and 10-32 screws and taps are the general repair standbys. Replacement screws and taps for kit are available.

Complete assortment $27.50

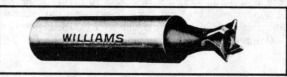

WILLIAMS SIGHT BASE CUTTER

This special four-fluted 3/8-inch dovetail cutter is of special high-speed cutting steel. Made .010 undersize with a plus or minus .005 tolerance so that the slot can be precision cut to the exact size on the second cut.

Each: $5.50

RICHLAND SHOTGUN CHAMBER REAMER

New type three-quarter cut chamber reamer and polishing tool with long forcing cone and brass pilot. Excellent for trimming chamber bushings and new ejectors and extractors to exact chamber size of 12 or 20 gauge.

Each: $15.00

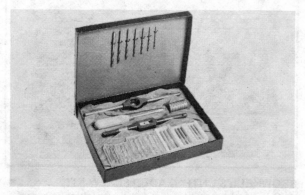

RICHLAND METRIC DRILL, TAP AND THREADING

With this kit, it is possible to make any screw used for European shotguns or for plugs covering the hinge bolt. Contains all necessary taps, dies, die wrenches, screw driver and drills : . . . . Per Kit: $29.95

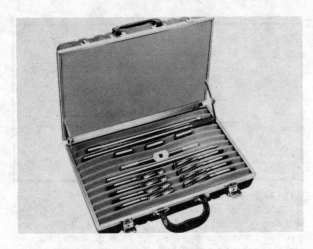

RICHLAND C-300 CHOKE REAMER KIT

For the advanced gunsmith, is available in 12 or 20 gauge. Each kit consists of eight choke reamers, three bore bushing guides, one two-piece rod and handle and carrying case. Left-hand spiral, right-hand cut. Assures that parallel planes of the choke are parallel to the bore.

Complete kit $85.00

WILLIAMS COUNTER BORE

For boring and counter boring sling swivel in stock and for machine swivel in forend.

Sling Swivel Counter Bore, with No. 17 drill. . . $6.50

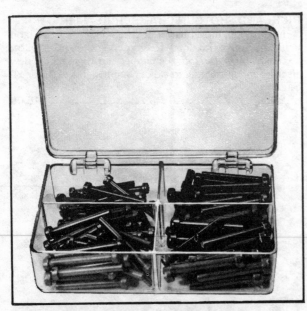

BROWNELL'S UNTHREADED SCREW KIT

One of the handiest kits for the working gun craftsman. Contains about 80 unthreaded screws in varying lengths and sizes, most adapted to gun work. Thread them yourself to proper size.

Complete kit $3.15

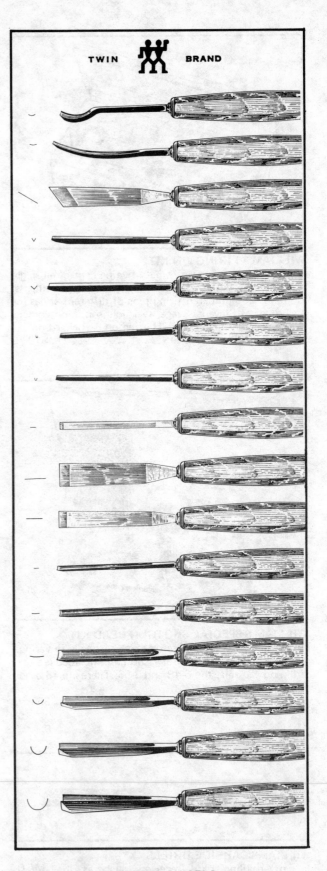

TWIN BRAND

BROWNELL'S INLETTING CHISELS

Twin Brand by J. A. Henckel of Germany, the Cadillac of inletting chisels. Preferred by leading gunsmiths. Price varies according to style needed.

$2.35 to $3.30